THE
GREAT AMERICAN
PLAYWRIGHTS
ON THE
SCREEN

A Critical Guide to
Film, Video and DVD

THE
GREAT AMERICAN
PLAYWRIGHTS
ON THE
SCREEN

A Critical Guide to
Film, Video and DVD

Jerry Roberts

APPLAUSE
THEATRE & CINEMA BOOKS

Jerry Roberts
Copyright © 2003 by Jerry Roberts

ISBN: 1-55783-512-8

Library of Congress Cataloging-in-Publication Data
Roberts, Jerry, 1956-
  Great American playwrights on the screen : a critical guide to film,
tv, video, and dvd / Jerry Roberts.
    p. cm.
  ISBN 1-55783-512-8
  1. American drama--Film and video adaptations. 2. Motion picture
plays--History and criticism. 3. Television plays, American--History
and criticism. 4. Film adaptations. I. Title.

PS338.M67R63 2003
791.43'6--dc21
                                    2003000060

British Library Cataloging in Publication Data
A catalogue record for this book is available from the British Library

Applause Theatre & Cinema Books
151 West 46th Street
New York, NY 10036
Phone: 212-575-9265
Fax: 646-562-5852
Email: info@applausepub.com

SALES AND DISTRIBUTION:

USA
HAL LEONARD CORP.
7777 West Bluemound Road
P.O. Box 13819
Milwaukee, WI 53213
Phone: 1-414-774-3630
Fax: 1-414-774-3259
Email: halinfo@halleonard.com
Internet: www.halleonard.com

UK
COMBINED BOOK SERVICES LTD.
Units I/K, Paddock Wood Distribution Centre
Paddock Wood, Tonbridge, Kent TN12 6UU
Phone: (44) 01892 837171
Fax: (44) 01892 837272
United Kingdom

Cover and interior book design by Mulberry Tree Press, Inc.
www.mulberrytreepress.com

Acknowledgments

Unlike my other books, this one was written on a deadline that was met. Encouragement and support came from my great friend, Julie Carlson. Kevin Cody allowed me the free use of his newspaper, *Easy Reader*, in Hermosa Beach, California, as a base of operations to coordinate and write the book. Instrumental in its jumpstart was my agent, Scott Sawyer.

Encouragement came sometimes from strange angles at odd hours, but among those whose witting and unwitting kind words, visits, telephone calls, jokes, insults, free beers, flung objects, and good-lucks helped inspire this project include Richard Andrews, Randy Angel, Ron Bailey, Rayford Berrymon, Chris and Ralph Bolgiano, Torin Burgess, Rich Chappell, Jessica Chou, Roger Creighton, Erin Danlasky, Ted Elrick, Dell Franklin, Robb Fulcher, Howard Gellerman, Cindy Gifford, Sam Gnerre, Dr. Carol Grabowski, Sr. Maureen Grabowski, Walter Grabowski, Victoria Gustafson, Stephen Hansen, Andrea Hayashi, Vic Haychi, Wil Haygood, Lynn Holladay, Darrell Hope, Sheila Hopkins, Randy Iwasaka, Peter Jackson, Steve Jett, Stuart Johnson, Lyle Kessler, Boots and JoAnn LeBaron, Don and Pat Lechman, David Lechman, Stuart Levine, Reverend Levy, Dick Loftus, Elisa Losson, Irene Loud, Doug List, Richard Loncraine, Leonard Maltin, Teri Marin, Ronald F. Maxwell, Mark McDermott, Julie Miller, Missouri Cal, Curt Morris, Ian Morris, Kevin and Dana Morris, Seth Morris, Benjamin Morse, Bev Morse, James Robert Parish, Heather Parnock, John Perry, Pittsburgh Pete, Tami Quattrone, Audrey Ralston, Alvin Rambo, Dr. Jerry Reich, Alex and Ann Roberts, Mark and Patty Roberts, Kevin Sanders, Kari Sayers, Dr. Jerry Reich, Mary Jane Schoenheider, Jake and Janet Shafer, Brian Simon, Adrienne Slaughter, Judy Smith, Craig Stephens, Richard Stephens, Dan Sullivan, John Tawa and Bondo Wyszpolski.

Library research was aided and expedited by the staffs of the Margaret Herrick Library at the Academy of Motion Picture Arts & Sciences, the UCLA Arts Library, and public libraries in the following California locations: Long Beach, San Diego, Palos Verdes Peninsula, Redondo Beach, Torrance, and Manhattan Beach. The immediate and extensive archives of the Internet Movie Database and the Internet Broadway Database were invaluable resources.

For Alexander and Ann L. Roberts

Introduction

Some of the greatest plays in the history of the American theatre have also made some of the most provocative and rewarding movies and television shows of all time, from A *Streetcar Named Desire* to *The Front Page* to *The Miracle Worker*; *Long Day's Journey Into Night*, *Death of a Salesman*, *Picnic*, *The Iceman Cometh*, *The Little Foxes*, *A Raisin in the Sun*... These productions on film and tape represent a treasure trove of great drama, much of it available to the public for home viewing, some of it languishing in vaults. Some titles also represent Oscar and Emmy award-winning history. Some are great teaching tools for theatre and film and television production courses. Some are pinnacles of success for the greatest star actors of their generations—Katharine Hepburn, Cary Grant, Henry Fonda, Walter Matthau, Paul Newman, Meryl Streep, Jack Nicholson, Robert Duvall, Kevin Spacey.

This book is the collation of these time-honored works by playwrights—from Eugene O'Neill and Tennessee Williams, to Beth Henley and David Rabe, to Wendy Wasserstein and A.R. Gurney—with historical perspective and contemporary and retrospective criticism.

Playwrights reach their widest audiences whenever their plays are filmed or made for television, sometimes as letter-faithful productions literally filmed on the stage, oftentimes as severely altered visions earning the ire of the authors. When Tennessee Williams saw the first film made from one of his plays, *The Glass Menagerie* (1950), by Warner Bros., he called it "the most awful travesty of the play I've ever seen...horribly mangled by the people who did the film script." Eugene O'Neill was satisfied with few films made from his canon, but notably admired the very first, *Anna Christie*, a 1923 silent starring Blanche Sweet.

While Broadway was the place to find vital performance art in the first half of the 20th century, cinema soon became the most important art form, and received a boost in prominence in the last three decades from the advent of cable TV and home-viewing media. While many prominent playwrights looked down on movies or refused to embrace the medium prior to World War II, many postwar playwrights found the movies and TV suitable and lucrative. Two-time Academy Award-winning screenwriter and Pulitzer Prize-winning playwright Horton Foote, who moved easily between the stage, films, and TV, expressed great concern for getting his plays on either screen to preserve the works. In the 1980s and 1990s, playwrights such as David Mamet, Sam Shepard, and Michael Cristofer began to direct films based on their plays and avidly embraced the far-reaching power of the film-captured image.

Plays may end up in many media—published version, on the stage, as TV, film, ballet, or opera. And they change, sometimes drastically, from version to version. Williams reworked and re-titled some of his plays reusing titles from his own canon. Many of the different versions were staged and filmed or taped, and various incarnations ended up on video. While many viewers are aware of the films of Williams's plays *The Fugitive Kind*, starring Anna Magnani and Marlon Brando, and *Summer and Smoke* with Geraldine Page and Laurence Harvey, the renamed TV versions remain much more obscure—*Orpheus Descending* with Vanessa Redgrave and *The Eccentricities of a Nightingale* with Blythe Danner, respectively. Both TV versions were more well-received critically than the films.

With dozens of homogenous video guides on the market, this guide collates the critical records of the bodies of cinema and TV works by more than 200 American playwrights with five goals:

- Establish a record of the great playwrights' filmed or taped works

- Compare and contrast the versions via critical treatments by the prominent film and TV critics of the times as well as revisionist critics

- Show which versions are available for home viewing and in which media

- Point out unheralded treasures and forgotten performances by the great actors of the times, who were often in the service of the great directors

- Resurrect the memories of TV productions of plays at a critical time when many of them are deteriorating in vaults, including many Emmy Award winners and nominees

Overall, this book is the home viewer's handbook to the filmed and taped American theatre, as well as the stage scholar's handy reference. To discover which Arthur Miller plays have been filmed or are available on video, and are valuable to seek out, involves a long process. One might be surprised to discover that, even though *All My Sons* and *Death of a Salesman* were theatrical films in the immediate postwar era, television did greater justice to these plays with its own versions (the former in 1986 with Aidan Quinn, the latter in 1966 with Lee J. Cobb and 1985 with Dustin Hoffman). In addition to this, TV versions of Miller's *The Price* and *The Crucible*, both with George C. Scott, and *A Memory of Two Mondays* with an ensemble including Jack Warden, were all critically lauded in the 1970s.

The book is composed alphabetically by playwright with brief biographical entries. It is then compiled alphabetically by each of his or her adapted plays, then chronologically if more than one treatment of a particular play exists—as is the case with several important works by Eugene O'Neill, Tennessee Williams, William Inge, Clifford Odets, Maxwell Anderson, Thornton Wilder, Ben Hecht, and others. The book covers every Pulitzer Prize-winning playwright and every Tony Award-winner for best play whose works have been adapted. Prolific, popular, and diverse playwrights such as August Wilson, Neil Simon, Philip Barry, Sam Shepard, and Sidney Kingsley are, of course, included. The book also deals with oddities and one-shots, such as Ernest Hemingway's one play, *The Fifth Column*, which was adapted for TV in 1960 by A.E. Hotchner, with John Frankenheimer directing Richard Burton and Maximilian Schell.

Broadway might as well have been on the moon for most fans of great comedy, musical theatre, and drama through the 20th century, and the prospects of traveling to New York, or even supporting regional theatre were invariably prohibitive. But the movies and the advent of TV helped several generations of Americans to see what the stage had to offer. And TV often has been a medium that is able to improve upon the intimacies of the stage, bringing the emotions of the actors to us in close-up. Movies and TV, in many cases, have preserved the ideas and poetics of the great American playwrights, and video has brought them into our homes and classrooms. Some of this recorded wealth of American stage culture has been resurrected from TV vaults to expand the video shelves and help fill domestic and foreign TV and cable airtime. The Broadway Theatre Archive is one commercial project that has undertaken the video restoration of more than 300 taped and filmed plays from the 1950s, 1960s, and 1970s.

Unlike Academy Award-winning and nominated films, many Emmy-winning and Emmy-nominated shows have aired once or twice and been forgotten with the passage of time. Despite the creation of such arts-friendly cable networks as Bravo and the Arts & Entertainment Network, demand for vintage award-winning TV movies and TV plays remains low. Broadway Theatre Archive is one avenue for the home-viewing theatre fan. For instance, the legendary 1960 production of O'Neill's *The Iceman Cometh*, which aired only on New York's educational Channel 13 in two two-hour installments a week apart on *The Play of the Week* series, starred Jason Robards in one of the theatre's benchmark performances, along with Robert Redford in one of his first TV appearances. The show was directed by Sidney Lumet, and achieved what Variety deemed "a reference point for greatness in TV drama." Virtually unseen since 1960, *The Iceman Cometh* has been brought to video by Broadway Theatre Archive.

Also available on video are such resurrected classics as the Emmy-winning Best Program of 1970-71, *The Andersonville Trial*, the adaptation of Saul Levitt's play with George C. Scott directing Richard Basehart, Jack Cassidy, and Martin Sheen; Shirley Booth's Emmy-nominated performance in Tennessee Williams's *The Glass Menagerie*; *The Royal Family* with Eva LaGalliene; Dustin Hoffman in *Journey of the Fifth Horse* from 1966, a year before *The Graduate*, and Faye Dunaway in 1971's *Hogan's Goat*. These and others now released on video or DVD were produced for the PBS series *American Playhouse*, *Great Performances*, and *Theatre in America*, as well as New York-based WNET *Playhouse* and the Los Angeles-based, KCET-produced *Hollywood Television Theatre*. *Theatre in America* produced three O'Neill plays in the 1970s that are now preserved on video—*Ah, Wilderness!* and *Beyond the Horizon*, both with Geraldine Fitzgerald, and *A Touch of the Poet* featuring Fritz Weaver and Nancy Marchand.

The book solely concerns plays written by American playwrights, produced on film or tape in the English language. It covers only productions that were adapted from plays that were seen first on the stage. TV dramas that began their performance life as TV shows, and are invariably called "plays" by their authors and others, are not included here. For instances, two of Horton Foote's dramas, *The Trip to Bountiful*, an original, and *Tomorrow*, based on a William Faulkner story, began their performance lives as TV presentations, the former with Lillian Gish in 1953 on *Philco Television Playhouse*, the latter with Richard Boone on *Playhouse 90* in 1960. Both then became plays, then movies. The movies are detailed with break-out studies here, but the TV shows are not. Had the works begun as plays, then became movies and TV presentations, any and all movies or TV productions would be considered with individual studies.

The book is a study in three media that looks first to the written word and the writer. The play's the thing, and whether it has been transferred to film or videotape doesn't matter—the performance on record is what matters. In this regard, video is occasionally the great leveler, illustrating that interpretations of playwrights' intents and dramatic success have nothing to do with size, money, and prestige. A 1973 small-screen, virtually one-set stab at Arthur Miller's *Incident at Vichy* by director Stacy Keach on PBS's *Hollywood Television Theatre* with a cast of character actors led by Harris Yulin and Richard Jordan was just as effective as the Technicolor, big-studio treatment of N. Richard Nash's *The Rainmaker*, which Paramount Pictures made with Burt Lancaster and Katharine Hepburn in 1956.

While the book primarily concerns the works of playwrights, it illuminates film and TV history—particularly TV history and what is often called the "Golden Age of Television." This includes the slew of drama anthology shows of the 1950s and early 1960s: *Philco Television Playhouse*, *Studio One*, *Ford Theatre Hour*, *Kraft Television Theatre*, *Playhouse 90*, *The United States Steel Hour*, *The Hallmark Hall of Fame*, *The Play of the Week*, *Celanese Theatre*, *Robert Montgomery Presents*, *The DuPont Show of the Month*, *Omnibus*, *DuPont Show of the Month*,

Producers' Showcase, and other programs that proliferated on the airwaves before the networks mainstreamed their schedules. By the 1970s, performing arts fare had moved almost exclusively to PBS.

A side issue in the book concerns sticking up, so to speak, for TV. Many of our greatest playwrights' works were adapted for TV and long forgotten. Early TV heritage is stowed away in a few dozen reference works, none of which fully collates and studies the tube's treatment of classic plays—which were a readymade staple of material for the voraciously growing medium in the 1950s. Catalogued, discussed, and critiqued will be productions that many theatre and TV aficionados may not know existed. Some are gone forever, some are in kinescope form in vaults.

No small selling point for the book is that it digs from the vaults the memory of great performances by the great stars and actors—portrayals forgotten in the passage of time. The nature of this book, which merges films with TV presentations, affords the public and scholars the opportunity to contemplate many great star actors' forgotten work in TV with their more well-chronicled movie roles.

Academy Award winners who worked in TV adaptations of plays with some regularity include Laurence Olivier, Fredric March, Helen Hayes, George C. Scott, Jessica Tandy, Melvyn Douglas, Jason Robards, Martin Balsam, Thomas Mitchell, Jack Lemmon, Ed Begley, Teresa Wright, Ethel Barrymore, Paul Newman, Joanne Woodward, Faye Dunaway, Maximilian Schell, Martin Landau, Kim Hunter, Jo Van Fleet, Shirley Jones, Ruth Gordon, Anne Bancroft, and Shirley Booth. Yet when the books, feature stories, and obituaries get written, these outstanding players' sterling TV efforts receive short shrift, even though the small-screen portrayals invariably required the actors' dedication and effort as much as much as the films did and were, by and large, seen by more people than the films.

The book also illuminates the careers of directors and adapters of the works. Some of the adapters were playwrights who cross-pollinated other playwrights' works. For instance, Phoebe and Henry Ephron adapted Maxwell Anderson and Laurence Stallings' *What Price Glory* for John Ford's 1952 remake, and Jay Presson Allen adapted Ira Levin's *Deathtrap* for Sidney Lumet's 1982 film with Michael Caine.

The principle sources for the critical quotes are *Variety*, *The New York Times*, *Los Angeles Times*, *The New Yorker*, *The Nation*, *The New Republic*, Chicago *Sun-Times*, *Time*, *Newsweek*, *The Saturday Review*, *Esquire*, and various genre books, biographies, and critical compilations. Four film critics were consulted on a regular basis: James Agee, Pauline Kael, Manny Farber, and Andrew Sarris. Some of the TV presentations from the early 1950s won't have critical quotes, because *Variety* overlooked the productions and, like *The New York Times* and

New York *Herald-Tribune*, didn't get into TV criticism in full force until the mid-to-late 1950s.

This brief glossary explains the abbreviations:

100m = 100 minutes
 bw = black-and-white
  c = color
Sc: = screenwriter
Tp: = teleplay writer
 D: = director
Cam: = cinematographer (or cameraman)

The star ratings are on a five-star basis (☆☆☆☆☆) and based on both the author's judgment and/or that of the quoted critic(s). Anything that has been critiqued will be judged by a star rating.

With the theatre and film arts remaining popular on college campuses and more students entering film and television schools than ever before, this book is a readymade companion reference for college courses and libraries. It merges scholarship with popular culture and keeps alive the literary heritage of the great playwrights even as the Great White Way has declined and many of its mainstays have shifted to movies and TV. Yet, the great playwrights are the great authors of our performing arts. Their works formulate a large part of the American literary tradition, and the filmed versions remain the only way that every person interested in them can see them performed. The intent here is to remember and honor their legacies.

THE
GREAT AMERICAN
PLAYWRIGHTS
ON THE
SCREEN

A Critical Guide to
Film, Video and DVD

George Abbott

George Francis Abbott
Born: June 25, 1887, Forestville, NY. **Died:** 1995.

As a writer, director, and producer of comedies, dramas, and musicals on-stage and for films and TV, George Abbott was one of the most diverse talents in 20th century entertainment. He was one of the most ubiquitous and versatile figures in musical comedy, as active and successful in 1957 as 1927. He was in demand as an adapter in the early sound era, retooling such stage plays for the screen as *Why Bring That Up?* (1929), *Manslaughter* (1930), *Stolen Heaven* (1931), and *Secrets of a Secretary* (1931). He also shared the Academy Award nomination for Best Writing Achievement of 1929–30 with Maxwell Anderson and Del Andrews for director Lewis Milestone's *All Quiet on the Western Front.* He produced such films as *Room Service* (1938), with the Marx Brothers, *Brother Rat* (1938), with Wayne Morris, *The Primrose Path* (1940), with Ginger Rogers, and *Kiss and Tell* (1945) with Shirley Temple. As a playwright, he almost always worked in collaboration. Abbott died at the age of 107 after consulting on a hit revival of *Damn Yankees* with Jerry Lewis.

Beat the Band (1947, RKO, 67m/bw) ☆☆ **Sc:** Lawrence Kibble. **D:** John H. Auer. **P:** Michel Kraike. **Cam:** Frank Redman. **Cast:** Frances Langford, Ralph Edwards, Phillip Terry, Gene Krupa, June Clayworth, Mabel Paige, Andrew Tombes, Donald MacBride, Mira McKinney, Harry Harvey, Grady Sutton. In this standard-brands musical, a country girl travels to the big city to follow through on her opera-singing aspirations, and an unscrupulous bandleader sets his sights on her money. It was based on the 1942 Broadway musical that Abbott wrote with John Green and George Marion, Jr., which starred Susan Miller (as a Caribbean girl, changed for the film), Jack Whiting, Jerry Lester, and Joan Caulfield. The Krupa band belts out the title tune and others, including "I'm in Love" and "I've Got My Fingers Crossed."

- *"...a witless musical...that contained enough sour notes to dampen half a dozen 'B' musicals...ultimately climaxed in a hotel boiler room where Gene Krupa and his band get really 'hot' when the steam is turned on." (Richard B. Jewell, Vernon Harbin, The RKO Story)*

The Boys From Syracuse was a farce loosely based on William Shakespeare's *A Comedy of Errors*, in which two sets of twin brothers are mistaken for their married siblings, making for sexcapade mixups. Eddie Albert led a cast including Burl Ives in the 1938 play, with music by Richard Rodgers and lyrics by Lorenz Hart.

The Boys From Syracuse (1940, Universal, 74m/bw) ☆☆½ **Sc:** Leonard

Spigelgass, Charles Grayson, Paul Gerard Smith. **D:** A. Edward Sutherland. **P:** Jules Levey. **Cam:** Joseph Valentine. **Cast:** Allan Jones, Martha Raye, Joe Penner, Charles Butterworth, Rosemary Lane, Irene Hervey, Alan Mowbray, Eric Blore, Samuel S. Hinds, Tom Dugan, Spencer Charters, Eddie Acuff, Bess Flowers. The writing credit for this wise-cracked-up version of *A Comedy of Errors* reads: "After a play by William Shakespeare...long, long after!" Among the songs that were added for the film version were "Who Are You?" and "The Greeks Had a Word for It."

- *"The...screenplay eliminated all traces of the original's satire, substituting anachronistic vulgarities in place of true humor. Musically, the Rodgers and Hart classics—numbers such as 'Sing for Your Supper,' 'Falling in Love with Love,' 'He and She' and 'This Can't be Love'—were bowdlerized almost to the point of extinction..."* (Clive Hirschhorn, The Universal Story)

The Boys From Syracuse was also made by the CBC in 1986 and aired in America on PBS, directed by Douglas Campbell and produced by Norman Campbell with a cast led by Colm Feore, Geraint Wyn Davies, Keith Thomas, Benedict Campbell, Susan Wright, and Goldie Semple.

Broadway is the 1926 Broadway play that Abbott wrote with Philip Dunning and Jed Harris about a nightclub dancer who becomes involved in the murder of racketeer Scar Edwards. Harris produced and Abbott and Dunning co-directed a cast topped by Lee Tracy and Sylvia Field.

Broadway (1929, Universal, 105m/bw) ☆☆☆½ **Sc:** Edward T. Lowe, Jr., Charles Furthman. **D:** Paul Fejos. **P:** Carl Laemmle, Jr. **Cam:** Hal Mohr. **Cast:** Glenn Tryon, Evelyn Brent, Merna Kennedy, Thomas Jackson, Robert Ellis, Otis Harlan, Paul Porcasi, Marion Lord, Fritz Feld, Leslie Fenton, Arthur Housman, George Davis, Betty Francisco, Edythe Flynn, Florence Dudley, Ruby McCoy, Gus Arnheim and His Cocoanut Grove Ambassadors. This movie's take on racketeers and speakeasies was considered brash and daring for the times, and its use of showbiz as-pirants and arm-in-arm chorines were archetypes and soon-to-be stereo-types of the fledgling movie musical. The songs include "Hot Footin' It" and "Sing a Little Love Song."

- *"A camera was devised by...Fejos which was able to travel at every con-ceivable angle at a speed of 600 feet a minute, thus giving greater fluidity than was usual in movie musicals of the time...As backstage musicals went, it was tense and hard-hitting, even though the elaborate nightclub settings were at odds with the intended sleaziness of the original."* (Clive Hirschhorn, The Universal Story)

- *"...modernistic decorations, impressive photography and other frills...a handsome entertainment in which much of the drama of the original sur-vives..."* (The New York Times)

Broadway (1942, Universal, 90m/bw) ☆☆☆ **Sc:** Felix Jackson, John

Bright. **D:** William A. Seiter. **P:** Bruce Manning. **Cam:** George Barnes. **Cast:** George Raft, Pat O'Brien, Janet Blair, Broderick Crawford, Marjorie Rambeau, Anne Gwynn, S.Z. Sakall, Edward S. Brophy, Marie Wilson, Gus Schilling, Arthur Shields, Iris Adrian, Dorothy Moore, Nestor Paiva, Abner Biberman, Tom Kennedy, Jennifer Holt, Mack Grey. The material was retooled to Raft's persona as he played himself, a former Broadway dancer who, during a stroll along the Great White Way, recalls his past during the Prohibition Era, when bootleggers and racketeers provided a certain flavor.

- *"Raft gave an adequate account of himself as himself, although he was eclipsed in the acting stakes by Pat O'Brien as a detective. Felix Jackson and John Bright's pacy script provided a number of featured roles which were done full justice to by Marjorie Rambeau, S.Z. Sakall, Edward Brophy...14 popular 1920s tunes were utilized, largely as background music..."* (Clive Hirschhorn, The Universal Story)

- *"Although full of songs and some action, the 1942 Broadway did not fully develop Raft's screen character, which seemed to stay in the background, although he and Blair did dance the tango. Despite the relatively rich trappings, the remake of Broadway could not escape its now hackneyed formula."* (James Robert Parish, Michael Pitts, The Great Gangster Pictures)

Broadway (1955, CBS, 60m/c) *The Best of Broadway* ☆½ **Tp:** Philip Dunning. **D:** Franklin J. Schaffner. **P:** Felix Jackson. **Cast:** Piper Laurie, Joseph Cotten, Gene Nelson, Keenan Wynn, Akim Tamiroff, Martha Hyer, Carol Matthews, Frank McGrath, Don Gordon, Beverly Bozeman, Helene Ellis, Iggie Wolfington, David Sheiner. The attractive cast floundered, and the production is one of hundreds forgotten from the so-called "Golden Age of TV" anthology drama. This was Laurie's TV debut.

- "Best of Broadway's *last play of its series...was an event all concerned in would prefer to believe never happened."* (William Torbert Leonard, Theatre: Stage to Screen to Television)

- *"...has none of the spark nor fire of the original melodrama...Stereotyped gangsters, flappers, a hoofer and sleuth went through their motions...The televersion simply failed to capture the spirit of flamboyant 1920s, painting Broadway people as caricatures rather than characters...only Martha Hyer performed very well...hokey teleplay and inept direction by Franklin Schaffner."* (Variety)

Coquette (1929, Mary Pickford, 75m/bw, **VHS**) ☆☆ **Sc:** John Grey, Allen McNeil, Sam Taylor. **D:** Sam Taylor. **P:** Mary Pickford. **Cam:** Karl Struss. **Cast:** Mary Pickford, Johnny Mack Brown, Matt Moore, William Janney, John Sainpolis, Henry Kolker, Louise Beavers, George Irving. Abbott wrote this piece—about a 1920s Southern flapper who's responsible for a long trail of broken hearts—with Ann Preston Bridgers and specifically for Helen Hayes. Hayes played it in a Jed Harris production in 1927 at the Maxine Elliott Theatre in New York, directed by Abbott. The major change in the film adaptation was that the father of the central flirt commits suicide instead of her. The film was both Pickford's failed attempt to change her image as "America's sweetheart" and her first of only four sound pictures before she retired from the screen. A founder of the Academy of Motion Picture Arts and Sciences, Pickford won the Academy Award for Best Actress for this performance in the second year of the Oscars' existence.

- "Considering the calibre of her performance, the Oscar would have been incomprehensible were it not for her social position within Hollywood. Mary's Oscar for her inferior work for Coquette surely qualifies at the first Lifetime Achievement Award to be handed out by the Academy." (Scott Eyman, Mary Pickford: America's Sweetheart)

Damn Yankees was co-written by Abbott with Douglass Wallop, deriving its Faustian tale about a Washington Senators fan who sells his soul to the devil for a long-ball hitter, then conjures the temptress Lola to lead the power hitter astray. The writers adapted the play from Wallop's novel, *The Year the Yankees Lost the Pennant*. This smash hit of 1955, directed by Abbott, starred Gwen Verdon, Ray Walston, and Stephen Douglass. Bob Fosse handled the choreography.

Damn Yankees (1958, Warner Bros., 110m/c, **VHS**) ☆☆☆☆ **Sc:** George Abbott. **D/P:** George Abbott, Stanley Donen. **Cam:** Harold Lipstein. **Cast:** Gwen Verdon, Tab Hunter, Ray Walston, Russ Brown, Shannon Bolin, Jean Stapleton, Jimmie Komack, Nathaniel Frey, Rae Allen, Albert Linville, Bob Fosse, Robert Shafer. Gwen Verdon's performance as the hyper-sexy and shrewdly comedic Lola is the highlight of this outstanding musical, which holds up very well, aided in its theme of the Yankees' dominance in this age. The songs include "You've Gotta Have Heart," "Whatever Lola Wants," and "Shoeless Joe from Hannibal, Mo." It was released in baseball-bereft England as *What Lola Wants*.

- "[Verdon's] sizzling performance...is one of the hottest and heartiest we've seen in a musical movie in years...wondrously repeating the role she played on the stage — and doing it in a fashion that is rare and refreshing on the screen...Like the George Abbott stage show before it, it has class, imagination, verve and a good many of the same performers who did so charmingly by it on Broadway...improvements...are genuine outdoor baseball sequences...and an overall speedup of movement and flexibility. If you can't get to see the World Series, get to see Damn Yankees. It's some show." (Bosley Crowther, The New York Times)

Damn Yankees (1967, NBC, 120m/c) ☆☆½ **Tp:** George Abbott. **D/P:** Kirk Browning. **Cast:** Lee Remick, Jerry Lanning, Phil Silvers, Linda Lavin, Jim Backus, Ray Middleton, Fran Allison, Bob Dishy, Lee Goodman, Gene Troobnick, Joe Garagiola, Lou Bods. Remick, whose sexuality was usually used by directors in subtle ways, didn't quite push herself here, in one of her few chances to portray brassy, all-out sauciness, but Silvers was in his element. Lavin, in one of her first TV roles, played a sportswriter.

• *"Criticized for cinematography excesses in the use of animated cartoons amd newsreels, the telecast uncertainly wavered between Faustian fantasy, comic strips, baseball and infrequent brushes with reality. But the vigorous playing of the cast and Kirk Browning's brisk pacing of the show gave the home viewers a pleasant two hours."* (William Torbert Leonard, Theatre: Stage to Screen to Television)

The Fall Guy (1930, RKO, 66m/bw) ☆☆½ **Sc:** Tim Whelan. **D:** Leslie Pearce. **P:** William Le Baron. **Cam:** Leo Tovar. **Cast:** Jack Mulhall, Mae Clarke, Ned Sparks, Pat O'Malley, Tom Jackson, Wynne Gibson, Ann Brody, Elmer Ballard, Alan Roscoe. This play by Abbott and James Gleason (who later became a ubiquitous Hollywood supporting actor) concerns a gullible New York druggist's fight to foil the pranksters in his neighborhood. It starred Ralph Sipperly on Broadway in 1925. The film was released in England as *Trust Your Wife*. Mulhall played the sap clever enough to con a confession out of the mobster trying to frame him.

• *"All their performances were adequate, but director Leslie Pearce's stage-bound direction robbed the comedy-drama of any true vitality."* (Richard B. Jewell and Vernon Harbin, The RKO Story)

Four Walls, an Abbott writing collaboration with Dana Burnet, debuted on the New York stage in 1927 with Abbott directing Muni Wisenfrend (Paul Muni) as Benny Horowitz, a Jewish ex-gangster released from Sing Sing after five years and determined to stay out—after he murders the Italian rackets boss who's romancing his girl. Jeanne Greene co-starred.

Four Walls (1928, MGM, 70m/bw/silent) ☆☆☆ **Sc:** Joe Farnham. **D:** William Nigh. **Cam:** James Wong Howe. **Cast:** John Gilbert, Joan Crawford, Vera Gordon, Carmel Myers, Robert Emmett O'Connor, Louis Natheaux, Jack Byron. Gilbert's popularity made this first version a hit. Crawford played the "bad girl," Frieda, the old girlfriend who takes up with the rival mobster, and Myers was the "good girl."

• *"...due to Gilbert's extreme popularity, the movie enjoyed considerable box-office success...Variety labeled the picture as 'well done' and especially liked Nigh's direction '...for its reality, restraint and knowledge of his element.' Like many films made in the late silent period, Four Walls had no dialogue, but it did have a theme song of the same title which was co-written by Al Jolson. Jolson recorded the tune for Brunswick Records, which may well be the only real memorable result of the film."* (James Robert Parish, Michael Pitts, The Great Gangster Pictures)

Straight Is the Way (1934, MGM, 59m/bw) ☆☆ **Sc:** Bernard Schubert. **D:** Paul Sloane. **P:** Lucien Hubbard. **Cam:** Lucien Androit. **Cast:** Franchot Tone, May Robson, Karen Morley, Gladys George, Nat Pendleton, Jack LaRue, Raymond Hatton, William Bakewell, C. Henry Gordon.

- "*A totally unconvincing gangster film which has Tone trying to play a Jewish gangster from New York's East Side.*" (J.P. Ross, S.R. Nash, The Motion Picture Guide)

Heat Lightning was written by Abbott with Leon Abrams and produced by Abbott and Philip Dunning. It debuted on Broadway in 1933, and starred Jean Dixon as a woman presiding over a combined filling station and auto camp in the rural Southwest.

Heat Lightning (1934, Warner Bros., 63m/bw) ☆☆ **Sc:** Brown Holmes, Warren Duff. **D:** Mervyn Le Roy. **P:** Sam Bischoff. **Cam:** Sid Hickox. **Cast:** Aline MacMahon, Ann Dvorak, Preston Foster, Lyle Talbot, Glenda Farrell, Frank McHugh, Ruth Donnelly, Theodore Newton, Willard Robertson, Edgar Kennedy, Jane Darwell, Chris-Pin Martin, Harry C. Bradley, James Durkin, Jill Bennett, Margareta Montez.

- "*Drab background, little sex appeal and not enough tension. It's a sluffo for deluxers, but can get by elsewhere.*" (Variety)
- "*Only of interest for its dusty highway view of the Southwest, putting its filling station in perspective as a piece of Americana.*" (J.P. Nash, S.R. Ross, The Motion Picture Guide)

Highway West (1941, Warner Bros., 62m/bw) ☆½ **Sc:** Allen Rivkin, Charles Kenyon, Kenneth Garnett. **D:** William McGann. **P:** Edmund Grainger. **Cam:** Ted McCord. **Cast:** Brenda Marshall, Arthur Kennedy, William Lundigan, Olympe Bradna, Slim Summerville, Willie Best, Frank Wilcox, John Ridgely, Dorothy Tree, Noel Madison, Pat Flaherty, Victor Zimmerman, Dick Rich, James Westerfield, William B. Davidson. Kennedy, in one of the "B" programmers he was given in his early Warner Bros. days, played a bank robber hidden by the innocent Marshall. When the police find him, Marshall has to go back to running the roadside diner until he breaks out of prison.

- "*...an undernourished melodrama.*" (Clive Hirschhorn, The Warner Bros. Story)
- "*A weak remake...The tale ends when Kennedy finally gets his just desserts from policeman Summerville.*" (J.P. Nash, S.R. Ross, The Motion Picture Guide)

Hills of Peril (1927, Fox, bw/silent) ☆☆½ **Sc:** Jack Jungmeyer. **D:** Lambert Hillier, Reginald Lyons. **P:** William Fox. **Cam:** Reginald Lyons. **Cast:** Buck Jones, Georgia Hale, Charles R. Althoff, Marjorie Beebe, Buck Black, Duke Green, Bob Kortman, Albert J. Smith, William

Welsh. Abbott's play *A Holy Terror* was snapped up by Fox and turned into a B western.

- *"...a fast-moving, two-fisted little western drama in which the love interest runs a definite second to the all-important business of hard riding and fast shooting between the upright Mr. Jones and an ornery assortment of cut-throats. Buck pretends to be an outlaw in order to aid the authorities to round up a gang of bootleggers."* (Buck Rainey, The Life and Films of Buck Jones: The Silent Era)

Lilly Turner (1933, Warner Bros., 65m/bw) ☆☆ **Sc:** Gene Markey, Kathryn Scola. **D:** William A. Wellman. **P:** Hal B. Wallis. **Cam:** Sid Hickox. **Cast:** Ruth Chatterton, George Brent, Frank McHugh, Ruth Donnelly, Guy Kibbee, Robert Barrat, Hobart Cavanaugh, Grant Mitchell, Mayo Methot, Gordon Westcott, Arthur Vinton. Abbott and Philip Dunning's 1933 play concerns the wife of a carnival magician who has a baby, learns her husband is a bigamist, then marries a drunk so the baby can have a father.

- *"Chatterton is the only saving grace in this mess of a film...The film has no logic, veering off on too many turns to be believable. Hardly one of Wellman's finer efforts."* (J.P. Nash and S.R. Ross, The Motion Picture Guide)
- *"...miscast Ruth Chatterton as Lilly...Miss Chatterton was too sophisticated an actress for this sort of role, and, as a result, the finished product lacked conviction."* (Clive Hirschhorn, The Warner Bros. Story)

Love 'Em and Leave 'Em was a collaboration between Abbott and John V.A. Weaver about sisters who are department store clerks with opposite personalities, both in love with the same guy. The "bad girl" sister, Janie, steals the company's welfare fund money and loses it at the horse track. The 1926 play was produced by Jed Harris, directed by Abbott, and featured Donald Meek and Thomas Chalmers in the ensemble.

Love 'Em and Leave 'Em (1926, Paramount, 62m/bw/silent, **VHS**) ☆☆½ **Sc:** George Abbott, Townsend Martin. **D:** Frank Tuttle. **P:** William LeBaron. **Cam:** George Webber. **Cast:** Louise Brooks, Lawrence Gray, Evelyn Brent, Osgood Perkins, Jack Egan, Marcia Harris, Edward Garvey, Vera Sisson, Joseph McClunn, Arthur Donaldson, Anita Page, Elise Cavanna, Dorothy Mathews. Brent was the "good girl" of the sisters, Mame, and the star of the picture, while Brooks was Janie. This flapper-era comedy was resurrected by video due to the latter-day fascination with Brooks.

- *"'This Miss Brooks is beginning to act,' said* Photoplay. *And it was true...Her performance in* Love 'Em and Leave 'Em *is an example of how little a 1926 film actress needed to know—and how much. 'Frank Tuttle was a master of easy, perfectly timed comedy which demanded that kind of acting rather than the wild, energetic style popular in Hollywood,' Louise later wrote...'An intelligent man, he never interfered with two classes of actors—great actors and nonactors. In the first class was Osgood Perkins, who needed no direction. In the second class was I, who, had he directed me to be funny, would have become an immobilized personality. Lawrence Gray belonged in the ham class. He required gobblets of comic appreciation to keep him functioning.'"* (Barry Paris, Louise Brooks)

The Saturday Night Kid (1929, Paramount, 62m/bw) ☆☆½ **Sc:** Lloyd Corrigan, Ethel Doherty, Edward E. Paramore, Jr. **D:** A. Edward Sutherland. **Cam:** Harry Fishbeck. **Cast:** Clara Bow, James Hall, Jean Arthur, Charles Sellon, Jean Harlow, Ethel Wales, Edna May Oliver, Frank Ross, Irving Bacon, Hyman Meyer, Eddie Dunn, Leone Lane, Getty Bird, Alica Adair, Mary Gordon. Bow and Arthur played the sisters—both in love with co-worker Hall, who lives in their rooming house. This pleasant and contrived comedy—which turns on Arthur trying to implicate Bow in stealing the store's welfare fund to bet on a horse—is interesting in retrospect for the actresses, including Harlow in a small part and particularly Arthur in a corrupt and sleazy role.

- *"...commonplace...were it not for Jean Arthur, who plays the catty sister with a great deal of skill...a thoroughly believable and natural portrayal, in contrast with her sister's, whose every other scene is shot through with heavy dramatics and thick sentiment."* (Mordaunt Hall, The New York Times)

Night Parade (1929, RKO, 72m/bw) ☆½ **Sc:** James Gruen, George O'Hara. **D:** Malcolm St. Clair. **P:** William LeBaron. **Cam:** William Marshall. **Cast:** Hugh Trevor, Lloyd Ingraham, Dorothy Gulliver, Eileen Pringle, Robert Ellis, Lee Shumway, Ann Pennington, Charles Sullivan, Walter Kane, Marie Astaire, James Dugan, Barney Furey, Nate Slott. Abbott's 1928 play *Ringside*, written with Edward Paramore, Gene Buck, and Hyatt Daab, is about a femme fatale in cahoots with racketeers, who uses her wiles to lead middleweight prizefighter Bobby Murray into throwing a bout. It starred Richard Taber, Harriett MacGibbon, and Brian Donlevy on Broadway, and the film was entitled *Sporting Life* in Great Britain.

- *"A familiar trip to the battleground of boxing...The mouldy tale...was not helped by James Gruen and George O'Hara's punch-drunk screenplay, Malcolm St. Clair's sluggish direction, or the notably dismal performances of Ingraham, Pringle and Ellis."* (Richard B. Jewell and Vernon Harbin, The RKO Story)

On Your Toes (1939, Warner Bros., 94m/bw) ☆☆½ **Sc:** Jerry Wald, Richard Macaulay. **D:** Ray Enright. **P:** Robert Lord. **Cam:** James Wong

Howe. **Cast:** Vera Zorina, Eddie Albert, Alan Hale, Frank McHugh, James Gleason, Donald O'Connor, Gloria Dickson. Abbott's 1936 play, which featured Tyrone Kearney and Tamara Geva, was enriched with the music and lyrics of Richard Rodgers and Lornez Hart. It concerns the youngest of the dancing Dolans, who grows up to become a music teacher while secretly wanting to uphold the family dancing tradition. When his student submits a ballet, he meets an earthy ballerina and steps into the vacated lead role to save the show.

- *"Warners lost interest in musicals and bought only one,* Naughty But Nice *(1939) in the period 1939–42. They bought* On Your Toes *(1939), and tossed out the superb Rodgers and Hart score with the exception of 'Slaughter on Tenth Avenue' and its hit tune, 'There's a Small Hotel,' the latter heard only in the background. The result, as directed by Enright, is an odd comedy about a hoofer (Albert) caught up with the exponents of Russian ballet."* (David Shipman, The Story of Cinema)

The Pajama Game (1957, Warner Bros., 101m/c, **VHS/DVD**) ☆☆☆☆½ **Sc:** George Abbott, Richard Bissell. **D:** Stanley Donen. **P:** George Abbott. **Cam:** Harry Stradling. **Cast:** Doris Day, John Raitt, Eddie Foy, Jr., Carol Haney, Reta Shaw, Barbara Nichols, Jack Straw, Ralph Dunn, Thelma Pelish, Owen Martin, Buzz Miller, Jack Waldron. Choreographed by Bob Fosse. The 1954 stage musical, about labor unrest at a pajama factory in Iowa, was one of the smash hits of the 1950s, opening in 1954 at Broadway's Schubert Theatre and running for 1,063 performances, with Janis Paige and John Raitt as the leads and support from Eddie Foy, Jr., Carol Haney, and a young dancer named Shirley MacLaine. Most of the cast was retained for the film, with Day replacing Paige for box-office clout. The songs include "Steam Heat," "There Once Was a Man," and "Once-a-Year Day."

- *"…a wholly cinematic and successful version…All the fun, songs, dances and laughs of the hit Broadway musical were brought to the screen with the added attraction of Bob Fosse's choreography. The key to its success, however, was in the choice of the stars…John Raitt…and…Doris Day…"* (Thomas G. Aylesworth, History of Movie Musicals)
- *"…Warners…brought George Abbott from Broadway to restage* The Pajama Game *(1957) and* Damn Yankees *(1958)…These are the best records we have of Broadway shows, since in spite of a mobile camera and much reshaping, often for the open air, their origins shine through, especially in the musical numbers. The effect is frequently exhilarating, and credit must be shared with Bob Fosse, reworking his Broadway choreography…Both books were based on the premise, then current, that the most suitable subject for a musical was the least likely…"* (David Shipman, The Story of Cinema)

Those We Love (1932, KBS/World Wide, 76m/bw) ☆☆☆ **Sc:** F. Hugh Herbert. **D:** Robert Florey. **Cam:** Arthur Edeson. **Cast:** Mary Astor, Kenneth MacKenna, Lilyan Tashman, Hale Hamilton, Tommy Conlon, Earle Foxe, Forrester Harvey, Virginia Sale, Pat O'Malley, Harvey Clark, Cecil Cunningham, Edwin Maxwell. The 1930 play by Abbott and S.K. Lauren concerns a straying husband who is found out by his 13-year-old son, then struggles to regain the boy's respect. Astor played the wife and Tashman the homewrecker.

- *"Although Astor still condemns Tashman, the viewer's reaction is one of understanding, if hardly moral acquittal. This sympathetic treatment of a woman who victimizes others as she has been herself victimized adds an extra level of depth and complexity to the characters and emotional drama...while following the general expectations of the genre, the picture offers a few original touches (along with some satiric injections of humor) that maintain interest throughout and allow for more universal audience appeal."* (*Brian Taves*, Robert Florey: The French Expressionist)

Three Men on a Horse was written by Abbott with John Cecil Holm and staged by Abbott at New York's Playhouse Theatre in 1935. It concerns a Brooklyn milquetoast who interests racketeers when they learn that he always predicts winners at the track. William Lynn starred with Millard Mitchell, Shirley Booth, Garson Kanin, and Sam Levene.

Three Men on a Horse (1936, Warner Bros., 85m/bw, **VHS**) ☆☆☆½ **Sc:** Laird Doyle. **D:** Mervyn Le Roy. **P:** Sam Bischoff. **Cam:** Sol Polito. **Cast:** Frank McHugh, Sam Levene, Joan Blondell, Guy Kibbee, Carol Hughes, Teddy Hart, Allen Jenkins, Edgar Kennedy, Eddie Anderson, Harry Davenport. A lot of wisecracks are dispensed out of the sides of mouths in this snappy bit of nonsense, with plum roles for the principal cast, particularly Blondell, Jenkins and Levene.

- *"Frank McHugh played the clairvoyant-handicapping-poet...Sam Levene reprised his stage role as Patsy in the film and Teddy Hart was imported from Broadway to repeat his performance as Frankie...a fast-paced, scrambling entry in which Teddy Hart practically won the race for laughs."* (*William Torbert Leonard*, Theatre: Stage to Screen to Television)

- *"...a likable farce...Mervyn LeRoy directed this amiable nonsense amiably...There were lots of funny scenes, which produced lots of action at the box office."* (Variety)

Three Men on a Horse (1957, CBS, 90m/bw) *Playhouse 90* ☆☆☆ **Tp:** J.W. Russell. **D:** Arthur Hiller. **P:** Martin Manulis. **Cast:** Johnny Carson, Frank McHugh, Jack Carson, Carol Channing, Edward

Everett Horton, Arnold Stang, Mona Freeman, Jane Darwell, Allen Jenkins, Larry Blyden. Rarely was such a distinctive and flavorful supporting cast rounded up for a mid-1950s Broadway comedy. But Johnny Carson, one of the great TV personalities (who preferred to call himself a humorist and not a comic), was never that successful at playing others. McHugh, who played Erwin in the 1936 version, played a racketeer in this one.

- *"There were enough pros in this production of the old stage howler to practically insure its success on TV, but it all came perilously close to naught because the main character was a misfit in the role...the miscasting of Johnny Carson as Erwin, the greeting card verifier, who had a 'system' of picking winners while riding to and from work. The whimsical quality, the fey aura of the daffy poet could not be developed by Carson through no fault of his...he's no Wally Cox...Apart from this debit, the play had its hilarious moments propelled with Runyonesque flavor..."* (Variety)

- *"...played and saved by an impressive cast of farceurs..."* (William Torbert Leonard, Theatre: Stage to Screen to Television)

Three Men on a Horse was also seen in 1952 on *Broadway Television Theatre*, with Orson Bean as the poet/prognosticator, Ann Thomas, and Mervyn Vye.

Where's Charley? (1952, Warner Bros., 97m/c) ☆☆☆ **Sc:** John Monks, Jr. **D:** David Butler. **P:** Ernest Martin, Cy Feuer. **Cam:** Erwin Hillier. **Cast:** Ray Bolger, Robert Shackleton, Allyn (Ann) McLerie, Mary Germaine, Margaretta Scott, Horace Cooper, Howard Marion, Henry Hewitt, H.G. Stoker, Martin Miller. Coreographed by Michael Kidd and shot in Great Britain, this great stage success for Bolger featured him — at age 48 — as a student at Oxford University. Abbott and Frank Loesser based their 1948 musical on the 1893 comic play, *Charley's Aunt*, which had been filmed under the same title in versions that starred Sydney Chaplin in 1925, Charlie Ruggles in 1930, and Jack Benny in 1941, and as *Charley's Big Hearted Aunt* (1940) with Arthur Askey. In Victorian England, two college roommates are in love the same girl, and, as mixups ensue, Bolger's Charley dresses up as his aunt to save the day. Among "drag" performances, Bolger's is outstanding, if a bit lost due to the picture's obscurity because of slipshod production values. The songs include "Once in Love with Amy," "Make a Miracle," and "My Darling, My Darling."

- *"The picture itself is not that good. The sets are cheesy, the dialogue often creaky and the chorus ordinary. What makes the experience extraordinary is the incredible performance by Bolger..."* (S.R. Ross, J.P. Nash, The Motion Picture Guide)

Zoe Akins

Born: October 30, 1886, Humansville, MO. **Died:** 1958.
Pulitzer Prize-winning play: *The Old Maid* (1935)

Zoe Akins came to New York to write plays for the Washington Square Players and had her first stage successes with *Declassee* in 1919 and *Daddy's Gone A-Hunting* in 1921. Akins's plays include *The Varying Shore* (1921), *Greatness* (1923), and the smash hit *The Greeks Had a Word for It* (1930). Akins wrote or contributed to the screenplays for *Ladies Love Brutes* (1930), *Once a Lady* (1931), *Working Girls* (1931), *Christopher Strong* (1933), *Accused* (1936), *Camille* (1937), *Zaza* (1939), and *Desire Me* (1947). An original she wrote for TV was *The Koshetz Story* in 1957 (for the anthology series *Telephone Time*) with Nina and Marina Koshetz as themselves. *Bitter Waters* was Akins's adaptation of the Henry James short story "Louis Pallant," which aired on *Screen Directors' Playhouse* in 1956, with George Sanders and Constance Cummings.

Daddy's Gone A-Hunting (1925, MGM, bw/silent) ☆☆ **Sc:** Kenneth B. Clarke. **D/P:** Frank Borzage. **Cam:** Chester A. Lyons. **Cast:** Percy Marmont, Holmes Herbert, James O. Barrows, Ford Sterling, Edythe Chapman, Charles Crockett, Helena D'Argy, Alice Joyce, Virginia Marshall. The 1921 Arthur Hopkins production staged at New York's Plymouth Theatre starred Frank Conroy and Marjorie Rambeau. The play is about Julien Fields's return to his American family from studies in Paris. He is a decidedly changed man who wants to be free of familial obligations—even after the death of his daughter.

- "*The primary stages of the film version of Zoe Akins's play...are thoughtfully directed, with the action pictured from interesting angles. Unfortunately, this good work does not atone for the weakness of the story as it appears on the screen.*" (The New York Times)

Declassee concerns Lady Haden, who's in love with Ned Thayer. When Ned is accused of cheating at cards, Lady Haden sells her jewelry and heads to the United States to wait for him, where a new suitor seeks her hand. This 1919 hit at New York's Empire Theatre starred Ethel Barrymore, with Vernon Steel, Harry Plimmer, and Clare Eames.

Declassee (1925, First National, bw/silent) ☆☆½ **Sc:** Bradley King, Charles E. Whittaker. **D:** Robert G. Vignola. **P:** Corinne Griffith. **Cam:** Tony Gaudio. **Cast:** Lloyd Hughes, Corinne Griffith, Clive Brook, Rockliffe Fellowes, Lilyan Tashman, Hedda Hopper, Bertram Johns, Gale Henry, Louise Fazenda, Eddie Lyons, Mario Carillo, Clark Gable, Paul Weigel.

- "Corinne Griffith's radiant beauty, enhanced by bewitching gowns and sparkling head-dress, is apt to make one quite charitable when gazing upon some of the banal sequences and cumbersome captions in the picturization of Zoe Akins's brilliant play...While the film does not approach the artistic stage production, it is nevertheless an entertaining effort, which might have been infinitely more worthy if the producers had not pandered to what they believe is provincial popular taste." (Mordaunt Hall, The New York Times)

Her Private Life (1929, Warner Bros., bw/silent) **Sc:** Forrest Halsey. **D:** Alexander Korda **Cast:** Billie Dove, Walter Pidgeon, Holmes Herbert, Montagu Love, Thelma Todd, Roland Young, Mary Forbes, Brandon Hurst, ZaSu Pitts.

The Furies (1930, First National, 69m/bw) ☆½ **Sc:** Forrest Halsey. **D:** Alan Crosland. **Cam:** Robert Kurrle. **Cast:** Lois Wilson, H.B. Warner, Theodore Von Eltz, Natalie Moorhead, Jane Winton, Tyler Brooke, Alan Birmingham, Purnell Pratt, Byron Sage, Ben Hendricks, Jr., Carl Stockdale. The play debuted in 1928 with a cast featuring Alan Campbell, Laurette Taylor, and Estelle Winwood. This flimsy parlor murder investigation seems almost like a send-up of such schematic plays.

- "Who murdered Wilson's husband? The answer is somewhere in the continual stream of entrances and exits this unexciting adaptation of a stage play brings forth. The only entertainment is provided by the district attorney's investigation that produces a lot of laughs when it is discovered that the lawyer for Mrs. Wilson has coached the servants to fib, and her son discovers the ruse." (J.P. Nash and S.R. Ross, The Motion Picture Guide)

The Greeks Had a Word for It was Akins's major Broadway smash, a 1930 play about three golddiggers living it up on Broadway—a favorite theme ever since Avery Hopwood's earlier The Gold Diggers. The trio was played by Dorothy Hall, Verree Teasdale, and Murial Kirkland in a production staged by William H. Harris, Jr. at the Sam H. Harris Theatre.

The Greeks Had a Word for Them (1932, UA, 77m/bw, **VHS**) ☆☆☆ **Sc:** Sidney Howard. **D:** Lowell Sherman. **P:** Samuel Goldwyn. **Cam:** George Barnes. **Cast:** Joan Blondell, Madge Evans, Ina Claire, David Manners, Lowell Sherman, Betty Grable, Phillips Smalley. This film, which was a big hit for the wisecrack-friendly Blondell and Broadway legend Claire, is also known as Three Broadway Girls on VHS.

- "An enormously likable sophisticated comedy...This was one of the few movies in which [Claire] was able to show some of the tricky high style that made her the most fashionable stage comedienne of her time." (Pauline Kael, 5001 Nights at the Movies)

Three Blind Mice (1938, 20th Century-Fox, 75m/bw) **Sc:** Brown Holmes, Lynn Starling. **D:** William A. Seiter. **P:** Raymond Griffith,

Darryl Zanuck. **Cam:** Ernest Palmer. **Cast:** Loretta Young, Joel McCrea, David Niven, Stuart Erwin, Marjorie Weaver, Pauline Moore, Binnie Barnes, Jane Darwell, Leonid Kinsky. A remake, with the trio going from Kansas to New York City looking for well-heeled husbands.

Three Little Girls in Blue (1946, 20th Century-Fox, 100m/bw) **Sc:** Valentine Davies. **D:** H. Bruce Humberstone. **P:** Mack Gordon. **Cam:** Ernest Palmer. **Cast:** June Haver, George Montgomery, Vivian Blaine, Celeste Holm, Vera-Ellen, Frank Latimore, Charles Smith, Charles Halton.

How to Marry a Millionaire (1953, 20th Century-Fox, 96m/c, **VHS/DVD**) ☆☆☆½ **Sc/P:** Nunnally Johnson. **D:** Jean Negulesco. **Cam:** Joe MacDonald. **Cast:** Lauren Bacall, Marilyn Monroe, Betty Grable, William Powell, Cameron Mitchell, Rory Calhoun, David Wayne, Alex D'Arcy, Fred Clark. The trio of stars band together to magnetize millionaires, pooling their resources, so to speak, to share and overlook the man each one attracts. A thoroughly posh 1950s artifact, with Powell in good form as a tycoon who hooks Bacall, then dumps her.

- *"The script draws for partial source material on two plays, Zoe Akins's* The Greeks Had a Word for It *and* Loco *by Dale Eunson and Katherine Albert. Nunnally Johnson has blended the legiter ingredients with his own material for snappy comedy effect...as the predatory sex game unfolds, the chuckles are constant...Certain for audience favor is Monroe's blonde with astigmatism who goes through life bumping into things, including men, because she thinks glasses would detract."* (Variety)

Ladies Love Brutes (1930, Paramount, 83m/bw) ☆☆ **Sc:** Waldemar Young, Herman J. Mankiewicz. **D:** Rowland V. Lee. **Cam:** Harry Fischbeck. **Cast:** George Bancroft, Mary Astor, Fredric March, Margaret Quimby, Stanley Fields. This film was based on Akins's play, *Pardon My Glove.*

- *"Zoe Akins's play written down to a presumptive neighborhood fan grade of taste, and what it might have held as a class screen production discounted. Result is just pretty good program material...Picture has many slow spots where story progress lags badly; comedy incidents have been inexpertly written in...What the title has to do with the story is another puzzle. This particular lady didn't love this particular brute anyway, but that's the least of this poorly translated stage play."* (Variety)

Mrs. January and Mr. X, Akins's 1944 play, which starred Barbara Bel Geddes and Frank Craven, was produced on TV in 1950 on *The Pulitzer Prize Playhouse*, with Penny Singleton and Melvyn Douglas.

O Evening Star, Akins's 1936 flop featuring Grace Fox and Frank Conroy, was given a TV revival in 1952 on *Robert Montgomery Presents* with a cast headed by Fay Bainter and Robert H. Harris.

The Old Maid was adapted from Edith Wharton's novel about a woman widowed by the Civil War who allows her cousin to raise her illegitimate daughter, igniting a lifelong rivalry for affections. The play ran for 305 performances on Broadway in 1935, and starred Judith Anderson, Helen Menken, and future film director John Cromwell.

The Old Maid (1939, Warner Bros., 95m/bw, **VHS**) ☆☆☆½ **Sc:** Casey Robinson. **D:** Edmund Goulding. **P:** Henry Blanke. **Cam:** Tony Gaudio. **Cast:** Bette Davis, Miriam Hopkins, George Brent, Jane Bryan, Donald Crisp, Henry Stephenson, Louise Fazenda, Jerome Cowan, William Lundigan, Rand Brooks, Cecilia Loftus, Janet Shaw, Rod Cameron, Doris Lloyd, William Hopper, Marlene Burnett. The rivalry between the leads played by Davis and Hopkins extended to their offstage selves as well, no doubt fueling the superb performances of both actresses.

- *"It is better than average and sticks heroically to its problem, foresaking all delights and filling a whole laundry bag with wet and twisted handkerchiefs."* (*Otis Ferguson*, The New Republic)

- *"For a bad play it makes a surprisingly good drama; or, if you feel that way about it, for a good play, it fits surpringly well on the screen."* (*Frank S. Nugent*, The New York Times)

The Old Maid was twice made for TV: in 1954 on ABC's *Kraft Television Theatre* with Nancy Marchand, Jayne Meadows, Eva Marie Saint, Bill Lundmark, and Addison Richards, and again in 1956 on NBC's *Matinee Theatre* with Sarah Churchill.

Edward Albee

Edward Franklin Albee
Born: March 12, 1928, Washington, DC.
Pulitzer Prize-winning play: *A Delicate Balance* (1967)
Tony Award-winning play: *Who's Afraid of Virginia Woolf?* (1963)
New York Drama Critics Circle's Best Play: *Who's Afraid of Virginia Woolf?*

All Over (1976, PBS, 66m/c, **VHS**) *Theatre in America.* ☆☆☆☆ **Tp/Commentary:** Edward Albee. **D:** John Desmond, John Edwards, Paul Weidner. **P:** Jac Venza, Phyllis Geller. **Cast:** Myra Carter, William Prince, Anne Shropshire, Anne Lynn, Pirie MacDonald, David O. Peterson, Margaret Thomson. A famous man is dying in his elegant sitting room as reporters wait downstairs. The medicos attend to him while his wife squabbles with her children, his mistress, and his lawyer. This

Hartford Stage Company production in Connecticut was also later broadcast by PBS under that network's *Great Performances* umbrella.

- "*...a superb production of a flawed but intriguing play...The violence, a commodity that Mr. Albee handles with astonishing skill, is removed to the interior, to the quiet fluctuations of words and phrases...The conception is fascinating, and Mr. Albee's execution commands serious attention. But the play's weaknesses are gradually apparent. Mr. Albee has been widely praised for his precise and poetic use of language, for his almost musical construction of words. In All Over, however, the language often becomes not precise but self-conscious.*" (John J. O'Connor, The New York Times)

The Ballad of the Sad Cafe (1991, Merchant Ivory, 110m/c, **VHS**) ☆☆½ **Sc:** Michael Hirst. **D:** Simon Callow. **P:** Ismail Merchant. **Cam:** Walter Lassally. **Cast:** Vanessa Redgrave, Keith Carradine, Cork Hubbert, Rod Steiger, Austin Pendleton, Beth Dixon, Anne Pitoniak, Lanny Flaherty, Mert Hatfield, Earl Hindman. Carson McCullers's novel about a tiny rural Southern hamlet is dominated by Miss Amelia, a tall, tomboyish, laconic figure who still has the best healing herbs and makes the best moonshine around. She receives a visit from two mysterious figures—a dwarf who claims kinship with her, and Marvin Macy, her husband of 10 days, years ago. The latter hopes for a reckoning with Miss Amelia, which results in a bare-knuckles fistfight. Quirky Southern Gothic in capital letters in the slow, deliberate Merchant-Ivory style. Michael Dunn and Colleen Dewhurst starred on Broadway in 1963.

- "*...comes wrapped in cultural glory...McCullers...Albee, and yet it persists in sounding like a sketch for* Saturday Night Live*...I suppose there was once a time when* The Ballad of the Sad Cafe *was thought to contain truths about life as lived. I can no longer relate to it that way. It now plays more like a prose opera, in which jealousy and passion inflame the characters, who are trapped in the sins of the past. To see the movie for its story is an exercise in futility. But it works well as gesture and flamboyance, a stage for outsize tragic figures.*" (Roger Ebert, Chicago Sun-Times)

A Delicate Balance (1973, American Film Theater, 132m/c) ☆☆ **Sc:** Edward Albee. **D:** Tony Richardson. **P:** Ely Landau. **Cam:** David Watkin. **Cast:** Katharine Hepburn, Paul Scofield, Lee Remick, Joseph Cotten, Kate Reid, Betsy Blair. The excellent cast is the best reason to take in this adaptation of Albee's Pulitzer Prize winner about the neurotic mother of an alcoholic daughter, and a neighboring couple that barges in for an extended stay. It's all tense talk with little payoff in spite of its pedigree as one of Landau's prestige pieces for his financially unsuccessful AFT, a series of movies adapted from plays.

- "*...the film was one of the least successful of the American Film Theatre productions. An oppressive series of close-ups, it has enough verbiage to* *sink three or four movies. All the actors look ill at ease, especially Kate, who opens and closes the film with the same speech, a high-flown tongue-twister that is nearly (in both senses of the word) unspeakable."* (Gary Carey, Katharine Hepburn: A Biography)

Who's Afraid of Virginia Woolf? (1966, Warner Bros., 129m/bw, **VHS/DVD**) ☆☆☆☆☆ **Sc/P:** Ernest Lehman. **D:** Mike Nichols. **Cam:** Haskell Wexler. **Cast:** Elizabeth Taylor, Richard Burton, George Segal, Sandy Dennis. Older and younger college professors and their wives have drinks and dinner amid impromptu and full-throttle spillings of their emotions in this benchmark in both the theatre and films. The acidic dialogue was preserved by Lehman and Nichols in this masterpiece, with Burton delivering his greatest performance as the seemingly mousy George, brought to a roaring, sardonic pitch by booze and resentment. The film won Oscars for Best Actress (Taylor), Supporting Actress (Dennis), Cinematography, Art Direction/Set Decoration and Costume Design, and was nominated for Best Picture, Actor (Burton), Supporting Actor (Segal), Director, Screenplay, Sound, Score (Alex North), and Film Editing.

- *"...a film of landmark significance. Today, its language — 'God damn you' and 'hump the hostess' — fails to have shock value...But in July 1966 it was shocking. More than the language, the film's vision of marriage...was startling. Before this, no movie had ever shown anything quite like the destructive frenzy of George and Martha, each tearing the other apart, screaming and taunting and drinking and embroiling a younger couple (who had problems of their own) as pawns in their wars of emotional attrition...unprecedented acting out of rage, frustration and degradation, a trip to the lower depths of the soul. It was all that...the beginning of a different era in American movies..."* (Charles Champlin, The Movies Grow Up 1940–1980)

- *"Richard Burton gave a good performance; Elizabeth Taylor was monotonously shrill; Sandy Dennis was excruciatingly mannered; George Segal was excessively bland. The film seemed to preen itself on its honesty."* (Andrew Sarris, The American Cinema: Directors and Directions 1929–1968)

- *"One of the most scathingly honest American films ever made."* (Stanley Kauffmann, The New Republic)

William Alfred

Born: August 16, 1922, Brooklyn, NY. **Died:** 1999.

William Alfred was a longtime professor at Harvard University who achieved his greatest recognition for *Hogan's Goat*, a play in blank verse about the bitter political maneuvering among Irish-Americans in Brooklyn in the late 19th century. It was a surprise success Off Broadway in 1965 at the American Place Theater, where critics acclaimed it, audiences flocked for 607 performances, and Faye Dunaway was first noticed. She returned to Alfred's subsequent Irish-American play, *The Curse of an Aching Heart*, in 1982. He collaborated with Albert Marre on *Cry for Us All*, a musical version of *Hogan's Goat*. Among Alfred's students were Tommy Lee Jones, Stockard Channing, and John Lithgow.

Hogan's Goat (1971, PBS, 117m/c, **VHS**) ☆☆☆½ *Theatre in America: Special of the Week* **Tp:** William Alfred. **D:** Glenn Jordan. **P:** Glenn Jordan, Jac Venza. **Cast:** Robert Foxworth, Faye Dunaway, George Rose, Philip Bosco, Rue McClanahan, Margaret Linn, Kevin Conway. This presentation was reprised in 1974 for PBS's *Theatre in America*. In 1890, an Irish immigrant's political loyalty puts him in line to be the Mayor of Brooklyn, while his wife's convent upbringing and her sensual side battle for control within her. Meanwhile, his drive for power puts him at odds with the women in his life and the Catholic Church. Dunaway originated the role of Kathleen Stanton Off Broadway in 1965, and it led to her casting in *Bonnie and Clyde* (1967).

- "*Beautifully mounted and painstakingly acted by a distinguished cast...nevertheless a rather tiresome two hours of heavy-handed melodrama...What was missing was a contemporary application that the viewer could apply to the humorless developments...Foxworth's hero was gradually turning into a sanctimonious young fool. Rose's mayor was a deep-eyed villain with kinship to the old gaslight era's rapscallions—and all along the the line the black and white virtues were laid on with a trowel, curiously couched in that delightfully delicate Irish speech. Alfred's obviously planted harbingers of future plot development were dropped on the viewer in unsubtle ways...*" (Variety)

Jay Presson Allen
Jacqueline Presson
Born: March 3, 1922, Fort Worth, TX.

Jay Presson Allen was nominated twice for screenwriting Oscars, for Bob Fosse's *Cabaret* (1972, as Jay Allen) and Sidney Lumet's *Prince of the City* (1981). Her first screenplay was for Alfred Hitchcock's psychological study, *Marnie* (1964). She collaborated with Lumet on two more films by adapting her own Hollywood novel, *Just Tell Me What You Want* (1980), and Ira Levin's play *Deathtrap* (1982). She followed up the success of *The Prime of Miss Jean Brodie* (1969) with an adaptation of Graham Greene's novel *Travels With My Aunt* (1972), for Maggie Smith and director George Cukor. Other screenplays include *Funny Lady* (1975) with Barbra Streisand, the remake of *The Lord of the Flies* (1990), John Frankenheimer's *Year of the Gun* (1991), and *Copycat* (1995) with Holly Hunter and Sigourney Weaver.

Allen's TV work includes adapting *The Borrowers*, Mary Norton's novel about small people living under a family's stairs, into a 1973 installment of *The Hallmark Hall of Fame*, and creating the long-running 1970s ABC series *Family*. Allen is married to eclectic producer Lewis M. Allen, whose films include the original *Lord of the Flies* (1963), Francois Truffaut's *Farenheit 451* (1966), *Fortune and Men's Eyes* (1971), *Never Cry Wolf* (1983), Horton Foote's *1918* (1985), and Spalding Gray's *Swimming to Cambodia* (1987). She had great Broadway success writing and directing the one-man show, *Tru* (1990), which starred Robert Morse in a Tony Award-winning performance as Truman Capote.

The Big Love was filmed in 1994 and shown on HBO. It was a one-woman show by Tracey Ullman, written for the stage by Brooke Allen and her mother, Jay Presson Allen, who directed. Ullman played Florence Aadland, who co-authored the book on which the play is based with Tedd Thomey. Jay Allen directed the 1991 play, which ran for 41 performances at the Plymouth Theatre. Flo Aadland was the mother of Beverly Aadland, who, at 15, had an affair with Errol Flynn. Flo's account of the affair was published in book form in 1961, then re-issued in the 1990s as a camp classic with an introduction by William Styron. Ullman is superb as both Flo and Bev.

Forty Carats (1973, Columbia, 110m/c, **VHS**) ☆☆ **Sc:** Leonard Gershe. **D:** Milton Katselas. **P:** M.J. Frankovich. **Cam:** Charles B. Lang, Jr. **Cast:** Liv Ullmann, Edward Albert, Gene Kelly, Binnie Barnes, Deborah Raffin, Nancy Walker, Rosemary Murphy, Billy Green Bush, Natalie Schaefer, Don Porter. Allen based her 1968 Broadway hit on the successful Parisian stage play by Pierre Barillet and Jean-Pierre Gredy. A 40-year-old divorcée on a Greek vacation has a fling with a 22-year-old man, returns to New York and finds that he has taken up with her daughter, but still has designs on her. Awkward casting took some of the luster off this sophisticated tussle of the sexes.

- *"The sort of strained,wisecracking frivolity that can be a hit on Broadway but all too often congeals on the screen…meant to be romantic and slightly daring, but the miscast Ullmann doesn't have the dryness for comedy. She's much too touching and anxious for her superficial role, and she and the wet-lipped looking young Albert are a dismaying pair. At this point, Ullmann's English was heavily accented, and she articulates her colloquial lines with*

considerable difficulty. You sympathize with her instead of laughing."
(*Pauline Kael*, 5001 Nights at the Movies)

The Prime of Miss Jean Brodie (1969, 20th Century-Fox, 116m/c, **VHS**) ☆☆☆☆ **Sc:** Jay Presson Allen. **D:** Ronald Neame. **P:** Robert Fryer. **Cam:** Ted Moore. **Cast:** Maggie Smith, Robert Stephens, Pamela Franklin, Celia Johnson, Gordon Jackson, Jane Carr. Allen adapted Muriel Spark's 1961 short novel into the 1968 play at New York's Helen Hayes Theatre. The play starred Zoe Caldwell and featured support from Catharine Burns and Amy Taubin. Vanessa Redgrave originated the role on the London stage. Allen adapted the period piece into this film, which won Smith the Oscar for Best Actress for the role of the titular Edinburgh teacher, who seeks to inspire her girls instead of instructing them. In 1979, Allen was credited as the story consultant for a six-part Scottish Television miniseries called *The Prime of Miss Jean Brodie*, which starred Geraldine McEwan. The presentation was written by others and shown on PBS in America.

• *"The elitist Edinburgh schoolteacher, talking of the life force but actually frigid and authoritarian, is a meal of a part based on the theatrical division of unhappy woman and actress relishing flamboyance. In fact, the part is more touching than she made it; sheer comic technique made Smith's Brodie seem a calculating phony, whereas she could be a true hysterical virgin."* (*David Thomson*, A Biographical Dictionary of Film)

• *"Maggie Smith, with her gift for mimicry and her talent for mannered comedy, makes Jean Brodie very funny—snobbish, full of affectations, and with a jumble shop of a mind. Miss Brodie is so entertaining that you can't accept it when the plot becomes melodramatic and you're asked to take her seriously as a dangerous influence."* (*Pauline Kael*, 5001 Nights at the Movies)

Wives and Lovers (1963, Paramount, 103m/bw) ☆☆½ **Sc:** Edward Anhalt. **D:** John Rich. **P:** Hal B. Wallis. **Cam:** Lucien Ballard. **Cast:** Van Johnson, Janet Leigh, Shelley Winters, Ray Walston, Martha Hyer, Jeremy Slate, In the adaptation of Allen's play, *The First Wife*, a suddenly successful author moves his family to Connecticut, where his wife can stand only so much upper-crust fraternizing.

• *"The old 'will success spoil marriage' theme is handled with a certain amount of flair...It's old hat, but stylishly refurbished by way of bright dialogue and spry performances. Miss Leigh's and Mr. Johnson's sincerity as the young couple, Ray Walston's efficiency as a manufacturer of antiques, and Shelley Winters's superb portrayal of a sardonic divorcee with subsurface warmth are among the pros that gloss over the cons."* (*Judith Crist*, Judith Crist's TV Guide to the Movies)

Woody Allen

Allen Stewart Konigsberg
Born: December 1, 1935, Brooklyn, NY.

At the beginning of his career, Allen was a stand-up comedian and a joke writer for others. He was also known as a prose humorist, particularly in *The New Yorker*, and eventually became a successful playwright. His two hit plays (below) now get lost in the discussions of the most Oscar-nominated screenwriter in history. *Deconstructing Harry* (1997) gave Allen his 13th nomination for Best Screenplay, besting former record holder Billy Wilder's even dozen (for writing only). Allen has been nominated for Oscars six times as a director. He won Oscars for writing and directing *Annie Hall* (1977), and also was nominated for Best Actor for that film for his performance as comedian Alvy Singer. An intensely private individual whose relationships with actresses Diane Keaton and (especially) Mia Farrow often became public fodder, Allen mined those relationships for his art. A completely New York-based filmmaker, he was the most successful former playwright to realize the cinema's power to relay his relationship-obsessed stories, and he found unparallelled success in that medium for a person who is manifestly a writer.

Don't Drink the Water opened on Broadway in 1966 at the Morosco Theater, produced by David Merrick and directed by Stanley Prager. Lou Jacobi starred as Walter, a Newark caterer who's vacationing with his family in a nation behind the Iron Curtain. They take refuge in the American embassy after officials believe he's taking illegal photos. Kay Medford and Anita Gillette also starred.

Don't Drink the Water (1969, Avco Embassy, 98m/c, **VHS**) ☆☆ **Sc:** R.S. Allen, Harvey Bullock. **D:** Howard Morris. **P:** Charles Joffe. **Cam:** Harvey Genkins. **Cast:** Jackie Gleason, Estelle Parsons, Ted Bessell, Joan Delaney, Richard Libertini, Michael Constantine, Avery Schreiber, Howard St. John, Danny Mehan, Pierre Olaf, Phil Leeds, Mark Gordon, Dwayne Early, Joan Murphy, Howard Morris, Martin Danzig. Libertini was the only cast member drafted from the Broadway original. Allen's agent, Joffe, sold the project and produced the movie. Allen once said that the bad reviews the film got never bothered him—but he did his own version for TV (below).

- "*Overall* Water *is a bland and mildly pleasant viewing experience, although the final third of the film does bog down thanks to a somewhat convoluted plot that has to get the Hollanders out of Vulgaria, but doesn't quite know how to go about it...Howard Morris's direction is very cartoonish...He uses many exaggerated close-ups, and directs the cast to play very broadly. The film deteriorates into a typical, lame, wacky 1960s comedy/chase/costume movie for the last 15 minutes." (Stephen J. Spignesi,* The Woody Allen Companion*)*

Don't Drink the Water (1994, ABC, 120m/c, **VHS**) ☆☆☆½ **Tp/D:** Woody Allen. **P:** Robert Greenhut. **Cast:** Woody Allen, Michael J. Fox, Mayim Bialek, Julie Kavner, Edward Herrmann, Rosemary Murphy, Josef Sommer, Dom DeLuise, Taina Elg, Austin Pendleton, Ed Herlihy, Robert Stanton, Ed Van Nuys, Skip Rose. In an effort to do his play his own way, Allen managed to gather TV funding and an attractive cast to give the old gag-filled chestnut another try.

• *"When seeking asylum, beware the inmates who run it. On this farcical premise, Woody Allen wrote his first play, the Cold War spoof* Don't Drink the Water, *in 1966. Now, as a treat for those who yearn for the old Woody, for the shameless gag-meister concerned with no greater purpose than piling on the laughs, he has remade this dated property into a giddy TV movie...It's no great shakes, more of a minor mirthquake. But with a charmingly hammy cast led by the Woodman himself in full neurotic rant,* Drink *is dandy refreshment, a welcome respite from the TV-movie mill of fact-based yawners and soggily sentimental holiday fables." (Matt Roush,* USA Today*)*

Play It Again, Sam (1972, Paramount, 85m/c, **VHS/DVD**) ☆☆☆½ **Sc:** Woody Allen. **D:** Herbert Ross. **P:** Arthur P. Jacobs. **Cam:** Owen Roizman. **Cast:** Woody Allen, Diane Keaton, Tony Roberts, Jerry Lacy, Susan Anspach, Jennifer Salt, Joy Bang, Viva, Suzanne Zenor, Diana Davila, Mari Fletcher, Michael Green, Ted Markland. In his second hit full-length play, a vehicle for himself, Allen played Allan Felix, a film critic whose wife leaves him. To revive his sex life, Allan tries to immitate the smooth moves of his screen idol, Humphrey Bogart, played in fantasy conversations by Lacy. But Felix's efforts backfire ludicrously. The film also featured Keaton, Roberts, and Lacy from the 1969 Broadway production. The play marked the beginning of Allen's relationship with Keaton.

• *"...a deeply satisfying adaptation. The most obvious change was caused by a film technicians' strike in New York—the setting is switched to San Francisco...Allen's screenplay also adds a few quips that show Felix responding with morbid gloom to the beauty of the seaside...'I don't tan. I stroke.'...This sensitive, adventurous adaptation is true to the original play even when it departs from it." (Maurice Yacowar,* Loser Take All: The Comic Art of Woody Allen*)*

• *"...slightly less mad than the usual Woody Allen comedy, maybe because* Play It Again, Sam *is based on Woody's Broadway play, and with a play it's a little hard to work in material like Howard Cosell play-by-play of an assassination in South America. Still, as comedies go, this is a very funny one...The notion of using a Bogart character is surprisingly successful. The Bogie imitation by Jerry Lacy is good, if not great...That and the movie's rather conventional Broadway plot structure give it more coherence than the previous Woody Allen films..."* (Roger Ebert, Chicago Sun-Times)

Maxwell Anderson

Born: December 15, 1888, Atlantic, PA. **Died:** 1959.
Pulitzer Prize-winning play: *Both Your Houses* (1933)
New York Drama Critics Circle Award, Best Play: *Winterset* (1935),
   High Tor (1937)

Anderson grew up the son of a railroad fireman who became a Baptist preacher. The family lived for periods of time in Andover, Ohio, and, in Pennsylvania at Richmond Center, Townville, Edinboro, McKeesport, New Brighton, and Harrisburg—then back to Ohio, followed by Iowa and North Dakota. Anderson attended graduate school at Stanford and taught high school in San Francisco and at Whittier College before moving to New York, where he was a writer and editor on *The New Republic, New York Evening Globe,* and *New York World.*

In 1924 *What Price Glory,* written in tandem with Laurence Stallings, began its run as one of the great stage hits of the 1920s. It captivated audiences with its antiwar theme and initiated the theme of male bonding in American popular entertainment. The play concerns the knockabout camaraderie between two U.S. Marines—Captain Flagg and Sergeant Quirt—who fight over the same girl in World War I-era France. Anderson then began working in other media—on screenplays in the 1920s, and teleplays when television became established in the 1950s.

The playwright's blank verse style confounded some screen adapters and his work was seen as arcane only a few years after it had been staged. His series of plays about European royalty—*Elizabeth the Queen, Mary of Scotland, Anne of the Thousand Days, Joan of Lorraine*—found ready audiences in all formats. One of Anderson's originals for TV was *The Trial of Ben Jonson* in 1952 on *Omnibus* starring June Lockhart and Alexander Scourby. He also wrote the libretto for a musical version of Charles Dickens's *A Christmas Carol,* scored by Bernard Herrmann in a 1954 production on *Shower of Stars,* with Fredric March and Basil Rathbone.

Among Anderson's plays that haven't been made into films or TV are *Gods of the Lightning, Both Your Houses, The Masque of Kings, The Feast of Ortolans, Candle in the Wind, Miracle of the Danube, Storm Operation,* and *Truckline Cafe.* His screenplays include those for Lewis Milestone's *All Quiet on the Western Front* (1930), *Rain* (1932), *Death Takes a Holiday* (1934), Howard Hawks's *We Live Again* (1934), *So Red the Rose*

(1935), and Alfred Hitchcock's *The Wrong Man* (1956). The James Cagney vehicle *Never Steal Anything Small* (1959) was based on Anderson's unproduced play *The Devil's Hornpipe*.

Anne of the Thousand Days told the story of Anne Boleyn's stormy relationship with King Henry VIII of England. The mother of Elizabeth I, the feisty and resilient Anne becomes a tiresome bore to the indulgent and corrupt monarch, so he makes himself the head of the Church of England, accuses her of adultery, and has her beheaded in 1536. The play was initially produced in 1948 and starred Rex Harrison and Lilli Palmer.

The Trial of Anne Boleyn (1952, CBS, 30m/bw) *Omnibus* ☆☆½ **Tp:** Maxwell Anderson. **D:** Alex Segal. **P:** Alan Anderson. **Host:** Alistair Cooke. **Cast:** Rex Harrison, Lilli Palmer. One of five segments on the debut installment of the prestigious series featured the married couple of Harrison and Palmer enacting the trial sequence from the play, which Harrison performed on Broadway for two years.

- *"Rex and Lilli...appeared together in the first show in the* Omnibus *series...short play written by Maxwell Anderson...derived from his play,* Anne of the Thousand Days. *Rex reprised his interpretation of Henry VIII, this time playing opposite Lilli as Anne Boleyn. On all fronts, whether it be film, stage or television work, Rex and Lilli were appearing almost exclusively as a team."* (Rex Harrison, The First Biography)

Anne of the Thousand Days (1969, Universal, 146m/c, **VHS**) ☆☆½ **Sc:** John Hale, Bridget Boland, Richard Sokolove. **D:** Charles Jarrott. **P:** Hal B. Wallis. **Cam:** Arthur Ibbetson. **Cast:** Richard Burton, Genevieve Bujold, Anthony Quayle, Irene Papas, John Colicos, Michael Hordern, Katharine Blake, Esmond Knight, Peter Jeffrey, Roland Squire, Nora Swinburne, Denis Quilley, T.P. McKenna, Gary Bond, Vernon Dobtcheff. This movie was greenlighted by Wallis after *The Lion in Winter* became such a hit the previous year. Though overlong, overdressed, and at a sluggish and stately pace, this passion pageant does attain levels of substance and charm in Bujold's best moments. The film won an Oscar for Costume Design and was nominated for Best Picture, Actor (Burton), Actress (Bujold), Supporting Actor (Quayle), Screenplay, Cinematography, Score (Georges Delerue), Art Direction/Set Decoration, and Sound.

- *"...turned by Charles Jarrott into a dull and pedestrian film, only partially redeemed by Genevieve Bujold's playing of the unhappy queen, and Richard Burton...the only Oscar it won was for the best costumes...cold comfort for over-inflated hopes and expectations."* (Jerzy Toeplitz, Hollywood and After: The Changing Face of Movies in America)

- *"...intelligent from line to line, but the emotions that are supplied seem hypothetical, and the conception lacks authority....The adapters sharpened*

Maxwell Anderson's play, and the dialogue is often much crisper than one anticipates, but the script has a structural weakness: It does not convince us that after all those years of waiting for Anne, the king would turn against her when she gives birth to a daughter. And at the end we're left with Maxwell Anderson's glowing, fatuous hindsight: a final shot of Anne's posthumous triumph — the baby Elizabeth wandering about, deserted, as her foolish father, who doesn't know what we know, goes off to beget a male heir." (Pauline Kael, 5001 Nights at the Movies)

The Bad Seed concerns a mother's gradual discovery that her eight-year-old daughter is a murderer who dispatched a classmate to steal a penmanship medal. The mother gradually decides to kill the child and commit suicide. A shocking piece for its take on the unfounded notion of hereditary evil, the 1954 Broadway play starred Nancy Kelly as the mother, Patty McCormick as the insidiously precious Rhoda, and Eileen Heckart.

The Bad Seed (1956, Warner Bros., 129m/bw, **VHS**) ☆☆☆ **Sc:** John Lee Mahin. **D/P:** Mervyn LeRoy. **Cam:** Harold Rosson. **Cast:** Nancy Kelly, Patty McCormick, Henry Jones, Eileen Heckert, Evelyn Varden, William Hopper, Paul Fix, Jesse White, Gage Clarke, Joan Croydon, Frank Cady. The film caused as much of a shockwave as the play, even with a Production Code-conscious ending (virtually the only difference in Mahin's adaptation from Anderson's original). After the murderess is struck by lightning, the filmmakers show her getting severely spanked. Anderson adapted the play from William March's novel. The high profile of the film brought the three principals of the stage version Oscar nominations, Kelly for Best Actress, McCormick and Heckart for Supporting Actress. Rosson also earned a nomination for Best Cinematography.

- *"For anyone interested in child-rearing, here is the ultimate cautionary tale: Maxwell Anderson's story of Rhoda, the sweet-faced eight-year-old with a way of creating fatal accidents for those who cross her. Mervyn LeRoy's film version of the stage hit has a B-movie-ish melodramatic side, but it remains enjoyable as a period piece. The happy family of the mid-1950s seems especially quaint, as does the discussion of psychiatry as the latest rage. Performances vary greatly in quality, but they're all oversized; Eileen Heckart has some particularly overblown drunk scenes. This kind of exaggeration is certainly more fun at home than it would be in a theater." (Janet Maslin, The New York Times, 1986)*

The Bad Seed (1985, ABC, 120m/c, **VHS**) ☆☆½ **Tp/P:** George Eckstein. **D:** Paul Wendkos. **Cast:** Blair Brown, Carrie Wells, Lynn Redgrave, David Carradine, Richard Kiley, David Ogden Stiers, Anne Haney, Weldon Bleiler, Carol Locatell, Chad Allen, Eve Smith. A starry TV cast was assembled for this remake, in which Wells played the eight-year-old murderess and Kiley played the gender-switched role of the parent whose son was drowned by the girl. The show won the Emmy Award for Best Photography (Ted Voightlander).

- *"This television remake…emerged as an equally frightening contemporary thriller…Richard Kiley (in a sex-switched part) had the role taken in both the play and the earlier film by Eileen Heckart as the parent of the schoolmate drowned by the 'angelic' young girl…"* (Alvin H. Marill, Movies Made for Television)

Barefoot in Athens (1966, NBC, 90m/c, **VHS**) *The Hallmark Hall of Fame* ☆☆☆½ **Tp:** Robert Hartung. **D/P:** George Schaefer. **Cast:** Peter Ustinov, Geraldine Page, Anthony Quayle, Salome Jens, Christopher Walken, Sheppard Strudwick, Eric Berry, Lloyd Bochner, John Heffernan. The play presents the erudite philosopher Socrates on trial after the Trojan War for his criticisms of the corrupt Athenian regime. Unkempt and put upon by his shrewish wife, he argues informally and at his trial that democratic justice should be upheld above all other virtues. The play debuted on Broadway in 1951 at the Martin Beck Theatre and starred Barry Jones as Socrates, with Lotte Lenya in support. Like the lofty themes evoked in many of Anderson's historical pageants, the advocacy of democracy needs mighty talents to put over the drama and whimsy. Here, Peter Ustinov delivered one of his most brilliant turns, combining a sort of contemporary take on sitcom husbands with the role and ideals of one of the great philosophers. He won the Emmy Award for Best Actor of the 1966–67 season.

- *"It had the feel of dramatic importance if not the content, which presumably is just the ticket for* Hallmark. *The cast was worthy of a more consequential show, though in isolated scenes Peter Ustinov, Geraldine Page and Anthony Quayle were responsible for some excellent television moments…But the climactic scene in court was only an intellectual exercise without an emotional lining, leading to the realization that there never had been any real involvement with the characters. And that exposed a shortcoming of the author that the players had till then successfully masked."* (Variety)

The Buccaneer, by Anderson and Laurence Stallings, played on Broadway in 1925 for only 20 performances and starred William Farnum. It aired in 1951 on ABC's *Pulitzer Prize Playhouse* with a cast headed by Brian Aherne and Nina Foch.

Elizabeth the Queen was first produced in 1930 by the Theatre Guild with Lynn Fontanne and Alfred Lunt as Elizabeth and the Lord Essex respectively. It studied the historically accurate affair between the 35-year-old Essex and Queen Elizabeth of England, who was 33 years his senior. She entertains his ardor; he fluctuates between lust and greed. Her loyalty to her nation wins out and she has him beheaded.

The Private Lives of Elizabeth and Essex (1939, Warner Bros., 106m/c, **VHS**) ☆☆☆ **Sc:** Norman Reilly Raine, Aeneas Mackenzie. **D:** Michael Curtiz. **Cam:** Sol Polito. **P:** Robert Lord. **Cast:** Bette Davis, Errol Flynn, Olivia DeHavilland, Vincent Price, Donald Crisp, Alan Hale, Nanette Fabares (Fabray), Leo G. Carroll, Henry Daniell, Henry Stephenson, Robert Warwick, John Sutton, Ralph Forbes, Doris Lloyd. Anderson's play afforded Warners another go at British historical pageantry via Technicolor—on the order of their great hit *The Adventures of Robin Hood* (1938). The film owes more to the Warners/Flynn tradition than to the source material, even though the swashbuckling is held to a minimum. Davis contributed a mighty performance as Queen Bess, a character she reprised in *The Virgin Queen* (1955).

• *"Bette Davis, well painted and dressed for the role of the shrewd old queen, looks the part and gives a magnetic, tough performance, but an impossible task was set for her, since as Essex, Errol Flynn couldn't come halfway to meet her. His talents were in other directions; the role was totally outside his range, and the poor man seemed to know it."* (Pauline Kael, 5001 Nights at the Movies)

• *"...[Flynn's] speeches rang with insincerity; his avowals of love are declaimed with all the conviction of a high school debater's support of the proposition that homework is ennobling...Still, the Maxwell Anderson dialogue is good to hear and the staging has been magnificent."* (Frank S. Nugent, The New York Times)

Elizabeth the Queen (1968, NBC, 90m/c) *The Hallmark Hall of Fame* ☆☆☆☆ **Tp:** John Edward Friend. **D/P:** George Schaefer. **Cast:** Judith Anderson, Charlton Heston, Alan Webb, Harry Townes, Michael Allinson, Anne Rogers, Dana Elcar, Frederick Worlock, Herbert Voland, Harvey Jason, Alan Caillou, Donald Marlatt, Peter Church. The show was impeccably and regally dressed with grand sets and costumes and the performers delivered inspired work. The show won the Emmy Award for Outstanding Dramatic Program of the 1967–68 season and Anderson was nominated for Best Actress.

• *"...requires an actor who can move between the subtleties of sexual lust and lust for power, and Charlton Heston carried off this portrayal [with] considerable depth. For Judith Anderson, it was another tour de force in a long skein...a virtuoso performance..."* (Variety)

• *"...a clumping bore, but I was amused by the way Judith Anderson played the title role, like some sort of monstrous cactus. Good support by Alan Webb and Charlton Heston and George Schaefer's customarily well organized and controlled direction helped take my mind off the sad fact that Maxwell Anderson's script is beginning to show wrinkles in its skin. But it was Dame Judith's night, and although she still looks like the Statue of Liberty, it was good to see her back at the old ax handle."* (Rex Reed, Big Screen, Little Screen)

The Eve of St. Mark concerns a stateside teenager worried about her country-boy sweetheart overseas in the service during World War II, and her efforts to remain true to him. First produced in 1942, the play included the boy's death. It featured Grover Burgess, Aline MacMahon, William Prince, and future film director Martin Ritt.

The Eve of St. Mark (1944, 20th Century-Fox, 95m/bw) ☆☆½ **Sc:** George Seaton. **D:** John M. Stahl. **Cam:** Joseph LaShelle. **Cast:** William Eythe, Anne Baxter, Michael O'Shea, Vincent Price, Ruth Nelson, Ray Collins, Stanley Prager, Dickie Moore, Henry Morgan. This sentimental film—which Seaton wrote with a happy ending—was one of several that established Baxter as the girl to come home to during the war years.

- "...smooth, careful, and full of decent intentions, it depresses me. It has a good deal of that flavor of corn syrup...The sufferings of wartime love and the difficulties of celibacy are conveyed in gentle glimmers by the drafted hero...and his sweetheart...but never frankly or painfully enough to trouble the audience." (James Agee, The Nation)

High Tor was first staged in New York's Martin Beck Theatre in 1937. The show was produced and directed by Guthrie McClintic and featured Burgess Meredith as Van Van Dorn, with Peggy Ashcroft and Hume Cronyn.

High Tor (1956, CBS, 90m/c) *Ford Star Jubilee* ☆½ **Tp:** Maxwell Anderson, John Monks, Jr. **D:** James Neilson. **P:** Arthur Schwartz. **Cast:** Bing Crosby, Julie Andrews, Nancy Olson, Everett Sloan, Hans Conried, Lloyd Corrigan, John Picaroll. This musical version features music by Arthur Schwartz and lyrics by Anderson. By this stage in his career, Crosby didn't know what to do about his fading popularity. His return to tried-and-true stage pieces that had worked previously—*High Society* and *Anything Goes*—failed at the movie box office, and this attempt at der-Bingle-bungled Anderson was woeful.

- "Bing Crosby badly miscast himself in undertaking a filmed musical version...embarassingly awkward and inept, a dismaying 'quickie' unworthy of the Old Groaner's time and talents...it was a case of a misplaced Bing. Mr. Crosby brought only his characteristically casual and experienced sophistication. It played havoc with the delicate spirit and meaning of the Anderson work. With Mr. Crosby emotionally aloof from the fantasy's pivotal character, the narrative, in turn, became only bewilderingly confused and cold." (Jack Gould, The New York Times)

- "Somewhere in the double translation—from stage to TV-pix terms and from dramatic to musical-comedy form, much of what made High Tor a B'way success seems to have got lost...essentially a listless exercise, with *rather undistinguished musical numbers and murky philosophizing, leavened only by the stingiest pinches of comedy. A strangely subdued Bing Crosby walks through his role with little conviction..."* (Variety)

High Tor was also produced in 1950 on *Philco Television Playhouse* in a version with Felicia Montealegre, Alfred Ryder, Vinton Hayworth, and Edgar Stehli.

Joan of Arc (1948, RKO, 145m/c, **VHS/DVD**) ☆☆☆ **Sc:** Maxwell Anderson, Andrew Solt. **D:** Victor Fleming. **Cam:** Joe Valentine. **P:** Walter Wanger. **Cast:** Ingrid Bergman, Jose Ferrer, George Coulouris, Ray Teal, Richard Derr, Roman Dohnen, Robert Barrat, Jimmie Lydon, Rand Brooks, Selena Royale, Francis Sullivan, Irene Rich, Hurd Hatfield, Nestor Paiva, Gene Lockhart, Ward Bond, Leif Erickson, John Ireland, J. Carroll Naish, Cecil Kellaway, Sheppard Strudwick, Morris Ankrum, Herbert Rudley, George Zucco, Houseley Stevenson, Alan Napier. This famously overproduced epic was based on Anderson's play, *Joan of Lorraine*, a tribute to Joan of Arc, the young French heroine known as the "Maid of Orleans," whose courageous military and moral leadership led to France's reversal of fortune over the invading English during the Hundred Years War. Ingrid Bergman played the title role on Broadway in 1946. The epic film bombed at the box office during a downward-spiraling point in Bergman's career; it also was the final film for Fleming, the director of *Gone With the Wind* and *The Wizard of Oz*. Bergman's reverent and saintly portrayal and the deeply religious nature of the film were way over the top. Its brilliantly saturated color cinematography won an Oscar, and the film also earned nominations for Best Actress (Bergman), Supporting Actor (Ferrer), Score (Hugo Friedhofer), Film Editing, and Art Direction/Set Decoration.

• *"...an expensive disaster, costing and losing a fortune. Ingrid Bergman...reduc[ed] the Maid's stature to that of a chain-clad cheerleader. A tedious, ponderous two and a half hours, the film had...two points in its favor: the coronation sequence in a magnificently recreated Rheims Cathedral and Jose Ferrer impressively making his screen debut as the Dauphin."* (Charles Higham and Joel Greenberg, Hollywood in the Forties)

• *"For the greater part of its two-and-a-half hour length,* Joan of Arc *presents many stirring sequences of pageantry. But too much of the film is merely empty spectacle and almost comic-strip progression from one historical highlight to the next. Where Anderson had provided an intellectually provocative, if not classic, play in* Joan of Lorraine, *the script for the film offers long stretches of flat, banal, and uninspired dialogue."* (Curtis F. Brown, Ingrid Bergman)

Key Largo deals with a disillusioned Spanish Civil War veteran who returns to the title island to meet the family of a comrade killed in the fighting. Finding that a gambler and his minions have taken over the family's small hotel, he grudgingly agrees to risk helping the owners as a hurricane brews. Written in blank verse, it was first produced on Broadway in 1939 at the Ethel Barrymore Theatre with Paul Muni, Uta Hagen, Jose Ferrer, James Gregory, and Karl Malden.

Key Largo (1948, Warner Bros., 101m/bw, **VHS/DVD**) ☆☆☆☆ **Sc:** Richard Brooks, John Huston. **D:** John Huston. **Cam:** Karl Freund. **Cast:** Humphrey Bogart, Edward G. Robinson, Lauren Bacall, Lionel Barrymore, Claire Trevor, Thomas Gomez, Harry Lewis, John Rodney, Marc Lawrence, Monte Blue, Jay Silverheels, Dan Seymour, William Haade, Rodric Redwing. A reluctant Huston directed his final picture under contract to Warner Bros. and updated and transformed the source material with Brooks, making the gambler a dangerous deported Cuban racketeer on the lam and turning the film into one of the better-remembered Bogart vehicles. Bogie is a World War II returnee in the film. The cast was in excellent form, particularly Robinson as the cigar-chomping Johnny Rocco and Trevor, who won the Oscar for Best Supporting Actress as Rocco's booze-craving, over-the-hill floozy Gaye Dawn.

- *"The soporific Maxwell Anderson play is an unlikely subject for John Huston but he steers a shrewd course, bailing Anderson out in order to stay afloat. What the play was supposed to be about—which was dim enough in the original—is even more obscure in the script that he and Richard Brooks...prepared, but the movie is so confidently and entertainingly directed that nobody is likely to complain. Huston fills the rancid atmosphere...with suspense, ambiguous motives, and some hilariously hammy bits, and the cast all go at it as if the nonsense about gangsters and human dignity were high drama."* (Pauline Kael, 5001 Nights at the Movies)

- *"John Huston and Richard Brooks have almost completely rewritten Maxwell Anderson's play, and I think that in almost every way they have improved on it...it is exceedingly well acted, and as picture-making most of it is as well worth watching as anything you will see this year."* (James Agee, The Nation)

Key Largo (1956, NBC, 60m/bw) *Alcoa Playhouse* ☆☆ **Tp:** Alvin Sapinsky. **D/P:** Alex Segal. **Cast:** Alfred Drake, Anne Bancroft, Victor Jory, Lorne Greene, J. Carroll Naish, Gerald Saccarini, John Morley, Don Hammer, William Kemp, John Vivyan, Bob Sheerer. Sapinsky adapted the original Spanish Civil War-era play into this pared-down version.

- *"Much of Anderson's blank verse was retained...and if it came through at times with a weighty ponderousness, it also had moments of strong poetic beauty...on the whole, the moralistic tale of a conflict between idealism and brute force came through more the battle of philosophies intended by Anderson, than the derring-do screen version. A strong cast responded well to Segal's direction. Alfred Drake, as the doomed soldier who regains his courage to face death bravely was especially outstanding, with J. Carroll Naish, as the gangster, equally compelling. Anne Bancroft demonstrated anew her growing stature as an actress."* (Variety)

- *"Time did not permit full development of the characters and much of the playwright's philosophy and theatrical theorizing was lost."* (William Torbert Leonard, Theatre: Stage to Screen to Television)

Knickerbocker Holiday was a 1938 smash hit musical comedy written with Kurt Weill that satirized Franklin Roosevelt's New Deal programs, via a story set in Peter Stuyvesant's New World colony of Nieuw Amsterdam (later New York). Joshua Logan directed Walter Huston as Stuyvesant at the Ethel Barrymore Theatre. The collaborators took their inspiration from Washington Irving's novel *Father Knickerbocker's History of New York.*

Knickerbocker Holiday (1944, United Artists, 84m/bw) ☆☆½ **Sc:** David Boehm, Harry Goldman, Roland Lee, Thomas Lennon. **D:** Harry Joe Brown. **Cam:** Phil Tannura. **Cast:** Charles Coburn, Nelson Eddy, Constance Dowling, Shelley Winters, Ernest Cossart, Otto Kruger. The crooning includes the film's highlight, Coburn singing "September Song." The film was nominated for an Oscar for its musical score by Werner Heymann.

- *"Knickerbocker Holiday uses the smirking mannerisms and attitudes of Gilbert and Sullivan as one might use Sanka dregs the fifth time."* (James Agee, The Nation)

Knickerbocker Holiday aired in 1950 on ABC's *Pulitzer Prize Playhouse,* and starred Dennis King, John Raitt, Doretta Morrow, Loring Smith, Jed Prouty, Philip Coolidge, Jack Manning, Stanley Carson, and Brooks Dunbar.

Lost in the Stars (1974, American Film Theatre, 114m/c) ☆☆ **Sc:** Alfred Hayes. **D:** Daniel Mann. **P:** Ely Landau. **Cam:** Robert Hauser. **Cast:** Brock Peters, Melba Moore, Raymond St. Jacques, Clifton Davis, Paul Rogers, Paulene Myers, Paula Kelly, John Williams, H.B. Barnam III, Ji-Tu Cumbuka, Alan Weeks, Ivor Barry, John Holland, Harvey Jason, Michael-James Wixted, John Hawker, Myrna White. Based on *Cry the Beloved Country,* Alan Paton's famous novel of South African turmoil, this musical play by Anderson and Kurt Weill concerns a black minister who loses his faith when he journeys to Johannesburg in search of his missing son. The songs include the titular one, "Trouble Man," "Train Go Now to Johannesburg," and "Bird of Paradise." The play was first directed by Rouben Mamoulian in 1949 at Broadway's Music Box Theatre with William Marshall in the ensemble.

- *"A poor adaptation…What could have been a powerfully moving film with a statement about segregation and racism falls far short in its attempt." (J.P. Nash, S.R. Ross,* The Motion Picture Guide)

Mary of Scotland (1936, RKO, 123m/bw, **VHS**) ☆☆☆ **Sc:** Dudley Nichols. **D:** John Ford. **P:** Pandro S. Berman. **Cam:** Joseph H. August. **Cast:** Katharine Hepburn, Fredric March, Donald Crisp, Florence Eldridge, Douglas Walton, John Carradine, Robert Barrat, Monte Blue, Moroni Olsen, Frieda Inescort, Alan Mowbray, William Stack, Gavin Muir, Ian Keith. One of Ford's more high-profile pictures in its day, this one seems to have slipped through the cracks, even among Ford aficionadoes and apologists. The film's convergence of talents is remarkable, even if the results are not. The story covers Mary Stuart's refusal to give the English throne to Elizabeth I. The Broadway play of 1933 starred Helen Hayes. Covering the same history was *Mary Queen of Scots* (1971), which starred Vanessa Redgrave and did not use the Anderson play.

- *"The tragedy of the most alluring of the Stuarts, which has fascinated dramatic poets from Schiller to Maxwell Anderson and every other sensible romantic since her reign, reaches the cinema in a moving, eloquent and distinguished transcription. Although Dudley Nichols, who made the screen adaptation of Mr. Anderson's excellent blank-verse play, has changed the poetry of the dialogue to prose. He has written speech that is both graceful and powerful, thus maintaining the lyric, as well as the theatrical, effectiveness of the drama...Fredric March has never been finer."* (Richard Watts, Jr., New York Herald-Tribune)

- *"...brought Ford into contact for the first and last time with Katharine Hepburn's radiantly brash beauty, Maxwell Anderson's pedestrian blank verse, and Fredric March's practiced hamminess in period roles...with...Hepburn cast as Mary and Florence Eldridge (Mrs. Fredric March) as Elizabeth, the dramatic one-sidedness of this historical pageant becomes oppressive...suffers from a form of sentimental masochism endemic in the 1920s and 1930s, decades in which paranoia was acted out literally and laboriously as interminable persecution."* (Andrew Sarris, The John Ford Movie Mystery)

Night Over Taos was produced by the Group Theatre in 1932, and starred Stella Adler, Robert Lewis, and Franchot Tone. *Pulitzer Prize Playhouse* presented it in 1951 with Riza Royce, Joseph Gallela and Murvyn Vye.

Saturday's Children presents the story of a poor and hard-working New York City girl; her boyfriend-cum-husband, who is less pragmatic than she is; and her staunch father, who stands by her. The younger man prefers to concoct impractical inventions while the older man adds philosophic commentary. The play was first produced on Broadway in 1927 under Guthrie McClintic's direction with a cast led by Ruth Gordon, Roger Pryor, and Beulah Bondi.

Saturday's Children (1929, First National, 90m/bw) ☆☆½ **Sc:** Forrest Halsey. **D:** Gregory La Cava. **P:** Walter Morosco. **Cam:** John Seitz. **Cast:** Corinne Griffith, Grant Withers, Marcia Harris, Alma Tell, Lucien Littlefield, Albert Conti, Charles Lane, Ann Schaeffer.

• *"The screen translation...is interspersed with dialogue passages that occasionally boom in a disquieting fashion and others that subside into abashed tones so low that the words of the players cannot always be heard. Although these audible sequences rather detract from the value of parts of the picture, it is a production that is directed with imagination, sympathy and restraint and therefore survives the periodical outbursts of speech."* (Mordaunt Hall, The New York Times)

Maybe It's Love (1934, First National, 74m/bw) ☆☆ **Sc:** Jerry Wald, Harry Sauber. **D:** Vincent Sherman. **P:** Jack L. Warner, Hal B. Wallis. **Cam:** Arthur Edeson. **Cast:** Gloria Stuart, Ross Alexander, Frank McHugh, Ruth Donnelly, Phillip Reed, Helen Lowell, Joseph Cawthorn, Henry Travers, Dorothy Dare, Maude Eburne, J. Farrell MacDonald.

• *"...beginning to look a wee bit frayed after all this handling. Blessed if the boys haven't gotten around to Maxwell Anderson's* Saturday's Children *again! Every time there's a little lull among Hollywood's pot-boilers, they dig the script out, turn it over to the writing staff for a new treatment, invent another title, and presto! Just like that, there's a picture."* (Frank S. Nugent, The New York Times)

Saturday's Children (1940, Warner Bros., 101m/bw) ☆☆½ **Sc:** Julius J. Epstein, Philip G. Epstein. **D:** Vincent Sherman. **Cam:** James Wong Howe. **P:** Jack L. Warner, Hal B. Wallis. **Cast:** Anne Shirley, John Garfield, Claude Rains, Lee Patrick, George Tobias, Roscoe Karns, Dennie Moore, Elizabeth Risdon, Berton Churchill, Frank Faylen, John Qualen, John Ridgely, Tom Dugan, Creighton Hale. Garfield accepted one of his most uncharacteristic assignments as the bespectacled and contemplative Rims Rosson, whose inventions leave much to be desired.

• *"...a small salary leads to tumultuous marital discord...by 1940 such Depression-drab tales had become too commonplace, and with the approach of World War II prosperity, the story was excessively quaint and archaic. Thus* Saturday's Children *received short shrift at the box office. In a typically sensitive portrayal, Rains claimed the best of the review notices with Anne [Shirley] scarcely mentioned in passing."* (James Robert Parish, The RKO Gals)

Saturday's Children (1950, CBS, 30m/bw) *Lux Video Theatre* ☆☆☆ **Tp:** Robert Cenedella. **D:** Fielder Cook. **P:** Cal Kuhl. **Cast:** Joan Caulfield, Dean Harens, John Ericson, Eileen Heckart, Una O'Connor, Ralph Riggs. This version was the debut installment of the long-running 1950s TV version of the famous *Lux Radio Theatre*.

• *"...camera, sets, and thesping were uniformly standout."* (Variety)

Saturday's Children (1952, ABC, 60m/bw) *Celanese Theatre* ☆☆ **Tp:** Alan Haskett. **D:** David Alexander. **Cast:** Shirley Standee, Mickey Rooney, Doro Merande, June Walker, Morrison Dowd, Patricia Bright, Freddy Wayne.

- *"...an ineffectual performance by Mickey Rooney."* (Variety)

Saturday's Children (1962, CBS, 60m/c) *Breck's Golden Showcase* ☆☆☆ **Tp:** Robert Emmett. **D:** Tom Donovan. **P:** Marshal Jamison, Leland Hayward. **Cast:** Cliff Robertson, Inger Stevens, Ralph Bellamy, Lee Grant, Doro Merande, Ted Beniades, Katherine Meskill, Ronnie Cunningham. *Breck's* was a brief run of monthly Sunday night dramas.

- *"The warmth of life was captured by the players...isn't a work of deep passions or major ideas. It's more of a dramatic vignette of young love trying to survive the winds of change wrought by marriage. Robert Emmett...brought the stage play up to date with topical references...There were static qualities in the [TV] version, a certain preoccupation with epigramatic philosophizing rather than a constant revelation of character and plot...All in all a pleasant hour, examining some marital problems with honesty, insight and optimism."* (Variety)

The Star Wagon, about a poor and eccentric inventor who escapes his wife's crankiness via his titular time machine, first played on Broadway in 1937 with Burgess Meredith and Lillian Gish. The inventor escapes to his youth, at a time when he feels he should have married a pretty rich girl rather than his wife. The evergreen theme is that if you could live your life over again, would you have made a better choice?

The Star Wagon (1957, CBS, 90m/bw) *Playhouse 90* ☆☆½ **Tp:** James P. Cavanaugh. **D:** Vincent J. Donehue. **Cast:** Eddie Bracken, Diana Lynn, Jackie Coogan, Maggie Hayes, Billie Burke, Steve Bishop. The casting trick here was that Lynn played both the older shrewish wife and the beautiful girl of three decades past.

- *"...while it succeeded in conveying some straightforward morality messages and some effectively touching scenes, it lacked the pacing and tightness so necessary to maintain living room interest. To put it simply, Star Wagon dragged through most of the 90 minutes, so that while the whole was extremely worthwhile, it far exceeded the sum of its parts, some of which were tedious...Miss Lynn was topnotch as the hot-tempered wife and the petulant but lovely girl of 30 years before, and Bracken instilled a sense of sweetness and uprightness to the role of the inventor."* (Variety)

The Star Wagon (1966, PBS, 150m/c) *NET Playhouse* ☆☆☆ **Tp:** Maxwell Anderson. **D/P:** Karl Genus. **Cast:** Orson Bean, Joan Lorring, Dustin Hoffman, Eileen Brennan, Jo Hurt, Hallie Arrington, Ed Zimmerman. This production, which was partially taped at exterior locations in Connecticut, is significant in retrospect as one of Dustin Hoffman's few screen performances prior to *The Graduate* (1967). He opens the play with a protracted belch. Lorring repeated the dual-role feat turned in by Lynn in the *Playhouse 90* production, above.

- "...*achieved a touching poignancy in the third act...For the first two acts the play was often arduous going...30 years after its Broadway presentation, stern editing would have been very much in order...Joan Lorring...was completely beguiling...as the inventor's constant friend throughout the two versions of their lives, Dustin Hoffman was exceptionally good...the difficulties lay in part with the Anderson script. The picnic scene in* The Star Wagon *is interminable.*" (*Jack Gould,* The New York Times)

- "...*rendered...as if it were a museum piece. Against today's theatre, the Anderson play is loosely knit, slow paced, amorphous and crowded with subsidiary characters. Had Genus been more daring, he could have edited smartly and hopefully brought the work more in tempo with the present...Orson Bean acquitted himself well...Dustin Hoffman as Bean's pal, a real oddball character, opened the play with a belch — the best controlled belch ever witnessed on the TV screen. Too many of the characters were caricatures. That was another failing of the Anderson work...*" (*Variety*)

Valley Forge tells the story the Continental Army's plight during the Revolutionary War, as it languished at General George Washington's headquarters in Pennsylvania during the bitter winter of 1777–78. Washington inventories the problems facing his bedraggled forces, including possible sedition, squabbles among adjutants, few supplies, and a Congress that secretly seeks a truce. His situation is contrasted with British General Howe's plush digs in Philadelphia. The play was first produced in 1934 at New York's Theatre Guild with Philip Merivale as Washington, Reginald Mason as Howe, George Coulouris, and Margalo Gillmore.

Valley Forge (1975, NBC, 90m/c) *The Hallmark Hall of Fame* ☆☆☆ **Tp:** Sidney Carroll. **D/P:** Fielder Cook. **Cast:** Richard Basehart, Harry Andrews, Simon Ward, Christopher Walken, Victor Garber, David Dukes, Kathryn Walker, Edward Herrmann, John Heard, Nancy Marchand, Lisa Pelikan. How much is history and how much is Anderson's sense of drama isn't very clear, especially Washington's doubts about his own Virginia company breaking camp and leaving, only to later learn that the troops simply left to forage for food.

- "...*handsomely-crafted...excellent in its separate parts and somewhat boring in total. The cast was great, the photography superb and the dialogue at once lyrical and incisive. That should have been enough, but it wasn't, and the central flaw appeared to be a lack of dramatic flow on the part of director Fielder Cook and adapter Sidney Carroll. It was loaded with historically fascinating episodes, periodic dramatic touches and compelling performances, but it lacked a cohesive plotline and point of focus. The superb characterization[s] by Richard Basehart as General Washington and Harry*

Andrews as General Howe suggest that it might have been a good idea to have used one of them for a focal point." (Variety)

Valley Forge also aired in 1950 on NBC's *Kraft Television Theatre* with E.G. Marshall, Judson Laire, and Vaughn Taylor, and the following year on ABC's *Pulitzer Prize Playhouse* with Albert Dekker, Victor Sutherland, Wright King, and Guy Aubrey.

What Price Glory? was written with Laurence Stallings and became one of the biggest Broadway hits of the late 1920s. Louis Wolheim and William Boyd starred in signature roles as Captain Flagg and Sergeant Quirt, U.S. Marines vying for the same girl while serving in France during World War I. The play is essentially a bitter anti-war treatise.

What Price Glory? (1926, Fox, 116m/bw/silent) ☆☆☆☆ **Sc:** Laurence Stallings, Maxwell Anderson. **D:** Raoul Walsh. **Cam:** Barney McGill, Jack Marta, John Smith. **P:** William Fox. **Cast:** Victor McLaglen, Edmund Lowe, Dolores Del Rio, Phyllis Haver, Leslie Fenton, Elena Jurado, Ted McNamara, Sammy Cohen, William V. Mong, August Tollaire, Mathilde Comont, Jack Pennick, Pat Rooney, Mahlon Hamilton. This seminal anti-war film and huge hit represented Anderson's introduction to movie work, Walsh's great leap as a filmmaker, and the ascendance of the production's three stars. The film's breezy bawdiness in the love triangle alternates between spectacular battles, particularly the fierce fighting at Belleau Wood, and sobering anti-war scenes, as when the soldiers huddle together for warmth and are all wiped out by artillery.

- *"Victor McLaglen stands out bigger than he ever has...As for the Charmaine of Dolores Del Rio, she registers like a house afire...To Raoul Walsh a great deal of credit will have to go. His handling of the war stuff is little short of marvelous."* (Variety)

- *"[Walsh] was given the film that represents the synthesis of his style and ability in the silent cinema,* What Price Glory?*...presented by means of a virile, robust, gutsy humor, with the two actors...fitting perfectly into Walsh's conception...the original was remade by John Ford [see below]...A comparison between the two versions underlines the difference between the two directors...Walsh's heroes were like two bulls in a China shop but then Walsh was concerned with their adventures while Ford uses their escapades and reactions to develop his point about the behavior patterns of men in war...Ford is also more concerned with the visual terms of reference in his film, outlining men against the sky in poetic images or representing the tragedy of war through the shots of deserted villages."* (Kingsley Canham, The Hollywood Professionals, Volume 1: Michael Curtiz, Raoul Walsh, Henry Hathaway)

What Price Glory? (1952, 20th Century-Fox, 111m/c, **VHS**) ☆☆½ **Sc:** Phoebe Ephron, Henry Ephron. **D:** John Ford. **Cam:** Joseph MacDonald. **P:** Sol C. Siegel. **Cast:** James Cagney, Dan Dailey, Corinne Calvet, William Demarest, Robert Wagner, Marisa Pavan, Craig Hill, Casey Adams, James Gleason, Wally Vernon, Paul Fix, Henry Morgan, Jack Pennick, Tom Tyler, Torben Meyer, Mickey Simpson, Paul Guilfoyle, Henry Letondal, Ray Hyke. In this remake, Ford lets Cagney roar and huff at will and appears to believe that Calvet is the most beautiful woman he or we will ever see. But the material was dated by 1952 and the film today holds no distinction in the Ford canon except for some striking images of battlefields.

- *"[Ford's] visual style had always been too elegantly premeditated and cere-monial for the sudden jolts of iconoclastic indiscretion. Ford's films are never to be laughed at in any sense. The seemingly interminable shouting matches of a Dan Dailey and a James Cagney in* What Price Glory?...*are not so much to be enjoyed as to be endured until Ford can lead us to the beating heart of the film...the moment in which Corinne Calvet comes down the stairs bathed in a filter like the Lady of Shalott and Cagney's Captain Flagg gazes at her as he recites his litany of the fighting man...In fact, the broad-ness of his humor is the price we must pay for the depth of his feelings."* (Andrew Sarris, The John Ford Movie Mystery)

Wingless Victory (1961, NET, 120m/bw) *The Play of the Week* ☆☆☆ **Tp:** Maxwell Anderson. **D:** Paul Nickell. **P:** David Susskind. **Cast:** Hugh O'Brian, Eartha Kitt, Jane Wyatt, Michael Tolan, Cathleen Nesbitt, Tim O'Connor, Barbara Lord. This play, which investigates the theme of interracial marriage, was produced on Broadway in 1936 by Katharine Cornell and staged by Guthrie McClintic. It starred Walter Abel as a cargo ship's captain in 1800 and Cornell as a former Maylay princess, Oparre, who bore his children. Another Anderson free-verse play, it's set in 19th century Salem, Massachusetts, where the white, for-merly Puritanical seafarer and his princess rely on their love to see them through community ostracism. The material was beyond TV horse opera star O'Brien's reach.

- *"...both an interesting and trying drama...O'Brien's name may have cor-raled some viewers...but his playing of the role lacked nuances and inner conviction. The Maxwell Anderson drama is a difficult piece in many re-spects. Eartha Kitt, however, in the other principal role...caught the tragedy of the piece, rendered greater meaning to Anderson's free verse, and pro-jected a wider range of feelings. For all its mannered accents, her role had conviction...There were golden nuggets of poetry that, on occasion, made the lines soar."* (Variety)

Winterset followed the quest of a New York waterfront drifter to find the witness to the crime for which his father, 15 years earlier, had been con-victed and electrocuted. Anderson's widely produced verse drama, based in part on the famous Sacco and Vanzetti murder trial, was a significant event of Depression Era Broadway, where it debuted in 1935, winning the Drama Critics Circle Award as Best Play. Produced and directed by Guthrie McClintic, it starred Burgess Meredith, Margo, and Eduardo Ciannelli.

Winterset (1936, RKO, 78m/bw, **VHS**) ☆☆☆ **Sc:** Anthony Veiller. **D:** Alfred Santell. **Cam:** J. Peverell Marley. **P:** Pandro S. Berman. **Cast:** Burgess Meredith, Margo, Eduardo Ciannelli, Paul Guilfoyle, John Carradine, Stanley Ridges, Myron McCormick, Willard Robertson, Edward Ellis, Mischa Auer, Alec Craig, Barbara Pepper, Paul Fix, Maurice Moscovitch, Murray Alper, Lucille Ball, Helen Jerome Eddy. The three Broadway leads repeated their roles, including Meredith in his film debut. Nathaniel Shilkret received an Oscar nomination for the score.

- "...[the play] was widely held to be the supremely eloquent last word on the unconquerable soul of man. Burgess Meredith, who mastered the cadences for Broadway, made his first screen appearnce as Mio, giving fine voice and excellent interpretation to the soaring banalities that one might—in a romantic mood—mistake for poetry. Even with Anderson's poetics slightly trimmed by the adaptor, Anthony Veiller, the play is still in a grand manner that just won't do on the screen. But there are fine moments in the performances, and there's something childishly touching in the florid dramatic effects." (Pauline Kael, 5001 Nights at the Movies)

- "We have had plenty of Scarfaces, of men whose trigger-fingers act like the conditioned reflexes of dogs who dribble when a bell sounds; Trock has more interest: the sick man who hates the healthy, who kills from envy because he has to die himself. In this character, acted with evil magnificence by Eduardo Ciannelli, there is some of the poety of a Renaissance tyrant, with basilisks in the eyes and the everlasting cold pinching the heart." (Graham Greene, The Spectator)

Winterset (1959, NBC, 90m/bw) The Hallmark Hall of Fame ☆☆☆½ **Tp:** Robert Hartung. **D/P:** George Schaefer. **Cast:** Don Murray, Piper Laurie, George C. Scott, Charles Bickford, Martin Balsam, George Mathews, Anotol Winogradoff, Tom Hatcher, Mercer McLeod, Bernie West, Robert P. Lieb. This was one of Schaefer's most personal productions of a play that influenced him early in his career. Laurie was a bit unsure, but Balsam, playing her brother, and Scott as Trock were superb.

- "...a first-rate television workover...Anderson's use of blank verse was only partially successful. At its best moments the poetic dialogue was charged with a poignancy that went beyond the meaning of the words. Too often, however, Anderson slipped into a groove of flabby and repetitious rhetoric which was made doubly conspicuous by the clarity of this TV presentation...Another first-rate performance was contributed by George C. Scott as the malevolent killer...George Schaefer's direction of this drama, done live, was fluid throughout." (Variety)

Winterset also aired in 1951 on ABC's *Celanese Theatre*, directed by Alex Segal, with Eduardo Ciannelli, Richard Carlysle, Joan Chandler, and Ralph Morgan.

Robert Anderson
Robert Woodruff Anderson
Born: April 28, 1917, New York, NY.

Robert Anderson was educated at Phillips Exeter Academy and Harvard University, and taught at the University of Iowa. His novels include *After* and *Getting Up and Going Home*, which he adapted for a 1992 TV movie about adultery with Tom Skerritt and Blythe Danner. Anderson's adaptations of others' works for TV include Oscar Wilde's *The Canterville Ghost* on *Actors' Studio* in 1949 with Wendy Barrie; James M. Barrie's *The Old Lady Shows Her Medals* in 1956 for a *United States Steel Hour* presentation that starred Gracie Fields and Jackie Cooper; and the CBS special *The Patricia Neal Story* in 1981, based on the book *Pat and Roald* by Barry Farrell, with Glenda Jackson and Dirk Bogarde. Jackson portrayed the title actress's actual stroke and earned herself an Emmy nomination.

Gilbert Cates, who directed the movie version of Anderson's most enduring and effective play, *I Never Sang for My Father* (see below), also directed the original TV movie by Anderson, *Absolute Strangers* (1991), a fact-based piece about a husband signing off on an abortion for his pregnant, comatose wife, which featured Henry Winkler and Patty Duke.

Anderson's plays explore the father/son dynamic in many ways, and most of them have been adapted into films or TV shows. His screenplay work includes *Until They Sail* (1957) with Paul Newman, Fred Zinnemann's *The Nun's Story* (1959) with Audrey Hepburn, and Robert Wise's *The Sand Pebbles* (1966) with Steve McQueen.

All Summer Long tells the story of a family of selfish individuals living in a house along a riverbank, and concentrates on the two sons. The 10-year-old voices his intuition that the river will flood and spends his summer vacation building a makeshift retaining wall along the bank while his older, crippled brother is the only one who heeds him. The play, which was an adaptation of Donald Wetzel's novel, *A Wreath and a Curse*, ran for 60 performances on Broadway in 1954 with a cast led by Clay Hall, John Kerr, June Walker, Carroll Baker, Ed Begley, and John Randolph.

All Summer Long (1956, NBC, 60m/bw) *The Goodyear Television Playhouse* ☆☆½ **Tp:** Robert Anderson. **Cast:** Raymond Massey, Malcolm

Broderick, William Shatner. Shatner's first major TV role was in this truncated version of the play.

- *"...generally absorbing...more poignant in scattered scenes than in the overall story. Through the playwright's penetrating character moldings, the Muson family...emerged as pitiful figures...There's the tender understanding given the sensitive lad by his older brother, the painful attempt at conversation between members of the family and the anguish suffered by the married daughter on learning she's to have a child, which she feels would destroy her only asset, her beauty."* (Variety)

All Summer Long (1961, NET, 120m/bw) *The Play of the Week* ☆☆½ **Tp:** Robert Anderson. **D:** Henry Kaplan. **P:** Jack Kuney, David Susskind. **Cast:** Keir Dullea, Philip Fox, Betty Field, Henderson Forsythe, Nina Wilcox, James Olson, Gloria Nelson. This was the 67th and final presentation of *The Play of the Week*.

- *"...at least attained a satisfying dramatic impact in its final scenes and was marked in its presentation by excellent performances all around. Theme is somewhat of a bromide with American dramatists and writers, being the familiar case of a bright kinder in dramatic clash with loutish parents...the fine thesping with a particularly convincing performance by Keir Dullea as the crippled brother, eased the dull stretches."* (Variety)

Double Solitaire (1974, PBS, 60m/c) *Conflicts* ☆☆☆ **D:** Paul Bogart. **P:** Norman Lloyd. **Cast:** Richard Crenna, Susan Clark, Harold Gould, Norma Crane, Nicholas Hammond. This piece concerns upscale spouses Charley and Barbara Potter in their 20th year of marriage after they're asked by his parents to renew their wedding vows along with the older couple, who will be celebrating 50 years of matrimony. The younger couple's doubts about their union surface in half of a 1971 Anderson Broadway double bill.

- *"What makes* Double Solitaire *work is that Anderson makes no great attempt to disguise the fact that these are set pieces, that each character will get a big scene and that while no vast new areas will be explored, some of the old familiar ground might just take on a new texture when it's through. 'Why should two people go along like railroad tracks — side by side into eternity?' asks Susan Clark. 'In every marriage more than a week old there are grounds for divorce — the trick is to find grounds for marriage,' says another character. Both thoughts aren't exactly newly minted, but they do have the sort of slightly askew familiarity that passes for — and often is — real wisdom."* (Dick Adler, Los Angeles Times)

I Never Sang for My Father chronicles an adult son's thorny relationship with his aging father, who rose from poverty to be a top executive and town mayor. Both men interact with each other based on lifetimes of instinct and stubbornness inbuilt into the contentious bond. The son,

Gene Garrison, must decide if he wants to stay close to home with his aging father or move to California and marry the woman he loves. Alan Webb and Hal Holbrook starred on Broadway in 1968.

I Never Sang for My Father (1970, Columbia, 90m/c, **VHS**) ☆☆☆☆☆
Sc: Robert Anderson. **D/P:** Gilbert Cates. **Cam:** Morris Hartzband, George Stoetzel. **Cast:** Melvyn Douglas, Gene Hackman, Dorothy Stickney, Estelle Parsons, Elizabeth Hubbard, Lovelady Powell, Daniel Keyes, Conrad Bain, Sloane Shelton, Carol Peterson. Relying almost solely on the lead actors for its impact, this film provides perhaps cinema's most honest examination of an adult offspring's feelings for his parents. Hackman's performance, a collage of frustration—the need for approval, pent-up anger, and familial love—is one of his finest. Both he and Douglas received Academy Award nominations, as did Anderson.

- *"The film is completely verbal, and since the subject matter is so touchy, it is a difficult film to watch…The performances are virtually perfect… Hackman…at his best…makes Gene something more than what is written; his naturalism transcends the lapses in Anderson's screenplay, and he gives us a Gene more fully rounded and more thought-out than the one in the script…Of course,* I Never Sang for My Father *shares its subject with an American classic, Eugene O'Neill's* Long Day's Journey Into Night, *a play conceived on a far greater scale than Anderson's, and one that by the very nature of its greatness is perhaps less forceful than Anderson's small, intimate drama. Cates's direction is crude, the lighting is poor, and there is no discernable visual style; yet the film is affecting. It refuses to show a way out of these individuals' dilemmas, to indulge in false reassurances…"* (Judith M. Kass, Magill's Survey of Cinema)

- *"…the theme is so very pertinent, and the performances so affecting…it used to be fashionable to label these adaptations 'uncinematic'…But it has truth, and heart, and a sensitivity to human relationships that lift it far beyond the more aggressively movie movies."* (Arthur Knight, Saturday Review)

I Never Sang for My Father (1988, PBS, 120m/c) American Playhouse ☆☆☆½ **Tp:** Robert Anderson. **D:** Jack O'Brien. **P:** Iris Merlis. **Cast:** Daniel J. Travanti, Harold Gould, Dorothy McGuire, Margo Skinner. O'Brien, employing the cast of a version that played the Ahmanson Theater in Los Angeles, opened up the proceedings with exterior shots and studio sets.

- *"Giving another of his subdued, sometimes recklessly understated performances, Mr. Travanti at times turns Gene into too much of a wimp. His goodness and compassion threaten to become exasperating. Tackling the father, Mr. Gould goes to the other extreme, doing an aggressive turn that captures the man's New York City roots but little of the shrewd corporate executive who wound up as something of a suburban lord…In the final confrontation scene, Mr. Travanti and Mr. Gould end up demonstrating just how powerfully effecting this play remains. Miss McGuire...is as charming and gently elegant as ever, and Miss Skinner manages to be both biting and sympathetic...*" (John J. O'Connor, The New York Times)

Silent Night, Lonely Night (1969, NBC, 120m/c, **VHS**) ☆☆ **Tp:** John Vlahos. **D:** Daniel Petrie. **P:** Jack Farren. **Cast:** Lloyd Bridges, Shirley Jones, Lynn Carlin, Carrie Snodgress, Cloris Leachman, Woodrow Parfrey, Jeff Bridges, Robert Lipton, Richard Eastham, Nydia Westman. Set in a New England college town on Christmas Eve, this drama details a tryst that begins in a university mental hospital, between a man visiting his inmate wife and a woman—who has recently discovered her husband's infidelity—there to visit her son, a student. The play was first produced on Broadway in 1959 with Henry Fonda and Barbara Bel Geddes. Filmed on location in Amherst, MA, this earnest and poignant piece is wintry in both set and tone. Even as the leads turn in appealing performances, the piece's emotional weather is always a gloomy horizon as the inevitable looms.

- "*All sorts of sighs are tried on for size before they return to their respective mates. At the time of its network premiere in 1969, this tailored-for-television movie was described as adult entertainment. For adult chimpanzees, no doubt.*" (Judith Crist, Judith Crist's TV Guide to the Movies)

Tea and Sympathy (1956, MGM, 122m/c, **VHS**) ☆☆☆ **Sc:** Robert Anderson. **D:** Vincente Minnelli. **P:** Pandro S. Berman. **Cam:** John Alton. **Cast:** Deborah Kerr, John Kerr, Leif Erickson, Edward Andrews, Darryl Hickman, Norma Crane, Dean Jones, Tom Laughlin, Jacqueline de Wit, Kip King. This was a Broadway event of 1953 as its controversial theme of a prep school boy accused of homosexuality was then a daring calling card. The play's homosexuality was changed for the film to the boy having an affair with a teacher's wife, altering entirely the main point, with Anderson's acquiescence—he wrote the screenplay. Both Kerrs repeated their stage roles and Berman and Minnelli infused the production with the full MGM treatmeant.

- "*...mounted for the screen as if it were a precious objet d'art in danger from rioting but miraculously saved. Besides being archaic the film is a prodgiously silly fable, pulling the realities with which it deals dishonestly, systematically out of whack.*" (Parker Tyler, Screening the Sexes)

- "*Since Anderson himself wrote the screenplay (with the censors looking over his shoulder), any bowdlerization must be attributed to him. Still, under such stringent bluenoses, he managed to get his point across.*" (J.R. Nash and S.R. Ross, The Motion Picture Guide)

- "*At its best, Tea and Sympathy is an inferior Candida, and, at its worst, pernicious propaganda for sexual degeneracy.*" (Veronica Hume, Films in Review)

Sherwood Anderson

Born: September 13, 1976, Camden, OH. **Died:** 1941.

In addition to his work for the stage and screen, Anderson's books include *Poor White*, *The Triumph of the Egg*, and *Many Marriages*. His novels and short stories extolled small-town life and the primal force of sexuality as a means of expressive individuality during the Industrial Revolution.

I'm A Fool began as a short story by Anderson about a Midwestern teenage boy who hopes to impress a town girl, and was produced twice for TV. Both versions are notable and venerable, due to respective casts involved and the quality of the productions. James Dean and Natalie Wood starred in a 1954 presentation on *General Electric Theatre*. Ron Howard and Amy Irving were featured in a 1978 *American Short Story* rendering on PBS.

Winesburg, Ohio (1973, PBS, 90m/c) *Hollywood Television Theatre* ☆☆ **Tp:** Sherwood Anderson. **D:** Ralph Senensky. **P:** Norman Lloyd. **Cast:** Jean Peters, William Windom, Joseph Bottoms, Albert Salmi, Norman Foster, Don Hammer, Alvin Hammer, George Winters, Chip Hand, Gary Barton, Curt Conway, Laurette Spang, Dabbs Greer, Arlene Stuart, Pitt Herbert. Anderson's most famous book is a diverse collection of pieces about the actions and concerns of everyday people in a small, fictional town. Anderson's stage adaptation of his stories was first produced in 1934 at the Hedgerow Theatre in Maylan-Rose Valley, Pennsylvania. It ran for only 13 performances on Broadway in 1958 and starred Dorothy McGuire, James Whitmore, Leon Ames, and Claudia McNeil.

- *"The first production I did [on* Hollywood Television Theatre*]. The production had Jean Peters coming out of retirement, which caused a great stir in the press;…Windom…Bottoms. The three played mother, father and son. Much to my amazement the play was very successful with the audience. This version of the material is a poor one because the adaptor introduced a great deal of material of his own; although it is based on* Winesburg, Ohio, *it is not authentic Sherwood Anderson. We reached into the heartland with that play. We had been accused of being elitist, but this was more down-to-earth." (Norman Lloyd,* Stages: Of Life in Theatre, Film and Television*)*

Robert Ardrey

Born: October 16, 1908, Chicago, IL. **Died:** 1980.

Robert Ardrey focused on prestigious and eclectic projects throughout his screenwriting career. His credits include the adaptation of Sidney

Howard's *They Knew What They Wanted* (1940), the singular John Wayne/Jean Arthur pairing of *A Lady Takes a Chance* (1943), *The Three Musketeers* (1948) with Gene Kelly, *Madame Bovary* (1949) with Jennifer Jones, *The Secret Garden* (1949) with Margaret O'Brien, *The Wonderful Country* (1959) with Robert Mitchum, *Four Horsemen of the Apocalypse* (1961) with Glenn Ford, and the epic-scaled *Khartoum* (1966) with Charlton Heston and Laurence Olivier.

Thunder Rock (1942, Charter, 112m/bw) ☆☆☆ **Sc:** Jeffrey Dell, Bernard Miles. **D:** Roy Boulting. **P:** John Boulting. **Cam:** Mutz Greenbaum (Max Greene). **Cast:** Michael Redgrave, Lilli Palmer, James Mason, Barbara Mullen, Finlay Currie, Frederick Valk, Frederick Cooper, Sybilla Binder. This was an anti-isolationist treatise about Charleston, a journalist who's fed up with the American policies of the 1930s, and retires to a lighthouse on Lake Michigan, where he's haunted by ghosts of immigrants who were drowned in past generations. The play was first presented in 1939 by The Group Theatre with Luther Adler as Charleston along with Myron McCormick, Morris Carnovsky, Lee J. Cobb, Frances Farmer, Ruth Nelson, and Robert Lewis. The Boulting brothers produced this American play in Great Britain with an English cast and crew at a time when the Brits welcomed the entrance of the United States into World War II.

- *"...this ambitious movie is spectacularly handsome (especially the scenes outside the lighthouse); yet the situation is very theatrical—those dead people seem an awfully theatrical contrivance just to re-invigorate the hero."* (*Pauline Kael, 5001 Nights at the Movies*)

Arthur Arent

Born: September, 29, 1904, Jersey City, NJ. **Died:** 1972.

Arthur Arent's footnote in history is the authorship of the below play, one of the most outstanding plays to come out of the Works Progress Administration's Federal Theatre's "Living Newspaper" presentations during the Great Depression. These works focused on social and economic issues affecting the masses, and utilized naturalistic acting.

One Third of a Nation (1939, Paramount, 79m/bw) ☆☆☆ **Sc:** Oliver H.P. Garrett, Dudley Murphy. **D:** Dudley Murphy. **P:** Harold Orlob. **Cam:** William Mellor. **Cast:** Sylvia Sidney, Lief Erickson, Myron McCormick, Hiram Sherman, Sidney Lumet, Muriel Hutchison, Percy Waram, Otto Hulitt, Horace Sinclair, Iris Adrian, Charles Dingle, Edmonia Nolley, Hugh Cameron, Baruch Lumet, Byron Russell. First presented by the Federal Theatre in 1938 as *...one third of a nation...*, this socially conscious play portrays big city slum life among disenfranchised and problem-burdened children. Though the metaphor is valid, the film is a poor man's version of William Wyler's *Dead End* (1937), with the Hollywood addition of a poor shop girl persuading the bad landlord to tear down his filthy buildings and put up new ones. Future directing great Sidney Lumet played a role as a slum teen.

- *"The first retrogravure section of The Living Newspaper rolled off the presses...As roto art, it has been considerably retouched. In fact, Arthur Arent, who wrote the play, probably would have difficulty in recognizing his brainchild. But that matters only to Mr. Arent and his Adelphians who saw the play. We uninstructed of the movie audience will take it for what it's worth, which is considerable...It is the building that dominates the picture, gives it terror, pity and despair...its destruction at the last is exhilerating beyond all reason."* (Frank S. Nugent, The New York Times)

Leopold Atlas

Leopold Lawrence Atlas
Born: October 19, 1907, Brooklyn, NY. **Died:** 1954.

For RKO Radio Pictures, Leopold Atlas wrote or co-wrote the scripts for the Robert Mitchum pictures *The Story of G.I. Joe* (1945) and *My Forbidden Past* (1951). Atlas also adapted Charles Dickens's *The Mystery of Edwin Drood* into the 1935 film with Claude Rains, and James Gow and Armand D'Usseau's play *Tomorrow the World!*, about the deprogramming of a Hitler youth in America, for the 1944 film starring Fredric March and Betty Field. Atlas also wrote *Her Kind of Man* (1946), with Janis Paige as a saloon singer, and the venerated Anthony Mann film noir *Raw Deal* (1948).

Wednesday's Child became one of the more prominent mid-century literary works dealing with children of broken homes. The play debuted in 1934 at Broadway's Longacre Theatre in an H.C. Potter production. The play has nothing to do with the 1971 Ken Loach film of the same name, which concerns abortion.

Wednesday's Child (1934, RKO, 69m/bw) ☆☆½ **Sc:** Willis Goldbeck. **D:** John Robertson. **P:** Kenneth Macgowan. **Cast:** Frankie Thomas, Karen Morley, Edward Arnold, Robert Shayne, Frank Conroy, Shirley Grey, Paul Stanton, David Durand, Richard Barbee, Mona Buns, Elsa Janssen, Tom Franklin (Frank M. Thomas). A small boy testifies in a divorce trial between his parents, and is then sent away to military school since neither parent has any room in their lives for him. Though the film is about as tough as movies got on the subject during the Great Depression, this one opts for a happy ending, and remains a virtually forgotten film. Frankie Thomas was the young son of Frank M. Thomas.

- "...*the pathetic story of a youth who is the victim of his parents' broken home...Despite this sentimentalized tag [ending], this was one of RKO's most affecting dramas of the year, sensitively directed by John Robertson.*" (Richard B. Jewell, Vernon Harbin, The RKO Story)

Child of Divorce (1946, RKO, 62m/c) ☆☆☆ **Sc:** Lillie Hayward. **D:** Richard Fleischer. **P:** Lillie Hayward, Sid Rogell. **Cam:** Jack MacKenzie. **Cast:** Sharyn Moffett, Regis Toomey, Madge Meredith, Walter Reed, Doris Merrick, Una O'Connor, Harry Cheshire, Selmer Jackson, Lillian Randolph, Pat Prest, Gregory Muradian, George McDonald, Patsy Converse, Ann Carter. Hayward told Atlas's story from a female point of view. Moffet dominates the film with an affecting performance as the psychologically bruised little girl, who is deposited in household after household. The divorce rate in immediate postwar America was 250,000 annually, which prompted RKO to give the play another chance.

- "...*there were lots of stars at RKO...Bing Crosby, Ingrid Bergman, Cary Grant, John Wayne, Fred Astaire, Ginger Rogers, you name them. When it came time for me to direct my first picture...I got as my star Sharyn Moffett. It could have been worse. She was a ten-year-old the studio hoped would turn into a Shirley Temple or a Margaret O'Brien, a metamorphosis devoutly to be wished. Actually, she was a good little actress, better than most of the adults around her. The Chrysalis, however, stubbornly refused to turn into a butterfly. She never did fly. The movie turned out remarkably well. In their book* The RKO Story, *Richard B. Jewell and Vernon Harbin comment: 'It is seldom that one finds an RKO picture whose only flaw was an excess of artistic integrity.*'" (Richard Fleischer, Just Tell Me When to Cry)

George Axelrod

Born: June 9, 1922, New York, NY.

George Axelrod's greatest contribution to the performing arts was adapting Truman Capote's novella *Breakfast at Tiffany's* into the 1961 Blake Edwards romantic classic with Audrey Hepburn and George Peppard. The film version of his play *The Seven-Year Itch* (1956) transmogrified a play with a dirty mind behind a crooked smile into 1950s iconography via one of Billy Wilder's more heavy-handed treatments. Immortalized in popular culture through the persona and body of Marilyn Monroe, it's now an antique of the moral ambiguity of 1950s America. The movies substituted Jayne Mansfield for Monroe in *Will Success Spoil Rock Hunter?* the following year and Axelrod's tour through the sexy blonde syndrome topped out. On Broadway, he co-produced his own play, *Goodbye Charlie*, as well as Gore Vidal's *Visit to a Small Planet*. Axelrod—who wrote, directed, and produced the films *Lord Love a Duck* (1966) and *The Secret Life of an American Wife* (1968)—alternated sex farce with international thrillers, including two for director John Frankenheimer: the classic *The Manchurian Candidate* (1962) and *The Holcroft Covenant* (1985) with Michael Caine.

Goodbye Charlie (1964, 20th Century-Fox, 116m/c, **VHS**) ☆☆½ **Sc:** Harry Kurnitz. **D:** Vincente Minnelli. **P:** David Weisbart. **Cast:** Debbie Reynolds, Tony Curtis, Pat Boone, Walter Matthau, Ellen McRae (Burstyn), Joanna Barnes, Laura Devon, Martin Gabel, Roger C. Carmel, Harry Madden, Myrna Hansen, Michael Romanoff, Michael Jackson, Donna Michelle, Jerry Dunphy, Jack Richardson, Anthony Eustrel, James Brolin. The 1959 Broadway presentation starred Lauren Bacall as the reincarnation of a murdered man and Sydney Chaplin as the dead man's former best friend, who's suddenly sexually attracted to the "new Charlie." In the film, an earthy mobster dies and comes back as Reynolds. This film is one of the standard, dull sleaze-fests of its day.

- *"Debbie Reynolds plays perversion for laughs…a lecherous male is reincarnated as a sexy female with his masculine mind and libido making the transmigration intact. Its double-sex entendres, sleazy smuttiness, and smarmy creepiness are enough to set straight sex and comedy back 20 years—let alone win the all-time Nasty Film Sweepstakes…slimy trash. Ugh."* (Judith Crist, Judith Crist's TV Guide to the Movies)

The Seven Year Itch (1956, 20th Century-Fox, 105m/c, **VHS/DVD**) ☆☆☆ **Sc:** Billy Wilder, George Axelrod. **D:** Billy Wilder. **P:** Charles K. Feldman, Billy Wilder. **Cam:** Milton Krasner. **Cast:** Marilyn Monroe, Tom Ewell, Evelyn Keyes, Sonny Tufts, Robert Strauss, Oscar Homolka, Marguerite Chapman, Victor Moore, Donald McBride, Carolyn Jones, Doro Merande. One of Monroe's most famous vehicles and Wilder's biggest hits, this seminal piece of 1950s-style sexploitation displays the star as the befuddled Ewell's upstairs neighbor during a sweltering summer when his wife takes a vacation on her own. Axelrod's 1955 hit starred Ewell and Vanessa Brown on Broadway.

- *"As the once amusing story drags on and on endlessly and Tom acts more and more like a fool, one begins to think the whole thing should have been called the seven year picture."* (Philip T. Hartung, Commonweal)
- *"…offers several stimulating views of Marilyn Monroe as a substitute for the comedy that George Axelrod got into the original version of this trifle…when Miss Monroe turns up as a young lady too substancial for dreams, the picture is reduced to the level of a burlesque show, and Mr. Ewell's efforts to be quietly funny are lost in the shuffle."* (John McCarten, The New Yorker)

Will Success Spoil Rock Hunter? (1957, 20th Century-Fox, 95/c, VHS) ☆☆½ **Sc/D/P:** Frank Tashlin. **Cam:** Joe MacDonald. **Cast:** Jayne Mansfield, Tony Randall, Betsy Drake, Joan Blondell, John Williams, Henry Jones, Mickey Hargitay. The 1955 play, produced by Jules Styne, starred Orson Bean and Mansfield. The play's central theme about an advertising executive trying to persuade a movie star to pitch Stay-Put lipstick was changed for the film, because 20th Century-Fox wouldn't stand for satire about the film business — so the target became its then arch-enemy, TV. The movie's other targets are 1950s American culture in general: its gadgets, sales campaigns, sexual attitudes, etc.

- *"Frank Tashlin manfully directing material unworthy of his talents..."* (Gordon Gow, Hollywood in the Fifties)
- *"Without animation's capacity for remaking its image, Tashlin was always in danger of disrupting human reality or of stopping his jokes short of their distorted logic. This tension is reflected in his unresolved love-hate at the excessiveness of such things as advertising, packaging, rock 'n' roll, TV, Jayne Mansfield's breasts, and the general pixillation of rat-racing. The tone of his satire is momentarily much more mordant than the sentimental form of the finished film allows."* (David Thomson, A Biographical Dictionary of Film)

John L. Balderston

John Lloyd Balderston
Born: October 22, 1889, Philadelphia, PA. **Died:** 1954.

A journalist who worked on Philadelphia newspapers before serving as the *New York World*'s London correspondent from 1924 to 1931, John L. Balderston wrote plays including *The Genius of the Marne* in 1919 and *Berkeley Square*, which was first performed in 1928. He and co-author J.C. Squire based it on an unfinished manuscript by Henry James. It became a hit in London, and Balderston and Sonya Levien adapted it for the American screen in 1933. Because of the success of *Dracula* as a play and a 1931 film, Balderston was fast-tracked through Universal's suddenly popular line of horror pictures, either writing the screenplays for or contributing some dialogue to the originals of *Frankenstein* (1931) and *The Mummy* (1932) as well as *The Mystery of Edwin Drood* (1935), *Mark of the Vampire* (1935), *Bride of Frankenstein* (1935), *Mad Love* (1935), *Dracula's Daughter* (1936), and *The Man Who Changed His Mind* (1936). He received an Oscar nomination for the screenplay of *Lives of a Bengal Lancer* (1936) and broke from the horror mold. He also wrote the screenplays for *The Last of the Mohicans* (1936), *The Prisoner of Zenda* (1937), *Little Old New York* (1940), Vic-

tory (1940), *Smilin' Through* (1941), and *Gaslight* (1944), which won Ingrid Bergman her first Oscar.

Berkeley Square debuted in 1929, co-directed by and starring Leslie Howard with Valerie Taylor. Howard played Peter Standish, who travels back in time, becomes one of his own ancestors, and falls in love with Taylor. The play was based on an unfinished novel by Henry James.

Berkeley Square (1933, Fox, 84m/bw) ☆☆☆½ **Sc:** John L. Barderston, Sonya Levien. **D:** Frank Lloyd. **P:** Jesse L. Lasky. **Cam:** Ernest Palmer. **Cast:** Leslie Howard, Heather Angel, Valerie Taylor, Lionel Belmore, Irene Browne, Juliette Compton, Ferdinand Gottschalk, Samuel S. Hinds, Olaf Hytten, Beryl Mercer Alan Mowbray, Colin Keith-Johnston, Betty Lawford. This handsome production was in the line of prestige pictures in which Howard was presented in his heyday. The British star received an Oscar nomination for this performance in this initial big-studio time-travel entry.

- *"The first major cinematic journey in time was a class act indeed…When he returns to 'modern' times, the lovers are separated by the greatest obstacle the movies had yet found to implement 'boy loses girl' — two centuries (give or take a year or so) The movie can best be described as 'poignant,' which may or may not be exactly what James had in mind."* (Baird Searles, Films of Science Fiction and Fantasy)

I'll Never Forget You (1951, 20th Century-Fox, 90m/c&bw) ☆☆ **Sc:** Ranald MacDougall. **D:** Roy Ward Baker. **P:** Sol C. Siegel. **Cam:** Georges Perinal. **Cast:** Tyrone Power, Ann Blythe, Michael Rennie, Dennis Price, Beatrice Campbell, Raymond Huntley Irene Browne, Kathleen Byron, Felix Aylmer, Victor Maddern, Jill Clifford, Ronald Adam. Also known as *The House in the Square* and *The Man of Two Worlds*, this Tyrone Power vehicle was pounded across in leaden style.

- *"Although there are obvious intimations of the lovely play* Berkeley Square *in the movie* I'll Never Forget You*…there is little of its poetry or magic in the latest rendering of it on the screen. Rather, there are…so many stiff and materialistic aspects of ponderous crudity that all the fragile charm and wistful pathos of the original are crushed beneath mass…Tyrone Power is stolid and moody, as though he had been tapped on the head."* (Bosley Crowther, The New York Times)

Berkeley Square (1959, NBC, 90m/c) *Hallmark Hall of Fame* ☆☆ **Tp:** Theodore Apstein. **D/P:** George Schaefer. **Cast:** John Kerr, Jeannie Carson, Edna Best, John Colicos, Frances Reid, Mildred Trares, Jerome Kilty, Janet Munro.

- *"This version…for a variety of reasons, not the least of which was the miscasting and ineffectuality of John Kerr in the central role, just didn't come off as a TV special. What few compensations there were in Theodore*

Apstein's adaptation...were no match for the lethargic pace and seemingly pointless approach...The business of racing back and forth in time, which is the pivotal point of the play, emerged vague and inconsistent...annoying for the viewer." (Variety)

Berkeley Square was also seen in TV's infancy in 1948 on *Kraft Television Theatre*, in 1949 on *Studio One* starring Leueen MacGrath (Mrs. George S. Kaufman) and William Prince and in 1951 on *Prudential Family Playhouse* with Richard Green and Grace Kelly.

Dracula, which Balderstone wrote with Hamilton Deane, was based on Bram Stoker's novel, which in turn was based on the legend of Vlad the Impaler, an actual regional feudal ruler in the Carpathian ranges. The play debuted on Broadway in 1927 and starred Bela Lugosi in his career-making role. It was revived in 1931, when the movie was released to great popularity. The play was sucessfully revived again in 1977, featuring Frank Langella as a much more dashing count. Other films and shows about Count Dracula didn't use the play.

Dracula (1931, Universal, 75m/bw, **VHS/DVD**) ☆☆☆½ **Sc:** Garrett Fort. **D:** Tod Browning. **P:** Tod Browning, Carl Laemmle, Jr. **Cam:** Karl Freund. **Cast:** Bela Lugosi, Helen Chandler, David Manners, Dwight Frye, Edward Van Sloan, Herbert Brunston, Frances Dade, Joan Standing, Charles K. Gerrard, Tod Browning, Moon Carroll, Dorothy Tree. A cultural event and a high-blood mark in the history of the horror film, this Universal classic now seems quaint, lugubrious, and talky.

- *"...never quite the definitive vampire film that it deserved to be, or that its opening two reels indicated it could have been. Those opening reels, sparse in dialogue and rich in visuals, are obviously dominated far more by the pictorial style of cameraman Karl Freund...than by the static and stage-bound style of Browning. The camera, almost like phantom itself, floats through the crypt of Dracula's castle in stately unhurried fashion. The atmospheric sets, the mobility of the camera, the skill of the glass-shots (particularly one of the coach entering Borgo Pass), and the composition of the individual frames (Dracula's three white-gowned wives gliding in to claim a victim) are all far more characteristic of Freund's work than Browning's...Whatever quality Freund instilled into the film was dissipated when the plot abandoned Transylvania and settled in London. From then on, it followed the play rather than Bram Stoker's difficult but chillingly rewarding novel. All the marvelous visual highlights of the book were merely talked about in the film..."* (William K. Everson, Classics of the Horror Film)

Dracula (1979, Universal, 109m/c, **VHS/DVD**) ☆☆½ **Sc:** W.D. Richter. **D:** John Badham. **P:** Walter Mirisch. **Cam:** Gilbert Taylor. **Cast:** Frank Langella, Laurence Olivier, Donald Pleasance, Kate Nelligan, Trevor Eve, Jan Francis, Tony Hagarth, Teddy Turner, Ted Carroll, Frank Birch, Frank Hensen, Kristine Howarth, Sylvester

McCoy, Joe Belcher. Langella's chance to repeat his popular stage success was supplemented by the casting of Olivier as Dr. Van Helsing, one of the master's late-career, Euro-vague contributions.

- *"...while it fails on many counts, is, nevertheless, of historic importance because in it Frank Langella plays Count Dracula as the fatally attractive sexual figure that filmgoers, ever since the 1922 Nosferatu, secretly knew him to be. The film is entirely Langella's. He is everything a Byronic figure ought to be: tall, handsome, dashing...and ominous...Langella, as he did when he interpreted the role on the stage in New York, moves with the cold authority of the vampire. But there is no way for him to hide the superabundant erotic energy and that works against his role in the film...What the film lacks is the one ingredient without which a horror film is a dud: It lacks the capacity to scare anyone."* (Leonard Wolf, Horror: A Connoisseur's Guide to Literature and Film)

Red Planet Mars (1952, UA, 87m/bw, **VHS**) ☆☆½ **Sc:** John Balderston, Anthony Veiller. **D:** Harry Horner. **P:** Donald Hyde, Anthony Veiller. **Cam:** Joseph Biroc. **Cast:** Peter Graves, Andrea King, Herbert Berghof, Walter Sande, Marvin Miller, Willis Bouchey, Morris Ankrum, Bayard Veiller, Robert Carson, Vince Barnett, Orley Lindgren, Wade Crosby. The 1932 play by Balderston and John E. Hoare ran for seven performances at Broadway's Cort Theatre with a cast that included Valerie Taylor. Graves, as a young American scientist, picks up TV transmissions from Mars and learns that God rules a utopian society there; this news throws the world into chaos as the religious right invades Iron Curtain countries and installs a priest as the new Czar.

- *"With few exceptions, humans are presented very badly in these films. No sooner is there a whiff of impending doom than the average citizen reverts to a cowardly, greedy, selfish and lustful animal...This trend reached its cinematic peak with Red Planet Mars...In Russia the Soviet government is defeated by a group of aged revolutionaries who restore the monarchy, making a priest the new Tsar."* (John Brosnan, Future Tense: The Cinema of Science Fiction)

Amiri Baraka

Everett LeRoi Jones, aka, Imamu Ameer Baraka and LeRoi Jones
Born: October 7, 1934, Newark, NJ.

Amiri Baraka was one of the most influential African American playwrights of the 1960s and 1970s, initially under the name LeRoi Jones, which he used until 1967. His plays include *The Toilet, The Death of*

Malcolm X, A Black Mass, Junkies Are Full of SHHH, A Recent Killing, Dim Cracker Party Convention, Boy and Tarzan Appear in a Clearing, and *Money: Jazz Opera.*

Dutchman (1967, Gene Persson, 55m/c) ☆☆☆ **Sc:** LeRoi Jones. **D/Cam:** Anthony Harvey. **P:** Gene Persson. **Cast:** Shirley Knight, Al Freeman, Jr. In this short, surrealistic nightmare piece on a New York subway train that never stops, an insane white woman and a harsh black man terrorize the passengers. The symbolic play was first performed in New York in 1964 at the Cherry Lane Theatre with Robert Hooks and Jennnifer West; Knight and Freeman played it in Los Angeles.

- *"It is a work that tries to be both naturalistic and symbolistic, but fails in both modes, individually and in concert...Though Al Freeman, Jr. gives a nicely tempered performance as Clay...Shirley Knight's Lula is another matter. Miss Knight, always a walking compendium of the worst Actors Studio inanities, is here allowed not to act insane, but to be insane—something that, by Diderot's well-known paradox of the actor, does not work...That LeRoi Jones should be steadily published, produced, awarded grants and applauded would, in view of his unceasing let's-massacre-the-whites tantrums and rabble rousing, is grotesque."* (John Simon, Movies Into Film)

- *"In* Dutchman *the failure is of the medium itself and not the filmmakers, who have attempted the transition with integrity. The bare bones of the LeRoi Jones parable can survive a transition...But put even the same actors...into the magnified realism of film, make it a real and roaring rattling subway train, and belief is shattered, the essential poetic incoherence of the interaction and response of what are essentially symbols disappear, and we are left with incredibles, in form and content."* (Judith Crist, The Private Eye, the Cowboy and the Very Naked Lady)

Philip Barry

Born: June 18, 1896, Rochester, NY. **Died:** 1949.

Born of Irish heritage and educated at Yale and Harvard, Philip Barry served for a time as a United States envoy in London. From the mid-1920s on he wrote about a play a year. *Paris Bound* (1927) was his first big box-office success, followed by *Holiday* (1928). *The Philadelphia Story* (1939) became his lasting touchstone in American culture, fronted on both the stage and screen by Katharine Hepburn. His plays include *John* (1927), about John the Baptist, *The Joyous Season* (1934), *Bright Star* (1935), *Here Come the Clowns* (1938), *Liberty Jones* (1941), and *Foolish Notion* (1945). Barry collaborated with Elmer Rice on the mystery play, *Cock Robin* (1928) and also converted *Here Come the Clowns* into a 1938 novel called *War in Heaven*. The largely completed play, *Second Threshold*, was dusted off by Robert E. Sherwood after Barry's death and produced in 1951. Barry's dialogues in his best plays sparkled with witty repartée concerning the battles and truces between the sexes.

The Animal Kingdom starred Leslie Howard on Broadway in 1932 as a publisher who believes that he can have the best of both worlds by maintaining his liaison with his mistress and sustaining his marriage and family life. Co-starring were Frances Fuller, Ilka Chase, and Lora Baxter.

The Animal Kingdom (1932, RKO, 90m/bw, **VHS**) ☆☆☆ **Sc:** Horace Jackson. **D:** Edward H. Griffith. **P:** David O. Selznick. **Cam:** George Folsey. **Cast:** Ann Harding, Leslie Howard, Myrna Loy, Neil Hamilton, William Gargan, Henry Stephenson, Ilka Chase, Leni Stengel, Donald Dillaway. Deftly playing his stars against type, Griffith deployed Loy, usually used as a sexy coquette, to play the wife, and used Harding's reputation as a well-mannered society matron in the role of the mistress. This was a big hit in the year before the major studios decided to adhere to the Production Code.

- *"The playwright's ideas have been adhered to faithfully. It has the subtlety and restraint of the stage work and the settings are always in good taste."* (Mordaunt Hall, The New York Times)
- *"Griffith directed [Harding] for a third time and again brought to the fore her finest screen qualities...The total production emerged both professionally slick and true to Barry's witty original. This picture proved to be the best liked and most successful of [Harding's] film career."* (James Robert Parish, The RKO Gals)

One More Tomorrow (1946, Warner Bros., 89m/bw) ☆☆½ **Sc:** Charles Hoffman, Catherine Turney, Julius J. Epstein, Philip G. Epstein. **D:** Peter Godfrey. **P:** Henry Blanke. **Cam:** Bert Glennon. **Cast:** Ann Sheridan, Dennis Morgan, Jack Carson, Alexis Smith, Jane Wyman, Reginald Gardiner, John Loder, Marjorie Gateson, Thurston Hall, John Abbott, William Benedict. Warner Bros. put its *Casablanca* (1943) team of Epsteins on this World War II-era update of Barry's play, with topical references, such as war profiteering, thrown in.

- *"It took four of Warner's best script writers to rewrite...*The Animal Kingdom...*Yet out of all of this effort...has come a film which only serves to prove how far superior Mr. Barry was at turning a sharp, meaningful phrase. The scenarists have retained only the basic framework of the play...the dialogue is blunted, whereas it needs to be razor-edged...just another romantic comedy drama with pretentions of social import."* (Thomas M. Pryor, The New York Times)

The Animal Kingdom (1957, NBC, 60m/bw) *The Alcoa Hour* ☆☆ **Sc/P:** Philip Barry, Jr. **D:** Alex Segal. **Cast:** Robert Preston, Meg Mundy,

Joanne Linville, Alan Hale, Jr. Segal and Mundy had plumbed this territory before (see below). The playwright's son, acting as producer, pared the play into the teleplay. The irrepressable Preston usually signified quality, but the results were mediocre at best.

- *"Philip Barry, Jr. has proven himself an able television producer since taking over the* Alcoa-Goodyear *mantle, but he's a long way to go to become a TV playwright. That was amply demonstrated Sunday...Barry's adaptation of his late father's* The Animal Kingdom *proved out as one of the most disastrous of this season's dramatic efforts. Most of the fault lies with Barry himself, for the adaptation suffered from sketchiness, mawkishness and an absence of establishing scenes and dialogue that left the viewer wondering what was going on most of the time."* (Variety)

The Animal Kingdom aired in 1952 on ABC's *Celanese Theatre* with Alex Segal directing Wendell Corey and Meg Mundy.

Foolish Notion, a 1945 Tallulah Bankhead vehicle on Broadway, aired in 1948 on NBC's *Kraft Television Theatre*.

Holiday was produced on Broadway in 1928 with Hope Williams as the rebellious society girl, Linda Seton. She rejects her banker father's conservative views and plots to disrupt her younger sister's wedding to the unconventional Johnny Chase, whom she loves on sight. His plan is to retire early in life and work later on, which she advocates. Williams was understudied by Katharine Hepburn, who helped make the 1938 film of the play into one of the 1930s most fondly remembered comedies.

Holiday (1930, RKO-Pathé, 89m/bw) ☆☆☆ **Sc:** Horace Jackson. **D:** Edward H. Griffith. **P:** E.B. Derr. **Cam:** Norbert Brodine. **Cast:** Ann Harding, Mary Astor, Edward Everett Horton, Robert Ames, Hedda Hopper, Monroe Owsley, William Holden, Hallam Cooley, Mabel Forrest, Creighton Hale, Elizabeth Forrester, Mary Elizabeth Forbes. Harding's star luster—her throaty voice commanding in the era of shaky early sound techniques—helped make Linda Seton's adventurousness more realistic and less mannered than Hepburn's (below). The film was Oscar nominated for Best Actress (Harding) and Jackson's script, which preserves almost all of the original play.

- *"...a stylish production...a solid hit, comparing most favorably—taking its still primitive sound techniques into consideration—with George Cukor's elegant 1938 remake...[Harding] solidified her screen image as a patrician beauty...at 28 years of age, she epitomized the well-bred young matron...Her aristocratic standoffishness and her at times icy deep voice often seemed more foreboding than Garbo's aloof screen presence."* (James Robert Parish, The RKO Gals)

Holiday (1938, Columbia, 93m/bw, **VHS**) ☆☆☆☆☆ **Sc:** Donald Ogden

Stewart, Sidney Buchman. **D:** George Cukor. **P:** Everett Riskin. **Cam:** Franz Planer. **Cast:** Katharine Hepburn, Cary Grant, Doris Nolan, Lew Ayres, Edward Everett Horton, Henry Kolker, Binnie Barnes, Jean Dixon, Henry Daniell, Charles Trowbridge, George Pauncefort, Charles Richman, Bess Flowers, Neil Fitzgerald, Mitchell Harris. This is one of the most enduring and emblematic sophisticated comedies of the 1930s, performed by a superior cast that was determined and arranged by Hepburn, who sold the idea to Columbia's Harry Cohn.

- *"In* Holiday, *she gave one of her best screen performances, making the role her own and creating this version as a first-rate comedy of manners...Polishing and updating (from the 1920s to the 1930s) the sophisticated comedy, Stewart (and Buchman) turned Linda Seton into the very epitmote of Hepburn: rich, literate, rebellious...Deftly amusing and gracefully played,* Holiday *succinctly captures the 1930s' cinema concepts of society and life among the idle rich."* (Alvin H. Marill, Katharine Hepburn, 1973)

- *"Donald Ogden Stewart's adaptation...bore such style and wit that Cukor and a handpicked cast could scarcely fail. Hepburn and Grant are at the top of their considerable form here...Literate, amusing, thought-provoking, and often very moving,* Holiday *is vintage 1930s comedy, and its failure to win even an Academy Award nomination in 1938 is difficult to fathom."* (Jerry Vermilye, The Films of the Thirties)

Holiday aired in 1947 on *Kraft Television Theatre,* in 1949 on CBS's *Studio One* with Valerie Bettis, and in 1956 as an NBC special with Kitty Carlisle and Tammy Grimes.

In a Garden (1961, PBS, 120m/bw) *The Play of the Week* ☆☆☆ **Sc:** Philip Barry. **D:** Henry Kaplan. **P:** Lewis Freedman. **Cast:** Roddy McDowall, George Grizzard, Frances Sternhagen, Barbara Cook, Laurie Main. The 1925 play, produced and staged by Arthur Hopkins and starring Frank Conroy, Laurette Taylor, and Louis Calhern, concerns a playwright with high standards of cultural taste, and the suffering of his wife, who yearns to be carefree and spontaneous. He tricks her into recreating her romantic past with her former beau, now a family house guest.

- *"...hardly the sturdiest of the late Philip Barry's plays, but has enough flashes of the Barry wit and brilliance to make this* Play of the Week *revival worthwhile. Certainly, it constitutes more stimulating fare, for all its weaknesses, than most of the drama available on TV today...Barry's characters aren't entirely believable, and in some respects are dated as well, but a fine performance and sensitive direction by Henry Kaplan nonetheless produce fine moments of high comedy."* (Variety)

The Joyous Season aired in 1951 on ABC's *Celanese Theatre* with Alex Segal directing Lillian Gish and Wesley Addy. The 1934 play, starring Gish and featuring Jane Wyatt and Alan Campbell, concerns a Catholic nun who is asked to consult on her recently deceased father's will after the family leaves the farm for Boston's fashionable Beacon Street.

Paris Bound (1929, Pathé, 73m/bw) ☆☆☆ **Sc:** Horace Jackson. **D:** Edward H. Griffith. **P:** Arthur Hopkins. **Cam:** Norbert Brodine. **Cast:** Ann Harding, Fredric March, Leslie Fenton, Ilka Chase, George Irving, Hallam Cooley, Juliette Crosby, Charlotte Walker, Carmelita Geraghty. The 1927 stage hit starred Madge Kennedy in the daring story (for its time) of a married couple who insist that two people can remain spiritually true to each other while dallying with other sexual partners. Pathé and Harding decided on this piece for the actress's film debut. Director Griffith's camera tricks, Harding's and March's smooth performances, and the racy material mesh agreeably.

- *"Quite a praiseworthy adaptation of Philip Barry's clever play. It is in most respects an effort that bears evidence of a restraining hand and the voices are exceptionally well-registered. E.H. Griffith, the director, often uses his camera to advantage, but there are discursive passages that become somewhat tedious, and so does the constant embracing of husband and wife..."* (Mordaunt Hall, The New York Times)

The Philadelphia Story was Barry's most enduring work, telling the Main Line story of C.K. Dexter-Haven, who divorces the haughty Tracy Lord, then tries to prevent her second marriage while magazine reporter Mike Connor, angling for a story on society marriage, has a serious flirtation with her on the eve of the vows. Barry tailored the play to Hepburn's strengths and she starred on Broadway in a run of 416 performances in 1939 and 1940.

The Philadelphia Story (1940, MGM, 112m/bw, **VHS/DVD**) ☆☆☆☆☆ **Sc:** Donald Ogden Stewart. **D:** George Cukor. **P:** Joseph L. Mankiewicz. **Cam:** Joseph Ruttenberg. **Cast:** Cary Grant, Katharine Hepburn, James Stewart, Ruth Hussey, John Howard, Roland Young, John Halliday, Virginia Weidler, Mary Nash, Henry Daniell, Lionel Pape, Rex Evans, Hilda Plowright, Russ Clark, Lee Phelps. One of the most sublimely sophisticated romantic comedies ever made, this film became the biggest box-office success of its day, solidifying the reputations of all its participants. It won the Academy Awards for Best Actor and Best Screenplay (the two Stewarts) and was nominated for Best Picture, Actress (Hepburn), Supporting Actress (Hussey), and Director.

- *"An exceptionally bright job of screenplay writing...though films like this do little to advance the art of motion pictures, they may help some of the more discerning among cultural slugabeds that when movies want to turn their hand to anything, they can turn it."* (Otis Ferguson, The New Republic)
- *"Shiny and unfelt and smart-aleck-commercial as the movie is, it's almost irresistibly entertaining—one of the high spots of MGM professionalism.*

There isn't much real wit in the lines, and there's no feeling of spontaneity, yet the engineering is so astute that the laughs keep coming. This is a paste diamond with more flash and sparkle than a true one. The director, George Cukor, has never been so heartlessly sure of himself." (Pauline Kael, 5001 Nights at the Movies)

The Philadelphia Story (1954, CBS, 60m/c) *The Best of Broadway* ☆☆½ **Tp:** Philip Barry, Jr. **D:** David Alexander. **P:** Martin Manulis. **Cast:** Dorothy McGuire, John Payne, Richard Carlson, Mary Astor, Dick Foran, Herbert Marshall, Neva Patterson, Charles Winninger, Jane Sutherland. A top-notch cast was rounded up for this live telecast.

- *"This 16-year-old play about Philly's Main Line snobs had seen its best days and also its best performances long before Westinghouse picked it as The Best of Broadway for last...It has been around through numerous stage revivals and on the screen since Katharine Hepburn created its central character. For her, it was a natural. Last night, in the reflection of her artistry, Dorothy McGuire was forced to extremes to manage only a carbon copy of the original...the fluffed lines and slow cues stunted the play's casual pace...Apparently the adapter, Philip Barry, Jr., was too family-proud to change or update it."* (Variety)

High Society (1956, MGM, 107m/c, **VHS**) ☆☆½ **Sc:** John Patrick. **D:** Charles Walters. **P:** Sol C. Siegel. **Cam:** Paul A. Vogel. **Cast:** Bing Crosby, Grace Kelly, Frank Sinatra, Celeste Holm, John Lund, Louis Calhern, Sidney Blackmer, Louis Armstrong, Margalo Gillmore, Richard Garrick, Lydia Reed, Gordon Richards, Richard Keene, Ruth Lee, Helen Spring, Paul Keast, Reginald Simpson, Hugh Boswell. The star trio rounded up for this musical remake outshone the results.

- *"The principals perform, most of the time, with a kind of glum cheeriness...There is one delightful duet, however, when Sinatra and Crosby get together for five minutes or so and show solid professionalism in their handling of 'What a Swell Party This Is.' If the rest of the movie were up to that level—but it isn't"* (Hollis Alpert, The Saturday Review)

- *"Looked at four decades on, High Society has a strangely remote, uninvolving feel to it, as if the events depicted were being viewed under a microscope...Walters's lackluster direction is absurdly static, with far too many dull long shots, making the film's stage origins more obvious than they were in The Philadelphia Story."* (Daniel O'Brien, The Frank Sinatra Film Guide)

The Philadelphia Story (1959, NBC Special, 90m/c) ☆☆ **Tp:** Jacqueline Babbin, Audrey Gellen. **D:** Fielder Cook. **P:** Fielder Cook, David Susskind. **Cast:** Diana Lynn, Gig Young, Christopher Plummer, Don DeFore, Ruth Roman, Mary Astor, Alan Webb, Gaye Huston, Leon Janney, Emory Richardson. This elaborate special went back to the well for a fifth time, the third on TV, but didn't have the sparkle of the previous versions.

- *"Barry's comedy belongs to another day in the theatre. 20 years ago it was fashionable to sit through the smart, semi-wacky, semi-romantic drawing room comedies that the Barrys, the Rachel Crotherses and the S.N. Behrmans were tossing off. In the cold light of 1959 few of them hold up, and* The Philadelphia Story *is no exception...All of the accepted rules of TV dramaturgy were complied with, from the inordinately elaborate production trappings to the skillful abbreviation in the adaptation by Jacqueline Bobbin and Audrey Gellen, two of the overworked reliables bearing the Talent Associates imprint."* (Variety)

The Philadelphia Story also aired in 1950 on *Robert Montgomery Presents* with Barbara Bel Geddes, Richard Derr, and Leslie Nielsen in the principal roles.

Second Threshold aired in 1951 on ABC's *Pulitzer Prize Playhouse* with the eclectic trio of Clive Brook, Betsy Von Furstenberg, and Hugh Reilly. The 1949 play concerned a man who estranges himself from friends and family so they won't feel the loss at his suicide, but then discovers that his daughter has decided to follow his cue.

Spring Madness (1938, MGM, 66m/bw) ☆☆☆ **Sc/P:** Edward Chodorov. **D:** S. Sylvan Simon. **Cam:** Joseph Ruttenberg. **Cast:** Maureen O'Sullivan, Lew Ayres, Ruth Hussey, Burgess Meredith, Joyce Compton, Ann Morriss, Jacqueline Wells (Julie Bishop), Frank Albertson, Truman Bradley, Sterling Holloway, Marjorie Gateson, Renie Riano. Barry's 1936 play, *Spring Dance*, updated a college-set play by Eleanor Golden and Eloise Barrangone. Louise Platt starred as Alex Benson, who hopes, near graduation time, for a marriage proposal from Sam. He instead plans to study in Russia for several years, until Alex's friends try to fuel Sam's jealousy. Richard Kendrick played Sam in the Jed Harris production at the Empire Theatre and the support included Jose Ferrer, Philip Ober, Mary Wickes, and Tom Neal. The film's actors were a bit long in the tooth to be on campus, but this fluff doesn't demand any sort of exactitude.

- *"The tragedy of young love, with a beautifully comic performance by Burgess Meredith, as a kind of anti-Cupid, to set it off, is not to be sneezed at...And with Lew Ayres (the cinema's best unappreciated actor) as the victim of a sorority house matrimonial plot involving Maureen (the dependable) O'Sullivan, it is practically irresistible."* (B.R. Crisler, The New York Times)

Tomorrow and Tomorrow (1931, Paramount, 73m/bw) ☆☆½ **Sc:** Josephine Lovett. **D:** Richard Wallace. **Cam:** Charles Lang. **Cast:** Ruth Chatterton, Paul Lukas, Robert Ames, Harold Minjir, Tad Alexander, Arthur Pierson, Walter Walker, Winter Hall, Margaret Armstrong. Barry took his title from *Macbeth* and his theme from The Bible. In the

1931 Barry play, an Earth-mother-styled wife decides to stay with the weaker man, her husband, instead of following her passions out of wedlock, which produces a child that she vows is her husband's. The point is that adultery and infidelity can be condoned to keep a marriage together in this pre-Production Code melodrama. Ames died before the film was released.

- *"Barry's drama didn't work nearly as well on screen as his high society comedies...but good dialogue and fine performances help to salvage this picture." (S.R. Ross, Nash, The Motion Picture Guide)*

Without Love (1945, MGM, 111m/bw, **VHS**) ☆☆½ **Sc:** Donald Ogden Stewart. **D:** Harold S. Bucquet. **P:** Lawrence A. Weingarten. **Cam:** Karl Freund. **Cast:** Spencer Tracy, Katharine Hepburn, Lucille Ball, Keenan Wynn, Carl Esmond, Patricia Morison, Gloria Grahame, Felix Bressart, Emily Massey, George Chandler, George Davis, Wallis Clark, Eddie Acuff, Clarence Muse, James Flavin, Hazel Brooks, Clancy Cooper. Barry and Hepburn huddled again after the stage success of *The Philadelphia Story*, and came up with this story of a widow in wartime Washington, DC, who agrees to a platonic sharing of her spacious home with a scientist working for the war effort. It ran for 113 performances. Stewart again reworked Barry for the screen and Hepburn starred with Tracy for the third time.

- *"Left to their own devices, Spencer comes on as a brick while Kate is very mannered—little of his simplicity has rubbed off on her...Every other line she exclaims, 'By gum!'...She's rarely been so arch and girlish, and for a woman of her age, this kind of affectation seems a bit old-maidish...Today, it seems the weakest of all the Tracy-Hepburn comedies, with nothing to recommend it but a pair of stylish, scene-stealing performances by Lucille Ball and Keenan Wynn." (Gary Carey, Katharine Hepburn, 1975)*
- *"...a satiny translation of a Philip Barry play; I like it all right and have very little to say for or against it. Unlike Mr. Barry, I don't find the expression 'by gum' charming on lips that use it for charm's sake...But a good deal of the dialogue is happy to hear and happier in its skill..." (James Agee, The Nation)*

You and I, first staged in 1923 by Robert Minton in New York's Belmont Theatre, concerns a wealthy businessman who passes up an artist's career early in life for the safer business world, and tries to see that his son doesn't make the same mistake. The play was Barry's first on Broadway.

The Bargain (1931, Warner Bros., 68m/bw) ☆☆ **Sc:** Robert Presnell. **D:** Robert Minton. **Cam:** Sol Polito. **Cast:** Lewis Stone, Evelyn Knapp, Charles Butterworth, Doris Kenyon, John Darrow, Oscar Apfel, Una Merkel, Nella Walker.

- *"...the comedy served up by Una Merkel and Charles Butterworth in com-*

paratively minor roles almost completely obscures the irony and pathos of the main theme. An uneven production, only the admirable acting of Lewis Stone and Doris Kenyon as the aging couple of the original title save it from a lopsided dive into ordinary father-and-son sentimentality. But the story remains one of genuine tenderness and warmth." (Andre Sennwald, The New York Times)

You and I aired in 1958 on NBC's *Matinee Theatre* starring Donald Woods.

S.N. Behrman

Samuel Nathaniel Behrman
Born: June 9, 1893, Worcester, MA. **Died:** 1973.

S.N. Behrman's screenplays in the early sound era included *The Sea Wolf* (1930), *Lilliom* (1930), *Lightnin'* (1930), *Daddy Long Legs* (1931), *The Brat* (1931), *Tess of the Storm Country* (1932), and *Rebecca of Sunnybrook Farm* (1932). He also wrote dialogue for the Greta Garbo vehicles *Queen Christina* (1933), *Anna Karenina* (1935), and *Two-Faced Woman* (1941); adapted Charles Dickens's *A Tale of Two Cities* into the 1935 Ronald Colman epic; wrote the expensive Clark Gable dud *Parnell* (1937); and adapted Robert E. Sherwood's *Waterloo Bridge* (1940) and the Roman epic *Quo Vadis?* (1951).

Behrman's plays include *Serena Blandish* (1929), *Meteor* (1929), *Rain From Heaven* (1934), *Amphitryon 38* (1937), *The Talley Method* (1941), *Jacobowsky and the Colonel* (1944 with Franz Werfel), and *But for Whom Charlie* (1964). Among his nonfiction are *Duveen* (1952), about the life of the art dealer, and *Portrait of Max* (1960), an intimate look at the life of Max Beerbohm.

For *Fanny*, see **Joshua Logan**.

Biography, Behrman's 1932 Broadway hit, starred Ina Claire as a celebrity portrait painter whose forthcoming biography reveals details of her love affairs, one with an important politician.

Biography of a Bachelor Girl (1934, MGM, 84m/bw) ☆☆ **Sc:** Anita Loos. **D:** Edward H. Griffith. **P:** Louis B. Mayer. **Cam:** James Wong Howe. **Cast:** Ann Harding, Robert Montgomery, Edward Everett Horton, Edward Arnold, Una Merkel, Donald Meek, Charles Richman, Greta Meyer, Willard Robertson. MGM bought the rights to the play for Marion Davies, who proved to be unavailable, and then cast Harding in the part.

- *"What Miss Harding does to the picture is to make the central and all-important character as artificial and unbelievable as are compatible with her trite and meaningless gestures." (Thornton Delehanty, New York Post)*

Biography was produced on TV in 1948 on *Kraft Television Theatre* with Virginia Gilmore and John Forsythe and in 1950 as the inaugural presentation on *Prudential Family Playhouse* starring Gertrude Lawrence and Kevin McCarthy.

Brief Moment was a hit of 1931, produced and staged by Guthrie McClintic at New York's Belasco Theatre with a cast topped by Robert Douglas, Alexander Woollcott, Louis Calhern, and Frances Rich. In it, a nightclub singer who's an advocate of hard work marries a rich society scion and becomes fed up with his do-nothing lifestyle, convincing his father to cut off the gravy train so he'll go to work.

Brief Moment (1933, Columbia, 69m/bw) ☆☆½ **Sc:** Brian Marlow, Edith Fitzgerald. **D:** David Burton. **Cam:** Ted Tetzlaff. **Cast:** Carole Lombard, Gene Raymond, Monroe Owsley, Donald Cook, Arthur Hohl, Reginald Mason, Jameson Thomas, Theresa Maxwell Conover, Florence Britton, Irene Ware, Herbert Evans.

- *"Miss Lombard and Mr. Raymond treat it as though it were entirely new. An audience cannot help being lured into a favorable reaction."* (Mordaunt Hall, The New York Times)

- *"A second-rate drama that could have been given some spirit if Lombard had felt up to turning in a clever, passionate performance instead of a merely entertaining one. The lackluster Raymond doesn't help much, either."* (Nash, S.R. Ross, The Motion Picture Guide)

Brief Moment also showed up in condensed form on a 1952 installment of *Celanese Theatre* directed by Alex Segal with Veronica Lake, Robert Sterling, and Burgess Meredith.

End of Summer aired in 1977 on PBS's *Theatre in America*, directed by Stephen Porter and produced by Ken Campbell, in a presentation hosted by Helen Hayes. Also starring were Lois Nettleton, Paul Shenar, Paul Rudd, Dennis Michael, Pamela Lewis, Alan Mixon, Robert Strane, and Bradford Wallace. The same production, a collaboration of the Charles MacArthur Center for the American Theatre and the Asolo State Theatre in Sarasota, Florida, also aired on PBS under the *Great Performances* banner. The play debuted in 1936 at New York's Guild Theatre and featured Ina Claire as Leonie Frothingham, who hopes that her daughter makes the right romantic choice between a fortune-hunting doctor and an adventurous young radical. Co-starring were Doris Dudley, Mildred Natwick, Osgood Perkins, Sheppard Strudwick, and Van Heflin.

He Knew Women (1930, RKO, 86m/bw) ☆☆½ **Sc:** Hugh Herbert, William Jutte. **D:** Hugh Herbert. **P:** Myles Connolly. **Cam:** Edward Cronjager. **Cast:** Lowell Sherman, Alice Joyce, David Manners, Frances Dade. The film was based on Behrman's play, *The Second Man*, about a novelist who leaves his sweetheart to bilk a widowed heiress until a savior comes along for both women.

- *"...better-than-average look at love...An intelligently scripted and alertly directed adaptation..."* (S.R. Ross, Nash, The Motion Picture Guide)

No Time for Comedy starred theatrical heavyweights Laurence Olivier and Katharine Cornell in a lightweight 1939 comedy at the Ethel Barrymore Theatre. Olivier played a playwright of popular lightweight farces who mopes about wanting to turn out something serious.

No Time for Comedy (1940, Warner Bros., 93m/bw) ☆☆☆½ **Sc:** Julius J. Epstein, Philip G. Epstein. **D:** William Keighley. **P:** Robert Lord. **Cam:** Ernest Haller. **Cast:** James Stewart, Rosalind Russell, Charles Ruggles, Genevieve Tobin, Allyn Joslyn, Clarence Kolb, Louise Beavers, Robert Greig, J.M. Kerrigan, Frank Faylen, Robert Emmett O'Connor, Selmer Jackson, Pierre Watkin, Herbert Heywood, John Ridgely. The Epsteins, who would write *Casablanca* three years later, rewrote Behrman to take advantage of Stewart's suddenly very popular downhome personality, and made him a naïve bumpkin all too susceptible to feminine wiles.

- *"Pundits insist the title told the whole story too well."* (James Robert Parish, The All-Americans)
- *"The Behrman dialogue was linked like precise, polished pearls. But the movie, with its change of equal time for both stars, was funny where the play was amusing. And the performances by the stars and by Charles Ruggles as the bemused husband of Stewart's 'patroness' (Genevieve Tobin), helped to make the film more spontaneously attractive than the caviar-flavored original."* (Howard Thompson, James Stewart, 1974)

No Time for Comedy was also seen twice on TV: in 1951 on *Celanese Theatre*, directed by Alex Segal, with Sarah Churchill and Jean-Pierre Aumont, and in 1957 on *Matinee Theatre*, again with Churchill.

The Pirate (1948, MGM, 102m/c, **VHS**) ☆☆☆☆ **Sc:** Albert Hackett, Frances Goodrich. **D:** Vincente Minnelli. **P:** Arthur Freed. **Cam:** Harry Stradling. **Cast:** Gene Kelly, Judy Garland, Walter Slezak, Gladys Cooper, Reginald Owen, George Zucco, the Nicholas Brothers. Originally written by Behrman for a 1942 play starring Alfred Lunt and Lynne Fontanne, it concerned a Latina girl who yearns to be swept off her feet by a pirate and sees that image in Kelly, the dashing member of a traveling troupe of actors. One of the top musicals of the 1940s.

- *"An unflawed MGM musical...now a cult favorite for its blend of dance- and story-musical forms...gorgeous costumes, superb use of Technicolor, a fine script...[Garland's] Manuela and Kelly's Serafin make one of the great musical teams, and Minnelli sets them off like jewels in a dream that does at length come true. Yet the film bombed." (Ethan Mordden, The Holly-wood Musical)*

- "*Color worth seeing, and Gene Kelly's very ambitious, painfully misguided performance, by John Barrymore out of elder Douglas Fairbanks. Judy Garland is good; and Vincente Minnelli's direction gives the whole business bulge and splendor...they're all really trying something—and in musical comedy..." (James Agee, The Nation)*

Stephen Vincent Benet

Born: July 22, 1898, Bethlehem, PA. **Died:** 1943.

Stephen Vincent Benet won Pulitzer Prizes in poetry for *John Brown's Body* (1928), a narrative of the Civil War, and *Western Star* (1943), a portion of a conceived epic about migration across the American West. His novels include *Jean Huguenot* (1923) and *Spanish Bayonet* (1926). His one-act folk operas with music by Douglas Moore include *The Headless Horseman* (1937) and *The Devil and Daniel Webster* (1939).

The Devil and Daniel Webster was written by Benet as a libretto for a 1939 folk opera with music by Douglas Moore. In 1840 New Hampshire, a farmer named Jabez Stone has fallen on hard times and sells his soul to the devil, known as Mr. Scratch, then has a lawyer defend him.

The Devil and Daniel Webster (1941, RKO, 106m/bw, **VHS**) **Sc:** Dan Totheroh. **D:** William Dieterle. **P:** William Dieterle, Charles L. Glett. **Cam:** Joseph August. **Cast:** Walter Huston, James Craig, Anne Shirley, Simone Simon, Edward Arnold, Jane Darwell, Gene Lockhart, John Qualen, H.B. Warner, Jeff Corey. Considered by many critics to be one of the best films of the 1940s, the movie is highlighted by the brilliant performance of Walter Huston as Mr. Scratch. He was nominated for a Best Actor Oscar and Bernard Herrmann won one for his haunting score. Perhaps Dieterle's best film, it benefits from his native German aesthetics and techniques and maybe even his acting role in F.W. Murnau's *Faust* (1926).

- "*...the film for which [Dieterle] is best remembered...Produced and directed by Dieterle under an obviously stringent budget, the film was a moody, ex-pressive piece of Americana with several haunting and powerful scenes, such as the ghostly ball at Jabez Stone's mansion and the climactic trial in the barn." (Ted Sennett, Great Movie Directors)*

- "*One of the season's best pictures...He [Dieterle] has succeeded in welding truth both timeless and timely in a picture which does not follow the lines of the old classic anymore than it adheres to the happy ending routine of Hol-lywood." (Archer Winsten, New York Post)*

- *"Theatre operators will have to be magicians to make this one stand up before any but the most naïve type of audiences...it is a very bad screenplay, not helped by Dieterle's slow-paced direction."* (Variety)

The Devil and Daniel Webster was pared to an hour for a 1960 NBC special adapted by Phil Reisman, Jr., directed by Tom Donovan, and produced by David Susskind. It starred Edward G. Robinson and David Wayne, along with Tim O'Connor, Betty Lou Holland, Royal Beal, Stuart Germain, and Howard Freeman.

Irving Berlin

Born: May 11, 1888, Mogilyov, Russia (now Belarus). **Died:** 1989.

Irving Berlin was one of America's greatest and most prolific songwriters, penning tunes at first for Broadway shows and Tin Pan Alley, then for Hollywood musicals. He was in demand throughout his lifetime for new material. He was awarded the Congressional Medal of Honor for writing "God Bless America" and among his hundreds of songs are "White Christmas," "Blue Skies," "Annie Get Your Gun," and "Always." He also spent some time as a stage book writer.

Mammy (1930, Warner Bros., 84m/bw&c, **VHS**) ☆☆☆ **Sc:** Joseph Jackson, Gordon Rigby. **D:** Michael Curtiz. **P:** Walter Morosco. **Cam:** Barney McGill. **Cast:** Al Jolson, Lois Moran, Lowell Sherman, Louise Dresser, Hobart Bosworth, Tully Marshall, Mitchell Lewis, Jack Curtis, Noah Beery, Ray Cooke, Stanley Fields, Danny Mac Grant. Warner Bros. changed the name of the original play, *Mr. Bones*, by Berlin and James Gleason, to take advantage of the great popularity of Jolson in the historical musical *The Jazz Singer* (1927), in which the star sang "Mammy." Jolson played an "endman" in a traveling minstrel show. The songs include "To My Mammy," "Looking at You," "Yes, We Have No Bananas," and "Let Me Sing and I'm Happy." The blackface shenanigans obviously make this film an artifact of its era.

- *"The combination of Al Jolson...and a musical score by Irving Berlin was a winning one...adapted by Gordon Rigby with more than a touch of the melodramatics about it, especially when Jolson is shot in a scene during the show after a rival has substituted real bullets for blanks. With Jolson around for most of the film's running time, the supporting players had a hard time making their presences felt."* (Clive Hirschhorn, The Warner Bros. Story)

Stop, Look and Listen (1926, Pathé, bw/silent) ☆☆ **Sc/D:** Larry Semon. **Cam:** James Brown, H.F. Koenekamp. **Cast:** Larry Semon, Dorothy Dwan, Mary Carr, William Gillespie, Lionel Belmore, Oliver

Hardy, Bull Montana, Curtis "Snowball" McHenry, Josef Swickard, Jack Earle, B.F. Blinn, Harry Sweet, Henry Murdock. Berlin wrote this play with Harry B. Smith, which in retrospect offers an early look at Hardy, who also served as Semon's assistant director.

- *"...as a musical stage play was a success. As a picture it means nothing...amusing at times...*(Variety)

This Is the Army (1943, Warner Bros., 121m/c, **VHS**) ☆☆☆ **Sc:** Casey Robinson, Claude Binyon. **D:** Michael Curtiz. **P:** Jack L. Warner, Hal B. Wallis. **Cam:** Bert Glennon, Sol Polito. **Cast:** George Murphy, Joan Leslie, George Tobias, Alan Hale, Rosemary De Camp, Charles Butterworth, Una Merkel, Dolores Costello, Stanley Ridges, Ruth Donnelly, Ronald Reagan, Kate Smith, Frances Langford, Joe Louis, Irving Bacon, Dorothy Peterson, Philip Truex, Ezra Stone, Pierre Watkin. Almost literally a revue, with only the vestiges of a story, this huge wartime hit, with its patriotic tunes belted out in great earnest, remains a one-of-a-kind. The 1942 stage show, on which the credited producer was "Uncle Sam," had a book by James McColl and Berlin and music and lyrics by Berlin, and the cast included Burl Ives and Gary Merrill.

- *"One of the most successful of the musicals in uniform...a super-duper musical that was a mélange of flag-waving, star-singing, fast-stepping hokum showmanship tied up in an unbeatable bundle of box-office allure with 17 smash-hit Irving Berlin songs."* (Thomas G. Aylesworth, The History of Movie Musicals)

Daniel Berrigan
Born: May 9. 1921, Two Harbors, MN.

Daniel Berrigan was one of the first Roman Catholic priests to receive a federal sentence in the United States as a peace agitator for the events described in his play *The Trial of the Catonsville Nine* (see below). His books of poetry include *No One Walks Waters*; *Love, Love at the End*; and *False Gods, Real Men*, which was a nominee for the National Book Award. He wrote the book *The Mission* (1986) about his experiences as a character actor making the Roland Joffe film of the same name in the Brazilian Amazon with stars Robert De Niro, Jeremy Irons, and Aidan Quinn.

The Trial of the Catonsville Nine (1972, Cinema 5, 85m/c, **VHS**) ☆☆ **Sc:** Saul Levitt. **D:** Gordon Davidson. **P:** Gregory Peck. **Cam:** Haskell Wexler. **Cast:** Ed Flanders, Richard Jordan, Peter Strauss, Nancy Malone, William Schallert, Douglas Watson, Gwen Archer, Barton Herman, Mary Jackson, Davis Roberts, Leon Russom, David Spielberg.

First presented by the Center Theatre Group in Los Angeles in 1971, the play concerns Berrigan, a Catholic priest, and the trial of several Jesuit priests and their allies who raided the draft board office in Catonsville, MD, in May 1968, stole records, and burned them with homemade napalm derived from Ivory Soap chips. They were convicted of destroying United States property that October in federal court in Baltimore.

- "...a rigorously faithful, immensely sincere adaptation...Unfortunately, it's not a very moving one. A terrible, self-defeating smugness seems to have taken hold, with the result that it won't appeal to any but the initiated, some of whom, possibly, may even be put off by it...more often piously intoned than acted...photographed by Haskell Wexler in long, slow, graceful, horizontal pan shots and zooms that look as if they were designed to canonize the characters, perhaps prematurely, than to reveal them." (Vincent Canby, The New York Times)

David Berry

Born: July 5, 1943, Denver, CO.

David Berry's 1979 Broadway play G.R. Point, about a U.S. infantryman in the Vietnam War whose morale is corroded by the assigned duty of handling body-bagged dead soldiers, was based on his own experience in the Army in Vietnam. Berry's play The Whales of August was first performed Off Broadway at the WPA Theatre in 1982.

The Whales of August (1987, Circle, 90m/c, **VHS**) ☆☆☆½ **Sc:** David Berry. **D:** Lindsay Anderson. **P:** Carolyn Pfeiffer, Mike Kaplan. **Cam:** Mike Fash. **Cast:** Bette Davis, Lillian Gish, Ann Sothern, Vincent Price, Harry Carey, Jr., Mary Steenburgen, Tisha Sterling, Margaret Ladd, Frank Grimes, Frank Pitkin, Mike Bush. Elderly widowed sisters Libby and Sarah reconvene for the summer at a seaside Maine cottage, the same one they have been coming to for generations.

- "With its two beautiful, very different, very characteristic performances by Miss Gish and Miss Davis, who, together, exemplify American films from 1914 to the present, Lindsay Anderson's The Whales of August is a cinema event...It's as moving for all of the history it recalls as for anything that happens on the screen...In its way, The Whales of August is tough, but it has a major flaw that David Berry's adaptation of his stage play isn't strong enough for the treatment it receives from the director and his extraordinary actors...Mr. Berry is no American Chekhov. Though minutely observed, the lives of Libby and Sarah evoke no landscape larger than this tiny Maine island to which they've been returning every summer...There are references to lost childhoods, dead husbands, wars survived and estranged children, but the ref-

erences are more obligatory than enriching. There's nothing really at stake in the course of the day." (Vincent Canby, The New York Times)

Donald Bevan & Edmund Trczinski

Bevan:
Born: 1920, Holyoke, MA.

Trczinski:
Born: January 2, 1921, New York, NY.

As an Air Force officer in World War II, Donald Bevan wrote, directed, and acted in monthly revues while imprisoned in the actual Stalag 17 as a prisoner of war in 1943 and 1944. Those wartime experiences were dramatized through his collaboration with Trczinski, a sergeant with the Army Air Corps who also spent time as a POW in Nazi Germany. The son-in-law of playwright Jack Kirkland and actress Nancy Carroll, Bevan was primarily an artist whose caricatures of theatrical celebrities adorned the walls of Sardi's Restauarant in New York City. Trczinski, who played a small role in the film of *Stalag 17* (see below), wrote one other produced play, *All Men Falling* (1949).

Stalag 17 (1953, Paramount, 119m/bw, **VHS/DVD**) ☆☆☆☆ **Sc:** Billy Wilder, Edwin Blum. **D/P:** Billy Wilder. **Cam:** Ernest Laszlo. **Cast:** William Holden, Otto Preminger, Don Taylor, Robert Strauss, Neville Brand, Peter Graves, Harvey Lembeck, Sig Rumann, Richard Erdman, Edmund Trczinski, John Mitchum, Michael Moore, Peter Baldwin, Robinson Stone, William Pierson, Robert Shawley, Gil Stratton, Jr., Jay Lawrence. Bevan and Trczinski based their 1951 Broadway hit, which starred John Ericson, on their own time spent as prisoners of war in a German stockade during World War II. The film won the Academy Award for Best Actor (Holden).

- *"Holden acts in quick, hard punches of character playing a realist who likes his own comforts and is willing to be an outcast or a hero in order to get them. He forms a kind of bridge between the humor and the drama in a solid performance."* (Otis L. Guernsey, Jr., New York Herald-Tribune)

Eric Bogosian
Born: April 24, 1953, Woburn, MA.

Eric Bogosian's career as a writer seems to have taken a back seat to his acting, at least publicly. His one-man performance pieces became well-known on Broadway in the 1980s, and Oliver Stone and cinematographer Robert Richardson revved up *Talk Radio* into a fascinating cinematic experience inside a radio studio. As an actor, Bogosian appeared in *Suffering Bastards* (1989), *Dolores Claiborne* (1995), and *Deconstructing Harry* (1997), among others, and on TV in Robert Altman's *The Caine Mutiny Court-Martial* (1988), Terry George's *A Bright Shining Lie* (1998), and Agnieszka Holland's *Shot in the Heart* (2001).

Funhouse (1986, PBS, 30m/c) *Alive From Off Center* ☆☆☆ **Tp/Cast:** Eric Bogosian. **D:** Jo Bonney, Lewis MacAdams. **P:** John Dorr, John Hayes. This solo performance piece was originally performed in New York at the Public Theatre, then the Actors Playhouse in 1983. Bogosian's gallery, which an announcer says illustrates "the underside of the American dream," includes an insurance telemarketer, a paranoid street person, and a death-row inmate.

- "*As usual, the Bogosian performance is an impressive tour de force, not much different than those solo acts that, before television, used to do quite well in the Broadway theatre. Was Joyce Grenfell a performance artist? In any event, while Mr. Bogosian may not be 'off-center' on the show business spectrum, he brings a refreshing sense of rage to the television screen.*" (*John J. O'Connor, The New York Times*)

Sex, Drugs, Rock & Roll (1991, Avenue, 96m/c, **VHS**) ☆☆☆ **Sc/Cast:** Eric Bogosian. **D:** John McNaughton. **P:** Frederick Zollo. **Cam:** Ernest Dickerson. Bogosian's 1990 concert performance was taped live at the Wilturn Theatre in Boston. In this monologue, he voices several characters besides what is assumed as his own wiseguy personality: party animal, rock 'n' roll star, panhandler, fatuous millionaire, and 1960s conspiracy theorist. The bite of satire throughout, the high quality of Bogosian's writing and acting, and then tragic nature of the characters coalesce into a unique show.

- "*It is perhaps the tragedy of Bogosian's career that it began after the collapse of radio. Today he could be a talk show host (maybe like the one he played in* Talk Radio...) *Watching* Sex, Drugs, Rock & Roll, *I wished I was listening to it. I closed my eyes for a time, and I was right: Bogosian's art depends on sound, not sight. This is terrific material, but it doesn't have to be a movie.*" (*Roger Ebert, Chicago Sun-Times*)

SubUrbia (1996, Sony Classics, 121m/c, **VHS**) ☆☆½ **Sc:** Eric Bogosian. **D:** Richard Linklater. **P:** Anne Walker-McBay. **Cam:** Lee Daniel. **Cast:** Giovanni Ribisi, Steve Zahn, Parker Posey, Nicky Katt, Jayce Bartok, Amie Carey, Dina Spybey, Ajay Naidu, Samia Shoaib. Five small-town teenage losers hang out thinking about the time they waste drinking and doing drugs when a guy who was a few years older than them returns to town as a pop music star. Bogosian based his 1994 play on his own youth, growing up in Woburn, MA. The original text was directed for the stage by Robert Falls at the Lincoln Center Theater in New York City during the summer of 1994.

• *"It's a shockingly banal view both of kids and the suburbs, but chronicling banality is Linklater's stock-in-trade. What's weird about* SubUrbia *is that Linklater's zoned-out technique is wedded to Bogoisian's in-your-face power-rant oratory. The result is like local anesthesia—you can see the incisions, but you can't feel them."* (Peter Rainer, New Times LA)

Talk Radio (1988, Universal, 109m/c, **VHS/DVD**) ☆☆☆☆ **Sc:** Eric Bogosian, Oliver Stone. **D:** Oliver Stone. **P:** Edward R. Pressman, A. Kitman Ho. **Cam:** Robert Richardson. **Cast:** Eric Bogosian, Alec Baldwin, Ellen Greene, Leslie Hope, John C. McGinley, John Pankow, Michael Wincott. Bogosian's writing and acting stage triumph as the sleepless and management-nagged nightime talk-radio shock-jock Barry Champlain, billed as "the man you love to hate," became an appropriately driving, restless film in the hands of Oliver Stone. The play and film are partially based on the 1984 murder of Denver talk-show host Alan Berg.

• *"...played with rasping, aggresive sarcasm by Eric Bogosian...*Talk Radio *is directed by Stone with claustrophobic intensity...the movie doesn't feel as boxed-in as many filmed plays do, perhaps because radio itself is such an intimate, claustrophobic medium. It's not over there inside the TV set; it's in your head...it was the right decision to star [Bogosian] in the movie, too, instead of some famous star. He feels this material from the inside out, and makes the character convincing. That's especially true during a virtuoso, unsettling closing monologue..."* (Roger Ebert, Chicago Sun-Times)

• *"Champlain is the same mixture of honesty and sleaze, high aspiration and character as James Woods's reporter in Stone's* Salvador. *Like that character, Champlain is a catalyst; he drags out the truth, the dark sides. But he's become a beast in public to win his ratings. And he's become a beast in private as well. He tears his life and his ideals to shreads. Honesty becomes a gig and cynicism a crutch."* (Michael Wilmington, Los Angeles Times)

Claire Boothe
Ann Boothe
Born: March 10, 1903, New York, NY. **Died:** 1987.

Claire Boothe took editorial positions at *Vogue*, then *Vanity Fair*, in the early 1930s. Her first play, *Abide With Me*, was produced on Broadway in 1935, and *The Women* debuted the following year to great acclaim and box-office success at the Ethel Barrymore Theatre. Her final produced play was *Child of the Morning*, which was produced Off Broadway in 1958. In 1935, she married *Time* publisher Henry Luce and became Claire Boothe Luce. A Republican and a Roman Catholic, she served as a U.S. Representative from Connecticut from 1943 to 1947, and became the first woman to serve as a U.S. ambassador, to Italy from 1953 to 1956. She wrote the book *Europe in the Spring* (1940), which recounted her travels and recommended a continued American crusade to establish democracy worldwide. Boothe also wrote the original story for *Come to the Stable* (1949) starring Loretta Young. She wrote magazine stories throughout her life and was a columnist and correspondent for *Life* and *Look*.

Kiss the Boys Goodbye (1941, Paramount, 85m/bw) ☆☆☆ **Sc:** Harry Tugend, Dwight Taylor. **D:** Victor Schertzinger. **P:** Paul Jones. **Cam:** Ted Tetzlaff. **Cast:** Don Ameche, Mary Martin, Oscar Levant, Eddie "Rochester" Anderson, Raymond Walburn, Connie Boswell, Virginia Dale, Barbara Jo Allen, Elizabeth Patterson. The 1938 play basically mined a similar satiric vein as *The Women*, this time in Hollywood, skewering the elaborate public-relations campaign that MGM launched in its nationwide search to find Scarlett O'Hara for *Gone With the Wind* (1939).

- *"In converting Clare Boothe's satirical comedy to films, Paramount made some major revisions of the original, substituting a group of tuneful songs for the playwreight's satirical barbs, and coming up with a light, humorous and breezy piece of entertainment. Picture effectively showcases the acting and vocal talents of Mary Martin, who ably carries the full burden of the picture with a top-notch performance."* (Variety)

Margin for Error (1943, 20th Century-Fox, 74m/bw) ☆☆½ **Sc:** Lillie Hayward. **D:** Otto Preminger. **P:** Ralph Dietrich. **Cam:** Edward Cronjager. **Cast:** Milton Berle, Joan Bennett, Otto Preminger, Carl Esmond, Howard Freeman, Poldy Dur, Hans Von Twardowski. The play, a melodrama about the investigation into the murder of a Nazi consul by a Jewish detective, was staged on Broadway by Preminger in 1940. When he was asked to play the Nazi, he insisted that he direct as well, and his film directing career was born.

- *"The well-known Austrian actor, Rudolf Forster...was engaged for the Nazi. When Forster had unexpectedly to leave America, Preminger assumed the role himself. For more than a decade thereafter, he was irritated by the legend that he played Nazis for a decade. In fact, he played only three others—in films. But as they were the only roles at all he played in this country, it is easy to see how the legend arose."* (Stanley Kauffmann, The New Republic)

The Women, which satirized the cattiness and backstabbing of wealthy society women in New York, debuted on Broadway in 1936 and ran for

657 performances. Among the cast were Margalo Gillmore, Ilka Chase, Arlene Francis, and Doris Day.

The Women (1939, MGM, 132m/c&bw, **VHS**) ☆☆☆☆ **Sc:** Anita Loos, Jane Murfin. **D:** George Cukor. **P:** Hunt Stromberg. **Cam:** Oliver T. Marsh, Joseph Ruttenberg. **Cast:** Norma Shearer, Joan Crawford, Rosalind Russell, Mary Boland, Paulette Goddard, Joan Fontaine, Lucile Watson, Margaret Dumont, Phyllis Povah, Virginia Weidler, Ruth Hussey, Marjorie Main, Muriel Hutchison, Esther Dale, Hedda Hopper, Mary Beth Hughes, Priscilla Lawson, Marjorie Wood, Virginia Grey, Vera Vague. The venom is hissed everywhere in this dextrous adaptation, with a raft of actresses who can be irritating soaring with the material. Boothe hit a nerve with the play and the film was also a big hit.

- *"Claire Boothe Luce's ode to wisecracking cattiness, given the full, expensive MGM treatment...It confirms rich men's worse suspicions and fantasies of what women want (money) and what they're like when they're together (clawing beasties)...George Cukor directed — surprisingly coarsely; it's a kicking, screaming, low comedy...Goddard is a standout — she's fun. And audiences at the time loved Russell's all-out burlesque of women as jealous bitches."* (Pauline Kael, 5,001 Nights at the Movies)

- *"'At this critical moment I set my sights on the part of Crystal, the hardboiled perfume clerk who uses every wile to catch another woman's husband in The Women.' In this, Crawford did well, a delicious vixen, overplaying with precision. She also did the part off screen, bitching Shearer and being bawled out by director George Cukor for unprofessionalism."* (David Shipman, The Great Movie Stars 1: The Golden Years)

The Women (1955, NBC, 90m) *Producers' Showcase* ☆☆☆ **Tp:** Sumner Locke Elliott. **D:** Vincent J. Donehue. **P:** Max Gordon, Fred Coe. **Cast:** Shelley Winters, Paulette Goddard, Ruth Hussey, Mary Astor, Nancy Olson, Mary Boland, Valerie Bettis, Cathleen Nesbitt, Nita Talbot, Bibi Osterwald, Pat Carroll, Pamela Lawrence, Jada Rowland, Mary Michael, Nan McFarland, Sybil Baker, Paula Bauersmith, Helen Raymond, Jeanne Murray, Agnes Doyle, Lennie Dunne, Brett Somers, Frances Woodbary, Sandra Church, Sara Mead. Producer Fred Coe spared nothing for this all-star TV treatment. Goddard and Boland were retained from the 1939 film.

- *"The 'alley cats' were still clawing away last night...Little of the bite and sting in the travesty on gossiping females and wrecked homes has been lost over the years, albeit this version was toned down for video's family audience. Superbly cast and brilliantly produced by Max Gordon and Fred Coe, it was a personal triumph for Ruth Hussey in the sympathetic role. Shelley Winters and Paulette Goddard scored impressively as scheming hussies..."* (Variety)

The Opposite Sex (1956, MGM, 116m/c, **VHS**) ☆☆½ **Sc:** Fay Kanin, Michael Kanin. **D:** David Miller. **P:** Joe Pasternak. **Cam:** Robert

Bronner. **Cast:** June Allyson, Dolores Gray, Joan Collins, Ann Sheridan, Agnes Moorehead, Joan Blondell, Charlotte Greenwood, Barbara Jo Allen, Ann Miller, Leslie Neilsen, Jeff Richards, Sam Levene, Bill Goodwin, Carolyn Jones, Dick Shawn, Jonathan Hale, Jim Backus, Juanita Moore, Dean Jones, Barrie Chase.

- *"[Sheridan] walked away with* The Opposite Sex; *the likes of June Allyson and Joan Collins were not in her class, but the film was a mess and did nothing for her career." (David Shipman,* The Great Movie Stars 1: The Golden Years)

George Emerson Brewer, Jr. & Bertram Bloch

Brewer:
Born: November 13, 1899, New York, NY.

Bloch:
Born: April 5, 1892, New York, NY. **Died:** June 19, 1987.

Brewer's one other Broadway play was *Tide Rising* (1937). He directed *An Enemy of the People* in 1938 for the Works Progress Administration's Federal Theatre Project. An avid outdoorsman, he produced the conservation-minded documentaries *Yours Is the Land* (1949), *The Web of Life* (1950), *The Making of the River* (1954), and *The House of Man* (1963). Bloch's plays in collaboration include *Glory Hallelujah* (1926) with actor Thomas Mitchell and *Spring Again* (1941) with Isabel Leighton. Bloch, who served as eastern head of the story departments for MGM (1928-39) and 20th Century-Fox (1941-56), also wrote the novels *Mrs. Hulett*, *The Little Laundress*, *The Fearful Knight*, and *The Only Nellie Fayle.*

Dark Victory was a 1934 Tallulah Bankhead vehicle that ran for 51 performances on Broadway. Bankhead played society girl Judith Traherne, who is doomed to an early death because of a brain tumor.

Dark Victory (1939, Warner Bros., 106m/bw, **VHS/DVD**) ☆☆☆☆ **Sc:** Casey Robinson. **D:** Edmund Goulding. **P:** Hal B. Wallis. **Cam:** Ernest Haller. **Cast:** Bette Davis, Humphrey Bogart, George Brent, Geraldine Fitzgerald, Ronald Reagan, Henry Travers, Cora Witherspoon, Virginia Brissac, Dorothy Peterson, Charles Richman, Herbert Rawlinson, Leonard Mudie, Fay Helm, John Ridgely, Diane Bernard. This play was transformed by Robinson into one of Davis's most memorable films.

- *"Bette Davis won an Academy Award last year for her performance in* Jezebel...Now it is more than ever apparent that the award was premature.*

It should have been deferred until her Dark Victory *came along...Miss Davis is superb. More than that, she is enchanting and enchanted...a great role—rangy, full-bodied, designed for a virtuosa...the eloquence, the tenderness, the heartbreaking sincerity with which she has played it."* (Frank S. Nugent, The New York Times)

Dark Victory (1976, NBC, 180m/c) ☆☆ **Sc:** M. Charles Cohen. **D:** Robert Butler. **P:** Jules Irving. **Cast:** Elizabeth Montgomery, Anthony Hopkins, Michele Lee, Janet MacLachlan, Michael Lerner, Herbert Berghoff, Vic Tayback, John Elerick, Mario Roccuzzo, Julie Rogers, Michael Thoma, James Ingersoll, Deborah White, Jack Manning. The new script turns Judith Traherne into Katherine Meskill, a driven TV talk show producer, and Hopkins played her physician, who falls in love with her.

• *"There's no getting around that the latest (and disastrously overlong) reworking of* Dark Victory*...recalls throughout a vivid memory of Bette Davis in one of her finest portrayals...Elizabeth Montgomery...has been illserved by a script that starts out in high gear but is allowed to slide gradually into tedious bathos...the drama goes on far too long, which is its most serious flaw...padded to fill out a three-hour time slot, indulges in relentless tear-jerking...In fact the film just stops making sense."* (Kevin Thomas, Los Angeles Times)

Dark Victory was trimmed by adapter Sanford Barnett for a 1957 installment of *Lux Video Theatre* that starred Shirley Jones, Jack Cassidy, Toni Gerry, and Keith Larsen.

Harry Brown

Born: April 30, 1917, Portland, ME. **Died:** 1986.

After Harry Brown adapted his novel *A Walk in the Sun*, about U.S. Infantry soldiers in Italy during World War II, into the successful film of the same name, Hollywood kept him. An expert in the action/adventure genres, his screenplays included those for the John Wayne movies *Wake of the Red Witch* (1948), *Sands of Iwo Jima* (1949), and *El Dorado* (1967). His screenplay for the Las Vegas/Rat Pack caper *Ocean's 11* (1960), was retooled for the 2001 remake. His films include *Kiss Tomorrow Goodbye* (1950), *A Place in the Sun* (1951), *Bugles in the Afternoon* (1952), *All the Brothers Were Valiant* (1953), *Many Rivers to Cross* (1955), and *D-Day, the Sixth of June* (1956). He also wrote for ABC's classic World War II series *Combat!* in the mid-1960s.

Eight Iron Men (1952, Columbia, 80m/bw) ☆☆☆ **Sc:** Harry Brown. **D:** Edward Dmytryk. **P:** Stanley Kramer. **Cam:** J. Roy Hunt. **Cast:** Richard Kiley, Bonar Coleano, Lee Marvin, Arthur Franz, Nick Dennis, James

Griffith, Dickie Moore, George Cooper, Barney Phillips, Robert Nichols, Mary Castle. The 1945 play, A *Sound of Hunting*, concerns a group of GIs holed up in a bombed-out building who ruminate on whether to go back out into the battlefield where one of their own lies, perhaps alive. Brown modeled the play on an incident that occurred near Monte Cassino, Italy, among members of General Mark Clark's 5th Army during World War II. The play was instrumental in bringing Burt Lancaster and Frank Lovejoy to Hollywood's attention.

• "'I kept my squad together,' replies Marvin airily, with defensible arrogance...the film, in the final analysis, is about fidelity and honor...not without inventive, classy moments...These dream sequences show Dmytryk at his best...The rest of the picture, alas, is deadeningly routine, and the machine gun fire and strained talk of men under pressure cannot redeem it from terminal torpor." (*Donald Spoto*, Stanley Kramer: Filmmaker)

Abe Burrows

Abram Solman Borowitz
Born: December 18, 1910, New York, NY. **Died:** 1985.
Pulitzer Prize-winning play: *How to Succeed in Business Without Really Trying* (1962)

A Borscht Belt comedian who went to Hollywood to write for *The Rudy Vallee-John Barrymore Show* in 1938, Abe Burrows became a witty force on the party and radio circuits and would regale even the likes of Groucho Marx, Robert Benchley, and S.J. Perlman with his barbs. His self-written songs included "Three Blue Eyes," "Green Christmas," and "I Looked Under a Rock and Found You." A radio star who made the transition to early TV, Burrows's first musical books in the 1950s for *Guys and Dolls*, *Can-Can*, and *Silk Stockings* were legendary hits and seemed tailor-made as big-screen material.

How to Succeed in Business Without Really Trying and *Cactus Flower* extended his stage success into the 1960s. His autobiography, *Honest Abe; or, Is There Really No Business Like Show Business?* was published in 1980. His other plays, all in collaboration with other authors, include *Three Wishes for Jamie*, *Say, Darling*, and *First Impressions*, based on Jane Austen's *Pride and Prejudice*. For the big screen, he also wrote a sketch for the episodic *Duffy's Tavern* (1945) and adapted the Kaufman/Teichman play *The Solid Gold Cadillac* into the 1956 screen version.

Cactus Flower (1969, Columbia, 103m.c, **VHS/DVD**) ☆☆½ **Sc:** I.A.L. Diamond. **D:** Gene Saks. **P:** M.J. Frankovich. **Cam:** Charles Lang. **Cast:** Ingrid Bergman, Walter Matthau, Goldie Hawn, Jack Weston, Rick Lenz,

Vito Scotti, Irene Hervey, Eve Bruce, Irwin Charone, Matthew Saks, Tani Guthrie. Burrows adapted his first nonmusical play from a French play by Pierre Barillet and Jean-Pierre Gredy about a dentist who poses as a married man to stall his mistress's dreams of marrying him. Hawn won the Best Supporting Actress Oscar for her performance as the ditsy mistress, a role that resembled her bubble-headed persona on TV's *Laugh-In*.

- *"As a play it wasn't much, but as a movie it's a hopeless disaster in which absolutely nothing goes right…Cactus Flower has no feel, no style, no tempo, no rhythm."* (Rex Reed, Holiday)

- *"Cactus Flower drags, which is probably the worst thing that can be said of a light comedy. It's due to sloppy direction by Gene Saks and the miscasting of Walter Matthau opposite Ingrid Bergman. The plot…is minimal and the lines are somewhat stilted and hollow…There are some laughs and Goldie Hawn, as the Greenwich Village kook…makes a credible screen debut."* (Variety)

Can-Can (1960, 20th Century-Fox, 131m/c, **VHS**) ☆☆☆ **Sc:** Dorothy Kingsley, Charles Lederer. **D:** Walter Lang. **P:** Jack Cummings. **Cam:** William H. Daniels. **Cast:** Shirley MacLaine, Frank Sinatra, Maurice Chevalier, Louis Jourdan, Juliet Prowse, Marcel Dalio, Leon Belasco, Nestor Paiva, John A. Neris, Jean Del Val, Ann Codee, Eugene Borden, Barbara Carter, Maurice Marsac. The play debuted at the Schubert Theatre in 1953 with songs by Cole Porter. MGM gave the movie a starry treatment with plenty of attractive showgirls to live up to its title. It was nominated for Oscars for its score (Nelson Riddle) and costumes. The songs include "I Love Paris," "C'est Magnifique," "Let's Do It," and "Just One of Those Things."

- *"Perhaps because his role was written specifically for him, Sinatra is Sinatra, ring-a-ding-ding and all. His naturalness makes him all the more effective, and his charm and self-assuredness ably complement a vocal style which fits hand-in-glove with the Porter tunes, particularly 'It's All Right With Me.'"* (Variety)

- *"The show itself…turns out to be lavish, easy to look at…the sort of sophisticated mediocrity not likely to excite anybody at all…Chevalier and Sinatra are entertaining with their individual, off-hand brands of charm, while the erratic Miss MacLaine acts as though she had a patent on personality, and clearly needs a hard-hearted director who would dare to disillusion her now and then."* (Newsweek)

Guys and Dolls (1955, Goldwyn, 149m/c, **VHS/DVD**) ☆☆☆½ **Sc/D:** Joseph L. Mankiewicz. **P:** Samuel Goldwyn. **Cam:** Harry Stradling. **Cast:** Marlon Brando, Frank Sinatra, Jean Simmons, Vivian Blaine, Stubby Kaye, B.S. Pully, Sheldon Leonard, Robert Keith, George E. Stone. Gambler Sky Masterson bets "floating crap game" organizer Nathan Detroit that he can get street mission director Sarah Brown to go to Havana with him. This famous and very poshly done musical, derived by Burrows and career screenwriter Jo Swerling from Damon Runyon's Broadway stories, was an attempt by Goldwyn to produce the ultimate studio musical. It fell short of that, but is entertaining throughout. Ten of Frank Loesser's songs were retained from the stage show and he added three more for this movie. The songs include "Sit Down, You're Rockin' the Boat," "Luck Be a Lady," and "If I Were a Bell." The film was nominated for Oscars for Best Cinematography, Art Direction/Set Decoration, Score (Jay Blackton, Cyril Mockridge), and Costumes.

- *"The biggest news is this: Goldwyn gambles and wins! It's more than 'a probable twelve to seven' that Guys and Dolls will be one of the most popular movies ever made. The film retains the purity of the Broadway musical (and) Joseph L. Mankiewicz...has kept most of the funny lines and added some of his own...Brando and Sinatra look too young for their roles as veteran gamblers...but this is quibbling."* (William K. Zinsser, New York Herald-Tribune)

- *"The two major flaws...are Oliver Smith's sets and Frank Sinatra's performance. Samuel Goldwyn, Joseph Mankiewicz and Mr. Smith apparently couldn't make up their minds whether the scenery should be realistic or stylized. As a result, they have the disadvantages of both, and these disadvantages work against the very special nature of Runyonesque storytelling...Sinatra ambles through his role as if he were about to laugh at the jokes in the script (and) sings on pitch, but colorlessly...Sinatra's lackadaisical performance, his careless and left-handed attempt at characterization, not only harm the picture immeasurably, but indicate an alarming lack of professionalism."* (Stephen Sondheim, Films in Review)

- *"The Broadway version is legendary; the movie provides no clue as to why."* (Pauline Kael, 5,001 Nights at the Movies)

How to Succeed in Business Without Really Trying (1967, UA, 121m/c, **VHS/DVD**) ☆☆☆½ **Sc/D/P:** David Swift. **Cam:** Burnett Guffey. **Cast:** Robert Morse, Michele Lee, Rudy Vallee, Anthony "Scooter" Teague, Maureen Arthur, Carol Worthington, John Myhers, Kay Reynolds, Sammy Smith, Ruth Kobart, Jeff DeBenning, Janice Carroll, Robert Q. Lewis, Paul Hartman, Dan Tobin, Murray Matheson, Patrick O'Moore, Hy Averback, Erin O'Brien-Moore, David Swift. The troika of Burrows, Jack Weinstock, and Willie Gilbert based their play on Shepherd Mead's Christmas-gift satire novel about a greedy businessman clawing his way to the top, complete with mock humility toward his superiors and gleeful glances at the camera when his ruses are successful.

- *"It may be that cinema audiences did not care for satire at this time...failed to repeat its success on the stage...not satire of a high order, as David Swift, directing, realized. His comic-book style works better here than in his previ-*

ous films, and this is one instance in which a Broadway musical, preserved and encapsulated, is invigorating on the screen. Its virtues are those of the original, and chief among them are Frank Loesser's witty score and lyrics and Robert Morse, as the little guy who will literally stop at nothing to get to the top." (David Shipman, The Story of Cinema)

Silk Stockings (1957, MGM, 117m/c, **VHS**) ☆☆☆ **Sc:** Leonard Gersche, Leonard Spigelgass. **D:** Rouben Mamoulian. **P:** Arthur Freed. **Cam:** Robert J. Bronner. **Cast:** Fred Astaire, Cyd Charisse, Janis Paige, Peter Lorre, George Tobias, Jules Munshin, Josef Buloff, Wim Sonneveld, Eugene Borden. The 1955 Cole Porter musical—with a book by Burrows, George S. Kaufman, and his wife, Leuween MacGrath—was based on the stage play *Ninotchka* by Melchior Lengyel that starred Hildegarde Neff and Don Ameche. Charisse played a Russian envoy who begins enjoying the freedoms offered in Paris.

- *"[Producer Arthur Freed] and director Ruben Mamoulian kept the story and songs pretty much the same except that—with Fred Astaire and Cyd Charisse in the leads—the emphasis became primarily choreographic. 'I had two of the best dancers in the world,' Mamoulian once said…'and what interested me was to give greater importance to the dancing than to the action proper. The psychological drive and dramatic development existed only in the dances.' Because of this, two minor songs were discarded in favor of two new ones created specifically as dance routines. 'Fated to Be Mated' was a joyous marriage proposal…'The Ritz, Roll and Rock' was a bouncy, angular, top-hatted Fred Astaire specialty, far more Ritz than rock."* (Stanley Green, Burt Goldblatt, Starring Fred Astaire)

- *"A paralyzed version of the Cole Porter Broadway musical…"* (Pauline Kael, 5,001 Nights at the Movies)

Arthur Carter

Arthur Carter's one other Broadway play was *The Number*, which ran for 87 performances in 1951–52 with George Abbott directing a cast including Martha Scott, Dane Clark, Luis van Rooten, and Murvyn Vye.

Operation Mad Ball (1957, Columbia, 105m/bw) **Sc:** Arthur Carter, Jed Harris, Blake Edwards. **D:** Blake Edwards. **P:** Jed Harris. **Cam:** Charles Lawton. **Cast:** Jack Lemmon, Ernie Kovacs, Kathryn Grant, Mickey Rooney, James Darren, Arthur O'Connell, Dick York, Jeanne Manet, Roger Smith. One of the more underrated service comedies of the 1950s concerned Allied forces in Normandy who circumvent orders that say they can't fraternize with the nurses.

- *"...whirls along, neatly and quickly developing some funny ideas...Jack Lemmon shows a nice gift for playing the ingenious low man on the military totem pole. Watching Mr. Lemmon and Mr. Kovacs run through a few reels together, I reflected fleetingly on the likes of Edmund Lowe and Victor McLaglen and Karl Dane and George K. Arthur, who played Marine and Army braves after the First World War, and reached the conclusion that the movies have made a couple of strides in the right direction."* (John McCarten, The New Yorker)

Mary Chase

Mary Coyle Chase
Born: February 25, 1907, Denver, CO. **Died:** 1981.
Pulitzer Prize-winning play: *Harvey* (1945)

This Colorado-born radio play writer gained her widest fame in the creation of *Harvey*, the upright, man-sized white rabbit that a boozy if infinitely friendly and jobless man claims as his best friend. Her other plays include *Now You've Done It*, *Next Half Hour*, *Bernardine*, and *Mrs. McThing*. She also wrote a fantasy for children entitled *Loretta Mason Potts*.

Bernardine (1957, 20th Century-Fox, 96m/c) ☆☆½ **Sc:** Theodore Reeves. **D:** Henry Levin. **Cam:** Paul Vogel. **P:** Samuel G. Engel. **Cast:** Pat Boone, Terry Moore, Janet Gaynor, Dean Jagger, James Drury, Dick Sargent, Walter Abel, Isabel Jewell, Ronnie Burns, Natalie Schafer, Val Benedict. A sort of old-school college try, the 1952 play is something of a precursor to the clean-cut teen sitcoms of the late 1950s, about a student who finally finds the girl of his dreams, then must cram for exams. He asks a friend's older brother to look after his comely newfound girlfriend for a few days with the expected results. Boone's pallid big-screen shot also allowed Gaynor time as an innocuous mom in her first screen role since 1939.

- *"Fox's answer to the Presley films...doesn't have much to recommend it. Boone says 'Gee' a lot and looks as though he's doing an imitation of himself."* (Jay Robert Nash and Stanley Ralph Ross, The Motion Picture Guide)

Harvey is Chase's greatest contribution to the theatre. The 1945 Pulitzer Prize winner is about the tippling Elwood P. Dowd, whose insistence on an imaginary companion, the invisible six-foot-tall white rabbit of the title, embarrasses his family. His sister tries to have him committed. Frank Fay originated Dowd on Broadway in 1944. James Stewart replaced him for a few months in 1947 as a trial run for the film, and returned to

Broadway in the part in 1970 opposite Helen Hayes. Stewart and Hayes also starred in a 1975 London stage revival.

Harvey (1950, Universal-International, 104m/bw, **VHS/DVD**) ☆☆☆☆ **Sc:** Mary Chase, Oscar Brodney. **D:** Henry Koster. **P:** John Beck. **Cam:** William Daniels. **Cast:** James Stewart, Josephine Hull, Peggy Dow, Charles Drake, Cecil Kellaway, Victoria Horne, Jesse White, Wallace Ford, Nana Bryant, William Lynn, Grace Mills, Clem Bevans, Ida Moore, Minerva Urecal. Chase's witty repartee is preserved on film with Stewart delivering one of his most easygoing signature parts in this pleasantly wacky interpretation. The lines are part of theatrical culture—Dowd: "I've wrestled with reality for 35 years, and I'm happy, doctor, I finally won out over it." One of the great sentimental favorites, and deservedly so.

- *"...loses little of its whimsical comedy charm in the screen translation...Stewart would seem the perfect casting for the character so well does he convey the idea that escape from life into a pleasant half-world existence has many points in its favor. Josephine Hull...is immense, socking the comedy for every bit of its worth."* (Variety)

- *"...it was Stewart...who pulled audiences closer than ever to the heart and spirit of the play with an endearingly wistful portrait of the whimsical, imaginative alcoholic, Elwood P. Dowd. Rather surprisingly, the movie version added a dimension, a sweetness and perhaps even a kind of credibility that the play did not have, and Stewart's performance had much to do with that. Mrs. Chase and Oscar Brodney wrote a most sensible movie adaptation and the supporting cast was exceptionally appealing...As touching and amusing as Frank Fay's original performance was, Stewart's work on the screen somehow added a more personal, meaningful glow."* (Howard Thompson, James Stewart)

Harvey (1958, CBS, 90m/bw) *The DuPont Show of the Month* ☆☆☆ **Tp:** Jacqueline Babbin, Audrey Gellen. **D:** George Schaefer. **P:** David Susskind. **Cast:** Art Carney, Marion Lorne, Loring Smith, Larry Blyden, Fred Gwynn, Charlotte Rae, Ruth White, Elizabeth Montgomery, Jack Weston, Katherine Raht, Ray Bramley. The prestige series's second season's debut installment became a unique benchmark in the medium as far as critics were concerned. Susskind beamed via closed-circuit TV the previous night's dress rehearsal to critics across the nation, whose pieces were then printed in their papers on the day of the night it aired (10/22/58). "It worked in the sense that the reviews were fantastic and the rating was unbelievably high...the number one show that week and CBS was ecstatic," wrote Schaefer. "It didn't work for me because the performance that the critics saw and reviewed was better than the one the audience saw."

- *"Viewers this evening can anticipate a softly winning and fey performance by Art Carney in the role of Elwood P. Dowd and [an] uproarious cameo by Marion Lorne as Dowd's fluttery sister, Veta. Miss Chase's Pulitzer Prize work seems immune to the passage of time...remains an imaginative gem of fantasy...Mr. Carney was very touching...If viewers ultimately find reviewing in advance a service, it should not matter that the system puts both sponsors and critics on the spot." (Jack Gould,* The New York Times*)*

Harvey (1972, NBC, 90m/c) *The Hallmark Hall of Fame* ☆☆☆☆ **Tp:** Jacqueline Babbin, Audrey Gellen Maas. **D:** Fielder Cook. **P:** David Susskind. **Cast:** James Stewart, Helen Hayes, Arlene Francis, Martin Gabel, Fred Gwynn, John McGiver, Richard Mulligan, Jesse White, Madeline Kahn, Marian Halley, Dorothy Blackburn. By this time, Stewart had perfected and aged into the role—some 1950 criticism claimed him too young then (42) for Dowd. This production used a further honed version of the 1958 TV adaptation by Babbin and Gellen Maas (above).

- *"...the basic material is pleasant enough but the [1970] Broadway production was a bit too cute for its own fragile good. The TV version...is better. Mr. Stewart is noticeably more assured in front of a camera than he was in front of a live audience. Miss Hayes tones down some of the more outrageous mugging she had concocted to manipulate the stage proceedings. While trimming the play, the adaptation dilligently retains its basic message. Elwood and his invisible friend...are pitted against ordinary citizens concerned with a more mundane sense of responsibility and duty. And, of course, Elwood and Harvey win the hearts and minds of the audience. It's all very gentle and Mr. Stewart is superb." (John J. O'Connor,* The New York Times*)*

Harvey (1996, CBS, 120m/c) ☆☆½ **Tp:** Joseph Dougherty. **D:** George Schaefer. **P:** Don Gregory, Lisa Towers. **Cast:** Harry Anderson, Leslie Nielsen, Swoosie Kurtz, Jessica Hecht, Jonathan Banks, William Schallert, Lisa Akey, Jim O'Heir, Robert Wisden, Lynda Boyd, Sheila Moore, Alex Ferguson. Great television director Schaefer made this fresh production, shot in Vancouver, the last show of his career. Anderson and Neilsen played the lines nearly straight, allowing the humor to flow through the dialogue.

- *"Whether or not I direct again [he didn't] depends on what and when and my health, but should this be the last of a long line of films for home viewing, it would make a most happy ending." (George Schaefer,* From Live to Tape to Film: 60 Years of Inconspicuous Directing*)*

Mrs. McThing (1958, NBC, 60m/bw) *Omnibus* ☆☆½ **Tp:** Walter Kerr. **P:** Fred Rickey. **Cast:** Helen Hayes, Sam Levene, Eddie Hodges, Alexander Wager, Iggie Wolfington, Irwin Corey, Minette Barrett. This McThing was Chase's comic fantasy of life among the well-to-do with a bit of gamboling from spirits and witches. Helen Hayes starred as Mrs. Larue, whose son has run away from home to become a racketeer, in the Broadway version of 1952. Much of the original Broadway cast repeated their roles in this adaptation by Kerr, then drama critic for the *New York Herald-Tribune.*

- "...the TV variation was a most disappointing charade...somewhere in the translation to TV the spell of make-believe was mislaid. The inevitable need for editing in part may have been responsible. But one wonders if Mrs. McThing was not another example of the difficulty of doing fantasy on TV. From a distance, with footlights intervening, perhaps Mrs. Chase's work had all the hilarity claimed for it. In the intimate medium of TV it seemed contrived beyond the pale. Miss Hayes had some supreme comedy moments..." (Jack Gould, The New York Times)

Sorority House (1939, RKO, 64m/bw) ☆☆½ **Tp:** Dalton Trumbo. **D:** John Farrow. **Cam:** Nicholas Musuraca. **P:** Robert Sisk. **Cast:** Anne Shirley, James Ellison, Barbara Reed, Pamela Blake, J.M. Kerrigan, Helen Wood, Doris Jordan, June Storey, Elisabeth Risdon, Margaret Armstrong, Selmer Jackson, Chill Wills, Veronica Lake, Marge Champion. Coyle's play *Chi House*, first produced in her home town of Denver in 1939, was the basis for this Anne Shirley vehicle for the "B" movie mill at RKO. The behind-the-camera pedigree of future players is impressive. Shirley (as Anne) attends Talbot University on the money her father raised by selling his country store. Wide-eyed, she bumps into the big man on campus, who helps her adjust socially and she momentarily strays to snobbiness as a pledge to join the Gamma Sorority.

- "[Shirley] proves again she is one of the ablest actresses on Hollywood's long roster." (Regina Crewe, New York American)

Paddy Chayefsky
Sidney Aaron Chayefsky
Born: January 29, 1923, The Bronx, NY. **Died:** 1981.

Perhaps the most famous and admired writer of the so-called Golden Age of Television, Chayefsky found success in three performance media. Several of his teleplays were turned into films or stage plays, most notably *Marty* (1953 on *Philco Television Playhouse*, 1955 on film), *The Bachelor Party* (1953 on *Philco*; 1957 on film), and *The Catered Affair* (1955 on *The Goodyear Theatre*, 1956 on film). He was nominated for an Emmy Award in 1954 for his contributions to *Philco*.

He won Academy Awards for the screenplays of *Marty* (1955), which also won Oscars for Best Picture, Actor (Ernest Borgnine), and Director (Delbert Mann); *The Hospital* (1971) with George C. Scott; and *Network* (1976), which also won Oscars for Peter Finch, Faye Dunaway, and Beatrice Straight (and nominations for William Holden and Ned Beatty). Chayefsky was nominated for the screenplay of *The Goddess* (1958), in which Kim Stanley gave a brilliant Marilyn Monroe-styled performance. The writer also adapted William Bradford Huie's satirical Army novel *The Americanization of Emily* into an exceptional 1964 film, and adapted Alan Jay Lerner and Frederick Loewe's stage musical *Paint Your Wagon* into the overproduced 1969 film starring Lee Marvin and Clint Eastwood. Chayefsky's novel, *Altered States*, was turned into a 1981 film by director Ken Russell. Shaun Considine's biography, *Mad as Hell: The Life and Work of Paddy Chayefsky*, was published in 1994.

Chayefsky's plays include *No T.O. for Love* (1944), *Fifth from Garibaldi* (1944), *The Tenth Man* (1959), *The Passion of Josef D* (1964), and *The Latent Heterosexual* (1967).

Gideon (1971, NBC, 90m/c) *Hallmark Hall of Fame* ☆☆☆ **Tp:** Robert Hartung. **D/P:** George Schaefer. **Cast:** Peter Ustinov, Jose Ferrer, Arnold Moss, Little Egypt, Eric Christmas, Harry Davis, Harry Ellerbe, Alfred Dennis, Booth Coleman, Logan Ramsey, Gregory Morton, Priscilla Morrill, William Hansen, Robert Casper, Sarah Seegar. Chayefsky retells the Biblical tale of a simple hill farmer who's chosen by God to lead the Israelites in triumph against the Midianites, but with the titular character more dissenting and argumentative than the obedient servant in the good book. Fredric March and Douglas Campbell played it with religious overtones on Broadway in 1961, but Schaefer and Ustinov limbered up the wit and humor in this piece for *Hallmark*.

- "...*under the intelligent guidance of...Schaefer, it provided one of the better hour-and-a-half segments on the television horizon these days...It's in the details of character that Mr. Chayefsky brings his own mischieviousness into play. His Gideon, played delightfully this time around by Peter Ustinov, is something of a pompous dolt. His angel, played by Jose Ferrer, is an even more pompous egomaniac, much given to momentous announcements...Neither very deep nor especially sweeping, Gideon is a modest achievement, but its very modesty can be charming...The play and everyone concerned couldn't have been better served.*" (John J. O'Connor, The New York Times)

Middle of the Night (1959, 20th Columbia, 118m/bw) ☆☆☆☆ **Sc:** Paddy Chayefsky. **D:** Delbert Mann. **Cam:** Joseph Brun. **P:** George Justin. **Cast:** Fredric March, Kim Novak, Glenda Farrell, Jan Norris, Lee Grant, Martin Balsam, Lee Philips, Albert Dekker, Rudy Bond, Effie Afton, Lee Richardson, Joan Copeland. Originally, this story of a 50-year-old garment industry executive who tragically falls in love with his young secretary was broadcast on *Philco Television Playhouse* in 1954 starring E.G. Marshall and Eva Marie Saint. Joshua Logan directed the Broadway version in 1955, which starred Edward G. Robinson and Gena Rowlands. This film version attains a level of classical tragedy through March's brilliant portrayal, which is surely among his best movie work.

- "...*transforms an honest but clumsy play...into a cruely beautiful and mov-*

ing film...what most strikingly meets the eye in this movie is the profound and professional performance of Fredric March..." (Time)

- *"The Chayefsky school of TV writing tends to dwell on the small moment in the small life, as if the author's mind were cramped by the narrow screen into concentration on naturalistic minutiae. Crises are often built of accumulated naggings rather than large conflicting forces...The Chayefskians pose a small instance and try to reach larger implications through it. Too often they have merely stated the instance and not evoked the widespread implications. But Middle of the Night, though lapped in verism, goes on to touch a universal quick nerve. It has all the trappings of stenographic dialogue and reportorial detail, it has the usual air of emasculated Odets (that is, social drama without social purpose); but the subject matter is larger than humdrum life, and both major characters rise to it."* (Stanley Kauffmann, The New Republic)

Frank Chin

Frank Chew, Jr., aka Francisco de Menton
Born: February 25, 1940, Berkeley, CA.

Frank Chin was one of the most important postwar Asian-American writers, contributing plays, fiction, teleplays, essays, and comic books. His fiction includes the novels *Donald Duk* and *Gunga Din Highway* and the collection of short stories *The Chinaman Pacific & Frisco R.R. Co.* Chin's plays include *The Chickencoop Chinaman*, *America More or Less*, and *Peek-a-Boo Kabuki, World War II, and Me*. He wrote *Chinaman's Chance* for an NET airing in 1971, edited several anthologies, and published a collection if essays, *Bulletproof Buddhists*.

The Year of the Dragon (1975, PBS, 90m/c) *Theatre in America* ☆☆☆½ **Tp:** Frank Chin. **D:** Russell Treyz, Portman Paget. **P:** Matt Herman. **Cast:** George Takei, Conrad Yama, Tina Cheng, Pat Suzuki, Doug Higgins, Lilah Kan, Keenan Shimizu. First produced at New York's American Place Theater in 1974, this play concerns a middle-aged travel agent's Chinese American family's foibles, including a younger brother who runs with a bad crowd, his father's perfect English diction (especially when he tells people that he can't understand a word they're saying), and a successful and famous sister who married a white guy.

- *"It is not a completely successful play, its intense energies finally dissipated in a confused area between painful realism and theatrical absurdity. But as a portrait of an Asian-American's struggle for identity, the play is a searing statement, a powerful cry...barges through the comfortable stereotypes of Asian Americans...It is not an 'easy' play. The language is frequently strong and the bitterness, even when wrapped in some very funny comedy, is unrelenting...this TV version is excellent. George Takei...is a mass of explosive energy and feeling..."* (John J. O'Connor, The New York Times)

Edward Chodorov

Born: April 17, 1904, New York, NY. **Died:** 1988.

Edward Chodorov was a Brown University graduate whose first major theatrical experiences were as a stage manager for *Abie's Irish Rose* in 1922 and in South Africa on a production of *Is Zat So* in 1928. He wrote screenplays for most of the major studios, many of them derived from major plays, including those for *The Mayor of Hell* (1933) with James Cagney, *The World Changes* (1933), Howard Hawks's *Barbary Coast* (1935), *Craig's Wife* (1936), *Yellow Jack* (1938), *Spring Madness* (1938), *Undercurrent* (1946), *The Hucksters* (1947) with Clark Gable, and *Road House* (1948) with Richard Widmark.

Chodorov had production responsibility on at least 18 films, some of which he wrote. He also doctored many screenplays and worked uncredited on such films as *The Story of Louis Pasteur* (1935) with Paul Muni and *Macao* (1952) with Robert Mitchum. Chodorov's TV writing included *The Billy Rose Show* in 1952. Chodorov's plays include *The Spa*, *Listen to the Mockingbird*, *Cue for Passion*, and *Common Ground*. Like his brother, playwright Jerome Chodorov, whose best-known plays were collaborations with Joseph Fields, Edward Chodorov was blacklisted during the McCarthy Era. For Jerome Chodorov, see **Joseph Fields & Jerome Chodorov**.

Gentlemen Are Born (1934, Warner Bros., 75m/bw) ☆☆½ **Sc:** Robert Lee Johnson, Eugene Solow. **D:** Alfred E. Green. **Cam:** James Van Trees. **Cast:** Franchot Tone, Jean Muir, Margaret Lindsay, Ann Dvorak, Ross Alexander, Dick Foran, Charles Starrett, Russell Hicks, Henry O'Neill, Robert Light, Addison Richards, Arthur Aylesworth, Marjorie Gateson, Bradley Page, Carlyle Blackwell, Jane Darwell. Four college graduates are disappointed about not getting jobs during the Great Depression.

- *"Unfortunately, the new drama, after a brave and stirring advance on the somewhat vague phantoms of social evils, contents itself with a good deal of tentative shadow-boxing around its subject. After a succession of morose and violent climaxes,* Gentlemen Are Born *solves the problem to its own satisfaction by permitting Franchot Tone to marry Margaret Lindsay, thereby conquering not only life, but the depression, and also the difficulties of raising a family on $20 a week."* (Andre Sennwald, The New York Times)

Kind Lady, which Chodorov adapted from the Hugh Walpole short story "The Silver Casket," was first produced on Broadway at the Booth Theatre in 1935 with a cast that included, Florence Britton, Francis Compton, and Henry Daniell. A larcenous artist plays on the sympathy of a wealthy, elderly Londoner and makes her a prisoner in her own bedroom while he sells off her furniture and paintings from the rooms downstairs.

Kind Lady (1935, MGM, 76m/bw) ☆☆½ **Sc:** Bernard Schubert. **D:** George B. Seitz. **P:** Lucien Hubbard. **Cam:** George J. Folsey. **Cast:** Aline MacMahon, Basil Rathbone, Mary Carlisle, Frank Albertson, Dudley Digges, Donald Meek, E.E. Clive, Doris Lloyd, Nola Luxford, Murray Kinnell, Eily Malyon, Justine Chase, Barbara Shields, C. Montague Shaw. Released in Great Britain as *House of Menace.*

- *"Stands out as one of Miss MacMahon's best acting contributions...Chief flaw is the tedious build-up to a fairly intriguing plot...blackmail via doping...Implausible..."* (Variety)

Kind Lady (1951, MGM, 78m/bw) ☆☆☆ **Sc:** Jerry Davis, Charles Bennett, Edward Chodorov. **D:** John Sturges. **P:** Armand Deutsch. **Cam:** Joseph Ruttenberg. **Cast:** Maurice Evans, Ethel Barrymore, Betsy Blair, Keenan Wynn, Angela Lansbury, John Williams, Doris Lloyd, John O'Malley, Sally Cooper, Henri Letondal, Moyna MacGill, Phyllis Morris, Patrick O'Moore, Queenie Leonard.

- *"...a sedate thriller with the emphasis on characterization. Playing his first major screen part in some 20 years, Evans does a suavely villainous job as the impecunious artist, Elcott...Ethel Barrymore brings her customary authority to the role of Mary Herries...Actually, the hopelessness of Miss Herries's predicament is a little hard to swallow, and the new denouement is a fortuitous play for more believable action. But such is the excellent performance of the two stars and their supporting players that* Kind Lady *turns out to be a commendable exercise in melodrama."* (Newsweek)

Oh, Men! Oh, Women! (1957, 20th Century-Fox, 90m/c) ☆☆½ **Sc/D/P:** Nunnally Johnson. **Cam:** Charles G. Clarke. **Cast:** Ginger Rogers, David Niven, Dan Dailey, Tony Randall, Barbara Rush, Franklin Pangborn, Joel Fluellen, Cheryll Clarke, Clancy Cooper, Les Raymaster, Monty O'Grady. The play was first produced on Broadway at Henry Miller's Theatre in 1953. Niven plays a psychiatrist whose patients begin to believe that they can solve their problems on their own. Randall throws temper tantrums, while Rogers must live up to the expectations that come with being the wife of a movie star (Dailey).

- *"...still is a three-sided presentation that can't shake the legit beginnings, and is lacking in the movement that is expected of the big CinemaScope screen. Also there is an inclination to step on the lines, meaning that considerable of the writing wit plays second fiddle to the physical antics..."* (Variety)

Those Endearing Young Charms (1945, RKO, 81m/bw) ☆☆ **Sc:**

Jerome Chodorov. **D:** Lewis Allen. **P:** Bert Granet. **Cam:** Ted Tetzlaff. **Cast:** Robert Young, Laraine Day, Ann Harding, Marc Cramer, Anne Jeffreys, Lawrence Tierney, Glen Vernon, Norma Varden, Bill Williams, Vera Marshe, Tom Dugan, George Anderson. The production at the Booth Theatre in 1943 starred Virginia Gilmore and Zachary Scott in a working girl romance. This is the only film on which the Chodorovs were both credited. Harding plays the captain of the 84th Street Auxilliary, who attempts to help her daughter deal with a new beau.

- "...*silly little film in which a virtuous shop-girl falls in love with an Air Force 'wolf.'...it is all a romantic cliché...the values are conventionally smug...And there's no point in passing critical judgement on an obviously artificial script, on slickly mechanical direction and performances in make-believe style...[it's] eyewash...*" (Bosley Crowther, The New York Times)

D.L. Coburn

Donald Lee Coburn
Born: August 4, 1938, East Baltimore, MD.
Pulitzer Prize-winning play: *The Gin Game* (1978)

A former advertising agent in Baltimore and Dallas, D.L. Coburn won the Pulitzer Prize for his first produced play, *The Gin Game*. First produced in Los Angeles in 1976, it premiered on Broadway the following year. Coburn is one of the great overnight-success, one-shot stories of the American theatre.

The Gin Game (1981, PBS, 82m/c, **VHS**) *American Playhouse* ☆☆☆☆
Tp: D.L. Coburn. **D:** Mike Nichols. **P:** Terry Hughes. **Cast:** Hume Cronyn, Jessica Tandy. This taped performance of the play with an audience in London is of Mike Nichols's 1978 Broadway production at the John Golden Theatre. The play follows a game of cards by an elderly couple, the cantankerous Weller and the apologetic Fonsia, who hash out their lives while they play a game, which she regularly wins, to his growing humiliation. The roles were taken over by E.G. Marshall and Maureen Stapleton.

- "*Hume Cronyn and Jessica Tandy are consummate actors, a fact that is self-evident when one watches them gracefully thread their art in and around and under the words of D.L. Coburn's* The Gin Game...*In tandem, the Cronyns offer special insights into acting and reacting, both of which are enhanced within the tight frame of television...The play could have, of course, been expanded and opened up...Mr. Hughes has taken, I think, the wiser course of stressing the theatricality rather than the nat-*

*uralism of the dialogue. The laughter underscores the spontaneity of an
unerring double performance." (Mel Gussow,* The New York Times*)*

George M. Cohan

Born: July 4, 1878, Providence, RI. **Died:** 1942.

The great tribute to Cohan was, of course, the Michael Curtiz film
Yankee Doodle Dandy (1942), which won James Cagney his Academy
Award for the portrayal of the grand showman. TV paid tribute to
Cohan numerous times over the years for being the American enter-
tainment giant that he was, with a tribute narrated by Peter Lind
Hayes called *Regards to George M. Cohan* in 1962 on the *DuPont Show
of the Week*, and portrayals by Mickey Rooney in *Mr. Broadway*, a 1957
NBC Special, and by Joel Grey, repeating his 1968 Broadway role in
George M!, a 1976 CBS Special.

For derivations of *Elmer the Great*, see **Ring Lardner**.

45 Minutes From Broadway (1920, bw/silent) ☆½ **Sc:** Isabel Johnston,
Bernard McConville. **D:** Joseph DeGrasse. **Cam:** Chester A. Lyons.
Cast: Charles Ray, Dorothy Devore, Hazel Howell, Eugenie Besserer,
May Foster, Donald McDonald, Harry Myers, William Courtright.

• *"The story is badly cut, in some instances causing the characters to move so
  rapidly that it resembles slapstick comedy. Too, the continuity is bad and the
  picture is half over before the characters are clearly placed in your mind."*
  (Motion Picture)

45 Minutes From Broadway aired on *Omnibus* in 1959 with Tammy
Grimes and Larry Blyden.

Gambling (1934, Fox, 82m/bw) ☆☆ **Sc:** Garret Graham. **D:** Rowland
V. Lee. **P:** Howard B. Franklin. **Cam:** Jack MacKenzie. **Cast:** George M.
Cohan, Wynne Gibson, Dorothy Burgess, Theodore Newton, Walter
Gilbert, Percy Ames, Cora Witherspoon, Harold Healy, David Morris,
E.J. De Varney, Robert Strange, John T. Doyle, Joseph Allen, Fred
Miller, Hunter Gardner. The 1929 play, which was produced by and
starred Cohan, ran for 152 performances at Broadway's Fulton Theatre.
An illicit gambling house operator, who converts the joint to a knitting
circle when the police come inquiring, becomes a sleuth after his
adopted daughter is murdered and the gent tried in the case is acquitted.
It was Cohan's second sound film performance as well as his swan song
on the silver screen.

• *"Having his own tart opinion of the mentality of the cinema maharajas in
  Hollywood, based upon his experiences during the production of* The Phan-

tom President *several years ago, George M. Cohan has elected to make his second talking picture on Long Island far from the doltish interference of the feeble-minded film supervisors. It is an unpleasant duty…to report that he has provided his enemies with unexpected fodder for their cannon…Gambling is unfortunately deficient in many of the technical fundamentals in which the usual Hollywood product manages to be so unobtrusively suave…qualifies as a photographed stage play rather than a brilliant example of cinematic technique."* (Andre Sennwald, The New York Times)

George Washington Jr. (1924, 60m/bw/silent) ☆☆ **Sc:** Rex Taylor. **D:** Mal St. Clair. **Cam:** Ed Du Par. **Cast:** Wesley Barry, Gertrude Olmstead, Léon Bary, Heinie Conklin, Otis Harlan, William Courtright, Eddie Phillips.

- *"…was suggested, probably remotely so, by George Cohan's musical comedy of that name…a cross between crude farce and cruder melodrama…never reaches the humorous heights one anticipates."* (The New York Times)

Get-Rich-Quick Wallingford (1921, Paramount, bw/silent) ☆☆½ **Sc:** Luther Reed. **D:** Frank Borzage. **Cam:** Chester A. Lyons. **Cast:** Sam Hardy, Norman Kerry, Doris Kenyon, Diana Allen, Edgar Nelson, Billie Dove, Mac Barnes, William T. Hayes, Horace James, John Woodford, Mrs. Charles Willard, Eugene Keith. George Randolph Chester's stories about a rascally financial wizard who skirts the law were collected into the above-titled book in 1908, and Cohan dramatized some of them under the same title in 1910 at the Gaiety Theatre and a year later at George M. Cohan's Theatre.

- *"…the picture is practically a duplicate of the play to the extent that the stage can be duplicated on the screen…Those who are content to take the screen as a mere substitute for the stage ought to have no fault to find with the filmed Wallingford, while those who enjoy the screen for its motion pictures must regret that many opportunities to really picturize, and thereby to revivify, Wallingford, have been thrown away."* (The New York Times)

Hit-the-Trail Holliday (1918, bw/silent) ☆☆☆ **Sc:** John Emerson, Anita Loos. **D:** Marshall A. Neilan. **Cam:** Walter Stradling. **Cast:** George M. Cohan, Marguerite Clayton, Robert Broderick, Pat O'Malley, Russell Bassett, Richard Barthelmess, William Walcott, Estar Banks. Cohan's play and the film try to replicate an evangelical likeness to Billy Sunday, who here goes after bootleggers.

- *"The subject is up-to-the-minute and George M. Cohan's breezy impersonation of Billy carries the performance along at a lively rate…The story is very human and leaves an excellent impression."* (Edward Weitzel, The Moving Picture World)

The Home Towners was written and produced by Cohan in 1926 at Broadway's Hudson Theatre in a production starring William Elliott, Robert McWade, and Chester Morris. It depicted a visitor to New York City from South Bend, Indiana, who disdains the city and its natives and intends to foil his millionaire friend's wedding to a woman half his age.

The Home Towners (1928, Warner Bros., bw) ☆☆ **Sc:** Addison Burkhard, Murray Roth. **D:** Bryon Foy. **Cam:** Barney McGill, Willard Van Enger. **Cast:** Richard Dennett, Doris Kenyon, Robert McWade, Robert Edeson, Gladys Brockwell, John Miljan, Vera Lewis, Stanley Taylor, James T. Mack, Patricia Caron.

• *"It is perhaps the first feature-length production, in which there is no singing, that actually holds the interest throughout the story. It has its quota of amusement as well as suspense...The director is a little too fond of jangling telephone bells and a buzzer that sounds abnormally loud...If these sounds were more subdued, it would add to the general realistic idea of the picture."* (Mordaunt Hall, The New York Times)

Times Square Playboy (1936, 62m/bw) ☆☆ **Sc:** Roy Chanslor. **D:** William McGann. **P:** Hal B. Wallis, Jack L. Warner. **Cam:** L. William O'Connell. **Cast:** Warren William, June Travis, Barton MacLane, Gene Lockhart, Dick Purcell, Craig Reynolds, Granville Bates, Dorothy Vaughan Also known by the titles *Broadway Playboy*, *The Gentleman From Big Bend*, and *His Best Man*.

• *"The talky screenplay (it bickered more than it talked) was by Roy Chanslor...It was not an improvement on the earlier version or even on the stage play, despite its fidelity to the original."* (Clive Hirschhorn, The Warner Bros. Story)

Ladies Must Live (1940, Warner Bros., 58m/bw) ☆☆ **Sc:** Robert E. Kent. **D:** Noel M. Smith. **Cam:** Ted D. McCord. **Cast:** Wayne Morris, Rosemary Lane, Roscoe Karns, Lee Patrick, George Reeves, Ferris Taylor, Lottie Williams DeWolfe Hopper, Cliff Saum, Billy Dawson, Mildred Grover, Dana Dale, Mildred Coles. Also known by the title *The Bridegroom Misbehaves* and by the title of Cohan's original play, *The Home Towners*.

• *"...the Warners are repeating almost word for word the story of the garrulous country know-it-all which George M. Cohan was telling back in 1926...Or, perhaps, Warners are repeating themselves, since they first looked into this matter in 1928. Anyway, the fact is that* Ladies Must Live *offers, even in its best moments, only tolerable entertainment...even Mr. Cohan was warming over a cold stew when he wrote about the Main Streeter who viewed New Yorkers as charlatans..."* (Thomas M. Pryor, The New York Times)

Little Johnny Jones debuted in 1904 at Broadway's Liberty Theatre in a Sam H. Harris production starring Cohan, who also directed and wrote the book, lyrics, and music. It was revived three times in the first decade of the 20th century, then in 1982 starring Donny Osmond in a production that closed after one performance. The title character is a jockey who is to ride the Earl of Bloomsberg's horse in the English Derby, but is framed as a thief by racketeers, who also kidnap his girlfriend.

Little Johnny Jones (1923, Warner Bros., bw/silent) ☆☆ **Sc:** Raymond L. Schrock. **D:** Johnny Hines, Arthur Rosson. **Cam:** Charles E. Gilson. **Cast:** Johnny Hines, Margaret Sedden, Wyndham Standing, Robert Prior, Molly Malone, Mervyn LeRoy, George Webb, Nat Carr, Pauline French, Harry Myers.

- *"...absurdity...the Earl of Bloomsberg...of course...has a monocle and wears his handkerchief up his sleeve. He is the Warner Bros.'s conception of all that an earl should be. The acting in this production is about on the level of the story. Johnny Hines, with well made-up eyelids, is the jockey and Wyndham Standing writhes as the Earl of Bloomberg."* (The New York Times)

Little Johnny Jones (1929, 74min/bw) ☆☆☆ **Sc:** Edward Buzzell. **D:** Mervyn LeRoy. **Cam:** Faxon M. Dean. **Cast:** Edward Buzzell, Alice Day, Edna Murphy, Robert Edeson, Wheeler Oakman, Ray Turner, Donald Reed.

- *"Eddie 'Have-You-Heard-This-One' Buzzell, one of Broadway's most determined storytellers...makes his major film introduction in this old Chan quasi-epic of the turf. Oshkosh and Podunk won't know much about Eddie, but the picture should deliver general satisfaction on its intrinsic entertainment. It's a nice, agreeable and well-done feature."* (Variety)

Little Nellie Kelly (1940, MGM, 100m/bw, **VHS**) ☆☆½ **Sc:** Jack McGowan. **D:** Norman Taurog. **P:** Arthur Freed. **Cam:** Ray June. **Cast:** Judy Garland, George Murphy, Charles Winninger, Douglas MacPhail, Arthur Shields, Rita Page, Forrester Harvey, Milton Kibbee, Robert Emmet Keane. A garrulous Irish grandfather doesn't want his daughter to marry her beau and tries to foil his granddaughter's budding romance. Garland is the sole reason to see it, and presumably the sole reason for its availability on video. The original play ran for 248 performances beginning in 1922 with book, lyrics, and music by Cohan, who also produced and directed. The songs include "Danny Boy," "Singing in the Rain," and "Nellie Is a Darling."

- *"...a little bit of Irish chauvinism...only passing fare...The title of it is derived from an 18-year-old musical comedy [by] George M. Cohan, but the story is pieced together out of all the comic and sentimental Irish-American clichés that have been knocking around for years...much kicking around of the brogue by all and sundry, much interminable ripping and snorting by Charles Winninger as Grandpa and a sprinkle of pretty singing of several songs by Judy Garland. And that's about all."* (Bosley Crowther, The New York Times)

The Meanest Man in the World is about a kind-hearted lawyer who has to get tough to get clients.

The Meanest Man in the World (1923, bw/silent) **Sc:** Austin McHugh. **D:** Edward F. Cline. **Cam:** Arthur Martinelli. **Cast:** Bert Lytell, Blanche Sweet, Bryant Washburn, Marion Aye, Lincoln Stedman, Helen Lynch, Ward Crane, Frances Raymond, Carl Stockdale, Tom Murray, Forrest Robinson, Robert Dunbar, Victor Potel, William Conklin.

The Meanest Man in the World (1943, 20th Century-Fox, 57m/bw) ☆☆½ **Sc:** Allan House, George Seaton. **D:** Sidney Lanfield. **P:** William Perlberg. **Cam:** Peverell Marley. **Cast:** Jack Benny, Priscilla Lane, Eddie "Rochester" Anderson, Edmund Gwenn, Matt Briggs, Anne Revere, Margaret Seddon, Helene Reynolds, Donald Douglas, Harry Hayden, Arthur Loft, Andrew Tombes, Paul E. Burns, Lyle Talbot, Hobart Cavanaugh, Jan Dugan.

• *"An old play...has been adapted to the screen ...There is, of course, nothing vitally timely about this picture...but it should hand you a couple of laughs, especially if Benny customarily kills you."* (David Landner, The New Yorker)

The Miracle Man debuted on Broadway in 1914 as Cohen's adaptation of Frank L. Packard's novel. It concerned a gang of lowlifes—scheming leader, pretty waitress, dope fiend, and the hideous "Frog," who impersonates cripples—in New York's Chinatown who viciously prey on any and all victims.

The Miracle Man (1919, Famous Players-Lasky, 8reels/bw/silent) ☆☆☆☆☆ **Sc/D/P:** George Loane Tucker. **Cam:** Philip E. Rosem, Ernest Palmer. **Cast:** Thomas Meighan, Betty Compson, Lon Chaney, J.M. Dumont, W. Lawson Butt, Elinor Fair, F.A. Turner, Lucille Hutton, Joseph J. Dowling, Frankie Lee. In his book *Lost Films*, Frank Thompson writes, "Some of the films in this book were not particularly treasured in their own times...But *The Miracle Man* was almost universally acclaimed...In an era when motion pictures were nearly always discussed in terms of stories and stars instead of directors...*The Miracle Man* was praised primarily for the direction of George Loane Tucker." Chaney created one of his first grotesque, attention-getting parts as the Frog.

• *"As a study in genuine human beings, as an exhibition of the instinctive triumph of the better nature when that better nature has a chance, as a per-*

fect fabric of life as it is lived—alternately funny as a Chaplin and pathetic as a Warfield scene—and as an adroitly constructed drama, rising from climax to climax and never missing a telling point, I do not recall that the silver sheet has ever offered anything better than this and few pieces as good." (Julian Johnson, Photoplay)

The Miracle Man (1932, Paramount, 85m/bw) ☆☆½ **Sc:** Waldemar Young, Samuel Hoffenstein. **D:** Norman Z. McLeod. **Cam:** David Abel. **Cast:** Sylvia Sidney, Chester Morris, Irving Pichel, John Wray, Robert Coogan, Boris Karloff, Hobart Bosworth, Ned Sparks, Lloyd Hughes, Virginia Bruce, Florine McKinney, Frank Darien, Lew Kelly.

- *"...as a silent film 13 years ago it was the outstanding contribution of its day, and is now...a talking picture...It is a good production, but one in which familiarity with the plot rather detracts from its general interest."* (The New York Times)

Officer 666 (1916, bw/silent) ☆☆☆ **Sc:** George M. Cohan, W.J. Lincoln. **D:** Fred Niblo. **Cam:** Maurice Bertel. **Cast:** Enid Bennett, Mattie Brown, George Bryant, Pirie Bush, Marion Marcus Clarke, Reine Connelly, Marice Dudley, Edwin Lester, Henry Matsumoto, Fred Niblo, Sydney Stirling.

- *"For sheer rollicking fun, Officer 666 has few equals...has been done in the spirit of farce comedy—differentiating from the theatrical performance to the extent that the latter rather tended to emphasize the melodramatics...Howard Estabrook is superb...delightfully ridiculous..."* (Variety)

Pigeons and People was written and produced by Cohan on Broadway in 1933, and also starred the renowned showman. It aired in truncated versions on *Studio One* in 1955 with Edward Andrews and on *Matinee Theatre* in 1957 via a Joseph Shrank teleplay.

A Prince There Was (1922, Paramount, bw/silent) **Sc:** Waldemar Young. **D:** Tom Foreman. **P:** Adolph Zukor. **Cam:** Harry Perry. **Cast:** Thomas Meighan, Mildred Harris, Charlotte Jackson, Nigel Barrie, Guy Oliver, Arthur Stuart Hull, Sylvia Ashton, Fred Huntley.

Seven Keys to Baldpate first appeared in 1913 as a novel by Earl Derr Biggers, who created the Charlie Chan novels. Cohan adapted and produced the play derived from it the same year and it ran for 320 performances. The mysterious story follows a writer at the lonely, mountaintop, and supposedly haunted Baldpate Inn trying to win a $25,000 bet by writing a full-length novel within 24 hours. He gets interrupted.

Seven Keys to Baldpate (1917, Artcraft, 66m/bw/silent, **VHS**) **D:** Hugh Ford. **Cast:** George M. Cohan, Hedda Hopper, Anna Q. Nilssen,

Corene Uzzell, Joseph W. Smiley, Armand Cortes, C. Warren Cook, Purnell Pratt, Frank Losee, Eric Hudson, Carleton Macy, Robert Dudley. Cohan starred in this film version, though he had not appeared in the original stage production.

Seven Keys to Baldpate (1925, Paramount, 66m/bw/silent) ☆☆½ **Sc:** Wade Boteler, Frank Griffin. **D:** Fred Newmeyer. **P:** Douglas MacLean. **Cam:** Jack MacKenzie. **Cast:** Douglas MacLean, Edith Roberts, Anders Randolf, Crauford Kent, Ned Sparks, William Orlamonde, Wade Boteler, Edwin Sturgis, Betty Francisco, Mayme Kelso, Fred Kelsey.

- *"There are long stretches without much in the way of genuine fun and Mr. MacLean is rather stiff and his clothes are much too well pressed. He looks as if he had come to life from a men's fashion advertisement, without a characterizing crease."* (Mordaunt Hall, The New York Times)

Seven Keys to Baldpate (1929, RKO, 72m/bw, **VHS**) ☆☆½ **Sc:** Jane Murfin. **D:** Reginald Barker. **P:** Louis Sarlecky. **Cam:** Edward Cronjager. **Cast:** Richard Dix, Miriam Seegar, Crauford Kent, Margaret Livingston, Joseph Allen, Lucien Littlefield, DeWitt Jennings, Carlton Macy, Nella Walker, Joe Herbert, Alan Roscoe, Harvey Clark, Edith Yorke.

- *"More effective than it was in Douglas MacLean's silent picture of three years ago. It is one of those fanciful flights that compels one to withhold criticism until the denoument. In fact it is an adventure which virtually defies derogatory comment. Richard Dix gives an agile and pleasing performance..."* (Mordaunt Hall, The New York Times)

Seven Keys to Baldpate (1935, RKO, 80m/bw, **VHS**) ☆☆½ **Sc:** Anthony Veiller, Wallace Smith. **D:** William Hamilton, Edward Killy. **P:** William Sistrom. **Cam:** Robert De Grasse. **Cast:** Gene Raymond, Margaret Callahan, Eric Blore, Erin O'Brien-Moore, Moroni Olsen, Grant Mitchell, Ray Mayer, Henry Travers, Murray Alper, Harry Beresford, Emma Dunn, Walter Brennan, Erville Alderson, Monte Vandegriffe.

- *"...palatable despite your familiarity with every nook and corner of Baldpate Inn. Even though you might pardon the screenwriters for attempting to erase the years by inserting a few choice lines of dialogue mentioning G-men among other things, the producers have neglected to explain that the mysterious goings-on were prearranged carefully to thwart [the] writer...While it contains more action that you normally will find in a dozen pictures, the film's chief handicap is that it ambles along at too leisurely a pace."* (Thomas M. Pryor, The New York Times)

Seven Keys to Baldpate (1947, RKO, 64m/bw) ☆☆ **Sc:** Lee Loeb. **D:** Lew Landers. **P:** Herman Schlom. **Cam:** Jack MacKenzie. **Cast:** Phillip Terry, Jacqueline White, Eduardo Ciannelli, Arthur Shields, Margaret Lindsay, Jason Robards Sr., Jimmy Conlin, Tony Barrett, Tom Keane, Harry Harvey, Robert Bray, Pierre Watkin.

- *"Philip Terry acts as though he were a bit uncomfortable in the role of the boob-like writer...Director Lew Landers might have had more success with writer Lee Loeb's rather confusing screenplay if he could have decided whether to play it for humor or mystery. The blend wasn't too happily accomplished.*" (The Hollywood Reporter)

House of Long Shadows (1983, Cannon, 100m/c) ☆☆½ **Sc:** Michael Armstrong. **D:** Pete Walker. **P:** Jenny Craven, Menahem Golan, Yorum Globus. **Cam:** Norman G. Langley. **Cast:** Vincent Price, Christopher Lee, Peter Cushing, John Carradine, Desi Arnaz, Jr., Sheila Keith, Richard Todd, Julie Peasgood, Louise English, Richard Hunter, Norman Rossington. Cannon put together a cast of old horror icons and placed them in an old horror plot, in an attempt at promotional-friendly filmmaking.

- "*...a kind of kidding-on-the-square homage to the bygone Gothic chiller. Pic could have been...scarier, wittier and more mocking, but clever promotion of its nostalgia value could spell OK returns...Michael Armstrong's screenplay is an affectionate, elaborate red herring with not one but two trick endings...*" (Variety)

Seven Keys to Baldpate also aired in an experiemental TV version in 1946 over WNBT-TV-New York with a cast that included Vinton Haworth, Eva Condon, Vaughn Taylor, and George Mathews; on *Broadway Television Theatre* in 1952 with Buddy Ebsen; and on *DuPont Show of the Week* in 1962 with Fred Gwynn, Joe E. Ross, Joyce Meadows, and Bruce Gordon.

So This Is London is a travelogue-style adventure with Cohan starring in his own play as a fish out of water in Great Britain.

So This Is London (1930, Fox, 92m/bw) ☆☆☆ **Sc:** Owen Davis, Sonia Levien. **D:** John G. Blystone. **P:** William Fox. **Cam:** Charles G. Clark. **Cast:** Will Rogers, Irene Rich, Maureen O'Sullivan, Frank Albertson, Lumsden Hare, Mary Forbes, Bramwell Fletcher, Dorothy Christy, Ellen Woonston, Martha Lee Sparks. The play was converted into a Rogers vehicle.

- "*In theme and treatment closely follows Fox's previous and recent Will Rogers talker,* They Had to See Paris...*is brimful of laughs...[Rogers's] comical stuff is 100 percent up to the minute and the puns on current topics all sharp, comprehendable and amusing.*" (Variety)

So This Is London (1940, 20th Century-Fox, 70m/bw) ☆☆☆ **Sc:** William M. Counselman. **D:** Thornton Freeland. **P:** Robert Kane. **Cam:** Otto Kanturek. **Cast:** Robertson Hare, Alfred Drayton, George Sanders, Berton Churchill, Fay Compton, Carla Lehman, Stewart Granger, Lily Cahil, Mavis Claire, Gracie West.

- "*George M. Cohan's original stage comedy has been converted to suit the personalities of Alfred Drayton and Robertson Hare, English farceurs, and their craftsmanship is worthy...the dialogue is crisp and pungent...*" (Variety)

Song and Dance Man presents a Broadway love triangle developing between dancers. The 1923 smash was produced by and starred Cohan, with Mayo Methot in the cast. Cohan revived one of his great successes in 1930 and again starred and produced.

Song and Dance Man (1926, Paramount, bw/silent) ☆☆ **Sc:** Paul Schofield. **D:** Herbert Brenon. **Cam:** James Wong Howe. **Cast:** Tom Moore, Bessie Love, Harrison Ford, Norman Trevor, Bobby Watson, Josephine Drake, George Nash, William B. Mack, Helen Lindroth, Jane Jennings.

- *"The black-face comedian's burden...just about what one might expect from the title. It contains spongy sentiment without much that could be construed as suspense...Tom Moore is capital as Farrell and Bessie Love is good as Leola."* (The New York Times)

Song and Dance Man (1936, 20th Century-Fox, 72m/bw) ☆☆ **Sc:** Maud Fulton. **D:** Allan Dwan. **P:** Sol M. Wurtzel. **Cam:** Barney McGill. **Cast:** Claire Trevor, Paul Kelly, Michael Whelan, Ruth Donnelly, James Burke, Helen Troy, Lester Matthews, Ralf Harolde, Gloria Roy, Margaret Dumont, Billy Bevan, Lynn Bari, Sonny Bupp.

- *"...without Mr. Cohan and with no singing and dancing to write home about...Wherever they have been keeping Mr. Cohan's play all these years, it seems to have been improperly camphorated and the moths of time have got into its trunks and backdrops. Moreover, not only is Mr. Cohan out, but even his famous part is no longer the lead part. Actors' trouble used to intrigue the public; now it is girls, girls, girls, and in line with this soft, decadent change, Miss Claire Trevor...has been made virtually the whole show."* (B.R. Crisler, The New York Times)

Wilson Collison

Clyde Wilson Collison
Born: November 5, 1893, Glouster, OH. **Died:** 1941.

Aside from the works cited below, Wilson Collison's plays produced on Broadway include *The Girl With the Carmine Lips* (1920), *A Bachelor's Night* (1929), and *Desert Sands* (1922). Collison's novel *Dark Dame* was the basis for the Maisie character played in a series of films in the 1930s and 1940s by Ann Sothern. *Congo Maisie* (1940) actually used elements from Collison's play *Red Dust* (see below). Collison contributed the original stories for the films *There's Always a Woman* (1938), *The Mad Miss Manton* (1938), and *Moon Over Burma* (1940). Collison occasionally used the pseudonym Willis Kent.

For *Getting Gertie's Garter*, see **Avery Hopwood**.

Divorce Made Easy (1929, Paramount, bw/silent) **Sc:** Alfred A. Cohn. **D:** Neal Burns, Walter Graham. **P:** Al Christie. **Cam:** Gus Peterson, Alex Phillips, William Wheeler. **Cast:** Douglas MacLean, Marie Prevost, Johnny Arthur, Frances Lee, Dot Farley, Jack Duffy, Buddy Wattles, Hal Wilson.

The Girl in the Limousine, a Farce (1924, First National, bw/silent) **Sc:** G. Graham Baker. **D:** Larry Semon, Noel Mason Smith. **P:** Larry Semon. **Cam:** Hans F. Koenkamp. **Cast:** Larry Semon, Claire Adams, Charles Murray, Oliver Hardy, Lucille Ward, Larry Steers, Florence Gilbert. This film was based on the play by Collison and Avery Hopwood.

- *"Naturally enough, liberties had to be taken with the story in building a comedy of this type, but on the whole it provided a good vehicle for Semon. Laughs are plentiful. Many of the gags are distinctly original."* (L.C. Moen, Motion Picture News)

Red Dust was a Broadway flop that played for eight performances in 1928 at Daly's 63rd Street Theatre. It concerns a torrid affair at a Malaysian rubber plantation between the foreman and the local free spirit.

Red Dust (1932, MGM, 83m/bw, **VHS**) ☆☆☆☆ **Sc:** John Lee Mahin, Donald Ogden Stewart (uncredited). **D/P:** Victor Fleming. **Cam:** Harold Rosson. **Cast:** Clark Gable, Jean Harlow, Mary Astor, Donald Crisp, Gene Raymond, Tully Marshall, Forrester Harvey, Willie Fung. Gable and Harlow conduct a torrid affair on an Indochinese rubber plantation. The film is notable for its snappy lines and pre-Production Code suggestiveness, but marred by its racism toward Asians.

- *"The flagrantly blonde Miss Harlow, who hitherto has attracted but intermittent enthusiasm from this capacious department, immediately becomes one of its favorites by her performance in* Red Dust...*In the new film she is called upon for the playing of...sardonic comedy and, by managing it with shrewd and engagingly humorous skill, she proves herself a really deft comedienne...transformed* Red Dust *into an entertaining photoplay."* (Richard Watts, Jr., New York Herald-Tribune)

- *"Given* Red Dust's *brazen moral values, Gable and Harlow have full play for their curiously similar sort of good-natured toughness. The best lines go to Harlow. She bathes hilariously in a rain barrel, reads Gable a bedtime story about a chipmunk and a rabbit. Her effortless vulgarity, humor and slovenliness make as noteworthy a characterization in the genre as the late Jeanne Eagles's Sadie Thompson."* (Time)

Mogambo (1953, MGM, 115m/c, **VHS**) ☆☆☆½ **Sc:** John Lee Mahin. **D:** John Ford. **P:** Sam Zimbalist. **Cam:** Robert Surtees, Freddie Young. **Cast:** Clark Gable, Ava Gardner, Grace Kelly, Donald Sinden, Laurence

Naismith, Eric Pohlman, Philip Stainton, Denis O'Dea, Asa Etula. The setting for the adultery and the catfight over Gable was moved to Africa for this remake, an unusual circumstance for Ford. Kelly is the ice princess and Gardner the fun-loving wisecracker. Both actresses were nominated for Oscars.

- *"Gable certainly doesn't have the animal magnetism he had in the earlier version, but when Gardner and Kelly bitch at each other, doing battle for him, they're vastly entertaining anyway."* (Pauline Kael, 5,001 Nights at the Movies)

Sing, Sinner, Sing (1933, Majestic, 70m/bw) ☆☆ **Sc:** Edward T. Lowe, Jr.. **D:** Howard Christie. **P:** Phil Goldstone. **Cam:** Ira H. Morgan. **Cast:** Paul Lukas, Leila Hyams, Donald Dillaway, Ruth Donnelly, George E. Stone, Joyce Compton, Jill Dennett, Arthur Hoyt, Gladys Blake, Arthur Housman, Pat O'Malley, John St. Polis. Inspired by the Smith Reynolds/Libby Holman case, this murder melodrama is about a torch singer who marries a wealthy playboy who's later found dead, the victim of a gunshot wound to the head.

- *"Leila Hyams is strangely cast as the singer and Paul Lukas as Carida seems bewildered by his sudden reformation as prescribed by the script. Donald Dillaway gives the best performance as Rendon, the playboy. Ruth Donnelly is not particularly amusing as Margaret Flannigan, one of Leila's friends."* (Frank S. Nugent, The New York Times)

Marc Connelly

Marcus Cook Connelly
Born: December 13, 1890, McKeesport, PA. **Died:** 1980.
Pulitzer Prize-winning play: *The Green Pastures* (1930)

While reporting on the theatre beat for the New York *Morning Telegraph*, Marc Connelly began collaborating with another newsman he met on Broadway, George S. Kaufman, Jr. The play they wrote together was *Dulcy*, about a bumbler who comes through in the end, a theme to which Connelly returned several times. Connelly received an Academy Award nomination along with James Lee Mahin and Dale Van Every for adapting the Rudyard Kipling fishermen's tale, *Captains Courageous*, into the 1937 MGM classic starring Spencer Tracy and Lionel Barrymore.

Other films made from his screenplays include *Cradle Song* (1933), *I Married a Witch* (1942), and *Reunion in France* (1943). He wrote the original stories for the films *Whispers* (1920) starring Elaine Hammerstein, *Exit Smiling* (1926) starring Beatrice Lillie, and *Elmer and Elsie*

(1934) with George Bancroft. Connelly also provided additional dialogue for the film *Crowded Paradise* (1956) starring Hume Cronyn. As an actor later in life, he played on several episodes of *The Defenders* and in the 1961 presentation of Horton Foote's original *The Night of the Storm* on *DuPont Show of the Month*.

Beggar on Horseback (1925, Paramount, 84m/bw/silent) ☆☆☆ **Sc:** Anthony Coldeway. **D/P:** James Cruze. **Cam:** Karl Brown. **Cast:** Edward Everett Horton, Esther Ralston, Erwin Connelly, Gertrude Short, Betty Compson, Ethel Wales, Theodore Kosloff, Jim Mason, Frederick Sullivan. The Broadhurst Theatre staging of the 1924 Kaufman/Connelly Broadway collaboration starred Richard Barbee, Kay Johnson, Osgood Perkins, Roland Young, and Spring Byington. Cruze, one of the most interesting filmmakers of the 1920s, was amid a period of unbridled experimentation.

- *"The camera showed people unnaturally large or small, overdressed, over-jewelled, stuck to chairs. Rooms appeared absurdly large; ostentatious settings were greatly exaggerated; the courtroom scene was stylized and fantastic throughout; actors' movements and gestures were sharp and grotesque."* (Lewis Jacobs, Rise of the American Film)

Dulcy was Connelly's first collaboration with George S. Kaufman, Jr., about a well-meaning but ditsy young woman who decides to throw a party to advance her boyfriend's career without understanding that it could backfire. The 1921 Broadway play starred Lynn Fontanne, John Westley, Elliott Nugent, H.B. Warner, and Howard Lindsay at the Frazee Theatre.

Dulcy (1923, Warner Bros., bw/silent) ☆☆☆½ **Sc:** John Emerson, Anita Loos, C. Gardner Sullivan. **D:** Sidney Franklin. **Cam:** Norbert Brodine. **Cast:** Constance Talmadge, Johnny Harron, Claude Gillingwater, Jack Mulhall, May Wilson, Anne Cornwall, George Beranger, Gilbert Douglas, Fred Esmelton, Milla Davenport.

- *"A splendid picture has been made of the stage's Dulcy. Cynical souls were never doubtful of the ability of the silent drama to do justice to this particular play. The play, they argued, required, as its central figure, merely an adorable nitwit to give it life. Surely, they said, this was one requirement the movies would be able to meet...A delightful and charming actress bring[s] the full perfection of her talents to a most ungrateful part...Constance Talmadge...showed a hitherto almost unrevealed sense for delicate light comedy..."* (The New York Times)

Not So Dumb (1929, MGM, 80m/bw) ☆☆☆ **Sc:** Edwin Justus Mayer, Lucille Newmark, Wanda Tuchock. **D:** King Vidor. **P:** King Vidor, Marion Davies. **Cam:** Oliver T. Marsh. **Cast:** Marion Davies, Elliott

Nugent, Raymond Hackett, Franklin Pangborn, William Holden, Donald Ogden Stewart, Sally Starr, George Davies, Julia Faye.

- *"Marion Davies, who is always at her best under the direction of King Vidor, shines in the role of Dulcy...This picture is a bright affair, with singular and unexpected twists. Miss Davies, often wide-eyed and, with her shock of flaxen hair, gives a spirited portrayal of the girl who mixes her words and has strange ideas about the compatibility of week-end guests."* (Mordaunt Hall, The New York Times)

Dulcy (1940, MGM, 73m/bw) ☆☆ **Sc:** Jerome Chodorov, Joseph A. Fields, Albert Mannheimer. **D:** S. Sylvan Simon. **P:** Edgar Selwyn. **Cam:** Charles Lawton, Jr. **Cast:** Ann Sothern, Ian Hunter, Roland Young, Reginald Gardiner, Billie Burke, Lynne Carver, Dan Dailey, Guinn "Big Boy" Williams, Hans Conreid, Jonathan Hale, Donald Huie.

- *"Ann Sothern must be awfully tired of displaying her particular talent for acting nit-wit dames, especially in second-rate films. But apparently Metro-Goldwyn-Mayer isn't weary of having her do it, for here she is, cast again in another of those screw-loose comedies conducted along the lines of a rotating squirrel cage."* (Bosley Crowther, The New York Times)

The Farmer Takes a Wife was co-written for the stage by Connelly and Frank Ball Elser and first performed in 1934 starring June Walker and Henry Fonda. It was derived from the novel, *Rome Haul* by Walter D. Edmonds, whose fiction illuminated the history of his native New York State. The play takes place in 1820 and follows a wandering girl's romance with an the Erie Canal worker who's saving to buy a farm.

The Farmer Takes a Wife (1935, 20th Century-Fox, 91m/bw, **VHS**) ☆☆☆ **Sc:** Edwin Burke. **D:** Victor Fleming. **P:** Winfield Sheehan. **Cam:** John Seitz. **Cast:** Janet Gaynor, Henry Fonda, Charles Bickford, Slim Summerville, Andy Devine, Jane Withers, Roger Imhoff, Margaret Hamilton, Sig Rumann, John Qualen, Kitty Kelly, Dick Foran, Jim Thorpe, Irving Bacon, Iron Eyes Cody, Chief Thundercloud, J.M. Kerrigan. This film was significant in Hollywood star lore as a comeback vehicle for Janet Gaynor and as the first film for Henry Fonda, who had starred in the Broadway production.

- *"If The Farmer Takes a Wife is a satisfactory film, then the screen debut of Henry Fonda seems something more than that...One of Mr. Fonda's most outstanding assets is his appearance of sincerity."* (Eileen Creelman, New York Sun)

- *"Charm and atmospheric color are two qualities that it is difficult for the screen to capture successfully and because* The Farmer Takes a Wife *manages both of them attractively, it deserves approval as an excellent motion picture…both charm and atmosphere are so sanely manipulated that you forget the unnecessary length of the picture, the absence of a sturdy story and the excessive amount of dialogue employed…The producers of the film were wise enough to retain Henry Fonda…"* (Richard Watts, Jr., New York Herald-Tribune)

The Farmer Takes a Wife (1953, 20th Century-Fox, 81m/c, **VHS**) ☆☆ **Sc:** Walter Bulloch, Sally Benson, Joseph Fields. **D:** Henry Levin. **P:** Frank P. Rosenberg. **Cam:** Arthur E. Arling. **Cast:** Betty Grable, Dale Robertson, Thelma Ritter, Eddie Foy, Jr., John Carroll, May Wynn, Charlotte Austin, Kathleen Crowley, Merry Anders, Gwen Verdon, John Butler, Kermit Maynard, Emile Meyer, Lee Phelps. The play was dusted off to extend Betty Grable's already flagging musical career. Harold Arlen and Dorothy Fields wrote the tunes and Cyril Mockridge the score for this colorful if sluggish and pedestrian treatment.

- *"To give it the zest it so pitifully lacked, it needed a screenplay far racier than the one…provided, and performances of more conviction than its leads were capable of. Its redeeming feature was its score by Harold Arlen and Dorothy Fields, especially a number called 'We're in Business,' sung by Grable and Robertson…"* (Clive Hirschhorn, The Hollywood Musical)

The Farmer Takes a Wife aired in 1938 over W2XBS, an experimental New York NBC station, with a teleplay by Frank Elser and Marc Connelly and included filmed inserts, miniature models, authentic period costumes, and sound effects "ranging from train whistles to insect noises," according to TV historian Brian G. Rose. The play also aired in 1949 on CBS's *The Ford Theatre Hour* with a cast headed by Dane Clark and Geraldine Brooks.

The Green Pastures tells the story of The Bible re-imagined by black Sunday school children as their teacher relates them the good book's basic stories. Connelly derived the essence of his theatrical triumph and Pulitzer Prize-winning play from *Ol' Man Adam An' His Chillun*, which collected the Southern sketches of Roark Bradford. In this telling of the Old Testament, "De Lawd" created man at a fish fry. Depicted are the sagas of Adam and Eve, Cain, Noah, Moses, and Babylon, with a side choir providing familiar spirituals between the dramatized events.

The Green Pastures (1936, Warner Bros., 93m/c, **VHS**) ☆☆☆ **Sc:** Marc Connelly, Sheridan Gibney. **D:** Marc Connelly, William Keighley. **P:** Jack L. Warner, Hal B. Wallis. **Cam:** Hal Mohr. **Cast:** Rex Ingram, Oscar Polk, Frank Wilson, Ernest Whitman, Eddie "Rochester" Anderson, George Reed, George Randol, Billy Cumby, Edna M. Harris, Slim

Thomson, Myrtle Anderson, Fred "Snowflake" Toone, Rosena Weston, Jimmy Fuller, Amanda Drayton, Dudley Dickerson. A musical from Warner Bros. (a rarity in the 1930s), this film, which Connelly co-directed, remains, as William Meyer pointed out in *Warner Bros. Directors* "occasionally embarrassing."

- "*Mr. Connelly is a sophisticated writer trying to see through the eyes of a negro preacher. He is on the outside looking in. The result is occasionally patronizing, too often quaint, and at the close of the film definitely false. For the end, Mr. Connelly deserts the Bible story and indulges in a little personal Protestant mysticism, and I do not think the author of* Dulcy, To the Ladies *and* Helen of Troy, N.Y. *is naturally a mystic...But Mr. Connelly deserves praise for his ingenious pathos...and his great technical dexterity...Rex Ingram's performance as De Lawd...is very moving...as good a religious play as one is likely to get in this age from a practised New York writer.*" (Graham Greene, The Spectator)

- "*That disturbance around the Music Hall yesterday was the noise of shuffling queues in Sixth Avenue and the sound of motion picture critics dancing in the street.*" (Bosley Crowther, The New York Times)

The Green Pastures (1957, NBC, 90m/bw) *Hallmark Hall of Fame* ☆☆½ **Tp:** Marc Connelly. **D/P:** George Schaefer. **Cast:** William Warfield, Eddie "Rochester" Anderson, Earle Hyman, Frederick O'Neal, Terry Carter, William Dillard, Avon Long, Estelle Hemsley, Richard Ward, Rosetta Le Noire, Sheila Guyse, Muriel Rahn, Helen Dowdy. At the time of a UCLA/TV Academy retrospective on the Hallmark shows in 1991, the program notes for this program read, "Even at the time it was first broadcast, *The Green Pastures*'s depiction of black life was recognized as naïve and limited, a fantasy-relic extant in a changing world." "It was a wild, wild show and one of the most controversial of the Hallmarks," Schaefer wrote. Some Southern TV stations refused to air it and *Ebony* magazine was one protesting entity, arguing against its depiction of blacks as primitive folks. Connelly hated it, and said, "If I had a million dollars, I'd buy it back so it wouldn't have to be seen."

- "*Any work about Negroes that's 27 years old is bound to appear dated in some respects, and* The Green Pastures *does not escape the ravages of time. The play's naïve viewpoint...is not in gear with the times...cloying in the play's depiction of the Negro as simple folk, either devoutly religious or thoroughly sinful...William Warfield was the dominant figure...playing the man-sized De Lawd with both power and humor...*" (Variety)

The Green Pastures (1959, NBC, bw) *Hallmark Hall of Fame* ☆☆½ **Tp:** Marc Connelly. **D/P:** George Schaefer. **Cast:** William Warfield, Eddie "Rochester" Anderson, Earle Hyman, Frederick O'Neal, Terry Carter, William Dillard, Avon Long, Estelle Hemsley, Richard Ward,

Sheila Guyse, Muriel Rahn, Helen Dowdy, Eulabelle Moore, Billie Allen, Butterfly McQueen. Three cast changes and an audio man change were the only differences between this *Hallmark Hall of Fame* live staging and the 1957 version. Hallmark restaged the play because the first production, despite great reviews, aired opposite a ratings-grabbing gala thrown in Madison Square Garden by producer Mike Todd to celebrate the release of his film *Around the World in Eighty Days.*

- *"…glorious viewing…must rate as one of the most luminous achievements of television…a debt of gratitude is owed to NBC and Hallmark for this 're-turn engagement.'…presented with deep love and humility…The all-Negro cast was, without exception, magnificent, but principally it was William Warfield in the role of the Lord who set the tone and the pace. His charm and warmth never for a moment slopped over into melodrama or ever bordered on the cloying or on the stereotype…It was a performance long to be remembered."* (Variety)

Merton of the Movies was one of Connelly's successful writing collaborations with George S. Kaufman, Jr. "Kaufman and Connelly did very well," wrote the former's biographer, Howard Teichmann. "As collaborating playwrights, Connelly was a whimsical optimist and Kaufman was a cynical pessimist." They adapted Harry Leon Wilson's novel about a naïve midwesterner who comes to Hollywood in hopes of becoming a serious western star. He's played for a sap by filmmakers who use his sincerity in a send-up of westerns.

Merton of the Movies (1924, Paramount, bw/silent) ☆☆☆☆ **Sc:** Walter Woods. **D/P:** James Cruze. **Cam:** Karl Brown. **Cast:** Glenn Hunter, Sadie Gordon, Charles Sellon, Gale Henry, Luke Cosgrave, Viola Dana, DeWitt Jennings, Ethel Wales, Elliott Rothe, Charles Ogle, Frank Jonasson, Eleanor Lawson.

- *"…represents the astounding spectacle of the movie industry making fun of itself…as far above the rank and file of the features as New York City is beyond Kalamazoo…so well done, thanks to James Cruze and Glenn Hunter and everyone connected with it, that the laughs roll along with the ease of a waterfall and the the staccato frequency of a machine gun."* (Variety)

Make Me a Star (1932, Paramount, 80m/bw) **Sc:** Sam Mintz, Walter De Leon, Arthur Kober. **D:** William Beaudine. **P:** Lloyd Sheldon. **Cam:** Allen Siegler. **Cast:** Stuart Erwin, Joan Blondell, ZaSu Pitts, Ben Turpin, Florence Roberts, Tallulah Bankhead, Clive Brook, Gary Cooper, Maurice Chevalier, Claudette Colbert, Fredric March, Jack Oakie, Charles Ruggles, Sylvia Sidney, Ruth Donnelly, Philips Holmes, Snub Pollard. Paramount turned out a few of its stars for cameos to punch up the box office, but Erwin was exceptional as Merton. Blondell was his equal in the tough role of the woman who both dupes him and sympathizes with his plight, and the production doesn't take an easy "out" for his predicament.

Merton of the Movies (1947, MGM, 82m/bw, **VHS**) **Sc:** Lou Breslow, George Wells. **D:** Robert Alton. **P:** Albert Lewis. **Cam:** Paul C. Vogel. **Cast:** Red Skelton, Virginia O'Brien, Gloria Grahame, Leon Ames, Alan Mowbray, Charles D. Brown, Hugo Haas, Douglas Fowley, Harry Hayden, Tom Trout, Morris Ankrum, Dick Wessell, Billy Benedict, Jim Davis, Phil Arnold. MGM scoured the vaults to find a vehicle for Skelton.

- *"The years have made few alterations in the story which George Kaufman and Marc Connelly dramatized 25 years ago, but a great many in audience reactions to it. Aware of the problems of trying to wring laughs from ancient situations Red Skelton knocks himself out in the effort to surmount them. The result...is a frenzied but unspontaneous kind of comedy, with long dull patches between the straining gags."* (Virginia Wright, New York Daily News)

Merton of the Movies made its TV debut the same year as the above Skelton picture on NBC's *Kraft Television Theatre*.

To the Ladies (1923, Paramount, bw/silent) **Sc:** Walter Woods. **D/P:** James Cruze. **Cam:** Karl Brown. **Cast:** Edward Everett Horton, Theodore Roberts, Helen Jerome Eddy, Louise Dresser, Z. Wall Covington, Arthur Hoyt, Jack Gardner, Mary Astor. The play was originally produced at New York's Liberty Theatre with Helen Hayes and Otto Kruger.

The Wild Man of Borneo (1941, MGM, 78m/bw) ☆☆½ **Sc:** Waldo Salt, John McClain. **D:** Robert B. Sinclair. **P:** Joseph L. Mankiewicz. **Cam:** Oliver T. Marsh. **Cast:** Frank Morgan, Mary Howard, Dan Dailey, Billie Burke, Donald Meek, Bonita Granville, Marjorie Main, Connie Gilchrist, Walter Catlett, Joe Yule, Phil Silvers, Andrew Tombes, Irving Bacon, Tom Conway, Karen Verne, James Flavin. In 1902, medicine show con man Dan Thompson settles down with the daughter he hardly knows in a New York theatrical boarding house full of eccentric characters. Forced to take a job in an sideshow, he tries to con daughter Mary and his fellow boarders into thinking he's on the legitimate stage.

- *"...a hokey little affair...fair audience hokum with some better-than-average comedy momements and some really good performances."* (The Hollywood Reporter)

The Wisdom Tooth, Connelly's 1926 play that starred Thomas Mitchell, aired in back-to-back years in hour-long versions on fledgling TV: in 1950 on CBS's *Studio One* with Jack Lemmon and Barbara Bolton, and in 1951 on ABC's *Pulitzer Prize Playhouse* with Jean Parker and John Beal.

Betty Comden & Adolph Greene

Comden:
Born: May 31, 1919, New York, NY.

Green:
Born: December 2, 1914, The Bronx, NY. **Died:** 2002.

Their screenplays include those for *Good News* (1947), *The Barkleys of Broadway* (1949), the all-time classic musical *Singin' in the Rain* (1952), *The Band Wagon* (1953), *Auntie Mame* (1958) with Rosalind Russell, and the all-star *What a Way to Go!* (1964). They also re-wrote *Applause* in 1973, and *I'm Getting Married* for ABC Stage '67, a two-character musical satire about a young businessman about to marry who can't stop thinking about getting ahead in the world.

Bells Are Ringing (1960, MGM, 127m/c, **VHS**) ☆☆½ **Sc:** Betty Comden, Adolph Green. **D:** Vincente Minnelli. **P:** Arthur Freed. **Cam:** Milton Krasner. **Cast:** Judy Holliday, Dean Martin, Jean Stapleton, Frank Gorshin, Fred Clark, Gerry Mulligan, Eddie Foy, Jr., Ruth Storey. The 1959 original, about the humanity of a switchboard operator, ran for three years on Broadway. It starred Judy Holliday and Sydney Chaplin with the book and lyrics by Comden, Green, and Sammy Cahn, music by Jules Styne, direction by Jerome Robbins, and choreography by Robbins and Bob Fosse. The film is a bit sluggish, with Dino phoning in his performance next to Holliday excelling in the repeat of her stage success.

- *"It is a daffy piece about a meddling telephonist, and was written for their old colleague, Judy Holliday (1922–65), with lyrics by Sammy Cahn and an excellent score by Jules Styne. Both Cahn and Comden have said that the film should have been much better, and Cahn said of the leading man, Dean Martin, 'He blew it away. They should have got a better singer or a better actor.' The CinemaScope camera sets before obvious sets recording too-broad performances, and as we watch them we may decide that the real culprits are Freed and Minnelli...That [Holliday] remains marvelous is no credit to anyone but herself."* (David Shipman, The Story of Cinema)

On the Town features three sailors on a 24-hour leave in the Big Apple, meeting three girls who they take on a whirlwind tour of the city. The 1944 musical at Broadway's Adelphi Theatre had music by Leonard Bernstein and the book and lyrics by, and two main roles played by, Comden and Green.

On the Town (1949, MGM, 98m/c, **VHS/DVD**) ☆☆☆☆ **Sc:** Betty Comden, Adolph Green. **D:** Gene Kelly, Stanley Donen. **P:** Arthur Freed. **Cam:** Harold Rosson. **Cast:** Gene Kelly, Frank Sinatra, Betty

Garrett, Ann Miller, Vera-Ellen, Jules Munshin, Florence Bates, Judy Holliday, Alice Pearce, George Meader, Murray Alper, Bea Beneradet, Don Brodie, Hans Conreid, Tom Dugan, Carol Haney, Milton Kibbee. One of Hollywood's better musicals, the film benefited from Kelly's athletics, Sinatra's singing, and location shooting—one of the first big musicals to move outside sound stages. The songs include "New York, New York" and "Some Other Time." The film won the Oscar for Best Score (Roger Edens, Lennie Hayton).

- "On the Town *brings air imagination and solid showmanship to the kind of movie that needs it most: the musical. The film avoids such standard cinemusical trappings as hothouse splendor, the lumbering backstage story and the curious notion that the script ought to give performers a pseudo-logical excuse to burst into song & dance. Instead, by combining a fluid cinematic approach and slick Broadway professionalism, co-directors Gene Kelly and Stanley Donen have turned out a film so exuberant that it threatens at moments to bounce right off the screen."* (Time)

- "...has one ingredient no musical should be without, and that is pace. It has it in unbelievable quantity...it packs the high spots of those 24 hours into an hour and a half of film that leaves you spinning and breathless." *(Ann Helming, Hollywood Citizen-News)*

Susan Cooper & Hume Cronyn

Cooper:
Born: 1935, Burnham, Buckinghamshire, England.

Cronyn:
Hume Blake
Born: July 18, 1911, London, Ontario, Canada.

Pulitzer Prize-winning play: *Foxfire* (1987)

Susan Cooper and Hume Cronyn also wrote the TV movie *The Dollmaker* (1984), for which Jane Fonda won the Emmy Award for Outstanding Actress as an illiterate Kentucky woman who takes her four kids and follows her husband to Detroit. Cooper also wrote the teleplays for *A Promise to Keep* (1990) with Dana Delaney, *To Dance With the White Dog* (1993) with Jessica Tandy and Cronyn, and *Jewel* (2001) with Farrah Fawcett and Cicely Tyson.

Hume Cronyn's distinguished film career as an actor began in 1943 with Alfred Hitchcock's *Shadow of a Doubt*. He won Emmy Awards for his performances in *Age-Old Friends* (1989), Neil Simon's *Broadway Bound* (1992), and *To Dance With the White Dog*, and was nominated for *Christmas on Division Street* (1991) and the TV remake of *12 Angry*

Men (1997). He was nominated for an Oscar as Best Supporting Actor for *The Seventh Cross* (1944). He has starred opposite his late wife Jessica Tandy dozens of times in the theatre and on TV, including in *The Gin Game* (1981) and *Cocoon* (1982). As a writer, Cronyn wrote the adaptations of Patrick Hamilton's play *Rope* (1948) and John Coltin and Margaret Lindon's play *Under Capricorn* (1949)— both for Hitchcock.

Foxfire (1987, CBS, 120m/c, **VHS/DVD**) *Hallmark Hall of Fame* ☆☆☆☆½ **Sc:** Susan Cooper. **D:** Jud Taylor. **P:** Dorothea G. Petrie. **Cast:** Jessica Tandy, Hume Cronyn, John Denver, Harriet Hall, Gary Grubbs, Joshua Bryson, Collin Wilcox Paxton, Jenny Whitter. Elderly Annie Nations ruminates on her and her family's Appalachian lives through the 20th century as developers want to buy her mountaintop home. The original 1982 play starred Tandy, Cronyn, Keith Carradine, and Trey Wilson. This TV production received an Emmy Award for Best Actress (Tandy), Taylor won the DGA's annual award for Best TV Feature Direction and Cooper the WGA's award in the same category. Both husband and wife were in superb form.

- *"Hector Nations has no use for television. It's 'sin furniture.' He might change his mind if he took a look at* Foxfire...*This movie about Hector and his kin, based on the play of the same name, is immensely affecting. If it were set in December, it would be the perfect holiday heart-warmer. Unfortunately, it's set in the summertime. But the holidays are when many people pause to ponder the themes of then and now, holding on and letting go, living and dying. And* Foxfire *illuminates these themes with an irresistible glow...Best of all, this* Hallmark Hall of Fame *presentation preserves the gorgeously tuned performances of Cronyn and Tandy. You can have your adorable kiddies and jolly Santas; Tandy's Annie is my idea of a character to cherish during the holidays—and beyond." (Don Shirley, Los Angeles Times)*

Michael Cristofer

Michael Procaccino
Born: November 22, 1945, Trenton, NJ.
Pulitzer Prize-winning play: *The Shadow Box* (1977)
Tony Award-winning play: *The Shadow Box*

Michael Cristofer's plays include *The Mandala* (1968), *Plot Counter Plot* (1971), *Americomedia* (1973), *Ice* (1976), *Black Angel* (1978), C.C. *Pyle and the Bunyon Derby* (1978), and *The Lady and the Clarinet* (1980). A sometime actor, Cristofer played in *Hamlet* and *The Cherry*

Orchard on Broadway and made appearances in the TV productions of *The Entertainer* (1976) with Jack Lemmon, *The Last of Mrs. Lincoln* (1976) with Julie Harris, *Knuckle* on PBS, and the ill-advised *An Enemy of the People* (1976) with Steve McQueen. Cristofer wrote the screenplays for *Falling in Love* (1986) with Robert DeNiro and Meryl Streep, *The Witches of Eastwick* (1987) with Jack Nicholson, the infamous *The Bonfire of the Vanities* (1990) with Tom Hanks, and *Mr. Jones* (1993) with Richard Gere. Cristofer began screen directing with *Gia* (1998), starring Angelina Jolie as a New York model consumed by the fast life. He also directed *Body Shots* (1999) with Amanda Peet and *Original Sin* (2001) with Antonio Banderas and Jolie.

Breaking Up (1997, Warner Bros., 90m/c, **VHS/DVD**) ☆☆☆ **Sc:** Michael Cristofer. **D:** Robert Greenwald. **P:** Robert Greenwald, George Moffly. **Cam:** Mauro Fiore. **Cast:** Russell Crowe, Salma Hayek, Abraham Alvarez. A couple go through the heated passions involved in several breakups and reunions until, finally, they decide to tie the knot. The film seeks to portray the unspoken character conflicts between mates. The two-character play was filmed in 1995 and shelved by Warner Bros.; it was only released after the stars' bankability was maximized. Hayek's portrayal of fiery sexuality is one of the film's drawing cards.

- *"Anyone who has ever been through the dissolution of a serious relationship will be able to identify with* Breaking Up, *a film that pulls the covers off movie-fed fantasies that the heady bliss of l'amour will last forever. Adapting his own play for the screen, Michael Cristofer retains the claustrophobic atmosphere of two people in a world where only the other exists. On stage, the pas de deux alternated vignettes from the relationship with the characters speaking directly to the audience, another device the film retains...."* (Phil Riley, Cinebooks)

The Shadow Box (1980, ABC, 125m/c, **VHS**) ☆☆☆☆½ **Tp:** Michael Cristofer. **D:** Paul Newman. **P:** Jill Marti, Susan Kendall Newman. **Cast:** Joanne Woodward, Christopher Plummer, Valerie Harper, James Broderick, Sylvia Sidney, Melinda Dillon, Ben Masters, John Considine, Curtiss Marlowe. Three terminally ill cancer patients face their ends as their families cope in different ways. The Newmans launched one of their occasional forays into TV with Cristofer's own uncompromising adaptation. The show was nominated for Emmys for Best Drama Special, Director, and Writer.

- *"The holiday season's most outstanding production—indeed, one of the best presentations of the entire year—is about death....a production that, in many respects, is superior to the original Broadway version. Michael Cristofer, the playwright, treads delicately but incisively over the undeniably*

*disturbing subject of terminal illness...Directed by Paul Newman, this pro-
duction has obviously been assembled with extraordinary care...this is a
splendidly controlled realization of Mr. Cristofer's play...The performances
are uniformly superb. Miss Woodward reveals still new layers of expertise
as the nasty wife. Mr. Plummer turns the impossible writer into a terribly
moving character. Miss Dillon is incredibly on target as the neglected daughter."* (John J. O'Connor, The New York Times)

Rachel Crothers

Born: 1878, Bloomington, IL. **Died:** 1958.

Rachel Crothers's plays formed one of the most perennially sturdy, insightful, and lasting feminist viewpoints in the front half of the 20th
century. Her women were often on missions of discovery about marriage
and "in the vanguard of public opinion," according to *The Oxford Companion to the Theatre*. She grappled with unconventional notions about
religion, class, and infidelity, and her characters, down to the smaller
parts, were invariably well observed. She played in many of her own
stage works at the outset of her career and directed some productions as
well, including *A Man's World* (1909), which was a significant event in
the theatre as an attack on "the double standard of morality."

As Husbands Go captures the ennui and dread of two Iowa housewives
who ponder their returns to their humdrum home lives after an invigorating and enlightening trip to Europe. Things get complicated when one
of their lovers becomes friends with one of their husbands. The play was
first staged on Broadway in 1931 at the Golden Theatre.

As Husbands Go (1934, Fox, 65m/bw) ☆☆☆ **Sc:** Sam Behrman, Sonia
Levien. **D:** Hamilton McFadden. **P:** Jesse L. Lasky. **Cast:** Warner Baxter, Helen Vinson, Warner Oland, G.P. Huntley, Jr., Catherine Doucet.

- *"Pleasant entertainment all the way, but a lack of action will bore children
  and annoy that not inconsiderable body of Americans who violently resent
  too much suavity of speech and manner."* (Variety)

As Husbands Go aired twice on NBC's *Kraft Television* Theatre: in 1949
with Ruth Matteson and Tonio Selwart, and in 1950 in a restaging that
featured Mary Alice Moore and Donald Briggs.

Let Us Be Gay (1930, MGM, 71m/bw) ☆☆ **Sc:** Frances Marion,
Lucille Newmark. **D:** Robert Z. Leonard. **Cast:** Norma Shearer, Marie
Dressler, Rod La Rocque, Sally Eilers, Raymond Hackett, Hedda
Hopper, Gilbert Emery, Tyrell Davis, William O'Brien. An unattractive
wife decides to do a physical makeover to win back her husband, who

has moved on to greener pastures. Not particularly politically correct, this one earned some latent notoriety because of its title. Dressler's society matron convinces Shearer to saucily vamp the latter's ex-husband in Paris. It's dated in nearly every possible way, despite the racy subject.

- *"[Dressler] was the high spot...as the society matron who persuades Norma Shearer to vamp her ex-husband (to prevent him from ruining her granddaughter)..."* (David Shipman, The Great Movie Stars 1: The Golden Years)

A Man's World (1918, Metro Pictures, bw/silent) **Sc:** June Mathis. **D:** Herbert Blache. **P:** Maxwell Kruger. **Cast:** Emily Stevens, John Merkyl, Frederick Truesdell, Florence Short, Baby Ivy Ward, Walter Hiers, Sidney Bracey, Vinney Binns.

Mother Carey's Chickens, based on the popular Kate Douglas Wiggin novel, was adapted by Crothers and Wiggin for a 1917 Broadway staging that was used as the basis for the 1938 screenplay. The folksy proceedings concern the seriocomic travails of a woman widowed by the Spanish American War. She scrapes to get by with her four children and turns the crumbling family manor home in 1912 Boston into a boarding house for teachers, a circumstance that unwittingly provides suitors for two of her girls.

Mother Carey's Chickens (1938, RKO, 82m/bw) ☆☆☆ **Sc:** S.K. Lauren, Gertrude Purcell. **D:** Rowland V. Lee. **Cam:** J. Roy Hunt. **P:** Pandro S. Berman. **Cast:** Anne Shirley, Ruby Keeler, Fay Bainter, James Ellison, Walter Brennan, Ralph Morgan, Donnie Dunagan, Frank Albertson, Alma Kruger, Margaret Hamilton, Jackie Moran, Lucille Ward, Virginia Weidler, Phyllis Kennedy. Katharine Hepburn's refusal to play the role that went to Keeler in this film famously terminated her RKO contract.

- *"Right down to its pin-feathers,* Mother Carey's Chickens *is a good show. The old Kate Douglas Wiggin novel has been brightened immeasurably by its screen adapters, by its director, by the cast...old fashioned it may be. Probably it deserves that priggish adjective 'wholesome.' But it's a rollicking, folksy comedy for all its vintage and as delightful an entertainment as one dare hope to meet..."* (Frank S. Nugent, The New York Times)

Summer Magic (1963, Disney, 104m/c, **VHS**) ☆☆ **Sc:** Sally Benson. **D:** James Neilson. **Cam:** William Snyder. **P:** Ron Miller. **Cast:** Hayley Mills, Dorothy McGuire, Burl Ives, Darren McGavin, Una Merkel, Deborah Walley, Eddie Hodges, Michael J. Pollard. The emphasis is on the children helping the widowed mother, centering on Mills, Disney's young star of the time. Benson retooled the material after RKO sold the rights and, by this time, with the slick 1960s Disney treatment of the old chestnut, it's unlikely that much of Crothers's contributions journeyed this far. The film was nominated for an Oscar for Snyder's camerawork. Buddy Baker scored the film and the Sherman Brothers added the songs.

- *"Under the sugar-coated pen of Sally Benson, Kate Douglas Wiggins's turn-of-the-century widow and three little orphans emerge as a ragtime quartet, one of those obnoxious families who are perpetually gathering around the piano and singing their hearts out in time of crisis."* (Judith Crist, New York Herald-Tribune)

Nice People (1922, Paramount, bw/silent) **Sc:** Clara Beranger. **D:** William C. de Mille. **P:** Adolph Zukor. **Cam:** Guy Wilky. **Cast:** Wallace Reid, Bebe Daniels, Conrad Nagel, Julia Faye, Claire McDowell, Edward Martindel, Eve Southern, William Boyd, Bertram Johns. Daniels played a hard-drinking flapper not unlike herself and Reid was the westerner interested in her in one of his last roles before dying of drug addiction.

Old Lady 31 was adapted for the stage by Crothers from Louise Forsslund's novel. Emma Dunn starred on Broadway at the 39th Street Theatre in 1916. The play examines life in an old ladies' home where the husband of one of the wards disguises himself as a woman to be near his spouse.

Old Lady 31 (1920, Metro, bw/silent) ☆☆☆ **Sc:** June Mathis. **D:** John E. Ince. **Cam:** William Beckway. **Cast:** Emma Dunn, Henry Harmon, Clara Knott, Carrie Clark Ward, Sadie Gordon, Winifred Westover, Antrim Short, Lawrence Underwood, Graham Pettie, Ruby Lafayette.

- *"This carefully crafted story of humor and sentimentality, despite the obvious artificiality of its arrangement, will undoubtedly have much of the popularity it enjoyed on the stage, and mainly through the unerring performance of Emma Dunn and Henry Harmon...Both their characters are marked with sincerity and cannot fail to appeal."* (The New York Times)

The Captain Is a Lady (1940, MGM, 65m/bw) ☆☆☆ **Sc:** Henry Clark. **D:** Robert B. Sinclair. **P:** Frank Stephani. **Cam:** Leonard Smith. **Cast:** Charles Coburn, Beulah Bondi, Virginia Grey, Helen Broderick, Billie Burke, Dan Dailey, Helen Westley, Marjorie Main, Clem Bevans, Cecil Cunningham, Earle Hodgins. In one of the largely forgotten cross-dressing pictures, sea captain Coburn hits on hard times and puts his wife in an old folks' home, then visits her by disguising himself as a woman.

- *"Absurd-sounding comedy not without a certain lunatic charm."* (Leslie Halliwell, Halliwell's Film Guide)

Splendor (1935, Goldwyn, 77m/bw) ☆☆½ **Sc:** Rachel Crothers. **D:** Elliott Nugent. **Cam:** Gregg Toland. **P:** Samuel Goldwyn. **Cast:** Joel McCrea, Miriam Hopkins, Helen Westley, Katherine Alexander, David Niven, Billie Burke, Arthur Treacher, Paul Cavanagh. A drawing room artifact of its time, about the scion of a once powerful Park Avenue dynasty on the skids. He falls in love with a nice, poor Southern girl to the family's chagrin. As the reviews pointed out, this tame film doesn't nearly resemble its title.

- *"A model of dramatic exposition, but it suffers from inaction and its theme is too commonplace."* (The New York Times)

Susan and God relates the story of a flighty, upper-crust wife who returns from Europe having been converted to a new faith that she feels she must impose on her family and friends. Gertrude Lawrence won acclaim in the role of Susan Trexel on Broadway at the Plymouth Theatre in 1937.

Susan and God (1940, MGM, 117m/bw) ☆☆ **Sc:** Anita Loos. **D:** George Cukor. **Cam:** Robert Planck. **P:** Hunt Stromberg. **Cast:** Joan Crawford, Fredric March, Rita Hayworth, John Carroll, Ruth Hussey, Nigel Bruce, Constance Collier, Marjorie Main, Bruce Cabot, Dan Dailey, Rose Hobart. The religious theme woven through comic badinage was certainly daring for MGM's heyday, but Crawford is ill-suited for the role and March enacts another of his driven-to-drink hubbies. The supporting cast, especially Marjorie Main, is excellent. The film was released in Great Britain as *The Gay Mrs. Trexel.*

- *"...not really in Joan Crawford's range...when Crawford is being intellectually frivolous, it's merely tiresome...Cukor and...Loos must certainly have been aware of the problem, because Loos supplied some new characters, and Cukjor lavished affection on the actresses — Marjorie Main and Constance Collier — who played them...It's not a good comedy, but it has a certain fascination, because the theme is such an odd one for Hollywood to have attempted at all."* (Pauline Kael, 5001 Nights at the Movies)

Susan and God (1951, ABC, 60m/bw) *Celanese Theatre* ☆☆☆ **Tp:** Lawrence Hazard. **D:** Alex Segal. **P:** Burke Crotty. **Cast:** Pamela Brown, Wendell Corey, Albert Dekker, Helen Craig, Polly Rowles, Edmon Ryan, Elizabeth Johnson, Donald Keyes.

- *"Miss Brown scored solidly, bringing to her role of the flighty socialite on the crest of a new religious fad the same warm personality, charm and thesping ability which featured her work on Broadway last season in* The Lady's Not for Burning. *And with co-star Albert Dekker and a fine supporting cast contributing equally good performances, the show represented video drama at its best."* (Variety)

Susan and God was broadcast in 1938 over New York's NBC affiliate W2XBS in a 22-minute experimental excerpt version starring Gertrude Lawrence. The original Broadway cast recreated their roles in full costume for this abridgement of the play, broadcast to show how TV production values could be boosted. The play also showed up on NBC's *Matinee Theatre* in 1956 from a Laurence Hazard teleplay and starred Sarah Churchill and Lenore Shanewise.

39 East (1920, Realart, bw/silent) **Sc:** Kathryn Stuart. **D:** John S. Robertson. **Cam:** Roy F. Overbaugh. **Cast:** Constance Binney, Reginald Denny, Alison Skipworth, Lucia Moore, Blanche Frederici, Edith Gresham, Mildred Arden, Luis Alberni, Albert Carroll.

The Three of Us (1914, Alco Film, bw/silent) **Sc:** Susan Crothers. **D:** John W. Noble. **Cam:** H.O. Carleton. **Cast:** Edwin Carewe, Madame Claire, Irving Cummings, Creighton Hale, Mayme Kelso, Harry Smith, Master Stuart, Mabel Taliaferro. This was Crothers's first involvement with the movies.

When Ladies Meet was one of Crothers's more daring upper-class comedies of manners, about a female novelist who falls in love with her married publisher. Both film versions were shown on television under the title *Strange Skirts*.

When Ladies Meet (1933, MGM, 73m/bw) ☆☆☆ **Sc:** John Meehan, Leon Gordon. **D:** Harry Beaumont. **P:** Lawrence Weingarten. **Cam:** Ray June. **Cast:** Ann Harding, Robert Montgomery, Myrna Loy, Alice Brady, Frank Morgan, Martin Burton, Luis Alberni, Sterling Holloway. This brisk and faithful adaptation relied on Crothers's witty repartee and the performances of an attractive cast. Also known as *Truth Is Stranger.*

- "...here the adapters have preserved the savor of the original while producing a generally mobile atmosphere...it soon steadies down into a nicely-paced action punctuated by plenty of laughs that arise from the lines instead of the horseplay...It's interesting and holds quiet attention, which is unusual." (Variety)

When Ladies Meet (1941, MGM, 108m/bw, **VHS**) ☆☆½ **Sc:** S.K. Lauren, Anita Loos. **D:** Robert Z. Leonard. **P:** Robert Z. Leonard, Orville O. Dull. **Cam:** Robert Planck. **Cast:** Joan Crawford, Robert Taylor, Greer Garson, Herbert Marshall, Spring Byington, Rafael Storm, Olaf Hytten. After their attempt with *Susan and God*, MGM, Loos, and Crawford went back to the Crothers canon, but this time with proven material that had made a hit in 1933 (see above). The powerhouse cast can't completely put over the material, which was somewhat dated in its liberal feminism theme.

- "When the ladies in question are the supremely vulgar Joan Crawford and the svelte-but-deadly Greer Garson, quite a lot happens...The screenplay by Anita Loos ensures maximum bitch-factor. Crawford, playing a sophisticated (and ridiculously well-dressed) novelist, loses Marshall but gets Robert Taylor as a kind of consolation prize." (Adrian Turner, Time Out)

When Ladies Meet aired in 1952 on ABC's *Celanese Theatre* with a cast that featured Claudia Morgan, Patricia Morison, and Richard Carlson.

Wine of Youth (1924, Metro-Goldwyn, bw/silent) ☆☆☆ **Sc:** Carey Wilson. **D/P:** King Vidor. **Cam:** John J. Mescall. **Cast:** Eleanor Boardman, James Morrison, Johnnie Walker, Niles Welch, Creighton Hale, Ben Lyon, William Haines, William Collier, Pauline Garon, Eulalie Jensen, Jean Arthur, ZaSu Pitts. The film, which was made two years before Boardman and Vidor married, was entitled *Mary the Third* onstage. A group of young adults drink and frolic as they take a trip to rough it at a camp. The 1923 play featured Ben Lyon and Beatrice Terry.

- *"Those with whom the recent series of flapper films found favor will be entertained by* Wine of Youth...*as usual in such efforts the doings of the young people are exaggerated. No such picture would be considered properly finished without a number of scenes depicting the shaking up and drinking of cocktails and their resultant effect on those who partake of them...Eleanor Boardman...is charming and thoroughly natural."* (The New York Times)

Mart Crowley
Born: August 21, 1935, Vicksburg, MS.

Since the play and film of *The Boys in the Band*, Mart Crowley has made his living in TV, adapting James Kirkwood's book and play, *There Must Be a Pony* (1986) with Elizabeth Taylor; the Barbara Taylor Bradford epic *Remember* (1993), and the sequel movie to a series, *Hart to Hart: Harts in High Season* (1996). He produced the series for a time. He has also been an actor in the films *Somebody Up There Likes Me* (1956) and *Nijinsky* (1980), and appeared as himself in the documentary *The Celluloid Closet* (1995).

The Boys in the Band (1970, Cinema Center, 120m/c, **VHS**) ☆☆ **Sc:** Mart Crowley. **D:** William Friedkin. **P:** Mart Crowley, Kenneth Utt. **Cam:** Arthur J. Ornitz. **Cast:** Cliff Gorman, Leonard Frey, Frederick Combs, Kenneth Nelson, Laurence Luckinbill, Reuben Greene, Robert La Tourneaux, Keith Prentice, Peter White. Crowley's once groundbreaking play in the mainstream theatre concerned a birthday party thrown by New York homosexuals (gay wasn't yet in the language in its present context), who vent their indvidual stories, then are aghast that one attendee happens to be straight.

- *"...it's like the gathering of bitchy ladies in* The Women, *but with a 1940s-movie bomber-crew cast: a Catholic, a Jew, a Negro, a hustler, one who is butch, and one who is nellie, and so on. They crack jokes while their hearts are breaking. The message appears to be that the spirit of MGM in the 1940s still lives in the hearts and jokes of homosexuals...Crowley preserves the text as if the quips were ageless." (Pauline* Kael, 5001 Nights at the Movies)

Ossie Davis

Raiford Chatman Davis
Born: December 18, 1917, Cogdell, GA.

A ubiquitous post-World War II actor, Ossie Davis forged an outstanding career across the performing media. His dozens of films as an actor include Spike Lee's *School Daze* (1988), *Do the Right Thing* (1989), *Jungle Fever* (1991), and *Malcolm X* (1992), in which Davis, an influential theatrical figure, played himself. Davis's films as a writer/director include *Cotton Comes to Harlem* (1970) and *Countdown at Kusini* (1976), based on a story by John Storm Roberts. For TV, he also wrote *For Us the Living* (1983), the *American Playhouse* adaptation of Myrtle Evers's biography about her husband, the Civil Rights activist Medgar Evers, who was slain by the Ku Klux Klan in 1963. Davis has appeared in hundreds of TV shows, occasionally with his wife, Ruby Dee, and was a regular in the 1990s on the Burt Reynolds sitcom, *Evening Shade*. Davis's other plays include *Goldbrickers of 1944; The Big Deal in New York; Curtain Call, Mr. Aldridge, Sir; Escape to Freedom: A Play About Frederick Douglass; Langston: A Play*, and *Bingo*, a musical based on the novel *The Bingo Long Traveling All Stars and Motor Kings* by William Brasher.

Purlie Victorious was first staged in 1961 with Davis as the oracular title minister whose powers of persuasion help confound a racist white Southern plantation owner so the neighborhood folks can convert an old barn into an integrated church. Davis starred in the satire as the Reverend Purlie with Ruby Dee, Alan Alda, Sorrell Booke, Godfrey Cambridge, Beah Richards, Roger C. Carmel, and Helen Martin.

Purlie Victorious (1963, Trans Lux, 99m/bw) ☆☆ **Sc:** Ossie Davis. **D:** Nicholas Webster. **P:** Brock Peters, Nicholas Webster. **Cam:** Boris Kaufman. **Cast:** Ossie Davis, Ruby Dee, Alan Alda, Godfrey Cambridge, Sorrell Booke, Hilda Haynes, Beah Richards, Charles Welch, Ralph Roberts. The theatre's immediacy and the intellectualization of the parody of the segregationist white southerner's view of black folks as lawdy-lawdy-low class didn't translate well to the big screen, and this film is virtually forgotten. Originally released in 1963 as *Gone Are the Days*, but retitled *Purlie Victorious* for video release.

- *"The style of the film is entirely farcical; it is not very far removed from a prolonged vaudeville sketch. Davis's intention was to make audiences laugh, from a sophisticated distance, at the stereotyped image of the Negro held by the white Southerner. There are many amusing lines, indeed, but the film is not very laughable. There is too much self-consciousness about this deliberate attempt at parody. Gone Are the Days only intensifies the Negro spectator's reluctance to laugh at himself on the screen, even when he is trying very hard to do so...Davis and his cast are guilty of overplaying their farce."* (Lindsay Patterson, Black Films and Film-makers)

Purlie, the musical version, was presented in 1981 on PBS, from a teleplay by Peter Udell, direction by Rudi Goldman and a cast that included Robert Guillaume, Sherman Hemsley, Melba Moore, Rhetta Hughes, Clarice Taylor, Brandon Maggart, Don Scardino, Linda Hopkins, Loretta Abbott, Tanya Gibson, Michael Goring, Herbert Rawlings, Ted Ross, David Weatherspoon, and Renee Rose. The stage musical was first performed at New York's Broadway Thetre in 1970.

Owen Davis

Owen Gould Davis, Sr.
Born: January 29, 1874, Portland, ME. **Died:** 1956.
Pulitzer Prize-winning play: *Icebound* (1923)

Davis's first play, *Through the Breakers*, opened in 1897 in Bridgeport, Connecticut, and ran for three years. In the next decade, he wrote more than 100 melodramas. In the 1910s, he began writing comedies. Although he sold plays to film studios throughout his working life, he was a staff screenwriter for Paramount Pictures from 1927 to 1930. His screenplays included the Will Rogers vehicles *They Had to See Paris* (1929) and *So This Is London* (1930). The most significant films to be made from his plays were the Oscar-winning *The Good Earth* (1937) and *Jezebel* (1938). He was also the producer of the film *Julius Caesar* (1950), with Marlon Brando top-lining an all-star cast.

Davis's autobiography was entitled *My First Fifty Years in the Theatre*, which was subtitled "The Plays, the Players, the Theatrical Managers and the Theatre Itself as One Man Saw Them in the Fifty Years Between 1897 and 1947."

Big Jim Garrity (1916, Pathé, bw/silent) **Sc:** Ouida Bergere. **D:** George Fitzmaurice. **Cast:** Robert Edeson, Eleanor Woodruff, Carl Harbaugh, Lyster Chambers, Charles Compton, Carlton Macy. This film was based on Owens's 1914 play.

Blow Your Own Horn (1923, Film Booking, bw/silent) **Sc:** Rex Taylor. **D:** James W. Horne. **Cam:** Joseph A. DuBray. **Cast:** Warner Baxter, Ralph Lewis, Derelys Perdue, Eugene Acker, William H. Turner, Ernest C. Warde, Johnny Fox, Mary Jane Sanderson, Eugenie Forde, Dell Boone, Billy Osborne, Stanhope Wheatcroft.

Broadway After Dark (1924, Warner Bros., 7reels/bw/silent) **Sc:** Douglas Doty. **D:** Monta Bell. **Cam:** Charles Van Enger. **Cast:** Adolphe Menjou, Norma Shearer, Anna Q. Nilsson, Edward Burns, Carmel Myers, Vera Lewis, Willard Louis, Mervyn Le Roy, Jimmy Quinn, Edgar Norton, Gladys Tennyson, Ethel Miller, Otto Hoffman, Michael Dark, Fred Stone. Davis's play became a Menjou vehicle in which the star plays a society playboy who tires of his pithless girlfriend. He takes up with boarding-house actress Shearer, introduces her to the good life, and squires her around town until a detective frames her with her jailbird past.

The Detour was a 1921 Davis play staged at the Astor Theatre with Harry Andrews and Eva Condon. It aired on *Kraft Television Theatre* twice: in 1948 with Curtis Cooksy, Isabel Price, and Joan Stanley, and in 1950, restaged with Ethel Remy, Ames Coates, and Blair Davies. The following year, *Pulitzer Prize Playhouse* aired it with Dorothy Gish and William Harrigan.

The Donovan Affair (1929, Columbia, 83m/bw) ☆☆½ **Sc:** Howard Green, Dorothy Howell. **D:** Frank Capra. **Cam:** Ted Tetzlaff. **Cast:** Jack Holt, Dorothy Revier, William Collier, Jr., John Roche, Fred Kelsey, Agnes Ayres, Hank Mann, Wheeler Oakman, Virginia Brown Faire, Alphonse Ethier, Edward Hearn, Ethel Wales, John Wallace. This murder mystery was Columbia's first all-talking picture, made from the 1926 Davis play about a self-assured but bumbling detective who recreates a murder scene in a darkened dining room, resulting in a second murder.

- *"Capra has manipulated his story and people with restraint and intelligence. Recording and technical details all nicely taken care of. Production looks good. In short, Columbia has rung the bell."* (Variety)
- *"It is a yarn that sustains the interest, and because of its farcical quality it affords good entertainment."* (Mordaunt Hall, The New York Times)

Driftwood (1916, bw/silent) **Sc:** Anthony Paul Kelly. **D:** Marshall Farnum. **Cast:** Vera Michelena, Clarissa Selwynne, Dora Heritage, Harry Springler, Leslie Stowe, Charles Graham, Joseph Daley, Vida Johnson, David McCauley, Etta Mansfield.

Easy Come, Easy Go was initially staged in 1925 at George M. Cohan's

Theatre, produced by Sam H. Harris with Victor Moore, Edwin Maxwell, and Edward Arnold in the cast

Easy Come, Easy Go (1928, Paramount, bw/silent) **Sc:** George Marion, Jr., Florence Ryerson. **D:** Frank Tuttle. **P:** Jesse L. Lasky, Adolph Zukor. **Cam:** Edward Cronjager. **Cast:** Richard Dix, Nancy Carroll, Charles Sellen, Frank Currier, Arnold Kent, Christian J. Frank, Jean Arthur, Joseph Franz, Guy Oliver.

Only Saps Work (1930, Paramount, 77m/bw) ☆☆ **Sc:** Sam Mintz, Percy Heath, Joseph L. Mankiewicz. **D:** Cyril Gardner, Edwin H. Knopf. **Cam:** Rex Wimpy. **Cast:** Leon Errol, Richard Arlen, Mary Brian, Stuart Erwin, Anderson Lawler, Charley Grapewin, George Irving, Nora Cecil, Fred Kelsey, George Chandler, Jack Richardson, Pat Collins. Errol grows from a kleptomaniac to a bank robber once he gets the hang of pilfering. He has a few funny scenes in which he explains to a bellhop how to be a private detective.

- *"The great title reflects the effort of a few in this cast."* (*J.R. Nash, S.R. Ross*, The Motion Picture Guide)

The Family Cupboard (1915, World Pictures, bw/silent) **Sc/D:** Frank Hall Crane. **Cast:** Holbrook Blinn, Grace Henderson, Johnny Hines, Jessie Lewis, Estelle Mardo, Frances Nelson, Clinton Preston, Stanhope Wheatcroft. Davis's play was originally produced at Broadway's Playhouse Theatre in 1913 by William A. Brady and starred Alice Brady.

Gambler of the West (1915, bw/silent) **Sc:** Owen Davis. **Cast:** Linda Arvidson, Clara T. Bracy, Jack Brammall, William J. Butler.

The Good Earth (1937, MGM, 138m/bw, **VHS**) ☆☆☆☆ **Sc:** Talbot Jennings, Tess Schlesinger, Claudine West, Frances Marion (uncredited). **D:** Sidney Franklin, George Hill (uncredited). **P:** Irving Thalberg, Albert Lewin. **Cam:** Karl Freund. **Cast:** Paul Muni, Louise Rainer, Walter Connolly, Tilly Losch, Charley Grapewin, Keye Luke, Jessie Ralph, Harold Huber, Roland Got, Soo Young, Chingwah Lee, Philip Ahn, Richard Loo, Mary Wong, Charles Middleton, Olaf Hytten, Suzanna Kim. Davis adapted his play from Pearl S. Buck's 1931 Pulitzer Prize-winning novel, and the screenwriters used portions of it for the film. It concerns Chinese peasant farmers who loot wealth and are corrupted by it. They are brought back to (the good) earth by the destruction of a locust plague, which is impressively replicated. This was the last film Irving Thalberg produced before his death and it's dedicated to him. The film won Oscars for Best Actress (Rainer) and Cinematography. It was also nominated for Best Picture and Director. The film was a huge production for its time, while remaining somber in tone.

- *"Some of* The Good Earth *is magnificent...This film is one of the su-*

perb visual adventures of the period…The clean-swept feeling of the images and the uncluttered performances give credibility to the simple story, and contrast effectively with the occasional moments of fantasy—Tilly Losch's dance…an embodiment of lust and decadence…locust plague…revolutionary riots…Flawed by its simple-mindedness…The Good Earth is nevertheless a striking and original film." (John Baxter, Hollywood in the Thirties)

- *"It's a melodramatic sermon—a glorification of the passive, selfless, suffering mother, O-Lan. (There isn't a shred of sympathy for [the sensual, home-wrecking] Lotus [Tilly Losch], who is bought and sold.) The film domesticates exoticism: it's as predictable as an Andy Hardy picture, but much more sober, and much, much longer."* (Pauline Kael, 5001 Nights at the Movies)

The Great Gatsby (1949, Paramount, 90m/bw, **VHS**) ☆☆½ **Sc:** Richard Maibaum, Cyril Hume. **D:** Elliott Nugent. **P:** Richard Maibaum. **Cam:** John Seitz. **Cast:** Alan Ladd, Macdonald Carey, Betty Field, Barry Sullivan, Howard Da Silva, Ruth Hussey, Shelley Winters, Henry Hull, Carole Mathews, Ed Begley, Elisha Cook, Jr., Nicholas Joy, Jack Lambert, Jack Gargan. Davis's 1926 play arrived a year after F. Scott Fitzgerald's novel, produced by William A. Brady at New York's Ambassador Theatre with James Rennie as Jay Gatsby and Florence Eldridge as Daisy Fay.

- *"An electric, gaudily graceful figure in action movies, [Ladd] has to stand still and project turbulent feelings, succeeding chiefly in giving the impression of an isinglass baby-face in the process of melting…As a matter of fact, he gives a pretty good impression of Gatsby's depressed, non-public moments."* (Manny Farber, The Nation)

The Haunted House (1928, bw/silent) **Sc:** Richard Bee, Lajos Biros, Cornell Woolrich (as William Irish). **D:** Benjamin Christensen. **P:** Wid Gunning. **Cam:** Sol Polito. **Cast:** Larry Kent, Thelma Todd, Edmund Breese, Sidney Bracey, Barbara Bedford, Flora Finch, Chester Conklin, William V. Mong, Montagu Love, Eve Southern, John Gough.

The Haunted House also aired on TV in 1951 on *Pulitzer Prize Playhouse* with Barbara Britton and Howard St. John.

Her Marriage Vow (1924, Warner Bros., bw/silent) **Sc/D:** Millard Webb. **Cast:** Monte Blue, Willard Lewis, Beverly Bayne, Margaret Livingston, John Roach, Priscilla Moran, Mary Grabhorn, Martha Patelle, Aileen Manning, Arthur Hoyt. This film is based on Davis's play, *At the Switch, or Her Marriage Vow.*

Hold 'Em Yale (1928, DM/Pathé, 8reels/bw/silent) ☆☆½ **Sc:** George Dromgold, Sanford Hewitt. **D:** Edward H. Griffith. **P:** Cecil B. DeMille.

Cam: Arthur Miller. **Cast:** Rod LaRoque, Jeannette Loff, Joseph Cawthorn, Tom Kennedy, Jerry Mandy, Hugh Allan. Based on Davis's play *Life at Yale*, this conventional 1920s college-life souffle follows a student who falls for a faculty member's daughter and then wins the big football game in the final minute.

- *"Kennedy, as a comic cop, steals the show."* (J.R.Nash, S.R. Ross, The Motion Picture Guide)

Icebound was the Pulitzer Prize-winning play of 1923. In it a young man flees his New England home after accidentially burning down the barn. He returns after his mother's death to find that she left everything to a young woman who looked after her. The two fall in love, but he soon strays from the combine. The stage production starred Lotta Linthicum and John Westley and featured Edna May Oliver and Phyllis Povah.

Icebound (1924, FP/Paramount, bw/silent) **Sc:** Clara Beranger. **D:** William de Mille. **Cast:** Richard Dix, Lois Wilson, Helen Du Bois, Edna May Oliver, Vera Reynolds, Mary Foy, Ethel Wales, Alice Chapin, Joseph Depew, John Daly Murphy, Frank Shannon.

Icebound also aired three times on early TV, in 1948 on *Kraft Television Theatre*, and twice in 1951 on *Prudential Family* Playhouse with Jessica Tandy and Kevin McCarthy, and on *Pulitzer Prize Playhouse* with Edmond O'Brien and Nina Foch.

Jezebel was produced on the Broadway stage in 1933 by Katharine Cornell and Guthrie McClintic and directed by McClintric. Miriam Hopkins starred as the selfish antebellum Southern belle who's in love with her cousin. Co-starring were Joseph Cotten, Owen Davis, Jr., and Reed Brown.

Jezebel (1938, Warner Bros., 104m/bw, **VHS/DVD**) ☆☆☆☆½ **Sc:** Clements Ripley, Abem Finkel, John Huston. **D:** William Wyler. **P:** Henry Blanke. **Cam:** Ernest Haller. **Cast:** Bette Davis, Henry Fonda, Fay Bainter, George Brent, Margaret Lindsay, Donald Crisp, Spring Byington, Richard Cromwell, Eddie Anderson, Henry O'Neill, Gordon Oliver, John Litel. Bette Davis delivered her second Academy Award-winning performance (following *Dangerous*, 1935) as the titular temptress. The film won Oscars for Best Actress (Davis) and Supporting Actress (Bainter) and was nominated for Best Picture, Cinematography, and Musical Score (Max Steiner).

- *"It's hard to know which is Davis's 'big scene' — the painful flamboyant error of her appearance in red, or the breathtaking moment of her apology in white. She took the Academy Award of 1938 for this role, and rarely has it been awarded so justly."* (Pauline Kael, Kiss Kiss Bang Bang)

Jezebel was adapted by Catherine Turney for a 1956 *Lux Video Theatre* installment that starred Martha Hyer.

The Lash (1934, RKO, 63m/bw) **Sc:** Brock Williams, Vera Allinson, H. Fowler Mear. **D:** Henry Edwards. **P:** Julian Hagen. **Cam:** Ernest Palmer. **Cast:** Lyn Harding, John Mills, Joan Maude, Leslie Perrins, Mary Jerrold, Aubrey Mather, D. J. Williams, Roy Emerton, S. Victor Stanley, Peggy Blythe. This violent Davis play concerns an industrialist who beats his son with a whip over the latter's devil-may-care attitude, and his wish to follow a married woman to Australia. Davis wrote it with Sewell Collins and Cyril Campion.

Lighthouse by the Sea (1924, Warner Bros., bw/silent) **Sc:** Darryl F. Zanuck. **D:** Malcolm St. Clair. **Cam:** H. Lyman Broening. **Cast:** Rin Tin Tin, William Collier, Jr., Louise Fazenda, Charles Hill, Douglas Gerrard, Matthew Betz. The pooch and his master save the lives of a lighthouse keeper and his daughter, who are put upon by rum runners.

Lola (1914, Schubert/World, bw/silent) **Sc/D:** James Young. **Cast:** Clara Kimball Young, Frank Holland, Alec B. Francis, James Young. Clara Young played the sweet daughter of an inventor who creates a machine that revives corpses. When Lola is accidentally killed, he uses the machine to give her life again, but she returns as a carnally voracious strumpet, leaves him, and embarks on a hedonistic path. A sensual performance by Clara Young is the highlight of this unusual artifact, based on Davis's 1911 science-fiction melodrama. The film was re-released in 1916 as *Without a Soul*.

Marry the Poor Girl (1921, bw/silent) **Sc:** Rex Taylor. **D:** Lloyd Ingraham. **Cast:** Flora Parker De Haven, Carter De Haven. A scandal erupts when house guest Jack Tanner gets drunk on Prohibition Era booze and wakes up seated in house guest Julia's bedroom. Oliver Morosco produced Davis's 1920 stage farce, which starred William Roselle and Isabel Love.

Mile-a-Minute Kendall (1918, Paramount, bw/silent) **Sc:** Gardner Hunting. **D:** William Desmond Taylor. **P:** Jesse L. Lasky. **Cam:** Frank E. Garbutt. **Cast:** Jack Pickford, Louise Huff, Charles Arling, Jane Wolfe, Casson Ferguson, Lottie Pickford, John Burton, Jack McDonald, W.E. Lawrence.

Mr. and Mrs. North played Broadway in 1941 and starred Albert Hackett and Peggy Conklin, with support from Owen Davis, Jr., Millard Mitchell, and Philip Ober. It concerns the title couple, who find a corpse in their closet. The Belasco Theatre presentation was based on stories by Frances and Richard Lockridge.

Mr. and Mrs. North (1941, MGM, 68m/bw) **Sc:** S.K. Lauren. **D:** Robert B. Sinclair. **P:** Irving Asher. **Cam:** Harry Stradling, Sr. **Cast:** Gracie Allen, William Post, Jr., Paul Kelly, Rose Hobart, Virginia Grey, Tom Conway, Felix Bressart, Porter Hall, Millard Mitchell, Keye Luke, Jerome Cowan.

Mr. and Mrs. North was directed and produced by Fred Coe in 1946 for NBC Television Theatre.

Nellie, the Beautiful Cloak Model (1924, Goldwyn, bw/silent) **Sc:** H.H. Van Loan **D:** Emmet J. Flynn. **Cam:** Lucien N. Andriot. **Cast:** Claire Windsor, Betsy Ann Hisle, Edmund Lowe, Mae Busch, Raymond Griffith, Lew Cody, Hobart Bosworth, Lilyan Tashman, Dorothy Cumming, Will Walling, Mayme Kelso, William Orlamond, Arthur Houseman, David Kirby. In this version of Davis's play, a rich girl is mistreated by her father and raised in poverty. She grows up to be a fashion model, and is prevented from knowing her true heritage by her disturbed nephew. Near the end, she's tied to train tracks.

The Nervous Wreck, the adaptation of a 1921 *Argosy/All Story* magazine serial by Edith J. Rath and G. Howard Watt called "The Wreck" concerns a pill-popping Pittsburgh hypochondriac who takes his restful vacations at an Arizona ranch. He helps a damsel in distress escape an arranged marriage, and he becomes the title. Edward Everett Horton and Frances Howard starred onstage in 1922 in Atlantic City, New Jersey.

The Nervous Wreck (1926, Christie/PDC, 7reels/bw/silent) **Sc:** F. McGrew Willis. **D:** Scott Sidney. **Cam:** Alec Phillips. **Cast:** Harrison Ford, Phyllis Haver, Chester Conklin, Mack Swain, Hobart Bosworth, Paul Nicholson, Vera Steadman, Charles Gerrard, Clarence Burton. Cinema's first Harrison Ford starred in the title role and his adventures include robbing a gas station with a wrench, getting hired by the man he robbed, and a climactic auto wreck on a mountainside.

Whoopee! (1930, Goldwyn, 94m/c, **VHS**) ☆☆☆½ **Sc:** William Conselman. **D:** Thornton Freeland. **P:** Samuel Goldwyn, Florenz Ziegfeld. **Cam:** Lee Garmes, Ray Rennahan, Gregg Toland. **Cast:** Eddie Cantor, Eleanor Hunt, Paul Gregory, Jack Rutherford, Betty Grable, Ethel Shutta. This early Hollywood musical took its cues from the 1929 musical play, *Whoopee!*, by Anthony McGuire, which was adapted from Davis's smash hit of 1922. Cantor was in his element as a timid soul who's terrified during a series of adventures as he's supposed to be taking a rest cure in the west. Busby Berkeley supervised the musical numbers in his first screen assignment, deploying the Goldwyn Girls. Almost all of the original stage cast was hired for the movie. The most expensive musical of its time, it quadrupled regular costs to $1 million.

• "Good as Whoopee! *was on the stage, some felt the film was better. Goldwyn shot in color...The story was tightened and score actually im-*

proved...with Betty Grable leading the Goldwyn Girls in a rip-roaring opening number, Ethel Shutta...launching "Stetson," a hat number with much Berkeleyesque arrangements of the girls' white cowboy hats, and a better-than-average run of choral settings for wedding and Indian scenes, Whoopee! is a musical in the fullest sense, its only drawback being the poor quality of the sound..." (Ethan Mordden, The Hollywood Musical)

Up in Arms (1944, Goldwyn, 106m/c, **VHS**) ☆☆½ **Sc:** Don Hartman, Robert Pirosh, Allen Boretz. **D:** Elliott Nugent. **P:** Samuel Goldwyn. **Cam:** Ray Rennahan. **Cast:** Danny Kaye, Dinah Shore, Dana Andrews, Constance Dowling, Louis Calhern, Lyle Talbot, George Mathews, Benny Baker, Walter Catlett, Margaret Dumont, Virginia Mayo, Harry Hayden. Kaye's film debut finds him as a hypochondriac drafted for World War II duty. He and best friend Andrews end up on the same troop ship as girlfriend Dowling. An empty-headed mess, to be sure, dusted off by Goldwyn, it nevertheless became a hit and made Kaye, formerly a Catskill Mountains comic, an immediate movie star. The film was nominated for the Academy Award for Best Song ("Now I Know") and Musical Score (Louis Forbes, Ray Heindorf).

• *"...puts Danny Kaye through a Sam Goldwyn war, ought logically to leave me as cold, but I enjoyed it...The Goldwyn Girls look like real, live women instead of the customary radio-cap sculptures. There are some pleasant, silly gags...Kaye is the whole show, and everything depends on whether or not you like him. I do."* (James Agee, The Nation)

Whoopee! aired in 1950 on *Musical Comedy Time* with a teleplay by William A. McGuire, and *The Nervous Wreck* was aired in 1952 on *Broadway Television Theatre* with Buddy Ebsen.

Nine Forty-Five (1934, Warner Bros., 59m/bw) **Sc:** Brock Williams. **D:** George King. **P:** Irving Asher. **Cast:** Binnie Barnes, Donald Calthrop, Violet Farebrother, Malcolm Tod, James Finlayson, Cecil Parker, Janice Adair, George Merritt, Ellis Irving, Margaret Yarde, Rene Ray. Director King, aka "King of the Quickies," processed this patchwork British suspense melodrama with an agreeable pace. The new life for Davis and Sewell Collins's 1919 play, *At 9:45*, dovetailed to the 1930s needs of the British screen, where murder melodramas were popular. Three people, covering for each other, confess to the murder of a roundly hated rascal as a police inspector and a doctor pore over their stories.

No Way Out became one of the first titles to air on *Kraft Television Theatre* in 1948. The original 1944 play was produced by Robert Keith and co-directed by Davis and Keith at the Cort Theatre.

The Shamrock and the Rose (1927, bw/silent) **Sc:** Isadore Bernstein. **D:** Jack Nelson. **Cam:** Ernest Miller. **Cast:** Mack Swain, Olive

Hasbrouk, Edmund Burns, Maurice Costello, William H. Strauss, Dot Farley, Rosa Rosanova, Leon Holmes, Leon Watson, Otto Lederer.

Sinners (1920, Realart, bw/silent) **Sc:** Eve Unsell. **D:** Kenneth S. Webb. **Cam:** George J. Folsey. **Cast:** Alice Brady, Agnes Everett, Augusta Anderson, Lorraine Frost, Nora Reed, James Crane, William T. Carleton, Frank Losee, Crauford Kent, Robert Schable.

Spring Is Here (1930, First National, 65m/bw) ☆☆ **Sc:** James A. Starr. **D:** John Francis Dillon. **Cam:** Lee Garmes. **Cast:** Bernice Claire, Lawrence Gray, Alexander Gray, Ford Sterling, Louise Fazenda, Inez Courtney, Natalie Moorehead, Frank Albertson, Gretchen Thomas, Wilbur Mack, The Brox Sisters. The 1929 play featured music by Richard Rodgers and lyrics by Lorenz Hart. It starred Charles Ruggles in the story of two suitors for a pretty girl, one of which is disapproved of by her father. In the movie, the Grays vie for Claire. The songs include "With a Song in My Heart" and "Bad Baby."

• *"Silly musical…When the no-good Alexander Gray tries to elope with Claire, the other Gray arrives and carries her off." (N.R. Nash, S.R. Ross,* The Motion Picture Guide)

Tonight at Twelve (1929, Universal, 78m/bw) **Sc:** Matt Taylor, Harry A. Pollard, Owen Davis. **D/P:** Harry A. Pollard. **Cam:** Jerome Ash. **Cast:** Madge Bellamy, George Lewis, Robert Ellis, Madeline Seymour, Margaret Livingston, Donald Douglas, Vera Reynolds, Hallam Cooley, Josephine Brown, Norman Trevor, Mary Doran, Louise Carver, Nick Thompson. In this adaptation of Davis's 1928 play, a boy claims that a love letter to his philandering father was actually sent to him, causing the boy to lose his girlfriend.

Up the Ladder (1925, Universal, 61m/bw/silent) **Sc:** Grant Carpenter, Tom McNamara. **D:** Edward Sloman. **Cam:** Jackson Rose. **Cast:** Virginia Valli, Forrest Stanley, Margaret Livingstone, Holmes Herbert, George Fawcett, Priscilla Moran, Olive Ann Alcorn, Lydia Yeamans Titus.

The Wishing Ring: An Idyll of Old England (1914, Shubert/World, 60m/bw/silent) ☆☆☆☆ **Sc/D:** Maurice Tourneur. **Cam:** John van den Broek. **Cast:** Vivian Martin, Alec B. Francis, Chester Barnett, Simeon Wilsie, Walter Morton, Johnny Hines, James Young, Holbrook Blinn. A high-born ne'er-do-well is expelled from college and not accepted back into his family until he earns half a crown, which he endeavors to do by gardening for a minister who happens to have a pretty daughter. One of

Davis's first plays, it was first staged in 1910, and its realization as a film by Tourneur has been recently treated by historians as a rediscovered classic.

- *"...major landmark in both its lyricism and its attempts to weld the diverse elements of cinema and theatre...Tourneur, in particular, tried to evolve a language of film built rather more on pictorialism rather than grammar. He certainly understood the principles of editing, and there is some extremely subtle cutting in* The Wishing Ring *—so subtle that it disguises rather than calls attention to itself...* The Wishing Ring *owes [D.W.] Griffith no particular allegiance, and in fact is a more sophisticated film than any of the pre-*The Birth of a Nation *features made by Griffith. Its performances are charmingly relaxed and casual, and the atmosphere of England is so well created that for many years many astute historians assumed it was a British film."* (William K. Everson, The American Silent Film)

The Woman Next Door (1915, bw/silent) **Sc:** Owen Davis. **D:** Walter Edwin. **Cast:** Della Connor, Irene Fenwick.

Phillip Hayes Dean
Born: Chicago, IL.

Philip Hayes Dean's *Paul Robeson*, about the legendary early-century African-American singer, actor, athlete, and attorney, was played on Broadway in 1978 by James Earl Jones and in revivals in both 1988 and 1995 by Avery Brooks. *Time* magazine cited *The Sty of the Blind Pig* as one of the 10 best plays of 1971. Dean's trilogy of plays under the umbrella title of *American Night Cry* are *Thunder in the Index, This Bird of Dawning Singeth All Night Long*, and *Minstrel Boy*.

The Sty of the Blind Pig (1974, PBS, 90m/c) Hollywood Television Theatre **Tp:** Phillip Hayes Dean. **D:** Ivan Dixon. **P:** George Turpin. **Cast:** Mary Alice, Scatman Crothers, Richard Ward. First presented by New York's Negro Ensemble Company in 1971, the play is set in the Chicago ghetto in the early 1960s and focuses on an elderly woman and her frayed relationship with her depressed daughter and the impromptu visit of an old blind singer.

- *"Mr. Dean's rapid shifts between slice-of-life naturalism and a kind of heightened symbolism are more awkward than illuminating. The mother gets lost between sassy diatribes, startlingly similar to some Redd Foxx routines in* Sanford and Son, *and cold viciousness...The result is one magnificent scene resting on a rickety dramatic superstructure. That scene, however, and Miss Alice's performance throughout the production are strongly recommended."* (John J. O'Connor, The New York Times)

Christopher Durang

Born: January 2, 1949, Montclair, NJ.

Christopher Durang's Broadway plays include the musical *A History of the American Film* starring Swoosie Kurtz in 1978, and *Sex and Longing* with Dana Ivey in 1996. He is an actor as well as a writer and has appeared in such films as *Mr. North* (1988), *Penn & Teller Get Killed* (1989), *A Shock to the System* (1990), *Joe's Apartment* (1996), and the remake of *The Out-of-Towners* (1999).

Beyond Therapy (1987, New World, 93m/c, **VHS**) ☆☆ **Sc:** Robert Altman, Christopher Durang. **D:** Robert Altman. **P:** Steven M. Haft. **Cam:** Pierre Mignot. **Cast:** Glenda Jackson, Jeff Goldblum, Tom Conti, Julie Hagerty, Christopher Guest, Genevieve Page. A parody of psychology, the 1982 play debuted on Broadway and ran for 21 performances at the Brooks Atkinson Theatre with John Madden directing a cast led by John Lithgow and Dianne Wiest. The plot concerns a woman and a bisexual man who meet through personal ads, and the advice they're being given by their respective shrinks—his an absent-minded comforter, hers a Freudian letch. This may be the preeminent example of Robert Altman's abilities to secure money and draw casts to film eclectic stage pieces.

- *"Robert Altman doesn't make movies like anybody else, so I suppose it makes sense that his stinkers are as one-of-a-kind as his great films.* Beyond Therapy…*isn't like other bad movies. But make no mistake, it's a nose-pincher…you can't even take the movie's lack of seriousness seriously."* (*Peter Rainer,* Los Angeles Herald-Examiner)

Sister Mary Explains It All (2001, Showtime, 77m/c) **Sc:** Christopher Durang. **D:** Marshall Brickman. **P:** Ron Bozman. **Cast:** Diane Keaton, Laura San Giacomo, Brian Benben, Jennifer Tilly, Victoria Tenant, Jon Davey, Martin Mull, Jordan Allison, Edie Inksetter, Wallace Langham, Max Morrow, Hunter Scott, Colleen Williams.

Margaret Edson

Born: 1954, Washington, DC.
Pulitzer Prize-winning play: *Wit* (1999

Margaret Edson was a 37-year-old kindergarten teacher in Atlanta, Georgia, when she learned that she had won the 1999 Pulitzer Prize for her only produced play, *Wit*. Written in 1991, the stark, straightforward, and moving portrait of an ovarian cancer patient was based on Edson's experience as a volunteer social worker and hospital clerk in her native Washington. The play was originally mounted in Connecticut in 1997, then moved to an off-off Broadway company, and finally made it to the Off Broadway Union Square Theatre in December 1998.

Wit (2001, HBO, 98m/c, **VHS/DVD**) ☆☆☆☆☆ **Tp:** Emma Thompson, Mike Nichols. **D:** Mike Nichols. **P:** Simon Bosanquet. **Cast:** Emma Thompson, Christopher Lloyd, Aileen Atkins, Audra McDonald, Harold Pinter, Jonathan M. Woodward, Rebecca Laurie, Su Lin Looie, Miguel Brown, Harry Dillon, Benedict Wong, Alex Gregor. The play debuted in 1995 at the South Coast Repertory in Costa Mesa, California, starring Kathleen Chalfant as cancer victim Vivian Bearing. Judith Light succeeded her in the role. This superb TV production, with Thompson delivering one of her greatest performances, won Emmys for Best Movie or Miniseries, Director and Camera Editing, and was nominated for the Adaptation, Best Actress (Thompson), Supporting Actress (McDonald), and Casting.

- *"...drama at its mightiest.* Wit *fractures the funny bone first, then the heart, locating just the right emotional pitch when somehow finding comedy as well as poignancy in dying. It triumphs on every level, from Emma Thompson's commanding, shaven-head performance...to the adaptation she wrote with director Mike Nichols to his staging that draws viewers into the sterile, enclosing whiteness of the hospital where this brilliant scholar's redemption takes place as her plume of life steadily shrinks...The story's intimacy and interior quality, too, are ideal for television, as Bearing returns to earlier flashbacks, and makes the audience her only confidant with dark, often wickedly wry asides to the camera...This is bravura television. The full dose."* (John J. O'Connor, The New York Times)

Sherman Edwards & Peter Stone

Edwards:
Born: April 3, 1919, New York, NY. **Died:** 1981.

Stone:
Born: February 27, 1930, Los Angeles, CA.

A TV writer who wrote shows for *The Defenders* and *Espionage* series, Peter Stone made the leap to features with a pair of Cary Grant vehicles, *Charade* (1963) and *Father Goose* (1964), then a pair of Gregory Peck thrillers, *Mirage* (1965) and *Arabesque* (1966), using the nom de screen of Pierre Marton. His other screenplays include those for *Sweet Charity* (1968), *Skin Game* (1971), *The Taking of Pelham One Two Three*

(1974), *Silver Bears* (1977), *Who Is Killing the Great Chefs of Europe?* (1978), and *Just Cause* (1995). Stone's TV work included a special 1967 presentation of *Androcles and the Lion*, the 1973 series *Adam's Rib*, and the 1984 movie *Woman of the Year* with Barbara Eden.

Sherman Edwards wrote songs for the Elvis Presley vehicle *Flaming Star* (1960) and worked uncredited on the star's *Kid Galahad* (1962).

1776 (1972, Columbia, 142m/c, **VHS/DVD**) ☆☆ **Sc:** Peter Stone. **D:** Peter H. Hunt. **P:** Jack L. Warner. **Cam:** Harry Stradling, Jr. **Cast:** William Daniels, Howard Da Silva, Ken Howard, Donald Madden, Blythe Danner, John Cullum, Roy Poole, David Ford, Ray Middleton, Howard Caine, Ron Holgate, William Hansen, Virginia Vestoff, Emory Bass, William Duell, Daniel Keyes. The Second Continental Congress gathers to sign the Declaration of Independence. The play ran for 1,217 performances on Broadway with largely the same cast for this film. The tunes include "But, Mr. Adams," "The Lees of Old Virginia," and "Piddle, Twiddle and Resolve."

• *"It's shameless: first it exploits them as clodhopping fools, and then it turns pious and reverential, asking us to see that their compromise on the issue of slavery may look like a sellout but was the only way to win the unity needed to break away from England—that what they did we would have done, too. Yocks and uplift—that's the formula. We get toilet jokes, frisky anachronisms, double entendres and the signing of the Declaration of Independence; the insulting, dumb, crusty jocularity may have you shrinking in your seat...The actors are like kids dressed up...director Peter H. Hunt's idea of camera movement is to follow them all as they scamper about. His camera is as busy as a nervous puppy chasing its master."* (Pauline Kael, 5,001 Nights at the Movies)

Lonne Elder III
Born: December 26, 1927, Americus, GA. **Died:** 1996.

Lonne Elder III wrote the screenplays for director Martin Ritt's watershed films about African American sharecroppers in the Depression Era South, *Sounder* (1972), and *Sounder, Part 2* (1976), as well as for the violent blaxploitation programmer *Melinda* (1972) with Calvin Lockhart. He also wrote scipts for such series as *Camera Three* in 1956 and *McCloud* in 1971, and for the TV movies *A Woman Called Moses* (1978), an adaptation of Marcy Heldish's novel about Harriet Tubman's exploits founding the "underground railway" to help slaves escape to freedom in the antebellum South, and *Thou Shalt Not Kill* (1982) with Lee Grant as a lawyer defending an innocent of murder. Elder also originated the role of Bobo in the 1959 debut of Lorraine Hansberry's *A Raisin in the Sun*, starring Sidney Poitier at the Ethel Barrymore Theatre.

Ceremonies in Dark Old Men (1975, ABC, 120m/c) *ABC Theatre* ☆☆☆½ **Tp:** Lonne Elder III. **D:** Michael S. Schultz, Kirk Browning. **P:** Jacqueline Babbin. **Cast:** Douglas Turner Ward, Glynn Turman, Godfrey Cambridge, Robert Hooks, Rosalind Cash, J. Eric Bell, Michele Shay. Members of the Negro Ensemble Company performed this family drama of 1958 Harlem, in which the patriarch, an unsuccessful barber, regales the youngsters of his days as a vaudeville dancer. The fine cast pumps some heart into this rare all-black 1970s prime-time network show. Elder's play debuted in 1969 with the NEC performance at New York's St. Mark's Playhouse and starred Douglas Turner Ward and Rosalind Cash.

- *"...has several moving moments and at least two excellent performances. As a whole, however, this video version seems even more of a dramatic muddle than it did onstage — part Saroyan, part O'Neill (with the weak-nessness of both), a touch of Hansberry and a flash of old-fashioned melo-drama...The best things...are the performances of Glynn Turman and Douglas Turner Ward. Ward has some rough edges that might stick out in slicker pieces, but here they make his performance as the father extremely convincing."* (Dick Adler, Los Angeles Times)

Phoebe & Henry Ephron

Phoebe:
Born: January 26, 1914, New York, NY. **Died:** 1971.

Henry:
Born: May 26, 1911, The Bronx, NY. **Died:** 1992.

Phoebe and Henry Ephron's plays include *My Daughter, Your Son* (1969). Phoebe also wrote the play *Howie* (1958). Among the films for which they received joint screen credit are *Look for the Silver Lining* (1949), *Jackpot* (1950), *What Price Glory?* (1952), *There's No Business Like Show Business* (1954), *Daddy Long Legs* (1955), *Desk Set* (1957), and *Captain Newman, M.D.* (1963). The pair were the parents of writers Amy, Delia, and Nora Ephron. Nora Ephron's films as a director include *Sleepless in Seattle* (1993) and *You've Got Mail* (1998).

Take Her, She's Mine (1963, 20th Century-Fox, 98m/c) ☆☆ **Sc:** Nunnally Johnson. **D/P:** Henry Koster. **Cam:** Lucien Ballard. **Cast:** James Stewart, Sandra Dee, Audrey Meadows, Robert Morley, Robert (Bob) Denver, John McGiver, Philippe Forquet, Cynthia Pepper, Maurice

Marsac, Jenny Maxwell, Irene Tsu, Monica Moran, Marcel Hilaire, Eddie Quillan, Charla Doherty, Francesca Bellini. Directed by George Abbott and produced by Harold Prince, this comedy ran for 404 performances in 1961–62 and starred Art Carney as the father. The Ephrons' play follows a lawyer's odyssey in tracking his college freshman daughter's liberal escapades at sit-ins, protests, and coffeehouses.

- "...drawn with broad, heavy strokes as to make it grossly and dismayingly exaggerated. The people here aren't real; they're caricatures of what they once were [in the play], and what they should be." (Leo Mishkin, New York Morning Telegraph)

- "Let's all be thankful that society is generally, if not entirely, free of such farcical types as the doting father played by James Stewart...And let's hope the screen will not be burdened for too much longer with such drivel as this old-hat Hollywood picture." (Bosley Crowther, The New York Times)

Three Is a Family (1944, RKO/UA, 81m/bw) ☆☆ Sc: Harry Chandlee, Marjorie Pfaelzer. D: Edward Ludwig. P: Sol Lesser. Cam: Charles Lawton, Jr. Cast: Marjorie Reynolds, Charles Ruggles, Fay Bainter, Arthur Lake, Helen Broderick, Hattie McDaniel, Jeff Donnell, John Philliber, Walter Catlett, Clarence Kolb, Warren Hymer, Elsa Janssen, Christian Rub, William Terry, Cheryl Walker. During World War II, with husbands off in the service, young mothers and expectant future mothers during the housing shortage in New York converge on the household of an elderly couple with an imbibing maid. The film was nominated for an Oscar for its sound. The 1944 play, which was entitled *Three's a Family*, ran for 497 performances under the direction of Henry Ephron, and starred Ethel Owen, Edwin Philips, and William Wadsworth.

- "...not only have this film's authors crowded 10 or 12 frantic occupants into a four-room New York apartment originally inhabited by three, but they also have packed in around them a lot of inferior jokes...the new tenants have either had—or are going to have—babies, and that accounts for the endless flow of perturbation and alarm. Charlie Ruggles, Fay Bainter and Helen Broderick are as droll as a weak script will allow..." (Bosley Crowther, The New York Times)

Jules Feiffer
Jules Ralph Feiffer
Born: January 26, 1929, New York, NY.

Better known as an editorial cartoonist who won the Pulitzer Prize for that specialty in 1986, Jules Feiffer wrote the 1971 screenplays for Carnal Knowledge—an unproduced play that was directed for the screen by Mike Nichols and became a cinema touchstone of the battle of the sexes —and Little Murders, which was first produced on Broadway in 1967. His cartoon collections include Feiffer on Nixon: The Cartoon Presidency (1974) and Marriage Is an Invasion of Privacy and Other Dangerous Views (1984). His plays often deal with New Yorkers' musings on the violence of urban life. They include Crawling Arnold (1961), The White House Murder Case (1970), and Anthony Rose (1990).

Grown Ups (1985, PBS, 120m/bw) Broadway on Showtime **Tp:** Jules Feiffer. **D:** John Madden. **P:** Patrick Whitley. **Cast:** Martin Balsam, Charles Grodin, Jean Stapleton, Marilu Henner, Paddy Campanaro, Kerry Segal. First produced at the Loeb Drama Center in Cambridge, MA in 1981, the play debuted on Broadway, directed by Madden, the same year at the Lyceum Theatre. A miserable middle-aged political writer for The New York Times deals with the problems of his aging parents, wife, and daughter in Queens, New York.

• "Mr. Feiffer's humor is far darker and more unsettling than, say, Neil Simon's...The performances are never less than adept at treading the thin Feiffer line between hilarious caricature and truly uncomfortable reality. Mr. Feiffer, whose satirical cartoon strips have blossomed into new life with the administration and policies of President Reagan, has been served well in this adaptation." (John J. O'Connor, The New York Times)

Little Murders (1971, 20th Century-Fox, 108m/c, **VHS**) **Sc:** Jules Feiffer. **D:** Alan Arkin. **P:** Jack Bodsky. **Cast:** Elliott Gould, Marcia Rodd, Elizabeth Wilson, Vincent Gardenia, Alan Arkin, Donald Sutherland, Lou Jacobi, Jon Korkes. This satiric look at the violence and apathy inherent in life in New York City opened on Broadway in 1967 and ran for five performances with Gould. A British production was well received, so Arkin revived the play Off Broadway in 1969 and the principals turned out this film two years later.

• "Perhaps the most terrifying aspect of Little Murders is that today it seems neither grotesque nor absurd but rather an only mildly distorted mirror of our times. To be sure, the film is black enough, but the comedy is no longer funny because we happen to be living with its tag lines...On the stage, the perils of New York crept in through the interstices of barricaded windows and cautiously opened doors. In the film, they are omnipresent...Lights fail...conversation goes on as if nothing happened... buildings burn and corpses are carried out on stretchers. There are muggings, bombings, riots...all part of daily routine. The cast, recruited in the main from Arkin's Off Broadway production, is almost beyond reproach, and the film is relevant, risible—and profoundly disturbing." (Arthur Knight, Saturday Review)

David Feldshuh

Born: 1944.

Dr. David Feldshuh has been artistic director at the Center for Theatre Arts at Cornell University since 1984. His play *Miss Evers' Boys* has been produced throughout the U.S., received the New American Play award and was nominated for the Pulitzer Prize. He co-produced the video *Susceptible to Kindness*, for which he interviewed observers as well as survivors of the Tuskegee syphilis study, the basis for *Miss Evers' Boys*. Feldshuh's television script *Harmony* was written for an educational television project dedicated to teaching science to children and sponsored in part by the National Science Foundation.

Miss Evers' Boys (1997, HBO, 118m/c, **VHS/DVD**) **Tp:** Walter Bernstein. **D:** Joseph Sargent. **P:** Derek Kavanagh. **Cast:** Alfre Woodard, Laurence Fishburne, Craig Sheffer, Joe Morton, E.G. Marshall, Ossie Davis, Obba Babatunde, Von Coulter, Thom Gossom, Jr., Robert Benedetti, Peter Stelzer, Joan Glover, Kiki Shepard. In 1932 in Macon County, Alabama, the federal government infected 412 black men with syphilis to diagnose whether there were any differences between whites and blacks infected with the disease. Despite the existence of an antidote, the men were never treated. The story is told from the viewpoint of the nurse caring for the survivors. After ten years in regional theatres, the play made its New York debut in 2002 through the Melting Pot Theatre Company at the McGinn-Cazale Theatre. This production won Emmy Awards for Best Movie, Actress (Woodard), Cinematography, and Editing, and was nominated for Best Actor (Fishburne), Supporting Actor (Davis, Babatunde), Teleplay, Casting, Choreography, and Make-up. Sargent won the Directors Guild of America Award for Best TV Directing.

Edna Ferber

Born: August 15, 1887, Kalamazoo, MI. **Died:** 1968.

Most of Edna Ferber's popular novels were turned into films, and most of her plays in collaboration with George S. Kaufman became benchmarks in American theatre. She was a staff reporter on the *Milwaukee Journal*, followed by a stint with the *Chicago Tribune*. Her first novel, *Dawn O'Hara*, was about a female reporter. She wrote four volumes of stories from 1911 to 1914, most of them featuring Emma McChesney. She moved to New York and dramatized Mrs. McChesney's adventures in the play *Our Mrs. McChesney* with George V. Hobart. In 1924, *So Big*, about a farm wife who makes a success of her land after the death of her husband, became a critical and popular success.

Her novels that followed often illuminated specific pockets of American history and industry. Among her works that were transformed into epic movies were *Show Boat* (three times), *Cimarron* (twice), Howard Hawks's and William Wyler's *Come and Get It* (1936), *Saratoga Trunk* (1945), George Stevens's *Giant* (1956), and *Ice Palace* (1960) with Richard Burton and Robert Ryan. Her plays with Kaufman were *Minick, The Royal Family, Dinner at Eight, Stage Door, The Land Is Bright*, and *Bravo!* Ferber only wrote one play on her own, *The Eldest: A Drama of American Life*. For TV, she dramatized three of her short stories—"The Pen," "You're Not the Type," and "The Weak Spot"—for a 1951 installment of *Pulitzer Prize Playhouse*.

Dinner at Eight was a 1932 Broadway hit by Ferber and George S. Kaufman. In it, the Jordans throw a dinner party for several well-heeled members of New York society who all face personal crises during the Great Depression. The ensemble featured Constance Collier, Marguerite Churchill, and Cesar Romero.

Dinner at Eight (1933, MGM, 113m/bw, **VHS**) ☆☆☆☆ **Sc:** Frances Marion, Herman J. Mankiewicz, Donald Ogden Stewart. **D:** George Cukor. **P:** David O. Selznick. **Cam:** William H. Daniels. **Cast:** John Barrymore, Wallace Beery, Marie Dressler, Jean Harlow, Lionel Barrymore, Billie Burke, Lee Tracy, Madge Evans, Jean Hersholt, Edmund Lowe, May Robson, Karen Morley, Phoebe Foster, Grant Mitchell, Elizabeth Patterson, Phillips Holmes, Harry Beresford, Hilda Vaughn. The trio of notable screenwriters removed much of the acid inherent in Ferber and Kaufman's original to make the show more palatable to moviegoers.

- *"It lives up to every occasion…It is one of those rare pictures which keeps you in your seat until the final fade-out, for nobody wants to miss one of the scintillating lines."* (The New York Times)

- *"It seems to me that Miss Harlow, an increasingly delightful actress with each picture, plays…with such high spirits, comic gaiety and shrewd knowledge—or perhaps instinct—that…she is quite the hit of the evening."* (Richard Wattis, New York Herald-Tribune)

Dinner at Eight (1948, NBC, 60m/bw) *Philco Television Playhouse* ☆☆☆ **D/P:** Fred Coe. **Cast:** Peggy Wood, Dennis King, Mary Boland, Vikki Cummings, Matt Briggs, Royal Beal, Joyce Van Patten, Judson Laire, Philip Loeb, Jane Seymour. This was the very first installment of the time-honored *Philco*, airing on October 3, 1948. This show had an impact on the future of plays on TV. When it aired on WNBT, NBC's New York station was directly linked with three other stations by coaxial cable (Philadelphia, Washington, DC, and Baltimore) and three by microwave relay (Boston, Schenectady and Richmond). At the time, NBC's other eight stations could only air shows by means of kinescopes.

- *"Film studios owning the rights to plays such as* Dinner at Eight *and Rebecca blocked NBC from airing kinescopes of them, successfully arguing in court that kines were not delayed broadcasts as the network claimed, but films to which studios owned the rights. Movie-studio intransigence would spur the growth of the new medium, however, by forcing it to develop its own writing talent. Given the unavailability of studio-owned plays, Coe would nurture writers like Paddy Chayefsky, Horton Foote, and Tad Mosel. This made the film company lawyers, in author Max Wilk's memorable phrase, 'so many grains of sand, responsible for a multitude of future pearls on Coe's seedbed.'"* (Jon Krampner, The Man in the Shadows: Fred Coe and the Golden Age of Television)

Dinner at Eight (1955, CBS, 60m/c) *Front Row Center* ☆☆ **Sc:** Whitfield Cook. **D/P:** Fletcher Markle. **Cast:** Pat O'Brien, Mary Beth Hughes, Mary Astor, Everett Sloane, Marion Ross, Tristram Coffin, John Emery, Eleanore Audley. Advertised as "a color spread special," this first installment of Markle's series of live shows was produced in Hollywood in the years before almost all live TV drama was staged in New York.

- *"…debuted inauspiciously…suffering chiefly from a dated aura and some inferior direction by Fletcher Markle…Whitfield Cook's tele adaptation had a tendency to fix characters into a cliché mold…there wasn't enough sustenance in* Dinner *on TV. Pat O'Brien was badly directed as the loudmouth, shouting so continuously that when a crisis actually arose his shattering voice had lost all its effect."* (Variety)

Dinner at Eight (1989, TNT, 100m/c, **VHS**) ☆☆☆½ **Tp:** Tom Griffin. **D:** Ron Lagomarsino. **P:** Bridget Terry. **Cast:** Lauren Bacall, Charles Durning, Ellen Greene, Marsha Mason, John Mahoney, Harry Hamlin, Tim Kazurinsky, Stacy Edwards. Griffin used the best of the original play and also drew on the 1933 screenplay by Marion, Mankiewicz, and Stewart while he updated the story to contemporary times. Hamlin, for instance, plays a TV series star wired on cocaine.

- *"Lauren Bacall sets the tone for the occasion with her elegance and sophistication…Ron Lagomarsino's direction is more theatrical than cinematic, and that suits the material and the medium just fine. Durning and especially Greene play broadly, but that's just part of the fun. Mahony emerges as a figure of dignity and sympathy, and Mason gets to show us that the wife has some substance after all. This* Dinner at Eight *is a very stylish affair…"* (Kevin Thomas, Los Angeles Times)

Minick was originally produced by Winthrop Ames in 1924 at New York's Booth Theatre and starred Antoinette Perry, Phyllis Povah, Beatrice Moreland, O.P. Heggie, and Sydney Booth. It concerned a family man who takes his father out of a veterans home and into his own, annoying his wife. Ferber and Kaufman based it on Ferber's short story, "Old Man Minick."

Welcome Home (1925, Paramount, bw/silent) ☆☆ **Sc:** F. McGrew Willis, Walter Woods. **D/P:** James Cruze. **Cam:** Karl Brown. **Cast:** Warner Baxter, Lois Wilson, Luke Cosgrave, Ben Hendricks Sr., Margaret Morris, Josephine Crowell, Adele Watson.

- *"In New York [on the stage]...Minick owed the greater part of its success to the...performance of O.P. Heggie...in the film it has no such exponent...It's well made and all that, but the story just isn't there for movies and the casting hasn't helped any."* (Variety)

The Expert (1932, Warner Bros., 62m/bw) ☆½ **Sc:** Julian Josephson, Maude Howell. **D:** Archie Mayo. **Cam:** Bob Kurrie. **Cast:** Charles "Chic" Sale, Dickie Moore, Lois Wilson, Earle Foxe, Ralf Harolde, Adrienne Dore, Walter Catlett, Noel Francis, Louise Beavers, Clara Blandick, Zita Moulton, Dorothy Wolbert.

- *"Sale is talented, but he can't hold his ground against a script this hapless."* (J.R. Nash, S.R. Ross, The Motion Picture Guide)

No Place to Go (1939, Warner Bros., 57m/bw) ☆☆☆ **Sc:** Lee Katz, Lawrence Kimble, Fred Niblo, Jr. **D:** Terry Morse. **P:** Bryan Foy. **Cam:** Arthur Edeson. **Cast:** Dennis Morgan, Gloria Dickson, Fred Stone, Sonny Bupp, Aldrich Bowker, Charles Halton, Georgia Caine, Frank Faylan, Dennie Moore, Alan Bridge, Joe Devlin, Bernice Pilot, Greta Meyer, Wright Kramer, Christian Rub. In one of his better recycling jobs, Bryan "Brynie" Foy, the head of Warners's B-movie line, who once boasted that he remade *Tiger Shark* seven times, turned out a winsome comedy.

- *"...adaptation of a minor play by the great writers Kaufman and Ferber. Stone is marvelously funny with good support from Morgan and from Dickson as Morgan's social climbing wife. Bupp is an absolute delight as the young bootblack befriended by the old soldier."* (J.R. Nash, S.R. Ross, The Motion Picture Guide)

Minick was also staged in 1948 on *Kraft Television Theatre*.

Our Mrs. McChesney (1918, Metro, 5reels/bw/silent) ☆☆☆½ **Sc:** Luther Reed. **D:** Ralph Ince. **P:** Maxwell Karger. **Cam:** William J. Black. **Cast:** Ethel Barrymore, Huntley Gordon, Wilfrid Lytell, Lucille Lee Stewart, John Daly Murphy, Walter Percival, William H. St. James, Ricca Allen, Fred Walters, George S. Trimball, Sammy Cooper. Ferber's "Emma McChesney" stories were published in three volumes that became the basis for a 1915 play by Ferber and George V. Hobart. The title character is a department store buyer who invents a new dress style, which, before becoming a fashion sensation and turning her daughter-in-law into a successful newfound model, hurdles several family problems.

- *"Barrymore brings her stage success to the screen with equally satisfying results...The movie's big punch comes when the model who is set to show Barrymore's design collapses, and her daughter-in-law takes over."* (Nash, S.R. Ross, The Motion Picture Guide)

The Royal Family, first produced on Broadway in 1927 by Jed Harris, was a hit and remains one of the great lampoons of theatrical life. It satirizes the larger-than-life theatrical legends of John, Lionel, and Ethel Barrymore and the whole Barrymore/Drew clan. The play starred Otto Kruger as Tony Cavendish, Ann Andrews, Roger Pryor, and Sylvia Field.

The Royal Family of Broadway (1930, Paramount, 82m/bw) ☆☆☆☆
Sc: Herman J. Mankiewicz, Gertrude Purcell. **D:** George Cukor, Cyril Gardner. **Cam:** George Folsey. **Cast:** Fredric March, Henrietta Crosman, Ina Claire, Mary Brian, Charles Starrett, Frank Conroy, Arnold Korff, Royal G. Stout, Murray Alper, Elsie Edmonds, Wesley Stark. March's portrayal of the egotistical Tony Cavendish, the facsimile of John Barrymore, is the highlight of this stagebound but worthwhile comedy, which was Cukor's third film.

- *"[Mr. March] gives a performance that is positively brilliant. [His] impersonation is, it seems to me, one of utter perfection, sensitively drawn, true to life, immensely amusing...the projection of a personality at once preposterous and glamorous, lunatic and tremendously vital."* (Quinn Martin, New York World)

- *"Fredric March gives the performance of the year as the mad matinee idol, Tony, in this hilariously amusing movie about the private life of stage aristocrats. He completely dominates the picture and five minutes of his comedy are worth the whole price of admission...Witty dialogue, brisk action, eloquent direction give the comedy a brilliant polish."* (Bland Johaneson, New York Daily Mirror)

The Royal Family (1954, CBS, 60m/bw) *The Best of Broadway* ☆☆☆☆
Tp: Ronald Alexander. **D:** Paul Nickell. **P:** Martin Manulis. **Cast:** Fredric March, Claudette Colbert, Helen Hayes, Charles Coburn, Nancy Olson, Kent Smith. March repeated his role on the small screen in one of early TV's prestige presentations.

- *"That the years haven't rusted its comedy joints was amply evident with the raucous display of rowdy humor given new life by a cast of stage and screen notables...Withal it was a pleasant visitor to grown-up television...It's an easy play for hamming but with these sterling performers it passed as artistry because of their polished techniques...Miss Hayes was her superb self...March's swagger and bluster set the play's swift tempo...He played it like a Barrymore possessed."* (Jack Gould, The New York Times)

The Royal Family (1977, PBS, 120m/c) *Great Performances* ☆☆☆ **Tp:**

Edna Ferber, George S. Kaufman. **D:** Ellis Rabb, Kirk Browning. **P:** Ken Campbell. **Cast:** Eva LeGallienne, Rosemary Harris, Ellis Rabb, Mary Layne, Sam Levene, Keene Curtis. Rabb's revival of the play on Broadway in 1976 directly led to this TV production. LeGallienne's portrayal of the Barrymoore matriarch became an occasion for highlighting her long and illustrious stage career.

- *"But aside from the occasional sticky moments and a belaboring of the obvious, it's a lively two hours on the little screen, largely because of Rabb's inspired hamming and LeGallienne's glorious tribute to the theatre as Fanny, though the sentiments, I imagine, come as much out of LeGallienne's 63 years on the stage as from the script."* (Cecil Smith, Los Angeles Times)

The Royal Family was also presented on *The Pulitzer Prize Playhouse* in 1951 with Florence Reed.

Stage Door concerns a boarding house full of aspiring Broadway actresses with all of their tribulations and romances. The 1936 play by Ferber and Kaufman starred Margaret Sullavan.

Stage Door (1937, RKO, 93m/bw, **VHS**) ☆☆☆☆½ **Sc:** Morrie Ryskind, Anthony Veiller. **D:** Gregory La Cava. **P:** Pandro S. Berman. **Cam:** Robert de Grasse. **Cast:** Katharine Hepburn, Ginger Rogers, Adolphe Menjou, Constance Collier, Gail Patrick, Lucille Ball, Jack Carson, Samuel S. Hinds, Franklin Pangborn, Andrea Leeds, William Corson, Pierre Watkin, Grady Sutton, Eve Arden, Ann Miller, Peggy O'Donnell. The playwrights' story was transformed by the screenwriters, La Cava, and a terrific cast into this classic film, which has been deemed much better than the original, even though MacArthur was supposed to have famously remarked, "Why didn't they call it *Screen Door?*" The performances were uniformly excellent, especially Hepburn, Rogers, and Leeds. The film received Oscar nominations for Best Picture, Director, Screenplay, and Supporting Actress (Leeds), and La Cava won the Best Director honor from the New York Film Critics Circle.

- *"What with Katharine Hepburn, Ginger Rogers, Andrea Leeds, Constance Collier, Gail Patrick, Lucille Ball and all the others, it is a long time since we have seen so much feminine talent so deftly handled. When you think of Miss Rogers's former song-and-dance appearances, it seems as though this is the first chance she has had to be something more than a camera object and stand forth in her own right, pert and charming and just plain nice, her personality flexible in the actor's expression."* (Otis Ferguson, The New Republic)

Stage Door (1955, CBS, 60m/bw) *The Best of Broadway* ☆☆☆ **Tp:** Gore Vidal. **D:** Sidney Lumet. **P:** Felix Jackson. **Cast:** Diana Lynn, Peggy Ann Garner, Rhonda Fleming, Nita Talbot, Dennis Morgan, Charles

Drake, Elsa Lanchester, Victor Moore, Virginia Vincent, Jack Weston. Vidal and Lumet cranked up the pace for this hourlong version.

- *"...a rapidly paced, sometimes ragged but generally entertaining production...Mr. Vidal crammed a lot of script into the one-hour show...He permitted a minimum of loitering...The girls rushed up and down the staircase, the bell rang continually and men visitors made frequent entrances and departures. The activity was suggestive of the dizzy pace provided by George Abbott in a long line of productions he has staged on Broadway. Sometimes this quick tempo was distracting...Miss Lynn did not break the spell. She was convincing and admirable...To keep* Stage Door *from creaking, Mr. Vidal injected references to television shows, Mike Todd's discovery of* War and Peace *and other present-day manifestations of culture."* (J.P. Shanley, The New York Times)

- *"Something more than the intervening years has dulled the edge that once excited playgoers in this serio-comic tale...As one of the* Best of Broadway, *it didn't act that way."* (Variety)

Stage Door was also produced in 1948 as an NBC special directed by Edward Sobol with a cast including Louisa Horton, Harvey Stephens, Mary Anderson, John Forsythe, Enid Markey, and Mary Alice Moore.

Dorothy & Herbert Fields

Dorothy:
Born: July 15, 1905, Allenhurst, NJ. **Died:** 1974.
Herbert:
Born: July 26, 1897, New York, NY. **Died:** 1958.

Dorothy Fields wrote 400 songs, including the tunes she composed for 25 movies. Her most famous songs are "On the Sunny Side of the Street," "I'm in the Mood for Love," "The Way You Look Tonight," and "I Can't Give You Anything But Love." She collaborated with both of her brothers onstage musicals, most notably with Herbert on *Annie Get Your Gun*, and most of those were converted to films (see below). She also was the librettist with Neil Simon on *Sweet Charity* and with Cy Coleman on *Seesaw*, a musical derived from William Gibson's *Two for the Seesaw*. Dorothy also scored such stage musicals as *Hello, Daddy*; *Rhapsody in Black*; *Singin' the Blues*; and *Redhead*, for which she won Tony and Grammy awards. Her film scores include those for *The Farmer Takes a Wife*, *I Dream Too Much*, and *Mr. Imperium*.

Aside from the titles listed below, Herbert Fields also collaborated with Dorothy on the stage titles *Arms and the Girl*, *By the Beautiful Sea*, and *Redhead*. The Fields siblings' father was the legendary Lew Fields, born Lewis Maurice Shanfield, a theatrical impresario who made a name for himself in the 1890s as one half of Weber and Fields, who contributed "Dat vas no lady; dat vas my wife" to the enduring American joke lexicon.

See also **Joseph Fields**.

Annie Get Your Gun was first produced on Broadway in 1946 with Ethel Merman, supported by Ray Middleton and William O'Neal as Buffalo Bill, and ran for 1,147 performances. It's the story of Annie Oakley's adventures with Buffalo Bill's Wild West Show, where she joins Frank Butler in his sharpshooting act, then his love life.

Annie Get Your Gun (1950, MGM, 107m/c, **VHS/DVD**) ☆☆☆☆ **Sc:** Sidney Sheldon. **D:** George Sidney. **P:** Arthur Freed. **Cam:** Charles Rosher. **Cast:** Betty Hutton, Howard Keel, Louis Calhern, J. Carroll Naish, Edward Arnold, Keenan Wynn, Clinton Sundberg, James H. Harrison, Benoy Venuta, William Tannen, Bradley Mora, Diana Dick, Chief Yowlachie, Elizabeth Flournoy, Marjorie Wood. This may be Hutton's most vigorous and athletic performance in a big, gaudy, colorful production with an equally game performance by Keel and a lot of heaving and hollering. The songs include "Anything You Can Do," "Doing What Comes Naturally," "Colonel Buffalo Bill," and "There's No Business Like Show Business." This is a notable film for its many replacements—Hutton for Judy Garland, who fell ill; Calhern for Frank Morgan, who died; and Sidney for Charles Walters, who had taken over from Busby Berkeley.

• *"Though sometimes overlooked in critical surveys of the great MGM musicals, it was the biggest money-maker of them all in its time. And no mere photographed stage show: Freed's production opened out the Dorothy and Herbert Fields 'book' of the Broadway record-breaker, giving added scope to Irving Berlin's 11 songs...Sidney directed Miss Hutton to her best performance as Annie, and Howard Keel to instant movie stardom. The whole cast...performed throughout as if inspired by their finale, 'There's No Business Like Show Business.'"* (John Douglas Eames, The MGM Story)

Annie Get Your Gun (1957, NBC Special, 120m/c) ☆☆½ **Tp:** Herbert Fields. **D:** Vincent J. Donehue. **P:** Richard Halliday. **Cast:** Mary Martin, John Raitt, William O'Neal, Rita Shaw, Donald Burr, Norman Edwards, Susan Luckey, Zachary Charles, Robert Nash, Stuart Hodes, Jan Skidmore, Patricia Morrow, Shelley Windsor, Luke Halpin. Martin gave it her all in this lavish and well-received TV version.

• *"The production lacked for nothing in sumptuous mounting, but the electric spirit of the infectious and gay theatre was disappointingly missing...The book by Herbert and Dorothy Fields never was quite a masterpiece...long and wearing stretches...To disguise this structural weakness it takes a robust Annie to breathe hilarity into the musical. In the romantic moments...Miss Martin was a delicate vision. These interludes made for happy viewing. But it is to be feared that Miss Martin did not project the quality of brassy insouciance that Annie must have. Instead of being a boisterous hick from the sticks she was more the genteel elf." (Jack Gould,* The New York Times)

Annie Get Your Gun (1967, NBC Special, 120m/c) ☆☆☆ **Tp:** Herbert Fields. **D:** Clark Jones, Jack Sydow. **P:** Clark Jones. **Cast:** Ethel Merman, Bruce Yarnell, Rufus Smith, Jerry Orbach, Beany Venuta, Harry Bellaver, Wayne Hunter, Jack Dabdoub, Tony Catanzaro. This was a taped version of the Lincoln Center's 1966 revival rendition, which reunited Merman, the original stage Annie, with one of her signature stage parts.

• *"Ethel Merman rendered the Irving Berlin score with a buoyancy and verve that made it hard to believe she first appeared in the show more than 20 years ago. It could have been wished, however, that she had been allowed to play to a live audience...Miss Merman and the spectator need a feeling of electric rapport...special was distinctly cold and distant...The staging was obviously a compromise between the requirements of television and the theatre and was not quite one or the other, which did not help to draw the attention from a book that is by now understandably dated." (Jack Gould,* The New York Times)

A Connecticut Yankee in King Arthur's Court is Mark Twain's story of Martin Barret, who, after suffering a head injury, is propelled to the sixth century and impresses the primitive English with certain bits of modern knowledge. It played Broadway as a Richard Rodgers/Lorenz Hart musical in both 1927 and 1943. The film versions—in 1920 with Harry Myers, 1931 with Will Rogers, and 1949 with Bing Crosby—used other adapters, as did other TV versions.

A Connecticut Yankee in King Arthur's Court (1955, NBC Special, 90m/c) **Tp:** William Friedberg, Neil Simon, Will Glickman, Al Schwartz. **D:** Max Liebman, Bill Hobin. **P:** Max Liebman. **Cast:** Eddie Albert, Janet Blair, Leonard Elliott, Boris Karloff, Gale Sherwood, John Conte.

Du Barry Was a Lady (1943, MGM, 112m/c, **VHS**) ☆☆☆½ **Sc:** Irving Brecher. **D:** Roy Del Ruth. **P:** Arthur Freed. **Cam:** Karl Freund. **Cast:** Red Skelton, Gene Kelly, Lucille Ball, Virgina O'Brien, Zero Mostel, Rags Ragland, Donald Meek, Douglas Dumbrille, Louise Beavers, George Givot, Tommy Dorsey and His Orchestra. The 1939 play written by Herbert Fields and B.G. De Sylva was supplemented with a Cole Porter score and starred Bert Lahr, Ethel Merman, Betty Grable, Ronald Graham, and Charles Walters. MGM tailored the film version as a Skelton vehicle. It tells the tale of a nightclub's washroom attendant who wins $75,000 in the Irish Sweepstakes. Hoping to lure away the floor-show queen, May, he plans to use knock-out drops in her boyfriend's drink, but accidentally downs the stuff himself. In his stupor, he dreams he's Louis XIV and May is his mistress, Du Barry.

- *"DuBarry...was an out-and-out 'showcase' picture. It was one of many made primarily for the sake of establishing and/or exploiting stars or would-be stars. In this instance, it was 'icing on the cake,' and the cake was Lucille Ball. It was also tailor-made to establish Red Skelton as a great comic. The old formula of stacking a film with nothing but entertainment proved correct: It paid off at the box office ($3,496,000) in spite of an outrageous amount of money spent on it, $1,239,222.56."* (Hugh Fordin, The Movies' Greatest Musicals: Produced in Hollywood USA by the Freed Unit)

Leathernecking (1930, RKO, 80m/bw&c) ☆☆½ **Sc:** Alfred Jackson, Jane Murfin. **D:** Edward Cline. **P:** Louis Sarecky. **Cam:** J. Roy Hunt. **Cast:** Irene Dunne, Ken Murray, Eddie Foy, Jr., Louise Fazenda, Ned Sparks, Lilyan Tashman, Benny Rubin, Rita La Roy, Fred Santley, William von Brinken, Carl Gerrard, Werther Weidler, Wolfgang Weidler. Jackson and Murfin adapted *Present Arms*, the 1928 Broadway musical by Herbert Fields, Richard Rodgers, and Lorenz Hart, into a straightforward comedy when musicals began tanking at the box office. The play starred Charles King and Flora LeBreton with Busby Berkeley and Fuller Mellish, Jr. The fluffy and predictable film concerns a Honolulu socialite who cozies up to a soldier she thinks is a high-ranking U.S. Marine, until she discovers he's just a buck private.

- *"If a Marine's life is anything like...Leathernecking...then it must be one continual round of parties, yachting trips and pillow fights among the boys in the barracks...The film's chief virtue is its failure to take itself seriously, and in so doing frolics along to a slapstick beat..."* (The New York Times)

Let's Face It (1943, Paramount, 76m/bw) ☆☆½ **Sc:** Harry Tugend. **D:** Sidney Landfield. **P:** Fred Kohlmar. **Cam:** Lionel Lindon. **Cast:** Bob Hope, Betty Hutton, ZaSu Pitts, Phyllis Povah, Eve Arden, Dave Willock, Cully Richards, Marjorie Weaver, Dona Drake, Andrew Tombes, Raymond Walburn, Joe Sawyer, Joyce Compton, Barbara Pepper, Emory Parnell, Yvonne De Carlo, Grace Hayle, Brook Evans. The 1941 play by Dorothy and Herbert Fields and Cole Porter starred Danny Kaye and Eve Arden on Broadway, and was adapted from the 1925 play *The Cradle Snatchers* by Norma Mitchell and Russell G. Medcraft, which starred Humphrey Bogart and Mary Boland. The film is a screwball comedy about three wives who, fed up with their cheating husbands, date soldiers. The wives, soldiers, husbands, and their dates all end up in the same nightclub, and things get out of hand. The songs include "Let's Not Talk About Love," "Let's Face It," and "Who Did? I Did."

- *"...an acceptable bit of monkeyshines...As a vehicle for Bob Hope it is a rather feeble and outdated contraption...if it weren't for Mr. Hope himself,* Let's Face It *would be a very sad affair indeed."* (The New York Times)

Melody Man (1930, Columbia, 68m/bw) **Sc:** Howard J. Green. **D:** Roy William Neill. **P:** Harry Cohn. **Cam:** Ted Tetzlaff. **Cast:** John St. Polis, Alice Day, William Collier, Jr., Johnnie Walker, Mildred Harris, Albert Conti, Anton Vaverka, Major Nichols, Tenen Holtz, Lee Kohlmar.

- *"Taken from a thinly plotted play, Columbia has managed to strengthen the continuity and music. That the picture doesn't make the top grade lies mainly in the subject matter...Direction is unadorned..."* (Variety)

Mexican Hayride (1948, Universal, 77m/bw, **VHS**) ☆☆ **Sc:** Oscar Brodney, John Grant. **D:** Charles Barton. **P:** Robert Arthur. **Cam:** Charles Van Enger. **Cast:** Bud Abbott, Lou Costello, Virginia Grey, John Hubbard, Pedro de Cordoba, Fritz Feld, Luba Malina, Tom Powers, Pat Costello, Frank Fenton, Chris Pin Martin. This is the instance of a Cole Porter stage musical being transformed into an Abbott and Costello movie without the music. The play, by Herbert and Dorothy Fields and Porter, concerned a mobster on the lam in Mexico attempting to organize a numbers racket to mark time. Bobby Clark and June Havoc starred in a 1944 Michael Todd production at New York's Winter Garden Theatre. The film was crafted to capitalize on Bud and Lou's popularity and the source material was bowdlerized.

- *"There was only one really funny moment...when Costello walks into a bull ring south of the border and completely subdues the snorting animal's ferocity. For the rest it was a depressingly routine A&C comedy..."* (Clive Hirchhorn, The Universal Story)

Panama Hattie was a Broadway hit of 1940 with Ethel Merman in the title role of a "Canal Zone girl" who reforms and marries Nick Bullett of Philadelphia society and tries to forge a relationship with his eight-year-old daughter. The play by Herbert Fields and B.G. De Sylva, with Cole Porter's music, also featured Pat Harrington, Joan Carroll, Rags Ragland, Betty Hutton, James Dunn, Phyllis Brooks, and Arthur Treacher.

Panama Hattie (1942, MGM, 79m/bw, **VHS**) ☆☆ **Sc:** Jack McGowan, Wilkie Mahoney. **D:** Norman Z. McLeod. **P:** Arthur Freed. **Cam:** George Folsey. **Cast:** Ann Sothern, Dan Dailey, Red Skelton, Marsha Hunt, Rags Ragland, Virginia O'Brien, Alan Mowbray, Ben Blue, Carl Esmond. This draggy musical is enlived when a trio of sailors played by Skelton, Ragland, and Blue are on screen, but it's otherwise a dud. Sothern reportedly hated doing it, and that shows in her performance.

- *"The screenplay of* Hattie *was in essence the book of the Broadway show, transferred to the screen without any cinematic development. Ann Sothern wasn't Ethel Merman; Virginia O'Brien wasn't Betty Hutton. Cole*

Porter's score was mutilated and the added new songs did not fit into the style in which the book was originally conceived. George Murphy was in one day and out another, and the role went to Dan Dailey, Jr. Shirley Temple's contract was bought out and she was replaced by Jackie Horner...The film was just too overladen with dialogue and too light on entertainment." (Hugh Fordin, The Movies' Greatest Musicals: Produced in Hollywood USA by the Freed Unit*)*

Panama Hattie (1954, CBS, 60m/bw) *The Best of Broadway* **Tp:** Ronald Alexander. **D:** David Alexander. **P:** Martin Manulis, Jule Styne. **Cast:** Ethel Merman, Art Carney, Ray Middleton, Jack E. Leonard, Karin Wolfe, Betty O'Neil, Neil Hamilton, Tony Mottola, Osceola Archer, Mort Marshall, John Pelletti, Joseph Macauley. Merman returned to her old hit for this truncated and very sanitized TV rendition, which no longer suggested what a "Canal Zone girl" might do.

Something for the Boys (1944, 20th Century-Fox, 87m/c) ☆☆☆ **Sc:** Robert Ellis, Helen Logan, Frank Gabrielson. **D:** Lewis Seiler. **P:** Irving Starr. **Cam:** Ernest Palmer. **Cast:** Carmen Miranda, Michael O'Shea, Vivian Blaine, Phil Silvers, Sheila Ryan, Perry Como, Judy Holliday, Glenn Langan, Cara Williams, Roger Clark, Thurston Hall, Clarence Kolb, Andrew Tombes, Murray Alper, Eddie Acuff. The 1943 play was another collaboration between Dorothy and Herbert Fields, Cole Porter, and Ethel Merman. Allen Jenkins and Paula Lawrence also starred in the tale of a carnival pitchman and a nightclub entertainer who find that they've inherited a Texas ranch near an Army base. This fluff marked Como's film debut. The spirited cast helps put over another backstage musical-from-scratch story. The songs include "Wouldn't It Be Nice" and "I Wish I Didn't Have to Say Goodnight."

- *"20th Century-Fox's estimation of the current consumer taste in masculine entertainment is rather clearly — and lusciously — displayed...a superabundance of beautiful girls...so winsomely and generously revealed that the senses pulsate at such extravagance. Tall girls, small girls, fair girls, redheads and raven brunettes, all in lovely Technicolor — and all of them shapely...as for tempestuous Miss Miranda, she is still rather fearful to behold, but she sings 'Samba Boogie' with superb snap..." (Bosley Crowther,* The New York Times*)*

Up in Central Park (1948, Universal, 88m/bw, **VHS**) ☆☆½ **Sc/P:** Karl Tunberg. **D:** William A. Seiter. **Cam:** Milton Krasner. **Cast:** Deanna Durbin, Dick Haymes, Vincent Price, Albert Sharpe, Tom Powers, Hobart Cavanaugh, Thurston Hall, Howard Freeman, Mary Field, Tom Pedi, Moroni Olsen, Curt Bois, William Skipper, Nelle Fisher. The hit play by Herbert and Dorothy Fields and Sigmund Romberg was a Michael Todd production at New York's Century Theatre starring

Wilbur Evans as a *New York Times* reporter and Maurice Burke as a *Harper's Weekly* cartoonist. They save New York taxpayers thousands of dollars when they investigate Tammany Hall and Boss Tweed, played by Noah Beery Sr. The film was Durbin's next to last movie; she retired in 1948.

- *"After a run of 504 performances, the studio wouldn't leave well enough alone and removed much of the tuneful Romberg score in favor of an attempt at a story. Big mistake. The paper-thin plot had Haymes, a* New York Times *reporter, teaming up with Durbin, a beauteous Irish immigrant (who was oddly devoid of any Irish accent)...Nothing much helped and this turn-of-the-century story fell flat."* (J.R. Nash, S.R. Ross, The Motion Picture Guide)

Joseph Fields & Jerome Chodorov

Fields:
Joseph Albert Fields
Born: February 21, 1895, New York, NY. **Died:** 1966.

Chodorov:
Born: August 10, 1911, New York, NY.

Fields spent time in Hollywood before collaborating with Jerome Chodorov on the stage spoof *Schoolhouse on the Lot*. The pair then penned two big Broadway hits about young women, *My Sister Eileen* (1940) and *Junior Miss* (1941). The musical version of *My Sister Eileen* (1955) inspired a TV series that ran from 1960 to 1961 and starred Elaine Stritch. Jerome Chodorov was blacklisted during the McCarthy Era.

For Fields's collaboration on *Flower Drum Song*, see **Oscar Hammerstein II**; and on the book for *Gentlemen Prefer Blondes*, see **Anita Loos**.

The Doughgirls (1944, Warner Bros., 102m/bw) ☆☆☆ **Sc:** Sam Hellman, James V. Kern, Wilkie C. Mahoney. **D:** James V. Kern. **P:** Mark Hellinger. **Cam:** Ernest Haller. **Cast:** Ann Sheridan, Alexis Smith, Jack Carson, Jane Wyman, Irene Manning, Charles Ruggles, Eve Arden, Craig Stevens, John Ridgely, Alan Mowbray, Donald MacBride, Regis Toomey, John Alexander, Joe DeRita, Fred Kelsey, Barbara Brown, Stephen Richards. The George S. Kaufman-directed play ran for 671 performances beginning in 1942 with Arlene Francis, Virginia Field, and Doris Nolan in the ensemble. Collected in this screwball wartime comedy set in a Washington, DC, hotel suite are, among others, a Russian sniper, a man who hasn't slept in a month, and the ditzy Vivian (Wyman), who thinks that FDR gave a great performance in *Yankee Doodle Dandy*.

- *"There are times when it seems that the dialogue, especially when it has been too finely distilled from the stage dialogue, misses the mark. Some of the lines have become so refined they twirl out to nothingness and others seem quite pointless. But on the whole the lines are broad enough and well enough planted to assure the desired reaction. The picture as a whole sets out to make no sense, and it accomplishes that negative aim beautifully and delightfully." (Paul P. Kennedy, The New York Times)*

Happy Anniversary (1959, UA, 83m/bw) ☆☆ **Sc:** Joseph Fields, Jerome Chodorov. **D:** David Miller. **P:** Ralph Fields. **Cam:** Lee Garmes. **Cast:** David Niven, Mitzi Gaynor, Carl Reiner, Loring Smith, Monique van Vooren, Phyllis Povah, Elizabeth Wilson, Patty Duke, Kevin Coughlin, David Doyle, William Dwyre, Sam Locante. The 1954 Fields/Chodorov play, entitled *Anniversary Waltz* and directed by Moss Hart, starred Macdonald Carey and Kitty Carlisle as the celebrating couple who recall their sexual history together before their marriage. The film was one of its era's legion of sex farces that defy its subject.

- *"It is too bad that the movies' Code custodians had to bother to make a fuss about the moral values of* Happy Anniversary*...For the consequences of this attention has been to give an illusion of substance to a conspicuously hollow little picture that is about as wicked as an adolescent joke...it made light of the sacredness of marriage by allowing that a husband and wife had partaken of connubial bliss before their wedding and had no remorse about same...[This] is the picture's basic joke, and it is on this one intimate detail that the whole try at comedy hangs...David Niven and Mitzi Gaynor behave as if they were plastic mechanisms operated elaborately by strings." (Bosley Crowther, The New York Times)*

Junior Miss, derived from Sally Benson's stories, was staged in 1941 by Moss Hart at Broadway's Lyceum Theatre. It concerns a teenage girl's coming of age, and was something of a touchstone theatre piece, recognizing and portraying teen themes with some astuteness (even if it was a fairly straightforward comedy).

Junior Miss (1945, 20th Century-Fox, 94m/bw) ☆☆☆½ **Sc/D:** George Seaton. **P:** William Perlberg. **Cam:** Charles Clarke. **Cast:** Peggy Ann Garner, Stephen Dunne, Sylvia Field, Allyn Joslyn, Faye Marlowe, Mona Freeman, Barbara Whiting, Stanley Prager, Connie Gilchrist, Mel Torme, John Alexander, Lillian Bronson, Scotty Beckett. Garner made a huge impression in 1945, winning a special Academy Award as Outstanding Child Actress for her roles in this and *A Tree Grows in Brooklyn*.

- *"...a captivating comedy...The film version has even more pointed and antic definition. With Peggy Ann Garner playing the title role to perfection, and Scott Beckett playing her adolescent vis-à-vis with remarkable authority, the picture has substance and meaning in addition to amusement." (Howard Barnes, New York Herald-Tribune)*

Junior Miss was given a stellar musical treatment on TV in 1957 with songs by Burton Lane and lyrics by Dorothy Fields on *The DuPont Show of the Month*, directed by Ralph Nelson, produced by Richard E. Levine and with a cast that starred the young Carol Lynley with Don Ameche, Joan Bennett, Paul Ford, Jill St. John, Diana Lynn, David Wayne, and Susanne Sidney.

My Sister Eileen was originally based on stories in *The New Yorker* by Ruth McKenney, which related the adventures of two Ohio sisters who move into a Greenwich Village flat and are charmed, interested, and put off by the neighborhood's "fringe dwellers." The play was adapted into a stage musical in 1953 called *Wonderful Town*, which ran for 559 performances.

My Sister Eileen (1942, Columbia, 96min/bw) ☆☆☆ **Sc:** Joseph Fields, Jerome Chodorov. **D:** Alexander Hall. **P:** Max Gordon. **Cam:** Joseph Walker. **Cast:** Rosalind Russell, Brian Aherne, Janet Blair, George Tobias, Allyn Joslyn, Elizabeth Patterson, Richard Quine, June Havoc, Jeff Donnell, Grant Mitchell, Donald MacBride, Gordon Jones, Forrest Tucker, Ann Doran, Moe Howard, Curly Howard, Arnold Stang, Walter Sande. The film was nominated for an Oscar for Best Actress (Russell).

- *"There is no denying the obvious. This film is largely a farcical juggling act in which the authors…keep their characters spinning more through speed than grace. Some of it is forced almost to snapping; some of it drags heavily on the screen. And Alexander Hall, the director, did little with his camera in that small [Greenwich Village] room. But Rosalind Russell plays the smart sister with a delightfully dour and cynical air, and Janet Blair is disarmingly naïve as the pretty, desirable one."* (Bosley Crowther, The New York Times)

My Sister Eileen (1955, Columbia, 108m/c, **VHS**) ☆☆☆ **Sc:** Blake Edwards, Richard Quine. **D:** Richard Quine. **P:** Fred Kohlmar. **Cam:** Charles Lawton, Jr. **Cast:** Janet Leigh, Jack Lemmon, Betty Garrett, Bob Fosse, Kurt Kasznar, Dick York, Tommy Rall, Lucy Marlow, Barbara Brown, Horace McMahon, Henry Slate, Hal March, Richard Deacon, Ken Christy, Queenie Smith.

- *"As adapted by Blake Edwards and Richard Quine, My Sister Eileen presented the bizarre, often humorous encounters between the young innocents Leigh and Garrett and the 'criminal element' of Greenwich Village. Although the score by Jule Styne and Leo Robin was not one of the film's best assets, Fosse's choreography bolstered even the weaker songs. His vaudeville antecedents surface in the dances for 'Conga,' while Broadway's razzmatazz exuberance shines in 'Give Me a Band and My Baby.'"* (Kevin Boyd Grubb, Razzle Dazzle: The Life and Work of Bob Fosse)

Wonderful Town (1958, 60m/bw) **Tp:** Joseph Fields, Jerome Chodorov. **D:** Herbert Ross. **Cast:** Rosalind Russell, Sydney Chaplin, Jacquelyn McKeever. This adaptation of Fields and Chodorov's 1953 stage musicalization of *My Sister Eileen* featured music by Leonard Bernstein and lyrics by Betty Comden and Adolph Green. Russell reprised her know-it-all performance of 16 years earlier.

A Talent for Murder (1984, Showtime, 80m/c) **Tp:** Jerome Chodorov, Norman Panama. **D:** Alvin Rakoff. **P:** Peter Abrams, James Rich, Jr. **Cast:** Laurence Olivier, Angela Lansbury, Hildegarde Neil, Charles Keating, Garrick Hagon, Tracey Childs, Tariq Yunus. The 1981 Chodorov/Norman Panama play ran for 77 performances at New York's Biltmore Theatre starring Jean-Pierre Aumont and Claudette Colbert.

The Tunnel of Love (1958, MGM, 98m/bw, **VHS**) ☆☆½ **Sc:** Joseph Fields. **D:** Gene Kelly. **P:** Joseph Fields, Martin Melcher. **Cam:** Robert Bronner. **Cast:** Doris Day, Richard Widmark, Gig Young, Gia Scala, Elisabeth Fraser, Elizabeth Wilson, Vikki Dougan, Doodles Weaver, Charles Wagenheim, Robert Williams, Esquire Trio. The 1957 play by Fields and Peter De Vries was based on De Vries's novel of the same name, about the red tape encountered by a couple who wish to adopt a baby, a situation complicated by his sudden attraction to a social worker. Tom Ewell, Nancy Olson, and Darren McGavin starred on Broadway.

- *"Well, it isn't quite as shocking as it is made to sound and appear. Indeed, it boils down at the finish to a wholesome and virtuous little tale. After flirting around the edges of that seemingly scandalous affair and giving everybody opportunity to drop shocking innuendoes, it turns out that the agency lady is secretly married all the time, the baby she has is her own husband's and the wife of our hero is finally blessed…it all fits neatly into the frame of the Production Code…Under the direction of Gene Kelly, they have played it competently."* (Bosley Crowther, The New York Times)

Harvey Fierstein
Born: June 6, 1954, Brooklyn, NY.

Harvey Fierstein's *Torch Song Trilogy* became one of the higher-profile gay-themed plays to jump from Broadway to the movies. Fierstein's many appearances as an actor include in *Mrs. Doubtfire* (1993), *Bullets Over Broadway* (1994), *Independence Day* (1996), and *Death to Smoochy* (2002). For documentaries, the raspy-voiced Fierstein also narrated *The Life and Times of Harvey Milk* (1984) and was interviewed for *The Celluloid Closet* (1995).

Tidy Endings (1988, HBO, 60m/c) ☆☆☆ **Tp:** Harvey Fierstein. **D:** Gavin Millar. **Cast:** Stockard Channing, Harvey Fierstein. In the adaptation of the final segment of Fierstein's 1987 Broadway trilogy *Safe Sex*, the ex-wife of a man who died of AIDS and his male lover meet to divide up his belongings and debate their roles in the deceased's life. Millar opened up the piece to include a funeral sequence.

- *"Both characters are almost too exemplary; there isn't a venal bone in either of them. But Fierstein's speeches are pumped up to showcase his ability to shift moods suddenly. One minute, he's lacerating his listener with righteous indignity; the next, he's cracking little jokes about his weight. It's a tad showy and self-indulgent. Nonetheless, Fierstein and Channing bring conviction to the play, and eventually it becomes a passionate appeal for reconciliation and respect in the face of the plague."* (*Don Shirley*, Los Angeles Times)

Torch Song Trilogy (1988, New Line, 119m/c, **VHS**) ☆☆☆ **Sc:** Harvey Fierstein. **D:** Paul Bogart. **P:** Howard Gottfried. **Cam:** Mikael Salomon. **Cast:** Harvey Fierstein, Anne Bancroft, Matthew Broderick, Brian Kerwin, Karen Young, Eddie Castrodad, Ken Page, Charles Pierce, Axel Vera, Benji Schulman, Geoffrey Harding, Tracy Bogart. The gay love life of a gravel-voiced female impersonator was made popular on Broadway by Fierstein in a production that ran for 1,222 performances, beginning in 1982. It made a mostly smooth, if occasionally arch, transition to film.

- *"I'm glad they let Fierstein star in the movie himself...I have not seen anyone quite like Harvey Fierstein in the movies before, and the fact that he is a specific individual gives this material a charm and weight it might have lacked if an interchangeable actor had just played the role...some passages don't work very well. The whole business of the adopted son feels unconvincing and tacked on, and Eddie Castrodad plays the teen-ager like the precocious host of his own party...I also believed Arnold when he finally told [his mother] exactly what he thought about his sexuality and her attitude toward it, and when he said, 'There are two things I demand from the people in my life: love and respect.' He could have been speaking for anybody."* (*Roger Ebert*, Chicago Sun-Times)

Fred F. Finklehoffe & John Monks, Jr.

Finklehoffe:
Born: February 16, 1910, Springfield, MA. **Died:** 1977.

Monks:
Born: February 24, 1910. **Died:** 1982.

Brother Rat (1938, Warner Bros., 98m/bw) **Sc:** Richard Macaulay, Jerry Wald. **D:** William Keighley. **P:** Hal B. Wallis. **Cam:** Ernest

Haller. **Cast:** Wayne Morris, Priscilla Lane, Eddie Albert, Ronald Reagan, Jane Wyman, Jane Bryan, Johnnie Davis, Henry O'Neill, Larry Williams, William Tracy, Gordon Oliver, Olin Howland, Louise Beavers, George O'Hanlon, Don DeFore, William Orr, Jessie Busley. The play had been a hit of the 1936 Broadway season and starred Eddie Albert, Jose Ferrer, and Frank Albertson as troublemakers at the Virginia Military Institute. A sequel followed the success of this film, entitled *Brother Rat and a Baby* (1940).

- *"...a natural for the movies. The spirit of military life is ever present, but the cadets seem to reside in a comical fraternity house rather than a staid barracks...still an amusing and diverting farce...briskly directed by the forgotten, underrated Warners's contract director William Keighley..."* (*Rob Edelman*, Magill's Survey of Cinema)

About Face (1952, Warner Bros., 94m/c) ☆☆½ **Sc:** Peter Milne. **D:** Roy Del Ruth. **P:** William Jacobs. **Cam:** Bert Glennon. **Cast:** Gordon MacRae, Eddie Bracken, Dick Wesson, Phyllis Kirk, Joel Grey, Virginia Gibson, Aileen Stanley, Jr., Larry Keating, James Best, Cliffe Ferre, John Baer, Donald Kerr. At military school, one of a trio of pals hides his marriage from the other two.

- *"A light-hearted, pleasant musical...makes little pretense at plot, director Roy Del Ruth adroitly keeping the emphasis on comedy and the tuneful melodies of Peter De Rose...keeps the tempo racing ahead skillfully setting a puckish mood..."* (The Hollywood Reporter)

Martin Flavin

Martin Archer Flavin
Born: November 2, 1883, San Francisco, CA. **Died:** 1967.

Martin Flavin won the Pulitzer Prize for Fiction in 1944 for *Journey in the Dark*. His screenplays during his stint as a studio script writer for MGM and Paramount from 1930 to 1934 include those for *The Big House* (1930) with Wallace Beery and Chester Morris, *Passion Flower* (1930), and *Three Who Loved* (1931). His plays included *Children of the Moon, Cross Roads, The Cock Crowed,* and *The Tapestry in Gray*. Columbia filmed his popular play *Broken Dishes* three times, and Warner Bros. did the same with *The Criminal Code.*

Broken Dishes, which was staged in 1929 with Bette Davis and Donald Meek in the ensemble, concerns put-upon Cyrus Bumpsted, who is henpecked by two daughters and his wife. The wife pines away for the long-lost love of the man she thinks she should have married. Meanwhile, a third daughter has fallen in love with someone of whom her mother disapproves.

Too Young to Marry (1931, Warner Bros., 67m/bw) ☆☆½ **Sc:** Francis Edward Faragoh. **D/P:** Mervyn LeRoy. **Cam:** Sid Hickox. **Cast:** Loretta Young, Grant Withers, O.P. Heggie, Emma Dunn, J. Farrell MacDonald, Lloyd Neal, Richard Tucker, Virginia Sale, Aileen Carlyle, John Sheehan. Young and Withers (who was suing for a divorce from his wife at the time) eloped by airplane to Yuma, Arizona, during this picture. Warner Bros. cranked up its publicity machine accordingly.

- "...one of the most amusing domestic comedies—a grand satire on family life." (Photoplay)

- "If O.P. Heggie, who plays Cyrus Bumpstead, the henpecked husband...had kept within reasonable bounds of restraint in his performance, instead of clowning the part, this production...might have been a far more successful one. Aside from Mr. Heggie's somewhat painful overacting...it is a fair entertainment, for the producers have adhered closely enough to the original work, and therefore it does tell a tale and point a moral." (Mordaunt Hall, The New York Times)

Love Begins at Twenty (1936, Warner Bros., 58m/bw) ☆☆ **Sc:** Tom Reed, Dalton Trumbo. **D:** Frank McDonald. **P:** Bryan Foy. **Cam:** George Barnes. **Cast:** Hugh Herbert, Warren Hull, Patricia Ellis, Hobart Cavanaugh, Mary Treen, Dorothy Vaughn, Clarence Wilson, Robert Gleckler, Anne Nagel, Arthur Aylesworth, Milton Kibbee. The play quickly became fodder for Foy's B picture unit at Warners—the studio waited only five years before recycling it.

- "Martin Flavin's play...had been memorable only in that it featured a newcomer by the name of Bette Davis. The screen version, retitled Love Begins at Twenty...did not, alas, have that particular distinction. The tedious story...was a pretty ineffectual entertainment." (Clive Hirschhorn, The Warner Bros. Story)

Calling All Husbands (1940, Warner Bros., 64m/bw) ☆☆ **Sc:** Robert E. Kent. **D:** Noel M. Smith. **P:** William Jacobs. **Cam:** Ted D. McCord. **Cast:** George Tobias, Lucille Fairbanks, Ernest Truex, George Reeves, Florence Bates, Charles Halton, Virginia Sale, John Alexander, Clem Bevans, Sam McDaniel, Spencer Charters.

- "An inconsequential production without much merit as entertainment...will slip by...without creating any stir. An overload of dialogue, and so little of it good, is too much of a burden for seasoned players to carry successfully." (The Hollywood Reporter)

Broken Dishes was produced for TV in 1948 on Kraft Television Theatre and in 1951 on Pulitzer Prize Playhouse starring James Dunn.

The Criminal Code is about a hotshot district attorney who convicts a young man for a killing he knew was committed in self-defense. The DA then becomes the warden of the prison holding that convict, who subsequently becomes the warden's driver. A murder occurs inside the prison, and the driver must decide whether to break the title code of silence to tell the truth. The 1929 play at Broadway's National Theatre featured Arthur Byron.

The Criminal Code (1931, Columbia, 97m/bw, **VHS**) ☆☆☆½ **Sc:** Seton I. Miller, Fred Niblo, Jr. **D:** Howard Hawks. **P:** Harry Cohn. **Cam:** James Wong Howe, Ted Tetzlaff. **Cast:** Walter Huston, Constance Cummings, Boris Karloff, Phillips Holmes, De Witt Jennings, Mary Doran, Ethel Wales, Clark Marshall, Arthur Hoyt, John St. Polis, Paul Porcasi, Otto Hoffman, Andy Devine, Russell Sheehan. One of Hawks's first sound pictures received first-rate work from the cast, and the director always said that Huston was his favorite actor.

- *"...the first major studio prison picture, George Hill's* The Big House, *cowritten by Flavin, which had been released in June and to which* The Criminal Code *has always been compared. An exciting film until its cop-out ending,* The Big House *is impressive for its size and near-architectural qualities, but scenes from* The Criminal Code *stick in mind more indelibly: Huston's repeated displays of arrogant confidence as he faces the prisoners in the yard, yells back at them in their own crude manner, and defiantly lights his cigar and stares down their hate for him; Karloff's implacable stalk as he corners the sadistic guard for the kill while the other prisoners cover the act with their shouting, and the surprising humor Hawks draws from grim surroundings and character...* The Criminal Code *doesn't seem as timeless or congenial as many of Hawks's later films, and it is damaged by an uncharacteristic sappiness in the scenes with the romantic youngsters." (Todd McCarthy,* Howard Hawks)*

Penitentiary (1938, Columbia, 74m/bw) ☆☆☆ **Sc:** Seton I. Miller, Fred Niblo, Jr. **D:** John Brahm. **P:** Robert North. **Cam:** Lucien Ballard. **Cast:** Walter Connolly, John Howard, Jean Parker, Robert Barratt, Ward Bond, Stanley Andrews, Ann Doran, Paul Fix, James Flavin, Bess Flowers, Marc Lawrence, Thurston Hall, Charles Halton, Marjorie Main, Lee Shumway.

- *"Geared to the 'Class B' ratio, Columbia Pictures continues to embarrass critical judgment, every now and then, by turning out a soundly constructed film in the dependable categories below the fashionable 'A' ratings. A good example of this gratuitous largesse is* Penitentiary...borne *on the wings of some mysterious hack-inspiration, has made of it an unexpectedly exciting piece of pulpwood fiction." (B.R. Crisler,* The New York Times)*

Convicted (1950, Columbia, 91m/bw) ☆☆½ **Sc:** William Bowers, Seton I. Miller, Fred Niblo, Jr. **D:** Henry Levin. **P:** Jerry Bresler. **Cam:** Burnett Guffey. **Cast:** Glenn Ford, Broderick Crawford, Millard Mitchell, Dorothy Malone, Carl Benton Reid, Frank Faylen, Will

Geer, Martha Stewart, Henry O'Neill, Ed Begley, Douglas Kennedy, Roland Winters, Frank Cady, Whit Bissell, John Doucette, John Butler, Harry Harvey, Ray Teal. Crawford's warden comes to believe that Ford's inmate is innocent. The remake, which is less complicated than the above film, retains the romantic angle of the convict falling for the warden's daughter (Malone).

- *"...lacks originality. Its overworked themes and obvious amelioration are opposed to the noir framework; but there is a noir quality in the film due primarily to the presence of Glenn Ford. Ford's presence in many of the noir films of Columbia Pictures during that period...established a screen personality that, of itself, articulated a close affinity to the noir world." (Carl Macek in* Film Noir: An Encyclopedic Reference to the American Style *by Alain Silver and Elizabeth Ward)*

The Criminal Code played TV in a 1956 *Lux Video Theatre* installment starring Dewey Martin.

Horton Foote

Born: March 14, 1916, Wharton, TX.
Pulitzer Prize-winning play: *The Young Man From Atlanta* (1995)

One of America's most versatile, prolific and enduring dramatists, Horton Foote has achieved great success in three media, winning the Pulitzer Prize at age 79 for *The Young Man From Atlanta* (1995). He also earned Academy Awards for adapting Harper Lee's Pulitzer Prize-winning novel *To Kill a Mockingbird* (1962) and for his original screenplay of *Tender Mercies* (1983), and an Emmy Award for the adaptation of William Faulkner's novella, *Old Man*, into the 1997 *Hallmark Hall of Fame* presentation starring Arliss Howard as a Mississippi convict. Foote adapted the same story in 1958 for a large-scale *Playhouse 90* production that starred Sterling Hayden, which garnered the writer his first Emmy nomination.

Many of Foote's plays, screenplays and teleplays have been autobiographical, reflecting his roots in his native Wharton, Texas. His illuminations of the rural Southern past and of family matters in Texas have some parallels to the rustic and volatile tangles afflicting Faulkner's characters in Mississippi. Many of Foote's teleplays and plays are interrelated, including the nine plays in his ambitious masterwork, *The Orphan's Home Cycle*, which is comprised of *Roots in a Parched Ground*, *Convicts*, *Lily Dale*, *The Widow Claire*, *Courtship*, *Valentine's Day*, *1918*, *Cousins*, and *The Death of Papa*.

Six of the cycle have been filmed. The slightly retitled *On Valentine's Day*, *1918*, and pieces of *Courtship* (see individual entries below) made up a five-hour miniseries that was retitled *Story of a Marriage* and broadcast in April 1987 on PBS's *American Playhouse*. Another four-part cycle of Foote's Southern family mood plays became jewels of the live-TV era, even though their connections weren't apparent to viewers: *The Trip to Bountiful* with Lillian Gish and *The Midnight Caller* with Catherine Doucet, both in 1953 on *Kraft Television Playhouse*, and two with Kim Stanley, *Tears of My Sister* in 1953 on *First Person Playhouse* and *Flight* three years later on *Playwrights '56*.

As one of the great dramatists of that so-called "Golden Age" of TV, Foote also penned originals that were later produced as plays, including *A Young Lady of Property* with Kim Stanley and Joanne Woodward in 1953 on *Philco Television Playhouse*, *The Roads to Home* with James Daly and Beatrice Straight in 1955 on *The United States Steel Hour*, and *Tomorrow* with Richard Boone and Stanley in 1960 on *Playhouse 90*. Other TV productions written by Foote include *Drugstore Sunday Noon* with Helen Hayes in 1956 on *Omnibus*, *A Member of the Family* with Hume Cronyn in 1957 on *Studio One*, *The Shape of the River* about Mark Twain in 1960 on *Playhouse 90*, and *Horton Foote's Alone* with Cronyn in a 1997 Showtime presentation.

One of the top interpreters of other Southern writers, Foote also adapted Flannery O'Connor's *The Displaced Person* starring John Houseman in 1978 and Faulkner's *Barn Burning* with Tommy Lee Jones in 1980, both for PBS's *American Short Story*. Foote's screenplays include the adaptations of Clinton Seeley's *Storm Fear* (1956) with Cornell Wilde, K.B. Gilden's *Hurry Sundown* (1967), with Jane Fonda and John Steinbeck's *Of Mice and Men* (1992) with John Malkovich.

Among Foote's plays, most of which are situated in the Wharton facsimile of Harrison, Texas, are *Texas Town* (1941), *In My Beginning* (1944), *Night Seasons* (1977), *In a Coffin in Egypt* (1980), *The Man Who Climbed Pecan Trees* (1981), *The Prisoner's Song* (1985), *Blind Date* (1985), *Dividing the Estate* (1989), *Talking Pictures* (1990), *The Day Emily Married* (2000), *Getting Frankie Married—and Afterwards* (2002), and *The Carpetbagger's Children* (2002).

The Chase (1966, Columbia, 135m/c, **VHS**) ☆☆☆ **Sc:** Lillian Hellman. **D:** Arthur Penn. **P:** Sam Spiegel. **Cam:** Joseph La Shelle. **Cast:** Marlon Brando, Jane Fonda, Robert Redford, Robert Duvall, E.G. Marshall, Miriam Hopkins, James Fox, Janice Rule, Angie Dickinson, Henry Hull, Martha Hyer. This hothouse drama of loyalties, betrayals, deals and liaisons, among the gentry in a small Southern town centers one swelting evening on the sheriff's efforts to track prison escapee Bubber Reeves. Originating as a Broadway play in 1952 that starred Kim Stanley—in the first of her many Foote collaborations—then published as Foote's only novel in 1956, *The Chase* was adapted rather famously for this richly pedigreed, all-star melodrama by Hellman. "But she said quite openly that she was using it as a departure," Foote said. "And she departed so far that, you know, I didn't know why they bought the work to begin with."

- *"In the queen bee of vignette scenes, in which two or three moralistic scolds bitch [at] each other in interesting dialogue, Miss Hellman has...chopped her script into a mass of small town filigrees, miniature versions of* The Little Foxes. *Some of her 100 percent masochists and sadists drive in from the most distant reaches...This diced conglomeration of middle class theater that forces its director to mimic scenes from* On the Waterfront *and* Ice Palace *is pure department store...Miss Hellman has written three or four of everything: Two near ghosts who walk uninvited into anyone's office or living room just to kibitz the action; three Robin Hoods in reverse who beat up anyone who looks awful; two sexpots who have little flesh but manage to divide the good and bad males between them..."* (Manny Farber, Negative Space)

- *"...the town isn't merely corrupt: it has an appetite for violence, it's a blood-lusting Texas town in the mythical United States of message movies. It's evil. Lillian Hellman wrote the screenplay...and the little foxes really took over. Our vines have no tender grapes left in this hellhole of wife swapping, nigger hating, and nigger-lover hating, where people are motivated by dirty sex or big money, and you can tell which as soon as they say their first lines..."* (Pauline Kael, Kiss Kiss Bang Bang)

Convicts (1991, MCEG, 95m/c, **VHS**) ☆☆☆½ **Sc:** Horton Foote. **D:** Peter Masterson. **P:** Sterling Van Wagenen, Jonathan D. Krane. **Cam:** Toyomichi Kurita. **Cast:** Robert Duvall, Lukas Haas, James Earl Jones, Starletta DuPois, Carlin Glynn, Calvin Levels, Gary Swanson, Mel Winkler, Lance E. Nichols, Jerry Biggs, Robert Edmundson, Walter Breaux, Jr., Duriel Harris. The second play in *The Orphan's Home Cycle, Convicts* depicts 13-year-old Horace Robedaux's Christmas Eve in 1902, as he serves as a Texas plantation store clerk after his father died of alcoholism. He toils to buy his father a tombstone, lives with black sharecroppers, abides the aging plantation boss's senility and watches as one of the convicts who work the plantation escapes and is killed. The performances of Duvall and Jones carry this mood piece, which was originally performed in 1983 at the Ensemble Studio in New York.

- *"Mr. Duvall is terrific as old Soll. He is the towering figure in Convicts...Peter Masterson...directs...in the plain, unadorned style that best suits the Foote material and doesn't upstage the performers. Mr. Duvall is a very special actor in that he doesn't have to be noisily (or quietly) busy to assert his control over character and the audience's attention. The camera sees everything he does, which, when one tries to describe it, seems to be nothing at all. The behavior becomes somehow riveting...Convicts is scarcely more than a fragment. Its realities are harsh but its conflicts are muted. The dramatic line is without big conventional revelation. Yet the film creates its own elegiacal mood, which has a special poignancy when one is aware of what is to come after. Watching Mr. Foote's memory films is like being gifted with eerie foresight, as well as with the forgiveness that only comes with time." (Vincent Canby, The New York Times)*

Courtship (1986, Angelika Films, 84m/c, **VHS**) ☆☆½ **Sc:** Horton Foote. **D:** Howard Cummings. **P:** Lillian V. Foote. **Cam:** George Tirl. **Cast:** Hallie Foote, Matthew Broderick, William Converse-Roberts, Amanda Plummer, Steven Hill, Carol Goodheart, Michael Higgins, Richard Jenkins, Horton Foote, Jr., Rochelle Oliver. Young Elizabeth is courted by Horace Robedaux, but her deeply conservative parents disapprove of the relationship. This is the first of the marriage trilogy at the center of *The Orphan's Home Cycle*, and is followed by *[On] Valentine's Day* and *1918*. The play was first performed in 1984 at the Actors' Theatre in Louisville, Kentucky.

- *"There is an almost dreamlike quality to their relatively placid existences while, around them, a young woman dies and an old, crazed man commits suicide. The periphery of Mr. Foote's world seems to be more interesting than the very center, which is perceived in almost elegiac tenderness. A powerful performance can bring that world shimmering to life. Witness Robert Duvall in the writer's* Tender Mercies *and Geraldine Page in his* The Trip to Bountiful. *This...sorely lacks that galvanizing asset. Most of the cast, especially Mr. Converse-Roberts, are just fine...but the pervasive tone of rather smug gentility gradually defeats them." (John J. O'Connor, The New York Times)*

The Habitation of Dragons (1992, TNT, 100m/c, **VHS**) *TNT Screenworks* ☆☆☆ **Tp:** Horton Foote. **D:** Michael Lindsay-Hogg. **P:** Donald P. Borchers. **Cast:** Brad Davis, Hallie Foote, Frederic Forrest, Maureen O'Sullivan, Hawthorne James, Jean Stapleton, Elias Koteas, Pat Hingle, Joanna Miles, Roberts Blossom, David Smith, Blake Stokes, Lucinda Jenney. This 1930s period piece resembles one of the playwright's earliest plays, *Out of My House* (1942). Both plays feature adult brothers battling each other amid a disintegrating family in the small-town South. *The Habitation of Dragons* was first performed at the Pittsburgh Public Theatre in 1988, directed by Foote.

- *"There is an extramarital affair, an anonymous letter, an extortion effort, the death of two children, a murder. Someone actually says, 'If it is ever discovered that you destroyed evidence, it'll go hard on you.' Mr. Foote's practiced way with down-home dialogue gets fancy as one of his characters casts about for significance: 'I thought to myself, "Here lies power. Here lies ambition."' For all the commotion, even the characters become bored...Most of the actors...go down in the heavy emotional weather. The exception is Jean Stapleton...she is too busy saving herself from lines like: 'Have we committed some terrible sin? Are we being punished?' 'Fraid so, ma'am." (Walter Goodman, The New York Times)*

Lily Dale (1996, Showtime, 98m/c, **VHS**) ☆☆☆ **Tp:** Horton Foote. **D:** Peter Masterson. **P:** John Thomas Lenox. **Cast:** Mary Stuart Masterson, Sam Shepard, Stockard Channing, Tim Guinee, Jean Stapleton, John Slattery, Sean Hennigan, Chamblee Ferguson, Horton Foote, Elbert Lewis. In 1910 Texas, 19-year-old Horace Robedaux is asked by his mother to visit her and his little sister, Lily Dale, in Houston. His father died of alcoholism when he was 12, and his mother remarried a railroader who agreed to raise Lily Dale, but not him. This is the third play in *The Orphan's Home Cycle* and was first performed Off Broadway in 1986.

- *"...rummages once again through an exquisitely neurasthenic past, its taut emotions stretched almost painfully beneath flutterings of propriety...There are some casting glitches. Ms. Masterson, daughter of Mr. Masterson, the director, is 30, and just not terribly convincing as a hopelessly naïve 18-year-old. And some characters remain irritatingly vague. Ms. Channing manages to make the ambiguous Corella quite moving, but the lanky Mr. Shepard can do little with Mr. Davenport other than make him look as if he has just wandered in from* The Grapes of Wrath...*Mr. Foote...painstakingly remembers a world poised between cold practicality and the sudden warmth of a John McCormack recording of 'Mother Macree.' It's a fragile world and, in this production, demanding. Patience is essential."* (John J. O'Connor, The New York Times)

1918 (1985, Cinecom, 94m/c, **VHS**) ☆☆☆½ **Sc:** Horton Foote. **D:** Ken Harrison. **P:** Lillian V. Foote, Ross Milloy, Peter Newman. **Cam:** George Tirl. **Cast:** Hallie Foote, William Converse-Roberts, Matthew Broderick, Belinda Jackson, Lisa Howard, Michael Higgins, Rochelle Oliver, Horton Foote, Jr., Jeannie McCarthy, L.T. Felty, Bill McGhee. Horace Robedaux feels the pressure to enlist in the Army during World War I, but he doesn't want to leave his young wife, Elizabeth, and their young child, Jenny. But Elizabeth's family, particularly her father, plans to take care of his daughter and the child so Horace can fight for his country. However, the influenza epidemic is sweeping the town; this historically devastating "Spanish flu" eventually killed more than 25 million people worldwide. The play debuted Off Broadway in 1982.

- *"...[a] writer's movie...one that, for better or worse, pays no attention to the demands for pacing and narrative emphasis that any commercially oriented Hollywood producer would have insisted on. The very flatness of its dramatic line is its dramatic point."* (Vincent Canby, The New York Times)

On Valentine's Day (1986, Angelika Films, 106m/c, **VHS**) *American Playhouse* ☆☆☆½ **Sc:** Horton Foote. **D:** Ken Harrison. **P:** Lillian V. Foote, Calvin Skaggs. **Cam:** George Tirl. **Cast:** Hallie Foote, William Converse-Roberts, Matthew Broderick, Steven Hill, Michael Higgins,

Carol Goodheart, Irma P. Hall, Richard Jenkins, Jeannie McCarthy, Bill McGhee, Rochelle Oliver. The title changed from *Valentine's Day* on stage for this middle work of the marraige trilogy inside the nine-play *Orphan's Home Cycle*. This film captures the flavor of Foote's Harrison through ensemble playing, setting the stage for the events of *1918*. The play was first performed Off Broadway in 1980.

- *"If anyone has a chance of reclaiming the word 'auteur' for authors — after years of seeing it used as a synonym for movie directors — it's certainly this soft-spoken Southerner, who's never afraid to reject the Hollywood rule book in favor of his own insights and instincts." (David Sterritt,* Christian Science Monitor*)*

Only the Heart concerns a small-town businesswoman and the effect of her materialism on the people around her — she eventually becomes both wealthy and lonely. The play premiered Off Broadway at the American Actor's Theater in 1942, and eventually had a short Broadway run. It became Foote's first adaptation for TV in 1948 on NBC's *Kraft Television Theatre. Kraft* restaged the play in 1951 with a cast that included Jack Ewing, Isobel Price, Isobel Robins, and Dorothy Sands.

Tomorrow (1972, Filmgroup, 102m/bw, **VHS**) ☆☆☆☆☆ **Sc:** Horton Foote. **D:** Joseph Anthony. **P:** Gilbert Pearlman, Paul Roebling. **Cam:** Alan Green. **Cast:** Robert Duvall, Olga Bellin, Sudie Bond, Richard McConnell, Peter Masterson, William Hawley, Johnny Mask, James Franks, Dick Dougherty, Effie Green, R.M. Weaver. William Faulkner's original short story was published in the *Saturday Evening Post* in 1940, then adapted by Foote for TV's *Playhouse 90* in 1960. Duvall then starred in the 1968 Off Broadway play that Foote adapted from his teleplay, which became the basis for this film. It's the story of Jackson Fentry, a former Mississippi sawmill worker serving as a jurist in a murder trial. The film flashes back to the incidents from Fentry's past that include his marriage and his new wife's death in childbirth. A great character study with brilliant performances by Duvall and Bellin, this film is possibly the best screen work ever derived from Faulkner's fiction.

- *"...one can hardly fail to praise the film on its own terms.* Tomorrow *is simply one of the best independent productions in the recent history of American narrative film." (Bruce F. Kawin,* Faulkner and Film, *1977)*

- *"The special beloveds are the unexpected films, the 'sleepers' that arrive without fanfare, are viewed without expectations, and make an indelible mark on memory and heart.* Tomorrow *is such a film." (Judith Crist, foreword,* Tomorrow & Tomorrow & Tomorrow, *edited by G. Yellin and Marie Connors, 1985)*

The Traveling Lady was originally performed onstage in New York in 1954 by Kim Stanley, Jack Lord, and Lonny Chapman. It concerns Georgette, the wife of a recently released Texas ex-con. The couple hit the road, with their pre-school daughter in tow, as the husband tries to make a living as a country and blues singer in bars and nightclubs. It was first filmed in 1957 for CBS's *Studio One*, with a teleplay by Foote and a first-rate cast led by Kim Stanley, Robert Loggia, Mildred Dunnock, Wendy Hiller, and Steven Hill.

Baby, the Rain Must Fall (1965, Columbia, 100m/bw, **VHS**) ☆☆½
Sc: Horton Foote. **D:** Robert Mulligan. **P:** Alan J. Pakula. **Cam:** Ernest Laszlo. **Cast:** Steve McQueen, Lee Remick, Don Murray, Paul Fix, Josephine Hutchinson, Ruth White, Charles Watts. While McQueen got top billing in this slow-moving and ultimately disappointing character study, Mulligan gave this quiet movie over to Remick, who elicits the worries of young motherhood faced with disappointment and the unknown in an unforced yet poignant portrayal of everyday courage. The title came from the Glenn Yarborough hit song over the title sequence. The writer, director, and producer of *To Kill a Mockingbird* tried to strike oil twice with this adaptation of a Foote original.

- *"...aside from the hit song, watching this 1965 disaster offers absolutely nothing except the futile speculation on what a couple of nice kids (let alone fine actors) like Lee Remick and Steve McQueen are doing in an artsied-up melodramatic mishmash like this one."* (Judith Crist, Judith Crist's TV Guide to the Movies)

The Trip to Bountiful (1985, Allied/FilmDallas/Island, 106m/c, **VHS**) ☆☆☆☆½ **Sc:** Horton Foote. **D:** Peter Masterson. **P:** Sterling Van Wagenen, Horton Foote. **Cam:** Fred Murphy. **Cast:** Geraldine Page, John Heard, Carlin Glynn, Rebecca De Mornay, Richard Bradford, Kevin Cooney, Norman Bennett, Kirk Sisco. In another case of a TV production coming first, this Foote original aired in the spring of 1953 on *Philco Television Playhouse* in a production starring Lillian Gish, John Beal, Eileen Heckert, and Eva Marie Saint. It inspired producer Fred Coe to bring the work, with Gish attached, to Broadway later that year. Three decades later, this film version became a tour de force for Foote's old friend, Geraldine Page, winning her the Academy Award for Best Actress for her performance as Carrie Watts. Carrie is an aging woman living in the stifling environment of her son's Houston apartment in 1953, and longs to return to the rural Texas Gulf Coast farm of her youth. She does in this beautifully realized film, which also brought Foote his third Oscar nomination.

- *"...funny, exquisitely performed...Geraldine Page has never been in better form, nor in more firm control of that complex, delicate mechanism that makes her one of our finest actresses...Her Mrs. Watts is simultaneously hilarious and crafty, sentimental and unexpectedly tough...a strong, shrewdly willful woman who also happens to be decent. It's a wonderful role...Mr. Foote and Mr. Masterson have seen to it that the movie doesn't have the constricted manner of a play that's been filmed...works perfectly as a small, richly detailed film that, in turn, realizes Mr. Foote's particular visions." (Vincent Canby, The New York Times)*

- *"...the Golden Age of TV...seemed even then the Age of Golden Syrup. The main impulse of that age was anti-Hollywood: the small screen was used to celebrate the unbeautiful people, in contrast to the perfection-worship of Hollywood. So we got on TV the pathetic types from big cities (Marty, Queen of the Stardust Ballroom) and we also got, among other small-town confections, Foote's Texan wistfulness. These TV plays, which seemed the predominent types, were carpentered as traps for tears. The very title of* The Trip to Bountiful *suggests that it's a sight for moist eyes. The new 1950s realism, which in fact reduced realism to facile pathos, is almost cartooned in Foote's title." (Stanley Kauffmann, The New Republic, 1986)*

Donald Freed & Arnold M. Stone

Freed:
Born: May 13, 1932, Chicago, IL.

Donald Freed's writings include intellectual books — *Freud and Stanislavsky: New Directions in the Performing Arts* — and well-received liberal-to-radical political treatises: *Agony in New Haven: The Trial of Bobby Seale, Ericka Huggins and the Black Panther Party*, and *Big Brother and the Holding Company (The World Behind Watergate)*. His book *Executive Action: Assassination of a Head of State* was the basis for the political thriller *Executive Action* (1973) starring Burt Lancaster and Robert Ryan. Freed's play *Inquest: The U.S. vs. Julius and Ethel Rosenberg* was first produced in 1970 on Broadway at the Music Box Theatre with Anne Jackson, George Grizzard, and James Whitmore.

Secret Honor (1986, Cinecom, 90m/c, **VHS**) ☆☆☆☆½ **Sc:** Donald Freed, Arnold M. Stone. **D/P:** Robert Altman. **Cam:** Pierre Mignot. **Cast:** Philip Baker Hall. Richard M. Nixon, raving to himself alone in his study, boozes, tapes his memories, and neurotically inventories the success and failures, believed and imagined, of his lifetime. A fabulous, hilarious one-man show with Hall in the performance of his life. The play, which debuted in 1984 at the Provincetown Playhouse as *Secret Honor: The Last Testament of Richard M. Nixon*, also starred Hall.

- *"...one of the funniest, most unsettling, most imaginative, and most surprisingly affecting movies of its very odd kind I've ever seen...Mr. Altman recoups his reputation with* Secret Honor, *a most unlikely work —*

a one-character movie, set entirely within a single set...The result is something of a cinematic tour de force, both for Mr. Altman and for the previously unknown Philip Baker Hall, whose contribution is a legitimate, bravura performance, not a Saturday Night Live *impersonation...an extremely skillful, witty, dramatic work with an extraordinary character at its center. Mr. Altman serves it beautifully. He never undercuts the material or Mr. Hall's immense performance, which is astonishing and risky — for the chances the actor takes and survives..."* (Vincent Canby, The New York Times)

Bruce Jay Friedman

Born: April 26, 1930, New York, NY.

Movies based on Friedman stories include Elaine May's *The Heartbreak Kid* (1972), *Stir Crazy* (1980), and *Doctor Detroit* (1983). Friedman worked with Lowell Ganz and Babaloo Mandel on the screenplay for Ron Howard's *Splash* (1984) and his book, *The Lonely Guy's Book of Life*, was turned into Carl Reiner's *The Lonely Guy* (1984) starring Steve Martin. Friedman has also acted in films, most notably in the Woody Allen's *Another Woman* (1988) and *Celebrity* (1998).

Steambath (1973, PBS, 90m/c, **VHS/DVD**) *Hollywood Television Theatre: Special of the Week* ☆☆☆☆ **Tp:** Bruce Jay Friedman. **D:** Burt Brinckerhoff. **P:** Norman Lloyd. **Cast:** Bill Bixby, Jose Perez, Valerie Perrine, Herb Edelman, Stephen Elliott, Kenneth Mars, Art Metrano, Biff Elliott, Neil Schwartz, Patrick Spohn, Peter Kastner, Shirley Kirkes. One of the most scandalous shows in TV history, with rough language and nudity, this production caused a national uproar. It concerns a prison teacher (Bixby) who wakes up in a steambath that serves as detention center for souls waiting to enter the afterlife. The original play was performed Off Broadway.

- *"...it was much better on television than in the theatre...[Perez] was superb. This figure of God with a Puerto Rican accent offended many people all over the country. Of the approximately 208 stations on the PBS network, only 28 initially played the show. To most of the stations, the play was sacrilegious and its language and nudity unacceptable...Jim Loper, who was then the head of KCET, insisted pubic hair was visible...I removed the public hair. Nevertheless, the show was an utter scandal...We were castigated by ministries all over the country...I think it's fair to say that* Steambath *has remained a classic in television drama. It is timeless in its concept."* (Norman Lloyd, Stages: Of Life in Theatre, Film and Television)

Charles Fuller

Born: March 5, 1939, Philadelphia, PA.
Pulitzer Prize-winning play: *A Soldier's Play* (1982)

Charles Fuller's most significant TV work was the teleplay for the movie *A Gathering of Old Men* (1987) about a Louisiana murder with Civil Rights implications, starring Louis Gossett, Jr., Holly Hunter, and Richard Widmark. He also adapted Ernest Gaines's *The Sky Is Gray* for a 1980 installment of *American Shory Story* starring Olivia Cole, Cleavon Little, and James Bond III.

A Soldier's Story (1984, Columbia, 101m/c, **VHS/DVD**) ☆☆☆☆ **Sc:** Charles Fuller. **D:** Norman Jewison. **P:** Patrick Palmer, Norman Jewison. **Cam:** Russell Boyd. **Cast:** Howard E. Rollins, Jr., Adolph Caesar, Denzel Washington, Art Evans, David Alan Grier, David Harris, Larry Riley, Robert Townsend, Wings Hauser, Trey Wilson, Patti LaBelle, Dennis Lipscombe. In his own adaptation of his play, *A Soldier's Play*, Fuller tells the story of a black U.S. Army attorney who's sent to a Southern base in 1944 Louisiana to investigate the shooting murder of an unpopular black sergeant. The play featured Caesar in the first performance in 1981 by the Negro Ensemble Company. The film received Oscar nominations for Best Picture, Screenplay, and Supporting Actor (Caesar).

- *"...Jewison has handled the white antagonists so ham-handedly that they seem to demand being hissed off the screen...Small, slight Adolph Caesar plays [Sgt. Waters] like a whip dipped in vinegar, with a harrowing strength that projects to the back row of a theatre...Art Evans...Denzel Washington...Robert Townsend...David Harris...are simply extraordinary...Fuller and Jewison give the film a fine John Wayne finish—patriotism, militarism and civil rights all marching off together—in a flourish which is only one example of what went wrong at Fort Neal."* (Sheila Benson, Los Angeles Times)

Zooman (1995, Showtime, 95m/c, **VHS**) ☆☆☆½ **Tp:** Charles Fuller. **D:** Leon Ichaso. **P:** Michael Manheim, James B. Freydberg. **Cast:** Louis Gossett, Jr., Charles S. Dutton, CCH Pounder, Khalil Kain, Cynthia Martells, Vondie Curtis-Hall, Hill Harper. Based on Fuller's 1978 play, *Zooman and the Sign*, performed Off Broadway by the Negro Ensemble Company, this tough inner-city drama focuses on the estranged father of a young girl killed in gangbangers' crossfire and the witnesses to the horrid act who won't come forward to identify the killer—because of their fear for their own safety. The drama centers around the title character, the killer, who tells the audience, "Be honest. You don't care about me, and I don't care about you, neither."

- *"On one level,* Zooman *is about a family groping for reconciliation in the midst of a tragedy. On another, it's about a neighborhood's struggle to survive its fear...powerfully disturbing as it confronts apathy in the face of growing violence fueled by handguns. And a fine cast, directed by Leon Ichaso...makes this production singularly compelling."* (John J. O'Connor, The New York Times)

Zona Gale

Born: August 26, 1874, Portage, WI. **Died:** 1938.
Pulitzer Prize-winning play: *Miss Lulu Bett* (1920)

Two other films were made from Gale's writings, *Faint Perfume* (1925) from her novel and starring William Powell, and director Christy Cabanne's *When Strangers Meet* (1934). Gale often wrote about repressed, complex characters beneath seemingly simple veneers that evoked bleak life in her native Wisconsin. Her novels include *Birth, Mr. Pitt, Borgia, The Secret Way,* and *When I Was a Little Girl.* Her biography, *Still Small Voice* (1940) was written by August Derleth.

Miss Lulu Bett (1921, Paramount, bw/silent) ☆☆☆☆ **Sc:** Clara Beranger. **D:** William C. de Mille. **P:** Adolph Zukor. **Cam:** L. Guy Wilky. **Cast:** Lois Wilson, Milton Sills, Theodore Roberts, Helen Ferguson, Clarence Burton, Mae Giraci, Taylor Graves, Charles Ogle, Mabel Van Buren, Ethel Wales. Gale adapted her 1920 novel of the same name into the Pulitzer Prize-winning play, which was in turn made into this film. The play was produced by Brock Pemberton at Broadway's Belmont Theatre and ran for 198 performances with a cast that featured Catherine Calhoun Doucet, William E. Holden, and Willard Robertson. In the film, Wilson plays a Midwestern spinster who's considered unattractive and works as a drudge for her sister's family.

- *"Lost in the clamor is Cecil's older brother, William, who spelled de with a small d. Unhappily most of the films of William C. de Mille have disappeared. Only Miss Lulu Bett survives...shows de Mille to have been a man of great warmth and perceptiveness. He cared more for psychological reality than melodramatic action, and his style was as different from Cecil's as a miniaturist's from an epic painter...brilliantly directed film...The opening title indicates the unusual approach: 'The greatest tragedy in the world, because it is the most frequent, is that of a human soul caught in the toils of the commonplace.' The sense of observation reaches a standard very seldom excelled, and the de Mille compassion and his realistic treatment give every scene a truthfulness still rare in the cinema. It retains its magic, and this fragile, delicate little story can still move its audience to tears."* (Kevin Brownlow, The Parade's Gone By...)

Samuel Gallu

Born: March 21, 1918. **Died:** 1991.

In addition to authoring *Give 'Em Hell, Harry!*, Samuel Gallu directed the films *Theatre of Death* (1966) with Christopher Lee, *The Man Outside* (1967) with Van Heflin, *The Limbo Line* (1968), and *Arthur! Arthur!* (1969) with Donald Pleasance.

Give 'Em Hell, Harry! (1975, Avco Embassy, 104m/bw, **VHS**) ☆☆☆½ **Sc:** Samuel Gallu. **D:** Steve Binder. **P:** Joseph E. Bluth, Al Ham, David Permut, Bill Sargent, John J. Tenant. **Cam:** Ken Palius. **Cast:** James Whitmore. This became the most famous of Whitmore's one-man theatrical shows as famous folks (he also impersonated Will Rogers and Theodore Roosevelt in similar productions), receiving an Oscar nomination for Best Actor in his role as Harry Truman. Gallu fleshed out his script from Truman's speeches, letters, and other writings about the former president, and Whitmore gave his impersonation gusto, warmth, intelligence and command. The first performance of the play was in 1975 under the direction of Peter H. Hunt at the Community Theatre in Hershey, Pennsylvania, with President Gerald Ford and Mrs. Ford in attendance. The film performance is outstanding, covering many significant historical events, but Binder's cameras basically recorded a stage show. Whitmore earned his Oscar nomination in part due to the film being shown in the Los Angeles area on the Z Channel, a cable forerunner to HBO, shortly before the Academy's nominations deadline. (The same year, Maximilian Schell earned a Best Actor nomination for another film shown on the Z Channel, *The Man in the Glass Booth*, which had a similarly stagy filmization.)

Herb Gardner

Born: 1934, Brooklyn, NY.
Tony Award-winning play: *I'm Not Rappaport* (1986)

Herb Gardner's feel-good comedies set in New York City have identified him with many critics as the second-division Neil Simon, status that he occasionally transcended. His two big hits, *A Thousand Clowns* (1962) and *I'm Not Rappaport* (1986), turned on showy central characters full of individualism, and vigorous protestation and wisecracks, enlivening otherwise static presentations. In a checkered career, Gardner also contributed a story to a Marlo Thomas TV special, *Free to Be...You & Me* (1974) and wrote and produced Dustin Hoffman's most impossibly titled film flop, *Who Is Harry Kellerman and Why Is He Saying Those Terrible Things About Me?* (1971). He's the credited director on two adaptations of his plays, and was an uncredited co-director of another two.

The Goodbye People (1985, Embassy, 104m/c, **VHS**) ☆☆ **Sc/D:** Herb Gardner. **Cam:** John Lindley. **P:** David V. Picker. **Cast:** Martin Balsam, Pamela Reed, Judd Hirsch, Ron Silver, Gene Saks, Michael Tucker. Max Silverman, an aging former Coney Island hot dog stand owner, and Arthur Korman, a bored toy-making executive, decide to re-open the stand after 22 years. Reed plays an oddball who decides to help them in their shared dream. This sentimental play flopped on Broadway in the 1960s. Balsam, in a return to Gardner material, which won him an Oscar in 1965 (see below), and Reed illuminate their characters with game performances, but the playwright's slack direction makes this a static beach experience.

- *"...neither time nor the transferral of media has improved the story of three eccentric losers who band together in hopes of changing their luck...The uneasy alliance between the characters is treated in a glib fashion by Gardner."* (Variety)

I'm Not Rappaport (1996, Grammercy, 135m/c, **VHS**) ☆☆ **Sc/D:** Herb Gardner. **Cam:** Adam Holender. **P:** John Penotti, John Starke. **Cast:** Walter Matthau, Ossie Davis, Amy Irving, Martha Plimpton, Craig T. Nelson, Guillermo Diaz, Boyd Gaines, Ron Rifkin, Elina Lowensohn, Irwin Corey. Set mostly in Central Park, this is a character study of the octogenarian Nat, a cantankerous political radical and put-on who rants on and on to Midge, another old man who still works as a building superintendent and lends a skeptical ear. The 1988 Broadway original starred Judd Hirsch as the 81-year-old Nat Moyer and Cleavon Little as Midge, with Mercedes Rheul and Jace Alexander in support.

- *"...Mr. Matthau has one of the richest characters of his career...gives Mr. Matthau free rein as a storyteller, verbal pugilist and character actor. But Mr. Matthau's wonderfully engaged performance can't conceal the glaring weaknesses of the play...suffers mightily from its translation into a more realistic medium...essentially an extended two-man vaudeville routine...It is with an almost vengeful glee that Mr. Matthau brings home the play's message: Imagination is the best defense."* (Stephen Holden, The New York Times)

Thieves (1977, Paramount, 92m/c) ☆ **Sc:** Herb Gardner. **D:** John Berry, Al Viola, Herb Gardner (uncredited). **Cam:** Andrew Laszlo, Arthur J. Ornitz. **P:** George Barrie. **Cast:** Marlo Thomas, Charles Grodin, Mercedes McCambridge, Gary Merrill, Hector Elizondo, Irwin Corey, John McMartin, Ann Wedgworth, Bob Fosse. This piece depicts the Cramers, Sally and Martin, whose marriage is on the rocks as she decides whether to abort her pregnancy. Meanwhile, several mentally disturbed people try to recapture their innocence on the pointedly unfriendly streets of New York City. Virtually undistributed, unseen, long forgotten and not transferred to home video, this sticky piece of unfocused sentimentality dashed TV star Thomas's big-screen aspirations.

• "Thieves *may not be the worst movie I ever saw, but it may well be the most annoyingly cloying. Herb Gardner...is one of those horrible examples of how extremely limited, intensely self-satisfied, repetitious and predictable cleverness can become—within minutes—more offensive than extended witlessness...Gardner has been turning out plays and movies of increasing self-indulgence, cutesiness and indigestibility...on screen, his archness— really fallen archness—has reached the limits of human endurance.* Thieves *goes beyond them."* (John Simon, New York)

A Thousand Clowns (1965, UA, 115m/bw, **VHS**) ☆☆☆☆½ **Sc:** Herb Gardner. **D/P:** Fred Coe, Herb Gardner (uncredited). **Cam:** Arthur J. Ornitz. **Cast:** Jason Robards, Jr., Barry Gordon, Martin Balsam, Barbara Harris, William Daniels, Gene Saks. Murray Burns is the former writer of a children's show who tries to escape the conformities of society while he serves as the guardian to his nephew, the 12-year-old Nick. The New York school system's child welfare department visits to see if Nick is being cared for properly. Jason Robards, Jr. and Barry Gordon originated Murray and Nick on Broadway in Gardner's first great stage success, which was also directed by Coe. The snappy material overcomes the limitations of essentially a sitcom-style, one-room apartment set and Robards delivers one of his best performances as Murray. The film was nominated for four Academy Awards, including Best Picture and Screenplay. Balsam won for his performance as Murray's stuffy brother, Arnold.

• "A Thousand Clowns *tells its audience what it craves to hear—that every man, woman and child is a treasure-trove awaiting discovery."* (Newsweek)

• "*One of the most surprising box-office successes...laid some claims to being about nonconformity, and it, too, went more and more out of control, becoming redundant and embarrassing and gross that same they-don't-know-what-they're-doing way. It [took] its hero...only to romantic crackpotism—harmless American nonconformity. The hero's idea of freedom was to wander in Central Park with a kid and make TV-style jokes about TV before going back to do it for money. Basically, it was about as nonconformist as Mom's apple pie, and it even fudged on that much, by giving the Madison Avenue spokesman the audience-pulling speech...*" (Pauline Kael, Kiss Kiss Bang Bang)

Michael V. Gazzo

Michael Vincente Gazzo
Born: 1923, Hillside, NJ. **Died:** 1995.

A bartender's son trained at the Actors Studio, Michael V. Gazzo eventually realized fame when he received an Academy Award nomination as Best Supporting Actor playing mobster Frankie DiPentangeli in Francis Ford Coppola's *The Godfather Part II* (1974). Gazzo subsequently played character roles on TV and in *Black Sunday* (1977), *King of the Gypsies* (1979), *Alligator* (1980), *Fear City* (1984), *Cookie* (1989), and other films. *A Hatful of Rain* was his one great success as a writer.

A Hatful of Rain concerns the Pope family's travails, centering on Johnny Pope's heroin addiction at a time when increased narcotics trafficking was a new issue in American urban culture. The 1955 play starred Ben Gazzara as the addict, Anthony Franciosa as his beer-guzzling brother, Polo, and Shelley Winters as Johnny's wife, Celia. It was hard-hitting for its day, with concentrations on Polo's attempts to help Johnny, Polo's lust for Celia, her sorrows, and the two boys' father's inability to handle the matter.

A Hatful of Rain (1957, 20th Century-Fox, 109m/bw) ☆☆☆☆½ **Sc:** Michael V. Gazzo, Alfred Hayes. **D:** Fred Zinnemann. **P:** Buddy Adler. **Cam:** Joe MacDonald. **Cast:** Don Murray, Eva Marie Saint, Anthony Franciosa, Lloyd Nolan, Henry Silva, William Hickey, Gerald S. O'Loughlin, Art Fleming, Tom Ahearn, Michael Vale, Gordon B. Clark, Norman Willis, Jason Johnson, Rex Lease, Ralph Montgomery. The film received an Oscar nomination for Best Actor (Franciosa, repeating his stage role).

- *"Significantly, Mr. Gazzo and Alfred Hayes...have played down the more spectacular aspects of personal enslavement to narcotics—the fearful spasms...the way the stuff is got into the blood. Obviously, they and Mr. Zinnemann have calculated that these are the things of which sensational melodramas, not straight and thoughtful tragedies, are made...a tremendously taut and true description of human agony and shame, of solicitude and frustration and the piteousness of tangled love. Though Don Murray as the addict is most impressive in the versatility with which he rings a 'junkie's' baffling changes, the surest acting is done by Eva Marie Saint. Her portrait of the pregnant wife is tender, poignant, brave and haunting..."* (Bosley Crowther, The New York Times)

A Hatful of Rain (1968, ABC, 120m/c) ☆☆☆ **Tp:** Michael V. Gazzo. **D:** John Llewellyn Moxey. **P:** David Susskind. **Cast:** Michael Parks, Sandy Dennis, Peter Falk, Herschel Bernardi, John Ryan, Don Stroud, Jack Kehoe, Toni Bull. This version was resurrected after heroin addiction and trafficking became recognized as prevalent social, health, and criminal problems.

- *"11 years ago, when A Hatful of Rain was first produced on Broadway, it may have been something of a pioneer in dramatizing the proliferation of problems from an individual's addiction to narcotics. But last night's revival...was a primitive and tedious telling of a problem that in the interim has become all too prevalent and vividly substantiated in innumerable documentaries. John Moxey, the director, must have had his problems in preparing Michael V. Gazzo's adaptation. The central figures in the cast— Michael Parks, as the junkie, Peter Falk, as the brother...and Sandy Dennis...—played their roles like so many introverted wooden figures. Moreover, the dialogue moved at a snail's pace and skirted most of the deeper tragic emotional values now associated with addiction...surface theatre for two hours, not helped in the slightest, incidentally, by stereotyped portraits of pushers and family concerns that were relentlessly contrived rather than compelling."* (Jack Gould, The New York Times)

- *"...meaningful television drama...(no, nobody expected Jack Gould to like it), two hours of solid dramatic thunder...Updated to include references to hippies, LSD, the Beatles, Michael Gazzo's play remained one of those rare, unbeatable dramas in which everything works, but more important, it has never seemed more pertinent in its exploration of America's drug-addled youth..."* (Rex Reed, Big Screen, Little Screen)

Larry Gelbart

Born: February 25, 1928.

Larry Gelbart grew up the son of a Beverly Hills barber and was writing comedy for radio's *Duffy's Tavern* in his teens. He also wrote material for such diverse stars as Bob Hope, Jack Paar, Joan Davis, and Red Buttons. Gelbart joined the loony bin of Sid Caesar's *Your Show of Shows* in the 1950s and worked with such other greats as Neil Simon, Woody Allen, Carl Reiner, and Imogene Coca. Among his early plays was My L.A. His first film was Blake Edwards's *The Notorious Landlady* (1962). After the 1962 Broadway smash of *A Funny Thing Happened on the Way to the Forum*, which he wrote with Bert Shevelove, Gelbart spent nine years in England after the play opened in London.

After contributing to several spaghetti westerns, he returned to the U.S. and achieved widespread fame as a guiding force behind the TV version of M*A*S*H in the 1970s. He was nominated for Academy Awards for the screenplays of *Oh, God!* (1977) and *Tootsie* (1982). He received seven Emmy nominations, including for the TV movies *Barbarians at the Gate* (1993) and *Weapons of Mass Destruction* (1997), and won an Emmy in 1974 for M*A*S*H. His screenplays include those for *The Wrong Box* (1966), *Movie, Movie* (1978), *Neighbors* (1981), *Blame It on Rio* (1984), and *Bedazzled* (2000).

Gelbart wrote 97 episodes of M*A*S*H, one of TV's most consistently thought-provoking and funny shows. He adapted Ben Jonson's *Volpone* into a Broadway success, *Sly Fox*, directed by Arthur Penn and starring George C. Scott. The writer was the subject of the 1998 PBS special, *M*A*S*H, Tootsie & God: A Tribute to Larry Gelbart*.

A Funny Thing Happened on the Way to the Forum (1966, UA, 99m/c, **VHS/DVD**) ☆☆☆ **Sc:** Melvin Frank, Michael Pertwee. **D:** Richard Lester. **P:** Melvin Frank. **Cam:** Nicolas Roeg. **Cast:** Zero Mostel, Phil Silvers, Michael Crawford, Jack Gilford, Michael Hordern, Buster Keaton, Patricia Jessel, Leon Greene, Annette Andre, Beatrix Lehmann. Gelbart wrote this bawdy Roman Empire farce with a decidedly New York Jewish flavor with Bert Shevelove and Stephen Sondheim. The smash hit ran for 962 performances beginning in 1962 and starred Zero Mostel, David Burns, John Carradine, and Jack Gilford.

• *"Richard Lester's short-term camera magic keeps cutting into and away from the comedians..., who never get a chance to develop a routine or to bring off a number. They're rushed pell-mell through this fractured version of the wonderful musical farce...We get the sense that Lester thinks it would be too banal just to let us see a dance or a pair of burlesque clowns singing a duet...He proceeds in fits and starts and leaves jokes suspended in mid-air; as if he'd forgotten what it's all for...the experience becomes one of impatience and irritation—like coitus interruptus going on forever."* (*Pauline Kael*, 5001 Nights at the Movies)

Mastergate: A Play on Words (1992, Showtime, 120m/c) ☆☆☆½ **Tp:** Larry Gelbart. **D:** Michael Engler. **P:** David Jablin. **Cast:** Richard Kiley, David Ogden Stiers, Bruno Kirby, Ed Begley, Jr., Tim Reid, Marcia Strassman, James Coburn, Burgess Meredith, Darren McGavin, Henry Jones, Ken Howard, Dennis Weaver, Pat Morita, Jerry Orbach, Buck Henry, Ron Vawter, Mark L. Taylor, Ben Stein, Louis Giambalvo, Robert Guillaume. The 1989 play *Mastergate: A Play on Words* featured an ensemble that included Wayne Knight, Tom McDermott, and Jeff Weiss at New York's Criterion Center. Gelbart's sardonic take on governmental rhetoric focuses on a Congressional investigation into the death of a CIA director during the making of an epic war film, *Tet: The Movie*, which is suspected of laundering $800 million for right-wing guerrillas in Central America. Showtime assembled a superb cast for the occasion.

• *"...accurately subtitled...As weaseling witnesses confront unctuous Congressmen, ordinary words become meaningless in a jumble of twisted platitudes*

('Ethics and morality aside, I felt I had a higher duty to obey orders') and surreal logic ('No one else was in a position not to know as much as the President didn't know') A splendid cast...offers invaluable tips on how to be steadfastly evasive and selectively honest." (John J. O'Connor, The New York Times)

Jack Gelber

Born: April 12, 1932, Chicago, IL.

Jack Gelber created a sensation with the play and film of *The Connection* (see below), which is seen as a galvanizing experience of the American alternative theatre, and a door-opener to the cultural experimentation of the 1960s. But his subsequent, greatly experimental plays enraged certain critics. His plays include *The Apple, Square in the Eye,* and *Sleep.* Gelber's novel, *On Ice,* received tepid reviews. The playwright, who was awarded Guggenheim and Rockefeller fellowships, played one of the party guests in Woody Allen's *Another Woman* (1988).

The Connection (1961, Shirley Clarke/Lewis Allen, 110m/bw, **VHS**) ☆☆½ **Sc:** Jack Gelber. **D:** Shirley Clarke. **P:** Shirley Clarke, Lewis Allen. **Cam:** Arthur J. Ornitz. **Cast:** Warren Finnerty, Jerome Raphael, Jim Anderson, Carl Lee, Roscoe Lee Browne, William Redfield, Garry Goodrow, Jackie McLean, Freddie Redd. Several drug addicted jazz musicians hang out in a New York City apartment waiting for the pusher to deliver their fixes while a documentary filmmaker records their conversations and actions. The film became noted for the censorship problems it faced because of its four-letter words. The play, which Kenneth Tynan called "the most exciting new American play that Off Broadway has produced since the war," debuted in 1959 Off Broadway at the Living Theatre.

• *"It's painfully obvious that the dialogue is dramatic writing, and this doesn't jibe too well with the conceit of the documentary's being made. And there are characters (such as a Salvation Army sister) who carry a whiff of antique dramaturgy."* (Pauline Kael, 5001 Nights at the Movies)

William Gibson

Born: November 13, 1914, New York, NY.

William Gibson's lasting achievement is *The Miracle Worker.* His other plays include *Dinny and the Witches: A Frolic on Grave Matters, A Cry of Players, John and Abigail, The Body and the Wheel, The Butterfingers Angel, Mary and Joseph, Herod the Nut,* and the *Slaughter of*

12 Hit Carols in a Pear Tree, Golda, Goodly Creatures, Handy Dandy, and *Raggedy Ann.* He converted Clifford Odets's *Golden Boy* into a 1964 musical. Gibson's novel, *The Cobweb,* written under the pseudonym of William Mass, was adapted into a 1955 movie starring Lauren Bacall and Charles Boyer.

The Miracle Worker originally debuted on CBS's *Playhouse 90* in 1957, directed by Arthur Penn, and produced by Fred Coe. Teresa Wright and Patty McCormack starred respectively as the determined tutor Annie Sullivan and the unruly blind girl, Helen Keller. Gibson, who originally conceived the adaptation of Keller's 1902 autobiography, *The Story of My Life,* as a ballet in 1953, retooled it for the TV production. He, Penn, and Wright all received Emmy nominations for their work. The storied initial TV production, set in Keller's home town of Tuscumbia, Alabama, also featured Burl Ives, Akim Tamiroff, and John Barrymore, Jr., and directly led to a 1959 Penn/Coe Broadway production, for which Anne Bancroft and Patty Duke created their signature roles.

The Miracle Worker (1962, UA, 106m/bw, **VHS/DVD**) ☆☆☆☆☆
Sc: William Gibson. **D:** Arthur Penn. **P:** Fred Coe. **Cam:** Ernesto Caparros. **Cast:** Anne Bancroft, Patty Duke, Victor Jory, Inga Swenson, Andrew Prine, Beah Richards, Kathleen Comegys, Jack Hollander, Michael Darden, Peggy Burke, Dale Ellen Bethea. The film emphasizes the physical as well as emotional efforts exercised by Sullivan in enlisting the child's senses of exuberance and wonder. The performances of Bancroft and Duke are sublime under Penn's sure touch. The film won Oscars for Best Actress (Bancroft) and Supporting Actress (Duke) and was nominated for Best Director, Screenplay, and Costumes.

- *"The absolutely tremendous and unforgettable display of physically powerful acting that Anne Bancroft and Patty Duke put on in William Gibson's stage play…is repeated by them…shown in close-ups…dump[s] the passion and violence right in your lap, the sheer rough-and-tumble of the drama becomes more dominant than it was on the stage. Indeed, one may well leave this picture with the feeling that the triumph achieved by Annie Sullivan with the child Helen Keller…was more a matter of muscle over sinew than of a strong mind over a raw, young, uncurbed will…Mr. Penn…directed with great vigor…"* (Bosley Crowther, The New York Times)

- *"Using very long takes, Penn achieved an audience involvement in the confrontation of emotional teacher and wild child that is physically and morally draining. The sentimentality that lies in wait is avoided with the insistence that Annie and Helen are stubborn, private creatures, the one with a message of civilization, the other a savage. And it is crucial to Penn's development that Helen's education is not just deeply moving when it succeeds, but also aware of a natural solitariness that has been lost. Education is vindi-*

cated, but not whitewashed, because we see how far Annie teaches to soothe her own emotional wounds...Penn's romanticism is clear in his treatment of Helen as a noble savage restrained by culture." (David Thomson, A Biographical Dictionary of Film)

The Miracle Worker (1979, NBC, 98m/c, **VHS**) ☆☆☆½ **Tp:** William Gibson. **D:** Paul Aaron. **P:** Fred Coe. **Cast:** Patty Duke Astin, Melissa Gilbert, Diana Muldaur, Charles Siebert, Anne Seymour, Stanley Wells, Hilda Haynes. Astin, who had played Hellen Keller on Broadway and the above movie, took on the role of Annie Sullivan that Anne Bancroft played opposite her night after night. This was the final show supervised by the legendary Coe, who died during the production.

• *"...an excellent new production of the famous play...If the young Melissa does not quite achieve the emotional fervor of the young Patty Duke, the older Patty Astin plays Annie Sullivan...to a passionate turn — she is absolutely splendid...Exceedingly well made under the direction of Paul Aaron." (Cecil Smith, Los Angeles Times)*

• *"[The only point] was to give Patty Duke Astin a chance on the other side of the food...careless casting...William Gibson's play...remains, even when not perfectly done, a nearly perfect joy, one of the most assuredly affirmative dramatic works to come out of the optimistic 1950s." (Tom Shales, Washington Post)*

The Miracle Worker (2000, ABC, 90m/c, **VHS/DVD**) ☆☆½ **Tp:** Monte Merrick. **D:** Nadia Tass. **P:** Suzy Beugen-Bishop. **Cast:** Alison Elliott, Hallie Kate Eisenberg, David Strathairn, Lucas Black, Kate Greenhouse, Stuart Arnott, Damir Andrei, Neville Edwards, Patricia Gage. The eight-year-old Eisenberg had become iconic as the face of Pepsi on commercial TV.

• *"...the biggest obstacle for Helen the character to overcome is the casting of Hallie Kate Eisenberg...It isn't that Miss Eisenberg does a bad job. She is professional throughout and at moments quite moving. But she isn't powerful enough to erase the memory of her familiar guise as the cute huckster of a less-than-nutritional drink. She also can't erase the memory of her predecessor, Patty Duke...While Miss Eisenberg brings intelligence and an appealing fragility to the part, Ms. Duke brought to life the animal terror of a bright child trapped behind a wall of sensory deprivation. Miss Eisenberg conveys the idea of Helen's pain and fury, but Ms. Duke made you feel it." (Julie Salamon, The New York Times)*

Monday After the Miracle (1998, CBS, 120m/c) ☆☆½ **Tp:** Deena Goldstone. **D:** Daniel Petrie. **P:** Vanessa Greene. **Cast:** Roma Downey, Moira Kelly, Christina Pickles, Mike Doyle, Tom Bower, Bill Campbell, Peggy Freisen, Jennifer Mays, Timothy Graham, David Rees Snell, Glenn Q. Pierce. The bond between teacher Annie Sullivan and the adult Helen Keller is explored in this sequel play, set during the time the latter became a national celebrity and toured on the vaudeville stage. The play was first produced in Charleston, South Carolina, then at Broadway's Eugene O'Neill Theatre in 1982. This movie shouldn't be confused with *Helen Keller, the Miracle Continues* (1984) starring Mare Winningham as Keller and Blythe Danner as Sullivan and adapted by John McGreevey from Joseph P. Lash's book, *Helen and Teacher*.

- *"If Helen Keller were alive today, she would probably have her own daytime talk show. That is one of the messages of* Monday After the Miracle...*This is a grossly sentimental movie posing as irreverent. The real miracle in Keller's life, apparently, was that love never turned to duty for Annie Sullivan. This one-layered film never gets beyond the surface of that phenomenon, but at least it makes the point."* (Anita Gates, The New York Times)

Two for the Seesaw (1962, UA, 120m/bw, **VHS**) ☆☆½ **Sc:** Isobel Lennart. **D:** Robert Wise. **P:** Walter Mirisch. **Cam:** Ted McCord. **Cast:** Robert Mitchum, Shirley MacLaine, Edmon Ryan, Elisabeth Fraser, Eddie Firestone, Billy Gray, Vic Lundin, Shirley Cytron, Virginia Whitmore. The play concerned a Nebraska lawyer who's estranged from his wife and meets and romances a bohemian free-spirit in Greenwich Village. The 1958 Broadway version starred Henry Fonda and Anne Bancroft at the Booth Theatre. The Mitchum/MacLaine alliance for the movie started one of the more notable Hollywood extramarital affairs, but this stodgy film just doesn't have the magic that the stage version had, and many critics blamed Mitchum. The film was nominated for Oscars for its cinematography and the song "Second Chance."

- *"Mitchum—plump, hard-boiled and looking more disbarred than domestically harried—is altogether out of place. Indeed, the perfection of the miscasting prompts one to speculate on how wonderful Miss MacLaine might have been as a sensitive girl from Omaha and how wonderful Mr. Mitchum would have been as a tough guy from the Bronx."* (Brendan Gill, The New Yorker)

Frank D. Gilroy

Frank Daniel Gilroy
Born: October 13, 1925, The Bronx NY.
Pulitzer Prize-winning play: *The Subject Was Roses* (1964)

Gilroy, educated at Darmouth and the Yale Drama School, became a prolific writer of early television, particularly for the series *Studio One*, *The Rifleman*, *The United States Steel Hour*, and *The Dick Powell Theater*.

He later became a director of a series of eclectic movies that he also wrote, from the Shirley MacLaine indictment of the ills of New York, *Desperate Characters* (1971), to the Charles Bronson western, *From Noon Till Three* (1976), to the jazz-band sleeper *The Gig* (1985). His first stage success was the Off Broadway *Who'll Save the Plowboy?* (1962). He conceived the 1960s ABC series *Burke's Law* starring Gene Barry. Gilroy's 1993 autobiography was entitled *I Wake Up Screening!*

The Only Game in Town (1969, 20th Century-Fox, 113m/c) ☆☆ **Sc:** Frank D. Gilroy. **D:** George Stevens. **P:** Fred Kohlmar. **Cam:** Henri Decae. **Cast:** Elizabeth Taylor, Warren Beatty, Hank Henry, Charles Braswell. A musician deep into the gambling habit and a chorus girl hook up in Las Vegas in this rambling version of Gilroy's 1968 play, which starred Tammy Grimes, Barry Nelson and Leo Genn and was directed by Nelson. For some reason, this Vegas movie was shot in Paris. It's stunning in its wrongheaded misallocation of the two charismatic icons' talents, and Taylor is simply too old to play a chorus girl.

- *"To paraphrase Groucho's 'Either this man is dead or my watch has stopped,' either Frank D. Gilroy...has a barely visible talent or I have a blind spot. His script...has the wrong kind of simplicity, and his attempts at sprightly badinage have that leaden jocularity...George Stevens's attentiveness to the actors might have shown to some advantage if the script weren't so transparent; there's nothing behind the dialogue, no sense of the texture of peoples' lives. It's a movie that never should have been made...long sequences of...blinding banality..."* (Pauline Kael, Deeper Into Movies)
- *"...neither [Taylor] nor 20th Century-Fox nor George Stevens nor anyone else should expect anyone who hasn't been permanently brain damaged to believe for one minute that she could be a dancer in a chorus line!"* (Rex Reed, Holiday)

The Subject Was Roses (1968, MGM, 107m/c, **VHS**) ☆☆☆☆ **Sc:** Frank D. Gilroy. **D:** Ulu Grosbard. **Cam:** Jack Priestley. **P:** Edgar Lansbury. **Cast:** Patricia Neal, Martin Sheen, Jack Albertson, Don Saxon, Eliane Williams, Grant Gordon. Gilroy's first Broadway success won the Pulitzer Prize and became a showcase for Neal and Albertson as the bickering Irish-American parents of a returning World War II veteran to the Bronx, played by Sheen in his second film. Both he and Alberston were recreating their Broadway roles and the picture returned Neal to the screen after her stroke. Grosbard's first film, it's stagy for sure, but the three assured, superb performances carry the production. Albertson won the Academy Award for Best Supporting Actor and Neal was nominated for Best Actress.

- *"This seemingly small family portrait achieves its universals in the gesture, the stance, the unspoken word; this is an inarticulate family that loves but can voice only its jealousies, its suspicions and its resentments...the crowning glory of the screen version is Patricia Neal's portrait of the frigid wife and overpos-sessive mother...When this trio of fine actors is trapped in the cluttered con-fines of their Bronx apartment, the screen comes to life with all the 'small'— and soul-searching—truths of human drama, and the movie attains classic stature." (Judith Crist, Judith Crist's TV Guide to the Movies)*

Susan Glaspell
Born: July 1, 1882, Davenport, IA. **Died:** 1948.
Pulitzer Prize-winning play: *Alison's House* (1930)

Susan Glaspell was a premiere satirist of the American stage after the turn of the 20th century—her *Suppressed Desires* (1914) skewered psy-choanalysis. She and her husband, George Cram Cook, were founders and administrators of both the Provincetown Players and the Play-wrights' Theatre. Glaspell's early short plays, such as *Trifles* (1916), often dealt realistically with women characters at a time when the stage treated them mostly as side characters. Glaspell's other major plays in-clude *Bernice* (1919), *The Inheritors* (1921), and *The Verge* (1921). Her novels include *The Glory of the Conquered* (1909), *Fidelity* (1915), *The Morning Is Near Us* (1940), and *Judd Rankin's Daughter* (1945).

Alison's House, Glaspell's Pulitzer Prize-winning play, was about the ef-fects of a deceased prominent poet's life on her surviving family, and sup-posedly was inspired by the life of Emily Dickinson. It debuted in 1930 starring Eva Le Gallienne, Alma Kruger, and Howard da Silva. It be-came a postwar TV mainstay on *Kraft Television Theatre* in 1948; on *The Play's the Thing* in 1950 with Flora Campbell, John Merivale, and Regi-nald Mason; *The Pulitzer Prize Playhouse* in 1951 with Madge Evans, Otto Kruger, and Patricia Quinn O'Hara; *The Pulitzer Prize Playhouse* in 1952 with Ruth Chatterton and Otto Kruger; and *Matinee Theatre* in 1956 with an adaptation by Richard McCracken.

Ruth Goetz & Augustus Goetz
Ruth:
Born: January 11, 1908, Phildelphia, PA. **Died:** 2001.
Augustus:
Born: c. 1901. **Died:** 1957

The Heiress was adapted by the Goetzes from the Henry James novel, *Washington Square*, about Catherine Sloper, a New York heiress in 1850 who is forbidden by her wealthy but embittered father from marrying a young man who appears to only be after the family fortune. The 1947 play, directed by Jed Harris, starred Wendy Hiller, Basil Rathbone, and Peter Cookson. In a late-1940s London production, John Gielgud directed Ralph Richardson as the controlling Dr. Sloper.

The Heiress (1949, Paramount, 115m/bw, **VHS**) ☆☆☆☆ **Sc:** Ruth Goetz, Augustus Goetz. **D/P:** William Wyler. **Cam:** Leo Tover. **Cast:** Olivia De Havilland, Montgomery Clift, Ralph Richardson, Miriam Hopkins, Vanessa Brown, Mona Freeman, Ray Collins, Betty Linley, Selena Royle, Paul Lees, Harry Antrim, Russ Conway, David Thursby. This immaculate Wyler version contains superb performances from all the principals and he and Tovar opened up the play into a cinematic jewel. The film won Oscars for Best Actress (De Havilland), Score (Aaron Copland), Art Direction, and Costumes, and was nominated for Best Picture and Director.

• *"Mr. Wyler has taken this drama, which is essentially of the drawing room and particularly of an era of stilted manners and rigid attitudes, and has made it into a motion picture that crackles with allusive life and fire in its tender and agonized telling of an extraordinary characterful tale."* (Bosley Crowther, The New York Times)

The Heiress (1961, CBS Special, 60m/c) *Family Classics* **Tp:** Jacqueline Babbin, Audrey Gellen. **D:** Marc Daniels. **P:** David Susskind. **Host:** Joan Fontaine. **Cast:** Julie Harris, Barry Morse, Farley Granger, Murial Kirkland, Barbara Robins, Suzanne Stores, David O'Brien, Mary Van Fleet.

James A. Goldman

Born: June 30, 1927, Chicago, IL. **Died:** 1998.

James Goldman's career was launched in 1961 when *Blood, Sweat and Stanley Poole*, written with his younger brother, William Goldman, was produced on Broadway. The brothers co-wrote the 1962 musical *A Family Affair*. James also wrote the book that inspired Stephen Sondheim's *Follies*, which debuted in 1971.

The Goldman brothers eventually became successful screenwriters. James won an Academy Award for the adaptation of his play, *The Lion in Winter* (1968, below), and William alternated between adapting his own novels (*Soldier in the Rain*, *Marathon Man*, *The Princess Bride*) and doing other screenplays (including Oscar winners *Butch Cassidy and the Sundance Kid*, 1969, and *All the President's Men*, 1976). James's other screenplays include those for *Nicholas and Alexandra* (1971), *Robin and Marian* (1976), and *White Nights* (1985); and his TV reworkings of classics include *Oliver Twist* (1982), *Anna Karenina* (1985), and *Anastasia: The Mystery of Anna* (1986).

The Lion in Winter (1968, Avco Embassy, 134m/c, **VHS**) ☆☆☆☆½
Sc: James Goldman. **D:** Anthony Harvey. **P:** Martin Poll. **Cam:** Douglas Slocombe. **Cast:** Katharine Hepburn, Peter O'Toole, Anthony Hopkins, Jane Merrow, John Castle, Timothy Dalton, Nigel Terry. Goldman's 1966 play starred Robert Preston and Rosemary Harris on Broadway as King Henry II and Eleanor of Acquitaine, engaging in a 12th century marital battle royale of epic proportions during the Christmas season while a variety of family members weigh in on the crown's succession. A veritable masterpiece, it won Oscars for Best Actress (Hepburn, her third of four), Screenplay, and Musical Score (John Barry). It was also nominated for Best Picture, Actor (O'Toole), Director, and Costumes.

- *"Miss Hepburn certainly crowns her career as Eleanor, triumphant in her creation of a complete and womanly queen, a vulture mother who sees her sons too clearly, an aging beauty who can look her image in the eye, a sophisticate whose shrewdness is matched only by her humor."* (Judith Crist, New York)

- *"...the kind of play to delight Walter Kerr: vaguely literate, somewhat historical yet saucily anachronistic, and as stuffed with suburbanly suburbane epigrams as a Victorian sofa with horsehair...presented as TV domestic comedy, dilutedly Freudian and Shavian, and concentratedly middle-class Jewish. The film version, from Goldman's own screenplay, sticks closely to the original and suffocatingly in our craw."* (John Simon, The New Leader)

- *"James Goldman wrote the script...and if it's talky, the talk is interesting and character-revealing...The dialogue, often poetic in its choice of words and imagery, is an engaging mixture of medieval and modern. James Goldman is not writing a factual movie about the Plantagenets, but an interpretation in which he successfully combines their language and ours."* (Philip T. Hartung, Commonweal)

They Might Be Giants (1971, Universal, 88m/c, **VHS/DVD**) ☆☆☆☆
Sc: James Goldman. **D:** Anthony Harvey. **P:** Paul Newman, John Foreman. **Cam:** Victor J. Kemper. **Cast:** George C. Scott, Joanne Woodward, Jack Gilford, Lester Rawlins, Kitty Wina, M. Emmet Walsh, Al Lewis, Rue McClanahan, F. Murray Abraham, Paul Benedict, Theresa Merritt. After their success with *The Lion in Winter*, Goldman and Harvey reteamed, this time with the Newmans. Scott played a New York City judge and widower who believes he's Sherlock Holmes, and Woodward is a psychiatrist named Watson who treats him. The wrinkle is that the judge's brother wants him put away in a looney bin so the family fortune can be his. Alternately funny and touching, this odd film was a superbly written and acted box-office failure—Scott's followup to his Oscar-winning *Patton* (1970).

- *"The failure of* Giants *is a mystery, if only because of the compassion and skill with which it portrays a modern archetype, the decent man driven to delusion. For Scott, this character is directly in line with* The Hospital *and, while neither film smacks of a director, they both glow with his own personality." (David Thomson,* A Biographical Dictionary of Film)

Frances Goodrich & Albert Hackett

Goodrich:
Born: December 21, 1890, Belleville, NJ. **Died:** 1984.

Hackett:
Born: February 16, 1900, New York, NY. **Died:** 1995.

Pulitzer Prize-winning play: *The Diary of Anne Frank* (1955)

One of the most successful screenwriting teams of the mid-century, Frances Goodrich and Albert Hackett haven't had the profile among writers that other pen teams have enjoyed. Hackett started in films as an actor and appeared on screen as late as 1930 in *Whoopee!* The following year, the husband-and-wife team's first credited film as writers, *Up Pops the Devil*, was released. They became highly-prized studio scribes via a succession of hits beginning with transcendent *The Thin Man* (1934), starring William Powell and Myrna Loy as the wisecracking, cocktail-imbibing sleuthing couple, Nick and Nora Charles, who first appeared in Dashiell Hammett's stories.

From there Goodrich and Hackett produced hits in succession with films about romance and domesticity, musicals and comedies, adaptations and originals: *Naughty Marietta* (1935), *Ah, Wilderness!* (1935), *Rose-Marie* (1936), *After the Thin Man* (1936), *Another Thin Man* (1939), *The Hitler Gang* (1944), and *The Virginian* (1946). Their *It's a Wonderful Life* (1946) wasn't what postwar Americans wanted to see from James Stewart, but the film has since become an annual yuletide rite. The hits kept rolling: the Judy Garland musicals *The Pirate* (1948) and *Easter Parade* (1948); the paeans to Spencer Tracy's patriarchal grimaces *Father of the Bride* (1950) and *Father's Little Dividend* (1951); the exuberant *Seven Brides for Seven Brothers* (1954), and *Gaby* (1956) with Leslie Caron.

As Donald W. McCaffrey wrote, "Goodrich and Hackett still remain the most eclectic screenwriters that Hollywood has produced. Their scope has not yet been matched by any other team." Hackett and Goodrich's one main play was *The Diary of Anne Frank*, which they were asked to rewrite from the original adaptation of *The Diary of a Young Girl* (see below).

The Diary of Anne Frank starred Susan Strasberg on Broadway in 1955, supported by Joseph Schildkraut, Jack Gilford, and Lou Jacobi. Via reprintings of the original diary, the play, the subsequent movie, and several TV remakes, the story of a Jewish family hiding from Nazis in an Amsterdam attic during World War II became a widely recognized and uncommonly poignant story of everyday courage in the face of a horrific reality. Anne Frank began the diary on July 6, 1942, and two years later, the Franks were discovered and sent to concentration camps. Only the father, Otto Frank, survived. He died in 1979 in Switzerland at the age of 91. Two other TV productions, a 1987 British production called *The Diary of Anne Frank* and a 2001 American TV movie, *Anne Frank* (2001), starring Ben Kingsley as Otto Frank, were not based on the play.

The Diary of Anne Frank (1959, 20th Century-Fox, 180m/bw, **VHS**) ☆☆☆½ **Sc:** Frances Goodrich, Albert Hackett. **D/P:** George Stevens. **Cam:** William C. Mellor. **Cast:** Millie Perkins, Joseph Schildkraut, Shelley Winters, Richard Beymer, Diane Baker, Ed Wynn, Lou Jacobi, Gusti Huber, Douglas Spencer, Dodie Heath. This quietly modulated Stevens production, which caught the inherent beauty and severe poignancy of the tragic story, won Oscars for Best Supporting Actress (Winters), Cinematography, and Art Direction/Set Decoration. It was also nominated for Best Picture, Director, Supporting Actor (Wynn), Score (Alfred Newman), and Costumes.

- "It merely plods through the routines and small events of the Frank and van Daan families hidden away in at the top of the warehouse in Amsterdam...The use of CinemaScope, albeit in black and white, contradicts the fundamental feeling of claustrophobia and intimacy, and a more serious error was the casting of Millie Perkins as Anne. This ex-model was chosen, sensibly, so as not to associate Anne with a known actress, but Miss Perkins has a jarring accent (even to American ears) and the gamine looks fashionable in 1959. The direction is expectedly careful and tasteful, but again lacking in feeling: a book which haunts all who have read it has become a forgettable film." (David Shipman, The Story of Cinema)

- "As a rule, of course, a play written initially for the stage is visually too confined to be transferred satisfactorily to the free-ranging medium of cinema unless a good deal of adaptation goes on, opening it out. In certain cases this might deprive the work of its very essence, and the only viable thing to do is to let well alone, as George Stevens demonstrated to the irritation of some of his admirers in his film of The Diary of Anne Frank..." (Gordon Gow, Hollywood in the Fifties)

The Diary of Anne Frank (1967, ABC, 124m/c) ☆☆☆½ **Tp:** James Lee. **D:** Alex Segal. **P:** David Susskind. **Cast:** Diana Davila, Max von Sydow, Lilli Palmer, Viveca Lindfors, Theodore Bikel, Marisa Pavan, Donald Pleasance, Suzanne Grossman, Peter Bieger, Wolfgang Zilzer. Lee's teleplay stuck closely to the circumstances of the original play.

- "...a powerful and deeply moving production...caught all the marvelously youthful, chimerical aspects of Anne's fine spirit—her gaity, peevishness, imagination, coquetry and bravery—and at the same time disclosed the girl struggling so tempestuously to grow into womanhood. It would be difficult to imagine a better choice than Diana Davila for the title role...enchanting...heartrending in its poignancy..." (George Gent, The New York Times)

The Diary of Anne Frank (1980, NBC, 120m/c) ☆☆☆½ **Tp:** Frances Goodrich, Albert Hackett. **D:** Boris Sagal. **P:** Arthur Lewis. **Cast:** Melissa Gilbert, Maximilian Schell, Joan Plowright, James Coco, Doris Roberts, Clive Reville, Scott Jacoby, Melora Marshall, Erik Holland, Anne Wyndham. Gilbert, the star of Little House on the Prairie, was instrumental in bringing this classic story back to TV, basing it line for line on the original play.

- "...continues to survive with remarkable strength...manages to convey with power the horror of the Nazi holocaust...the play captures the initial blossomings of a sensitive and beautiful young woman doomed for the simple fact that she was a Jew. The monstrousness of her inevitable murder is always palpable, gradually overwhelming. This television production sticks closely to the original script...Miss Gilbert is a touch too robust in the role...Miss Gilbert, though, captures the essential spirit of the youth. The rest of the cast is just about perfect." (John J. O'Connor, The New York Times)

Ruth Gordon

Ruth Gordon Jones
Born: October 30, 1896, Wollaston (Quincy), MA. **Died:** 1985.

Ruth Gordon shared Academy Award nominations with her second husband, Garson Kanin, for the screenplays of A Double Life (1947), which won Ronald Colman an Oscar, Adam's Rib (1949), and Pat and Mike (1952)—all three directed by George Cukor.

Known mostly as actress, Gordon made her debut on Broadway in Peter Pan (1915) and had her first starring role in Booth Tarkington's Seventeen (1918). She became a respected actress after the success of Ethan Frome (1936). As an actress, her films include Abe Lincoln in Illinois (1940), Action in the North Atlantic (1943), Inside Daisy Clover (1966), Harold and Maude (1971), and Every Which Way But Loose (1978). She won an Oscar for Best Supporting Actress for her portrayal of a Manhattan witch in Rosemary's Baby (1968).

Years Ago, Gordon's autobiographical play about her early life in the theatre, had its initial run in 1946 in Boston in a production starring Patricia Kirkland as Ruth Gordon Jones, Fredric March, and Florence Eldridge.

The Actress (1953, MGM, 91m/bw) ☆☆☆ **Sc:** Ruth Gordon. **D:** George Cukor. **P:** Lawrence Weingarten. **Cam:** Harold Rosson. **Cast:** Jean Simmons, Spencer Tracy, Teresa Wright, Anthony Perkins, Ian Wolfe, Mary Wickes, Jackie Coogan, Kay Williams, Norma Jean Nilsson, Dawn Bender. Considering the director and the stars assembled for this film—a nostalgia piece that was equal parts family squabbles, the stage life and coming-of-age issues—it wasn't well received by the public. This was the film debut of Perkins, the son of longtime stage star Osgood Perkins.

• *"...a pleasantly modest though disappointing picture by...Cukor. Jean Simmons plays the title role with grace, but the author has neglected to provide indications of talent and drive in the character; this girl seems too nice, too ordinary—she could never grow up to be that tough, indefatigable trouper Ruth Gordon...Tracy overdoes it, but he shows some energy, and the film is sadly short of it."* (Pauline Kael, 5001 Nights at the Movies)

Years Ago (1960, CBS, 90m/c) *DuPont Show of the Month* ☆☆½ **Tp:** Jacqueline Babbin, Audrey Gellen. **D:** Alex Segal. **P:** David Susskind. **Cast:** Robert Preston, Sandra Church, Peggy Conklin. The braintrust behind the camera—Segal, Susskind, Babbin, and Geller—were among the most important and ubiquitous adapters of plays to TV in the 20th century.

• *"Years ago, Years Ago was a reasonably fresh, reasonably touching experience. But now, in this heyday of the lovable TV family, it's little more than a king-sized Father Knows Best. Audiences are familiar to the point of exasperation with such average American domestic shenanigans as those that occur in Ruth Gordon's autobiographical 1946 play...the character clichés and the corn...all comes through virtually intact...Robert Preston displayed style and vigor. Sandra Church exhibited the proper starry-eyed exuberance as the 16-year-old Miss Gordon."* (Variety)

Over 21 starred Gordon on Broadway in 1944 for 221 performances at the Music Box Theatre. She played a Dorothy Parker-like wit and screenwriter who accompanies her liberal editor husband to officers' training camp during World War II. The play was staged by George S. Kaufman.

Over Twenty-One (1945, Columbia, 102m/bw) ☆☆½ **Sc/P:** Sidney Buchman. **D:** Charles Vidor. **Cam:** Rudolph Mate. **Cast:** Irene Dunne, Alexander Knox, Charles Coburn, Jeff Donnell, Lee Patrick, Phil Brown, Cora Witherspoon. Columbia paid $350,000 for the screen rights to the play, which was exorbitant by all standards of the era. Vidor and Columbia Pictures head Harry Cohn told Dunne to produce a carbon copy of Gordon's stage role, but the role didn't serve the star at all.

• *"Unfortunately, this heroine...is extremely articulate but not nearly as funny as she's meant to be; many of the jokes turn on the mad, charming inconsequence of the feminine mind, and the whole comedy is too obviously set up, and rather self-congratulatory. With Alexander Knox, effective as the husband until he reads us an editorial sermon on the brotherhood of man..." (Pauline Kael, 5,001 Nights at the Movies)*

Over Twenty-One aired in 1950 on *The Prudential Family Playhouse* starring Ruth Gordon and Paul Stewart. This is the only screen production in which Gordon appears in one of her plays.

Ed Graczyk

Ed Graczyk's plays include *Weeds, As Simple as Day Old Bread, Rainbow Dancing, S'Wonderful* with Stephen Hildebrand, *A Murder of Crows, Love, Janis* about Janis Joplin, and *My Time Ain't Long* written for a one-man show by Keith Carradine on the life of singer Jimmie Rodgers. Graczyk's children's plays include *Due to a Lack of Interest, Tomorrow Has Been Postponed.* He has worked with the Hartford Stage Company, Honolulu Community Theatre, and Erie Playhouse.

Come Back to the 5 & Dime, Jimmy Dean, Jimmy Dean (1982, Viacom, 110m/c, **VHS**) ☆☆☆½ **Sc:** Ed Graczyk. **D:** Robert Altman. **P:** Scott Bushnell. **Cam:** Pierre Mignot. **Cast:** Sandy Dennis, Cher, Karen Black, Kathy Bates, Sudie Bond, Marta Heflin, Mark Patton. Five women convene at a broken-down Texas drugstore for a 20-year reunion of the death of James Dean in 1975. The tour-de-force performances and the way Altman and Mignot move the camera to capture personality and emotion make this one of the most successful filmed plays of the 1980s. It was also one of Altman's "comeback" films and showcased Cher as an actress of substance. Graczyk's play debuted in 1982 at New York's Martin Beck Theatre with the above cast. The inspiration for the play came from the five years that Graczyk spent at the Midland Community Playhouse in Texas, near Marfa, the site of the ranch house built for George Stevens's film of Edna Ferber's *Giant* (1956), Dean's last film.

- *"Ed Graczyk's play itself is a humdrum if highly enjoyable affair, gradually proceeding from its comic observations about the way the women aren't quite friends anymore to a serious consideration of shattered dreams and saddened lives, all exposed in a gripping and familiar series of intimate revelations. But beyond the excellent performances and Altman's evident sympathy for his garrulous gathering of beautiful losers, what makes the film is the way he uses both the camera and the wall mirror (which periodically reflects us back to 1955) to explore and open up his single, dime-store set and the cracks in the masks of his deluded/deluding characters. Stunning stuff." (Geoff Andrew, Time Out)*

Spalding Gray

Born: June 5, 1941, Barrington, RI.

Monologist, actor, and novelist Spalding Gray co-founded the experimental theatrical company the Wooster Group in 1977. He performed his first major autobiographical monologue, *Sex and Death*, about life up to the age of 14, throughout the U.S. and Europe during the 1980s. His work Off Broadway and in films helped him land a small role in Roland Joffe's *The Killing Fields* (1984), an experience which became the basis of another monologue, *Swimming to Cambodia* (1987), a four-hour harrangue cut to 80 minutes for Jonathan Demme's film.

Monster in a Box (1991) concerned Gray's attempts to complete his epic novel, *Impossible Vacation*, published the following year. A third feature, the Steven Soderbergh-helmed *Gray's Anatomy*, followed in 1996. The audio edition of his monologue *It's a Slippery Slope* appeared two years later. Films in which Gray appeared as a character actor include *True Stories* (1986), *King of the Hill* (1993), *The Paper* (1994), *Beyond Rangoon* (1995), *Drunks* (1995), and *Kate & Leopold* (2001).

Gray's Anatomy (1996, Northern Arts, 80m/c, **VHS/DVD**) ☆☆☆ **Sc:** Spalding Gray. **D:** Steven Soderbergh. **P:** Jon Hardy. **Cam:** Elliot Davis. **Cast:** Spalding Gray, Buddy Carr, Alyne Hargroder, Alvin Henry, Mike McLaughlin, Kirk A. Patrick, Jr., Melissa Robertson, Chris Simms, Tommy Staub, Gerry Urso, Fat L. Woo. In middle age, Gray claims to have reached "the Bermuda Triangle of health," as various portions of his body have begun to break down, particularly an eye malady he calls "macular pucker." He discusses remedies from American Indian sweat lodges to nutritionists.

- "A *Spalding Gray film means equal parts humor and dread, digressions and absurdity, meditation and mania, personal confession and Yankee reserve. Add a desk, a mike and a glass of water, and you've got the basic formula. But there's at least as much different as there is the same about* Gray's Anatomy...*the most cinematic [Gray film]. This time, Steven Soderbergh takes Gray (who appeared in his little-appreciated gem* King of the Hill) *places he's never been on screen. Motion, color and brazen stylizing enhance what is at times a genuinely hysterical work on rationalized terror.*" (John Anderson, Los Angeles Times)

Monster in a Box (1991, Fine Line, 87m/c, **VHS**) ☆☆ **Sc:** Spalding Gray. **D:** Nick Broomfield. **P:** Jon Blair, Renee Shafransky. **Cam:** Michael Coulter. **Cast:** Spalding Gray. The monster is a 1,600-page manuscript for a novel that Gray can't seem to finish, and has been carrying around in a box. He talks about the frustrations of writer's block.

- *"To call Spalding Gray's autobiographical monologues self-indulgent is to underscore the obvious. A better question would be: Is Gray worth indulging?...Monster in a Box takes place on a spotlighted stage with a table and a chair and not much else. Director Nick Broomfield understands how to keep a monologue visually interesting—no small feat. He modulates the jabber with cuts and camera angles keyed to the shifts in Gray's charged verbiage. The results are involving without being particularly probing; Gray's stand-up performance never really deepens, perhaps because his persona doesn't. He's transfixed by his own limpid nuttiness, and his gift for self-enclosure sometimes keeps us at a distance. He often seems furthest from us when his close-ups fill the screen."* (Peter Rainer, Los Angeles Times)

Spalding Gray's The Terrors of Pleasure (1988, PBS, 60m/c) ☆☆½ **Tp/Cast:** Spalding Gray. **D:** Thomas Schlamme. Gray talks about the freedom and choices of irresponsible youth compared with the growing responsibilities of middle age.

- *"While he awaits assessment of his literary prowess [for his first book, Impossible Vacation], the Rhode Island native also has a few physical problems to contend with. 'I chipped my tooth on a bagel chip,' he said darkly. 'I'll never eat bagel chips again.' As for that pesky retina that keeps slipping over his pupil, Gray, 48, tries to be optimistic. 'The doctor says maybe it will fix itself,' he sighed. 'Or maybe not.'... a dark, comic journey into the contemplation of responsible adulthood and (gulp) home ownership."* (Janice Arkatov, Los Angeles Times)

Swimming to Cambodia (1987, Cinecom, 87m/c, **VHS**) ☆☆☆ **Sc:** Spalding Gray. **D:** Jonathan Demme. **P:** Peter Newman, Ira Deutchman. **Cam:** Ira Brenner. **Cast:** Spalding Gray. In this stagy monologue, Gray describes his experiences as a character actor making the film *The Killing Fields* (1984), about the mass murders by Pol Pot's Khmer Rouge regime in Cambodia. Gray gives the background of the events, the process of making the movie and his own experiences in the fleshpots of Bangkok. The film's star, Sam Waterston, is seen in archival footage. Gray sits at a table with a glass of water, delivering his monologue.

- *"Because he is a good talker, and because he has something to say, this curious idea for a movie actually works...[It] is, on some level, self-agrandizement. All actors might enjoy the thought of a feature film devoted entirely to their face and their voice, but few would have the nergve to go ahead with one...None of us can directly experience more than we actually see and hear. Everything else is hearsay. All we really know, for sure, is what happened to us. There's that story about the actor hired to play the gravedigger in Hamlet. Asked what the play was about, he replied, 'It's about this gravedigger, who meets a prince...' Swimming to Cambodia is about this actor, who meets this war."* (Roger Ebert, Chicago Sun-Times)

John Guare

Born: February 5, 1938, New York, NY.

John Guare's major movie involvement was writing the screenplay for Louis Malle's *Atlantic City* (1980), which offered Burt Lancaster one of his capstone performances as a seedy numbers runner during a bleak winter at the titular seaside resort. The writer received Best Original Screenplay awards from the National Society of Film Critics and from the critics groups in Los Angeles and New York for that film and also garnered an Oscar nomination for it. Guare also collaborated with Milos Forman, Jean-Claude Carriere, and John Klein on the screenplay for *Taking Off* (1971), expatriate Czech director Forman's revue-like take on American norms, and was a producer on *Marvin's Room* (1996).

The House of Blue Leaves (1987, PBS, 113m/c) *American Playhouse* ☆☆☆½ **Tp:** John Guare. **D:** Kirk Browning, Jerry Zaks. **P:** Iris Merlis, Michael Brandman. **Cast:** Swoosie Kurtz, John Mahoney, Julie Hagerty, Christine Baranski, Ben Stiller, Richard Portnow, Ian Blackman, Debra Cole, Patricia Falkenhain, Jane Cecil, Brian Evers. This performance was taped at a live presentation of the play at New York's Plymouth Theatre, which followed its 1986 debut at the Lincoln Center Theatre, winning several Tony Awards. Artie, a zookeeper, his deranged wife Bananas, would-be adulterer Bunny, and an assortment of other characters set out on October 4, 1965 to watch the Pope's motorcade through their neighborhood.

- *"The 'live-on-tape' approach, always tricky, is remarkably effective in this instance. The brilliant stage production, directed by Jerry Zaks...has the actors talking directly to the audience...The production needs an audience to bounce off and Mr. Browning wisely retains that essential element...Perhaps the best compliment that can be paid this television version...is that it captures with remarkable accuracy the tone and spirit of the stage production. The performances of Ms. Kurtz, Ms. Baranski, Ms. Hagerty and Mr. Mahoney splendidly survive the rigors of the television close-up. In the end, viewers will appreciate fully what all the shouts of 'bravo' were about."* (John J. O'Connor, The New York Times)

Six Degrees of Separation (1993, MGM, 112m/c, **VHS**) ☆☆☆½ **Sc:** John Guare. **D:** Fred Schepisi. **P:** Arnon Milchan, Fred Schepisi. **Cam:** Ian Baker. **Cast:** Stockard Channing, Will Smith, Donald Sutherland, Mary Beth Hurt, Bruce Davison, Ian McKellan, Heather Graham, Richard Masur, Anthony Michael Hall, Eric Thal, Kitty Carlisle Hart, Osgood Perkins II, Anthony Rapp, Catherine Kellner, Brooke Hayward. Channing was nominated for an Oscar for Best Actress for her performance as a wealthy New York art dealer who, with her husband, is bamboozled by a young man who claims to be a Harvard classmate of their children. They allow him to stay the night and, the next morning, discover he isn't who he has appeared to be, causing the couple to re-evaluate their lives.

- *"Guare's theatrical imagination has always had a cinematic freewheeling-ness, with improbable montages of mood and emotion. His knockabout ardor is the perfect instrument for capturing the slapstick black comedy of New York's high-low life. He doesn't just roll with the punches, he jitterbugs and tangos and waltzes. Even if you've already seen the play, the movie refreshes the experience, which has been 'opened up' by bringing much of the action into real Manhattan locations. The opening up extends the meaning of the play by employing the city in all its spangled ritz and grubbiness as a major character. The action moves from the Upper East Side to the Rainbow Room to scruffy police precincts and the homeless dales of Central Park. You never quite catch your bearings. Watching the movie is a bewildering experience, but bewilderment is the appropriate response to what Guare and Schepisi give you. What seems to start out as a burlesque against the rich—a satire of class-consciousness—ends up mutating into something stranger and richer and more ambiguous."* (Peter Rainer, Los Angeles Times)

A.R. Gurney

Albert Ramsdell Gurney, Jr.
Born: November 1, 1930, Buffalo, NY.

A.R. Gurney's plays often explain and satirize upper- and upper-middle-class East Coast family life. As Frank Rich noted in *The New York Times*, Gurney laid claim to the same socioeconomic territory on the stage that John Cheever claimed through prose. Several Gurney plays have endured as the favorites of regional and amateur troupes, particularly *The Dining Room*, *The Cocktail Hour*, and *Love Letters*. He adapted "O Youth and Beauty" as one of a trilogy of dramatized Cheever short stories for a 1984 segment of PBS's *Great Performances* entitled *3 by Cheever*. Gurney's other plays include *Love in Buffalo*, *The Rape of Bunny Stuntz*, *The David Show*, *Scenes From an American Life*, *The Old One-Two*, *The Middle Ages*, *What I Did Last Summer*, *Sylvia*, and *Labor Day*. Gurney's novels include *The Gospel According to Joe*, *Entertaining Strangers*, and *The Snow Ball*.

The Dining Room (1984, PBS, 90m/c) *Great Performances* ☆☆☆½ **Tp:** A.R. Gurney. **D:** Allan A. Goldstein. **P:** Howard K. Grossman, John H. Williams. **Cast:** Frances Sternhagen, William H. Macy, John Shea, Remak Ramsey, Pippa Peartree, Jeanne Ruskin. The play, which was originally produced at Playwrights Horizons and ran for 18 months Off Broadway, employs six actors playing more than 50 roles to satirize and portray upper-middle-class American values around the dining table. In this TV rendition, the camera never leaves its title room as characters, played by the original stage cast, make their entrances and exits through two doorways.

- *"Occasionally, the 'action' comes uncomfortably close to resembling an exercise in acting class—here an elegant hostess, there a little girl, here an adenoidal haughtiness, there a warm brogue. For the most part, however, the cast comes through these thickets in splendid shape...Mr. Gurney's message can get a touch heavy-handed...Finally, though, the play considers its subject with a tone falling somewhere between grudging respect and genuine fondness."* (Stephen Holden, The New York Times)

Far East (2000, PBS, 87m/c) **Tp:** A.R. Gurney. **D:** Daniel J. Sullivan. **P:** Casey Childs, Jac Venza, Steven Tabakin. **Cast:** Lisa Emery, Michael Hayden, Miou, Bill Smitrovich, Jo Yang, Connor Trinneer, John Speredakos, Clark Thorell, Leslie Lyles, Jessamyn Blakeslee. The play concerns a young Navy officer and heir to a Milwaukee beer fortune in 1954. While on duty in occupied Japan, he agonizes over his family's values, which wouldn't condone his love for a beautiful Japanese woman. Conflicts erupt between West and East, duty and love, family and individuality. The play opened in 1999 at Lincoln Center's Mitzi Newhhouse Theatre.

The Golden Fleece (1969, NET, 90m/c) *NET Playhouse* **Tp:** A.R. Gurney. The play was first produced in 1968 at the Mark Taper Forum in Los Angeles, then in New York the same year.

Love Letters (1999, ABC, 85m/c) ☆☆☆ **Tp:** A.R. Gurney. **D:** Stanley Donen. **P:** Leonard Goldberg, Martin Starger. **Cast:** Steven Weber, Laura Linney, Kirsten Storms, Emily Hampshire, Chas Lawther, Patrick Galligan, Jackie Richardson, Stephen Joffe, Eve Conroy, Marcia Diamond, June Whitman, Isabella Fink, Tim Redwine. The play was first performed in New York in 1989 by Kathleen Turner and John Rubenstein, and since then hundreds of pairs of actors have performed the two-character play of revelations among upper-class New Yorkers.

- *"It was probably a mistake to turn Andy and Melissa's two-character epistolary play,* Love Letters, *into a full-fledged television movie...But there are enormously talented people at work here:...Gurney...Stanley Donen, doing his first television project at the age of 75...in less gifted hands the result could have been much worse, given the inevitable loss of impact when described events are acted out and visible, rather than revealed a sentence at a time through the written word. And for those who missed the stage production, it's worthwhile seeing the film just to get to know the play…Ms. Linney makes every facial expression enchanting."* (Anita Gates, The New York Times)

My Brother's Wife (1989, ACI, 120m/c, **VHS**) **Tp:** Percy Granger. **D:** Jack Bender. **P:** David Byron, Robert Greenwald, Philip K. Kleinbart, Paul Lussier. **Cast:** John Ritter, Mel Harris, Dakin Matthews, Lee Weaver, David Byron, Polly Bergen, Glenn Dixon, Richard Marion, Ruth C. Engel.

James Hagan
Born: c. 1888. **Died:** 1947.

A former newspaperman and actor, and a stage manager for such directors as Arthur Hopkins and Henry Miller, James Hagan wrote two stage flops — *Trimmed* and *Guns* — before *One Sunday Afternoon* became a hit at the height of the Great Depression. It was the runner-up for the Pulitzer Prize to Maxwell Anderson's *Both Your Houses*, and eventually became one of the most enduring source stories in screen entertainment history.

One Sunday Afternoon opened on Broadway in 1933 and starred the virtually unknown Lloyd Nolan as Biff Grimes, a turn-of-the-century Brooklyn dentist who believes he may have married the wrong girl while the supposed "right girl" married his so-called best friend, Barnstead.

One Sunday Afternoon (1933, Paramount, 93m/bw) ☆☆½ **Sc:** William Slavens McNutt, Grover Jones. **D:** Stephen Roberts. **P:** Louis D. Lighton. **Cam:** Victor Milner. **Cast:** Gary Cooper, Frances Fuller, Faye Wray, Neil Hamilton, Roscoe Karns, Jane Darwell, Clara Blandick, Sam Hardy, James Burtis, Harry Schultz, A.S. Byron, Jack Clifford, Johnny St. Clair. Made during the upswings in Cooper's and Wray's careers, the film showcases both stars in thoughtful performances, with Cooper giving it both his best aw-shucks stuff as well as prevailing resolve.

- *"The role of the redoubtable Biff Grimes is played in the film by Gary Cooper, whose performance, like the picture as a whole, is praiseworthy in many respects but fails to impress one with the character's aggressive personality."* (Mordaunt Hall, The New York Times)

- *"It is still pitched in stage tempo for the screen and unfolds haltingly. Its substance is delicate character humor and elusive sentimental appeal and these are qualities that are difficult to translate from footlight to celluloid."* (Variety)

The Strawberry Blonde (1941, Warner Bros., 97m/bw, **VHS**) ☆☆☆☆ **Sc:** Julius J. Epstein, Philip G. Epstein. **D:** Raoul Walsh. **P:** Jack L. Warner, Hal B. Wallis. **Cam:** James Wong Howe. **Cast:** James Cagney, Olivia De Havilland, Rita Hayworth, Alan Hale, George Tobias, Jack Carson, Una O'Connor, George Reeves, Lucille Fairbanks, Edward McNamara, Herbert Heywood, Addison Richards, James Flavin, Susan Peters, Creighton Hale, Russell Hicks, Helen Lynd, Roy Gordon, Frank Mayo. This convergence of Warner Bros. talent, with Cagney injecting his customary gusto, made this the very best film version of the play—it goes beyond the play into a cinematic gusto and originality that the original never had. Walsh liked it so much that he remade it as a musical eight years later (below).

- *"...a quite remarkable study of ambition and its absence, with outstanding performances by Cagney, Olivia De Havilland, Rita Hayworth and Jack Carson..."* (David Thomson, A Biographical Dictionary of Film)

- "The Strawberry Blonde *is a blithe, turn-of-the-century buggy ride. Cagney makes the hero a tough but obviously peachy fellow...Rita Hayworth takes the picture away from him, and dark-eyed Olivia De Havilland takes it away from both of them."* (Time)

One Sunday Afternoon (1948, Warner Bros., 90m/c) ☆☆ **Sc:** Robert L. Richards. **D:** Raoul Walsh. **P:** Jerry Wald. **Cam:** Sid Hickox. **Cast:** Dennis Morgan, Dorothy Malone, Janis Paige, Don DeFore, Ben Blue, Oscar O'Shea, Alan Hale Jr., George Neise. This musical, with its unmemorable songs and second-rate cast, goes through the motions. A premium example of what remaking the remakes really means.

- *"Raoul Walsh seems to have slackened the directorial reins this time. And the cast, with the exception of Miss Malone, who is genuinely appealing, never fully projects the flavor of the people or the period. Theirs is a lackadaisical and uninspired jaunt down memory lane...age apparently did wither and custom did stale."* (Bosley Crowther, The New York Times)

One Sunday Afternoon (1949, CBS, 60m/bw) ☆☆☆ *Ford Theatre Hour* **D:** Marc Daniels. **P:** Garth Montgomery. **Cast:** Burgess Meredith, Hume Cronyn, Francesca Bruning, Augusta Roland, Pat Harrington. The new medium, with its live format, reinvigorated the old chestnut, leading to a run of five more TV productions in a decade.

- *"Sock all the way...Meredith was fine in the Biff Grimes role, shading his characterization to the correct degree to make the character believable. Cronyn was equally outstanding as the wily Hugo Barnstead, being surely and hateful for the part."* (Variety)

One Sunday Afternoon (1954, ABC, 60m/bw) ☆☆ *Kraft Television Theatre.* **Tp:** James Hagan. **Cast:** Claudia Morgan, Gene Persson, Kenneth Nelson, Valerie Cossart, John Shellie, Frank Albertson, Aina Niemela, Jeff Harris. Hagan's teleplay took both couples back to childhood, highlighting the young actors and young love that led to the lifelong friendly-enemies relationship of both couples.

The Strawberry Blonde (1959, NBC, 60m/c) ☆☆½ **Tp:** George Baxt. **D:** William Corrigan. **P:** David Susskind. **Host:** Edgar Bergen. **Cast:**

David Wayne, Janet Blair, Eddie Bracken, Dolores Dorn-Heft, Iggie Wolfington. Pared back to accommodate songs, the play served as a basic framework for this musical.

- *"Some magnificent acting has been spent on James Hagan's slight story...The piece hasn't deserved the kind of treatment it has received, yet because of the treament the story has become rather a small-town classic. The story is incredibly mono-dimensional and unbelievable as they come. Considering the story merely as a frame on which to hang a few songs—by Wayne and Miss Blair—it was fine."* (Variety)

One Sunday Afternoon also aired in 1951 on CBS's *Prudential Playhouse* with Richard Carlson, June Lockhart, and Virginia Gilmore; in 1952 on *Broadway Television Theatre* with Jack Warden, Gloria McGhee, Mimi Kelly, and Jimmy Sheridan, and also in 1957 on NBC's *Lux Video Theatre* with Gordon MacRea, Mary Healy, Peter Lind Hayes, and Sheila MacRea.

Oliver Hailey

Born: July 7, 1932, Pampa, TX. **Died:** 1993.

Oliver Hailey wrote the film *Just You and Me, Kid* (1979), which paired George Burns and Brooke Shields. He also wrote the TV movies *Sidney Shorr: A Girl's Best Friend* (1981) with Tony Randell, *Isabel's Choice* (1981) with Jean Stapleton, and the fact-based sequel *Adam: His Song Continues* (1986) with Daniel J. Travanti and JoBeth Williams as John and Reve Walsh, who after their son was murdered, lobbied Congress to pass the Missing Children's Bill. Hailey's plays include *First One Asleep, Whistle* (1966), *Father's Day* (1971), and *I Won't Dance* (1981).

For the Use of the Hall (1975, PBS, 90m/c) *Hollywood Television Theatre* ☆☆☆ **Tp:** Oliver Hailey. **D:** Lee Grant, Rick Bennewitz. **P:** Norman Lloyd. **Cast:** Aline MacMahon, Barbara Barrie, David Hedison, George Furth, Susan Anspach, Joyce Van Patten, John Barbour. This play was originally staged at the Trinity Theatre in Providence, Rhode Island, in 1971, but was rewritten by Hailey for this presentation.

- *"We did Oliver Hailey's lively play...which I think is the kind of project which should be done. Lee Grant directed with a good cast...The play...needed new life—with revised writing, a new cast and director—in short, an advancement towards the play's realization. Rick Bennewitz called the camera shots for this production."* (Norman Lloyd, Stages: A Life in Theatre, Film and Television)

Who's Happy Now? (1975, PBS, 90m/c) *Theatre in America* ☆☆☆ **Tp:** Oliver Hailey. **D:** Gordon Davidson. **Cast:** Betty Garrett, Rue

McClanahan, Albert Salmi, John Ritter, Guy Raymond, John Fiedler, Kirby Furlong. This play was first produced at the Mark Taper Forum in Los Angeles in 1967 with Betty Garrett as one of the two stars and Off Broadway in 1969 with Rue McClanahan, both of whom reprised their roles as the two leads. This version was a Hailey rewrite of the original play into what had been envisioned as a screenplay, but made it to TV instead. Hailey's autobiographical story concerns two decades in the eccentric and comical lives of a family in a small Texas town called Sunray, where his bartender father, Horse, is cheating on his mother with the waitress, Faye Precious.

- "...*not a successful play. The focus is blurry too frequently, and the tone swerves recklessly between raucous vulgarity and momentous sentimentality. But the characters and setting are sharply perceived, and many of the scenes capture an effective combination of outrageous humor and compassionate understanding. The production...is remarkably good...Albert Salmi's Horse is a marvelously appropriate mixture of menace and unconscious buffoonery, an unlikely cross between W.C. Fields and Neanderthal Man. And Miss McClanahan is superb as Faye Precious...remains experimental theatre. Its faults are exasperating. But for those willing...its quota of rewards is quite respectable.*" (John J. O'Connor, The New York Times)

William Wister Haines
Born: September 17, 1908, Des Moines, IA. Died: 1989.

William Wister Haines primarily wrote war pictures; specifically, screenplays about actual crippled former military figures such as Admiral John Hoskins in *The Eternal Sea* (1955) starring Sterling Hayden, and Frank "Spig" Weade in John Ford's *The Wings of Eagles* (1957), starring John Wayne. Haines contributed to the anti-Ku Klux Klan film *Black Legion* (1937), wrote the Robert Mitchum movies *The Racket* (1951) and *One Minute to Zero* (1952), and also *Torpedo Run* (1958) with Glenn Ford. He adapted his own novel *Slim* into a 1937 film starring a young Henry Fonda.

Command Decision (1949, MGM, 111m/bw, **VHS**) ☆☆☆½ **Sc:** William R. Laidlaw, William Wister Haines, George Froeschel. **D:** Sam Wood. **P:** Sidney Franklin. **Cam:** Harold Rossen. **Cast:** Clark Gable, Walter Pidgeon, Van Johnson, John Hodiak, Brian Donlevy, Charles Bickford, Edward Arnold, Marshall Thompson, Cameron Mitchell, Richard Quine, John McIntire, Ray Collins, Clinton Sundberg, Warner Anderson, Moroni Olsen. Haines's play about the war-room machinations of the U.S.

Eighth Army plotting bombing raids over Germany during World War II was given the full MGM treatment with a top-notch cast.

• *"...a perfect vehicle for Sam Wood's thoroughly masculine, no-nonsense style of filmmaking. The stage play...about the anguish of command in wartime aviation was transferred to the screen with little change and an admirable restraint on the part of MGM not to embellish it with combat footage...grimly humorous and fairly honest in revealing the almost dehumanizing function of operating a modern war machine. Wood gave the story the proper blend of tough-mindedness and sentiment, pulling no punches in showing the devious expediences and opportunism as well as heroism and heartfelt concern among the various militarists and politicians."* (Tony Thomas, The Hollywood Professionals, Volume 2: Henry King, Lewis Milestone, Sam Wood)

Oscar Hammerstein II

Born: July 12, 1895, New York, NY. **Died:** 1960.
Pulitzer Prize-winning musical: *South Pacific* (1949)

The grandson of New York theatrical impresario Oscar Hammerstein, Hammerstein II became the most important, accomplished, and awarded American author of stage musical books, collaborating famously with composers George Gershwin, Jerome Kern, and especially Richard Rodgers to the point where their tandem names, Rodgers and Hammerstein, practically said "American musical theatre." Hammerstein's musical plays were great Broadway successes and he contributed to more than 60 New York stage productions, including frequent revivals and posthumous renditions of his songs. Most often he functioned as both the book author and lyricist, often in tandem on the latter discipline. Many of these time-honored contributions to popular culture translated beautifully to cinema, including the touchstone classics *Oklahoma!*, *The King and I*, *South Pacific*, and *Show Boat*.

Among the stage productions written by Hammerstein that have yet to reach either the big or small screen are *Sweet Adeline*, *The Gang's All Here*, *East Wind*, *May Wine*, *Sunny River*, *Allegro*, *Burning Bright*, *Me and Juliet*, and *Pipe Dream*. Hammerstein also produced plays, including Samuel A. Taylor's *The Happy Time* and John Steinbeck's *Burning Bright*. Among the TV documentary glimpses at Hammerstein's illustrious career are *General Foods Anniversary Show: A Tribute to Rodgers & Hammerstein* (1954), *The World of Richard Rodgers: Part II* (1967), and *Rodgers & Hammerstein: The Sound of Movies* (1996) hosted by Shirley Jones and featuring Julie Andrews. For *Golden Dawn*, *Rose-Marie*, *The Song and the Flame*, and *Sunny*, see **Oscar Hammerstein II & Otto Harbach**; for *The*

Desert Song and *New Moon*, see **Oscar Hammerstein II & Frank Mandel**; for *The Sound of Music*, see **Harold Lindsay & Russel Crouse**; for *South Pacific* see **Joshua Logan**; for *Oklahoma!*, see **Lynn Riggs**.

Broadway Rhythm (1944, MGM, c, **VHS**) ☆☆½ **Sc:** Harry Clork, Dorothy Kingsley. **D:** Roy Del Ruth. **P:** Jack Cummings. **Cam:** Leonard Smith. **Cast:** George Murphy, Ginny Simms, Charles Winninger, Lena Horne, Gloria DeHaven, Ben Blue, Nancy Walker, Eddie "Rochester" Anderson, Hazel Scott, Tommy Dorsey, Kenny Bowers, Sidney Blackmer, Kay Medford. This film is based on Hammerstein's 1939 play, *Very Warm for May*, which was produced by Max Gordon, directed by Hammerstein and Vincente Minnelli with music by Jerome Kern and lyrics by Hammerstein. It ran for 58 performances with a cast that included June Allyson, Eve Arden, Vera Ellen, Richard Quine, and Max Showalter. Murphy played a Broadway producer looking to sign big talent for his next show when he begins to realize that his family and friends might be able to pull off the production themselves. Horne sings "Somebody Loves Me" and "Brazilian Boogie."

- *"...a typical backstage filmusical wheeled out in the usual Metro elaborate and colorful style. Displaying group of top-rank specialties and names among the entertainers, the fragile and hodge-podge yarn...stops periodically while the guest stars appear...run-of-mill formula for a backstager."* (Variety)

Carmen Jones (1954, 20th Century-Fox, 105m/c, **VHS/DVD**) ☆☆☆½ **Sc:** Harry Kleiner. **D/P:** Otto Preminger. **Cam:** Sam Leavitt. **Cast:** Harry Belafonte, Dorothy Dandridge, Pearl Bailey, Diahann Carroll, Olga James, Joe Adams, Roy Glenn, Brock Peters, LaVerne Hutcherson, Marilyn Horne, Alvin Ailey, Max Roach, Marvin Hayes. Prosper Merimee's story *Carmen* was adapted into an opera by Henri Meilhac and Ludovic Halevy. A brazen Gypsy lures a soldier with her charms, but then is unfaithful to him, romancing a bullfighter. Hammerstein crafted a book and lyrics from the opera and Georges Bizet applied the music for the 1943 smash hit, which ran for 502 performances. The film was nominated for Oscars for Best Actress (Dandridge) and Score (Herschel Burke Gilbert).

- *"The film starts magnificently, as the sauntering Carmen...goes into her Habanera—'Dat's Love'—and taunts Corporal Joe...by, at one point, brushing his pants, a peak of eroticism at the time; but from then on it proceeds at [a] ponderous pace. An all-black musical was still considered daring..."* (David Shipman, The Story of Cinema)

Carousel is based on Benjamin Glazer's adaptation of Ferenc Molnar's play *Lilliom*, from which Hammerstein fleshed out a book and lyrics.

The music for producer Billy Rose's 1945 smash hit, which ran for 890 performances, was composed by Richard Rodgers, directed by Rouben Mamoulian, and choreographed by Agnes De Mille. The large cast included Bambi Linn, John Raitt, and Murvyn Vye.

Carousel (1956, 20th Century-Fox, 128m/c, **VHS/DVD**) ☆☆☆½ **Sc:** Phoebe Ephron, Henry Ephron. **D:** Henry King. **P:** Henry Ephron. **Cam:** Charles G. Clarke. **Cast:** Gordon MacRae, Shirley Jones, Cameron Mitchell, Barbara Ruick, Gene Lockhart, Claramae Turner, Robert Rounseville, Audrey Christie, Susan Luckey, William Le Massena, John Dehner, Jacques d'Amboise, Richard Deacon, Marion Dempsey, Tor Johnson.

- "...didn't work out well, mostly through ho-hum casting. Sinatra, hired for the lead, ducked out just before shooting—a smart move as he's completely wrong for the part. But his replacement, Gordon MacRae, was correct, no more." (Ethan Mordden, The Hollywood Musical)
- "Gordon MacRae and Shirley Jones splendidly head the cast, but Carousel, like its source, Liliom, concludes in whimsy, which is rendered here with an arty and saccharine ballet likely to destroy the goodwill of all but the most indulgent audiences." (David Shipman, The Story of Cinema)

Carousel (1967, ABC) ☆☆☆ **P:** Norman Rosemont. **Cast:** Robert Goulet, Mary Grover, Pernell Roberts, Marilyn Mason, Charles Ruggles, Michael F. Blake, Jack DeLon, Linda Howe, Patricia Neway, Marge Redmond.

Flower Drum Song (1961, Universal, 133m/c, **VHS**) ☆☆½ **Sc:** Joseph Fields. **D:** Henry Koster. **P:** Ross Hunter, Joseph Fields. **Cam:** Russell Metty. **Cast:** Nancy Kwan, James Shigeta, Benson Fong, Miyoshi Umeki, Jack Soo, Juanita Hall, Reiko Sato, Kam Tong, Patrick Adiarte, Victor Sen Yung, James Hong, Harry Beau, Marilyn Horne. The 1958 stage original, with music composed by Richard Rodgers, ran for 600 performances. It was directed by Gene Kelly, choreographed by Carol Haney, and featured the performances of Miyoshi Umeki, Larry Blyden, Keye Luke, and Jack Soo. Hammerstein and Joseph Fields based their book on the novel by C.Y. Lee, about four young people of Chinese descent in San Francisco's Chinatown torn between Eastern and Western cultures.

- "Much of the [play's] fundamental charm, grace and novelty...has been overwhelmed by the sheer opulence and glamour with which Ross Hunter has translated it to the screen. As a film, it emerges a curiously unaffecting, unstable and rather undistinguished experience, lavishly produced but only sporadically rewarding." (Variety)

The King and I (1956, 20th Century-Fox, 133m/c, **VHS/DVD**) ☆☆☆☆ **Sc:** Ernest Lehman. **D:** Walter Lang. **P:** Charles Brackett, Darryl F. Zanuck. **Cam:** Leon Shamroy. **Cast:** Deborah Kerr, Yul Brynner, Rita Moreno, Martin Benson, Terry Saunders, Rex Thompson, Carlos Rivas, Patrick Adiarte, Alan Mowbray, Geoffrey Toone, Robert Banas, Reuben Fuentes. Debuting in 1951, the musical ran for 1,246 performances on Broadway and created a vital new star in Yul Brynner. It also supplied Gertrude Lawrence with her final hit as Anna; she died three weeks after her last performance in the part. Hammerstein adapted the book from Margaret Langdon's autobiography, *Anna and the King of Siam*, which chronicled her years tutoring Siam's royal family in Western manners. Richard Rodgers supplied the music, Jerome Robbins the choreography, and John Van Druten the direction. The film combined one of Kerr's most famous performances, Brynner's Oscar-winning, career-making portrayal of the Siamese king, and sumptuous settings to create one of the best movie musicals of the 1950s. The film also won Oscars for Art Direction/Set Decoration, Score (Alfred Newman, Ken Darby), Costumes, and Sound. "Getting to Know You," "Hello, Young Lovers," and "Something Wonderful" are among the show's enduring tunes.

• *"All the ingredients that made Rodgers and Hammerstein's [1951]* The King and I *a memorable stage experience have been faithfully transferred to the screen. The result is a pictorially exquisite, musically exciting and dramatically satisfying motion picture...the production has the talent to support the opulence of this truly blockbuster presentation."* (Variety)

New Toys (1925, bw/silent) ☆☆½ **Sc:** Josephine Lovett. **D:** John S. Robertson. **P:** Richard Barthelmess, Mary F. Hay. **Cam:** Roy Overbaugh. **Cast:** Richard Barthelmess, Mary F. Hay, Katherine Wilson, Clifton Webb, Francis Conlon, Bijou Fernandez, Tammany Young, Baby Pat O'-Connor, Jules Jordan, Jacob Kingsbury, Laura Lacillade. Based on the 1924 play by Hammerstein and Milton Herbert Gropper, produced by Sam H. Harris, with Vivienne Osborne, Robert McWade, and Frances Nelson.

Show Boat began as an Edna Ferber novel in 1926, which was first translated to the screen in 1929 via a Charles Kenyon adaptation that starred Laura La Plante and Joseph Schildkraut. That film was a mostly silent rendition during Hollywood's fitful adoption of sound techniques; however, a couple of songs were last-minute additions. Oscar Hammerstein II translated the novel into a 1927 stage musical at New York's Ziegfeld Theatre. This successful production was first adapted to the screen in 1936 by Hammerstein, and was remade by MGM in equally lavish fashion in 1951.

Show Boat (1936, Universal, 113m/bw, **VHS**) ☆☆☆☆½ **Sc:** Oscar Hammerstein II. **D:** James Whale. **P:** Carl Laemmle Jr., James Whale. **Cam:** John J. Mescall. **Cast:** Irene Dunne, Allan Jones, Charles Winninger, Helen Morgan, Paul Robeson, Helen Westley, Queenie Smith,

Sammy White, Donald Cook, Hattie McDaniel, Franis X. Mahoney, Charles Middleton, Clarence Muse, Eddie "Rochester" Anderson, E.E. Clive, Edmund Cobb.

- *"This is by far the best of the three* Show Boat *films, though it emphasizes the sentimentality of the Kern-Hammerstein epic (love lasts a lifetime) rather than its salient idea (human strivings fall away to nothing; the natural world outlasts us all) The casting is superb: Dunne as the heroine, Allan Jones as her gambler love, Helen Morgan as Julie...Except for Westley and Smith, all had played their roles onstage...The film is a quite faithful adaptation—Hammerstein wrote the screenplay himself—so the performers' experiential ease with their characters makes it rich in personal depth."* (Ethan Mordden, The Hollywood Musical)

- *"For a rare change the elastic screen medium was used to nearly full advantage in this* Show Boat, *recapturing the grandeur of the showboat era with the lachrymose flavor and lilting score that made the stage show such a perennial crowd-pleaser. Irene, albeit a mature Magnolia, was accomplished, beautiful and versatile. Her shuffling and trucking during the 'Can't Help Lovin' Dat Man' number remains a joyous scene with Irene at her liberated screen best."* (James Robert Parish, The RKO Gals)

Show Boat (1951, MGM, 107m/c, **VHS/DVD**) ☆☆☆☆ **Sc:** John Lee Mahin. **D:** George Sidney. **P:** Arthur Freed. **Cam:** Charles Rosher. **Cast:** Kathryn Grayson, Ava Gardner, Howard Keel, Joe E. Brown, William Warfield, Marge Champion, Gower Champion, Agnes Moorehead, Leif Erickson, Robert Sterling, Chick Chandler, Boyd Ackerman, Bette Arlen, Linda Christian, Adele Jurgens, Anna Q. Nilsson, Emory Parnell, Earle Hodgins. Made at the height of MGM's musical superiority, this version contains one of Gardner's best performances.

- *"...very handsome...notable shots of the show boat as it moves down the Mississippi, has felicitous contributions from Charles Rosher, the cinematographer, and the designer, Jack Martin Smith. The orchestrations are by Adolph Deutsch, and though the score has been curtailed the songs seem to come up at five minute intervals...Despite the presence of Miss Grayson as magnolia, it is the way Kern's music is used which makes this the best of the three film versions—and it has howard Keel to sing his share of the lyrics. Ava Gardner is a magnificent Julie...The book has also been better compressed—by John Lee Mahin—than in Whale's version, and Sidney makes it move along with a certain charm."* (David Shipman, The Story of Cinema)

Show Boat (1989, PBS, 165m/c) *Great Performances* ☆☆☆½ **Tp:** Oscar Hammerstein II. **D:** Robert Johanson. **Cast:** Eddie Bracken, Rebecca Baxter, Richard White, Marsha Bagwell, P.L. Brown, Shelly Burch, Ellia English, Lenora Nemetz, Lee Roy Reams. This performance was videotaped at the Paper Mill Playhouse in New Jersey.

Song of the West (1930, Warner Bros., 82m/bw) ☆☆☆ **Sc:** Harvey F. Thew. **D:** Ray Enright. **Cam:** Devereaux Jennings. **Cast:** John Boles, Vivienne Segal, Joe E. Brown, Marie Wells, Sam Hardy, Marion Byron, Eddie Gribbon, Edward Martindel, Rudolph Cameron, Ann Sothern. This picture was based on the 1928 play *Rainbow* by Hammerstein and Laurence Stallings, which ran for only 29 performances at New York's Gallo Opera House choreographed by Busby Berkeley with an ensemble including Brian Donlevy, Libby Holman, and Charles Ruggles.

• *"Seemingly all the weaknesses, without the strength, of stage operettas get transferred to the screen so that despite shrewd and costly production, as in the case of* Song of the West, *the finished result is less than completely satisfying. As unreeled, this film is just a nice-looking program feature. No more—no less."* (Variety)

Oscar Hammerstein II & Otto Harbach

See individual entries for biographical information.

Golden Dawn (1930, Warner Bros., 81m/bw) ☆½ **Sc:** Walter Anthony. **D:** Ray Enright. **Cam:** Frank B. Good, Devereaux Jennings. **Cast:** Walter Wolf King, Vivienne Segal, Alice Gentle, Noah Beery, Lupino Lane, Dick Henderson, Marion, Byron, Edward Martindel, Nina Quartero, Otto Matieson. The 1927 play, produced by Arthur Hammerstein and directed by Dave Bennett and Reginald Hammerstein, is notable as the first of only four Broadway appearances by Archie Leach, who later went to Hollywood and became Cary Grant. The Germans capture a portion of British East Africa, then release their captives into service to help them put down a "native" uprising. A subplot involves Dawn (Segal), a white girl who is passing as a native.

• *"...only seems to prove that a tuneful piece of this type, while it is acceptable in a flesh and blood portrayal, is less effective on the screen, being a hybrid of pasteboard realism and a romantic musical background that do not seem to dovetail...Noah Beery, who chants in a deep bass voice and frightens the children into rapid retirement by simply putting in an appearance, speaks his lines with a Southern darkey accent probably utterly foreign in East Africa."* (The New York Times)

Rose-Marie was first produced at Broadway's Imperial Theatre by Arthur Hammerstein in 1924 with book and lyrics by both Oscar Hammerstein II and Otto Harbach. With Lela Bliss and Eduardo

Ciannelli in the opening night cast, it ran for 311 performances. The title Canadian lass must choose between a free-spirited, forest roving Robin Hood type and his archenemy, a Canadian Mounted Policeman. The songs include "Indian Love Call," "Rose-Marie, I Love You," and "Song of the Mounties."

Rose-Marie (1928, MGM, 70m/bw/silent) ☆☆☆ **Sc/D:** Lucien Hubbard. **Cam:** John Arnold. **Cast:** Joan Crawford, James Murray, House Peters, Creighton Hale, George Cooper, Gibson Gowland, Lionel Belmore, William Orlamond, Polly Moran, Gertrude Astor, Harry Gribbon, Sven Hugo Borg, Lou Costello, Ralph Yearsley.

• *"Filming a musical comedy narrative seldom results in any marked success, and the present transcription of* Rose-Marie*...is no exception to the rule. The praiseworthy passages of this effort are more than offset by the muddled story, the ridiculous suspicions and the tedious and frequently absurd incidents...Joan Crawford is most prepossessing as Rose-Marie, but she seems like a girl who quickly flings the past behind her..."* (Mordaunt Hall, The New York Times)

Rose-Marie (1936, MGM, 113m/bw, **VHS**) ☆☆☆☆ **Sc:** Frances Goodrich, Albert Hackett, Alice Duer Miller. **D:** W.S. Van Dyke. **P:** Hunt Stromberg. **Cam:** William Daniels. **Cast:** Jeanette MacDonald, Nelson Eddy, James Stewart, Reginald Owen, Allan Jones, Alan Mowbray, Gilda Grey, George Regas, Robert Grieg, Una O'Connor, Lucien Littlefield, Herman Bing, David Niven, Iron Eyes Cody, Jimmy Conlin, Halliwell Hobbes, James Murray, Jack Pennick. This film was also released as *Indian Love Call*. A popular hit, it was the apex of Macdonald and Eddy's careers, and one of Stewart's first pictures. He played her brother, whom Eddy arrests.

• *"As blithely melodious and rich in scenic beauty as any picture that has come from Hollywood...a lyric recording of the...score that distinguished the operetta...If the three script writers were entrusted with its adaptation to the screen have dealt less respectfully with the original's book, they may be pardoned on the ground that here the song—and its singers—are the thing. To paraphrase Fletcher, let Jeannette MacDonald and Nelson Eddy sing an operetta's love songs and we care not who may write its book."* (Frank S. Nugent, The New York Times)

Rose-Marie (1954, MGM, 104m/c, **VHS**) ☆☆☆ **Sc:** George Froeschel, Ronald Miller. **D/P:** Mervyn LeRoy. **Cam:** Paul Vogel. **Cast:** Ann Blythe, Howard Keel, Fernando Lamas, Bert Lahr, Marjorie Main, Joan Taylor, Ray Collins, Chief Yowlachie, Robert Anderson, Robert Bray, Dabbs Greer, Lumsden Hare, Mickey Simpson. Keel was the forthright Mountie, Lamas the romantic roverboy.

• *"...slowly develops on the screen with a fearfully fixed deliberation under the direction of Mervyn LeRoy. The dialogue is long, the plot is ponderous and the occasional intrusions of Bert Lahr and Marjorie Main as comic re-*

lief (in small doses) are disappointingly brief. However, the principals manage, now and again, to catch hold of a cue, take a firm stand on a piece of scenery and then let go with a song. Mr. Keel booms the loudest and the longest with the memorable 'Rose-Marie,' but Miss Blythe and Mr. Lamas carry the farthest with the echoing 'Indian Love Call.'" (Thomas M. Pryor, The New York Times)

The Song of the Flame (1930, Warner Bros., 72m/bw) ☆☆☆ **Sc:** Gordon Rigby. **D:** Alan Crosland. **Cam:** Lee Garmes. **Cast:** Alexander Gray, Berneice Claire, Noah Beery, Alice Gentle, Inez Courtney, Bert Roach, Shep Camp, Ivan Linow, Gregory Gaye, Janina Smolinska. With music by Herbert Stothart and George Gershwin and libretto and lyrics by Harbach and Hammerstein, the Broadway original at the 44th Street Theatre featured Hugh Cameron and Louise Dahlberg in the cast. The Bolshevik Revolution is abetted by dashing action, romance, and warbling.

- *"...the songs come often and one can smile at the melodramatic action...The settings are magnificent and the crowds have been exceptionally well handled by Mr. Crosland...Perhaps those...seeking dramatic interest in a picture may find fault with the idea of Konstantin going before a firing squad in a singing mood...The soldiers are permitted to hold up the execution until the ballad is nearly finished and then comes the report of firearms."* (Mordaunt Hall, The New York Times)

Sunny debuted in 1925 at Broadway's New Amsterdam Theatre with both book and lyrics by Hammerstein and Harbach and music by Jerome Kern. It ran for 517 performances with a cast that included Marilyn Miller and Clifton Webb. A circus bareback rider stows away dressed as a boy on an ocean liner heading for New York City and marries on board to an American citizen to avoid immigration officials on Ellis Island.

Sunny (1930, First National, 78m/bw) ☆☆☆½ **Sc:** Henry McCarty, Humphrey Pearson. **D:** William A. Seiter. **Cam:** Ernest Haller, Arthur Reeves (uncredited). **Cast:** Marilyn Miller, Lawrence Gray, Joe Donahue, O.P. Heggie, Inez Courtney, Barbara Bedford, Clyde Cooke, Mackenzie Ward, Judith Vosselli, Harry Allan, Bill Elliott. The throaty Miller repeated her stage success via First National's Vitaphone recording process, and certainly drew the interest of Mordaunt Hall.

- *"Marilyn Miller is the stellar performer...Whether she is dancing, singing or just talking, Miss Miller is captivating...Miss Miller's dancing is fascinating. She trips the light fantastic in several costumes, including a nun's habit, and William A. Seiter, the director, has done splendid work in picturing these scenes."* (Mordaunt Hall, The New York Times)

Sunny (1941, RKO, 98m/bw) ☆☆½ **Sc:** Sig Herzig. **D/P:** Herbert Wilcox. **Cam:** Russell Metty. **Cast:** Anna Neagle, Ray Bolger, John

Carroll, Edward Everett Horton, Grace Hartman, Paul Hartman, Frieda Inescort, Helen Westley, Benny Rubin, Torben Meyer, Jeff York, Muggins Davies, Richard Lane, Bess Flowers, James Flavin, Halliwell Hobbes. This is one of the 32 career collaborations between Neagle and Wilcox.

• *"It is a thoroughly conventional story without a single surprise. That, we regret to conclude, is the sort of thing we must expect from these two [Neagle and Wilcox] when they are wooing the musical comedy muse. Every single one of their revivals has been conventional, sweet and humorless. Miss Neagle is a very pretty person and a pleasant dancer when she chooses to shake a leg. But she can't sing worth a nickel, her charm always seems slightly forced and her old-fashioned musical comedy mannerisms tend to monotony. However, she fills the bill for family entertainment, which is what* Sunny *is."* (Bosley Crowther, The New York Times)

Oscar Hammerstein II & Frank Mandel

Mandel:
Born: May 31, 1884, CA. **Died:** 1958.

Frank Mandel was one of Hammerstein's important collaborators. He saw his first play, *My Lady Friends*, adapted for films in 1921. He penned the work with Emil Nyitray, and it starred Carter De Haven and Flora Parker De Haven. Mandel's play with Lawrence Schawb, *Follow Thru*, became a 1930 film with Buddy Rogers and Nancy Carroll.

For biographical information on Hammerstein, see **Oscar Hammerstein II.**

The Desert Song debuted in 1926 and ran for 471 performances with music by Sigmund Romberg and a book by Hammerstein and Frank Mandel. The songs include "Long Live the Night," "Romance," "One Flower," and "Gay Parisienne." The plot involves the male lead heading a secret rebel force against the evil sheik.

The Desert Song (1929, Warner Bros., 123m/c&bw) ☆☆☆ **Sc:** Harvey Gates. **D:** Roy Del Ruth. **Cam:** Barney McGill. **Cast:** John Boles, Carlotta King, Louise Fazenda, Johnny Arthur, Myrna Loy, Jack Pratt, Roberto E. Guzman, Edward Martindel, Otto Hoffman, Marie Wells, Delk Elliott, John Miljan. This film is an artifact as the first Vitaphone-recorded operetta and, in retrospect, a look at Loy's early career, which capitalized on her beauty, here as an Arab vamp.

- *"With colorful settings, impressive scenes with Riffs ahorse on the undulating sands and some well-recorded singing, the first audible film operetta came to the screen...It is an interesting experiment and one wherein the story, even allowing for the peculiar license necessary for such offerings, lays itself open to chuckles rather than sympathy or concern regarding the events...The characters...seem to seize upon song at inopportune moments, which in fact might be all well on the stage but it is a weakness in a picture...The comedy offered...is really of too low an order to fit in with this type of musical offering..."* (The New York Times)

The Desert Song (1943, Warner Bros., 90m/c) ☆☆☆½ **Sc/P:** Robert Buckner. **D:** Robert Florey. **Cam:** Bert Glennon. **Cast:** Dennis Morgan, Irene Manning, Bruce Cabot, Victor Francen, Gene Lockhart, Lynne Overman, Marcel Dalio, Faye Ermerson, Curt Bois, Jack La Rue, Frank Arnold, Leah Baird, Eugene Borden, Wallis Clark, Noble Johnson, Gerald Mohr, Nestor Paiva. The Nazis are brought in for this wartime version as railroad builders who inspire the Riff uprising.

- *"Despite modernization...basic entertainment qualities of Desert Song are retained to provide most diverting audience reaction at this time. Morgan is neatly cast as the Red Rider, delivering both dramatic and vocal assignments in top style. Manning capably handles the girl spot as singer and actress."* (Variety)

The Desert Song (1953, Warner Bros., 96m/c, **VHS**) ☆☆☆ **Sc:** Roland Kibbee. **D:** H. Bruce Humberstone. **P:** Rudi Fehr. **Cam:** Robert Burks. **Cast:** Kathryn Grayson, Gordon MacRae, Raymond Massey, Steve Cochran, Allyn Ann McLerie, Ray Collins, Frank DeKova, William Conrad, Trevor Bardette, Dick Wesson, Paul Picerni, Mark Dana. McLerie did a sinuous dance, Massey enacted an evil sheik, and Wesson played a reporter for "the *New York Chronicle*."

- *"Those who still hold the score of The Desert Song to be as warm and beguiling as the Sahara, and a new generation who may have wondered why, will find the latest film version...on display...[with a] handsome, burnished Technicolor backdrop to Sigmund Romberg's sandy rhapsodies, which, as warbled by the two stars, never sounded prettier. A blessed good thing, too...mumbling production merely underlines the pedantic dialogue...At this point, The Desert Song may be considered dying of thirst."* (Howard Thompson, The New York Times)

The Desert Song (1955, NBC, 90m/c) **Cast:** Nelson Eddy, Gale Sherwood, Salvatorre Baccaloni, Otto Kruger, John Conte, Viola Essen.

The New Moon (1989) ☆☆½ **Tp:** Oscar Hammerstein II, Frank Mandel, Laurence Schwab. **Cast:** Richard White, Leigh Munro, Ivy Austin, James Billings, Gerald Isaac, Muriel Costa-Greenspon. This New York City Opera rendition was taped before a live audience and restored the

original plot and characters of the 1928 operetta, which had been bowdlerized for versions produced in 1930 and 1940.

Lorraine Hansberry

Born: May 19, 1930, Chicago, IL. **Died:** 1965.

Lorraine Hansberry's three produced plays on Broadway were *A Raisin in
the Sun* (1959), *The Sign in Sidney Brustein's Window* (1964) with Rita
Moreno, and *Les Blancs* (1970) with James Earl Jones and Cameron
Mitchell. She directed one play, *Kicks and Co.*, in Chicago in 1961.
After Hansberry died of cancer at the age of 35, her husband, Robert
Nemiroff, produced a documentary about her including a collage of her
writings called *To Be Young, Gifted and Black*, which was shown on *NET
Playhouse* with Ruby Dee playing the playwright in some passages. He
also produced *Raisin*, a musical based on *A Raisin the Sun*. It ran for more
than two years on Broadway, beginning in 1973 featuring Debbie Allen,
Joe Morton, and Ted Ross.

A Raisin in the Sun (1961, Columbia, 128m/bw, **VHS/DVD**) ☆☆☆☆
Sc: Lorraine Hansberry. **D:** Daniel Petrie. **P:** David Susskind, Philip
Rose. **Cam:** Charles Lawton Jr. **Cast:** Sidney Poitier, Claudia McNeil,
Ruby Dee, Diana Sands, John Fiedler, Ivan Dixon, Lou Gossett. The
landmark play about a black family's choice to move into a suburban
white Chicago neighborhood in the 1950s was delivered with four brilliant performances by a core cast—Poitier, McNeil, Dee, and Sands—
and broke new ground in mainstream American cinema's treatment of
African-Americans. This is the classic version.

- "…*a film transcription (not really an adaptation) by Lorraine Hansberry of
  her successful play and is…excellently acted. .. As for the script itself, Miss
  Hansberry's dialogue is generally commonplace and occasionally ridiculous…As the son, Sidney Poitier—tigerish, impassioned, moving with a
  marvelous sense of dramatic rhythm—enlarges the play, gives it an agony
  that is almost too big for it and stretches it at the seams. Ruby Dee is touching as the wife whose marriage and love are being corroded by her husband's
  frustrations."* (Stanley Kauffmann, The New Republic)

- "*If it stays pretty much in one room, if it seems to smack of multi-move-
  ment cinema, that is probably because its screenplay writer, Miss Hansberry, and its director, Daniel Petrie, have agreed that its drama takes place
  mainly in the hearts of its people, and they wanted to keep it as close to those
  vitals as they could…The effect is to make even clearer than what was done
  on the stage the natures of the members of a family…It is a wonderful,
  warm comprehension of a people's humor, strength and dignity under a mul-*

titude of sad and silly burdens. It should generate love, not hate." (Bosley Crowther, The New York Times)

A Raisin in the Sun (1989, PBS, 171m/c, **VHS**) *American Playhouse* ☆☆☆½ **Tp:** Lorraine Hansberry. **D:** Bill Duke. **P:** Jaki Brown, Chiz Schultz. **Cast:** Danny Glover, Esther Rolle, Starletta DuPois, Kim Yancy, John Fiedler, Lou Ferguson, Helen Martin, Joseph C. Phillips, Stephen Henderson. Duke allowed the actors wide latitude in building and sustaining their characters in this 171-minute version, set virtually in one apartment. This was the Roundabout Theatre's 25th anniversary production.

- *"The result is that this television version is every bit as accomplished and perhaps more vivid than its theatrical counterpart, thanks to the camera's probing eye and its ability to give us this family's turbulence at close range. The stage version billed itself (not incorrectly, as it turned out) as 'definitive,' this American Playhouse version is entitled to the same adjective for the same reason: It earns it...Hansberry weaves matters of personal and political conscience into a textured, vibrant piece...But it is Glover's insistent performance as Walter Lee...that is central to this production." (Sylvie Drake, Los Angeles Times)*

Otto A. Harbach

Otto Abels Hauerbach
Born: August 18, 1873, Salt Lake City, UT. **Died:** 1963.

One of the most successful librettists in American history, Otto Harbach became an English professor at Whitman College in Walla Walla, WA, then a newspaperman in 1901 for the New York *Daily News*, followed by a stint in advertising. His first Broadway success was *The Three Twins*, a collaboration with Karl Hoschna, with whom he wrote five more successful musicals until the latter's death in 1911. Harbach's musicals created a large section of the popular show tunes of the early 20th century, including "Cuddle Up a Little Closer," "Giannina Maria," "Indian Love Call," "One Alone," "She Didn't Say Yes, She Didn't Say No," and "Smoke Gets in your Eyes." The first film made from his work was a collaboration with Hoschna, *Madame Sherry* (1917), starring Gertrude McCoy.

Harbach's stage musicals that were never adapted for the movies include *Crinoline Girl* (1914), *The O'Brien Girl* (1921), *June Love* (1921), *The Blue Kitten* (1921), *Molly Darling* (1922), *Jack and Jill* (1923), and *Oh! Oh! Madeleine* (1924). Harbach set a record with five different works in production on Broadway during the 1926 season: *Kitty's Kisses, Wild Rose, Criss Cross, Oh! Please,* and the enduring *The Desert Song.* Harbach collaborated with such composers as Jerome Kern, Sigmund

Romberg, and Peter de Rose and co-wrote stage books with Oscar Hammerstein II. Both Kern and Hammerstein gave Harbach praise as the greatest writer in the history of the American light musical. The taste and tone of his best work was nonpareil in the genre. In 1950, Harbach was elected president of the American Society of Composers, Authors, and Publishers (ASCAP) after 30 years on its board of directors. In addition to the productions listed below, Otto Harbach wrote the screenplay for *Men of the Sky* (1931).

For *Golden Dawn*, *Rose-Marie*, *The Song and the Flame*, and *Sunny*, see **Oscar Hammerstein II & Otto Harbach.**

The Cat and the Fiddle (1934, MGM, 88m/c&bw, **VHS**) ☆☆☆ **Sc:** Bella Spewack, Sam Spewack. **D:** William K. Howard. **P:** Bernard H. Hyman. **Cam:** Charles G. Clarke, Ray Rennihan, Harold Rosson. **Cast:** Ramon Navarro, Jeanette MacDonald, Frank Morgan, Jean Hersholt, Charles Butterworth, Frank Conroy, Vivienne Segal, Harry Armetta, Adrienne D'Ambrcourt, Joseph Cawthorn, Herman Bing, Sterling Holloway, Arthur Hoyt, Paul Porcasi. With a book by Harbach and Jerome Kern, the 1931 stage musical produced by Max Gordon ran for 395 performances.

- *"Clean and wholesome throughout, the picture, skipping the lavish spectacle specialties common to the current musical trend, depends upon the dramatic and romantic story values, plus the Jeanette MacDonald and Ramon Navarro singing to put over its punches."* (Motion Picture Herald)

The Firefly (1937, MGM, 131m/bw, **VHS**) ☆☆☆ **Sc:** Ogden Nash, Frances Goodrich, Albert Hackett. **D:** Robert Z. Leonard. **P:** Robert Z. Leonard, Hunt Stromberg. **Cam:** Oliver T. Marsh. **Cast:** Jeanette MacDonald, Allan Jones, Warren William, Billy Gilbert, Douglass Dumbrille, Leonard Penn, Henry Daniell, Tom Rutherford, Belle Mitchell, George Zucco, Corbet Morris, Eugene Borden, Lane Chandler, Pedro de Cordoba, Jason Robards (Sr.), Ian Wolfe. The original 1931 play produced by New York's Civic Light Opera was an eight-performance flop. The songs for one of MacDonald's most popular pictures include "The Donkey Serenade," "Love Is Like a Firefly," and "A Woman's Kiss."

- *"...fails to shine with the brilliance one might reasonably expect of a screen presentation so convinced of its own importance that its very Napoleon is a mere extra...It is told, moreover, by such uninspired dialogue and transparency of intrigue that only the superb voices of Jeannette MacDonald and Allan Jones...save the production from downright, if beautifully photographed, dullness."* (Bosley Crowther, The New York Times)

Going Up was a musical with a book by Harbach based on James Montgomery's novel *The Aviator*, about a young author whose book about aviation wasn't based on any experience. The publisher, keen for publicity, tries to trick the youth into one air ride at a mountain resort and then an air-plane race with a French barnstormer, while the boy is keen on trying to romance a girl. The 1917 hit at Broadway's Liberty Theatre starred a youthful Ed(ward) Begley, Ruth Donnelly, Frank Craven, and Donald Meek.

Youth's Desire (1920, Forward, bw/silent) ☆☆ **Sc:** Philip H. White. **Cast:** Joseph Bennett, Doris Baker.

Going Up (1923, Associated Exhibiters, bw/silent) ☆☆☆ **Sc:** Raymond Griffith. **D:** Lloyd Ingraham. **P:** Douglas MacLean. **Cam:** Russ Fischer. **Cast:** Douglas MacLean, Hallam Cooley, Arthur Stuart Hull, Francis McDonald, Hughie Mack, Wade Boteler, John Steppling, Mervyn LeRoy, Marjorie Daw, Edna Murphy, Lillian Langdon. Future director LeRoy played a bellhop in a few scenes.

• *"Lloyd Ingraham directed this film, the action of which is swift and without a tedious instant...MacLean...Hallam Cooley...These two really get away from the ordinary motion-picture acting, and they seem quite natural, actually moved to mirth themselves by the story of the farce...This is a film that will appeal to everybody who wants a really good laugh."* (The New York Times)

Kid Boots (1926, Paramount, bw/silent) ☆☆☆½ **Sc:** Tom Gibson, Luther Reed, George Marion Jr. **D:** Frank Tuttle. **P:** B.P. Schulberg. **Cam:** Victor Milner. **Cast:** Eddie Cantor, Clara Bow, Billie Dove, Lawrence Gray, Natalie Kingston, Malcolm Waite, William Worthington, Aud Cruster, Harry von Meter, Fred Esmelton. This film debut for Cantor was the adaptation of his stage triumph as a bumbling haberdasher who runs afoul of a bodybuilder. He exchanges his legal largesse with a well-heeled type looking for a divorce for relief from strongman "Big Boyle."

• *"...brisk piece of buffoonery...Sometimes [the comedy] is accomplished through ingenious stunts and on other occasions, with no less success, by means of gags that are not exactly new...one has a feeling that Mr. Cantor would do well in a tamer sort of effort with a more coherent yarn. His physiognomy is one to bank on in a comedy...Mr. Cantor screens well, and he appears to be just as much at home before the camera as he is on the stage."* (Mordaunt Hall, The New York Times)

Madame Sherry (1917, bw/silent) **D:** Ralph Dean. **P:** M.H. Hoffman. **Cam:** David W. Gobbett. **Cast:** Gertrude McCoy, Frank L.A. O'Connor, H.J. Quealy, Jean Stuart, Alphie James, Lucy Carter, Jack Mundy, Alfred Deery, Robert Homans. Based on Harbach's 1910 musical.

No, No, Nanette was a smash hit of 1926, set amid the Smith household and the campus of Chickadee College, with Harbach sharing credit for the book with Frank Mandel and lyrics with Irving Caesar. The cast included Charles Winninger and Lucille Moore.

No, No, Nanette (1930, First National, 98m/c&bw) ☆☆☆½ **Sc:** Howard Emmett Rogers, Beatrice Van. **D:** Clarence Badger. **P:** Ned Marin. **Cam:** Sol Polito. **Cast:** Berneice Claire, Alexander Gray, Lucien Littlefield, Lilyan Tashman, Louise Fazenda, ZaSu Pitts, Henry Stockbridge, Bert Roach, Mildred Harris, Jocelyn Lee.

- *"The audible and periodically prismatic film version...proves to be quite a merry affair with tunes that are now well known and players whose activities were rewarded with gusts of laughter...It is a show that stirs up mirth from persons who might desire a more sophisticated type of entertainment, for the comedy of wives discovering the more or less harmless deceits of their husbands is invariably unfailing."* (Mordaunt Hall, The New York Times)

No, No, Nanette (1940, RKO, 96m/bw, **VHS**) ☆½ **Sc:** Ken Englund. **D/P:** Herbert Wilcox. **Cam:** Russell Metty. **Cast:** Anna Neagle, Victor Mature, Richard Carlson, Roland Young, ZaSu Pitts, Helen Broderick, Eve Arden, Billy Gilbert, Russell Hicks, Aubrey Mather, Tamara, Staurt Robertson, Dorothea Kent, Keye Luke, Mary Gordon, Benny Rubin, Torben Meyer. According to the consensus verdict on this version, someone should have headed off its plans with a "no-no—don't make it."

- *"The ways of film producers are indeed inscrutable. Anyone who remembers No, No, Nanette from way back in 1925 will recall that the most charming and commendable feature of it was its highly melodious score...Yet the current screen version of it...uses that airy score for little more than incidental background music, substitutes nothing in its place and meanders tediously through a typical silly musical comedy plot to an exceedingly silly conclusion."* (Bosley Crowther, The New York Times)

Tea for Two (1950, Warner Bros., 98m/c, **VHS**) ☆☆☆½ **Sc:** Harry Clork, William Jacobs. **D:** David Butler. **P:** William Jacobs. **Cam:** Wilfred M. Cline. **Cast:** Doris Day, Gordon MacRae, Gene Nelson, Eve Arden, Billy De Wolfe, S.Z. Sakall, Patrice Wymore, Virginia Gibson, George Baxter, Jack Daley, Bess Flowers, Carol Haney, Harry Harvey.

- *"Good music and snappy comedy—dialogue variety—combine to make* Tea for Two *a pleasant entertainment...quite a genial production."* (Thomas M. Pryor, The New York Times)

Roberta, which Harbach crafted into a stage book from the Alice Duer Miller novel, *Gowns by Roberta*, was a 1933 musical with tunes by Jerome Kern, and performances by Bob Hope, Sydney Greenstreet, George Murphy and Marion Ross. The plot follows a trio of wanna-be Broadway producers who travel to Paris to sell a half-interest in a chi-chi dress shop to raise money for their show.

Roberta (1935, RKO, 106m/bw, **VHS**) ☆☆☆☆ **Sc:** Sam Mintz, Jane Murfin, Allan Scott. **D:** William A. Seiter. **P:** Pandro S. Berman. **Cam:** Edward Cronjager. **Cast:** Irene Dunne, Fred Astaire, Ginger Rogers, Randolph Scott, Claire Dodd, Helen Westley, Victor Varconi, Luis Alberni, Torben Meyer, Bodil Rosing, William Frawley. Dunne starred in the title role and sings a memorable rendition of "Smoke Gets in Your Eyes," but the Astaire/Rogers team steals the show.

- "*Even when they [Astaire and Rogers] are shunted into secondary spots in their third film,* Roberta...*they dominate. Irene Dunne and Randolph Scott are the apparent heroine and hero...with the Paris fashion world the film's gummy setting (hideous clothes) and all the big Kern ballads going to Dunne. Dunne is no dancer and Scott is just a lump, and* The Gay Divorcee *has set a tempo for dance, so every time Astaire and Rogers appear the film forgets the clothes and the balalaikas and does what we want it to...Astaire and Rogers make 'I'll Be Hard to Handle' a challenge dance that looks improbably spontaneous...And whom does* Roberta *fade out on? Astaire and Rogers, in a last gleeful runthrough of 'I Won't Dance.'*" (*Ethan Mordden,* The Hollywood Musical)

Lovely to Look at (1952, MGM, 103m/c, **VHS**) ☆☆☆½ **Sc:** George Wells, Harry Ruby, Andrew Solt. **D:** Mervyn LeRoy, Vincente Minnelli (uncredited). **P:** Jack Cummings. **Cam:** George J. Folsey. **Cast:** Kathryn Grayson, Howard Keel, Red Skelton, Marge Champion, Gower Champion, Ann Miller, Zsa Zsa Gabor, Kurt Kasznar, Marcel Dalio, Diane Cassidy, Pierre Watkin.

- "*A generation has grown up since Jerome Kern and Otto Harbach first showed the many charms of* Roberta *to a paying public...So it is also pleasing to report...that the vehicle is a durable one and that the touch of Jerome Kern's hand is still magical...Although all of the dance numbers choreographed by Hermes Pan are not inspired, he has inventively devised spirited turns for 'I Won't Dance' and 'Smoke Gets in Your Eyes' to which Marge and Gower Champion contribute professional grace, verve and charm.*" (*A.H. Weiler,* The New York Times)

Roberta (1958, NBC Special, 90m/c) ☆☆½ **Tp:** Mort Lachman, Bill Larkin, Lester White, John Rapp, Charles Lee, Norman Sullivan. **D:** Dick McDonough, Ed Greenberg. **P:** Jack Hope. **Cast:** Howard Keel, Anna Maria Alberghetti, Bob Hope, Janis Paige, Sara Dillon, Lilli Valenti.

Roberta (1969, NBC Special, 90m/c) ☆☆ **Tp:** Mel Tolkin, Lester White, Charles Lee, Gig Henry, Bill Larkin, Mort Lachman. **D:** Dick McDonough, John Kennedy. **P:** Bob Hope. **Cast:** John Davidson, Michele Lee, Bob Hope, Janis Paige, Laura Miller, Ann Shoemaker, Irene Hervey, Eve McVeagh.

Up in Mabel's Room was based by Harbach and Wilson Collison on Collison's story, "Oh, Chemise"—similar to Collison and Avery Hopwood's play, *Getting Gertie's Garter*, which concerns an inscribed undergarment that could cause mistaken identity and imperil a pending marriage.

Up in Mabel's Room (1926, PDC, bw/silent) ☆☆☆ **Sc:** Tay Garnett, F. McGrew Willis. **D:** E. Mason Hopper. **P:** Al Christie. **Cam:** Alex Phillips, Harold Rosson. **Cast:** Marie Prevost, Harrison Ford, Phyllis Haver, Harry Myers, Sylvia Breamer, Paul Nicholson, Carl Gerard, Maude Truax, William Orlamond, Arthur Hoyt.

- *"This was one of a series of low-budget bedroom farces from when Marie Prevost was at the height of her career...Up in Mabel's Room is the best of the series...Prevost plays a wife who has divorced her husband, and realized she made a mistake. It is interesting to see how this complicated situation is finally resolved."* (Robert K. Klepper, Silent Films 1877–1996)

Up in Mabel's Room (1944, UA, 76m/bw, **DVD**) ☆☆ **Sc:** Tom Reed, Isobel Dawn. **D:** Allan Dwan. **P:** Edward Small. **Cam:** Charles Lawton Jr.. **Cast:** Marjorie Reynolds, Dennis O'Keefe, Gail Patrick, Mischa Auer, Charlotte Greenwood, Lee Bowman, John Hubbard, Binnie Barnes, Janet Lambert, Harry Hayden, Fred Kohler Jr.

- *"What's funny about a lot of actors rushing madly in and out of bedrooms, diving under beds and stifling sneezes in order not to be found? What's humorous about a limp-brained husband trying vainly to prevent his childish wife from thinking that he is making whoopee with a coyly seductive dame? Don't ask us, ladies and gentlemen."* (Bosley Crowther, The New York Times)

Robert Harling

Born: 1951.

Since *Steel Magnolias* was adapted into an all-star tear-jerker of a film, Robert Harling has stayed with star-studded women's pictures, writing the scripts for *Soapdish* (1991), *The First Wives Club* (1996), and *Evening Star* (1996), the sequel to James L. Brooks's Oscar-winning Best Picture, *Terms of Endearment* (1983).

Steel Magnolias (1989, Columbia/Tri-Star, 117m/c, **VHS/DVD**) ☆☆☆½ **Sc:** Robert Harling. **D:** Herbert Ross. **P:** Ray Stark. **Cam:** John A. Alonzo. **Cast:** Sally Field, Shirley MacLaine, Dolly Parton, Julia Roberts, Daryl Hannah, Sam Shepard, Olympia Dukakis, Tom Skerritt, Kevin J. O'Connor, Janine Turner, Dylan McDermott, Ann Wedgeworth, Bill McCutcheon. In a small Louisiana town in the 1980s, the womenfolk gather at the local beauty parlor to trade gossip and wisecracks. The cast makes it worthwhile, especially MacLaine as a kook in overalls. The film was nominated for Best Supporting Actress (Roberts).

- "Steel Magnolias *is essentially a series of comic one-liners leading up to a teary tragedy...At first we are not aware of impending tragedy...because the movie sticks so successfully to its comic dialogue. I doubt if any six real women could be funny and sarcastic so consistently (every line is an epigram), but I love the way these women talk, especially when Dukakis observes, 'What separates us from the animals is our ability to accessorize.'...this is a woman's picture...The principal pleasure of the movie is in the ensemble work of the actresses, as they trade one-liners and zingers and dish the dirt."* (Roger Ebert, Chicago Sun-Times)

Elmer Harris

Elmer Blaney Harris
Born: January 11, 1878, Chicago, IL. **Died:** 1966.

Elmer Harris adapted his play *Pretty Mrs. Smith* into the 1915 film of the same title, and immediately embarked upon a career in silent films. His scenarios and screen stories include *The Love That Dares* (1919), *The Sin of St. Anthony* (1920), *The Speed Girl* (1921), *Ducks and Drakes* (1921), *The Awful Truth* (1925), *The Siren* (1927), *The Spirit of Youth* (1929), *Society Girl* (1932), *The Barbarian* (1933), and *Three Wise Guys* (1935). His play *Johnny Belinda* has become one of the standard melodramas about the physically challenged.

Her Guilded Cage (1922, Paramount, bw/silent) **Sc:** Percy Heath. **D:** Sam Wood. **Cam:** Alfred Gilks. **Cast:** Gloria Swanson, David Powell, Harrison Ford, Anne Cromwell, Walter Hiers, Charles A. Stevenson. Based on the play *The Love Dreams* by Harris and Anne Nichols.

Johnny Belinda starred Helen Craig on Broadway in 1940. The mute daughter of a Nova Scotia farmer, deemed an idiot by her family, blossoms after a young doctor teaches her sign language. She's then raped by a local thug and carries the titular baby.

Johnny Belinda (1948, Warner Bros., 102m/bw, **VHS**) ☆☆☆☆ **Sc:** Irmgard Von Cube, Allen Vincent. **D:** Jean Negulesco. **P:** Jerry Wald. **Cam:** Ted McCord. **Cast:** Jane Wyman, Lew Ayres, Charles Bickford, Agnes Moorehead, Stephen McNally, Jan Sterling, Rosalind Ivan, Dan Seymour, Mabel Paige, Ida Moore, Alan Napier, Monte Blue, Douglas Kennedy, James Craven, Jeff Richards, Ian Wolfe, Holmes Herbert, Jonathan Hale, Creighton Hale, Richard Walsh. One of the all-time weepers benefits from Negulesco's superb direction and Wyman's career-making performance. The film won an Oscar for Best Actress (Wyman) and was nominated for Best Picture, Actor (Ayres), Supporting Actor

(Bickford), Supporting Actress (Moorehead), Director, Screenplay, Cinematography, Score (Max Steiner), Film Editing, Art Direction/Set Decoration, and Sound.

- *"Plucky girls with baby faces take heart: Jane Wyman was in movies more than 10 years before people began to cry over her...an evasive, slick sob story. The way in which, at age 34, she played a girl supposedly half her age, ostensibly deaf-mute but looking as neat and wholesome as a Mabel Lucy Attwell cherub, is evidence of make-believe becoming more artificial as it lumbers toward a subject that is 'authentic' and 'daring.' Johnny Belinda is uncut corn, but Wyman had a soulful, wide-eyed face (such as made handicap acceptable) and, under Negulesco's direction, it was no surprise that she won an Oscar. That film also established her as a stimulant to tears for another eight years."* (David Thomson, A Biographical Dictionary of Film)

- *"...might have been as exasperating as the Broadway play by Elmer Harris that it's based on, but the director, Jean Negulesco, managed to provide an atmosphere in which the hokey, tear-jerker elements are used for more than mere pathos—an example of technique over subject matter."* (Pauline Kael, 5001 Nights at the Movies)

Johnny Belinda (1958, NBC, 90m/c) *The Hallmark Hall of Fame* ☆☆☆☆ **Tp:** Theodore Apstein. **D/P:** George Schaefer. **Cast:** Julie Harris, Christopher Plummer, Victor Jory, Joanna Roos, Rip Torn, Betty Lou Holland, Beulah Garrick, John Cecil Holm, Boris Marshalov, Catherine Proctor.

- *"...had Julie Harris, Christopher Plummer, and Rip Torn playing the mean little villain. This saga of a deaf and dumb girl who is raped, has a baby, and finds a soul mate in the local doctor was a fine, play, a tremendous film and an absolutely first class TV show."* (George Schaefer, From Live to Tape to Film: 60 Years of Inconspicuous Directiing)

Johnny Belinda (1967, ABC Special, 120m/c) ☆☆½ **Tp:** Allen Sloane. **D:** Paul Bogart. **P:** David Susskind. **Cast:** Mia Farrow, Ian Bannen, Barry Sullivan, Ruth White, David Carradine, Jacques Aubuchon, Louise Latham, Carolyn Daniels, Stacy Keach, Mary Grace Canfield, Pitt Herbert, Glenn Langan, Jason Wingreen, Pat O'Hara. A formidable cast, in retrospect, was assembled for this special, fronted by Farrow, who was amid her uneasy marriage to Frank Sinatra and a year from film stardom in *Rosemary's Baby* (1968). Her work pales in comparison to Harris's acclaimed performance nine years earlier (above).

- *"Mia Farrow has the gentle and very young appearance the part requires but hardly the diversity of emotional expression to impart the deeper beauty and illumination that the assignment calls for; her range of response was statically narrow."* (Variety)

- *"For some strange reason, ABC felt the urge to repeat the Mia Farrow Johnny Belinda. Several Mia defenders have pointed out to me that this was her finest performance. They were absolutely right. She didn't say one word during the entire show."* (Rex Reed, Big Screen, Little Screen)

Johnny Belinda (1982, CBS Special, 120m/c, **VHS**) ☆☆☆ **Tp:** Sue Milburn. **D:** Anthony Page. **P:** Stanley Bass. **Cast:** Rosanna Arquette, Richard Thomas, Roberts Blossom, Dennis Quaid, Candy Clark, Fran Ryan, Robert Dryer, Billy Drago, Richard Linebeck, Mickey Jones, Penelope Windust, Wayne Heffley, Noni White.

- *"...uneven 1982 TV movie remake of Johnny Belinda, most notable for Rosanna Arquette's performance as a deaf-mute."* (Kevin Thomas, Los Angeles Times)

Johnny Belinda was also presented in 1955 on CBS's *Front Row Center* directed and produced by Fletcher Markle, and starred Katherine Bard, Eddie Albert, Tudor Owen, James Gavin, and Maudie Prickett.

Pretty Mrs. Smith (1915, Paramount, bw/silent) ☆☆½ **Sc:** Elmer Harris. **D:** Hobart Bosworth. **Cam:** George W. Hill. **Cast:** Louis Bennison, Leila Bliss, Owen Moore, Fritzie Scheff, Forrest Stanley. Based on the play by Elmer Harris and Oliver Morosco

- *"This was the first appearance of Miss Fritzie Scheff in pictures, and it was with great enthusiasm that the lovely star of the footlights commenced her work at the studio."* (Moving Picture World)

Sham (1921, Paramount, bw/silent) ☆☆ **Sc:** Douglas Doty. **D:** Thomas N. Heffron. **Cam:** Charles Edgar Schoenbaum. **Cast:** Ethel Clayton, Clyde Fillmore, Theodore Roberts, Sylvia Ashton, Walter Hiers, Helen Dunbar, Arthur Edmund Carewe, Tom Ricketts, Blanche Gray, Eunice Burnham, Carrie Clark Ward. The 1909 play by Harris and Geraldine Bonner lampooned false standards and pretenses in American society.

- *"The title implies that the picture is a solemn preachment...and in so far as it is that, it is unvaryingly dull, but occasionally it has light comedy touches, and then it is amusing...Theodore Roberts, Walter Heirs, Sylvia Ashton and occasionally Miss Clayton herself impart a breeziness to it now and then that makes one forget all about its sham title and mock moralizing, and just enjoy it."* (The New York Times)

So Long, Letty began as a collaboration between Harris and Oliver Morosco on the book for the 1916 musical, which featured music by Earl Carroll. A no-holds-barred comedy, it concerns an exchange of wives for a week, accompanied by prolonged mistaken identity. Charlotte Greewood starred as Letty in the original stage production.

So Long, Letty (1920, Robertson-Cole, bw/silent) ☆☆☆ **Sc:** W. Scott Darling. **D:** Al Christie. **Cam:** Anton Nagy, Steve Rounds. **Cast:** T. Roy Barnes, Colleen Moore, Walter Hiers, Grace Damond.

- "...*a very intelligent adaptation...with no attempt to improve on the plot, slender as it was, except to bring in the Christie bathing girls for a few scenes...splendid titles, most of them from the stage version...*" (Motion Picture News)

So Long, Letty (1927, Warner Bros., 64m/bw) ☆☆☆ **Sc:** De Leon Anthony, Arthur Caeser, Robert Lord. **D:** Lloyd Bacon. **Cam:** James Van Trees. **Cast:** Charlotte Greenwood, Claude Gillingwater, Grant Withers, Patsy Ruth Miller, Bert Roach, Marion Byron, Helen Foster, Hallam Cooley, Harry Gribbon, Lloyd Ingraham, Jack Grey.

- "*The film is raucous and broad and the idea of an exchange of wives for a period of a week is not entirely new. But with the playful Miss Grenwood to carry it along its frivolous route it manages to turn up as a cheery photoplay, with many entertaining moments...The picture itself goes almost insane at times, for it possesses so many irrational moments that its logical points seem strangely out of place.*" (The New York Times)

Moss Hart

Robert Arnold Conrad
Born: October 24, 1904, New York, NY. **Died:** 1961.
Pulitzer Prize-winning play: *You Can't Take It With You* (1937)

Moss Hart began his dramatic career as a secretary to a traveling theatre manager. As an actor, he played, among other roles, Smithers in Eugene O'Neill's *The Emperor Jones* to Paul Robeson's Jones in 1926. Hart was most significantly a writer, but he also directed and produced his own plays as well as those written by Norman Krasna, Alan Jay Lerner, and others. He won a New York Drama Critics Award in 1955 and a Tony Award in 1956, both for Best Director, for the staging of Lerner and Loewe's musical *My Fair Lady* with Rex Harrison and Julie Andrews. His playwriting partnership with George S. Kaufman is one of the great collaborations of American literature, producing most significantly *You Can't Take It With You* and *The Man Who Came to Dinner*.

All of Hart's Broadway plays written on his own have been adapted to films or TV and are inventoried below. Hart was also a significant screenwriter and his work in Hollywood received Academy Award nominations for the original story of *Broadway Melody of 1936* (1935) and the screenplay for the Oscar-winning Best Picture, *Gentlemen's Agreement* (1947). His other films as a screenwriter include John Ford's *Flesh*

(1932), *Hans Christian Andersen* (1952), the first remake of *A Star Is Born* (1954) with Judy Garland, and *Prince of Players* (1954).

Hart broke from Kaufman in 1940 after the theatrical failure of *George Washington Slept Here*, fearing that he would only be seen as half of a writing team. He was married to actress Kitty Carlisle and wrote one of the most critically acclaimed books about Broadway, *Act One: An Autobiography*, in 1959. Two years later, he was dead, and two after that, he was portrayed in the film adaptation of *Act One* by George Hamilton, with Jason Robards Jr. as Kaufman.

For collaborative works with Kaufman, see **George S. Kaufman**; for *Miss Liberty*, see **Robert E. Sherwood**.

The Climate of Eden was produced in 1960 for *The Play of the Week*. Hart originally adapted the play from Edgar Mittleholzer's story "Shadows Move Them Away." The cast included Kevin Coughlin, Diana Hyland, Roland Culver, Donald Harron, and Lynn Loring.

The Decision of Christopher Blake (1948, Warner Bros., 75m/bw) ☆☆☆½ **Sc/P:** Ranald MacDougall. **D:** Peter Godfrey. **Cam:** Karl Freund. **Cast:** Alexis Smith, Robert Douglas, Cecil Kellaway, Ted Donaldson, John Hoyt, Harry Davenport, Mary Wickes, Art Baker, Lois Maxwell, Douglas Kennedy, Bert Hanlon.

• *"...first class drama...the actors are uniformly good. Ranald Mac-Dougall...and Peter Godfrey have given Moss Hart's unusual preachment against divorce a sound and different motion picture." (Lynn Bowers,* Los Angeles Herald-Examiner)

The Great Waltz was originally produced on Broadway in 1934. Hart adapted the book by A.M. Willner, Heinz Reichert, Ernst Marischka, and Caswell Garth for producer Max Gordon's paean to the music of Johann Strauss Sr. and Jr. It was revived in 1955 for a 90-minute NBC special produced under the umbrella title of *Max Liebman Presents* with a teleplay by William Friedberg and Neil Simon. Liebman directed a cast including Keith Andres, Henry Sharp, Patrice Munsel, Jarmila Novotna, Bert Lahr, Lee Goodman, Gordon Dillworth, Sam Schwartz, and Mia Slavenska. Liebman's poshly done series of musical specials showcased classical music for a growing TV audience.

Lady in the Dark debuted on Broadway in 1941 and starred Gertrude Lawrence supported by Victor Mature, Macdonald Carey, Danny Kaye, and Bert Lytell. She played a fashion magazine editor whose psychological problems are solved when she gives up her job to a man—a move that dates the play horribly. The music was by Kurt Weill and the lyrics by Ira Gershwin.

Lady in the Dark (1944, Paramount, 100m/bw) ☆ **Sc:** Frances

Goodrich, Albert Hackett. **D:** Mitchell Leisen. **P:** Richard Blumenthal. **Cam:** Ray Rennahan. **Cast:** Ginger Rogers, Ray Milland, Warner Baxter, Jon Hall, Barry Sullivan, Mischa Auer, Phyllis Brooks, Mary Phillips, Edward Fielding, Mary Parker, Don Loper, Virginia Farmer, Catherine Craig, Billy Daniels, Rand Brooks, Tristram Coffin. Overblown, but with three imaginatively shot dream sequences, the film became a particularly hateful antique by the 1960s. Rogers was criticized for being inadequate for the part, but that issue became moot when the film was pulverized by critics.

- *"Monstrously overproduced musical...the content is insulting to women; the form is insulting to audiences of both sexes. It's a real botch."* (*Pauline Kael*, 5001 Nights at the Movies)

- *"Ziegfield Follies [is] rivalled only in ugliness by Mitchell Liesen's* Lady in the Dark...*There are the kinds of movies that Hollywood's enemies like to recall. And so, too, the dreadful* Lady in the Dark *was a vulgar and monstrous betrayal of the composer's genius."* (*Charles Higham & Joel Greenberg*, Hollywood in the Forties)

Lady in the Dark (1954, NBC Special, 90m/bw) *Max Liebman Presents* ☆☆ **Tp:** William Friedberg, Max Liebman. **D:** Jeffrey Hayden. **P:** Max Liebman. **Host:** Lee Bowman. **Cast:** Ann Sothern, James Daly, Paul McGrath, Sheppard Strudwick, Luella Gear, Carleton Carpenter, Bambi Linn, Robert Fortier, Rod Alexander. The star wasn't a singer, so Kurt Weill's score again wasn't well served. But in the 1950s, the housewives were still supposed to be housewives.

- *"Artistically, it was a triumph, for the production had taste and dignity, was wholly adult and had a grand sweep."* (*Variety*)

Light Up the Sky (1951, ABC, 60m/bw) *Pulitzer Prize Playhouse* ☆☆☆½ **Tp:** Felix Jackson. **Narrator:** Elmer Davis. **Cast:** Patricia Morison, Lee Tracy, Polly Rowles, William Terry, Tom Helmore, Phyllis Povah. Hart's satire of a Broadway show in the making took potshots at temperamental actresses, ice-skaters turned actresses, and artsy directors. The original was staged in 1948 by Hart at Broadway's Royale Theatre with a cast that included Barry Nelson, Audrey Christie, Sam Levene, and Simon Oakland.

- *"The comedy was given an extravagant reading which made for biting portrayals of the Broadway celebs that Hart was satirizing. Felix Jackson's adaptation had some good laughs, although in boiling it down to an hour-long vehicle, the play's well-worn situation, the coming-of-age of an idealistic young writer, was exposed. Additionally, the condensation made the characters' changes of heart seem too sudden. It added up, however, to a good picture of the way in which a show is hammered out after its Boston tryout."* (*Variety*)

Winged Victory (1944, 20th Century-Fox, 130m/bw) ☆☆☆½ **Sc:** Moss Hart. **D:** George Cukor. **P:** Darryl F. Zanuck. **Cam:** Glen MacWilliams. **Cast:** Lon McCallister, Jeanne Crain, Edmond O'Brien, Jane Ball, Mark Daniels, Don Taylor, Lee J. Cobb, Judy Holliday, Jo-Carroll Dennison, Peter Lind Hayes, Alan Baxter, Red Buttons, Barry Nelson, Gary Merrill, George Reeves, Alfred Ryder, Karl Malden, Martin Ritt, Don Beddoe, Geraldine Wall. Produced at Broadway's 44th Street Theatre in 1943 with the full cooperation of the U.S. Army Air Force, this flag-waver illustrated the power and enthusiasm of the Army Air Corps during World War II. The piece was a big hit on both stage and screen. The film ensemble played a group of fledgling airmen going through training.

- *"The Army Air Force show,* Winged Victory, *which was a big and deserving hit upon the stage, has now been transposed into the medium which was most appropriate to it all the time — the large-scale and swiftly fluid medium of the motion-picture screen…20th Century-Fox has put into it all the spectacle that the original so narrowly implied…all the wonder that the 'wild blue yonder' holds. Furthermore, George Cukor, the director, has kept all the poignancy and zeal that was tightly compacted in the episodes of Moss Hart's original play."* (Bosley Crowther, The New York Times)

Joseph Hayes

Born: August 2, 1918, Indianapolis IN.
Tony Award-winning play: *The Desperate Hours* (1955)

Joseph Hayes's other direct contribution to the screen was the adaptation of Arthur Hailey's novel *The Final Diagnosis* into *The Young Doctors* (1961), starring Fredric March and Ben Gazzara. *Bon Voyage!*, a comic novel written with his wife, Marrijane Hayes, about a Parisian vacation, was adapted into the 1962 Disney film starring Fred McMurray, and his novel *The Third Day* was made into a 1965 George Peppard thriller. Joseph Hayes should not be confused with John Michael Hayes, who wrote many Hollywood screenplays during the 1950s and 1960s, including several for Alfred Hitchcock.

The Desperate Hours was Hayes's adaptation of his own novel for a 1955 Broadway presentation that starred Karl Malden and Nancy Coleman as homeowners held hostage in their own house by a prison escapee and his gang — Paul Newman, George Grizzard, and company.

The Desperate Hours (1955, Paramount, 112m/bw, **VHS**) ☆☆☆☆

Sc: Joseph Hayes. **D/P:** William Wyler. **Cam:** Lee Garmes. **Cast:** Humphrey Bogart, Fredric March, Arthur Kennedy, Martha Scott, Dewey Martin, Gig Young, Mary Murphy, Richard Eyer, Robert Middleton, Alan Reed, Bert Freed, Ray Collins, Whit Bissell, Ray Teal, Don Haggerty, Beverly Garland, Ann Doran, Michael Moore, Ric Roman, Louis Lettieri. The casting couldn't have been better, with Bogart fleshing out his best latter-career gangster part. The film failed to be great, however; a fault of the play, which relies too much on the shocking (for the 1950s) premise.

- *"Wyler, a first-rate craftsman, has made a...polished production...His cast leaves little to be desired...the performances are good, the production solid, the settings reasonably believable...we are shown human nature reacting to an extreme sort of situation."* (Hollis Alpert, Saturday Review)

- *"The cast of the picture is splendid. Fredric March has an impressive dignity as the citizen whose house has suddenly been taken over and Humphrey Bogart is frightening as the principal convict."* (John McClain, The New Yorker)

The Desperate Hours (1967, ABC Special, 120m/c) ☆½ **Tp:** Clive Exton. **D:** Ted Kotcheff. **P:** Dan Melnick. **Cast:** Arthur Hill, Teresa Wright, Yvette Mimieux, George Segal, Michael Kearney, Barry Primus, Michael Conrad, Dolph Sweet, Mart Hulswit, Ralph Waite, Graham Jarvis. This astutely cast special concentrated on the threat of violence and was deemed by some to be too graphic for TV family audiences.

- *"This adaptation of Joseph Hayes's old play-meler should have been called* The Desperate Producers. *Clive Exton's adaptation destroyed the character evolution and turned the play into a two-bit thriller."* (Variety)

The Desperate Hours (1990, MGM, 105m/c, **VHS**) ☆☆½ **Sc:** Mark Rosenthal. **D:** Michael Cimino. **P:** Michael Cimino, Dino DeLaurentiis. **Cam:** Doug Milsome. **Cast:** Mickey Rourke, Anthony Hopkins, Mimi Rogers, Kelly Lynch, Lindsay Crouse, Elias Koteas, Shawnee Smith, David Morse, Danny Gerard, Matt McGrath, Gerry Bamman, Dean Norris.

- *"...updated, garbled remake...Hopkins...tears into lines as if he were King Lear on the heath. What has been lost is more than Bogart's gritty presence. The claustrophobia and the twisting false endings that allow William Wyler's original version to hold up today has been replaced by a house with distracting, ornate furnishings...It has been a long road down for Mr. Cimino from* The Deer Hunter *through* Heaven's Gate *and on to* The Sicilian. *It's hard to imagine that what comes next could be more misguided than* Desperate Hours. (Caryn James, The New York Times)

Ben Hecht

Born: February 28, 1894, New York, NY. **Died:** 1964.

Ben Hecht wrote, co-wrote, or re-wrote, with and without credit, at least 140 movies and 14 Broadway plays, as well as short stories, novels, and reminiscences. Most famously, he was partnered in both playwriting and screenwriting with another former Chicago newspaperman, Charles MacArthur. Their partnership on various stage, film, and TV renditions of *The Front Page* and *Twentieth Century* is more detailed in the dual entry with MacArthur below. Hecht's plays on his own include *To Quito and Back, Lily of the Valley,* and *A Flag Is Born.*

The short list of films that Hecht wrote with credit and without MacArthur includes *Scarface* (1932), *Design for Living* (1933), *Viva Villa!* (1934), *Nothing Sacred* (1937), *Angels Over Broadway* (1940), *Notorious* (1946), *Kiss of Death* (1947), *Monkey Business* (1952), and *A Farewell to Arms* (1957). Hecht also wrote as well as directed *Specter of the Rose* (1946) and *Actors and Sin* (1952) and often doctored scripts for directors Alfred Hitchcock and Howard Hawks. Hecht was nominated for six Academy Awards and won two, for creating the original stories for the gangster archetype *Underworld* (1927) and, with MacArthur, *The Scoundrel* (1935). Hecht also collaborated on screenplays with Charles Lederer, I.A.L. Diamond, and Gene Fowler.

Hecht's first TV offering was the adaptation of his story "The Rival Dummy" for a 1949 installment of *Studio One* starring Paul Lukas and Anne Francis; the same story had been the basis for the 1929 James Cruze film *The Great Gabbo* starring Erich von Stroheim. Hecht's *The Murder Club* aired in 1950 on *Billy Rose's Playbill* with Walter Hampden. *Robert Montgomery Presents* adapted Hecht and Charles Lederer's film scenario, *Ride the Pink Horse* (1947), which starred Montgomery in a 1950 show that gave the star another go at the demi-classic about blackmail. *Ben Hecht's Tales of the City* was a short-lived 1953 anthology series of 30-minute pieces on CBS, hosted by Hecht, who also performed in some of the pieces and wrote six of them. He also wrote the NBC pilot, *The Third Commandment,* starring Arthur Kennedy in 1959 for an intended series on the Ten Commandments.

Hecht also wrote 22 novels or collections of short stories, including several that were adapted into movies, such as *The Florentine Dagger* and *Miracle in the Rain.* His 1963 autobiographical account of newspaper work in early 20th century Chicago, *Gaily, Gaily,* was adapted into a 1969 film starring Beau Bridges. "Hecht's style at its best," wrote Doreen Bartoni, "was a delicate balance between cynicism and sentimentalism. His heroes tended to embody his own anti-middle-class bias, preferring a life of rugged individualism over the bland comforts of conformity. His unique brand of rapid-fire, overlapping dialogue often served to unmask the quick-witted cynic as a surprisingly caring humanitarian."

The Great Magoo was produced in 1932 by Billy Rose and staged by George Abbott. It ran for only 11 performances. It was written by Hecht, Wilkie C. Mahoney, and Gene Fowler, and concerns a sideshow barker who goes broke.

Shoot the Works (1934, Paramount, 64m/bw) ☆½ **Sc:** Claude Binyon, Howard J. Green. **D:** Wesley Ruggles. **Cam:** Leo Tover. **Cast:** Jack Oakie, Ben Bernie, Dorothy Dell, Arlene Judge, Alison Skipworth, Roscoe Karns, William Frawley, Paul Cavanaugh, Lew Cody, Jill Dennett, Ben Taggart. This film was known in the United Kingdom by the title *Thank Your Stars*.

- *"...when it was staged at the Selwyn in 1932, [it] produced in its auditors a pious ambition to cleanse its mouth with soap and water. This latter form of athletic purgation has duly taken place in the studio laundries, and* The Great Magoo *has now been scrubbed, rinsed and dried in the California sunshine with such heartiness that not only its stench but also its humor has been washed out...Their error resided not in their well-intentioned efforts to perform a major operation upon a bawdy play, but their attempt to transfer the guttersnipe population of* The Great Magoo *to the screen in the first place." (Andre Sennwald,* The New York Times*)*

Some Like It Hot (1939, Paramount, 65m/bw) ☆☆ **Sc:** Lewis R. Foster. **D:** George Archainbaud. **P:** William C. Thomas. **Cam:** Karl Struss. **Cast:** Bob Hope, Shirley Ross, Una Merkel, Gene Krupa, Richard Denning. This film was more about the studio building another Hope/Ross vehicle to follow *The Big Broadcast of 1938* and *Thanks for the Memory* (both 1938) than *The Great Magoo*. This has nothing to do with the classic 1959 Billy Wilder/I.A.L. Diamond comedy of the same name.

- *"Story itself is just an excuse on which to hang Krupa's musical display. It's built around the smart cracks and antics of Bob Hope as an ambitious, cocky and small-timey promoter..." (Variety)*

Living It Up (1954, Paramount, 95m/c) ☆☆☆ **Sc:** Jack Rose, Melville Shavelson. **D:** Norman Taurog. **P:** Hal B. Wallis. **Cam:** Daniel L. Fapp. **Cast:** Dean Martin, Jerry Lewis, Janet Leigh, Edward Arnold, Fred Clark, Sheree North, Sig Rumann. Hecht wrote the fully-barbed screenplay for William A. Wellman's *Nothing Sacred* (1937), derived from a William Street magazine story about the media circus caused by the erroneous news that a small-town beauty in New England has a short time to live. The film was adapted by Hecht into the 1953 Broadway musical *Hazel Flagg*, with music by Jule Styne and lyrics by Bob Hilliard. It starred Helen Gallagher, Thomas Mitchell and, in their Broadway debuts, John Howard, Sheree North and Ross Martin. In this version, Lewis played the dope supposedly dying from radium poisoning. This was one of Martin and Lewis's big hits of the mid-1950s.

- *"Nobody can look more radioactive than Jerry Lewis—and in* Living It Up *he is scarcely able to contain himself...intermittently amusing, as often plain silly and way overlength for comedy." (Philip K. Scheuer,* Los Angeles Times)

Spring Tonic (1935, Fox, 55m/bw) ☆ **Sc:** Patterson McNutt, H.W. Hanemann. **D:** S. Sylvan Simon. **P:** Robert Kane. **Cam:** L. William O'Connell. **Cast:** Lew Ayres, Claire Trevor, Walter Woolf King, ZaSu Pitts, Jack Haley, Sig Rumann, Talia Birell. Based on the play *Man Eats Tiger* by Hecht and Rose Caylor, the film concerns an escaped tigress that causes a gamut of expected comedic episodes.

- *"This picture has every appearance of having been ad-libbed by the cast while the director's back was turned...a total of inanity...conglomerated here for a gag man's picnic and zero entertainment...story and direction are exceptionally poor." (*Variety)

Ben Hecht & Charles MacArthur

See individual entries for biographical details.

Billy Rose's Jumbo (1962, MGM, 124m/c, **VHS**) ☆☆½ **Sc:** Sidney Sheldon. **D:** Charles Waters. **P:** Joe Pasternak, Martin Melcher. **Cam:** William H. Daniels. **Cast:** Doris Day, Stephen Boyd, Jimmy Durante, Martha Raye, Dean Jagger. The 1935 Hecht/MacArthur play *Jumbo* takes place in 1910, and concerns the daughter of a financially unsolvent circus rallying to prevent its takeover by shady financiers. The play was produced by Billy Rose, scripted by Hecht and MacArthur, and featured music and lyrics by Richard Rodgers and Lorenz Hart. This film converted the piece into a Doris Day vehicle.

- *"...directed by Charles Waters, getting the utmost from the material...especially in the production numbers from* Jumbo *(Billy Rose managed to get his name in the title because he produced the original show on Broadway). This has a Rodgers and Hart score, because of its circus setting had been at first bought by Freed as a possible follow-up to* Annie Get Your Gun; *the project was resurrected because Doris Day, then the reigning box-office queen, had indicated that she would like to sing again and owed a commitment to MGM. She is fine, but Stephen Boyd, an exceptionally dreary leading man, sinks the enterprise. The powers that be, however, decided that the film failed because audiences did not want to see Day in musicals..." (David Shipman,* The Story of Cinema)

The Front Page debuted on Broadway as a 1928 Jed Harris production and ran for 276 performances, with Lee Tracy as Hildy Johnson and Osgood Perkins as Walter Burns. With its fast and lowdown language and snappy comebacks, the play was lauded by Tennessee Williams as the one that "uncorseted the American theatre with its earthiness and two-fisted vitality."

The Front Page (1931, UA, 101m/bw, **VHS/DVD**) ☆☆☆☆½ **Sc:** Bartlett Cormack, Charles Lederer. **D:** Lewis Milestone. **P:** Howard Hughes. **Cam:** Tony Gaudio, Hal Mohr, Glen MacWilliams. **Cast:** Adolphe Menjou, Pat O'Brien, Mary Brian, Edward Everett Horton, Walter Catlett, George E. Stone, Mae Clarke, Slim Summerville, Matt Moore, Frank McHugh, Clarence H. Wilson, Fred Howard, Eugene Strong, Spencer Charters, Herman J. Mankiewicz, Lewis Milestone, Phil Tead. Menjou, who played supporting characters for most of his career, had perhaps his best sustained role as Burns (he replaced Louis Wolheim at the 11th hour when Wolheim died). The film was fast and furious for its day, but not as rapid-fire as *His Girl Friday* (see below). It was nominated for Oscars for Best Picture, Actor (Menjou), and Director.

- "*...a witty and virile talking picture. It is a fast-paced entertainment...*" (*Mordaunt Hall*, The New York Times)

- "*The action was driven along at a cracking pace, backed by sparkling dialogue and excellent acting by Pat O'Brien and Adolphe Menjou. Probably the most famous of all newspaper dramas, its hard, fast and ruthless pace also contained oblique references to the political and press chicaneries of the period...Milestone's control of dialogue and performances set a new 'house standard' for Warner Bros...and also sparked off a cycle of newspaper films...but the original play proved such a successful entity in itself that he was unable to impose much of himself on his material.*" (Kingsley Canham, The Hollywood Professionals, Volume 2: Henry King, Lewis Milestone, Sam Wood)

His Girl Friday (1940, Columbia, 92min/bw, **VHS/DVD**) ☆☆☆☆☆ **Sc:** Charles Lederer, Ben Hecht (uncredited), Morrie Ryskind (uncredited). **D/P:** Howard Hawks. **Cam:** Joseph Walker. **Cast:** Cary Grant, Rosalind Russell, Ralph Bellamy, Gene Lockhart, Helen Mack, Porter Hall, Ernest Truex, Cliff Edwards, John Qualen, Clarence Kolb, Roscoe Karns, Frank Jenks, Abner Biberman, Regis Toomey, Billy Gilbert, Alma Kruger, Frank Orth, Pat West, Edwin Maxwell. Hawks's decisions to make Hildy into a woman—and an excellent professional newspaperwoman at that—and push the actors to run the dialogue in overdrive produced an instant and enduring classic.

- "His Girl Friday *has remained in high regard...a Hawks classic of its period whose reputation was further strengthened by the revaluation of the di-*

rector's career from the 1950s on. Although theatre critics and historians have been curiously silent on the subject, a handful of film academics — Gerald Mast and Robin Wood in particular — who have bothered to closely analyze the differences between The Front Page *and* His Girl Friday *have come down decisively in favor of Hawks's film." (Todd McCarthy,* Howard Hawks: The Gray Fox of Hollywood*)*

- *"…His Girl Friday is still better than a clever, arch, extremely funny newspaper movie. It's hard to believe that anything in Chaplin or W.C. Fields has so many hard, workable gags, each one bumping the other in an endless interplay of high-spirited cynicism." (Manny Farber,* Negative Space*)*

The Front Page (1970, ABC, 90m/c) ☆☆☆½ **Tp:** Ben Hecht, Charles MacArthur. **D:** Harold J. Kennedy. **P:** Martha Scott, Plumstead Theatre. **Host:** Helen Hayes. **Cast:** Robert Ryan, George Grizzard, Estelle Parsons, Harold J. Kennedy, Susan Watson, John McGiver, Charles White, Doro Merande, Vivian Vance. Ryan and the Plumstead Theatre revived interest in the play and eventually took it to Broadway in the late 1960s, where it did brisk business under Kennedy's direction.

- *"This 40-year-old comedy classic of the Amereican theatre translated remarkably well to the TV screen." (Variety)*

The Front Page (1974, Universal, 105m/c, **VHS/DVD**) ☆☆☆½ **Sc:** Billy Wilder, I.A.L. Diamond. **D:** Billy Wilder. **P:** Paul Monash. **Cam:** Jordan S. Cronenweth. **Cast:** Jack Lemmon, Walter Matthau, Susan Sarandon, David Wayne, Carol Burnett, Vincent Gardenia, Allen Garfield, Herb Edelman, Charles Durning, Austin Pendleton, Harold Gould, Martin Gabel, Cliff Osmond, Doro Merande, Dick O'Neill, Lou Frizzell, Noam Pitlik, Paul Benedict, Jon Korkes. The pedigree of this production created enormous expectations. Wilder hadn't had a surefire hit in a decade. Parts are excellent at the expense of the whole, with the Lemmon/Matthau pairing supplying the most fuel.

- *"The sap and the snap are gone. This is a movie conceived with indifference and made with disinterest, like a piece of occupational therapy." (Jay Cocks,* Time*)*

- *"Lively, refreshingly caustic and easily one of the funniest films of the year." (Kathleen Carroll,* New York Daily News*)*

- *"Those of us who have been busy reappraising Wilder's career in the 1960s and 1970s must acknowledge* The Front Page *with gratitude. For one thing, it is refreshing to find a director who still makes talkies instead of gawkies, and who thus still believes in the spoken word as a vehicle of expression. For another, Wilder's unique blend of cynicism and passion seems much more profound than it once did. More profound and more contemporary." (Andrew Sarris,* The Village Voice*)*

Switching Channels (1988, Rank, 108m/c, **VHS**) ☆☆☆ **Sc:** Jonathan Reynolds. **D:** Ted Kotcheff. **P:** Martin Ransohoff. **Cam:** Francois Protat. **Cast:** Kathleen Turner, Burt Reynolds, Christopher Reeve, Ned Beatty,

Henry Gibson, George Newbern, Al Waxman, Ken James. This update was taken out of newspapers and put into a cable news operation where Reynolds was the producer, Turner the on-air anchor, and Reeve her hubby-to-be. It's fast and snappy, like the earlier editions, but somehow neither as funny nor satisfying.

- *"...Turner has perfect timing as the long-suffering anchor, and she and Reynolds work up a nice sweat and some good chemistry in their relationship, which seems to be based on a few good memories and a whole lot of one-liners...true to the obsessive-compulsive hostility that is the fuel for all good reporters."* (Roger Ebert, Chicago Sun-Times)

The Front Page was broadcast as a pioneering TV venture in 1945, then became a half-hour CBS series 1949–1950 with scripts by Alvin Sapinskey, direction by Franklin Heller and a cast headed by John Daly, Mark Roberts, Jan Shaw, Leona Powers, and Cliff Hall. *Broadway Television Theatre* offered a 90-minute version of the play in 1953 directed by Richard Larkin and starring Lew Parker and Edward Everett Horton.

Perfect Strangers (1950, Warner Bros., 87m/bw) ☆☆½ **Sc:** Edith Sommer, George Oppenheimer. **D:** Bretaigne Windust. **P:** Jerry Wald. **Cam:** J. Peverell Marley. **Cast:** Ginger Rogers, Dennis Morgan, Thelma Ritter, Margalo Gillmore, Howard Freeman, Paul Ford, Alan Reed, George Chandler, Anthony Ross, Harry Bellaver, Frank Conlan. Hecht and MacArthur's 1939 play *Ladies and Gentlemen*, which they derived from a Hungarian drama by Ladislaw Bush-Fekete, was adapted into this slim Rogers vehicle, about a woman juror who falls for a married fellow juror during a love-nest murder trial.

- *"...[Rogers and Morgan] are rather lightly and haphazardly mixed into the makings of this random little fiction without any real regard for their bright skills...the list of writers credited...is a pretty palsied lineage for an item which evidently didn't have too much vitality at the start...an obviously hacked out affair..."* (Bosley Crowther, The New York Times)

Twentieth Century, which was produced and directed by George Abbott in 1932, starred Eugenie Leontovich and Moffat Johnston as a novice actress and an overbearing Broadway producer. Their relationship flip-flops when she becomes the big-time film star Lily Garland. Hecht and MacArthur retooled an unproduced play called *Napoleon of Broadway* by a press agent named Charles Bruce Milholland, who had based the egomaniacal producer on actual Broadway financier Morris Gest. Another well-known flamboyant producer, Jed Harris, bought the work from Milholland and turned it over to Hecht and MacArthur. "Within three weeks," Todd McCarthy wrote, "the speedy team delivered the first two acts to Harris, who could now see that the character of Oscar Jaffe was based on Gest, David Belasco, and, naturally enough, him." In 1978, the play was converted into a musical called *On the Twentieth Century* with lyrics by Betty Comden and Adolph Green and music by Cy Coleman.

Twentieth Century (1934, Columbia, 91m/bw, **VHS**) ☆☆☆☆☆ **Sc:** Ben Hecht, Charles MacArthur. **D/P:** Howard Hawks. **Cam:** Joseph August. **Cast:** John Barrymore, Carole Lombard, Walter Connolly, Roscoe Karns, Ralph Forbes, Charles Levison, Etienne Girardot, Edgar Kennedy, Dale Fuller, Billie Seward, Clifford Thompson, James P. Burtis, Gigi Parrish, Edward Gargan, Snowflake, Herman Bing, Fred Kelsey, James Burke, Pat Flaherty, Mary Jo Matthews, Lee Kohlmar. This film is usually credited as Hollywood's first sophisticated comedy. As *Variety* noted at the time, the film was "probably too smart for general consumption." Both stars enjoyed what in retrospect were probably their best roles and film performances, beautifully timed and smartly delivered, especially in the second half aboard the transcontinental Twentieth Century passenger express.

• *"...a few years ahead of its time, and, as might be expected of a Hawks masterpiece, did not receive the popular and critical acclaim it deserved. Hawks can take credit not only for John Barrymore's best bravura comedy performance, but also for the film which first established Carole Lombard as the finest comedienne of the 1930s...*Twentieth Century *is notable as the first comedy in which sexually attractive, sophisticated stars indulge in their own slapstick instead of delegating it to their inferiors."* (Andrew Sarris, Films and Filming, 1962)

• *"...John Barrymore justifies in one role his immense reputation. Cajoling, demanding, even in one scene vamping the harassed Lombard, he projects a perfect image of Broadway panache and insanity."* (John Baxter, Hollywood in the Thirties)

Twentieth Century (1949, CBS, 60m/bw) *Ford Theatre Hour* ☆☆☆☆ **D:** Marc Daniels. **P:** Garth Montgomery. **Cast:** Fredric March, Lilli Palmer, Nancy Pollock, E.G. Marshall, Edgar Stehli, David White, Robert H. Harris, John Marriott, John Seymour, Henry Roscoe, Morris Shrog, Gayne Sullivan, Phil Tead.

• *"Performed with a skilled cast, topped with a brilliant portrayal by Fredric March. Amusing script and, above all, its ace production and direction brought this revival right up to par for 60 minutes of cockeyed fun."* (Variety)

Twentieth Century (1953, N/N, 90m/bw) *The Broadway Television Theatre* ☆☆ **Sc/D:** Robert St. Aubrey. **P:** Warren Wade. **Cast:** Fred Clark, Constance Bennett, Pat Harrington, Rex O'Malley, Robert Carroll, W.O. McWaters, Donald Foster, Morton Kingsley.

• *"...[has] none of the knockdown confusion and happy farce of the play."* (Variety)

Twentieth Century (1956, CBS, 90m/c) *Ford Star Jubilee* ☆☆½ **Tp:** Robert Buckner. **D/P:** Arthur Schwartz. **Cast:** Orson Welles, Betty

Grable, Keenan Wynn, Ray Collins, Olive Sturgess, Gage Clark, Steve Terrell.

- *"...enough laughs to rate it a hit in this medium as well. When Welles played with his accustomed flamboyance, he carried the play with him. Unfortunately, he did not maintain the pace. Betty Grable showed a part of the brassy quality that was needed for the role. She suggested the role rather than fulfilled it. Withal, it was still a funny show."* (Variety)

- *"...indicated that tastes in comedy with the passage of years certainly has changed, if not improved. Orson Welles and Betty Grable...did little to brighten Buckner's adaptation."* (Jack Gould, The New York Times)

Lillian Hellman

Born: June 20, 1905, New Orleans, LA. **Died:** 1984.

Lillian Hellman was one of the great lights of the American theatre, whose personal life became the stuff of celebrity legend and has threatened in later years to overtake her accomplishments as a writer, particularly as a playwright. Her on-and-off relationship with Dashiell Hammett, the pioneer of hard-boiled detective fiction, has become one of the seminal literary romances of American literature. Her first play, The Children's Hour (1934), was a sensation for both its lesbian subject matter and its artistry. Most of her completed plays have been converted to films or TV shows, and are inventoried below; her only two Broadway plays that haven't been converted are Days to Come (1936) and The Autumn Garden (1951). Hellman's first volume of autobiography was An Unfinished Woman (1969). Screenplays that she wrote or contributed to not based on her own works include those for Dark Angel (1935), Dead End (1937), The Westerner (1940, uncredited), The North Star (1943), and The Chase (1966). David Howe produced and directed five half-hour installments about Hellman on Profile for PBS in 1981. William Luce wrote the play Lillian, based on Hellman's autobiographical works, which ran for 45 performances in 1986 at Broadway's Ethel Barrymore Theatre starring Zoe Caldwell. Jane Fonda played Hellman most famously in the Fred Zinnemann-directed film Julia (1977), co-starring Jason Robards as Hammett and Vanessa Redgrave as the elusive title character; Fonda was nominated for an Oscar for her performance and Robards and Redgrave won supporting Oscars for their roles. Alvin Sargent adapted the screenplay for Julia from her autobiographical Pentimento.

Another Part of the Forest debuted on Broadway in 1946 fronted by Patricia Neal and Mildred Dunnock. It was the prequel to The Little Foxes, showing the dastardly deeds that shaped the past of the gentrified

Hubbard family in 1880 Alabama. Blackmailing, freebooting, betrayal, Ku Klux Klan organizing, and other heinous acts are all part of the Hubbard family way.

Another Part of the Forest (1948, Universal, 108m/bw) ☆☆☆ **Sc:** Vladimir Pozner. **D:** Michael Gordon. **Cam:** Hal Mohr. **P:** Jerry Bresler. **Cast:** Fredric March, Florence Eldridge, Ann Blythe, Edmond O'Brien, Dan Duryea, John Dall, Betsy Blair, Dona Drake, Fritz Leiber, Whit Bissell, Don Beddoe, Virginia Farmer, Libby Taylor. The performers excelled and the plots hatched by various family members made for a soaper of some impact. This film took the family from *The Little Foxes* back to their rotten roots. The cast was exemplary.

- *"The Hubbards, who are supposed to be rising Southern capitalists, are the greatest collection of ghouls since* The Old Dark House *of 1932. Hellman must combine witchcraft with stagecraft—who else could keep a plot in motion with lost documents, wills, poisonings and pistols, and still be considered a social thinker?...Mostly [the players] act as if they were warming up for an American version of* Ivan the Terrible." *(Pauline Kael, 5001 Nights at the Movies)*

- *"Lillian Hellman's saber-toothed play about the new-born New South [is] ardently acted and directed with sense and tension by Michael Gordon...Some alert intercutting of reactions around a smoldering dinner table. An unusually good hybridization of stage and screen drama." (James Agee, The Nation)*

Another Part of the Forest (1972, PBS, 140m/c) *Hollywood Television Theatre: Special of the Week* ☆☆½ **Tp:** Lillian Hellman. **D:** Daniel Mann. **P:** Norman Lloyd. **Cast:** Barry Sullivan, Dorothy McGuire, Tiffany Bolling, Robert Foxworth, Andrew Prine, Patricia Sterling, William H. Bassett, Kent Smith, Jack Manning, Maidie Norman, Bill Walker, Peter Brocco. "I heard that we offended Lillian Hellman by cutting it, and she inquired, through a third party, about what we had had the gall to take out," Lloyd wrote years later. "I sent word back that the version was the one her own touring company had used..."

- *"Miss Hellman plucks on the major chords, but she is no social historian...She is a dramatist and, more often than not, her theatrical virtuosity is enough to disguise the fact that the centers of her drama may be hollow. Another Part of the Forest is not one of her more convincing efforts...Bravura acting...would undoubtedly help...But bravura acting is precisely what this TV production lacks." (John J. O'Connor, The New York Times)*

The Children's Hour, Hellman's first play, caused a stir when it debuted in 1934. Its plot concerns a neurotic schoolgirl who defames two of her teachers by accusing them of conducting a lesbian affair.

These Three (1936, Goldwyn, 93m/bw, **VHS**) ☆☆☆☆ **Sc:** Lillian

Hellman. **D:** William Wyler. **Cam:** Gregg Toland. **P:** Samuel Goldwyn. **Cast:** Miriam Hopkins, Merle Oberon, Joel McCrea, Bonita Granville, Catherine Doucet, Alma Kruger, Marcia Mae Jones, Walter Brennan, Margaret Hamilton, Carmencita Johnson. Because of the Production Code, Hellman transferred the affair from a lesbian liaison to a heterosexual one. A smoothly acted and beautifully shot film, it is, despite the thematic change, much better than the faithfully adapted version with the original title (see below). For her performance as the despicable snot, Granville received an Academy Award nomination for Best Supporting Actress in that award's inaugural year.

- *"I have seldom been so moved by any fictional film as by These Three. After 10 minutes or so of the usual screen sentiment, quaintness and exaggeration, one began to watch with incredulous pleasure nothing less than life: a genuine situation, a moral realism that allows one of two school-mistresses, whose lives and careers have been ruined by the malicious lie of a child, to murmur before the rigid self-righteousness of the wealthy grandparent: 'It is the very young and the very old who are wicked.'...Never before has childhood been represented so convincingly on the screen..."* (Graham Greene, The Spectator)

- *"These Three has a vitality...all its own. Although the producer...and the exhibitors have been pledged to keep a dark secret the fact that this film was based on* The Children's Hour, *there are few moviegoers unaware of the picture's origin...an exceptionally absorbing and emotionally disturbing masterpiece."* (Helen Eager, Boston Traveler)

The Children's Hour (1961, UA, 108m/bw) ☆☆ **Sc:** Lillian Hellman. **D/P:** William Wyler. **Cam:** Franz Planer. **Cast:** Audrey Hepburn, Shirley MacLaine, James Garner, Miriam Hopkins, Fay Bainter, Karen Balkin, Veronica Cartwright. Wyler and Hellman reteamed to redo her play, this time with the lesbian theme intact. The result here was an unusually sterile piece, showy to watch but ultimately uneventful—one of Wyler's rare misfires. The film received Oscar nominations for Best Supporting Actress (Bainter) and Cinematography.

- *"...such a portentous, lugubrious dirge...that I developed a rather perverse sympathy for the rich old lady villainess—I thought the school-teachers treated her abominably...I've never understood Lillian Hellmanland, where rich people are never forgiven for their errors. But then, has Miss Hellman even recognized hers? I can't help thinking that she wouldn't waste any sympathy on sexual deviation among the rich...There has been some commiseration with Wyler about the studio hacking out the center of the film: that's a bit like complaining that a corpse has had a vital organ removed. Who cares?"* (Pauline Kael, I Lost It at the Movies)

The Lark (1957, NBC, 90m/bw) *The Hallmark Hall of Fame* ☆☆☆☆ **Tp:** James Costigan. **D/P:** George Schaefer. **Cast:** Julie Harris, Boris Karloff, Eli

Wallach, Basil Rathbone, Jack Warden, Denholm Elliott, Michael Higgins, Jan Farrand, Elspeth March, Gregory Morton, Bruce Gordon, Harry Davis. Hellman's English-language Broadway adaptation of Jean Anouilh's French play—about the inquisition into the rebellious actions of Joan of Arc—featured Julie Harris in one of her greatest stage triumphs. Harris and her brilliant supporting cast, many from the stage production, along with Schaefer's use of close-ups for intimate character studies, all contributed to one of the year's TV highlights, bringing *Hallmark* the George Foster Peabody Award for Programming Excellence.

- "*...a superb television accomplishment...Miss Harris...gave a performance of deep beauty, inspiration and excitement; the other parts were perfectly cast; the production had a majestic simplicity and cleanness of pictorial line that were striking...George Schaefer...capitalized fully on the potentialities of the home medium.*" (Jack Gould, The New York Times)

The Little Foxes was Hellman's third play, which was produced to acclaim on Broadway in 1939 with Tallulah Bankhead as the villainous matriarch, Regina Hubbard Giddens. It introduced the internecine plots of the Hubbard family in the post-Civil War South, a family saga of squabbling that the playwright later returned to in *Another Part of the Forest*.

The Little Foxes (1941, RKO, 116m/bw) ☆☆☆☆ **Sc:** Lillian Hellman, Dorothy Parker, Alan Campbell, Arthur Kober (the last three uncredited). **D:** William Wyler. **P:** Samuel Goldwyn. **Cam:** Gregg Toland. **Cast:** Bette Davis, Herbert Marshall, Teresa Wright, Richard Carlson, Dan Dailey, Patricia Collinge, Charles Dingle, Carl Benton Reid, Russell Hicks, Lucien Littlefield, Virginia Brissac, Kenny Washington. This film is clearly the best of Hellman's plays to make it to the screen. In the realms of filmed or taped plays and well-heeled Southern bitchology, it is held in high regard. Wyler fought with Davis over the conception of the role, and demanded that the actress attend a Bankhead performance. Toland's cinematography was sublime. Hellman allowed the three uncredited writers to add a new character for the film, Carlson's David Hewitt, because she was tired of rewriting the piece. The film received Oscar nominations for Best Picture, Actress (Davis), Supporting Actress (Collinge and Wright), Director, Screenplay, Art Direction/Set Decoration, Score, and Film Editing, yet won none.

- "*...the most bitingly sinister picture of the year...Miss Davis's performance, in the role Miss Tallulah Bankhead played so brassily onstage, is abundant with color and mood.*" (Bosley Crowther, The New York Times)
- "*The Wyler-Davis collaboration climaxed with the film version of Lillian Hellman's play* The Little Foxes. *Wyler directed Hellman's corrosive examination of a vicious Southern family with a dexterity and a precision that still impress, and Gregg Toland's deep-focus photography captured every nuance, every revealing detail. Once again, the acting was perfection, with*

Patricia Collinge leading all the other cast members as the cowed, alcoholic Birdie." (Ted Sennett, The Great Movie Directors)

- *"Cold and mechanical, though technically expert, it achieved a kind of frigid proficiency, acceptable enough as a rendering of the author's lines, but emotionally uninvolving. Bette Davis's performance as Regina Giddens was an unhappy one, never bringing the character into clear focus." (Charles Higham and Joel Greenberg, Hollywood in the Forties)*

The Little Foxes (1956, NBC, 90m/bw) *The Hallmark Hall of Fame* ☆☆☆ **Tp:** Robert Hartung. **D/P:** George Schaefer. **Cast:** Greer Garson, Franchot Tone, E.G. Marshall, Sidney Blackmer, Eileen Heckart, Georgia Burke, Mildred Treras, Peter Kelley, Lloyde G. Richards, Lauren Gilbert. The miscasting of Greer Garson as Regina was the central criticism of this production.

- *"Lillian Hellman's opus of the decadent South…came to TV Sunday, offering many electrifying moments and slices of honest tragedy, but for reasons of casting missed being the solid, hair-raising drama and social commentary of the stage and screenplay. Greer Garson as Regina Giddens, the bitter, power-hungry, unscrupulous woman, did not have the needed authority and subtlety for the role. Miss Garson…struggled valiantly to meet the challenge of portraying the woman of consummate evil and design…" (Variety)*

Montserrat (1971, PBS, 120m/bw) *Hollywood Television Theatre* ☆☆ **Tp:** Lillian Hellman. **D:** David Friedkin. **P:** Lewis Freedman. **Cast:** Keir Dullea, Rip Torn, Geraldine Page, Earl Holliman, Jack Albertson, Hurd Hatfield, Martin Sheen, Jess Walton, Scott Colomby, Paul Stevens, Michael Baseleon. Another Hellman adaptation from the French, this being a version of Emmanuel Robles's play about an officer in the Spanish occupation army in 1812 Venezuela. He's being threatened with the firing-squad killings of innocents unless he gives up the whereabouts of revolutionary leader Simon Bolivar. Hellman was quoted as saying that the piece had relevancy for all foreign military occupations, including the then-current United States intervention in South Vietnam.

- *"International Business Machines [the sponsors], sad to relate, could have provided a more enticing readout…the political reasons for the murder of the innocents are bereft of fire and persuasion. Keir Dullea, as the converted follower of Bolivar, suggests Montserrat is a refugee from* The Student Prince, *a handsome lad more ready for the waltz than the cause." (Jack Gould, The New York Times)*

The Searching Wind (1946, Paramount, 107m/bw) ☆☆½ **Sc:** Lillian Hellman. **D:** William Dieterle. **Cam:** Lee Garmes. **P:** Hal B. Wallis. **Cast:** Robert Young, Sylvia Sidney, Douglas Dick, Ann Richards, Dudley Digges, Albert Basserman, Dan Seymour, Norma Varden. Originally produced for the stage in 1944 and written at the height of World War II, this film took the United States to task for its pre-war isolationist stance, through the character of a 1930s American envoy with marital problems. Sidney played a correspondent who's passionate about the role the U.S. can have in stemming fascism.

- *"A smooth and surprisingly sharp-tongued version of Lilian Hellman's play berating America for its persistently blinkered isolationism...The weakness it never quite overcomes is the taint of soap opera apparent in every major political crisis, from Mussolini's march on Rome in 1922 to the Munich Pact by way of the Spanish Civil War, is trotted out as yet another stage in the diplomat hero's domestic troubles between wife...and Other Woman."* (Tom Milne, Time Out)

- *"...Lillian Hellman's horribly superficial play about a crusading journalist examining the advances of European dictators in the 1930s...was meant to be an important production..."* (David Shipman, The Great Movie Stars 1: The Golden Years)

Toys in the Attic (1963, UA, 90m/bw, **VHS**) ☆☆½ **Sc:** James Poe. **D:** George Roy Hill. **Cam:** Joseph Biroc. **P:** Walter Mirisch. **Cast:** Geraldine Page, Wendy Hiller, Dean Martin, Yvette Mimieux, Gene Tierney, Larry Gates, Frank Silvera. The three-way relationship between two aging spinster sisters and their playboy brother in their crumbling New Orleans home is examined in another of Hellman's contemplations on sexuality. Martin's shabby brother's money-motivated marriage to a dimwitted girl may be his comeuppance as his older sister overly dotes on him. With its overtones of possessiveness and incest, it was a Broadway hit in 1959. Poe changed Hellman's ending, which *Variety* thought was "artificial."

- *"Toys in the Attic, a terrible picture, raises two matters worth discussing. It is another example of the occasional phenomenon — the film that exposes the inflated reputation of a play. Lillian Hellman is the most overrated American dramatist of the century because she has chosen serious subjects and plated a serious-seeming covering over generally hokey melodrama. Here she has no subject. None. She has grasped at several en route; repressed incest, true love despised, persistent immaturity, race prejudice, the grind of greed, and others. But her grasp has been weak as they floated by, and they do not save her from drowning...The casting of Dean Martin, the night-club singer and comic, as Julian, is an offense to Miss Page, Miss Hiller, and us."* (Stanley Kauffmann, The New Republic)

Watch on the Rhine (1943, Warner Bros., 114m/bw, **VHS**) ☆☆☆½ **Sc:** Dashiell Hammett. **D:** Herman Shumlin. **Cam:** Merritt Gerstad,

Hal Mohr. **P:** Hal B. Wallis. **Cast:** Bette Davis, Paul Lukas, Lucille Watson, Geraldine Fitzgerald, George Coulouris, Donald Woods, Beulah Bondi, Henry Daniell. This very popular 1941 play concerned the struggle between an anti-Nazi family man and his betrayer, a Rumanian aristocrat living with the hero's mother-in-law in a mansion near Washington, DC. Paul Lukas won the Academy Award for Best Actor for his performance as a German refugee whose family is pursued by Nazi spies. The film was also nominated for Best Picture, Supporting Actress (Watson), and Screenplay (for Hammett, Hellman's longtime lover).

- "...Lukas never had a better role...quite stagy under Broadway producer-director Herman Shumlin's guidance. Today, Watch on the Rhine *is too static, too verbose and pedantic in its beware of fascism polemic. In 1943 its power was considerable.*" (*Jerry Vermilye*, Bette Davis, 1973)

- "...I join with anyone whose opinion of Paul Lukas's performance is superlative...a carefully screened play about which, cinematically, I feel little beyond respect for Paul Lukas's beautiful performance...among the finest I have seen." (*James Agee*, Agee on Film, Volume 1)

Ernest Hemingway
Born: 1899, Oak Park, IL. **Died:** 1961.

The Nobel Prize winner for Literature in 1954, Ernest Hemingway wrote many novels and short stories that were made into films and TV shows, including *The Sun Also Rises* (1932), *For Whom the Bell Tolls* (1943), *To Have and Have Not* (1944), *The Old Man and the Sea* (1956), and *Islands in the Stream* (1976). He wrote one full-length play, *The Fifth Column*, which was published in 1938 and first staged in 1940 after an adaptation by Benjamin Glazer.

The Fifth Column (1960, CBS, 90m/c) *Buick Electra Playhouse* ☆☆☆☆ **Tp:** A.E. Hotchner. **D:** John Frankenheimer. **P:** Gordon Duff. **Cast:** Richard Burton, Maximilian Schell, Sally Ann Howes, Betsy von Furstenburg, George Rose, Sydney Pollack, Milton Seltzer, Shai K. Ophir, Elisa Loti, Tonio Selwart, Robert Dowdell, Alfred De La Fuente, R.G. Brown, Philip Kenneally, Andreas Voutsinas, Clifford David. Spanish Civil War correspondent Philip Rawlings poses as a bored playboy while working as a counterespionage agent for the loyalists in 1938 Madrid. Hemingway's one known play was produced in New York by the Theatre Guild in 1940 and starred Lee J. Cobb and Franchot Tone. This production was marked by Frankenheimer's exacting insistence on achieving realism.

• *"To write my television adaptation, I had gone back to Hemingway's original script, and although I had to make changes, adding scenes and dialogue, I made every effort to stay true to the characters and events created by Hemingway."* (A.E. Hotchner, Choice People: The Greats, Near-Greats and Ingrates I Have Known)

Beth Henley

Elizabeth Becker Henley (Caldwell)
Born: May 8, 1952, Jackson, MS.
Pulitzer Prize-winning play: *Crimes of the Heart* (1978)

Both of Henley's adaptations of her quirky Southern plays are more involving than the pictures made from her original screenplays— *True Stories* and *Nobody's Fool*—which are even more quirk-driven and schematic. The attempts to bring her world to the screen have drawn excellent casts to collections of eccentric characters. But that world has remained oblique and half-distant on film, except in the performancess of Sissy Spacek in *Crimes of the Heart*, and Holly Hunter in *Miss Firecracker*.

The playwright's stage alter ego has been Hunter, who has starred in seven Henley plays, including *The Wake of Jamey Foster, Crimes of the Heart*, and *Control Freaks* as well as the stage and film versions of *The Miss Firecracker Contest*. Hunter also played a supporting part as Jeannie with Henley (playing the Bible Pusher) in *Swing Shift* (1984). The playwright's husband, Stephen Tobolowsky, co-wrote the film *True Stories* with her and David Byrne, and acted in the film *Nobody's Fool*, which she wrote and Evelyn Purcell directed. Among the notable Henley plays not yet filmed are *Am I Blue?*, *The Wake of Jamey Foster, Control Freaks, Impossible Marriage, The Debutante Ball, The Lucky Spot*, and *Abundance*.

Crimes of the Heart (1986, DeLaurentiis, 105m/c, **VHS**) ☆☆☆ **Sc:** Beth Henley. **D:** Bruce Beresford. **Cam:** Dante Spinotti. **P:** Freddie Fields, Burt Sugarman. **Cast:** Jessica Lange, Diane Keaton, Sissy Spacek, Sam Shepard, Tess Harper, Hurd Hatfield, Beeson Carroll, David Carpenter. Henley's great stage triumph, which starred Holly Hunter on Broadway in 1981, concerns the Magraths, three idiosyncratic sisters in small-town Mississippi. They reunite after one of them, Babe Magrath, is arrested for shooting her husband, while their father succumbs to grave illness. Quirky and well-observed on Mississippi locations, the film plumbs the intimacies and idiosyncracies of the siblings, who are excavating their pasts and dealing with their father's pending death. The film received Academy Award nominations for Best Actress (Spacek), Supporting Actress (Harper), and Adapted Screenplay.

- *"You might think the extravagant ups and downs of the Magrath sisters would be so self-sustaining that not even a second-rate production could effectively suffocate them—but you'd be dead wrong. The film version...has the dubious distinction of calling attention to just about everything the play isn't, and was never meant to be. As adapted by Ms. Henley and directed by Bruce Beresford, this Crimes of the Heart has been turned into a majestic, totally humorless star turn for three individually splendid, collectively lost actresses. What went wrong? A little bit of everything. Under Mr. Beresford...details aren't seen out of the corner of the eye but in the same larger-than-life closeups that destroy any sense of an ensemble performance by the actresses."* (Vincent Canby, The New York Times)

Miss Firecracker (1989, Corsair, 102m/c, **VHS**) ☆☆☆ **Sc:** Beth Henley. **D:** Thomas Schlamme. **Cam:** Arthur Albert. **P:** Fred Berner. **Cast:** Holly Hunter, Alfre Woodard, Mary Steenburgen, Tim Robbins, Scott Glenn, Ann Wedgeworth, Trey Wilson, Amy Wright, Veanne Cox, Christine Lahti, Kathleen Chalfant, Bert Rensen. *The Miss Firecracker Contest* was a 1984 Off Broadway play starring Holly Hunter as Carnelle Scott, the blazingly red-haired tart of Yazoo City, Mississippi, who yearns for a measure of respect by capturing the title banner at the annual Fourth of July celebration. As an adult orphan known to the boys in town as "Miss Hot Tamale," Carnelle is driven by sheer will, because her woeful twirling routine showcases a distinct lack of talent. This was the opportunity for Henley and Hunter to repeat their stage success. The actress dominates an ensemble piece filled with comic eccentrics.

- *"...a superficial and sporadically witty piece aimed at such easy targets as family squabbles, small-town folk and beauty contests. The film is not actively awful; just dull and banal. Ms. Hunter, who originated this role at the Manhattan Theatre Club, clearly knows Carnelle and knows how to modulate a performance for the camera...But even someone as talented as Ms. Hunter cannot give her character the depth Ms. Henley's script does not."* (Caryn James, The New York Times)
- *"It's all a little depressing because Ms. Henley clearly has a feel for the oddities and poignancy of small-town life, but she reduces it to its quirks. The cast is game. The performances by Tim Robbins, Mary Steenburgen and Holly Hunter periodically pump blood into the caricatures they've been given to play. Their gumption isn't enough."* (Julie Salamon, The Wall Street Journal)

F. Hugh Herbert

Frederick Hugh Herbert
Born: May 29, 1897, Vienna, Austria. **Died:** 1958.

A Hollywood screenwriter since the silent era, F. Hugh Herbert contributed to 80 widely varied movies and directed one in three different decades: *He Knew Women* (1930), *Scudda Hoo! Scudda Hay!*
(1948), and *The Girls of Pleasure Island* (1953). He received his most
notoriety for Otto Preminger's screen version of his play *The Moon Is
Blue* (1953), but also wrote or co-wrote Howard Hawks's *Air Circus*
(1928), *Danger Lights* (1930) with Jean Arthur, *Vanity Fair* (1932)
with Myrna Loy, Raoul Walsh's *Dark Command* (1940) with John
Wayne, and *Sitting Pretty* (1948) with Clifton Webb. Herbert's only
credit as a producer was for his own adaptation of the Andre
Roussin/Nancy Mitford play *The Little Hut* (1957), directed by Mark
Robson. A clunky and long forgotten desert-isle ménage-à-trois com-
edy, its lasting distinction is the cast: Ava Gardner, David Niven, and
Stewart Granger.

Kiss and Tell (1945, Columbia, 92m/bw) ☆☆½ **Sc:** F. Hugh Herbert.
D: Richard Wallace. **P:** Sol C. Siegel. **Cam:** Charles Lawton. **Cast:**
Shirley Temple, Robert Benchley, Walter Abel, Jerome Courtland,
Katherine Alexander, Porter Hall, Tom Tully.
• *"There is a plot held together only through the enormous stupidity, cow-
ardice, and mean-heartedness of as ugly a bunch of suburban parents as
have never yet got themselves done up brown, in any treatment worthy of
them. It is all brilliantly characteristic of the worst anyone could think of
American family life, and it is all clearly presented on the assumption that
you will find it charming, and sympathetic, and funny, because everyone in
it is so exactly like you."* (James Agee, The Nation)

The Moon Is Blue (1953, Otto Preminger, 99m/bw, **VHS**) ☆☆☆ **Sc:**
F. Hugh Herbert. **D/P:** Otto Preminger. **Cam:** Ernest Laszlo. **Cast:**
William Holden, Maggie McNamara, David Niven, Tom Tully, Dawn
Addams. The 1951 play, a lightweight romance that starred Barbara
Bel Geddes and Donald Cook, used words such as "virgin," "mistress,"
"seduction," and "pregnant," which were banned in films by the Production Code. Preminger skilfully manipulated the press and the public by presenting the film as vanguard for freedom of speech against
censorship. Joseph I. Breen, who had run the censorship board that
denied the film the Production Code Seal, resigned. "The commotion
fell as sharply as it had risen," Will Holtzman wrote, "and...Preminger
and Holden shrugged all the way to the bank." Holden played the

bachelor who hopes to "make" avowedly virginal McNamara, and Niven was a lecherous neighbor. It resembles an overlong 1970s sitcom. The film received Oscar nominations for Best Actress (McNamara), Song, and Film Editing.

- *"In fact, in 1951, sophisticated theatre audiences were given little cause to raise their eyebrows by this mildly entertaining piece, but the movie audience was further flung and hitherto sheltered from words like 'seduction.' The movie was even rebuked by Cardinal Spellman...the sheltered masses flocked to see and hear what all the fuss was about, and a pleasant but rather tame little comedy became historic as a major breakthrough against censorship."* (Gordon Gow, Hollywood in the Fifties)

This Happy Feeling (1958, Universal, 92m/c, **VHS**) ☆☆½ **Sc/D:** Blake Edwards. **P:** Ross Hunter. **Cam:** Arthur E. Arling. **Cast:** Curt Jurgens, Debbie Reynolds, John Saxon, Alexis Smith, Mary Astor, Troy Donahue, Estelle Winwood. This is an adaptation of Herbert's 1947 play *For Love or Money*, which starred June Lockhart. The action involves a retired stage actor, the Brooklyn girl who becomes his secretary and is sweet on him, and the next door boy who becomes enamored of her, all living in an upper-crust Connecticut neighborhood.

- *"...a rather fragile comedy that might afford you some mild amusement if you happen upon it in a tolerant mood...Obviously, as entertainment this sort of thing is about on a par with the fluffy novels prescribed for hammock reading, but quite a few of the participants in the endeavor have their engaging moments. I found the performance of Troy Donahue...something of a trial...It's unfortunate that* This Happy Feeling *was made to be shown on a CinemaScopic screen. The picture hasn't, I'm afraid, quite enough substance to cover that vast expanse."* (John McCarten, The New Yorker)

Smarty (1934, Warner Bros., 64m/bw) ☆☆½ **Sc:** Carl Erickson, F. Hugh Herbert. **D:** Robert Florey. **R:** Robert Presnell, Sr. **Cam:** George Barnes. **Cast:** Joan Blondell, Warren William, Edward Everett Horton, Frank McHugh, Claire Dodd, Joan Wheeler, Virginia Sale, Leonard Carey, Frederick Burton, Virginia Dabney, Frank Darien, Bill Elliott, Dennis O'Keefe. An odd comedy that managed to skirt the newly installed Production Code. Blondell, often cast as the sassy type, nags both of her husbands to the hilt, and the film espouses physical abuse as a means to romantic fulfillment.

There You Are! (1926, MGM, bw/silent) ☆☆½ **Sc:** Tay Garnett, F. Hugh Herbert, Ralph Spence. **Cam:** Ben F. Reynolds. **Cast:** Conrad Nagel, Edith Roberts, George Fawcett, Gwen Lee, Eddie Gribbon, Phillips Smalley, Gertrude Bennett.

- *"They elope with the usual chase by the pater and everything turns out hunky-dory. It really is quite amusing—and we can think of duller ways of spending your evening."* (Photoplay)

James Leo Herlihy
Born: February 27, 1927. **Died:** 1993.

Two of James Leo Herlihy's novels were well-served by Hollywood. *All Fall Down* was adapted by William Inge in 1962 and directed by John Frankenheimer with a blue-chip cast—Warren Beatty, Eva Marie Saint, and Karl Malden. But the Academy Award-winning Best Picture *Midnight Cowboy* became Herlihy's claim to fame in 1969, via the Oscar-winning screenplay by Waldo Salt and John Schlesinger's direction of a brilliant cast. The film created indelible images of New York City lowlifes in Dustin Hoffman's Ratso Rizzo and Jon Voight's Joe Buck.

Blue Denim (1959, 20th Century-Fox, 89m/bw) ☆☆☆ **Sc:** Edith Sommer, Philip Dunne. **D:** Philip Dunne. **P:** Charles Brackett. **Cam:** Leo Tover. **Cast:** Carol Lynley, Brandon de Wilde, Macdonald Carey, Marsha Hunt, Nina Shipman, Warren Berlinger. The 1958 play by Herlihy and William Noble starred Carol Lynley, Warren Berlinger, Burt Brinckerhoff, and Chester Morris. The film was significant in its day as a mainstream study of teenage pregnancy and the issue of abortion.

- *"Abortion was treated with kid gloves in Blue Denim...a disarming little study of teenagers...whose passion had got the better of them, and whose parents were easily shocked: a minor airing of a major matter, it holds retrospective interest because it was based on a play by James Leo Herlihy, whose novels All Fall Down and Midnight Cowboy were turned into consequential films of the 1960s."* (Gordon Gow, Hollywood in the Fifties)

DuBose & Dorothy Heyward
DuBose:
Born: August 31, 1885, Charleston, SC. **Died:** 1940.
Dorothy:
Born: June 6, 1890, Wooster, OH. **Died:** 1961.

DuBose Heyward and Dorothy Heyward's plays include the original *Porgy*, produced by the Theatre Guild in 1927 and revived two years later; the George Gershwin opera *Porgy and Bess* in 1935 (and its subsequent Broadway revivals in 1942, 1953, 1977, and 1983—all posthumous for DuBose); and the original Broadway presentation of *Mamba's Daughters* at the Empire Theatre with an ensemble including Jose Ferrer, Ethel Waters, and Canada Lee. Solo, DuBose wrote *Brass Ankle*, produced on Broadway at Theatre Masque in 1931 with Alice Brady and Joe Sweeney in the cast. DuBose also wrote the screenplay for Dudley Murphy's screen version of Eugene O'Neill's *The Emperor Jones* (1933) starring Paul Robeson. DuBose's story, "The Half-Pint Flask," was dramatized by South Carolina Educational Television Network in 1984 under the umbrella title of *Tales of the Unknown South*.

Porgy and Bess (1959, Columbia, 138m/c) ☆☆☆½ **Sc:** N. Richard Nash. **D:** Otto Preminger. **P:** Samuel Goldwyn. **Cam:** Leon Shamroy. **Cast:** Sidney Poitier, Dorothy Dandridge, Sammy Davis Jr., Pearl Bailey, Brock Peters, Diahann Carroll, Ivan Dixon, Leslie Scott, Ruth Attaway, Clarence Muse, Roy Glenn, Joel Fluellen, Earl Jackson, Everdinne Wilson, Moses LaMarr, Margaret Hairston, Helen Thigpen. First presented on Broadway as *Porgy* in 1927, the piece was turned into an opera in 1935, directed by Rouben Mamoulian, with the libretto by DuBose Heyward, lyrics by Heyward and Ira Gershwin, and music by George Gershwin. The song and dance sequences are excellent and the film is an opportunity to watch a great crossection of the best African American talent of the time, but the story panders to old "darkie" stereotypes in its portrait of life along Catfish Row in Charleston, SC. Poitier has always regretted doing the film. This is one of the very few available American event-styled big films not to be converted to home-viewing material. Previn's musical direction won an Oscar and the cinematography was nominated.

- "*Potentially the biggest event would be* Porgy and Bess...*There were several big considerations here*—*the filming of a too-long underrated American masterpiece, the eliciting stylization of the black idiom in music and dance, and the first American attempt at filming a major opera...Much more of the score than one had hoped to hear was there, and the casting was good...But Gershwin's line calls for extremely vital singing, the one thing dubbing can't deliver; and this film was* plenty *dubbed. Opera movies never work. That kind of big*—*the full-out mutuality of singer-public vocal communication*—*film cannot raise.*" (Ethan Mordden, The Hollywood Musical)

- "...*a rich and devoted filming...the work deserves the respect as one of the most ambitious and, frankly, one of the finest cinematic versions of an opera, and even its flaws ought to be seen in the light of the serious magnitude of the task its makers have set themselves.*" (Paul V. Beckley, New York Herald-Tribune)

- "...a truly magnificent motion picture and more than a credit to the original and oft-revived folk opera...a stunning, exciting, and moving film, packed with human emotions and cheerful and mournful melodies. It bids fair to be as much of a classic on the screen as it was on the stage." (Bosley Crowther, The New York Times)

Porgy and Bess (1993, PBS, 174m/c, **VHS/DVD**) ☆☆☆ **Tp:** Dorothy Heyward, DuBose Heyward. **D:** Trevor Nunn. **P:** Stephany Marks. **Cast:** Willard White, Cynthia Haymon, Gregg Baker, Cynthia Clarey, Marietta Simpson, Paula Ingram, Gordon Hawkins, Damon Evans, Harolyn Blackwell, Bruce Hubbard, Maureen Breatwaite, Barrington Coleman.

Porgy and Bess (2002, PBS, 160m/c) ☆☆½ **Tp:** Dorothy Heyward, DuBose Heyward. **D:** Tazewell Thompson. **Cast:** Marquita Lister, Alvy Powell, Timothy Robert Blevins, Sabrina Elaine Carten, Dwayne Clark, Angela Renee Simpson.

Roger O. Hirson

Roger O. Hirson's one true stage success was the book he wrote for *Pippin: His Life and Times*, famously directed and choreographed by Bob Fosse. Hirson's greatest achievements occurred on TV, where he became one of the more prolific if uncelebrated writers of the so-called Golden Age of Television and afterward. He wrote pieces for *Kraft Television Theatre*, *Philco Television Playhouse*, *Studio One*, *The Alcoa Hour*, *Playhouse 90*, and other drama anthologies of the 1950s and 1960s. He was nominated for an Emmy Award for the much celebrated *The Adams Chronicles* on PBS in 1976. He had an affinity for war drama, particularly in his *Playhouse 90* adaptation of William Styron's *The Long March*, a Korean War drama starring Sterling Hayden, and the original story for *The Bridge at Remagen* (1969) with George Segal. For TV, Hirson wrote *A Christmas Carol* (1984) with George C. Scott and Susannah York, *The Ted Kennedy Jr. Story* (1986) with Kimber Shoop, *The Old Man and the Sea* (1990) with Anthony Quinn, and *A Woman Named Jackie* (1991) with Roma Downey. Prior to *Pippin*, he wrote the musical *Walking Happy* (1966). He was married to actress Alice Hirson and is the father of playwright David Hirson, who wrote *Le Bete* and *Wrong Mountain*. Two of Hirson's most important TV shows aired on *Playhouse 90*: the war-themed *The Long March* in 1958 with Delbert Mann directing Sterling Hayden, and *Journey to the Day* in 1960, one of TV's early examinations of group therapy, with John Frankenheimer directing Mike Nichols, Mary Astor, Janice Rule, and Steven Hill. Hirson later converted *Journey to the Day* into a play.

Pippin: His Life and Times (1981, Showtime, 112m/c, **VHS/DVD**) ☆☆☆ **Tp:** Roger O. Hirson. **D/P:** David Sheehan. **Cast:** Ben Vereen, William Katt, Leslie Denniston, Benjamin Rayston, Martha Raye, Chita Rivera, Joannie P. Oneill, Debra Phelan, Linda Haberman, Allison Williams, John Mineo, Lee Mathis, Kate Ann Wright, Charles Lee Ward. Filmed before a live audience in Hamilton, Ontario, this version preserved the play with Bob Fosse's great choreography and Vereen's Tony Award-winning performance as Leading Player, who provides this tale of Charlemagne's son's search for true love and self worth with narration, asides, and dance solos.

- *"...Mr. Vereen is marvelously insinuating...The rest of the cast is considerably more uneven. Chita Rivera is delightful...But Martha Raye, as Pippin's grandmother, does enough mugging to get arrested...More disconcerting, the title role has been given to William Katt...and he is not quite up to it."* (John J. O'Connor, The New York Times)

Hal Holbrook

Harold Rowe Holbrook Jr.
Born: February 17, 1925, Cleveland, OH.

One of the most distinguished actors of his generation, in all three dramatic media, Hal Holbrook made one legendary public effort at writing or, rather, editing: *Mark Twain Tonight!*, adapted from the works of Samuel Langhorne Clemens (1835–1910), the literary pioneer who colloquialized American literature with his novels *The Adventures of Huckleberry Finn*, *Tom Sawyer*, *Life on the Mississippi*, and others, as he described the growing civilization along Old Man River. For Holbrook's work as an actor, he won Emmy Awards for *The Bold Ones: The Senator* (1971), playing U.S. Commander Lloyd Bucher in *Pueblo* (1973), and the role of the 16th president in *Lincoln* (1975). Holbrook was nominated for Emmys for *Mark Twain Tonight!* as well as *The Whole World Is Watching* (1969), *A Clear and Present Danger* (1970), *That Certain Summer* (1972), *Our Town* (1977), and *The Awakening Land* (1978). His films include *All the President's Men* (1976), in which he famously enacted White House snitch "Deep Throat," *Wall Street* (1987), *The Firm* (1993), and *Men of Honor* (2000).

Mark Twain Tonight! (1967, CBS, 90m/c, **VHS/DVD**) ☆☆☆☆½ **Tp/Cast:** Hal Holbrook. **D:** Paul Bogart. **P:** David Susskind. Holbrook culled speeches and passages from the folksy humorist's works and weaved them into this legendary one-man show, which he performed throughout the country. It was first presented on Broadway in 1959 at the 41st Street Theatre. This performance was filmed before an appreciative audience. Holbrook was nominated for an Emmy Award for this performance.

- *"What this country needs far more urgently than a good five-cent cigar...is another Mark Twain. Barring that happy eventuality, [CBS]...offered us the next best thing: Hal Holbrook recreating America's most famous humorist in his celebrated rendition of* Mark Twain Tonight!*...easily one of the highlights of this or any television season...He has been polishing and refining the characterization since 1959 until it now glitters with the art that conceals art. It has been said with some justice that Mark Twain owes as much to Hal Holbrook as Mr. Holbrook owes to Twain. Certainly no one in this generation who saw last night's performance (what an inadequate word!) will ever again be able to read the great humorist's works without summoning up an image of Holbrook's white-maned, mustachioed, cigar-smoking, vinegary Twain at 70."* (George Gent, The New York Times)

Arthur Hopkins & George Manker Watters

Hopkins:
Arthur Melancthon Hopkins
Born: 1878, Cleveland, OH. **Died:** 1950.

Watters:
Born: April 27, 1892, Rochester, NY. **Died:** 1943.

One of the great Broadway producers of the early 20th century, Arthur Hopkins was initially a newspaper reporter and was the first journalist to uncover information on Leon Czolgocz, the anarchist who assassinated President William McKinley. Hopkins left journalism to work as a vaudeville press agent and became associated with the dance team of Vernon and Irene Castle. He produced Eugene O'Neill's *Anna Christie* (1921) and *The Hairy Ape* (1922), the smash hit *What Price Glory?* (1924), Philip Barry's *Holiday* (1928), Robert E. Sherwood's *The Petrified Forest* (1935), and Emmet Lavery's *The Magnificent Yankee* (1946). He also produced several legendary Shakespearean productions that starred John, Lionel, and Ethel Barrymore. His own plays included *Conquest* (1933). His autobiography was entitled *How's Your Second Act?*

Burlesque was a 1927 play produced by Arthur Hopkins that featured Barbara Stanwyck, Hal Skelly, and Oscar Levant. Skelly played Skid

Johnson, a clown who can't refuse a drink and deserts his wife, yet she continues loving him. The public loved it, too, since it played on Broadway at the Plymouth Theatre for 372 performances.

The Dance of Life (1929, Paramount, bw) ☆☆☆½ **Sc:** George Manker Watters, Benjamin Glazer, Julian Johnson. **D:** John Cromwell, A. Edward Sutherland. **P:** David O. Selznick. **Cam:** J. Roy Hunt. **Cast:** Nancy Carroll, Hal Skelly, Dorothy Revier, Ralph Theodore, Charles D. Brown, Al St. John, May Boley, Oscar Levant, Gladys DuBois, James T. Quinn, James Farley, George Irving, John Cromwell, A. Edward Sutherland, Skeets Gallagher. *Burlesque* was considered too racy a title for a movie at the time. The film is interesting as an early talkie that portrays the backstage world of another brand of American entertainment.

- *"In many ways, it has more than the play…Skelly, who created the role on the stage, gives an excellent performance, doing his best work in the hysterical climax…Nancy Carroll comes in for a big share of the laurel wreath…The backstage atmosphere is well done…"* (Photoplay)

Burlesque (1955, CBS, 60m/c) ☆☆ **Tp:** Martin Fyne, David Friedkin. **D:** Seymour Berns. **P:** Nat Perrin. **Cast:** Dan Dailey, Marilyn Maxwell, Joan Blondell, Jack Oakie, Dick Foran, Jack Benny, Helen Stanley.

- *"…only the framework remained, but it came off as an acceptable replica…For Dan Dailey…it was a leisurely romp without too great a tax on his talents."* (Variety)

Burlesque was also produced for a 1949 TV special starring Bert Lahr and Vicki Cummings.

Avery Hopwood

Born: May 28, 1882, Cleveland, OH. **Died:** 1928.

Avery Hopwood was educated at the University of Michigan and became the New York correspondent for the *Cleveland Leader* in 1905. He wrote his first play, *Clothes*, with Channing Pollock. Hopwood cornered the market on the public's taste during the Roaring Twenties as he produced 18 smash hits in 15 years; at one point in 1920, he had four plays running simultaneously on Broadway. Most of his plays were sold to film studios through the silent era. His racy plays include *Our Little Wife* (1916), *Double Exposure* (1918), *The Demi-Virgin* (1921), *Spanish Love* (1920), *The Alarm Clock* (1923), *The Harem* (1924), and *The Garden of Eden* (1927). Among other stage credits, Hopwood wrote *The Bat* (1920) with Mary Roberts Rinehart.

For *The Girl in the Limousine*, see **Wilson Collison**. For *The Bat*, see **Mary Roberts Rinehart & Avery Hopwood**.

The Best People was co-authored by Hopwood and David Grey. It concerns well-heeled parents who believe they fit the title description, but feel their two offspring are straying by becoming romantically linked with socially unacceptable types. The play debuted in 1924 at New York's Lyceum Theatre with a cast that included Gavin Muir and Eva Condon.

The Best People (1925, Paramount, bw/silent) ☆☆ **Sc:** Bernard McConville. **D:** Sidney Olcott. **P:** Jesse L. Lasky, Adolph Zukor. **Cam:** James Wong Howe. **Cast:** Warner Baxter, Esther Ralston, Kathlyn Williams, Edward Davis, William Austin, Larry Steers, Margaret Livingston, Joseph Striker, Margaret Morris, Ernie Adams, Florence Roberts. Baxter played a chauffeur at the height of his silent film stardom.

• *"Except for an occasional touch of humor, the picturization...is a banal and rather muddled offering....There is a constant tendency to exaggerate in this production....Warner Baxter is much too calm and matter-of-fact as the infatuated chauffeur."* (Mordaunt Hall, The New York Times)

Fast and Loose (1930, Paramount, 70m/bw) ☆☆☆½ **Sc:** Preston Sturges, Jack Kirkland, Doris Anderson. **D:** Fred C. Newmeyer. **Cam:** William O. Steiner. **Cast:** Miriam Hopkins, Carole Lombard, Frank Morgan, Charles Starrett, Henry Wadsworth, Winifred Harris, Herbert Yost, David Hutchison, Ilka Chase, Herschel Mayall. In this version, a son of affluent parents wants to marry a chorus girl, while their daughter falls for a mechanic. The Sturges touch on this treatise in class-consciousness made a better picture than the original.

• *"...not only an example of brilliant camerawork, but also a highly amusing feature, with competent direction and clever acting. Preston Sturges...is to be congratulated on the adaptation, for, while it might be called 'Those Clever People,' it accomplishes its aim in being a thoroughly satisfactory entertainment of the higher order...the incidents are splendidly portrayed."* (Mordaunt Hall, The New York Times)

Clothes (1914, bw/silent) ☆☆½ **Sc:** Avery Hopwood, Channing Pollack. **D:** Francis Powers. **Cast:** Charlotte Ives, House Peters, Edward Mackay, Frederick Webber, Josephine Drake, Minna Gale.

Clothes (1920, bw/silent) ☆☆ **Sc:** Arthur J. Zellner. **D:** Fred Sittenham. **P:** Maxwell Karger. **Cam:** Arthur A. Cadwell. **Cast:** Olive Tell, Crauford Kent, Cyril Chadwick, Zeffie Tilbury, Ray Allen, Frank Currie, Mary Beaton.

• *"It appears to me as if a keen and satirical comedy might have been made from it—something in harmony with the original. Instead the action presents a deal of moralizing subtitles concerning clothes and the fact that women are apt to become mercenary in their desire to own them."* (Motion Picture News)

Fair and Warmer (1919, Metro, bw/silent) ☆☆☆ **Sc:** June Mathis, A.P. Younger. **D:** Henry Otto. **Cam:** Arthur Martinelli. **Cast:** Mary Allison, Pell Trenton, Eugene Pallette, Christine Mayo, William Buckley, Effie Conley.

Getting Gertie's Garter starred Hazel Dawn as Gertie Darling in Bertram Harrison's original 1921 staging of the play by Hopwood and Wilson Collison. This farce concerns a lawyer who doesn't understand the difference between a bracelet and a garter.

Getting Gertie's Garter (1927, PDC, bw/silent) ☆☆½ **Sc:** Tay Garnett, F. McGrew Willis. **D:** E. Mason Hopper. **P:** John C. Flinn. **Cam:** Harold Rosson. **Cast:** Marie Prevost, Charles Ray, Harry Myers, Sally Rand, William Orlanmond, Fritz Ridgeway, Franklin Pangborn, Del Henderson, Lila Leslie.

- *"No little trouble is caused in a picture entitled* Getting Gertie's Garter....*This comedy is of the slap-dash variety, in which it would be a terrible mistake to neglect to show a man with torn trousers. Virtually a chapter is given over to this edifying idea....Miss Prevost is charming as Gertie...pseudo amusement."* (Mordaunt Hall, The New York Times)

Night of the Garter (1933, UA, 86m/bw) ☆☆☆½ **Sc:** Marjorie Gaffney, Austin Melford. **D:** Jack Raymond. **P:** Herbert Wilcox. **Cam:** Freddie Young. **Cast:** Sydney Howard, Winifred Shotter, Elsie Randolph, Connie Ediss, Austin Melford, Jack Melford, Harold French, Marjorie Brooks, Arthur Chesney. This is a British version of Hopwood's play.

- *"...transplanted to the screen with great success...makes for hilarity..."* (Variety)

Getting Gertie's Garter (1945, UA, bw, **VHS/DVD**) ☆½ **Sc:** Karen De Wolf, Allan Dwan, Joe Bigelow. **D:** Allan Dwan. **P:** Edward Small. **Cam:** Charles Lawton Jr. **Cast:** Dennis O'Keefe, Marie McDonald, Barry Sullivan, Binnie Barnes, J. Carroll Naish, Jerome Cowan, Sheila Ryan, Vera Marsh, Don Beddoe, Frank Fenton, Richard LeGrand.

- *"Edward Small, to whom society owes nothing in the way of gratitude for his previous cinematic disinterments of* Twin Beds *and* Up in Mabel's Room, *has again raided the cupboard in which old stage farces are filed away and has hauled down* Getting Gertie's Garter, *which he has given a screen dusting off. The consequence...is no better (but may be worse) than you'd expect..."* (Bosley Crowther, The New York Times)

The Gold Diggers was originally produced for Broadway in 1919. Warner Bros. appropriated the title for *Gold Diggers of 1935* (1935) and

Gold Diggers in Paris (1938), which had nothing to do with Hopwood's source play. TV's *The Dean Martin Show* created a new line of similarly named chorus girls, who gained their own show—*The Golddiggers*—in the 1960s.

Gold Diggers (1923, Warner Bros., bw/silent) ☆☆☆ **Sc:** Grant Carpenter. **D:** Harry Beaumont. **P:** David Belasco. **Cast:** Hope Hampton, Wyndham Standing, Louise Fazenda, Gertrude Short, Alec B. Francis, Jed Prouty, Anita Gillman, Peggy Browne, Margaret Seddon, John Harron, Louise Beadet, Frances Ross, Louise Beavers.

Gold Diggers of Broadway (1929, Warner Bros., 98m/c) ☆☆☆½ **Sc:** Robert Lord. **D:** Roy Del Ruth. **Cam:** Barney McGill, Ray Rennahan. **Cast:** Nancy Welford, Conway Tearle, Winnie Lightner, Ann Pennington, Lilyan Tashman, William Bakewell, Nick Lucas, Helen Foster, Albert Gran, Gertrude Short, Neely Edwards, Lee Moran, Julia Swayne Gordon, Armand Kaliz. The songs by Al Dubin and Joe Burke include "Painting the Clouds With Sunshine," "Tip-Toe Through the Tulips," "Go to Bed," and "In a Kitchenette."

- *"...a delightful talking and singing natural color picture....The fun, coupled with the lovely pastel shades, the tuneful melodies, a sensible narrative, competent acting, and elaborate stage settings, resulted in an extraordinarily pleasing entertainment. It caused one to meditate in the end on the remarkable progress of the screen..."* (Mordaunt Hall, The New York Times)

Gold Diggers of 1933 (1933, Warner Bros., 96m/bw, **VHS**) ☆☆☆☆ **Sc:** Erwin Gelsey, James Seymour, David Boehm, Ben Markson. **D:** Mervyn LeRoy. **P:** Robert Lord, Jack L. Warner. **Cam:** Sol Polito. **Cast:** Warren William, Joan Blondell, Dick Powell, Ruby Keeler, Ginger Rogers, Aline MacMahon, Guy Kibbee, Ned Sparks, Sterling Holloway, Billy Barty, Hobart Cavanaugh, Busby Berkeley, Clarence Nordstrom, Robert Agnew, Tammany Young, Ferdinand Gottschalk. Harry Warren and Al Dubin's songs include "The Gold Diggers Song (We're in the Money)," "Pettin' in the Park," and "The Shadow Waltz." The film was nominated for an Oscar for Best Sound.

- *"It is an imaginatively staged, breezy show, with a story of no greater consequence than is to be found in this type of picture. Miss MacMahon adds another fine performance...Miss Blondell is lively...Ruby Keeler does quite well...Mr. Powell pleased the audience enormously...Ginger Rogers makes her numbers count for their full worth..."* (Mordaunt Hall, The New York Times)

- *"A funny, good-natured backstage musical, and a Depression period piece as well. It sums up what is meant by the phrase 'pure 1930s.'"* (Pauline Kael, 5,001 Nights at the Movies)

Painting the Clouds With Sunshine (1951, Warner Bros., 86m/c) ☆½ **Sc:** Harry Clark, Roland Kibbee, Peter Milne. **D:** David Butler. **P:**

William Jacobs. **Cam:** Wilfred Cline. **Cast:** Virginia Mayo, Gene Nelson, Dennis Morgan, S.Z. Sakall, Lucille Norman, Tom Conway. In this version, Las Vegas is the hunting ground for rich husbands.

• *"I think that was the worst of the whole bunch [of musicals] I made...I thought it was terrible, and I think the audience agreed with me. It didn't do much business. I've been very fortunate making pictures. I always said God had his arm on me because when you have to take a title and turn it into a picture, that's about as low as you can get, isn't it? The one thing I remember...we got a lot of good photography of Las Vegas."* (David Butler, David Butler)

Guilty of Love (1920, bw/silent) ☆☆½ **Sc:** Rosina Henley. **D:** Harley Knoles. **Cam:** Phillip Hatkin. **Cast:** Dorothy Dalton, Julia Hurley, Henry Carvill, Augusta Anderson, Edward Langford, Charles Lane, Douglas Redmond, Baby Ivy Ward, Lawrence Johnson. This film was based on Hopwood's play *This Woman — This Man*.

Her Wedding Night (1930, Paramount, 75m/bw) ☆☆☆½ **Sc:** Henry Myers. **D:** Frank Tuttle. **P:** E. Lloyd Sheldon. **Cam:** Harry Fischbeck. **Cast:** Clara Bow, Ralph Forbes, Charles Ruggles, Skeets Gallagher, Geneva Mitchell, Rosita Moreno, Natalie Kingston, Wilson Benge, Lillian Elliott. This was one of Bow's few talkies near the end of her career. After dozens of flapper roles in 1920s silents, she would make only five more films after this one.

• *"This hilarious contribution does not permit reasoning to interfere with its chances to arouse laughter. Persons dash in and out of rooms...It is a story that might be told in a quarter of its present length or, if fancy took a producer, it might be continued for days...Miss Bow does fairly well as Norma...Skeets Gallagher is capital..."* (Mordaunt Hall, The New York Times)

Judy Forgot (1915, bw/silent) ☆☆½ **Sc:** Raymond L. Schrock. **D:** T. Hayes Hunter. **Cast:** Marie Cahill, Sam Hardy.

Ladies' Night in a Turkish Bath (1928, First National, bw/silent) ☆☆ **Sc:** Al Boasberg, Henry McCarty, Gene Towne. **D:** Edward F. Cline. **Cam:** Jack MacKenzie. **Cast:** Dorothy Mackaill, Jack Mulhall, Sylvia Ashton, James Finlayson, Guinn "Big Boy" Williams, Harvey Clark, Reed Howes, Ethel Wales, Fred Kelsey. The play by Hopwood and Charlton Andrews concerns the efforts of Pa Slocum and his son-in-law-to-be, Speed, to get away from their mates and visit "a Salome dance."

• *"From the title one might get the idea that this is the picture above all others to interest the young man home for a vacation from preparatory school. He did not enjoy it, as a matter of fact, but not for the reasons indicated. The picture itself is amusing, and if it does slide a little near open water at one place, it soon moves on...Mr. Mulhall as Speed shifts his part (or is shifted by it) a little too often."* (The New York Times)

The Little Clown (1921, 5reels/bw/silent) ☆☆½ **Sc:** Eugene B. Lewis. **D:** Thomas N. Heffron. **Cam:** Faxon M. Dean. **Cast:** Mary Miles Minter, Jack Mulhall, Winter Hall, Helen Dunbar, Cameron Coffey, Nelly Edwards, Wilton Taylor, Lucien Littlefield, Zelma Maja, Laura Anson.

- *"...a reminder of Polly at the Circus...It is actually cut from the same pattern, relying upon a romance of the big tops which is stressed with sentiment and heart interest...the plot and characterization are almost identical...a mild but interesting little picture."* (Motion Picture News)

Little Miss Bluebeard starred Irene Bordoni in 1923 in a 175-performance stint at Broadway's Lyceum Theatre. The play and film are about a motion picture star and a music composer who, along with another couple, travel from Paris to the Italian Riviera and play fast and loose with their marital identities.

Miss Bluebeard (1925, 62m/bw/silent) ☆☆½ **Sc:** Townsend Martin. **D:** Frank Tuttle. **Cam:** J. Roy Hunt. **Cast:** Bebe Daniels, Robert Frazier, Kenneth MacKenna, Raymond Griffith, Martha O'Dwyer, Diana Kane, Lawrence D'Orsay, Florence Billings, Ivan F. Simpson.

- *"...alterations [on the play]...have been performed with much skill. Had Miss Bluebeard held in its cast a competent comedienne it undoubtedly would have been a comedy wallop of the highest type...But as it stands...is an average program picture of the better type."* (Variety)

Naughty Cinderella was a 1925 stage farce adapted by Hopwood from *Pouche*, a French play by Rene Peter and Henri Falk. The 1925 play starred Irene Bordoni as the wife of an Olympic athlete who has a dalliance amid Parisian society.

Good and Naughty (1926, Paramount, bw/silent) ☆☆☆ **Sc:** Pierre Collings. **D:** Malcolm St. Clair. **P:** Jesse L. Lasky. **Cam:** Bert Glennon. **Cast:** Pola Negri, Tom Moore, Ford Sterling, Miss DuPont, Stuart Holmes, Marie Mosquini, Warner P. Richmond.

- *"...not a little frisky in spots, nevertheless holds the attention. Miss Negri, in the opening chapters, demonstrates that she is willing to impersonate a sort of Ugly Duckling, provided, of course, she can appear startlingly beautiful in the ensuing scenes....Miss Negri gives the same facile and natural performance she has in other vehicles....Some of the humor is good, but in several episodes it is built on extraneous gags that do not help the continuity of the narrative."* (The New York Times)

This Is the Night (1932, Paramount, 80m/bw) ☆☆☆☆ **Sc:** Benjamin Glazer, George Marion Jr. **D:** Frank Tuttle. **P:** Benjamin Glazer. **Cam:** Victor Milner. **Cast:** Lila Damita, Charles Ruggles, Roland Young, Thelma Todd, Cary Grant, Irving Bacon, Davison Clark, Gino Corrado, Claire Dodd, Donald Novis, Tiny Sanford, Rolfe Sedon, Harry Semels. This travelogue takes in both Paris and Venice as Damita and Todd played wives who loiter with other suitors. Grant played the javelin-throwing Olympian in one of his early roles. The well-remembered gag has Todd losing her long skirt to a car door followed by a litany of announcements that "Madame has lost her dress," eventually broadcast from the Eiffel Tower.

- *"Clever farcical incidents and intriguing melodies make...a most enjoyable entertainment...an expert adaptation...it is a handsomely mounted and beautifully photographed picture. Mr. Young is a joy to behold. Miss Damita is vivacious and competent. Mr. Ruggles vies with Mr. Young in making the most of the humorous situations. Thelma Todd does splendidly as Claire and Cary Grant is efficient as the stalwart Stephan." (Mordaunt Hall, The New York Times)*

Nobody's Widow (1927, PDC, bw/silent) ☆☆½ **Sc:** Clara Beranger, Douglas Z. Doty. **D:** Donald Crisp. **P:** William de Mille. **Cam:** Arthur C. Miller. **Cast:** Leatrice Joy, Charles Ray, Phyllis Haver, David Butler, Dot Farley, Fritzie Ridgeway, Charles West. The play was produced by David Belasco in 1910 at Broadway's Hudson Theatre and ran for 215 performances.

- *"...an important incident happens much too early in* Nobody's Widow...*The plot...ought to have been filmed in much the same way as that of Oscar Wilde's play* The Importance of Being Earnest. *Instead...a supposed widow and her susceptible husband meet long before they ought to." (Mordaunt Hall, The New York Times)*

Our Little Wife (1918, bw/silent) ☆☆ **Sc:** Roy Somerville. **D:** Edward Dillon. **Cam:** David Abel, George W. Hill. **Cast:** Madge Kennedy, George J. Forth, Walter Hiers, William B. Davidson, Kempton Green, Marguerite Marsh, Wray Page. Based on Hopwood's 1916 play.

Sadie Love (1919, bw/silent) ☆☆☆½ **Sc:** Clara Beranger. **D:** John S. Robertson. **Cast:** Billie Burke, James Crane, Helen Montrose, Hedda Hopper, Jed Prouty, Shaw Lovett, Margaret A. Wiggin, May Rogers, Charles Craig, Ida Waterman. Based on Hopwood's 1915 play.

- *"The plot is light in texture and was taken from a not-very-compelling play...But it has good, light satirical touch and a few laughable comedy situations...The settings are pleasing and the cast is a good one throughout." (Robert C. McElravy, Motion Picture News)*

Why Men Leave Home (1924, First National, bw/silent) **Sc:** A.P. Younger. **D:** John M. Stahl. **P:** Louis B. Mayer. **Cam:** Sol Polito. **Cast:** Lewis Stone, Helene Chadwick, Alma Bennett, Mary Carr, Hedda Hopper, William V. Mong, Sidney Bracy, Lila Leslie, E.H. Calvert, Howard Truesdell. The play, about a couple who are depicted in bliss on their honeymoon, then in boredom after their first year of marriage, debuted on Broadway in 1922 with a cast including Theresa Maxwell Conover, Audrey Hart, and Minor Watson.

- *"...a competent piece of film work with which the censor has been rather lenient. It has its sighs and its laughs, its suspense and its satisfaction. It is an entertaining photoplay for adults, a serio-comedy in which allowances must be made for pantomimic license. There are certain touches...that border on vulgarity."* (The New York Times)

Why Was He Late for Work was produced by ABC in 1972 under the umbrella title of *Of Men and Women*, and starred Bill Bixby and Burgess Meredith.

Sidney Howard
Sidney Coe Howard
Born: June 26, 1891, Oakland, CA. **Died:** 1939.
Pulitzer Prize-winning play: *They Knew What They Wanted* (1924)

Best known as the writer who adapted Margaret Mitchell's epic Civil War novel, *Gone With the Wind*, into the 1939 MGM blockbuster, Sidney Howard actually culled a 400-page-plus script from the book that other writers—F. Scott Fitzgerald and Ben Hecht among them—chopped and embellished. Howard received sole screen credit and won the Academy Award, which his widow accepted a few months after he was killed in a tractor accident on his farm at Tyringham, MA. Howard worked mostly for MGM in the movies, and plays of his that weren't adapted into other media include *Paths of Glory*, *Ode to Liberty*, *Lucky Sam McCarver*, and *Alien Corn*.

Dodsworth starred Walter Huston in one of his great stage triumphs after Howard adapted a Sinclair Lewis novel for a second time. In 1931 the writer turned Lewis's *Arrowsmith* into one of John Ford's best, yet least remembered, movies. *Dodsworth* follows an idealistic industrialist's ocean voyage to Europe at his wife's behest, and his flirtations with another woman on board. The play debuted on Broadway in 1934, with Fay Bainter as Huston's co-star.

Dodsworth (1936, UA, 90m/bw, **VHS/DVD**) ☆☆☆☆½ **Sc:** Sidney

Howard. **D:** William Wyler. **P:** Samuel Goldwyn. **Cam:** Rudolph Mate. **Cast:** Walter Huston, Ruth Chatterton, Paul Lukas, Mary Astor, David Niven, John Payne, Maria Ouspenskaya, Gregory Gaye, Odette Myrtil, Kathryn Marlowe, Spring Byington, Harlan Briggs. Chatterton made her final film appearance as Fran Dodsworth.

- *"There's only one trouble, really, but it's central: Sidney Howard also did the screenplay, and the movie follows the stage version too closely. It looks programmed and underpopulated, though in an elegantly stylized way."* (*Pauline Kael*, 5001 Nights at the Movies)

- *"...an incisive, intelligent drama of a deteriorating marriage, with Wyler drawing peerless performances from Walter Huston, Ruth Chatterton and Mary Astor."* (*Ted Sennett*, The Great Movie Directors)

- *"Walter Huston, the most dependable of actors, gives a performance that makes you forget acting."* (*Archer Winsten*, New York Post)

Dodsworth (1956, NBC, 90m/c) *Producers' Showcase* ☆☆☆☆ **Tp:** David Shaw. **D:** Alex Segal. **P:** Fred Coe, Alex Segal. **Cast:** Fredric March, Claire Trevor, Geraldine Fitzgerald, Regis Toomey, Barbara Robbins, Olive Sturgess, Stephen Bekassy, Robert Boon, Celia Lovsky, William Swan, Geoffrey Toone. This program is a benchmark for bucking the TV code. Dodsworth walked out on his wife at the close of the play, an ending that Shaw preserved in the teleplay and NBC permitted to air.

- *"...a richly endowed, high-gloss performance...Never has* Dodsworth *been given finer interpretation or deeper values."* (Variety)

- "Producers' Showcase *registered another success...richly satisfying theatre — 90 minutes of adult drama beautifully and faithfully produced...The late Sidney Howard's play...has not suffered with the passage of years...Mr. March was altogether ideal as the businessman."* (*Jack Gould*, The New York Times)

Dodsworth *was also produced twice in 1950: first, on CBS's* Prudential Playhouse, *adapted by Robert Anderson, directed and produced by Donald Davis, and starring Walter Abel and Ruth Chatterton, reprising her role from the film of the play; then, on ABC's* Kraft Television Theatre, *directed and produced by Fielder Cook, with Anthony Ross, Irene Manning, Flora Campbell, and Nils Asther.*

Free Love (1930, Universal, 70m/bw) ☆☆½ **Sc:** Winifred Dunn, Edwin Knopf. **D:** Hobart Henley. **P:** Carl Laemmle Jr. **Cast:** Conrad Nagel, Genevieve Tobin, Monroe Owsley, Bertha Mann, Ilka Chase, George Irving, Slim Summerville, ZaSu Pitts, Sidney Bracey, Bert Roach. Based on Howard's play, *Half-Gods*.

- *"No action and extreme talkativeness make this marital twister belie its own* running time. Loses pace before the midway mark...Film early goes very much drawing room and stays there." (Variety)

The Late Christopher Bean concerns the works of an artist who has been dead for ten years, and the New York society mavens who swarm to his New England hometown when his paintings suddenly become the talk of the art world. In the original Broadway prodcution of 1932, Pauline Lord essayed the housemaid Abby, who comes into a minor fortune as the only person to have befriended Bean while he was alive.

Christopher Bean (1933, MGM, 80m/bw) ☆☆☆ **Sc:** Laurence Johnson, Sylvia Thalberg. **D:** Sam Wood. **P:** Harry Rapf. **Cam:** William Daniels. **Cast:** Marie Dressler, Lionel Barrymore, Beulah Bondi, Helen Mack, George Coulouris, H.B. Warner, Jean Hersholt, Russell Hardie, Helen Shipman, Ellen Lowe. MGM's propensity for beautifully produced small-town family entertainment helped put an appropriate shine on Howard's material. This was Dressler's final film; she died of cancer in 1934 after two years as the top box-office star in America.

- *"It is a vehicle admirably suited to Miss Dressler's unfailing ability to elicit laughter and sympathy...Lionel Barrymore is in fine fettle in this picture and he adds greatly to the general amusement."* (Mordaunt Hall, The New York Times)

- *"The painter had lived in a home in which Dressler was the maid and had painted a portrait of her, which her employers later attempted to cajole from her. The fluff was made buoyant by the expertise of Dressler."* (Tony Thomas, The Hollywood Professionals Volume 2: Henry King, Lewis Milestone, Sam Wood)

The Late Christopher Bean (1949, NBC, 60m/bw) *Philco Television Playhouse* ☆☆☆½ **D/P:** Fred Coe. **Cast:** Lillian Gish, Bert Lytell, Helen Carew, Clarence Derwent, Philip Coolidge, Louis Sorin, Ellen Cobb Hill, Perry Wilson. "A gifted young man, Fred Coe...sent me a script..." Gish wrote in her autobiography. "I have always been eager to try something new so I agreed to meet him, and soon I was playing in a vital new medium very much like the early movies. The main difference was that the performance was 'live'; you had only one chance and no one could prompt or help you."

- *"Lillian Gish made her television debut Sunday night with an excellent portrayal of the harassed housemaid, Abby...an entertaining hour...Sidney Howard's amicable little play engendered the same charm the original Broadway production had...Miss Gish was extremely appealing..."* (Variety)

The Late Christopher Bean (1950, ABC, 60m/bw) *The Pulitzer Prize Playhouse* ☆☆½ **Tp:** Edward Eliseu. **D:** Frank Telford. **P:** Edgar Peterson. **Narrator:** Elmer Davis. **Cast:** Helen Hayes, Charles Dingle, Elizabeth Patterson, Bethel Leslie, Logan Field, Hiram Sherman, Mikhail Rasumny, Ralph Bell. This was Hayes's TV debut.

- "...*[Hayes] scored a complete triumph as the maid...*" (Variety)

Death Paints a Legacy (1955, CBS, 60m/c) *The Twentieth Century-Fox Hour* ☆☆☆½ **Tp:** Mel Dinelli. **D:** Lewis Allen. **P:** Otto Lang. **Host:** Joseph Cotten. **Cast:** Thelma Ritter, Gene Lockhart, Mildred Natwick, Allyn Joslyn, Kip Hamilton, Les Tremayne, Philip Ober, Craig Hill. This truncated version of the play was released theatrically in Europe.

- "...*a worthy entry...emerging as a warm and tender drama, Mel Dinelli's adaptation is well written...Thelma Ritter's portrayal...dominates the entire film. Howard's drama is a simple yet appealing one...*" (Variety)

Ned McCobb's Daughter starred Claire Eames, Alfred Lunt, and Edward G. Robinson on Broadway in 1926.

Ned McCobb's Daughter (1928, Pathé, 71m/bw) ☆☆☆½ **Sc:** Beulah Marie Dix. **D:** William J. Cowen. **P:** John Rohlfs. **Cam:** David Abel. **Cast:** Irene Rich, Theodore Roberts, Robert Armstrong, George Barraud, Carol Lombard, George Hearn, Louis Natheaux.

- "*There are some excellent dramatic passages in the worthy pictorial translation...while this production differs in a number of respects from the stage version, the substance of the original is quite well preserved. The film loses nothing by being silent...suspense sustained in a way that is done none too frequently in motion pictures.*" (The New York Times)

Ned McCobb's Daughter aired in 1951 on ABC's *The Pulitzer Prize Playhouse*, adapted by Edward Eliseu, directed by Frank Telford, and starring Miriam Hopkins, Gig Young, Anthony Quinn, and Charles Dingle.

The Silver Cord might as well be called *The Umbilical Cord*, as it concerns a young wife's exasperation over her husband's obsessive preoccupation with pleasing his incredibly self-serving mother. For the 1926 Broadway debut, Laura Hope Crewes starred as the domineering, suffocating mother for director John Cromwell.

The Silver Cord (1933, RKO, 74m/bw) ☆☆☆☆ **Sc:** Jane Murfin. **D:** John Cromwell. **P:** Pandro S. Berman. **Cam:** Charles Rosher. **Cast:** Irene Dunne, Joel McCrea, Laura Hope Crews, Frances Dee, Eric Linden, Helen Cromwell, Gustav von Seyffertitz, Perry Ivins, Reginald Pasch. This examination of the oedipal complex was judged by *Photoplay* to "follow the play rigidly, and the result proves that fine 'theatre' does not necessarily make good 'movie.'"

- "...*a very daring play and film in that it attacked one of the sacred cows: motherhood. The excellent playing of a small cast is dominated by Laura Hope Crews's fidgety, monstrous mother, shifting ground from direct, fraudulently emotional and selfish appeals to bursts of outright aggression and pure outrageousness; it is a coupe de theatre from the moment she splits her newly-wed son and his bride into separate bedrooms; her eventual downfall when Dunne succeeds in taking McCrea from her is tempered by her retention of Linden…" (Kingsley Canham,* The Hollywood Professionals Volume 5: King Vidor, John Cromwell, Mervyn LeRoy)

The Silver Cord was broadcast on TV three times in four years: in 1948 on *Kraft Television Theatre*; in 1949 on *The Ford Theatre Hour*, adapted by Ted Mabeley, directed by Marc Daniels, with Mady Christians, Meg Mundy, Karl Webber, Will Hare, and Lois Wheeler; and in 1951 on *The Pulitzer Prize Playhouse*, with Judith Anderson, Jeffrey Lynn, Joanne Dru, and Joan Chandler.

They Knew What They Wanted opened on Broadway in 1924, starring Richard Bennett and Pauline Lord. It concerns a vintner who tricks a young waitress into a correspondence romance by sending her a picture of a younger and more handsome man.

The Secret Hour (1928, Paramount, bw/silent) ☆☆☆ **Sc/D:** Rowland V. Lee. **P:** Adolph Zukor, Jesse L. Lasky. **Cam:** Harry Fischbeck. **Cast:** Jean Hersholt, Pola Negri, Kenneth Thompson, George Kuwa, George Periolot, Christian J. Frank.

A Lady to Love (1930, MGM, 92m/bw) ☆☆☆ **Sc:** Sidney Howard. **D/P:** Victor Seastrom. **Cam:** Merritt B. Gerstad. **Cast:** Edward G. Robinson, Vilma Banky, Robert Ames, Richard Carle, Lloyd Ingraham, Anderson Lawler, Gum Chim, Henry Armetta, George Davis.

• *"Strong performance by the cast, especially Robinson, who evokes a lot of compassion." (J.R. Nash, S.R. Ross,* The Motion Picture Guide)

They Knew What They Wanted (1940, RKO, 96m/bw, **VHS**) ☆☆☆½ **Sc:** Robert Ardrey. **D:** Garson Kanin. **P:** Erich Pommer. **Cam:** (Kirk) Harry Stradling. **Cast:** Charles Laughton, Carole Lombard, William Gargan, Frank Fay, Harry Carey, Lee Tung-Foo, Karl Malden, Joe Bernard, Janet Fox, Victor Killian, Effie Anderson, Ricca Allen, Millicent Green, Grace Leonard, Tom Ewell, Bobby Barker, Nestor Paiva, Antonio Filauri. The film was nominated for an Oscar for Best Supporting Actor (Gargan).

• *"For dialogue. acting, background, and film creation, it's a honey." (Otis Ferguson,* The New Republic)

They Knew What They Wanted (1952, ABC, 60m/bw) *Celanese Theatre* ☆☆½ **Tp:** Don Ettlinger. **D:** Alex Segal. **P:** A Burke Crotty. **Cast:** Frank Puglia, Betty Field, Robert Stack, Frank McHugh, Theodore Newton.

The Most Happy Fella (1980, PBS, 180m/c) *Great Performances* ☆☆ **Tp:** Frank Loesser. **Cast:** Giorgio Tozzi, Sharon Daniels, Richard Muenz, Dennis Warning, Louisa Flaningham, Dan O'Sullivan, Adrienne Leonetti, Steven Alex-Cole, Dean Badolato, David Miles, Kevin Wilson, Joe McGrath, Lawrence Asher. Frank Loesser's musical version of the play opened on Broadway in 1956 and starred Norman Atkins and Barbara Meister. It won the New York Drama Critics Circle's award for Best Musical Production. When the musical was revived in 1980 by Detroit's Michigan Opera Theatre, PBS taped a dress rehearsal for this special. The songs include "Standing on the Corner," "Big D," and "Somebody Wants Me."

• *"...the closest thing to an opera that Loesser ever wrote. It was also his flabbiest show...When* Most Happy Fella *is serious, it's labored, and when it's light, it's condescending...a fair account of [the play], but doesn't make it live...The only sustaining interest is in the fact that we're watching a stage performance on TV and more or less accepting it...We can adapt to big-theatre conventions in the living room. That's important to know if Broadway intends to send out shows on cable or cassette. They'll have to be more interesting shows than this, however."* (Dan Sullivan, Los Angeles Times)

We're All Gamblers (1927, Paramount, bw/silent) ☆☆ **Sc:** John W. Conroy, Hope Loring. **D/P:** James Cruze. **Cam:** Bert Glennon. **Cast:** Thomas Meighan, Marietta Millner, Cullen Landis, Philo McCullough, Gertrude Claire, Gunboat Smith, Spec O'Donnell.

• *"Small time stuff. Doesn't seem to be any sense at all in so openly knifing a name like Meighan and this picture is nothing like another nail. In the tank towns, where Meighan still draws, it may be all right."* (Variety)

Yellow Jack, which Howard wrote with Paul de Kruif, dramatized Dr. Walter Reed's 1899 discovery of the cause of the title disease while caring for U.S. Marines in Cuba during the Spanish-American War. The play was based on a chapter in de Kruif's 1934 book, *Microbe Hunters.* The play was produced the same year by Guthrie McClintic with John Miltern as Reed, supported by James Stewart, Robert Keith, Lloyd Gough, Myron McCormick, and Sam Levene.

Yellow Jack (1938, MGM, 83m/bw) ☆☆☆ **Sc:** Edward Chodorov. **D:** George B. Seitz. **P:** Jack Cummings. **Cam:** Lester White. **Cast:** Robert Montgomery, Virginia Bruce, Lewis Stone, Andy Devine, Henry Hull, Charles Coburn, Buddy Ebsen, Henry O'Neill, Janet Beecher, Sam Levene, Stanley Ridges, Phillip Terry, William Henry, Alan Curtis, Jonathan Hale, Brick Sullivan, C. Henry Gordon, Harry Strang.

• *"...a fictional but fairly authentic account of their heroism and of the magnificent fight along the fever front. Although it lacks the unrelieved grimness of the play from which it was adapted,* Yellow Jack *hews close enough to its source to give the screen an exciting and superior drama."* (Newsweek)

Yellow Jack (1955, NBC, 90m/c) *Producers' Showcase* ☆☆☆☆ **Tp:** JP Miller. **D:** Delbert Mann. **P:** Robert Sherwood, Fred Coe. **Cast:** Lorne Greene, Rod Steiger, Eva Marie Saint, Jackie Cooper, Wally Cox, E.G. Marshall, Dane Clark, Dennis O'Keefe, Raymond Massey, William Redfield, Philip Abbott, Carlos Montalban, Fred Stewart. For one of NBC's bigger event-style programs of the year, Greene replaced Broderick

Crawford as Walter Reed at the 11th hour when Crawford backed away from the pressures of live TV. The play was never performed as magnificently as it was for this TV spectacular, making it one of the small-screen productions that is dramatically superior to a previous film.

- "...a heart-breaking play...was given a beautiful presentation...a costly and painstaking production...a gifted cast, intelligently directed..." (Harriet Van Horne, New York World Telegram)

- "...an excellent production and some of the finest acting this season...might very well have been written for TV." (Jack Gould, The New York Times)

Yellow Jack also aired in 1952 on Celanese Theatre with Alex Segal directing Richard Kiley, Macdonald Carey, and Walter Abel.

Tina Howe
Born: 1937.

Tina Howe's plays include Birth and After Birth, One Shoe Off, Approaching Zanzibar, Pride's Crossing, and Coastal Disturbances.

The Portrait (1993, TNT, 120m/c, **VHS**) ☆☆☆☆ **Tp:** Lynn Roth. **D:** Arthur Penn. **P:** Philip K. Kleinbart. **Cast:** Gregory Peck, Lauren Bacall, Cecelia Peck, Paul McCrane, Donna Mitchell, Joyce O'Connor, Mitchell Laurence, William Prince, Augusta Dabney, John Murphy, Marty McGaw, Colin Wilcox Paxton, Ed Lillard, Lucille Patton. An adult daughter returns to her elderly parents' home, amid the sale of that house to complete a portrait of the oldsters. This is an adaptation of Howe's Painting Churches, the runnerup for the Pulitzer Prize.

- "Peck and Bacall are radiant together, catching the afterglow of a lengthy, golden marriage that now, amid the couple's packing crates and empty bookcases, is moving on, gathering up its treasures for a quieter life in a cottage. But nobody's nodding off. The tail end of this life is a tangle of emotion. Director Arthur Penn draws moments from Peck and Bacall that are endearing and funny, especially as they sit before their exasperated artist daughter (Peck's real-life daughter Cecilia Peck) for a formal portrait and joke and tease one another. Peck has seldom been known for amusing roles, but here he's found an absent-minded literary character, on its surface not all that original, whom he layers with genuine warmth and humor. And Bacall's take-charge wife, rather than cliche-aggressive, is a sunny character who makes her love palpable, like the sound of chimes. This is the rare instance of a stage play...that looks more effective on the screen. The movie adaptation (by scenarist Lynn Roth) has structurally shored up the play while transforming it through the alchemy of its stars. (Ray Loynd, Los Angeles Times)

Hatcher Hughes

Born: February 12, 1881, Polkville, NC. **Died:** 1945.
Pulitzer Prize-winning play: *Hell-Bent for Heaven* (1924)

The youngest of 11 children in a sharecropper's family, Hatcher Hughes wrote mostly Southern folk plays. His first Broadway play was *A Marriage Made in Heaven* (1918). Hughes's Pulitzer Prize-winning play *Hell-Bent for Heaven* played for 122 performances at Broadway's Klaw Theatre in 1924 with a cast that included George Abbott and Clara Bandick. His other Broadway plays were *Ruint* (1925), *It's a Grand Life* (1930), and *The Lord Blesses the Bishop* (1934). He taught drama at Columbia beginning in 1909, and organized the school's drama department. He also wrote *Wake Up, Jonathan* (1921) in collaboration with Elmer Rise.

Hell-Bent For Heaven (1926, Warner Bros., bw/silent) ☆☆ **Sc:** Marion Constance Blackton. **D:** J. Stuart Blackton. **Cam:** Nicholas Musuraca. **Cast:** Patsy Ruth Miller, John Harron, Gayne Whitman, Gardner James, Wilfris North, Evelyn Selbie, James A. Marcus.

- *"As a picture it isn't going to win prizes anywhere, simply because the theme of religious fanaticism has been somewhat subdued in the picture, which has been handled along the lines of the average old fashioned screen meller..."* (Variety)

Frederic Hunter

Born: Los Angeles, CA.

Frederic Hunter is a former U.S. information officer in the Congo and Africa correspondent for the *Christian Science Monitor*. His plays include *Disposable Women* and *Subway*. His adaptation of his own *Hemmingway Play* was nominated for a Writers' Guild of America award. For PBS's *American Playhouse*, Hunter adapted Ring Lardner's story *The Golden Honeymoon* (1980). He also wrote *Lincoln and the War Within* and *Lincoln & Seward*, a pair of 1992 TV shows dramatizing episodes in the life of Abraham Lincoln. His TV movies include *Nazi Hunter: The Beate Klarsfeld Story* (1986) with Farrah Fawcett and *Nightmare in the Daylight* (1992) starring Jaclyn Smith. Hunter's book of stories, *Africa, Africa!*, was released in 1986. He began thinking about writing an incisive and critical play about Ernest Hemingway after reading the Nobel Prize winner's *The Green Hills of Africa*, which he felt falsely portrayed life on the Dark Continent.

The Hemingway Play (1976, PBS, 120m/c) *Hollywood Television Theatre* ☆☆☆☆ **Tp:** Frederic Hunter. **D:** Don Taylor. **P:** Norman Lloyd.

Cast: Alexander Scourby, Perry King, Tim Matheson, Mitch Ryan, Samantha Eggar, Biff McGuire, Kenneth Tigar, Miriam Colon, Pamela Sue Martin, Robert Carricart. First performed on the stage in 1968 at the Eugene O'Neill Foundation in Waterford, Connecticut, this play puts four Hemingways on the stage at once—the World War I ambulance driver, the 30-year-old expatriate in Paris, the 50-year-old of enormous fame and success, and the distrustful and senile old Papa.

- *"It's a brilliant theatrical device faultlessly executed in this production under the precise direction of Don Taylor. It probably works better on TV than it did on the stage as the cameras isolate and define the various times and levels of Hemingway's life...If you knew nothing of Hemingway, would this play be valid? Of course. The study of an undeniably great man grappling with his own myth and facing his past is fascinating—what is image and what real?"* (Cecil Smith, Los Angeles Times)

David Henry Hwang

Born: 1957, Los Angeles, CA.

David Henry Hwang's other screenplays include those for *Golden Gate* (1994) and *Possession* (2002). His plays include *Face Value* (1993), *Golden Child* (1998), and the musicals *Aida* (2000) and the revival of *Flower Drum Song* (2002).

M. Butterfly (1993, Warner Bros., 101m/c, **VHS**) ☆☆ **Sc:** David Henry Hwang. **D:** David Cronenberg. **P:** Gabriella Martinelli. **Cam:** Peter Suschitzky. **Cast:** Jeremy Irons, John Lone, Ian Richardson, Barbara Sukowa, Vernon Dobtcheff, Annabel Levanton, Shizuko Hoshi, Richard McMillan, Margaret Ma. The 1988 Broadway production initially starred John Lithgow, B.D. Wong, and Rose Gregorio and ran for 777 performances. Irons played a French diplomat in 1960s China who falls in love with an opera singer, but the singer may not be who she—or he—says she is. Hwang and Cronenberg made a Herculean effort to translate this play—a fact-based portrayal of a French attaché who was accused of spying in 1986—to the screen. But the literalness of movies makes the play's more ethereal side just seem impossible

- *"Dazzling and multicolored as a play, M. Butterfly has unaccountably been turned into a drab moth of a film. Despite starring Jeremy Irons and being directed by David Cronenberg, whose entire output from* Scanners *and* The Fly *to* Dead Ringers *and* Naked Lunch *has been an attempt to get one step beyond the ordinary, Butterfly is a determinedly pedestrian affair, sure to make anyone approaching the material for the first time wonder what the fuss was about...The problem is not the presence of anything sacred in the play, but that in the process of turning it upside down and reversing its focus Cronenberg and Hwang, who also wrote the screenplay, have managed to misplace all the considerable magic the original possessed." (Kenneth Turan, Los Angeles Times)*

William Inge

William Motter Inge
Born: May 3, 1913, Independence, KS. **Died:** 1973.
Pulitzer Prize-winning play: *Picnic* (1953)

William Inge dramatized the lives of seemingly ordinary Midwesterners, often involved in family rifts, romance, and detachment, as with the characters of Cherie in *Bus Stop* or Hal Carter in *Picnic*—two of Inge's works that have transcended stage, film, and TV culture. His first success as a playwright was *Farther Off From Heaven* in 1947, and although he never really took to Hollywood, he did write the original screenplays for two early Warren Beatty movies—Elia Kazan's *Splendor in the Grass* (1961) and John Frankenheimer's *All Fall Down* (1962)—after Beatty starred in the flop of Inge's 1959 play, *A Loss of Roses*. The movies eagerly adapted Inge's plays with considerable fidelity, but he took his name off the screenplay for *Bus Riley's Back in Town* (1965) for studio meddling, while retaining his cast credit as Walter Gage.

Inge was the script supervisor for the spin-off series *Bus Stop*. The show consisted of 25 hourlong episodes centering around the diner run by Grace Sherwood in Sunrise, Colorado, where guest stars would drift in each week with new adventures. Marilyn Maxwell and Rhodes Reason starred. The sixth episode, "Cherie," guest-starring Tuesday Weld, Gary Lockwood, and Joseph Cotten, was a boiling down of the original *Bus Stop*. The series's significance in retrospect is that it inspired a congressional hearing into TV violence. The episode in question, "A Lion Walks Among Us," aired in December 1961. It was Ellis Kadison's adaptation of Tom Wicker's novel *Told by an Idiot*, directed by one of the show's main guiding forces, Robert Altman. Pop singer Fabian Forte played a Mephistophelian serial killer who maniacally wields an axe on an old man.

Also for TV, Inge wrote at least two originals, *Glory in the Flower* for a 1953 installment of *Omnibus* starring Jessica Tandy, Hume Cronyn, and James Dean, and *Out on the Outskirts of Town* for a 1964 presentation on *The Bob Hope Chrysler Theatre* with Anne Bancroft and Jack Warden. Inge committed suicide in Los Angeles in 1973.

Bus Stop was a 1955 Broadway hit starring Kim Stanley, before it became so identified with Marilyn Monroe that the memory of the playwright almost vanished from its legacy. Cherie, a saloon singer with a promiscuous past, meets a young cowpoke in an Arizona rodeo town during a transportation-halting snowstorm, and he insists that they marry.

Bus Stop (1956, 20th Century-Fox, 96m/c, **VHS**) ☆☆☆☆ **Sc:** George Axelrod. **D:** Joshua Logan. **P:** Buddy Adler. **Cam:** Milton Krasner. **Cast:** Marilyn Monroe, Don Murray, Aurthur O'Connell, Betty Field, Hope Lange, Eileen Heckert, Hans Conreid, Robert Bray, Casey Adams, Henry Slate. Monroe's outstanding performance—judged by many to be her best—and her oozing sexuality dominate this overtly funny and surprisingly poignant film. Murray's occasionally loony bin-like ardor in his film debut is sometimes tough to take, but Monroe, fresh from her famous Actors Studio stint, was excellent as Cherie, who sings a saucy rendition of "That Old Black Magic." The film was nominated for an Academy Award for Best Supporting Actor (Murray).

- *"The character [of Cherie] was beautifully conceived initially by William Inge—and George Axelrod's screenplay opened out the action, incorporating scenes at a nightclub and at a rodeo before settling into the single location of the play, a bar-restaurant where a busload of people are compelled to wait for an unknown period....Axelrod preserved the sensitivity of Inge, and the delicate blending of knockabout mirth and fundamental insecurity. She resists. He persists. And from this absurdly simple promise, a wealth of human conflict arises. And beneath all the merriment, and the well-sustained twang to her voice, Marilyn Monroe was no longer the sex symbol. She had learned to inhabit a role, and she inhabited Cherie."* (Gordon Gow, Hollywood in the Fifties)

- *"...a wonderful role, and she plays it with a mixture of humor and pain that is very touching."* (William K. Zinsser, New York Herald-Tribune)

Bus Stop (1982, HBO, 120m/c) ☆☆½ **Tp:** William Inge. **D:** Peter H. Hunt. **P:** Peter H. Hunt, John Thomas Lenox. **Cast:** Margot Kidder, Tim Matheson, Claude Akins, Pat Hingle, Joyce Van Patten, Marilyn Jones. In cable's formative years, it began turning to the theatre for new material. At the time, its emphasis was on using the evergreens of the American stage as showcases for stars such as Kidder, who had recently played Lois Lane in the *Superman* movies. HBO reasoned that her identity would be a draw. Kidder hadn't done live theatre prior to this performance in front of a live audience at the Garrison Theatre on the Claremont College campus in Claremont, California. "I'm believing nobody's going to see it," she said.

- *"Just about everyone involved in staging plays for cable seems pleased with the greater freedom the cable networks allow than do the traditional broadcast networks. Director Hunt shattered one myth, however: the cable executives don't take a totally hands-off attitude. 'Once the thing is packaged there's more freedom,' said Hunt, 'but the cable people are very much involved in the putting together of the show....They believe very strongly in the power of the star....Their theory is that nobody's heard of* Bus Stop.' *If just half of HBO's audience watches* Bus Stop, Kidder's *performance would reach about four and a half million homes. That's equal to a play seen by 1,000 people a day for 12 years."* (David Crook, Los Angeles Times)

Come Back, Little Sheba details the long-suffering marriage between a delusionary small-town, middle-aged housewife, Lola, who pines for the return of the title family dog, and her recovering alcoholic chiropractor husband, Doc Delaney. They both rebound from torpor when a teenage girl boards with them. Shirley Booth won the 1950 Tony Award as Best Actress for her stage performance, and Sidney Blackmer essayed Doc.

Come Back, Little Sheba (1952, Paramount, 99m/bw, **VHS**) ☆☆☆½ **Sc:** Ketti Frings. **D:** Daniel Mann. **P:** Hal B. Wallis. **Cam:** James Wong Howe. **Cast:** Shirley Booth, Burt Lancaster, Terry Moore, Richard Jackel, Philip Ober, Edwin Max, Lisa Golm, Walter Kelley. Booth recreated her stage triumph in this faithful version of the play. Frumpy, sad-eyed, and with a sing-songy cadence, her Lola alternated between bloom and wilt, longing for the past, marking time in the present with Doc, who only married her decades ago because he got her pregnant. It was an auspicious film debut. Lancaster, cast against type as an aging and regretful drunk, turned in one of his better performances. The film won Booth the Academy Award for Best Actress and was also nominated for Best Supporting Actress (Moore) and Film editing.

• *"...Miss Booth's performance still has the feel of theatre in it, which is not surprising in view of the number of times she has played it on the stage, but this hardly mars the stunning virturosity with which her graceless waddle, that stumbling, nervous impetuosity of speech, that perpetually anxious sensibility of the eyes expose the mingled vulgarity, bedroom and tremendous pathos of the part."* (Lindsey Anderson, Sight and Sound)

• *"...the excellence of Mr. Lancaster as the frustrated, inarticulate spouse, weak-willed and sweetly passive, should not be overlooked."* (Bosley Crowther, The New York Times)

Come Back, Little Sheba (1977, NBC, 120m/c) ☆☆☆ **Tp:** William Inge. **D:** Silvio Narrizano. **P:** Derek Granger, Laurence Olivier. **Cast:** Joanne Woodward, Laurence Olivier, Carrie Fisher, Nicholas Campbell, Patience Collier. Olivier gave this production a mighty try, but this stagy, claustrophobic TV reworking depended upon his illustrious co-star's power, which wasn't in top form. The mores of the piece were dated by the 1970s, and it seemed more than ever mostly a showcase for the female lead rather than a resounding theatrical brenchmark. The network dumped it by airing it on New Year's Eve and it has never been seen since.

• *"Sir Laurence Olivier—a last minute replacement for Robert Mitchum —plays Doc, the MD fallen to chiropractor. He is about as credible in the part as Bob Mitchum would be as King Lear. Joanne Woodward, a lovely, gifted actress, gives an embarrassing performance...*" (Harriet Van Horne, New York Post)

- "*To be blunt as one can be, Miss Woodward...turns in a mediocre performance as the middle-aged wife of a man who felt trapped from the day she became pregnant, and he was forced to give up his medical career...[The play] is a work that calls for many levels of acting, something Olivier achieves and Miss Woodward does not.*" (Kay Gardella, New York Daily News)

The Dark at the Top of the Stairs (1960, Warner Bros., 123m/c) ☆☆☆ **Sc:** Irving Ravetch, Harriet Frank Jr. **D:** Delbert Mann. **P:** Michael Garrison. **Cam:** Harry Strading Sr. **Cast:** Robert Preston, Dorothy McGuire, Shirley Knight, Angela Lansbury, Eve Arden, Frank Overton, Lee Kinsolving, Robert Eyer, Penney Parker, Ken Lynch, Dennis Whitcomb, Addison Richards, Nelson Leigh. This slice-of-life piece, set in small-town Oklahoma in the 1920s, concerns a household headed up by an extroverted, unfocused, and unemployed traveling salesman, Rubin Flood. His wife, Cora, doesn't understand his sensibility and indolence. This drama of secrets, repression, and family foibles was first produced on the stage in 1957 with Pat Hingle as Rubin. Robert Preston's vigor and Shirley Knight's performance as his bashful daughter are the highlights of this almost too-quiet examination of marital discord. The period feel is effusive, as is the sense of place, and the film is well cast, but its focus meanders. It was nominated for an Oscar for Best Supporting Actress (Knight).

- "*Warners produced, and it might have been their way of preparing audiences for [Preston's] screen repeat as* The Music Man." (David Shipman, The Great Movie Stars: The International Years)

- "*A first-rate cast of carefully chosen players—and the kind of direction that blends, paces, and builds...into a sustained and glowing force. Matters are handled with good taste, common sense, and fine sensitivity.*" (Kay Proctor, Los Angeles Examiner)

Picnic was Inge's Pulitzer Prize winner of 1953, starring Ralph Mecker as the virile showoff and drifter, Hal Carter. On Labor Day, he stops in the small Kansas hometown of a former college fraternity brother, Alan Benson, and in the process stirs up the ardor of local women of all ages. The most enamored of him is Alan's girlfriend, Madge, the town beauty. The Broadway cast included Janice Rule as Madge, Paul Newman as Alan, and Kim Stanley.

Picnic (1955, Columbia, 113m/c, **VHS/DVD**) ☆☆☆☆½ **Sc:** Daniel Taradash. **D:** Joshua Logan. **P:** Fred Kohlmar. **Cam:** James Wong Howe. **Cast:** William Holden, Kim Novak, Rosalind Russell, Cliff Robertson, Betty Field, Susan Strasberg, Arthur O'Connell, Verna Felton, Nick

Adams, Reta Shaw, Phyllis Newman, Elizabeth Wilson. Logan executed a double victory with Inge works in his two major films as a director, this one a year before *Bus Stop*. It's a strong piece, one of the high-gloss and deeply effective sexual dramas of the 1950s—a benchmark. Inge's fascination with small-town lust and the emotions and needs that accumulate around it were never better served than in this classic. The top three stars delivered signature performances. The film won Oscars for Best Art Direction/Set Decoration and Film Editing and was nominated for Best Picture, Director (Logan), Supporting Actor (O'Connell), and Score (George Duning).

- *"Logan and [set decorator Jo] Mielziner shape their drama with hundreds of images and vignettes, meticulously chosen to capture not only the fun but [also] the sitting social climate of small-town life. It is ironic that all these passions erupt at the picnic which represents tradition and organized wholesomeness. The actors are excellent. Holden is handsome, weak, irresponsible, and, somehow, appealing in his enthusiasm."* (William K. Zinsser, New York Herald Tribune)

- *"Picnic was—something of a shock [to Logan watchers]: a stage play—given cinematic life and authentic rural atmosphere, with a sense of color and design, a better-than-average William Holden, and a quartet of exceptional female performances—Rosalind Russell, Betty Field, Susan Strasberg, and Kim Novak looking like confectioner's custard. There is no sham about* Picnic: *it wears well, especially the slumberous noctural dancing sequence..."* (David Thomson, A Biographical Dictionary of Film)

- *"Acting with his entire body and crafting a careful mosaic of a bewildered and jaded boy wonder, [Holden] effectively shaves years off his age. What is more, his characterization has such sweep that it carries the inexperienced Kim Novak...who wisely plays off Holden's studied cues. The two make a lusty pair, though it's a tossup for the more photogenic chest."* (Will Holtzman, William Holden)

Picnic (1986, Showtime, 120m/c) ☆☆☆½ **Tp/D:** Marshall W. Mason. **P:** Roger Berlind, Gregory Harrison. **Cast:** Gregory Harrison, Jennifer Jason Leigh, Michael Learned, Dana Hill, Timothy Shelton, Rue McClanahan, Dick Van Patten, Conchata Farrell. Harrison, recreating his stage revival role while also executive producing, is the weakest thing about this otherwise fine interpretation. It benefits greatly from the beautifully nuanced performance by Jason Leigh as the passive, then inspired Madge. Changes were made to the role of the schoolteacher boarder, Sydney, played by Learned, and her pathos doesn't approach Russell's in the original movie.

- *"Despite some misguided tinkering, the play comes through beautifully. This production is at its best when being most straightforward, when approaching the play's 1950s sensibilities without patronizing. Ms. McClanahan and*

Conchata Farrell as Helen Potts, the nextdoor neighbor, are especially successful on this score. And the famous 'dance scene,' in which Hal's partnering of Madge turns decidedly steamy, is captured brilliantly as 'Moonglow' plays insinuatingly in the background. As in most of Mr. Inge's work, the insights in Picnic are gentle, tender, and loving. There would still seem to be room for such qualities on the contemporary scene." (John J. O'Connor, The New York Times)

Picnic (2000, CBS, 100m/c) ☆☆ **Tp:** Shelley Evans. **D:** Ivan Passer. **P:** Bruce Hickey. **Cast:** Josh Brolin, Gretchen Mol, Bonnie Bedelia, Mary Steenburgen, Jay O. Sanders, Ben Caswell, Chad Morgan, J.D. Evermore, Christopher Bills, Rodger Boyce, E.J. Nolan. Some lyrical camerawork by Passer and director of photography Ousama Rawi on rural locations aided in this representation of the work, which was updated by the producers, for some unknown reason, to 1966.

• "If...you tune in to the remake of Picnic...be sure to keep a copy of William Inge's play handy, or a tape of the iconic William Holden-Kim Novak film. You're gonna need 'em....a cautionary tale about the quick passing of youth and opportunity, about cycles of mistakes and squandered lives, and about the eternal struggle between animal instinct and prudish civilizing restraint....the folks involved in the remake understand none of this." (Darryl H. Miller, Los Angeles Times)

The Stripper (1963, 20th Century-Fox, 95m/bw, **VHS**) ☆☆ **Sc:** Meade Roberts. **D:** Franklin J. Schaffner. **P:** Jerry Wald. **Cam:** Ellsworth Fredericks. **Cast:** Joanne Woodward, Richard Beymer, Carol Lynley, Claire Trevor, Robert Webber, Gypsy Rose Lee, Louis Nye, Michael J. Pollard. The original 1959 Broadway flop was called *A Loss of Roses*, about a down-on-her-luck showgirl. She returns to her small Kansas hometown and her mother's household, where she was once a babysitter to a boy who's become a 19-year-old mechanic. The fading beauty and the boy then consummate a seemingly inevitable tryst. Carol Haney, Betty Field, and Warren Beatty played the principal parts supported by Michael J. Pollard and Robert Webber in 25 performances at New York's Eugene O'Neill Theatre. Woodward's performance is the central reason to see this drab and undistinguished film, which was Schaffner's directorial debut in films. The film was nominated for an Oscar for Costume Design.

• "...has the dreary, liberal Freudian Sunday School neatness of second-rate series drama: it's necessary for the characters to be shallow so that the audience can see them learning their little life's lessons and changing. Still, Joanne Woodward is at the center of this picture, and everything she does here is worth watching." (Pauline Kael, 5001 Nights at the Movies)

Albert Innaurato

Born: June 2, 1948, New York, NY.

Albert Innaurato's teleplay for *Verna: USO Girl* (1978), based on a Paul Gallico story, which PBS aired on *Great Performances*, garnered the writer an Emmy Award nomination. It starred Sissy Spacek as a sweet and talentless entertainer who rejects the officer who loves her in favor of fan-magazine-style pipe dreams for her "career." Innaurato also wrote the "Underground" segment of *Subway Stories: Tales From the Underground* (1997). The playwright's followup to the wildly successful play *Gemini* was *Passione* (1980), which flopped after a few weeks. His plays include *Coming of Age in Soho* and *The Transfiguration of Benno Blimpie*. Innaurato and Christopher Durang appear as themselves in the documentary *Women in Black*.

Happy Birthday, Gemini (1980, UA, 107m/c, **VHS**) ☆½ **Tp/D:** Richard Benner. **P:** Bruce Calnan, Rupert Hitzig. **Cam:** James B. Kelly. **Cast:** Madeline Kahn, Rita Moreno, Robert Viharo, Alan Rosenberg, Sarah Holcomb, David Marshall Grant, Jeff Wincott, Timothy Jenkins, David MacIlwraith, Maura Swanson, Richard Easley, John William Kennedy, Michael Donaghue. A South Philadelphia man hits his 21st birthday and worries about his sexual orientation. An adaptation of Innaurato's long-running play of the 1970s, *Gemini* didn't translate well to the screen. The original 1977 production at New York's Little Theatre starred Robert Picardo, Danny Aiello, and Anne DeSalvo.

- *"Embedded in the grating artificiality of* Happy Birthday, Gemini...*are truths and insights of too much importance to be lost amid so much excess....Scarcely a breath of of reality has been allowed to permeate [the film]...an unrelenting staginess and improbability....Caricature is too puny a category to contain this grotesque...Benner is the culprit, through and through....His touch is leaden and graceless." (Kevin Thomas, Los Angeles Times)*

Preston Jones

Born: April 7, 1936, Albuquerque, NM. **Died:** 1979.

Preston Jones graduated from the University of New Mexico in 1960 and joined the Dallas Theatre Center in 1962 as an actor, director, and eventually a playwright with his 1974 *A Texas Trilogy*. The epic work includes *The Last Meeting of the Knights of the White Magnolia*, *Lu Ann Hampton Laverty Oberlander*, and *The Oldest Living Graduate*. The trilogy was later produced in 1976 at Kennedy Center in Washington, DC, and then under Alan Schneider's direction the same year in repertory on Broadway at the Broadhurst Theatre with an ensemble featuring Fred Gwynn, Diane Ladd, Henderson Forsythe, and Lee Richardson. Jones's other plays include A *Place on the Magdalena Flats* and *Santa Fe Sunshine*.

The Oldest Living Graduate (1980, NBC, 75m/c, **VHS**) ☆☆☆☆½ **Tp:** Preston Jones. **D:** Jack Hofsiss. **P:** David W. Rintels. **Cast:** Henry Fonda, Cloris Leachman, Timothy Hutton, George Grizzard, John Lithgow, Harry Dean Stanton, David Ogden Stiers, Penelope Milford. **Host:** Jane Fonda. This distinguished cast gathered around Fonda for NBC's first live drama telecast in 18 years, and did a terrific job from the Bob Hope Theatre at Southern Methodist University in Dallas. Fonda played Colonel J.C. Kinkaid, a crippled and cranky World War I veteran and patriarch whose family is at several crossroads in what one critic called "a sort of Texas *Cherry Orchard*." The play was originally performed in 1974 at the Dallas Theatre Center under the direction of Paul Baker.

- "...*elegant television and proud theatre....We both sympathized with poor old crippled-up Col. J.C. Kinkaid and loved Henry Fonda as Kinkaid, just as we would have in the theatre....Fonda going at it with Grizzard, or with Leachman, as Grizzard's shrewd-cookie wife, was beautiful stuff — high-risk, high-need acting, on both sides. But so were Fonda's solos....Not only did Fonda take energy from the colonel, he took it from the evening — the live audience, the good returns he was getting from the other actors, the momentum an actor can work up when no one keeps interrupting him to load the camera....Preston Jones would have loved this production..."* (Dan Sullivan, Los Angeles Times)

Tom Jones

Born: February 17, 1928, Littlefield, TX.
Tony Award-winning musical: *I Do! I Do!* (1967)

Tom Jones wrote the musical *110 in the Shade*, based on N. Richard Nash's *The Rainmaker*. His composing partner was Harvey Schmidt. Among their Broadway musicals was *Celebration*, and Off Broadway their work includes *The Bone Room* and *Grover's Corners*, based on Thornton Wilder's *Our Town*. Jones and Schmidt began collaborating while students at the University of Texas.

The Fantasticks was the long-running Off Broadway musical, which Jones and Schmidt based on *Les Romanesques* by Edmund Rostand. It was first staged in 1960 at New York's Sullivan Street Playhouse with Jerry Orbach in the lead. Two fathers conspire to marry one's son to the other's daughter, by having her kidnapped by members of the titular traveling carnival and getting the boy to play the hero.

The Fantasticks (1964, NBC, 60m/c) *The Hallmark Hall of Fame* ☆☆☆ **Tp:** Robert Hartung. **D/P:** George Schaefer. **Cast:** Ricardo Montalban, Bert Lahr, Stanley Holloway, Susan Watson, John Davidson. Future prominent film director Herbert Ross devised all of the musical stagings for this truncated version of the play.

- "...*translated nicely into what the trade likes to call family television...took to the tube rather well via cuts for time limitations. And against the line of video musical entertainment, it was tall stuff. Susan Watson and John Davidson, as the young lovers, gave their roles a well-modulated enthusiasm and both exhibited fine vocal gifts. Bert Lahr and Stanley Holloway had a ball....As on Off Broadway, the TV version of* The Fantasticks's *charm was in the unpretentiousness and cleverness of both the music and lyrics.*" (Variety)

The Fantasticks (1995, MGM, 86m/c, **VHS/DVD**) ☆☆☆½ **Sc:** Tom Jones, Harvey Schmidt. **D:** Michael Ritchie. **P:** Linne Radmin, Michael Ritchie. **Cam:** Fred Murphy. **Cast:** Jonathan Morris, Joel Grey, Barnard Hughes, Jean Louisa Kelly, Joe McIntyre, Brad Sullivan, Teller, Tony Cox, Victoria Stevens, Dyrk Ashton, Lee Bell, Arturo Gil. This film was completed in 1995 and shelved for five years because a test audience in Portland, Oregon, failed to appreciate the musical numbers, and because the studio was skittish about releasing a musical. Ritchie's original cut was shorn of 25 more minutes by Francis Ford Coppola, a move that Ritchie was reportedly happy with.

- "*A film in which settings and costumes play a major part in creating a unique world. Production designer Douglas W. Schmidt and his crew and costume designer Luke Reichle give us a rural 1920s as yet untouched by flapper clothes and Art Deco design, and a carnival that preserves its florid 19th century P.T. Barnum colors and baroque styling. They succeed flawlessly, with Fred Murphy's gloriously rich and fluid camera work capturing it all and expressing Ritchie's perceptive vision of what* The Fantasticks *could be on the screen....The Fantasticks is a gem, but so virtually extinct is the screen musical that the looming question remains as to whether people will care.*" (Kevin Thomas, Los Angeles Times)

I Do! I Do! (1982, Showtime, 116m/c, **VHS**) ☆☆☆☆ **Tp:** Tom Jones. **D:** Gower Champion. **Cast:** Lee Remick, Hal Linden. Taped before a live audience, this excellent performance of Jones's musical interpretation of Jan de Hartog's *The Fourposter* relied on the powerhouse talents of the two leads. Mary Martin and Robert Preston played the roles of a couple through 40 years of marriage on Broadway in 1966.

- "*Solid entertainment.*" (Mick Martin, Marsha Porter, Video and DVD Guide 2003)

Philemon (1976, PBS, 105m/c) *Hollywood Television Theatre* ☆☆ **Tp:** Tom Jones. **D/P:** Norman Lloyd. **Cast:** Dick Latessa, Michael Glenn-Smith, Howard Ross, Kathrin King Segal, Charles Blackburn, Lelia Martin. In A.D. 287 in the city of Antioch, an aging clown and actor is persuaded by a conquering Roman commander to impersonate and undermine the titular Christian leader. This was the next-to-last offering in the distinguished series.

- *"Produced and directed by Norman Lloyd, the play attempts to weave its curious spell through wily childlike charms. It fails. For one thing, the TV production is generally slack, unable to generate and maintain a base of dramatic tension. For another, the overall conception of the play is seldom more than irritating. The idea was suggested by a paragraph in the Allardyce Nicholl book* Masques, Mimes and Miracles....*The scenes are both sweeping and obvious....The style can be charming. The magic of theatre is conjured up with bare boards and a few yards of material...But the charm wears thin..."* (John J. O'Connor, The New York Times)

Fay Kanin

Born: May 9, 1917, New York, NY.

The sister-in-law of Garson Kanin, Fay Kanin often wrote in tandem with her husband, Michael Kanin. The couple was nominated for an Academy Award for their screenplay for *Teacher's Pet* (1958). She won Emmy Awards for *Tell Me Where It Hurts* (1974) and for producing the best program of the year in *Friendly Fire* (1979), for which she also received a writing nomination. Kanin's screenwriting credits include *My Pal Gus* (1952), *Rhapsody* (1954), *The Opposite Sex* (1956), and *The Right Approach* (1961). Her writing for TV includes *Heat of Anger* (1971) and *Hustling* (1975) with Lee Remick.

Goodbye, My Fancy (1951, Warner Bros., 107m/bw) ☆☆ **Sc:** Ivan Goff, Ben Roberts. **D:** Vincent Sherman. **P:** Henry Blanke. **Cam:** Ted D. McCord. **Cast:** Joan Crawford, Robert Young, Frank Lovejoy, Janice Rule, Eve Arden, Lurene Tuttle, Howard St. John, Ellen Corby, Morgan Farley, John Qualen, Creighton Hale, Viola Roache, Virginia Gibson. Journalist Agatha Reed returns to her alma mater for homecoming to renew an old romance with the guy who became the college president. But a rival for her charms shows up and the campus prez could be in hot water. The play was produced on Broadway in 1948 by Michael Kanin and directed by Sam Wanamaker with a cast including Madeleine Carroll, Joseph Boland, Shirley Booth, and Wanamaker.

- *"The scripts were becoming fewer and less attractive.* Goodbye, My Fancy *had been a provocative stage vehicle for Madeleine Carroll, but its political sting was removed in the Warners film. The result was a tepid triangle with Joan, Robert Young and Frank Lovejoy. When* Goodbye, My Fancy *failed to attract customers, Jack Warner sent on the script of a rancid melodrama,* This Woman Is Dangerous. *It was a familiar technique to avoid paying stars — submit scripts they had to refuse."* (Bob Thomas, Joan Crawford)

Rashomon became an industry term for a story told from several points of view after director Akira Kurosawa's great 1951 Japanese film received a worldwide audience. The screenplay by Kurosawa, about the rape of a noblewoman and the probable murder of her husband in ninth century Japan, acted out from four different points of view throughout the film, was originally derived from a story of Ryunosuke Akutugawa. The Kanins transported it to Broadway for a 1959 production staged at the Music Box Theatre by Peter Glenville and starring Rod Steiger, Claire Bloom, Akim Tamiroff, Oscar Homolka, and Ruth White — all in Asian facial makeup.

Rashomon (1960, NET Channel 13, 120m/bw) *The Play of the Week* ☆☆☆ **Sc:** Fay Kanin, Michael Kanin. **D:** Sidney Lumet. **Cast:** Ricardo Montalban, Carol Lawrence, Oscar Homolka, Michael Higgins, Osceolo Archer, James Mitchell, Michael Shille.

The Outrage (1964, MGM, 92m/c, **VHS**) ☆☆½ **Sc:** Michael Kanin. **D:** Martin Ritt. **P:** Michael Kanin, A. Ronald Lubin. **Cam:** James Wong Howe. **Cast:** Paul Newman, Laurence Harvey, Claire Bloom, Edward G. Robinson, William Shatner, Albert Salmi, Howard Da Silva, Thomas Chalmers, Paul Fix. Ritt transferred the tale to the American Southwest following the Civil War and used a blue-chip cast, top-lined by Newman as the eventually insidious Carrasco.

- *"In its original context, the ritualistic examination of the nature of truth was effective, but it seems ponderous, stilted, and ludicrous as a western. And Ritt's veering between realism and stylization, serious drama and farce, deprives us of a consistent focus. Except for the impressive photography of James Wong Howe…the film is a failure. Despite the message — that truth is relative — Newman plays Carrasco in almost the same way in all versions but the last. Sadistic, self-satisfied and defiant, Carrasco snarls, sneers, struts, and swaggers with macho arrogance….In the final, farcically played account, the three characters suddenly change. Carrasco becomes cowardly, groveling, whining, and willing to reform if the woman will marry him….Newman deserves credit for trying something boldly different, but it just doesn't work."* (Michael Kerbel, Paul Newman)

Garson Kanin

Born: November 24, 1912, Rochester, NY. **Died:** 1999.

Garson Kanin wrote, directed, and produced plays, movies, and TV shows,—sometimes in tandem with his wife, actress Ruth Gordon (see **Ruth Gordon**)—as well as wrote novels and histories. He attended the American Academy of Dramatic Arts from 1932 to 1933. In the 1930s, he became an assistant to George Abbot, and joined Samuel Goldwyn's staff shortly thereafter. He then signed on at RKO and directed *The Great Man Votes* (1939) and *Tom, Dick and Harry* (1941). A wartime documentary, *The True Glory* (1945), which he co-directed with Carol Reed, won the Oscar for Best Documentary. During the war years, Kanin began writing stories and plays as well. After the war, he directed his play *Born Yesterday* on Broadway.

Kanin and Gordon were nominated for Oscars for their screenplays for *A Double Life* (1947), which won Ronald Colman his Oscar, and the Katharine Hepburn/Spencer Tracy pairings of *Adam's Rib* (1949) and *Pat and Mike* (1952). They stopped working on scripts together for the sake of their marriage after 1952. They co-wrote one more, the TV film *Hardhat and Legs* (1980) with Kevin Dobson and Sharon Gless.

Born Yesterday debuted on Broadway in 1946 and ran for 1,642 performances through 1949. The original roles in the love triangle involving a Washington, DC, junk dealer, his brassy girlfriend, and the writer hired to "educate" her, were played by, respectively, Paul Douglas, Judy Holliday, and Gary Merrill. Holliday received what became her signature role when Jean Arthur backed out of the show during rehearsals.

Born Yesterday (1950, Columbia, 103m/bw, **VHS/DVD**) ☆☆☆☆ **Sc:** Albert Mannheimer. **D:** George Cukor. **P:** S. Sylvan Simon. **Cam:** Joseph Walker. **Cast:** Judy Holliday, William Holden, Broderick Crawford, Howard St. John, Frank Otto, Larry Oliver, Barbara Brown, Grandon Rhodes, Claire Carleton, Smoki Whitfield, Helyn Eby Rock, William Mays, David Pardoll, Mike Mahony, Paul Marion, John L. Morley, Ram Singh, Charles Cane. Holliday was showcased as a one-of-a-kind talent by Cukor, and she was sublime in pitch and poise, winning the Best Actress Oscar. The film also was nominated for Best Picture, Screenplay, Director, and Costumes.

- "...the picture sticks close to the Garson Kanin original....In the role of the junk dealer whom Miss Holliday learns to loathe because he is a Fascist, Broderick Crawford is appropriately tough, cruel, greedy, and self-centered, but even so he manages on occasion to be broadly comic. Against these two formidable principals, William Holden, as the tutor, has quite a time trying to stay in focus, and it's to his credit that the junkman and the lass, even *when in full cry, never blast him off the screen entirely."* (John McCarten, The New Yorker)

• *"Despite certain differences in emphasis which time and the Johnston office have necessarily injected, Garson Kanin's original comedy...comes off almost as freshly on the screen as it did on the stage....The indestructible if round-heeled Billie and her piercing gashouse inflections go on forever."* (Newsweek)

Born Yesterday (1956, NBC, 90m/c) *Hallmark Hall of Fame* ☆☆½ **Tp:** Garson Kanin, Hal Gerson. **D:** Garson Kanin, George Schaefer (uncredited). **P:** George Schaefer. **Cast:** Mary Martin, Paul Douglas, Arthur Hill, Otto Hulett, Larry Oliver, Belle Flower, Richard Taber, Laura Pierpont. By all accounts, the problem with this TV production was the fact that America couldn't get over their idea of Martin as Peter Pan.

• *"Mary Martin played the Judy Holliday role with a slight Texas accent and was very good, but the public didn't buy it. She was Peter Pan or Maria Von Trapp in* The Sound of Music *and the idea of her playing a hooker living with a crooked junk dealer didn't sit well....It was a mistake....Paul Douglas was perfect in his original part..."* (George Schaefer, From Live to Tape to Film: 60 Years of Inconspicuous Directing)

• *"[Martin] missed the brassy, earthy, and shrewd qualities of the girl who knew her man if not her grammar."* (Variety)

Born Yesterday (1993, Hollywood, 102m/c, **VHS**) ☆☆ **Tp:** Douglas McGrath. **D:** Luis Mandoki. **P:** D. Constantine Conte. **Cam:** Lajos Koltai. **Cast:** Melanie Griffith, John Goodman, Don Johnson, Edward Herrmann, Max Perlich, Fred Dalton Thompson, Nora Dunn, Benjamin C. Bradlee, Sally Quinn, Michael Ensign, William Frankfather, Celeste Yarnell, Meg Wittner, Ted Raimi. Griffith's persona and vocals fit in with the idea to remake the Holliday/Kanin classic, and she delivered one of her better performances, but the movie never gels and Goodman's performance was over-the-top obnoxious.

• *"Douglas McGrath's screenplay...modernizes the deal that Harry is trying to bring off. But two basic flaws couldn't be fixed. Billie herself is no longer a funny idea. Few would doubt that there are bird-brained beauties today who are well-paid concubines, but the subject simply isn't amusing anymore...a matter to deplore, not to chuckle at. Second, the play blends the* Pygmalion *story with a theme of Democratic surge, Billie as representative of the bamboozled populace rising at last to challenge and overthrow its corporate masters. This Norman Corwin-Henry A. Wallace idiom fit the immediate postwar atmosphere, but it wouldn't fit these more cynical times. McGrath has quite rightly eliminated almost all of it, but he hasn't replaced it with anything. The piece seems denuded."* (Stanley Kauffmann, The New Republic)

The Right Approach (1961, 20th Century-Fox, 92m/bw) ☆☆ **Sc:** Fay Kanin, Michael Kanin. **D:** David Butler. **P:** Oscar Brodney. **Cam:** Sam

Leavitt. **Cast:** Frankie Vaughan, Martha Hyer, Juliet Prowse, Gary Crosby, David MacLean, Jesse White, Jane Withers. The original play debuted on Broadway in 1950 as *The Live Wire*, a Michael Todd production with Kanin directing a cast including Peggy Cass, Heywood Hale Broun, Jack Gilford, and Elliott Reid. Of all the young musical actors who were thrust into backlot musicals in the wake Elvis Presley, Frankie Vaughan was one of the more talented, but he quickly fizzled. This musical, which was adapted by Kanin's brother and sister-in-law, is a pedestrian boys-seek-girls affair.

- *"I did it and I did it quick. And of course I was a hero....The fellows in the backlot that ran the studio...said, 'Geez, you've got to sign a seven-year contract...' Because I was fast. I wanted to finish the picture and get rid of it. Frankie Vaughan was very, very good, but he didn't catch on....When they previewed it,* The Right Approach *was just a mediocre picture...nothing happened. So that was the end of* The Right Approach." (*David Butler,* David Butler, *1993)*

The Rat Race (1960, Paramount, 105m/c, **VHS**) ☆☆☆ **Sc:** Garson Kanin. **D:** Robert Mulligan. **P:** William Perlberg, George Seaton. **Cam:** Robert Burks. **Cast:** Tony Curtis, Debbie Reynolds, Jack Oakie, Kay Medford, Don Rickles, Marjorie Bennett, Hal K. Dawson, Norman Fell, Lisa Drake, Joe Bushkin, Sam Butera, Gerry Mulligan, Dick Winslow, Wally Cassell, Jack (Tipp) McClure, Stanley Adams, Jacques Gailo. The original 1949 play, entitled *Live Wire*, starred Barry Nelson and Betty Field. The story concerns a Milwaukee saxophone player who is testing the Manhattan music scene, and falls for a jaded taxi dancer living in his boarding house.

- *"...a clear-eyed, pungently atmospheric view of two youngsters...caught in the savage, frenetic business of storming our town's slightly tarnished artistic and commercial towers....The point of view is standard and somewhat removed from genius...brisk, believable and entertaining...If the performances are generally on a high plane it must be attributed partly to the fact that Mr. Kanin has given his players lively lines to speak." (A.H. Weiler,* The New York Times*)*

George S. Kaufman

George Simon Kaufman
Born: November 16, 1889, Pittsburgh, PA. **Died:** 1961.
Pulitzer Prize-winning plays: *Of Thee I Sing* (1932) with Ira Gershwin and Morrie Ryskind, *You Can't Take It With You* (1937) with Moss Hart

George S. Kaufman, one of the 20th century's most exacting satirists, was, as Leonard Maltin wrote, also "one of the sharpest wits in the convocation of New York literary types known as the Algonquin Round Table," who "steadily resisted the siren call of Hollywood in the 1930s, making only two exceptions, contributing story only to 1933's Eddie Cantor vehicle *Roman Scandals* and co-scripting 1935's *A Night at the Opera* for old acquaintances the Marx Brothers, even as his colleagues like Dorothy Parker and S. J. Perelman flocked there to write film scripts for big bucks. (One Hollywood siren this notorious womanizer did heed, however, was star Mary Astor, whose diary praising Kaufman's sexual stamina was a hot item during Astor's bitter 1936 divorce.)"

Kaufman's plays, most of which were collaborations with other theatrical luminaries, have been filmed by Hollywood or produced for TV more than 50 times. All of Kaufman's celebrated collaborations with Moss Hart are listed under this entry. Other screen adaptations of his plays are cited elsewhere. For *June Moon*, see **Ring Lardner**. For *Dinner at Eight, Minick, The Royal Family*, and *Stage Door*, see **Edna Ferber**. For *Animal Crackers, Cocoanuts*, and *Of Thee I Sing*, see **Morrie Ryskind**. For *Dulcy, Beggar on Horseback, Merton of the Movies*, and *To the Ladies*, see **Marc Connelly**.

Kaufman's major plays that didn't make it to either screen include *Jacques Duval* (1919), *The 49ers* (1922), *Helen of Troy, New York* (1923), *Be Yourself* (1924), *The Channel Road* (1929), *Eldorado* (1931), *Let 'Em Eat Cake* (1933), *Bring on the Girls* (1934), *I'd Rather Be Right* (1937), *The Fabulous Invalid* (1938), *The American Way* (1939), *The Land Is Bright* (1941), *Dream on, Soldier* (1943), *Hollywood Pinafore* (1945), *Park Avenue* (1946), *School for Waiters* (1948), *Bravo!* (1948), and *Fancy Meeting You Again* (1952). He also co-wrote plays with his wife, Leueen MacGrath, including *The Small Hours*.

The Butter and Egg Man, about a cowboy in New York, is one of the most retooled and retitled fish-out-of-water shows in comedy film history as well as the only play that Kaufman, the "great collaborator," wrote on his own (although Herman J. Mankiewicz is said to have contributed to it). Gregory Kelly originated the cowpoke's role in the 1925 stage production directed by James Gleason. The title refers to legendary New York speakeasy hostess Texas Guinan's term for a hayseed out-of-towner.

The Butter and Egg Man (1928, First National, bw/silent) ☆☆ **Sc:** Adelaide Heilbron, Jack Jarmuth, Gene Towne. **D:** Richard Wallace. **Cam:** George J. Folsey. **Cast:** Jack Mulhall, Greta Nissen, Sam Hardy, William Demarest, Gertrude Astor. Hardy played a crooked Broadway producer who wants to get his hands on hayseed-in-New York Mulhall's cash.

- "*Kaufman's clever comedy…has been pulled down to a low level of intelligence, the producers having carefully excluded all the delightful nuances and adroit subtleties of the original. The skeleton of the story is left, but that is about all. Mr. Mulhall fails to sense what's wanted in the character, and he and the director, Richard Wallace, make the young man so silly that one wonders that he is even permitted at large....Now and again Mr. Kaufman's lines are used to advantage, but more often than not, Mr. Kaufman's bon mots are attached to scenes that render them ineffectual."* (Mordaunt Hall, The New York Times)

The Tenderfoot (1932, Warner Bros., 73m/bw) ☆½ **Sc:** Arthur Caesar, Monty Banks, Earl Baldwin. **D:** Ray Enright. **P:** Bryan Foy. **Cam:** Gregg Toland. **Cast:** Joe E. Brown, Ginger Rogers, Lew Cody, Vivian Oakland, Robert Greig. This Brown vehicle features the comic as a none-too-bright cowboy who gets mixed up with racketeers after he backs a Broadway musical (*Her Golden Sin*) starring Rogers's character. The piece apparently had appeal to Brown devotees, but was "excruciating" for others (see below).

- *"Bearing hardly any resemblance to the George S. Kaufman play...With a workmanlike screenplay...and direction by the reliable Ray Enright, its mediocre subject obviously appealed to someone in the studio's story department for it was remade five years later..."* (Clive Hirschhorn, The Warner Bros. Story)

- *"A belabored farce with inferior production values and a middling, long-spun narrative....Regrettably, Rogers is only ornamental in the proceedings, and Brown, he of the melon mouth and obnoxious cat-call, likewise flounders in an excruciating premise."* (Patrick McGilligan, Ginger Rogers, 1975)

Dance Charlie Dance (1937, Warner Bros., 64m/bw) ☆☆ **Sc:** Crane Wilbur, William Jacobs. **D:** Frank McDonald. **P:** Bryan Foy. **Cam:** Warren Lynch. **Cast:** Stuart Erwin, Jean Muir, Glenda Farrell, Allen Jenkins, Addison Richards, Charles Foy, Chester Clute.

- *"...bereft of George S. Kaufman's gift for satire...lifeless screenplay...equally moribund direction."* (Clive Hirschhorn, The Warner Bros. Story)

An Angel From Texas (1940, Warner Bros., 69m/bw) ☆☆½ **Sc:** Fred Niblo Jr., Bertram Millhauser. **D:** Ray Enright. **P:** Robert Fellows. **Cam:** Arthur L. Todd. **Cast:** Eddie Albert, Rosemary Lane, Wayne Morris, Ronald Reagan, Milburne Stone, Jane Wyman, Ruth Terry, John Litel, Hobart Cavanaugh, Ann Shoemaker, Tom Kennedy, Elliott Sullivan, Ferris Taylor, Paul Phillips, Emmett Vogan, George Irving.

- *"...a bright little farce about a couple of yokels...The story is neither new nor exciting and, except for the addtion of some modern slang, is pretty much the same as when George S. Kaufman told it in 1925...It has been smartly acted by a pleasant company...Ray Enright has directed in a breezy, farcical manner."* (Thomas M. Pryor, The New York Times)

Three Sailors and a Girl (1953, Warner Bros., 98m/bw) ☆☆ **Sc:** Roland Kibbee, Devery Freeman. **D:** Roy Del Ruth. **P:** Sammy Cahn. **Cam:** Carl Guthrie. **Cast:** Jane Powell, Gordon MacRae, Gene Nelson, Jack E. Leonard, Sam Levene, George Givot, Veda Ann Borg, Archer

MacDonald, Raymond Greenleaf. The songs included "Face to Face," "Kiss Me or I'll Scream," and "Oh So Right."

- *"An impoverished musical which attempted to marry off the Navy to Broadway in the story about the efforts of three sailors, an impecunious producer, and a singer to transform a nonentity of a revue into a Broadway smash. They succeed, of course, and the manner in which they do formed the water-thin substance of Roland Kibbee and Devery Freeman's screenplay....The film was directed—with a touch of desperation—by Roy Del Ruth..." (Clive Hirshhorn, The Warner Bros. Story)*

Hello Sweetheart was a 1935 filming of The Butter and Egg Man by Warner Bros.'s British production team based on a Brock Williams screenplay and starring Claude Hulbert, Gregory Ratoff, Jane Carr, Nancy O'Neil, and Felix Aylmer. It was never imported to the U.S.

Dancing in the Dark (1949, 20th Century-Fox, 92m/c, **VHS/DVD**) ☆☆½ **Sc:** Mary C. McCall Jr. **D:** Irving Reis. **P:** George Jessel. **Cam:** Harry Jackson. **Cast:** William Powell, Adolphe Menjou, Mark Stevens, Betsy Drake, Hope Emerson, Lloyd Corrigan, Walter Catlett, Jean Hersholt, Don Beddoe, Randy Stuart, Sid Grauman, Frank Ferguson, Helen Westcott, Charles Tannen. This occasionally mush-bucket story, Hollywood-style, could never diminish Powell's deepest resistance to thespian fraud. The play was called The Band Wagon, a showbiz special about a silent film star who makes a comeback as a talent scout and unwittingly "discovers" his own daughter. Kaufman wrote the play with Howard Dietz and Arthur Schwartz. It debuted on Broadway in 1931 starring Fred and Adele Astaire along with Helen Broderick.

- *"An improbable tale, but with good views of Hollywood, a stylish performance by Powell, and an interesting use of the Arthur Schwartz-Howard Dietz songs from The Band Wagon, which is the musical being considered for filming within this film." (Tony Thomas, Aubrey Solomon, The Films of 20th Century-Fox: A Pictorial History)*

The Dark Tower, written in collaboration with the critic and Broadway dandy Alexander Woollcott, was produced at New York's Morosco Theatre in 1933 with a cast including Margalo Gillmore, Margaret Hamilton, Basil Sydney, and William Harrigan. It concerned the murder of a truculent man by his brother-in-law.

The Man With Two Faces (1934, Warner Bros., 72m/bw) ☆☆☆½ **Sc:** Tom Reed, Niven Busch. **D:** Archie Mayo. **P:** Jack L. Warner. **Cam:** Tony Gaudio. **Cast:** Edward G. Robinson, Mary Astor, Ricardo Cortez, Mae Clarke, Louis Calhern, John Eldredge, Arthur Byron, Henry O'Neill, David Landau, Emily Fitzroy, Margaret Dale, Dorothy Tree, Arthur Aylesworth, Virginia Sale, Mary Russell, Milton Kibbee, Frank Darien, Dick Winslow. The fine cast shored up the melodrama.

- *"A suave bit of acting, done in the best tradition of good actors impersonating good actors."* (New York World Telegram)
- *"Occasionally the studio aimed at a somewhat higher literary level....Best of all was Archie Mayo's* The Man with Two Faces, *a film version of* The Dark Tower...*Its arresting, offbeat story of the murder of an obnoxious man by his brother-in-law...Calhern in particular was properly sinister if hammy as the victim, a self-confessed scoundrel with a mincing manner and a fondness for white mice."* (*Ted Sennett,* Warner Brothers Presents)

The Dark Tower (1942, Warner Bros., 93m/bw) ☆☆ **Sc:** Brock Williams, Reginald Purdell. **D:** John Harlow. **P:** Max Milder. **Cam:** Otto Heller. **Cast:** Ben Lyon, Anne Crawford, David Farrar, Herbert Lom, William Hartnell, Frederick Burtwell, Josephine Wilson. Lom, in his first film role, played a circus hypnotist who falls in love with his brother's trapeze partner and tries to hypnotize her into dropping him during their act.

The Dark Tower was also produced on NBC's *Kraft Television Theatre* in an hour-long version starring E.G. Marshall, Flora Campbell, and John Newland.

First Lady (1937, Warner Bros., 82m/bw) ☆☆☆ **Sc:** Rowland Leigh. **D:** Stanley Logan. **P:** Hal B. Wallis. **Cam:** Sid Hickox. **Cast:** Kay Francis, Preston Foster, Anita Louise, Walter Connelly, Verree Teasdale, Victor Jory, Marjorie Rambeau, Louise Fazenda, Marjorie Gateson. Kaufman co-wrote this 1935 comedy of Washington political life — in which the titular character is the real brains behind presidential decisions — with Katharine Dayton. This battle royale between two women, the wives of the Secretary of State and an ineffectual Supreme Court justice, reaches a fever pitch when one announces that she will be presenting America with a new Presidential candidate. The film became a showcase for Teasdale, who sailed on the film-preserved dialogue by Kaufman and Drayton, and practically wiped Francis off the screen.

- *"The difference between the stage and screen versions of* First Lady *is approximately the difference between Jane Cowl and Kay Francis. That distinction, like Mercutio's wound, may not be so deep as a well, nor so wide as a church door, but it serves. It serves, indeed, to blunt ever so slightly the cutting edge of the Katherine Drayton-George Kaufman play of two seasons ago, and it places Miss Francis's first lady...in the untenable position of running second to Verree Teasdale's second lady. For Miss Teasdale is the perfect mouthpiece for the Kaufman-Drayton insolences, while Miss Francis — even discounting her difficulty with the letter 'r' — has been trained far in the gentler school of drama. There is an art of insult, and Miss Francis has not mastered it....so closely follows the play that we are tempted lazily to refer you to Mr. [theatre critic Brooks] Atkinson's friendly report upon it on the morning of November 27, 1935."* (*Frank S. Nugent,* The New York Times)

George Washington Slept Here (1942, Warner Bros., 93m/bw, **VHS**) ☆☆☆½ **Sc:** Everett Freeman. **D:** William Keighley. **P:** Jerry Wald. **Cam:** Ernest Haller. **Cast:** Jack Benny, Ann Sheridan, Charles Coburn, Percy Kilbride, Hattie McDaniel, William Tracy, Lee Patrick, John Emery, Charles Dingle. The 1940 play starring Jean Dixon concerned a couple who move from Manhattan to a Pennsylvania farmhouse with the intent on fixing it up, while a greedy neighbor has ideas of his own.

- *"The leading comedy role in the play was the role of the wife, while the husband played the straight man. For the film, all they did was reverse the roles and Jack Benny took the comedy part, with Ann Sheridan as the wife who fed the lead lines. On Broadway the character actor Percy Kilbride had played the nasal down-east farmer and had been a comedic sensation....Kilbride did play the movie role and was a hilarious performer and did get tremendous laughs. But as Jack predicted, it only helped the picture, which turned out to be one of his better films."* (Irving A. Fein, Jack Benny: An Intimate Biography)

- *"...underwent major surgery in its transfer from the Broadway stage to the silver screen: Its comedy was amputated....it flatly refused to amuse, and nothing director William Keighley attempted, could inject life into Everett Freeman's screenplay."* (Clive Hirschhorn, The Warner Bros. Story)

The Good Fellows (1943, Paramount, 70m/bw) ☆☆½ **Sc:** Hugh Wedlock Jr., Walter Snyder. **D:** Jo Graham. **P:** Walter MacEwen. **Cam:** Theodor Sparkuhl. **Cast:** Cecil Kellaway, Helen Walker, James Brown, Mabel Paige, Patti Hale, Kathleen Lockhart, Douglas Wood, Norma Varden, Olin Howlin, Tom Fadden, Rod Cameron, Irving Bacon, Chester Clute. Co-written with Herman J. Mankiewicz, the 1926 play was directed by Kaufman and Howard Lindsay. It was known by the singular title *The Good Fellow* and closed after seven performances. The title of Grand Caesar in the Ancient Order of Noblest Romans of Wakefield, Indiana, so consumes Pop Helton that he forgets to pay bills, and absent-mindedly bungles a real estate deal and his daughter's romance.

- *"It was a small financial salvage for the play when Paramount bought the movie rights. But it took four years after the close of the play for Kaufman to be able to bring himself to regard the matter lightly. On October 27, 1930, finally recovered, and following the appearance of an article on Mankiewicz in [The New York] Times, he wrote a brief letter to the newspaper. 'You say,' he wrote, 'that he once collaborated with me on a "half forgotten" play. The reference is, of course, to The Good Fellow, produced about four years ago. I feel I must protest your use of "half forgotten." I have been conducting some inquiries, and I am pleased to say that I find no one who remembers it at all. I think you should be a little surer of your facts before rushing into print.' Certainly the play was more than half forgotten by Paramount. Though they acquired the rights in 1926, they didn't make a film based on the play until 17 years later, releasing it under the title of* The Good Fellows *in 1943." (Scott* Meredith, George S. Kaufman and His Friends*)*

The Late George Apley (1947, 20th Century-Fox, 98m/bw) ☆☆☆ **Sc:** Philip Dunne. **D:** Joseph L. Mankiewicz. **P:** Fred Kohlmar. **Cam:** Joseph LaShelle. **Cast:** Ronald Colman, Edna Best, Vanessa Brown, Richard Haydn, Peggy Cummins, Charles Russell, Richard Ney, Percy Waram, Mildred Natwick, Nydia Westman, Kathleen Howard, Paul Harvey, Mae Marsh, Francis Pierlot, Helen Freeman. Kaufman and John P. Marquand adapted the latter's novel about blue-blood Bostonians to the stage. Leo G. Carroll starred in the 1944 Max Gordon production at New York's Lyceum Theatre as the narrow-minded and arrogant patriarch, which Dunne's screenplay turned into a charming old-timer.

- *"...botched on the screen—but good!" (Bosley Crowther,* The New York Times*)*
- *"The film is handsomely produced, and the atmosphere of early 20th century Boston is faithfully reproduced. Mankiewicz catches all the necessary ambiance and his touches are sharp. Edna Best makes a charming Mrs. Apley...*The Late George Apley *greatly enhanced Colman's cinematic image, showcased him as an actor of solid range and attainments, and led directly to his major [Oscar-winning] triumph in* A Double Life *the following year." (Lawrence J. Quirk,* The Films of Ronald Colman*)*

The Man Who Came to Dinner was one of Kaufman and Hart's great triumphs, about a megalomaniac radio personality who breaks his hip on a lecture tour and must be confined to a suburban home for several weeks, as his acidic put-downs become the terror of the host family. The duo based the character on Broadway legend Alexander Woollcott. The play originated on Broadway in 1939 at the Music Box Theatre with Monty Woolley as Sheridan Whiteside and Mary Wickes in the ensemble.

The Man Who Came to Dinner (1942, Warner Bros., 112m/bw, **VHS**) ☆☆☆☆ **Sc:** Julius J. Epstein, Philip G. Epstein. **D:** William Keighley. **P:** Jack Saper, Jerry Wald. **Cam:** Tony Gaudio. **Cast:** Monty Woolley, Bette Davis, Ann Sheridan, Jimmy Durante, Reginald Gardiner, Richard Travis, Billie Burke, Grant Mitchell, Ruth Vivian, Mary Wickes, George Barbier, Elisabeth Fraser, Charles Drake, Laura Hope Crewes, Russell Arms, John Ridgely, Creighton Hale. This is usually regarded as the best adaptation, although Otis Ferguson didn't think so (see below). Sheridan Whiteside certainly was Woolley's signature part.

- *"...fidelity to the original is definitely a handicap. The picture is too long, too stuffy in its talk-talk and one main set, and in many respects just poorly done. In direction...it is often a case of overemphasis—big takes, exaggerated confusion, too much noise. It isn't hard to see why. Monty Woolley is in a central part he considers his own property, and while he manages all the attention-getting and point of the veteran stage man, he creates a character at once ill-defined and pushed outward with the emphasis of burlesque. These popping consonants, this practiced roar, this sarcasm without inner compulsion and ranting without the fire of rage...The camera eye picks this all up, shows relentlessly where it is false, and literally throws it at your head, back row or front." (Otis Ferguson,* The New Republic)

The Man Who Came to Dinner (1949, CBS, 60m/bw) *Ford Theatre Hour* ☆☆☆½ **Tp:** Max Wilk, Ellis Marcus. **D:** Marc Daniels. **P:** Garth Montgomery. **Cast:** Edward Everett Horton, Vicki Cummings, Judy Parrish, Kevin McCarthy, Beverly Carlton, Mary Wickes, Zero Mostel, Rex O'Malley, Whitford Kane, John Marlotte. Horton may not have given the Whiteside role the brass and egomaniacal quality that Woolley invested in the part, but it was a successful TV event in a year in which few Americans owned TV sets. Mostel played Banjo, a character based on Harpo Marx.

- *"...comedy which has already clicked in both legit and films, achieved almost as much success in its [TV] version. Tele script...managed to retain most of the original's best lines while still eliminating the blue remarks, and the cast, production and direction were top-notch."* (Variety)

The Man Who Came to Dinner (1954, CBS, 60m/bw) *The Best of Broadway* ☆☆ **Tp:** Ronald Alexander. **D:** David Alexander. **P:** Martin Manulis. **Cast:** Monty Woolley, Sylvia Field, Howard St. John, ZaSu Pitts, Margaret Hamilton, Reginald Gardiner, Merle Oberon, Joan Bennett, Buster Keaton, Bert Lahr, Catherine Doucet, Frank Twedell. Manulis rounded up an all-star cast for TV's second time around.

- *"...despite the bright performing...in the top-flight cast, took a pratfall on television." (William Torbert Leonard,* Theatre: From Stage to Screen to Television)

- *"One of the contemporary theatre's treasured viles of vitriol...was diluted...to a bottle full of stage 'pop.' Individual lines...came through in all their witty acidity...But the amusing whole failed to survive the drastic cutting of the script and the miscasting of several Hollywood stars....By their mere presence, the stars tended to throw the play further out of focus and detract from the dominance of Mr. Woolley's performance." (Jack Gould,* The New York Times)

The Man Who Came to Dinner (1972) *The Hallmark Hall of Fame* ☆☆☆½ **Tp/P:** Bill Persky, Sam Denoff. **D:** Buzz Kulik. **Cast:** Orson Welles, Lee Remick, Joan Collins, Peter Haskell, Edward Andrews, Mary Wickes, Marty Feldman, Don Knotts, Marcella Markham, Anita Sharp Bolster, Michael Gough, George Pravda, Kim Braden. A bit of Wellesian aggrandizement applied to Whiteside arrogance seemed almost an inevitability. The supporting cast was excellent.

- *"Everything was so individually good about this updated television version...that it is something of a puzzle as to why it didn't work better than it* did....the whole ambitious enterprise just didn't seem to gel. It is true that Orson Welles suffered from visible lapses of discipline and that they were not compensated for by a stronger hand by director Buzz Kulik. However, Welles has been playing this same Jovian role in various guises since he directed himself in Citizen Kane, and his overwhelming presence has usually made up in vitality for what it lacked in control and modulation." (Variety)

The Man Who Came to Dinner (2000, PBS, 176m/c) *Stage to Screen* ☆☆☆ **Tp:** Moss Hart, George S. Kaufman. **D:** Jay Sandrich. **P:** Todd Haimes, Judy Kinberg, Jac Venza. **Cast:** Nathan Lane, Jean Smart, Harriet Sansom, Jack Arendt, Jozef Fahey, William Duell, Stephen DeRosa, Ryan Torino, Linda Stephens, Julie Halston, Kit Flanagan, Mary Catherine Wright. This broadcast of a live performance of New York's Roundabout Theater Company's 2000 revival of the play displays a less acidic Sheridan Whiteside via Lane's not-so imperious take on the character.

- "Almost everything is played out to the audience. We want the audiences' laughs. I had gone to the final dress rehearsal, and Jean Smart is so wonderful. She has invented the most marvelous version of the famous actress Whiteside calls in to help bring an end to the relationship between his secretary and the young man of the town. Her arrival has great style." (Jac Venza to Susan King, Los Angeles Times)

Once in a Lifetime (1932, Universal, 80m/bw) ☆☆☆☆ **Sc:** Seton I. Miller. **D:** Russell Mack. **P:** Carl Laemmle Jr. **Cam:** George Robinson. **Cast:** Jack Oakie, Sidney Fox, Aline MacMahon, Gregory Ratoff, Russell Hopton, ZaSu Pitts, Louise Fazenda, Onslow Stevens, Walter Brennan, Jobyna Howland, Eddie Kane, Gregory Gaye, Johnnie Morris, Frank LaRue. This Kaufman/Hart Hollywood satire, one of the first major send-ups of Tinsel Town, follows the process of selling a screenplay to a studio. The play was a smash hit in 1930 and historic for being the first collaboration between Kaufman and Hart, brought together by producer Sam Harris. The pair labored through nine months of revisions on Hart's original idea, creating in their Hollywood producer a gullible but scheming know-nothing.

- "This particular play was considered too rough for Hollywood, but in 1932 Universal brought the enemy within the gates, and, of course, pulled some of its satirical teeth. With moon-faced Jack Oakie as the goodhearted imbecilic vaudevillian who in Hollywood is taken for a genius...The picture isn't particularly well-made, but it's a true period piece—a reminder of the beginnings of a type of Broadway lampoon-comedy, and it has a lovely corny triviality and innocence." (Pauline Kael, 5,001 Nights at the Movies)

- "...they seemed to enjoy poking fun at themselves. Carl Laemmle, the president of Universal Studios, signed his name to a short forward preceding the screen version of Once in a Lifetime to the effect that people in Hollywood did not mind a good laugh at their own expense....The leg-

end of the culturally moronic mogul became so pervasive in the industry that when a college-educated producer popped up in the front office, his intellectual pretensions were still good for a laugh, as in the caricature of a Walter Wanger-like arriviste in Sam and Bella Spewack's Boy Meets Girl, *which, like* Once in a Lifetime, *went from stage to screen with most of its anti-Hollywood satiric conceits intact. For a long time this apparent ability to take a joke was not recognized as a defense reaction against deep feelings of insecurity and self-hatred. The contempt for movies within the movie industry itself has never been properly chronicled." (Andrew Sarris,* You Ain't Heard Nothin' Yet)

The Small Hours, which Kaufman wrote with Leueen MacGrath, debuted onstage in 1951. It was reproduced in 1952 on *Kraft Television Theatre* with a cast led by Lauren Gilbert, Grace Kelly, and Katherine Meskill.

The Solid Gold Cadillac (1956, Columbia, 99m/bw, **VHS**) ☆☆½ **Sc:** Abe Burrows. **D:** Richard Quine. **P:** Fred Kohlmar. **Cam:** Charles Lang. **Cast:** Judy Holliday, Paul Douglas, Fred Clark, John Williams, Hiram Sherman, Neva Patterson, Ralph Dumke, Ray Collins, Arthur O'Connell, Richard Deacon, Marilyn Hanold, Anne Loos, Audrey Swanson, Larry Hudson, Madge Blake, Sandra White, Lulu Mae Bohrman. Based on the 1953 play by Kaufman and Howard Teichmann, which starred Josephine Hull and ran for 526 performances on Broadway, this comedy concerns Laura Partridge, who owns ten shares of stock in a huge corporation, forcing the directors of the company to be accountable.

- *"...with Abe Burrows's assistance as adapter, the invincible Miss Holliday has dared to project her youthful figure and personality...as the buzzing gadfly that pesters and tweaks and finally stings the directors of a mammoth corporation...Actually, she has very little to overcome...The problems set up by the playwrights are little barriers of cardboard farce...manned by...droll executives...cut from a fairly familiar stencil of Kaufmanesque farce....The Solid Gold Cadillac...will give you an entertaining ride, but don't expect it to take you or your intelligence very far." (Bosley Crowther,* The New York Times)

Someone in the House, which Kaufman wrote with Larry Evans and Walter Percival, was a flop in 1918, but produced what Kaufman's late-career collaborator and biographer, Howeard Teichmann, called the "first authentic Kaufman witticism." This was advertising copy for the tepid melodrama: "Beware of the flu, avoid crowds, see *Someone in the House.*"

Someone Must Pay (1919, State Rights, bw/silent) ☆☆ **Sc/D:** Ivan Abramson. **Cam:** John W. Brown. **Cast:** Edmund Lowe, Vola Vale, Howard Crampton, William Irving, Clara Lee, Lawrence Grant, Edward Connelly, Henry Miller Jr., Edward Jobson, Tom McGuire, Jack Levering.

Someone in the House (1920, Metro, bw/silent) ☆☆ **Sc:** Marc Robbins, Lois Zellner. **D:** John Ince. **Cam:** George K. Hollister. **Cast:** Edmund Lowe, Vola Vale, Howard Crampton, William Irving, Clara Lee, Lawrence Grant, Edward Connelly, Henry Miller Jr., Edward Jobson, Tom McGuire, Jack Levering.

You Can't Take It With You debuted on Broadway in 1936 and ran for 837 performances. Kaufman directed a cast led by Henry Travers and Josephine Hull in the story of the gregarious Sycamore family, which faces the Depression Era with eccentric charm.

You Can't Take It With You (1938, Columbia, 127m/bw, **VHS**) ☆☆☆☆ **Sc:** Robert Riskin. **D/P:** Frank Capra. **Cam:** Joseph Walker. **Cast:** Jean Arthur, James Stewart, Lionel Barrymore, Edward Arnold, Mischa Auer, Ann Miller, Spring Byington, Samuel S. Hinds, Donald Meek, Dub Taylor, H.B. Warner, Halliwell Hobbes, Mary Forbes, Lillian Yarbo, Eddie Anderson, Clarence Wilson, Ann Doran, Charles Lane, Harry Davenport, Russell Hicks, Byron Foulger, Ian Wolfe, Irving Bacon, James Flavin, Ward Bond, James Burke, Pert Kelton, Bodil Rosing, Josef Swickard. This film is as fondly remembered for the iconic performances of its stars. The film won the Academy Awards for Best Picture and Director and was nominated for Best Supporting Actress (Byington), Screenplay, Cinematography, Sound, and Film Editing.

- *"Mr. Deeds seems to have given writer (Robert Riskin) and director (Frank Capra) an idea of themselves as social philosophers that does them no good....There is an embarassing amount of space here given over to the spiritual poverty of riches, the wealth of the simple heart, the glory and pity of it all." (Otis Ferguson, The New Republic)*

- *"Pulitzer Prize plays do not grow on bushes, a circumstance which is bound to complicate their grafting onto the cinema. Columbia's film of the play...has had to justify that Pulitzer award. Simply because it is a motion picture, and not a play, it has had to explore the Kaufman-Hart characters more thoroughly than the playwrights had need to. It is a grand picture, which will disappoint only the most supeficial admirers of the play." (Frank S. Nugent, The New York Times)*

You Can't Take It With You (1950, ABC, 60m/bw) *Pulitzer Prize Playhouse* ☆☆☆ **Tp:** Nancy Moore. **D:** Alex Segal. **P:** Edgar Peterson. **Cast:** Charles Coburn, Ella Raines, Nydia Westman, E.G. Marshall, Joseph Buloff, Elliott Reid, Dora Clement, Glenn Discuss, Edith Wood, Ralph Bunker, Bond Taylor, Casey Allen, Ralph Stanley. To debut the prestigious series, Peterson and Segal decided on the Kaufman/Hart classic.

- *"...came off as one of the most gratifying stanzas adapted to the new medium. It was a slick piece of compressed staging, moving at a pace de-*

signed to extract maximum laugh values with seldom a lag in the hour presentation." (Variety)

- *"...a laudable production....the settings and staging were excellent and the camerawork flowed beautifully, without a ripple....this series holds much promise of helping television to grow out of its rompers."* (The New York Times)

You Can't Take It With You (1979, CBS, 120m/c) ☆☆☆ **Tp:** George S. Kaufman, Moss Hart. **D:** Paul Bogart. **P:** Lindsay Law, Paul Bogart. **Cast:** Art Carney, Jean Stapleton, Barry Bostwick, Blythe Danner, Harry Morgan, Mildred Natwick, Marla Gibbs, Howard Hesseman, Polly Holiday, Beth Howland, Robert Mandan, Kenneth Mars, Tim Reid, Paul Sand, Eugene Roche, Joyce Van Patten, Alan Oppenheimer.

- *"...suffered as much from the casting of TV series performers as it did from age. In fact, the play held up rather well as finely crafted theatrical fare, but the years have lessened the uniqueness of the Vanderhof family philosophy ...Bogart chose to use a contemnporary sitcom style, with its overabundance of close-up reactions — and thus tended to underscore the fact that the comedy was crafted for ensemble playing on a proscenium stage....Art Carney, as Grandpa Vanderhof, was the only player who seemed to be in complete command of his part...Stapleton, as Carney's daughter...gave the impression that she's determined to play every role as if she's Edith Bunker...play could have been a farcical treat, rather than the merely pleasant outing that it was."* (Variety)

You Can't Take It With You (1984, Showtime, 116m/c, **VHS**) **Tp:** Moss Hart, George S. Kaufman. **D:** Ellis Rabb, Kirk Browning. **P:** Daniel A. Bohr. **Cast:** Jason Robards, Elizabeth Wilson, Jack Dodson, Carol Androsky, Maureen Anderman, Colleen Dewhurst, George Rose, Arthur French, Nicholas Surovy, Bill McCutcheon, Christopher Foster, Rosetta Le Noire. After the revival of the play closed on Broadway, the same cast was reassembled for this production before an audience at New York's Royale Theatre. This splendidly directed production, which originally aired on the cable channel Showtime, was also shown later the same year on PBS's *Great Performances*.

- *"...its charm survives beautifully intact....Grandpa has learned that 'Life is pretty simple if you just relax.' That is precisely what Mr. Robards does and, in the process, gives one of his most appealing performances....The television cameras manage to capture a good deal of the play in close-up while never getting in the way of the tricky pacing. The production's most outstanding and beguiling asset is its sustained feeling of genuine warmth....a delightful vehicle for the very special talents of Mr. Robards, Miss Wilson, Miss Dewhurst, Mr. Rose and the rest. With this production, television also takes an important stride forward in the difficult craft of transferring a stage production to the electronic screen."* (John J. O'Connor, The New York Times)

George Kelly

George Edward Kelly
Born: January 16, 1887, Philadelphia, PA. **Died:** 1974.
Pulitzer Prize-winning play: *Craig's Wife* (1926)

Kelly, who in retrospect is most remembered as actress Grace Kelly's uncle, dabbled in Hollywood, wrote two screenplays for Bryan "Brynie" Foy in 1929: *The Flattering Word* with Helen Ferguson and *Finders Keepers* with the silent-era Harrison Ford. He also retooled a Will Rogers silent, *Honest Hutch* (1920), about a bum who finds $100,000, for the Wallace Beery vehicle *Old Hutch* (1936).

Craig's Wife was first produced in 1925 with Kelly directing a cast featuring Chrystal Herne, Charles Trowbridge, and Josephine Hull. It became one of the theatre's enduring chestnuts on greed and self-involvement. Harriet Craig values her standing, money, and home over everything else. Her husband, relatives, and servants all eventually come to bitterly understand this and subsequently leave her.

Craig's Wife (1928, Pathé, bw/silent) ☆☆½ **Sc:** Clara Beranger. **D:** William C. de Mille. **P:** Milton S. Whitehill. **Cam:** David Able. **Cast:** Irene Rich, Warner Baxter, Virginia Bradford, Carroll Nye, Lilyan Tashman, George Irving, Jane Keckley, Mabel Van Buren, Ethel Wales, Rada Rae.

- *"...a good carbon copy of the Mrs. Craig of the stage....although this carefully directed picture lacks the spontaneity and drama of the original, there is throughout its length an evident desire to do well by the author. The dramatic values in this production do not stir one as they did in the play."* (Mordaunt Hall, The New York Times)

Craig's Wife (1936, Columbia, 77m/bw, **VHS**) ☆☆☆ **Sc:** Mary C. McCall Jr., George Kelly. **D:** Dorothy Arzner. **P:** Edward Chodorov. **Cam:** Lucien Ballard. **Cast:** Rosalind Russell, John Boles, Billie Burke, Jane Darwell, Thomas Mitchell, Dorothy Wilson, Elisabeth Risdon, Alma Kruger, Raymond Walburn, Robert Allen, Nydia Westman. Russell delivered one of her more underrated and complex performances as she both exemplified Kelly's selfish theme and created sympathy for the character, in a way that wasn't anything like a Hollywood whitewash.

- *"...Hollywood appears to have the magic stone for converting good plays into better pictures. Columbia, to be quite quick about it, has been able to do quite well with Mr. Kelly's drama of domestic infelicity."* (Frank S. Nugent, The New York Times)

Harriet Craig (1950, Columbia, 94m/bw, **VHS**) ☆☆½ **Sc:** Anne Froelick, James Gunn. **D:** Vincent Sherman. **P:** William Dozier. **Cam:**

Joseph Walker. **Cast:** Joan Crawford, Wendell Corey, Allyn Joslyn, William Bishop, Lucille Watson, Raymond Greenleaf, K.T. Stevens, Ellen Corby, Virginia Brissac, Kathryn Card, Al Murphy. Columbia dusted off the play and converted it into this Crawford vehicle, retitling it with her character in the manner of her hits *Mildred Pierce* (1945) and *Daisy Kenyon* (1947). The venal, harsh, and self-centered Harriet was at least, on the surface, right down Crawford's narrow, cold-bricked alley.

- *"...as smooth as the silk in its namesake's well-guarded salon...[but with] a lack of warmth and personality by the presence of a star who does not know how to do anything except shine."* (Otis L. Guernsey Jr., New York Herald-Tribune)

- *"...the poisonous woman which the laquered Miss Crawford tries to play, under Vincent Sherman's direction, is not so much poisonous as just plain dull. Miss Crawford persists so intently in a harsh, mechanistic acting style that there is simply no reason or reality in the perfunctory shrew that she parades. It is as though an overdressed clotheshorse without character or sex were playing the role."* (Bosley Crowther, The New York Times)

Craig's Wife (1954, NBC, 60m/bw) *The Lux Video Theatre* ☆☆☆ **D:** Earl Ebi. **P:** Cornwell Jackson. **Cast:** Ruth Hussey, Philip Ober, Kathryn Givney, Lillian Bronson, Ezelle Poule, Margie Liszt, Eleanor Tanin, Paul Bryar, Ray Walker.

- "Lux came up with another winner in the tele version of this old stage play. The George Kelly story...has lost little of its potent force and needed little updating to sweeten its acceptance. For Ruth Hussey...and Philip Ober...it was a triumphant evening at the sets. Both were masterful in every facet of the emotional currents that swirled through the house of hate." (Variety)

Craig's Wife also aired on TV in 1947 on *Kraft Television Theatre* and in 1952 on *Broadway Television Theatre* in a version starring Ona Munson and Mildred Dunnock.

Daisy Mayme was a 1926 Kelly play that featured Josephine Hull and Madge Evans. It was televised in 1952 on the 52nd and last installment of *The Pulitzer Prize Playhouse* with June Havoc and Sheppard Strudwick, and again in 1958 on *Matinee Theatre* in a version starring Paul Hartman and Lurene Tuttle.

The Fatal Weakness (1976, PBS, 120m/c) *Hollywood Television Theatre* ☆☆☆½ **Tp:** George Kelly. **D/P:** Norman Lloyd. **Commentary:** Princess Grace of Monaco (Grace Kelly). **Cast:** Eva Marie Saint, John McMartin, Gretchen Corbett, Charlotte Moore, Dennis Dugan, Sara Seegar. The play was first launched on Broadway in 1946 with Ina Claire starring as a well-off woman who, after learning of her husband's affair, informs her daughter, who's having marital discord of her own. The play's historical significance lies in the fact that its reception made Kelly turn away from the theatre for good in disgust.

- *"…a very old fashioned kind of theatre in which Kelly, with a velvet scalpel, expertly reveals the inner workings of some very nice people in an adroit and glittering river of words. It's the theatre of language, once the glory of the stage but a rare bird today. What Kelly gives us—and Miss Saint plays beautifully—is a fragile, ethereal kind of woman…an incurable romantic.…By TV's machine-gun standards, the play is slow and talky, its pace methodical, its playing exquisite."* (Cecil Smith, Los Angeles Times)

Philip Goes Forth, a 1931 Kelly play, aired in 1952 and 1954 on *Kraft Television Theatre*. In both cases, the productions starred Roddy McDowell and Blanche Yurka.

The Reflected Glory, a 1936 Talllulah Bankhead vehicle produced by Lee Shubert, was redone on TV in 1954 on *Broadway Television Theatre* starring Clare Booth Luce.

The Show-Off (The Transcript of a Life) ran for nearly 600 performances on Broadway beginning in 1924 with Louis John Bartels as Aubrey Piper and co-starred Lee Tracy and Juliette Crosby. It concerns a clerk who pretends to be a railroad tycoon in order to win the affections of a girl, then loses everything, including his job.

The Show-Off (1926, Paramount, 82m/bw/silent, **VHS/DVD**) ☆☆☆ **Sc:** Pierre Collings. **D:** Malcolm St. Clair. **P:** William Le Baron, Malcolm St. Clair. **Cam:** Lee Garmes. **Cast:** Ford Sterling, Lois Wilson, Louise Brooks, Gregory Kelly, Claire McDowell, Charles Goodrich, Joseph W. Smiley. The chief attraction for the video resurrection of this silent version is the presence of Louise Brooks as, literally, the girl next door, who admonishes Aubrey Piper in one of the film's key scenes. Sterling, whose career was built on his presence as the leader of the Keystone Kops, delivered a fine performance.

- *"Most of the play's popularity had derived from its dialogue, but St. Clair added some fascinating exterior footage of Philadelphia, including a spectacular car chase, in order to liberate the drama from its drawing room. Overall, however, the film's silence was a drawback that Louise [Brooks] was expected to help offset. And she did her job. St. Clair later said that he had only to suggest a certain glance to Louise, and she produced it. A lightning flash of disapproval from her eyes, for instance, suffices to stop Aubrey from stealing a bite of chicken during a race."* (Barry Paris, Louise Brooks)

Men Are Like That (1930, Paramount, 105m/bw) ☆☆½ **Sc:** Marion Dix, Herman J. Mankiewicz. **D:** Frank Tuttle. **Cam:** Archie Stout. **Cast:** Hal Skelly, Doris Hill, Clara Blandick, Charles Sellon, Helene

Chadwick, Morgan Farley, George Fawcett, William B. Davidson, Eugene Pallette, E.H. Calvert.

The Show-Off (1934, MGM, 80m/bw) ☆☆½ **Sc:** Herman J. Mankiewicz. **D:** Charles F. Riesner. **P:** Lucien Hubbard. **Cam:** James Wong Howe. **Cast:** Spencer Tracy, Madge Evans, Lois Wilson, Grant Mitchell, Clara Blandick, Claude Gillingwater, Henry Wadsworth, Alan Edward, Richard Tucker, Charles Lane, Lee Phelps. Tracy makes the movie worthwhile, giving Aubrey Piper more humanity than other interpreters, who played up the farcical aspects of the part.

- *"Spencer Tracy has never given a bad screen performance. In the title role of this MGM comedy of family life, he gives one of his best. It is a filming of George Kelly's play...Both the screening and Tracy's acting compare favorably with the originals."* (Newsweek)

The Show-Off (1946, MGM, 83m/bw, **VHS**) ☆☆ **Sc:** George Wells. **D:** Harry Beaumont. **P:** Albert Lewis. **Cam:** Robert H. Planck. **Cast:** Red Skelton, Marilyn Maxwell, Marjorie Main, Virginia O'Brien, Eddie "Rochester" Anderson, George Cleveland, Leon Ames, Marshall Thompson, Jacqueline White, Lila Leeds, Emory Parnell, Kitty Murray, Wilson Wood, Grady Sutton, Byron Foulger, Wheaton Chambers.

- *"When Red returned from Army service, the studio decided to try a different approach for their comedy star and put him into remakes of two well-worn properties:* The Show-Off *and* Merton of the Movies. *Both had been filmed before and were considered surefire. But they misfired instead. The hero of* The Show-Off *is an obnoxious character, and this didn't serve Red terribly well, while all the possibilities of* Merton *were thrown out the window by a shoddy script that discarded every comic opportunity..."* (Leonard Maltin, The Great Movie Comedians)

The Show-Off (1955, CBS, 60m/bw) *The Best of Broadway* ☆☆☆☆ **Tp:** Ronald Alexander. **D:** Sidney Lumet. **P:** Martin Manulis. **Cast:** Jackie Gleason, Thelma Ritter, Cathy O'Donnell, Alice Ghostley, Carleton Carpenter, Russell Collins. The egotistical loudmouth Aubrey Piper was given perhaps his biggest, loudest mouth in Gleason, who superbly handled both the comic aspects and the pathos of the character under Lumet's direction.

- *"As Aubrey Piper, the title part, Gleason epitomized the kind of disruptive intruder that every family fears its daughter may marry: a nobody at work, a spendthrift at home, fancying himself helpful when he only muddles whatever he touches....the plot, predictably, turns this good-for-nothing loudmouth into a hero by the final scene. For audiences to believe that ending, they must want it to happen, and that dynamic requires an actor to be likable even while doing wholly unlikeable things. Gleason had that ability as Kramden and Reggie; he certainly exhibited it in* The Show-Off, *dominat-*

ing an all-star cast." (William A. Henry III, The Great One: The Life and Legend of Jackie Gleason*)*

The Show-Off was also seen in 1948 on *Kraft Television Theatre*.

The Torch-Bearers, a satire on the little-theater movement of the 1920s, premiered in 1922 at the Savoy Theatre in Asbury Park, New Jersey, in a production toplining Arthur Shaw, Mary Boland, and Alison Skipworth.

Doubting Thomas (1935, Fox, 78m/bw, **VHS**) ☆☆½ **Sc:** William Conselman, Bartlett Cormack. **D:** David Butler. **P:** Buddy G. DeSylva. **Cam:** Joseph A. Valentine. **Cast:** Will Rogers, Billie Burke, Alison Skipworth, Sterling Holloway, Andrew Tombes, Gail Patrick, Frank Albertson, John Qualen, Billy Benedict, Lynn Bari, Dennis O'Keefe. This was the final Rogers picture, which was in theaters when he died in an Alaskan plane crash with famous aviator Wiley Post. Rogers played a husband who doubts his wife's proficiency as an actress.

- *"There is one thing that Rogers knows, and that is how to get laughs with any sort of a situation, and he didn't learn that from reading the papers." (Variety)*

Too Busy to Work (1939, 20th Century-Fox, 64m/bw) ☆☆½ **Sc:** Robert Ellis, Helen Logan, Stanley Rauh. **D:** Otto Brower. **P:** Darryl F. Zanuck. **Cam:** Edward Cronjager. **Cast:** Jed Prouty, Spring Byington, Kenneth Howell, George Ernest, June Carlson, Florence Roberts, Billy Mahan, Joan Davis, Chick Chandler, Andrew Tombes, Irving Bacon, Eddie Acuff, Chester Clute. Elements from *The Torch-Bearers* were combined with those from the Howard Lindsay/Bertrand Robinson play *Your Uncle Dudley* for this B-programmer, in which Prouty played a mayoral candidate who's neglecting his family, so his brood neglects the housework. Another in a series of low-budget comedies about the Joneses.

- *"Both [plays] have been made as talkers…by Fox. Combining a few ideas from each, latest adventure of the Joneses covers plenty of ground in its 65 minutes of running time…above par…" (Variety)*

The Torch-Bearers also aired in 1948 on *Kraft Television Theatre*.

Joseph Kesselring

Born: June 21, 1902, New York, NY. **Died:** 1967.

One of Joseph Kesselring's plays that arrived on the screen before it ever hit the stage was *Aggie Appleby, Maker of Men* (1933) starring Wynne Gibson and Charles Farrell.

Arsenic and Old Lace ran for 1,444 performances on Broadway, beginning in 1941. Produced by Howard Lindsay and Russel Crouse, it was directed by Bretaigne Windust with a cast headed by Josephine Hull, Jean Adair, Boris Karloff, and Allyn Joslyn. The story concerns an aging pair of sisters who see themselves as euthanasia aids in times of pain, with a dozen bodies buried in the basement.

Arsenic and Old Lace (1944, Warner Bros., 118m/bw, **VHS/DVD**) ☆☆☆☆ **Tp:** Philip G. Epstein, Julius J. Epstein. **D:** Frank Capra. **P:** Howard Lindsay, Russel Crouse. **Cast:** Cary Grant, Priscilla Lane, Raymond Massey, Jack Carson, Edward Everett Horton, Peter Lorre, James Gleason, Josephine Hull, Jean Adair, John Alexander, Grant Mitchell, Edward McNamara, Chester Clute, John Ridgely, Charles Lane, Spencer Charters. One of the more memorable black comedies of the 1940s, this one also contains one of Grant's best performances, whether he agreed or not (see below).

- *"I was embarrassed doing it. I overplayed the character. It was a dreadful job for me, and yet the film was a very big success and a big moneymaker, perhaps because of the reputation it had as a play. The fellow who played the role onstage in New York, Allyn Joslyn, was much better than I was. Jimmy Stewart would have been much better in the film. One of the reasons I did it was because they could get me in and out in three weeks, and I wanted to give my salary to various charities, including the British War Relief."* (Cary Grant in Evenings With Cary Grant *by Nancy Nelson)*

Arsenic and Old Lace (1949, CBS, 60m/bw) *Ford Theatre Hour* ☆☆☆ **D:** Marc Daniels. **P:** Garth Montgomery. **Cast:** Josephine Hull, Ruth McDevitt, Boris Karloff, William Prince, Bert Freed, Edgar Stehli. Hull once again repeated her stage triumph, this time for the small screen.

- *"...remains the best video production with Josephine Hull and Boris Karloff reprising their stage roles."* (William Torbert Leonard, Theatre: From Stage to Screen to Television)

Arsenic and Old Lace (1955, CBS, 60m/c) *The Best of Broadway* ☆☆½ **Tp:** Howard Lindsay, Russel Crouse. **D:** Herbert Bayard Swope. **P:** Martin Manulis. **Cast:** Helen Hayes, Billie Burke, Boris Karloff, John Alexander, Orson Bean, Peter Lorre, Edward Everett Horton, Patricia Breslin, Alan Tower, King Calder, Bruce Gordon, Richard Bishop.

- *"That it creaked in the joints was but an admission of its age and what was high comedy 15 years ago has difficulty passing muster today. Tele-viewers demand a faster pace and a larger quota of laughs. It was the cast of well-knowns rather than the farce which was the main attraction....For the old-timers it still must pack a wallop."* (Variety)

Arsenic and Old Lace (1962, NBC, 90m/c) *The Hallmark Hall of Fame* ☆☆ **Tp:** Robert Hartung. **D/P:** George Schaefer. **Cast:** Dorothy Stickney, Mildred Natwick, Tony Randall, Tom Bosley, George Voskovec, Boris Karloff, Farrell Pelly, Dort Clark, Nathaniel Frey, Dody Heath,

Ralph Dunn. One of Schaefer, Hartung, and Hallmark's rare misfires had Karloff in the cast for the third time on TV.

- "I think the problem was that I failed to make the cast forget the home audience. If they had truly made believe — only communicated with each other and played the situation — the performance would have been much more amusing. Perhaps we should have been live, but we had gone to tape for all programs so they could be shown in advance for exploitation. I blame myself that somehow I did not throw the right switch." (George Schaefer, From Live to Tape to Film: 60 Years of Inconspicuous Directing)

- "In short, the wit and fantasy of the Kesselring original were swamped by several earthbound actors." (Variety)

Arsenic and Old Lace (1969, ABC Special, 120m/c) ☆☆☆ **Tp:** Luther Davis. **D:** Robert Scheerer. **P:** Hubbell Robinson. **Cast:** Helen Hayes, Lillian Gish, Fred Gwynn, David Wayne, Bob Crane, Jack Gilford, Sue Lyon, Billy De Wolfe, Frank Campanella, Bob Dishy, Victor Killian, Bernard West. The play was filmed before a live audience, which is seen at the outset and at the curtain call. Theatrical connoisseurs relished the chance to see Gish and Hayes together.

- "...still almost as good for laughs as it was 28 years ago when Howard Lindsay and Russel Crouse brought it to the Fulton Theatre back in 1941. Changes in the original sscript were limited to the necessary updating of a few topical gags to jive with the times plus turning the lead (Bob Crane) into a television critic and his fiancée into a TV actress. Acting was good and professional." (Variety)

Lyle Kessler

Born: April 11, 1942, Philadelphia, PA.

Lyle Kessler's one Broadway play was The Watering Place, which ran for one performance in 1969 starring William Devane, Shirley Knight, Vivian Nathan, and Ralph Waite. Kessler has written for St. Elsewhere and acted in Barnaby Jones and other series, as well as the movies Touched (1983), which he also wrote, Love in a Taxi (1980), and the TV movies To Heal a Nation (1988) and James Dean (2001), in which he played Lee Strasberg. His films as a screenwriter also include Gladiator (1992), a boxing movie, and The Saint of Fort Washington (1993) starring Danny Glover and Matt Dillon. The 1983 debut of his Orphans (see below) was a major event in the history of Los Angeles theatre.

Orphans (1987, Lorimar, 115m/c, **VHS**) ☆☆☆☆½ **Sc:** Lyle Kessler. **D:** Alan J. Pakula. **P:** Alan J. Pakula, Susan Solt. **Cam:** Donald McAlpine. **Cast:** Albert Finney, Matthew Modine, Kevin Anderson, John Kellogg,

Anthony Heald, Novella Nelson, Elizabeth Parrish, B. Constance Barry, Frank Ferrera, Clifford Fearl. Two orphaned brothers, living a psychotic existence of codependency in an abandoned house, are visited by a drunk racketeer, who helps them better their situation. The play premiered at the Matrix Theatre in Los Angeles in 1983 starring Paul Lieber, Joe Pantoliano, and Lane Smith.

- "...a tender, often beautifully acted film about violence and male bonding. The movie may play on the clichés of machismo, but there's a sweetness about it, a twisted, nervous delicacy, like a vein throbbing beneath bruised skin. It's suffused with Pakula's humane sensibility; it undermines the fantasies rather than indulging in them....The movie is not a total success. There's a nailed-tight, airless schema to its structure and, by the end, the spontaneity and drive slacken; sentimentality bleeds in. But it's still a moving experience. Kessler's argot-chocked lines, Pakula's directorial empathy, and the skill and passion of his superb cast...all make this dark fable pulse with life." (Michael Wilmington, Los Angeles Times)

Sidney Kingsley

Sidney Kirshner
Born: October 22, 1906, New York, NY. **Died:** 1995.
Pulitzer Prize-winning play: Men in White (1934)
New York Drama Critics Circle Award, Best Play: Darkness at Noon (1951)

Sidney Kingsley's plays include Ten Million Ghosts (1936), The World We Make (1940), Lunatics and Lovers (1954), and Night Life (1962), his last Broadway play, which he produced and directed with a cast including Neville Brand, Salome Jens, Carol Lawrence, and Jessica Walter. Kingsley's dramatization of The Outward Room, based on the Millen Brand novel about the cure of a psychopathic girl through sharing in the lives of poor people, aired in 1949 on Studio One starring Ruth Ford, Bramwell Fletcher, and John Forsythe. It was restaged eight months later as part of the same anthology series with Ford, Fletcher, and Charlton Heston.

Darkness at Noon (1955, NBC, 90m/c) Producers' Showcase ☆☆☆☆½
Tp: Robert Alan Aurthur. **D:** Delbert Mann. **P:** Fred Coe. **Cast:** Lee J. Cobb, Oscar Homolka, David Wayne, Joseph Wiseman, Keenan Wynn, Nehemiah Persoff, Ruth Roman, Henry Silva, Mikhail Rasumny. **Commentary:** Richard M. Nixon. Kingsley adapted Arthur Koestler's classic novel and staged it himself. The play became one of the Broadway events of the 1950–1951 season, starring Claude Rains, Kim Hunter, Walter (Jack) Palance, and Alexander Scourby. Aurthur cut down the

play to 90 minutes for TV. Cobb, who suffered an actual heart attack on the air during this live performance, enacted one of his finest TV roles, Rubashov, an idealistic Bolshevik whose efforts helped achieve Communism in the Soviet Union. During the Moscow Purge Trials of 1937, Rubashov was arrested by the State on phony charges, imprisoned, and executed by the regime he helped realize. *Producers' Showcase* won 1955 Emmy Awards for Best Dramatic Series (Kingsley's show was one factor in that), Producer (Coe), and Art Direction (Otis Riggs). Nixon provided a filmed postscript, praising the show for its anti-Communist stance. Critic Jack Gould wrote that it was like "following an impressive symphony concert with a harmonica solo."

- *"...television viewing is not often so stimulating...truly inventive stage craft...a triumph for the scenic designer [Otis Riggs]...and the director...the transitions back and forth between the cell and the flashback scenes were achieved almost by magic."* (Jack Gould, The New York Times)

- *"...an outstanding production...finely executed direction...one of the most arresting dramas of the season...a major dramatic achievement."* (Variety)

Dead End (1937, UA, 93m/bw, **VHS**) ☆☆☆☆ **Sc:** Lillian Hellman. **D:** William Wyler. **P:** Samuel Goldwyn. **Cam:** Gregg Toland. **Cast:** Sylvia Sidney, Joel McCrea, Humphrey Bogart, Wendy Barrie, Claire Trevor, Allen Jenkins, Marjorie Main, Nilly Halop, Huntz Hall, Bobby Jordan, Leo Gorcey, Gabriel Dell, Bernard Punsley, Charles Peck, Minor Watson, James Burke, Ward Bond, Elisabeth Risdon, Esther Dale, George Humbert, Marcelle Corday, Charles Halton. The 1935 play featured Dan Duryea, Marjorie Main, Martin Gabel, and several of the future Dead End Kids, including Gorcey and Hall. It was an attack on the social injustices of a New York City slum, where the kids are corrupted by both criminals and the well-heeled. Bogart played one of his more significant early gangster roles in the film as Baby Face Martin, who's upset that his girl has syphilis in the play, changed by the Production Code to her not having waited for him. The Dead End Kids were hatched here for future cinema escapades.

- *"...the best thing that could have been done at the last session of Congress would have been to show the film Dead End to the committees which crippled the Wagner Housing Act."* (Editorial, New York Post, 1937)

- *"Undeniably 'realistic' in many ways, Kingsley's play is nevertheless quite stylized. The conflict between winners and losers, between rich and poor, develops almost schematically, and characters (many of them types) only loosely associated criss-cross each other's path. Dead End's artificial mise-en-scene contributes to Kingsley's pessimistic evocation of human beings trapped within their narrow environment....The slum inhabitants are further closed in by the vertical and horizontal lines, by the bars and shadows created by Gregg Toland's low-key lighting and angled camera....the setting for* Dead End *becomes an energized and animated trap. Apart from Wyler's expressionistic manipulation of space,* Dead End *owes much of its impact to Humphrey Bogart's performance as the psychotic-sentimental killer, Baby Face Martin." (Michael A. Anderegg, William Wyler)*

Detective Story (1951, Paramount, 103m/bw, **VHS**) ☆☆☆½ **Sc:** Philip Yordan, Robert Wyler. **D/P:** William Wyler. **Cam:** Lee Garmes. **Cast:** Kirk Douglas, Eleanor Parker, William Bendix, Cathy O'Donnell, George Macready, Horace McMahon, Gladys George, Lee Grant, Joseph Wiseman, Gerald Mohr, Michael Strong, Frank Faylen, Craig Hill, Bert Freed, Warner Anderson, Luis Van Rooten, Burt Mustin, Catherine Doucet, Grandon Rhodes. In a bristling precinct house, New York's detectives face a barrage of problems not unlike those in episodes of TV shows decades later such as *Hill Street Blues* and *Law & Order.* One detective discovers his wife's (possible) infidelity. The play, which was staged on Broadway by Kingsley in a Howard Lindsay/Russell Crouse production, featured Ralph Bellamy, Edward Binns, Maurine Stapleton, and Joseph Wiseman. The film was nominated for Oscars for Best Actress (Parker), Supporting Actress (Grant), Director, and Screenplay.

- *"Long on graphic demonstration of the sort of raffish traffic that flows through a squadron of plainclothes detectives in a New York police station-house and considerably short on penetration into the lives of anyone on display, it shapes up as an impeccable mosaic of minor melodrama." (Bosley Crowther, The New York Times)*

- *"The cop dreamed up for us by Douglas, Wyler, and Kingsley is developed no more than an inch below the surface. For no other reason than that he has been uncharitably tough and just, he suddenly starts screaming and doing silly things like wanting to cut out his brain, take it in his hand and examine the 'dirty pictures' put in it by his wife. (The emptied skull is one of Kingsley's many images of hollowness; others are bells, graves, ticking meters, and, gaudiest of all, the cop's stomach)....What all this 'meaningful' color adds up to is total confusion, even unto the hammy death scene..." (Manny Farber, Negative Space)*

Men in White was first presented by The Group Theatre in 1933 at the Broadhurst Theatre in New York City with Lee Strasberg directing Alexander Kirkland and Margaret Barker, with a cast that included Luther Adler, Morris Carnovsky, Elia Kazan, Clifford Odets, and Robert Lewis. The play, which ran for 351 performances, concerns George Ferguson, an intern whose girlfriend demands his time. But he has an affair with a nurse who must then have an abortion. The operation is botched and George and his mentor try to save her life with another operation.

Men in White (1934, MGM, 80m/bw) ☆☆☆ **Sc:** Waldemar Young. **D:** Richard Boleslawski. **P:** Monta Bell. **Cam:** George Folsey. **Cast:** Clark

Gable, Myrna Loy, Jean Hersholt, Wallace Ford, Otto Kruger, Elizabeth Allan, Henry B. Walthall, Samuel S. Hinds, Lee Phelps, Berton Churchill, C. Henry Gordon, Russell Hardie, Russell Hopton, Frank Puglia. This film arrived just as Gable and Loy's stars were on the rise at MGM.

- *"It is a film long to be remembered—fine and honest. In the scene with the little sick girl, Gable does a remarkable acting job. And he has your sympathy all through the episode with the nurse who dies as a result of an operation that should not have been performed. Hersholt tops all previous performances."* (Motion Picture Herald)

Men in White (1960, CBS, 90m/c) *The DuPont Show of the Month* ☆☆
Tp: Jacqueline Babbin, Audrey Gellin. **D:** Don Richardson. **P:** David Susskind. **Cast:** Lee J. Cobb, Richard Basehart, Dina Merrill, Lois Smith, Peggy Feury, Dick Van Patten. Despite the strength of the cast, the reviewers weren't kind to this version of a play with a badly dated plot.

- *"...a complete soap opera in one sitting....must have given the [American Medical Association] shudders...at least it was an adult soap opera, if there is such a thing, and that is perhaps the best that can be said for it."* (Variety)

The Patriots dramatized Thomas Jefferson's differences with Alexander Hamilton, who believed that the United States shouldn't be entrusted to the people. Jefferson argued that democracy was all about trust. The 1943 cast at Broadway's National Theatre was led by Frances Reid and Raymond Edward Johnson.

The Patriots (1963, NBC, 90m/c) *The Hallmark Hall of Fame* ☆☆½
Tp: Robert Hartung. **D/P:** George Schaefer. **Cast:** Charlton Heston, John Fraser, Howard St. John, Peggy Ann Garner, Frank Schofield, Michael Higgins, Dana Elcar, Robinson Stone, John Karlen, William Le Massena, Frederick O'Neal, Wallace Englehardt, Laurinda Barrett, Herbert Nelson, Ted Van Griethuysen, John Gerstad, Paula Trueman.

- *"I was delighted to get a shot at playing Thomas Jefferson on live TV...with John Fraser, who'd been so good as the king in El Cid, as Alexander Hamilton. I didn't catch old Tom, but it was a learning experience trying. It's hard to play a genius; Jefferson was the only one to occupy the White House...one of the most significant of those old dead white guys who invented this country. I'd like another shot at him; men like that are too complicated to get right the first time around. That's my excuse anyway."* (Charlton Heston, In the Arena)

The Patriots (1976, PBS, 120m/c) *Theatre in America* ☆☆☆ **Tp:** Sidney Kingsley. **D:** Bob Hankal, Robert Strane. **P:** Ken Campbell, Jac Venza. **Cast:** Robert Murch, Philip Le Strange, Ralph Clanton, William Jay, Stephen Johnson, Bradford Wallace, Katherine Rao, David Kwait. This production, performed by the Florida Asolo State Theatre in Sarasota, also later aired on PBS's *Great Performances*. Clanton, a dead ringer for Washington, anchors the production while Murch (Jefferson) and LeStrange (Hamilton) spar verbally.

- "...*offers us a Thomas Jefferson too good to be true and an Alexander Hamilton too true to be good. I doubt seriously if Jefferson was as divine as Kingsley paints him or Hamilton as devious. No matter. Whatever its value as history, the play in this splendid production...is first-rate drama, as absorbing a two hours as the Bicentennial year has brought us....Kingsley's plays...are always highly theatrical, wedded to the stage. Wisely, Ken Campbell's production of* The Patriots *keeps us always aware we are watching a work on the stage in a theater."* (Cecil Smith, Los Angeles Times).

Jack Kirkland

Born: 1902, St. Louis, MO. **Died:** 1969.

Jack Kirkland authored and/or produced 10 plays on Broadway through the mid-century, including *Tobacco Road* (see below), one of the most popular productions of all time, running for 3,182 performances through the Depression era. His specialty was sensationalized stories. His one other successful play was 1939's *I Must Love Someone*, a fictionalization of the lives of the Florodora Girls that he wrote with Leyle Georgie. He also wrote either the story or screenplay for *Wall Street* (1929), *Fast and Loose* (1930), *Zoo in Budapest* (1933), *The Gilded Lily* (1935), *Wings in the Dark* (1935), and *Adventure in Manhattan* (1936).

Mandingo (1975, Paramount, 127m/c, **VHS**) ☆½ **Sc:** Norman Wexler. **D:** Richard Fleischer. **P:** Dino De Laurentiis. **Cam:** Richard H. Kline. **Cast:** Ken Norton, James Mason, Susan George, Perry King, Brenda Sykes, Richard Ward, Roy Poole, Lillian Hayman, Paul Benedict, Ji-Tu Cumbuka, Ben Masters. This overblown melodrama of miscegenation on a Southern plantation in 1840 qualifies as one of the most lurid and violent exploitation films of the 1970s, even as its setting, time, and idiom rarely have been portrayed—and portrayed interestingly—by the movies. Kirkland adapted the play from the novel by Kyle Onstott. The 1961 play, which ran for eight performances at New York's Lyceum Theatre, starred Franchot Tone, Dennis Hopper, Brooke Hayward, and Vinie Burrows.

- "*Mandingo is calculated to appeal to the broadest possible audience—sadists, masochists, bigots, sex fiends, and historians.*" (Paul D. Zimmerman, Newsweek)

Tobacco Road (1941, 20th Century-Fox, 84m/bw) ☆☆ **Sc:** Nunnally Johnson. **D:** John Ford. **P:** Darryl F. Zanuck. **Cam:** Arthur Miller. **Cast:** Charley Grapewin, Gene Tierney, Marjorie Rambeau, William Tracy,

Dana Andrews, Ward Bond, Elizabeth Patterson, Slim Summerville, Grant Mitchell, Russell Simpson, Spencer Charters, Zeffie Tilbury, Jack Pennick, Irving Bacon, Francis Ford, George Chandler. Erskine Caldwell's salacious 1933 novel was adapted by Kirkland for a stage production the same year at New York's Masque Theatre starring Sam Byrd, Margaret Wycherly, Dean Jagger, and Henry Hull. In its day, this was the most infamous play on Broadway. The saga of the shiftless sharecropping Lester family included the selling of a daughter for seven dollars, and a son who marries for the sole purpose of acquiring a car, only to later run over his mother in the same vehicle. The reviews were uniformly scathing, but the public flocked, making it the longest-running play on Broadway up to its time. The fact that Ford ended up making it for Zanuck is one of the anomalies of the director's career. Fortunately for his reputation, it hasn't been converted to video.

• *"Even Nunnally Johnson could not give a social purpose to the script, which showed Jeeter Lester's family as feckless and mindless, the true rural lumpenproletariat that even the Reds despaired of raising to political consciousness. Except for the sexuality of young Gene Tierney and the antics of Charley Grapewin, who seemed determined to bury his fine performance as Grampa Joad [in* The Grapes of Wrath *for Ford and Zanuck the same year] under the barnyard buffoonery of Jeeter Lester, there is little that is memorable about the film, and much that is embarrassing. The material encourages the audience to laugh at the indolence and supineness of the very poor....Even if a war boom was beginning...the memory of hard times was too recent to make* Tobacco Road *seem tolerable." (Andrew Sinclair,* John Ford)

James Kirkwood & Nicholas Dante

Kirkwood:
James Kirkwood, Jr.
Born: August 22, 1924, Hollywood, CA. **Died:** 1989.

Dante:
Conrado Morales
Born: November 22, 1941, New York, NY. **Died:** 1991.

Pulitzer Prize-winning play: *A Chorus Line* (1976)
Tony Award-winning Best Musical: *A Chorus Line*

James Kirkwood, Jr. was the son of actor James Kirkwood and actress Lila Lee. Among Kirkwood's novels is *There Must Be a Pony*, a fictionalized account of the 1936 murder of Russell Reid in Manhattan Beach, California, on the estate of socialite Gouverneur Morris, where Lila Lee was staying at the time. That novel was adapted by Mart Crowley into a 1986 TV movie starring Elizabeth Taylor.

Kirkwood's other novels include *Some Kind of Hero* (1981) and *P.S. Your Cat Is Dead* (2001), both of which were adapted for the screen, the latter from his own play adaptation (see below). An occasional actor, he also played small parts in *Oh, God! Book II* (1980) and *Mommie Dearest* (1981), and was a regular on the series *Valiant Lady* from 1953 to 1957. A close friend of Clay Shaw, the New Orleans businessman who was tried for the murder of President Kennedy, Kirkwood entitled his autobiography *Diary Of A Mad Playwright*, published in 1989, the year of his death.

Nicholas Dante, a Broadway dancer, died from complications of AIDS at the age of 49.

A Chorus Line (1985, Columbia, 113m/c, **VHS/DVD**) ☆☆ **Sc:** Arnold Schulman. **D:** Richard Attenborough. **P:** Cy Feuer, Ernest H. Martin. **Cam:** Ronnie Taylor. **Cast:** Michael Douglas, Alyson Reed, Vicki Frederick, Michelle Johnston, Janet Jones, Jan Gan Boyd, Audrey Landers, Cameron English, Yamil Borges, Gregg Burge, Blane Savage, Pam Klinger, Terrence Mann, Tony Fields. 16 singer-dancers are auditioned onstage by a theatrical choreographer, who listens to some of them reveal a few of their innermost thoughts and biographical details. Michael Bennett conceived, choreographed, and directed the original and shared its Pulitzer Prize with book authors Kirkwood and Dante, musician Marvin Hamlisch, and lyricist Edward Kleban. The unseen director in the stage version becomes conspicuously dominant in the person of Douglas. The play premiered on Broadway in 1975 at New York's Schubert Theatre.

- *"If you were one of the legion that saw* A Chorus Line *more than once in the theatre, the film is enough to make you doubt your judgment. If you've never seen the stage piece you may come out wondering what in the name of goodness all the fuss was about 10 years ago…In this stately and slavish representation…what pokes through with the pain of a broken bone is how thin the material really is. That secret was well-disguised by the exuberant theatricality of the original production…"* (Sheila Benson, Los Angeles Times)

P.S. Your Cat Is Dead (2001, Cargo, 92m/c) ☆☆☆ **Sc:** Steve Guttenberg, Jeff Korn. **D:** Steve Guttenberg. **P:** Steve Guttenberg, Kyle A. Clark. **Cam:** David A. Armstrong. **Cast:** Steve Guttenberg, Lombardo Boyar, Cynthia Watros, A.J. Benza, Frederick Lawrence, Tom Mesmer, Kenneth Moskow, Don Rosenberg. This comic drama about a man who doubts his heterosexuality when his wife leaves him ran for 16 performances in 1975 starring Keir Dullea, Tony Musante, and Jennifer Warren. TV show host Benza played a gay hairdresser who tries to rape Guttenberg.

- "A *workmanlike adaptation…a competent feature helming debut for star Steve Guttenberg. But the credulity straining core situation of a heterosexual man trapping a gay thief in his home one long night, with laughter and tears and possible romance resulting, was already contrived enough in James Kirkwood's original 1972 novel and his 1975 stage version…knockout lead performances or more whimsical tone…might have transcended the script's dubious logic…*" (Dennis Harvey, Variety)

There Must Be a Pony (1986, ABC, 120m/c) ☆☆½ **Tp:** Mart Crowley. **D:** Joseph Sargent. **P:** Howard Jeffrey. **Cast:** Elizabeth Taylor, Robert Wagner, William Windom, James Coco, Mickey Rooney, Ken Olin, Dick O'Neill, Edward Winter, Chad Lowe, Richard Bright, Richard Minchenberg, Robby Weaver, Helen J. Siff, Charles Stratton. Kirkwood's novel about a big Hollywood star making a comeback after a stay in a mental hospital was based on his life with his mother, the 1930s B-movie actress Lila Lee. It was adapted by the writer in the 1950s as a play, which toured with Myrna Loy as the facsimile of Lee.

- "*…strange little movie. [Taylor] triumphs, even as the production sinks….But each time the movie seems about to settle down to perhaps an illuminating analysis of Josh, the stories and camera shift to Marguerite and, with a svelte Miss Taylor done up in Nolan Miller costumes, nobody else stands a chance….disaster strikes. The problem is so unexpected that the effect is merely baffling. Suddenly, There Must Be a Pony—a title taken from a punchline of a kind of barnyard joke—becomes just another stale essay on Hollywood emptiness and the 'bitch goddess' success….in the end, the movie illustrates one of Marguerite's pearls of wisdom: 'Talk about grinding it out. TV brings new meaning to the words chopped liver.'*" (John J. O'Connor, The New York Times)

Arthur Kopit

Arthur Lee Kopit
Born: May 10, 1937, New York, NY.

Arthur Kopit, a Harvard alumnus, has a distinct tendency to "view the rotting underside of life from below," wrote George Wellwarth, "…Kopit's contribution lies in the wry imagination he brings to his description of life as he sees it." Kopit's plays include *The Day the Whores Came Out to Play Tennis* and *Chamber Music*. The playwright also wrote the TV movie *Hands of a Stranger* (1987), and "Promontory Point Revisited," a segment of *Foul*, a 1969 production of *New York Television Theatre* concerning pollution in America. His great contribution to the theatre is *Indians* (see below).

Buffalo Bill and the Indians, or Sitting Bull's History Lesson (1976, UA, 123m/c, **VHS**) ☆☆☆ **Sc:** Alan Rudolph, Robert Altman. **D/P:** Robert Altman. **Cam:** Paul Lohmann. **Cast:** Paul Newman, Burt Lancaster, Joel Grey, Kevin McCarthy, Harvey Keitel, Geraldine Chaplin, John Considine, Robert Doqui, Shelley Duvall, Denver Pyle, Bert Remsen, Will Sampson, E.L. Doctorow, Allan Nichols, Mike Kaplan, Bonnie Leaders, Noelle Rogers, Evelyn Lear, Frank Kaquitts, Pat McCormick, Ken Krossa. Kopit's play, *Indians*, had its American premiere in 1969 at the Arena Stage in Washington, DC, and then moved to New York's Brooks Atkinson Theatre with a cast led by Stacy Keach, Sam Waterston, Raul Julia, Charles Durning, and Ronny Cox. The film lampoons the Buffalo Bill legend—an easy target, especially for Altman's readily sardonic mien—but with a certain amount of style, wit, and pictorial handsomeness. Newman was on key as the boozy, fraudulent Bill and there were some superb supporting performances, especially by Lancaster as pulp western writer Ned Buntline.

- *"There is danger in trying to structure and control Altman. His films depend so much on the natural exuberance of his actors that the editing, in this case, seems to have killed much of the original excitement. Paul Newman gives a marvelously loose, often very funny performance as Buffalo Bill, even though the character still lacks definition and Newman is stuck with an impossibly dreary monologue that drags the whole picture down."* (Kathleen Carroll, New York Daily News)

- *"[Newman] tries hard, but is doomed. The Altman-Rudolph Buffalo Bill is two-dimensional, possibly biographically accurate but dramatically dull....Nothing Newman does can make him a satirical epitome, as was evidently hoped, of the American ability to transform harsh experience into emollient entertainment."* (Stanley Kauffmann, The New Republic)

Oh Dad, Poor Dad, Mama's Hung You in the Closet and I'm Feeling So Sad (1967, Paramount/Seven Arts, 86m/c, **VHS**) ☆☆ **Sc:** Ian Bernard. **D:** Richard Quine. **P:** Ray Stark, Stanley Rubin. **Cam:** Geoffrey Unsworth. **Cast:** Rosalind Russell, Robert Morse, Jonathan Winters, Hugh Griffith, Barbara Harris, Lionel Jeffries, Cyril Delavanti, Hiram Sherman. The Broadway original, which carried the subtitle, "A Tragifarce in a Bastard French Tradition," debuted in 1962 at the Phoenix Theatre with Jerome Robbins directing Hermione Gingold and Sam Waterston. This was another case of Hollywood not understanding how to convey the material.

- *"[Rosalind Russell] used to be funny, but she seems determined lately to destroy herself and her career by playing every role she touches like a cross between Auntie Mame and the Bride of Frankenstein."* (Rex Reed, Big Screen, Little Screen)

- *"Arthur Kopit's fresh-from-Harvard bit of I-hate-Momism was given sophisticated and beguilingly fantastic packaging by Jerome Robbins's staging and some impeccable performances [on the stage], so that the supermonstrosity of Mom became an amusement. But for the screen, the best of everything Hollywood can offer in the way of simplification and vulgarization—sublowbrow commentary, idiot title song, literal but illiterate gadgetry—is brought to bear on this fragile little black comedy, and annihation is inevitable for theme, performers...and audience."* (Judith Crist, The Private Eye, the Cowboy and the Very Naked Lady)

The Phantom of the Opera (1990, NBC, 200m/c, **VHS/DVD**) ☆☆☆
Tp: Arthur Kopit. **D:** Tony Richardson. **P:** Ross Milloy. **Cast:** Charles Dance, Burt Lancaster, Teri Polo, Ian Richardson, Adam Storke, Andrea Ferreol, Jean-Pierre Cassel. Gaston Leroux's 1911 novel has been transferred to film at least six times, including in 1925, 1943, 1962, 1989, and 1998. Kopit adapted this version from his own 1983 Off Broadway play. Dance was the disfigured and masked phantom loitering in the basement of the Paris Opera House, who falls in love with the young singer, Christine. Lancaster played the phantom's protective father.

- *"There are problems with this conception. How, viewers may well wonder, did this pathetic recluse become so cultivated and talented?...A strenuous sense of disbelief is also needed to cope with the international menu of accents....Jean-Pierre Cassel, playing Inspector Ledoux, gives us the real thing. Mr. Lancaster doesn't even try. When Carriere tells the frightened Christine, 'I'll get you a glass of water,' it comes out, 'I'll gedja a glass of woe-duh.'...Mr. Dance is elegant, Mr. Lancaster dignified, and Miss Polo, not yet 20 years old, strikingly beautiful....Throw in several opera arias, and this Phantom adds up to an odd but fascinating prime-time diversion."* (John J. O'Connor, The New York Times)

Joseph Kramm

Born: September 30, 1907, Philadelphia, PA.
Pulitzer Prize-winning play: *The Shrike* (1952)

Joseph Kramm was educated at the University of Pennsylvania. He began his career as a rewrite man on the *Philadelphia Inquirer* and acted for a local repertory company. He managed to secure roles in Broadway productions and turned to writing and directing after World War II. *The Shrike* was his first produced play.

The Shrike (1955, Universal, 88m/bw) ☆☆½ **Sc:** Ketti Frings. **D:** Jose Ferrer. **P:** Aaron Rosenberg. **Cam:** William Daniels. **Cast:** Jose Ferrer,

June Allyson, Joy Page, Jacqueline de Wit, Kendall Clark. The 1952 play, produced and directed by Ferrer at New York's Cort Theatre with Judith Evelyn as his co-star, concerned a theatrical director who is driven toward suicide because of the pestering of his obsessively nagging and vindictive wife. Ferrer and Allyson — in a huge change of pace from her girl-next-door pictures — meet the theatrical demands of the material, which generally seems stranded on the screen.

- *"The play had qualities which made it prizeworthy; the movie has not. Ferrer is memorably persuasive as a quiet man suffering almost unendurable strain, but after a few dozen long close-ups of Ferrer trembling on the verge of tears one begins to yearn for other fare. The other fare, when it interrupts, consists of negligently acted flashbacks and instructive little chats by psychiatrists, who speak to the camera as if they were selling a TV audience on the virtues of stomach powder. For dramatic climaxes, the movie leans heavily on background music which is intended to suggest incipient madness. The play ended with horrifying defeat for Ferrer. The makers of the movie, evidently wishing not to offend a soul with the price of admission, have given the same ending enough ambiguity to send the most possessive woman out of the theater feeling perfectly all right."* (Newsweek)

Norman Krasna

Born: November 7, 1909, Queens, NY. **Died:** 1984.

In Hollywood since the early sound era, Norman Krasna wrote or co-wrote the screenplays for more than 40 films, produced 12, and directed three: *Princess O'Rourke* (1943), for which he won an Academy Award for Best Original Story, *The Big Hangover* (1950), and *The Ambassador's Daughter* (1956). He received Oscar nominations for *The Richest Girl in the World* (1934), *Fury* (1935), and *The Devil in Miss Jones* (1940) with Jean Arthur.

Krasna's screenplays include those for *That's My Boy* (1932), *Bombshell* (1933), *Wife vs. Secretary* (1935), *Bachelor Mother* (1939), *Mr. & Mrs. Smith* (1941), *The Flame of New Orleans* (1941), *Practically Yours* (1944), *White Christmas* (1954), *Let's Make Love* (1960), and *I'd Rather Be Rich* (1964). Among Krasna's plays was *Time for Elizabeth*, a vehicle for Groucho Marx.

Dear Ruth (1947, Paramount, 95m/bw) ☆☆☆ **Sc:** Arthur Sheekman. **D:** William D. Russell. **P:** Paul Jones. **Cam:** Ernest Laszlo. **Cast:** Joan Caulfield, William Holden, Edward Arnold, Mary Philips, Mona Freeman, Billy De Wolfe, Virginia Welles, Marietta Canty, Kenny O'Morrison, Irving Bacon, Isabel Randolph. This was one of the few play adaptations that was followed by a movie sequel, *Dear Wife* (1949), also starring Holden and Caulfield. The second sequel, *Dear Brat* (1951), starred Mona Freeman and Billy DeWolfe. The original play, directed by Moss Hart in 683 performances on Broadway, starred Virginia Gilmore and John Dall. The younger of two sisters sends mash notes to a lonely lieutenant overseas during World War II and signs her sister, Ruth's, name.

- *"...another hilarious comedy hit...follows closely in spirit and pattern the Norman Krasna stage romp...here is one of those simon-pure excursions in fun, which bubbles and sparkles its way into your heart and completely disarms any resistence which an unadorned outline of its conventional plot might invoke....there is zest to the dialogue and it is played with the best of good humor by a small and expert cast."* (Thomas M. Pryor, The New York Times)

Four Hours to Kill! (1935, Paramount, 70m/bw) ☆☆☆ **Sc:** Norman Krasna. **D:** Mitchell Leisen. **P:** Arthur Hornblow Jr. **Cam:** Theodor Sparkuhl. **Cast:** Richard Barthelmess, Joe Morrison, Helen Mack, Dorothy Tree, Ray Milland, Henry Travers, Roscoe Karns, Gertrude Michael, Bodil Rosing, Charles C. Wilson, Lois Kent, Olive Tell. Krasna's play *Small Miracle*, staged on Broadway in 1934 by George Abbott with an ensemble cast including Ilka Chase and Myron McCormick, was adapted for this film. The action takes place at a theatre, where the staff and management have their own problems and the patrons are a motley lot. Barthelmess, in one of his best sound-era roles, played a captured thug under the watch of lawman Wilson, who has the title time to kill. One of Milland's first films.

- *"...transferred intact, except for its title, to the screen...gripping, though extremely theatrical, melodrama with a neatly dovetailed plot, uniformly excellent cast and well-paced direction. The film does not attempt to extend itself beyond the spatial limits of the stage play. The action, for the main, is confined to the lounge of the West Forty-third Street Theatre....Richard Barthelmess, as the convict, Tony Mako, contributes what is probably one of his finest performances."* (Frank S. Nugent, The New York Times)

John Loves Mary (1949, Warner Bros., 96m/bw) ☆☆ **Sc:** Phoebe Ephron, Henry Ephron. **D:** David Butler. **P:** Jerry Wald. **Cam:** J. Peverell Marley. **Cast:** Ronald Reagan, Patricia Neal, Jack Carson, Wayne Morris, Edward Arnold, Virginia Field, Katherine Alexander, Paul Harvey, Ernest Cossart, Irving Bacon, George B. Hickman, Nino Pepitone, Creighton Hale, Douglas Kennedy, Rodney Bell, Ray Montgomery. The 1947 Broadway play starred William Prince and Nina Foch in the story of a G.I. returning to the United States from World War II with a cockney girl, who he's escorting for a pal, confusing his bride-to-be. This was Neal's film debut.

- *"...translated to the screen with every evident endeavor to duplicate exactly the hilarity of the play. The story has been maintained in toto, the gags have been kept in proper line and, indeed, the bulk of the action has been presented in one conventional room. But somehow this Warner cut-up...does not have the natural spontaneity nor the artificial smoothness of the play. Something has been subtracted in the transmission to the screen, and this time* John and Mary *carries neither conviction nor charm." (Bosley Crowther, The New York Times)*

Kind Sir, which debuted on Broadway in 1954, was directed and produced by Joshua Logan and starred Mary Martin and Charles Boyer. It concerns two mutually attracted wealthy singles, an actress, and a diplomat/banker, who deceive each other, he with the ruse that he's married to avoid marriage, she with the counter of a fiancé after she finds him out and to save face.

Indiscreet (1958, Warner Bros., 100m/c, **VHS/DVD**) ☆☆☆½ **Sc:** Norman Krasna. **D/P:** Stanley Donen. **Cam:** Freddie Young. **Cast:** Cary Grant, Ingrid Bergman, Cecil Parker, Phyllis Calvert, David Kassoff, Megs Jenkins, Michael Anthony, Martin Boddey. As posh a production as could be dressed and turned out using such slight material, this glowing film is usually cited as a favorite among fans of the stars.

- *"...a somewhat leaden souffle...The movie displayed Bergman's still radiant beauty...Although the picture runs for more than an hour and a half, it seems much longer than that, despite the sprightly goings-on, the bright Technicolor world inhabited by the wsealthy characters, and the cast's animated performances. 'How dare he make love to me and not be a married man!' is the one outstanding line that Bergman is given to deliver. However, there is still pleasure in watching two professional actors at work." (Curtis Brown, Ingrid Bergman)*

Indiscreet (1988, CBS, 94m/c, **VHS**) ☆½ **Sc:** Walter Lockwood, Sally Robinson. **D:** Richard Michaels. **P:** John Davis. **Cast:** Robert Wagner, Lesley-Anne Down, Maggie Henderson, Robert McBain, Jeni Barnett, Fanny Carby, Derek Royle, Geoffrey Chater, Barry Woolgar, David Ashford, Barry Andrews. This production is bathed in a fake kind photographic glow, like a Lifetime production of a romance novel.

- *"Anyone who recalls Cary Grant and Ingrid Bergman in Norman Krasna's 1958 movie Indiscreet, will wince over the TV remake....The vapidity of both performances is magnified by come-hither camera shots that linger too long on their empty faces....When Wagner is called upon to crank up the charm, he smiles. Only his mouth moves; the rest of his face is frozen in a parody of suavity, and his voice is dead." (Lawrence Christon, Los Angeles Times)*

Sunday in New York (1963, MGM, 103m/c, **VHS**) ☆☆½ **Sc:** Norman Krasna. **D:** Peter Tewkesbury. **P:** Everett Freeman. **Cam:** Leo Tover. **Cast:** Rod Taylor, Jane Fonda, Cliff Robertson, Robert Culp, Jo Morrow, Jim Backus. The original 1961 New York production at the Cort Theatre had Garson Kanin directing Robert Redford, Pat Stanley, and Conrad Janis, in a sex farce about a single girl in the big city and the two men who complete her love triangle.

- *"...had been a minor, trite Broadway sex comedy. It was transformed for the screen by director Peter Tewkesbury into a stylish but still trite Hollywood sex gambol—a bit more daring than similar comedies of previous years, but cut from the same cloth....The story was necessarily short on frankness and long on innuendo, and the stock salaciousness of its dialogue gave the script whatever humor it had. In many respects, Jane's character of Eileen Taylor was the most difficult she'd ever had to play because of her one-dimensional mock innocence. The character was cousin to the cheerleader in* Tall Story...*but she managed to infuse it with an amusing credibility."* (Thomas Kiernan, Jane Fonda: Heroine for Our Time)

Who Was That Lady? (1960, Columbia, 115m/c) ☆☆½ **Sc/P:** Norman Krasna. **D:** George Sidney. **Cam:** Harry Stradling. **Cast:** Tony Curtis, Dean Martin, Janet Leigh, James Whitmore, John McIntire, Barbara Nichols, Simon Oakland, Larry Storch, Larry Keating, Joi Lansing, Barbara Hines, Marion Javits, Michael Lane, Kam Tong, William Newell, Mark Allen, Snub Pollard. Krasna's 1958 Broadway comedy, *Who Was That Lady I Saw You With?*, was directed by Alex Segal at the Martin Beck Theatre with Peter Lind Hayes, Mary Healy, Ray Walston, and Roland Winters. It concerns a married college professor who's prodded by his TV writer buddy into fooling around, and is caught by his wife with two showgirls. The fourth Curtis/Leigh movie pairing helped put over one of the standard sex farces of its era, with Dino somehow very comfortable as the quintessetial icon of leering.

- *"...a revealing sliver of the life and times. It ended up a respectable number 13 on the year's list of top box-office hits. No one can watch it today and dismiss Curtis and Leigh as anything other than the smoothest screen team of the decade."* (Barry Paris in Tony Curtis: The Autobiography)

James Lapine
Born: January 10, 1949, Mansfield, OH.

James Lapine's fortunate association with Stephen Sondheim has led to several successful Broadway musicals, three of which have been presented on TV (below). Lapine directed the films *Impromptu* (1991), a historical drama with Judy Davis as the 19th century author George Sand, and the comedy *Life With Mikey* (1993) starring Michael J. Fox. For TV, Lapine directed the 1999 movie *Earthly Possessions* featuring Susan Sarandon as a bored minister's wife taken hostage by bank robbers, and was the stage director of a William Hurt and Christine Baranski-fronted 1982 production of A *Midsummer Night's Dream*, filmed by director Emile Ardolino.

Into the Woods (1991, PBS, 120m/c, **VHS/DVD**) *American Playhouse* ☆☆☆½ **Tp/D:** James Lapine. **P:** Iris Merlis, Michael Brandman. **Cast:** Bernadette Peters, Chip Zien, Joanna Gleason, Tom Aldredge, Robert Westenberg, Kim Crosby, Ben Wright, Barbara Byrne, Danielle Ferland, Merle Louise, Chuck Wagner, Pamela Winslow, Philip Hoffman, Lauren Mitchell, Kay McClelland, Jean Louisa Kelly. Using the principals from the 1987 stage original, which he directed, Lapine preserved the Stephen Sondheim musical with this film. Cinderella, Little Red Riding Hood, Jack (who climbed the beanstalk), and a childless baker and his wife all make wishes that are realized.

- *"The musical...has rarely been more satisfying, particularly when you consider that since its earliest exposure at the San Diego Old Globe in 1986, this is a show that has never had more than a temperate critical reception. That reserve was engendered by the starkness of the change of mood between Acts I and II—a plunge off the high-diving board that still baffles an audience...The cast is terrific. And better than onstage, where our attention is of necessity more divided, the camera captures the show's pointillist juxtapositions of lyrics, events and mood, reminiscent of* Sunday in the Park [with George]." *(Sylvie Drake*, Los Angeles Times)

Passion (1996, PBS, 114m/c, **VHS**) *American Playhouse* ☆☆ **Tp/D:** James Lapine. **P:** Michael Brandman, Kimberly Myers. **Cast:** Donna Murphy, Jere Shea, Marin Mazzie, Tom Aldredge, Gregg Edelman, Linda Balgord, T.J. Meyers, William Parry, John Antony, Colleen Fitzpatrick. The 1994 musical, with music and lyrics by Stephen Sondheim, starred Donna Murphy and Jere Shea in the tale of a 19th century Italian soldier having an affair with a married woman. He's then assigned to a distant outpost where Fosca, a devious invalid girl, falls madly in love with him. Lapine based the story on the Ettore Scola film *Passione d'Amore* (1981) starring Bernard Girardeau and Laura Antonelli. Murphy recreated her role as the invalid girl, which won her the Tony Award for Best Actress.

- *"The one big problem: Fosca is perhaps the most irritating heroine ever devised for a musical. Even Ms. Murphy's powerful portrait isn't compensation enough for having to endure that character's ceaseless machinations."* (John J. O'Connor, The New York Times)

Sunday in the Park With George (1986, Showtime, 146m/c, **VHS/DVD**) ☆☆☆ **Tp:** James Lapine. **D:** Terry Hughes. **P:** Michael Brandman. **Cast:** Mandy Patinkin, Bernadette Peters, Charles Kimbrough, Barbara Byrne, Dana Ivey, Mary D'Arcy, Brent Spiner, Sue

Anne Gershenson, John Jellison, Judith Moore, Nancy Opel, Robert Westenberg. Most of the original 1985 Broadway cast was used for this Showtime presentation, which also aired on PBS the same year. An artist tries to capture his vision of a park on canvas, after which the play then shifts to 1984 and concentrates on the artist's need to connect with his family on an emotional level.

- *"Let's face it, and be glad of it—you can't fully capture a piece of musical theatre on the screen. The film version of* A Chorus Line *certainly didn't do so. Neither does Showtime cable's very decent presentation of...*Sunday in the Park With George...*The cameras try to show us what we would have seen at Broadway's Booth Theatre, but they must inevitably chop into separate shots—full shot, medium shot, close-up—what the eye can take in in one sweep on the stage. That's especially wrong for the first half of the show, where we shouldn't lose touch with the overarch of the green suburban park which painter Georges Seurat (Mandy Patinkin) is trying to arrange into significance. Like Seurat's pouting model, Dot (Bernadette Peters), the camera can't seem to settle down...needs the frame of the proscenium to lure the viewer all the way inside, but this isn't a bad reproduction at all."* (Dan Sullivan, Los Angeles Times)

Ring Lardner

Ringgold Wilmer Lardner.
Born: March 6, 1885, Niles, MI. **Died:** 1933.

Ring Lardner's novels and short stories were written in the conversational speech of his often sporting and average-joe characters, and he mercilessly provided sardonic undertones to their foibles and problems. His characters expressed themselves in slangy idioms that made his work ripe for the stage, yet quickly archaic. His two most well-known plays, the evergreen *June Moon* (1929) and *Elmer the Great* (1928), were written in collaboration, the former with the great Charles MacArthur, the latter with Broadway impressario James M. Cohan. Lardner's "playlets" or skits remain uncollected; they were so-called nonsense humor and precursors to the Theatre of the Absurd.

Robert E. Sherwood adapted one of Lardner's short stories, "The Love Nest," published in *The Love Nest and Other Stories* (1926), into a 1927 play of the same name. Lardner's novels include *You Know Me, Al* (1916) and *The Big Town* (1921), and his collections of stories include *Gullible's Travels* (1917) and *What of It?* (1925). Lardner's humorous autobiography was one of his best received books, *The Story of a Wonder Man* (1927). One of the most well-known sports writers of his era, he segued into a career as one of the most bitter satirists in

American letters. Lardner died at 48 of tuberculosis complicated by heart disease and alcoholism.

His stories adapted to the screen include *Zone of Quiet* three times for early TV, *Alibi Ike* for the 1935 Joe. E. Brown vehicle, and *Who Dealt?* for a 1993 British TV production with Juliet Stevenson as a wife who exposes her husband's philandering via a game of bridge. Lardner's acidic boxing classic *Champion* was converted by Robert Rossen into the 1949 Kirk Douglas movie. That story also became a 1950 installment of *Robert Montgomery Presents* with Richard Kiley, and a 1955 show on *Climax!* via an adaptation by Rod Serling, with Rory Calhoun as the greedy and pathologically driven pugilist Midge Kelly. Lardner's *The Golden Honeymoon* starred James Whitmore and Teresa Wright in 1980 on PBS's *American Short Story*. Lardner is the father of writers Ring Lardner, Jr. and John Lardner.

Elmer the Great concerned a cocky baseball star. The play, written with George M. Cohan and produced by him, starred Walter Huston as Elmer Kane, "solid bone above the ears," as the best pitcher in the Three-I League, who refuses to go to the big leagues because he secretly loves a girl in Gentryville, Indiana. Lardner based the character on Chicago White Sox Hall of Famer "Big Ed" Walsh, who was the most notorious spitballer of his time and still holds the record for the lowest lifetime earned run average (1.82).

Fast Company (1929, Paramount, 70m/bw) ☆☆☆ **Sc:** Walton Butterfield, Joseph L. Mankiewicz, Florence Ryerson. **D:** A. Edward Sutherland, Edwin H. Knopf (uncredited). **P:** Jesse L. Lasky. **Cam:** Edward Cronjager. **Cast:** Jack Oakie, Evelyn Brent, Richard "Skeets" Gallagher, Sam Hardy, Arthur Housman, Gwen Lee, Chester Conklin, Irish Meusel, E.H. Calvert, Eugenie Besserer, Bert Rome, Truck Hannah, Gus Sandberg, Red Rollings, Arnold "Jigger" Statz. The play dovetailed to Oakie's identity as an unaware sap. Here, he's a top home run hitter who foils racketeers.

• *"A thoroughly entertaining screen adaptation…Jack Oakie…proves himself a capable performer as well as 'bright boy' of the wise-cracking genre….The spirit of a baseball player's existence and the sort of drama that enters his life is here ably depicted. Mr. Oakie is splendid in his characterization…Ring wit is preserved for posterity in this film, which may or may not please the author. It certainly amused the audience…"* (The New York Times)

Elmer the Great (1933, Warner Bros., 74m/bw) ☆☆½ **Sc:** Tom Geraghty. **D:** Mervyn LeRoy. **P:** Ray Griffith. **Cam:** Arthur Todd. **Cast:** Joe E. Brown, Patricia Ellis, Claire Dodd, Preston Foster, Frank McHugh, Sterling Holloway, Berton Churchill, J. Carroll Naish, Douglas Dumbrille, Jesse Ralph, Russell Hopton, Emma Dunn, Charles Wilson. In one of several Brown films revolving around baseball, the comedian played a conceited, mule-headed all-star who foolishly falls in with the wrong element.

- *"...[A] worm-turning story became the prototype for many Joe E. Brown vehicles...casting Joe as a high-spirited braggart. Among these were two of his most successful films,* Elmer the Great *and* Alibi Ike. *Of the two,* Elmer *was Brown's favorite, because the central character, Elmer Kane, was based on a real-life baseball personality, 'Big Ed Walsh,' as observed by sportswriter Ring Lardner. The comic aspects of this back-patting pitcher were most enjoyable, although the perfunctory 'plot' owed something to Joe's baseball picture of the previous year,* Fireman, Save My Child *(in which the plot gimmick was a fire-extinguishing bomb Joe invented in the shape of a baseball)."* (Leonard Maltin, The Great Movie Comedians)

Cowboy Quarterback (1939, Warner Bros., 54m/bw) ☆½ **Sc:** Fred Niblo Jr. **D:** Noel M. Smith. **Cam:** Ted D. McCord. **Cast:** Bert Wheeler, Marie Wilson, Gloria Dickson, William Demarest, Eddie Foy Jr., William Hopper, William Gould, Charles C. Wilson, John Ridgely, Eddie Acuff, Clem Bevans, John Harran, Frederic Tozere. Transplanted to the world of football, the Lardner story's essential elements remain. Demarest played Rusty Walker, a Chicago Packers scout, who signs a legendary broken-field runner who doesn't want to leave his home-town girl and is secretly the object of Rusty's girlfriend's affections.

- *"Dull-witted football comedy...makes the inevitable last-minute push to extricate himself from [gamblers'] clutches in just enough time (40 seconds to be exact) to win the big game. Story is a poor remake..."* (J.R. Nash & S.R. Ross, The Motion Picture Guide)

June Moon satirizes the songwriters of Tin Pan Alley as a boneheaded master of malapropisms from Schenectady aspires to be a composer; he claims his big hit is "Paprika: The Spice of My Life." Written in tandem with Charles MacArthur, the play ran for 273 performances on Broadway, beginning in 1929, starring Norman Foster and Linda Watkins.

June Moon (1931, Paramount, 79m/bw) ☆☆☆ **Sc:** Vincent Lawrence, Joseph L. Mankiewicz, Keene Thompson. **D:** A. Edward Sutherland. **Cam:** Allen G. Siegler. **Cast:** Jack Oakie, Frances Dee, Wynne Gibson, Harry Akst, June MacCloy, Ernest Wood, Sam Hardy, Harold Waldridge, Ethel Kenyon, Frank Darian, Jean Barry, Eddie Dunn. Oakie's talent for enacting unaware patsies dovetailed to Lardner's and Kaufman's penchants for creating them.

- *"...a highly humorous talking picture...Jack Oakie turns to good account his opportunities for fun...may not be as well rounded out as the footlights version, but it can boast of excellent use of the camera and admirable vocal recording."* (The New York Times)

Blonde Trouble (1937, Paramount, 67m/bw) ☆☆½ **Sc:** Lillie Heyward.

D: George Archainbaud. **Cam:** Henry Sharp. **Cast:** Eleanor Whitney, Johnny Downs, Lynne Overman, William Demarest, Terry Walker, Benny Baker, El Brendel, John Patterson, Barlow Borland, Kitty McHugh, Helen Flint, Harvey Clark, Spec O'Donnell.

- "With charming diffidence, [the picture] may very well be...pleasant and profitable...if the picture can ever overcome the handicap of the...title, Blonde Trouble....Johnny Downs...and...Eleanor Whitney...do nicely with the naiveties asked of them, but the spice is provided by...Lynne Overman, William Demarest, Helen Flint, Benny Baker, Terry Walker, and good old El Brendel, and by the broad humor of the dialogue, a lot of which is carried over from the original stage play." (The New York Times)

June Moon (1974, PBS, 90m/c) Theatre in America ☆☆½ **Tp:** Burt Shevelove. **D:** Burt Shevelove, Kirk Browning. **P:** Bo Goldman, Jac Venza. **Host:** Hal Holbrook. **Cast:** Jack Cassidy, Estelle Parsons, Kevin McCarthy, Susan Sarandon, Stephen Sondheim, Austin Pendleton, Tom Fitzsimmons, Barbara Dana, Lee Meredith, Marshall Efron, Beatrice Colen. Shevelove's resurrection of the play coincided with one of Sondheim's rare acting stints and one of Sarandon's first notable roles.

- "There is little fascinating about June Moon...The humor is slight, heavy on grammatical manglings, and the story slighter, all about the budding young songwriter from the sticks on the verge of being corrupted by city slickers....Sondheim...deadpans his way through a third-rate Oscar Levant imitation. They all work hard, but the play just sits there." (John J. O'-Connor, The New York Times)

June Moon was also broadcast in 1948 on Kraft Television Theatre and in 1949 on Studio One in a version starring Glenda Farrell, Jack Lemmon, Eva Marie Saint, and Jean Carson.

Arthur Laurents

Born: July 14, 1918, New York, NY.

Arthur Laurents's screenplays include those for Alfred Hitchcok's Rope (1948), Max Ophuls's Caught (1949), Anna Lucasta (1949), Anastasia (1956) with Ingrid Bergman's Oscar-winning portrayal, Otto Preminger's film of Francoise Sagan's Bonjour Tristesse (1958) with Jean Seberg, Sydney Pollack's The Way We Were (1973), and Herbert Ross's The Turning Point (1977). Laurents's plays as a director include I Can Get It for You Wholesale in 1962, which jump-started Barbra Streisand's career, and the American stage version of La Cage aux Folles in 1983, which ran for 1,761 performances. Laurents's 2000 autobiography is Original Story By.

Gypsy, the musical about the life of celebrated stripper Gypsy Rose Lee, was based on Lee's biography and starred Ethel Merman and Jack Klugman at New York's Broadway Theatre in a production directed and choreographed by Jerome Robbins. A milestone in the history of the American musical for its balance of character, story, and musical elements, it featured a Jule Styne/Stephen Sondheim score and ran for 702 performances in the early 1960s.

Gypsy (1963, Warner Bros., 149m/c, **VHS/DVD**) ☆☆☆ **Sc:** Leonard Spigelgass. **D/P:** Mervyn LeRoy. **Cam:** Harry Stradling Sr. **Cast:** Natalie Wood, Rosalind Russell, Karl Malden, Paul Wallace, Betty Bruce, Parley Baer, Harry Shannon, Suzanne Cupito, Ann Jillian, Diane Pace, Faith Dane, Roxanne Arlen, George Petrie, Louis Quinn, Lois Roberts, Harvey Korman, Jean Willes, Burt Michaels. Wood was photographed to take every advantage of her beauty and Russell did a variation on her Auntie Mame role. The songs include "Some People," "Everything's Coming Up Roses," "Let Me Entertain You," and "You'll Never Get Away From Me." The film was nominated for Oscars for Best Cinematography, Score (Frank Perkins), and Costumes.

- *"Leonard Spigelgass's screenplay subtly added depth and texture to the characterizations, plus and immeasurable amount of substance and wit. Other plus factors...LeRoy's loving recreation of a bygone theatrical era, and his use of a perfect cast....where Merman had been volcanic [onstage], Rosalind Russell...was merely dynamic...Natalie Wood as the child-woman Louise...was at her loveliest..."* (Clive Hirschhorn, The Hollywood Musical)

Gypsy (1993, CBS, 142m/c, **VHS/DVD**) ☆☆☆½ **Tp:** Arthur Laurents. **D:** Emile Ardolino. **P:** Emile Ardolino, Cindy Gilmore. **Cast:** Bette Midler, Peter Riegert, Cynthia Gibb, Edward Asner, Christine Ebersole, Michael Jeter, Andrea Martin, Linda Hart, Anna McNeeley, Tony Shalhoub, Rachel Sweet, Jennifer Rae Beck, Jeffrey Broadhurst. Midler let it rip as the stage mother and completely dominates this show, which was nominated for 12 Emmys including Outstanding Miniseries or Special, Actress (Midler), and Director.

- *"While there may be no definitive Mama Rose, it is nonetheless crystal clear that Bette Midler was born to play her. Her Rose brings Gypsy to life as vividly as a flashing neon sign in a splendid...version. Midler is the complete Rose. She can be loud, vulgar, hilarious and larger than life, like Merman, but she's also as fine an actress as any woman who has ever played the part. Midler can be simultaneously voluptuous and maternal, and monster though her character may be, she makes it believable that the manager Herbie...would stick around as long as he does."* (Kevin Thomas, Los Angeles Times)

Home of the Brave (1949, UA, 85m/bw, **VHS**) ☆☆☆ **Sc:** Carl Foreman. **D:** Mark Robson. **P:** Stanley Kramer. **Cam:** Robert De Grasse. **Cast:** James

Edwards, Frank Lovejoy, Lloyd Bridges, Douglas Dick, Steve Brodie, Jeff Corey, Cliff Clark. Laurents's play, which was first produced on Broadway in 1945 at New York's Belasco Theatre featuring Eduard Franz and Joseph Pevney, concerned an ostracized Jew in a squad of soldiers on a Pacific atoll during World War II. Kramer changed the Jew to an African American for this movie. Bridges was forcefully effective as the main bigot.

- *"...the cycle of racial message movies began...not too much departing from the old stereotypes but creating a new one: that of Negroes who cannot be fulfilled without the sacrifice of, or the support of, white men. A case in point, James Edwards, the Negro in* Home of the Brave, *goes on a mission to a Japanese-held island where his best friend, a white man, is killed. Edwards feels a dual guilt at his friend's death, first, because he is glad that he personally survived, and second, because he had wished his friend dead after an argument in which he had been called a racial epithet. Falling victim to hysterical paralysis, he is taken to the base psychiatrist who induces Edwards to walk again by hurling the same epithets at him, symbolically implying that Negroes can be fulfilled only on white men's terms. At the end of the film the audience sees a fraternal scene in which Edwards and a one-armed white man depart, suggesting Negro-white equity only as long as the whites are not complete."* (*Thomas R. Cripps in* Black Films and Filmmakers *by Lindsay Patterson*)

Invitation to a March (1972, PBS, 120m/c) *Hollywood Television Theatre* ☆☆ **Tp:** Arthur Laurents. **D:** Marvin Chomsky. **P:** Lewis Freedman, Norman Lloyd. **Cast:** Blythe Danner, Cliff Potts, Pat Quinn, Louise Latham, Rosemary Murphy, Michael Sacks, Gordon Pinsent, Danny Bonaduce. The play was first staged on Broadway in 1960 at the Music Box Theatre with Laurents directing an ensemble including Celeste Holm, Jane Fonda, Madeliene Sherwood, Eileen Heckart, and James MacArthur. This TV version is faithful to Laurents's play about a fragile girl who has to decide between a charming beachcomber and a priggish, full-of-himself attorney.

- *"It is a touch dated; more than a touch predictable and surely some of its more obvious fantasy devices worked no better [in 1960] than they do now. For this is a contrived story of love and choice....Once the contrivance of the plot is overcome, if it can be, Laurents indulges in fairy-tale gimmicks designed to heighten the romantic aspects of the story, but remain improbable....Much of the dialogue is sparkling enough to cover up the self-indulgence of the play; but it, too, is self-conscious. See how clever I am, it says. Too clever. Too unreal."* (*Sylvie Drake, Los Angeles Times*)

Summertime (1955, London, 99m/c, **VHS/DVD**) ☆☆☆½ **Sc:** David Lean, H.E. Bates. **D:** David Lean. **P:** Ilya Lopert. **Cam:** Jack Hildyard. **Cast:** Katharine Hepburn, Rosanno Brazzi, Isa Miranda, Darren McGavin,

Mari Aldon, Jane Rose, MacDonald Parke, Gaetano Audiero, Andre Morrell, Jeremy Spencer, Virginia Simeon. This film is based on Laurents's 1952 play, *The Time of the Cuckoo*, which bowed at New York's Empire Theatre in 1952 with Harold Clurman directing Shirley Booth. After the movie, Laurents returned the story to the stage for the musical *Do I Hear a Waltz?* with music by Richard Rodgers and lyrics by Stephen Sondheim. Hepburn's traveling spinster who finds romance in Venice, Italy, became one of her signature roles and dominates this Lean production. The film was nominated for Oscars for Best Actress (Hepburn) and Director (Lean).

- *"I didn't like it at all....They jettisoned most of the play. It was an homage to Kate Hepburn who shed more water than there is in Venice. I did write a screenplay. She came in and ran the show. I met with David Lean a lot. I thought he was very upset because of his wife, Ann, whom he had left, and I thought he was mad for Kate. I found him a cold fish. We talked about the screenplay, and I came back to be told by a minion that it was over. I didn't even see him again. Talent is no excuse for bad behavior. I knew Kate. When it was all over, she told me, 'You won't like it. But I'm brilliant.'"* (Arthur Laurents in David Lean: A Biography by Kevin Brownlow)

- *"There is an element of embarrassment in this pining-spinster role, but Hepburn is so proficient at it that she almost—though not quite—kills the embarrassment. It's hard to believe that the coming together of a whithered Puritan and a middle-aged roué would light up the sky with the fireworks that the director, David Lean, provides, but this is one of those overwrought, understated romantic movies (like Lean's Brief Encounter) that many people remember with considerable emotion."* (Pauline Kael, 5,001 Nights at the Movies)

West Side Story (1961, UA, 155m/c, **VHS/DVD**) ☆☆☆☆☆ **Sc:** Ernest Lehman. **D:** Robert Wise, Jerome Robbins. **P:** Robert Wise. **Cam:** Daniel L. Fapp. **Cast:** Natalie Wood, Richard Beymer, George Chakiris, Rita Moreno, Tucker Smith, Tony Mordente, Joe De Vega, Simon Oakland, Ned Glass, Gus Trikonis, Gina Trikonis, Jay Norman, Eliot Feld, John Astin, Burt Michaels, Scooter Teague, David Winters. The initial 1957 Broadway musical starred Carol Lawrence, Larry Kert, and Chita Rivera under the direction and choreography of Robbins and ran for 732 performances before Wise was tapped to collaborate on the film. The film, which applies the *Romeo and Juliet* theme to gangs in New York's Hell's Kitchen, won Oscars for Best Picture, Director(s), Supporting Actor (Chakiris), Supporting Actress (Moreno), Cinematography, Art Direction/Set Decoration, Scoring (Saul Chapin, Johnny Green, Sid Ramin, Irwin Kostal), Sound, Film Editing, and Costume Design, and was nominated for Best Screenplay.

- *"...the decade's finest musical stage adaptation because it took all the elements of the Broadway version—a downbeat dramatic story, a stirring score, and inventive dances—and merged them in cinematic terms. With-*

out slavishly following the original, without altering the material to accommodate a star, the film creates its own world, a few necessary steps away from reality but never so stylized that the theatrical effects intrude on the emotional impact. Unlike many other musicals of the 1960s, it never falls prey to treating the property as a legend or an institution that must be handled reverently. It soars on its own wings, and it soars high." (Ted Sennett, Hollywood Musicals)

- "The irony of this hyped-up, slam-bang production is that those involved apparently don't really believe that beauty and romance can be expressed in modern rhythms, because whenever their Romeo and Juliet enter a scene, the dialogue becomes painfully old-fashioned and mawkish, the dancing turns to simpering, sickly romantic ballet, and sugary old stars hover in the sky." (Pauline Kael, 5,001 Nights at the Movies)

Emmet Lavery

Born: November 8, 1902, Poughkeepsie, NY. **Died:** 1986.

Emmet Lavery was president of the Screen Writers Guild from 1945 to 1947. *The Magnificent Yankee* (below) earned him his greatest acclaim as a writer. His other plays include *The Gentleman From Athens* (1947) and *Dawn's Early Light* (1959). His screenplays include those for Edward Dmytryk's then-shockingly sensational *Hitler's Children* (1942), the all-star *Forever and a Day* (1943), and, in two cases, films based on actual lives, *Guilty of Treason* (1949) with Charles Bickford as Joszef Cardinal Mindszenty and *The Court-Martial of Billy Mitchell* (1955) with Gary Cooper.

First Legion (1951, UA, 77m/c, **VHS**) ☆☆½ **Sc:** Emmet Lavery. **D/P:** Douglas Sirk. **Cam:** Robert De Grasse. **Cast:** Charles Boyer, William Demarest, Barbara Rush, Lyle Bettger, Leo G. Carroll, Wesley Addy, Walter Hampden, Taylor Holmes, H.B. Warner, George Zucco, John McGuire, Queenie Smith, Jacqueline de Wit. The 1934 play, which starred Charles Coburn and Whitford Kane, concerns an aging priest on his deathbed who recovers. Shortly thereafter a woman with a broken back also heals, and the consideration of these possible "miracles" by the priests at a Jesuit novitiate is met with the devil's advocacy, so to speak, of an agnostic physician.

- "Emmet Lavery's contemplations of religious faith and 'miracles'...have been brought to the screen in a faithful, temperate, and generally reasonable film...has a special fascination that should appeal to those of contemplative mind. For what Mr. Lavery is considering, in comparatively simple terms, *is the difference between the spiritual and materialist attitudes....a good literal production..." (Bosley Crowther, The New York Times)*

The Magnificent Yankee highlights the years that Oliver Wendell Holmes spent in Washington, DC, as the Chief Justice of the U.S. Supreme Court. The 1946 Broadway production starred Louis Calhern and Dorothy Gish, directed by Arthur Hopkins at the Royale Theatre.

The Magnificent Yankee (1950, MGM, 88m/bw, **VHS**) ☆☆½ **Sc:** Emmet Lavery. **D:** John Sturges. **P:** Armand Deutsch. **Cam:** Joseph Ruttenberg. **Cast:** Louis Calhern, Ann Harding, Eduard Franz, Philip Ober, Richard Anderson, Edith Evanson, Ian Wolfe, James Lydon, Haydn Roarke, Robert Sherwood, Hugh Sanders, Dan Tobin, Everett Glass, Holmes Herbert, Selmer Jackson, Todd Karns, Guy Anderson, Harlan Warde. Despite Calhern's fine portrayal and Sturges's no-nonsense direction, the film seems like it was produced in Biopic 101. Calhern received an Oscar nomination for Best Actor as Holmes.

• *"Obviously, this is in the pattern of the popular American ideal, which likes to shape our great heroes and statesmen in the comforting mold of just plain folks. And in diligently following this pattern Mr. Lavery has frankly allowed a good bit of sentimentality to invade and command his script. While the popular authority of the female is not as great in his film as in the play, while Mrs. Holmes does not originate the justice's phrases as much as she previously did, there is a great deal of cozy demonstration of the woman's commanding hand, all very cheerfully and sweetly laughed at and cluck-clucked about." (Bosley Crowther, The New York Times)*

The Magnificent Yankee (1965, NBC, 90m/c) *The Hallmark Hall of Fame* ☆☆☆☆ **Tp:** Robert Hartung. **D/P:** George Schaefer. **Cast:** Alfred Lunt, Lynn Fontanne, Eduard Franz, Robert Emhardt, James Daly, Brenda Forbes, Walter Moulder, Ion Berger, Lee Goodman, Dennis Cooney, Grover Dale, Gordon Charney, Donald Symington, Nan McFarland. The Lunts, performing at the top of their game, very late in their careers, delivered their most praised performances.

• *"In a 90-minute play that was neither a distinguished work nor dramatically absorbing, the Alfred Lunt and Lynn Fontanne portrayals of the aging justice and Mrs. Holmes were so spellbinding as to turn the George Schaefer production...into a vivid and memorable program....the love story was rare because the Lunts made it so." (Variety)*

• *"Just about anybody who saw it would probably rank Hallmark's production of* The Magnificent Yankee, *with Alfred Lunt and Lynn Fontanne, as one of the indelible viewing experiences of one's television lifetime." (Tom Shales, On the Air!)*

Jerome Lawrence & Robert E. Lee

Lawrence:
Jerome Lawrence Schwartz.
Born: July 14, 1915, Cleveland, OH.

Lee:
Robert Edwin Lee
Born: October 15, 1918, Elyria, OH. **Died:** 1994.

The Ohio-bred pair's stage collaborations include *Look, Ma, I'm Dancin'* in 1948, *Mame* in 1966, and *The Night Thoreau Spent in Jail*, a popular summer-stock and community theatre performance piece. The pair was nominated for an Emmy Award for Outstanding Writing in a Special Program Adaptation for *Actor*, a documentary based on Lawrence's biography of Paul Muni on PBS. Their big hit was *Auntie Mame* and their most enduring show has been the great performance piece *Inherit the Wind* (see below).

Auntie Mame was adapted by Lawrence and Lee from the best-selling Patrick Dennis novel about a free spirit who takes charge of her orphaned nephew and tries to instill a little vim and vigor into the lives of several eccentrics. The Morton Da Costa-directed play, which ran for 639 performances beginning in 1956, starred Rosalind Russell in her biggest stage triumph. Angela Lansbury played the part to great acclaim after the playwrights retooled the piece as the musical *Mame* in 1966, with music and lyrics by Jerry Herman.

Auntie Mame (1958, Warner Bros., 143m/c, **VHS**) ☆☆½ **Sc:** Betty Comden, Adolph Green. **D:** Morton DaCosta. **P:** Jack L. Warner. **Cam:** Harry Stradling. **Cast:** Rosalind Russell, Forrest Tucker, Coral Browne, Fred Clarke, Roger Smith, Patric Knowles, Peggy Cass, Jan Handzlik, Joanna Barnes, Pippa Scott, Lee Patrick, Connie Gilchrist, Yuki Shimoda, Henry Brandon, Margaret Dumont, Dub Taylor, Morton Da Costa, Willard Waterman, Rand Harper, Booth Colman. Russell recreated the title role from Da Costa's 1956 Broadway smash, and her performance dominates this overstuffed soufflé. The film was Oscar-nominated for Best Picture, Actress (Russell), Supporting Actress (Cass), Cinematography, Art Direction/Set Decoration, and Film Editing.

- "*Auntie Mame was the most expensive non-musical production to that date in Hollywood history, with a wondrous Travis Banton wardrobe, a gigantic cast and so much décor that noisemakers and projections were needed to simulate comic tempo in the lulls while the sets were being changed. The whole thing rested on Russell, as the den-mother of the avant-garde who raises an orphaned nephew....One line in the play, 'Life is a banquet, and most poor sons of bitches are starving to death!' lost some urgency in the film...forced to use 'suckers' in place of the no-no phrase....even bowdler-*

ized, it meant so much to Russell that she entitled her autobiography, Life Is a Banquet. *So, yes, Mame is Russell is Mame." (Ethan Mordden,* Movie Star: A Look at the Women Who Made Hollywood)

Mame (1974, Warner Bros., 131m/c, **VHS**) ☆½ **Sc:** Paul Zindel. **D:** Gene Saks. **P:** Robert Fryer, James Cresson. **Cam:** Philip Lathrop. **Cast:** Lucille Ball, Robert Preston, Beatrice Arthur, John Davidson, Joyce Van Patten, Don Porter, Audrey Christie, Jane Connell, Kirby Furlong, John McGiver. Often referred to as the largest misstep in Ball's career, this has been called one of the worst musicals ever made. The tunes include the title number, "We Need a Little Christmas," "My Best Girl," and "Open a New Window."

- *"The movie* Mame...*was her last theatrical film; its initial failure began a series of depressions and personal crises from which Lucille never really recovered. Ironically, in more recent years* Mame *has become something of a cult classic, and can be widely seen on cable television and on video." (Geoffrey Mark Fidelman,* The Lucy Book)

First Monday in October (1981, Paramount, 99m/c, **VHS**) ☆½ **Sc:** Jerome Lawrence, Robert E. Lee. **D:** Ronald Neame. **P:** Paul Heller, Martha Scott. **Cam:** Fred J. Koenekamp. **Cast:** Jill Clayburgh, Walter Matthau, Barnard Hughes, Jan Sterling, James Stephens, Joshua Bryant. The first woman to be appointed to the U.S. Supreme Court, a staunch conservative, soon begins winning over her critics even as she hotly debates her most liberal counterpart. The release of the picture arrived right around March 1981, when President Ronald Reagan appointed Sandra Day O'Connor to the highest court in the land. The leads give this production some needed liveliness amid a lot of legalese. The 1978 play starred Jane Alexander and Henry Fonda under Ed Sherin's direction.

- *"Not even the extras do anything right in* First Monday in October, *a movie in which a young man can't deliver the line, 'Excuse me, Mr. Chief Justice. Here are the files you asked for,' without sounding a false note. The screenplay...is the main source of difficulty. The authors' idea is to confront a crotchety liberal justice, Dan Snow, with the sprightly, more conservative Ruth Loomis and let the sparks fly. However, Mr. Lawrence and Mr. Lee have a way of mistaking hectoring, nagging, and all-out nastiness for the stuff of which sparks are made....directed by Ronald Neame, who also directed* The Poseidon Adventure, *but he sinks this one faster." (Janet Maslin,* The New York Times)

Inherit the Wind was the landmark dramatization of the famous anti-evolution "Monkey Trial" of 1925, when defense attorney Clarence Darrow defended Tennessee schoolteacher John T. Scopes against prosecutor William Jennings Bryan, who upheld the state's adherence to the fundamentalist Bible version of creation. The play was first performed at the National Theatre in New York City in 1955 with Ed Begley as Matthew Harrison Brady (a Bryan facsimile) and Paul Muni as Henry Drummond (the Darrow character).

Inherit the Wind (1960, UA, 128m/bw, **VHS/DVD**) ☆☆☆☆½ **Sc:** Nathan E. Douglas, Harold Jacob Smith. **D/P:** Stanley Kramer. **Cam:** Ernest Laszlo. **Cast:** Spencer Tracy, Fredric March, Gene Kelly, Florence Eldridge, Dick York, Harry Morgan, Donna Anderson, Claude Akins, Noah Beery Jr., Norman Fell, Elliott Reid, Philip Coolidge, Ray Teal, Paul Hartman, Jimmy Boyd, Gordon Polk, Hope Summers, Rene Godfrey. Nathan E. Douglas was a pseudonym for blacklisted screenwriter Nedrick Young, who had his credit restored on this film in 1992. The thespian duel between the great stars still makes for a mighty attraction as they worked, on the set, to upstage each other. The film was nominated for Oscars for Best Actor (Tracy), Screenplay, Cinematography, and Film Editing.

- *"These men were two of the finest actors of our time. Tracy was nominated...and I'll never understand why March was not equally honored....the reviews were extravagantly favorable — but that didn't translate into box-office success. At every theater...there were demonstrations against it and against me as being notoriously anti-God....United Artists refused to spend money on advertising....In lieu of support by our distributors, I toured the country doing my own promotion, but all this earned me was top billing as the Devil's first deputy."* (Stanley Kramer, A Mad, Mad, Mad, Mad World)

- *"Ingenious as it is, March's characterization puts too much stress on makeup and mannerisms. It is as though he was basically unsympathetic to the role, at least to the point of view it represents, and when making Bryan's better points had to smirk and overplay the man's vanity to keep from taking him too seriously."* (Paul V. Beckley, New York Herald-Tribune)

- *"Padded and heavily made up, Fredric March does an embarrassingly hollow imitation of the portly Bryan. Spencer Tracy, whose girth made him the more likely candidate for the role, is cast instead as the lean Darrow, and he plays the part in his patented wise, humane, meant-to-be-irresistible manner....it's a very crude piece of work, totally lacking in subtlety; what is meant to be a courtroom drama of ideas comes out as a caricature of a drama of ideas..."* (Pauline Kael, 5,001 Nights at the Movies)

Inherit the Wind (1965, NBC, 90m/c) *The Hallmark Hall of Fame* ☆☆☆☆ **Tp:** Robert Hartung. **D/P:** George Schaefer. **Cast:** Melvyn Douglas, Ed Begley, Diane Baker, Burt Brinckerhoff, Murray Hamilton, John Randolph, Roy Poole, Wallace Engelhardt, Leora Thatcher, Beulah Garrick, Joanna Roos, Truman Smith, John D. Irving, Harry Ellerbe, John McGovern, George Ebeling. Several critics felt that this was the superior version to the movie; Schaefer thought so, too (see below).

- *"I found the film directed by Stanley Kramer disappointing...The cast we* had was better. *Melvyn Douglas, who had played the Clarence Darrow role on the road, was stronger than Paul Muni had been in New York. Ed Begley, who was the original Broadway Brady and should have played it in the movie, was exactly right....It was one of those performances in which everything worked, and I never made a more completely realized translation of a play to TV. We have the color tape and it's gorgeous, but it's locked in a vault...*" (George Schaefer, From Live to Tape to Film: 60 Years of Inconspicuous Directing)

- "*It remains a timely and dramatically potent play even severely edited down as it was. It may be a while before video audiences are again treated to a performance as accomplished as that given by Melvyn Douglas.*" (Variety)

Inherit the Wind (1988, NBC, 96m/c) ☆☆☆½ **Tp:** John Gay. **D:** David Greene. **P:** Robert A. Papazian Jr., Peter Douglas. **Cast:** Kirk Douglas, Jason Robards, Darren McGavin, Jean Simmons, Megan Follows, John Harkins, Kyle Secor, Don Hood, Michael Ensign, Josh Clark, Scotch Byerly, Ebbe Roe Smith, Douglas Dirkson, Glenn Robards, Jason Marin, Richard Lineback. Douglas assaulted the Brady role as if he were harkening back to his tough pugilist in *Champion*.

- "*...still another revival of* Inherit the Wind, *the sturdy warhorse that's trotted out every few years to give actors of a certain age a chance to show off....The subject remains sensitive to this day. The creationists and evolutionists are still battling each other in courts.* Inherit the Wind *retains its emotional clout....this version attempts to make the Brady character more sympathetic...Mr. Douglas's portrayal, unfortunately, is of the scenery-chewing variety, leaving Brady something of a ranting oddity. It's still obvious that the play's indisputable hero is Drummond. His arguments for the 'individual human mind' are the heart of the matter, and Mr. Robards, restrained yet tough, brings them home convincingly.*" (John J. O'Connor, The New York Times)

Inherit the Wind (1999, Showtime, 127m/c, **VHS**) ☆☆☆☆ **Tp:** Nedrick Young, Harold Jacob Smith. **D:** Daniel Petrie. **P:** Dennis Bishop. **Cast:** Jack Lemmon, George C. Scott, Piper Laurie, Beau Bridges, Tom Everett Scott, John Cullum, Lane Smith, Kathryn Morris, Brad Greenquist, David Wells, Peter Mackenzie, Royce D. Applegate, Dirk Blocker, Russ Tamblyn. In the fourth marquee match-up between Brady and Drummond, the play got another successful going-over from another pair of masters.

- "*This time out, it's George C. Scott exuding a narrow and at moments ferocious piety, as Matthew Harrison Brady, facing off against Jack Lemmon, representing science and open argument as Henry Drummond....Mr. Scott and Mr. Lemmon make a strong pair of antagonists, right up there with Fredric March and Spencer Tracy...and are the main reason for tuning in...Mr. Scott and Mr. Lemmon invest their roles with a humanity that cuts deeper than ideology. The show flags whenever they are off camera, which happily is not often.*" (Walter Goodman, The New York Times)

Shangri-La (1960, NBC, 90m/c) *The Hallmark Hall of Fame* ☆☆☆ **Tp:** James Lawrence, Robert E. Lee, James Hilton. **D/P:** George Schaefer. **Cast:** Richard Basehart, Marisa Pavan, Claude Rains, Gene Nelson, Alice Ghostley, Helen Gallagher, John Abbott, James Valentine. The 1956 play ran for only 21 performances at Broadway's Winter Garden Theatre with Jack Cassidy, Carol Lawrence, Dennis King, Ghostley and Berry Kroeger. But Schaefer and the *Hallmark* regime gave the musical adaptation of Hilton's novel *Lost Horizon* another try. Frank Capra's 1937 film with Ronald Colman is still the superior interpretation. The ill-fated 1972 Ross Hunter musical production wasn't based on this musical.

• "*Jerome Lawrence and Robert E. Lee adapted this musical version from their ill-fated 1956 Broadway show. They must have learned a lot over the intervening years, for the production showed spirit, imagination and had a philosophical quality without being the least bit sermonizing....Richard Basehart gives a subdued, tender performance...George Schaefer produced and directed with a fine sense of believability and subtlety. Harry Warren's delicate score was for the most part non-intrusive...*" (Variety)

John Howard Lawson
Born: September 25, 1894, New York, NY. **Died:** 1977.

A controversial playwright whose left-wing politics were embedded in his work, John Howard Lawson's plays include *Roger Bloomer* (1923), *Processional* (1925), and *Success Story* (1932, see below). The Group theatre produced *Processional*—set against the background of a West Virginia miners' strike—and *Marching Song* (1937), both of which told stories of oppressed workers squaring off against strikebreakers. Lawson's films included two back-to-back in 1943 for director John Huston and Humphrey Bogart, *Sahara* and *Action in the North Atlantic*, as well as *Smash-Up: The Story of a Woman* (1947) with Susan Hayward and the adaptation of Alan Paton's *Cry, the Beloved Country* (1951) with Sidney Poitier and Canada Lee. Lawson was blacklisted during the McCarthy era, and was the author of *Theory and Technique of Playwrighting*.

Success at Any Price (1934, RKO, 74m/bw) ☆☆☆ **Sc:** John Howard Lawson, Howard J. Green. **D:** J. Walter Ruben. **P:** Merion C. Cooper, H.N. Swanson. **Cam:** Henry W. Gerrard. **Cast:** Douglas Fairbanks Jr.,

Genevieve Tobin, Frank Morgan, Colleen Moore, Edward Everett Horton, Nydia Westman, Henry Kolker. Based on Lawson's play, *Success Story*, this film depicts a driven businessman who uses and tramples everyone on the way to the top, then contemplates suicide when the stock market crashes. The 1932 play was staged on Broadway at Maxine Elliott's Theatre by the Group Theatre and starred Luther and Stella Adler with Franchot Tone and William Challee.

- *"With the connivance of the author, the screen version of John Howard Lawson's success story has been managed with considerable effectiveness....Although Mr. Lawson's account of a bitter youth's lust for power has become something of a cliché in recent years, his dialogue is adult. It lifts an episode story, always something of a bore in the cinema, to a high level of interest....Douglas Fairbanks Jr. reveals a surprising advance as a dramatic actor."* (Andre Sennewald, The New York Times)

Leslie Lee

Leslie E. Lee
Born: November 1935, Bryn Mawr, PA.

Leslie Lee received an Obie Award and a Tony nomination for *The First Breeze of Summer*. For *American Playhouse*, Lee wrote *The Killing Floor* (1984), directed by Bill Duke, and adapted James Baldwin's *Go Tell It on the Mountain* (1985) for director Stan Lathan. The recipient of Rockefeller and Schubert foundation grants, Lee is the author of the plays *Elegy to a Down Queen, As I Lay Dying, The Night of the Moon, Between Now and Then, Colored People's Time, Hannah Davis,* and others.

The First Breeze of Summer (1976, PBS, 90m/c) *Theatre in America* ☆☆☆☆ **Tp:** Leslie Lee. **D:** Douglas Turner Ward, Kirk Browning. **P:** Jac Venza. **Cast:** Moses Gunn, Frances Foster, Douglas Turner Ward, Carl Crudup, Charles Brown, Ethel Ayler, Bebe Drake, Janet League, Barbara Montgomery, Lou Myers, Petronia Reyno. During a sweltering stretch of summer, visiting "Grammar" celebrates her 75th birthday. Three generations of universal experiences in a middle-class African-American family are inventoried in this superbly acted show, which originated Off Broadway with the Negro Ensemble Company.

- *"...a lovely production of a lovely play...almost melodic structure...In its almost deceptively uncomplicated way,* The First Breeze of Summer *is about growing up, the black experience and the American experience, and every pertinent basic ingredient from economics to religion. The human experiences are cluttered and messy, composed of pride and shame, determination and compromise. A scene can be touching or terrifying or wonderfully moving....The entire cast...is splendid. But Frances Foster as Grammar and Janet League as Grammar in her youth deserve to be singled out...I did not see the play on-stage, but it is impossible to imagine a more effective production than this one tailored for television."* (John J. O'Connor, The New York Times)

Isobel Lennart

Born: May 18, 1915, Brooklyn, NY. **Died:** 1971.

Beginning with the World War II era, Isobel Lennart's eclectic list of 26 credited screenplays include those for *Anchors Aweigh* (1945) with Gene Kelly; *Love Me or Leave Me* (1955) with Doris Day as singer Ruth Etting and James Cagney as her brutal racketeer boyfriend; *The Inn of the Sixth Happiness* (1958) with Ingrid Bergman; the evocative and beautifully paced *The Sundowners* (1960) with Robert Mitchum leading a nomadic Australian family; and the adaptation of Tennessee Williams's *Period of Adjustment* (1962) starring Jane Fonda.

Funny Girl (1967, Columbia, 151m/c, **VHS**) ☆☆☆ **Sc:** Isobel Lennart. **D:** William Wyler. **P:** Ray Stark. **Cam:** Harry Stradling. **Cast:** Barbra Streisand, Omar Sharif, Kay Medford, Anne Francis, Walter Pidgeon, Lee Grant, Mae Qestel, Gerald Mohr, Frank Faylen, Mittie Lawrence, Gertrude Flynn, Penny Santon, John Harmon. This picture marked Streisand's D-Day on American entertainment as she threw herself into high gear as Fanny Brice, the Brooklyn girl who became a *Ziegfeld Follies* headliner and married gambler Nicky Arnstein. Streisand recreated her 1964 stage triumph opposite Sydney Chaplin as Arnstein. Streisand won the Best Actress Oscar (in a tie with Katharine Hepburn for *Guess Who's Coming to Dinner*) and the movie was nominated for Best Picture, Supporting Actress (Medford), Cinematography, Score (Walter Scharf), Song ("Funny Girl"), Sound, and Film Editing. Wyler's recreation of old New York and old Broadway is done with some charm and style.

- *"...elaborate, painstaking launching pad, with important talents of Hollywood, from the director, William Wyler, on down, treating Barbra rather fondly, improbably, and even patronizingly as though they were firing off a gilded broccoli."* (Renata Adler, The New York Times)

- *"Funny Girl is so much better than I thought it would be that I am almost tempted to recommend it....in all fairness to Miss Streisand, she might have fallen flat on her face after all the building, and she didn't. Practically every song number elicits spontaneous applause from the paying customers, and even this certified Barbraphobe found himself stirred on occasion by La Streisand's talent and energy."* (Andrew Sarris, Village Voice)

Alan Jay Lerner

Born: August 31, 1918, New York, NY. **Died:** 1986.

Alan Jay Lerner made Broadway musical history by writing books for some of the mid-century's biggest and most admired stage hits, primarily in tandem with composer Frederick Loewe, including *Brigadoon*, *Paint Your Wagon*, *My Fair Lady*, and *Camelot*. The team's music and songs were the subject of a 1962 NBC special, *The Broadway of Lerner and Loewe*, directed and produced by Norman Jewison and featuring performances by Richard Burton, Robert Goulet, and Stanley Holloway. Lerner wrote the original story for *Royal Wedding* (1951) and the story and screenplay for the Academy Award-winning Best Picture *An American in Paris* (1951), which put him on Hollywood's map for good. His second Oscar was for writing the screenplay for another Oscar-winning Best Picture, *Gigi* (1958).

   He was nominated for Oscars on four other occasions, including for the screenplays for *My Fair Lady* (1965) and *The Little Prince* (1974). He was generally regarded as peerless in the arena of highly literate and elegantly witty dioalogue. Lerner's autobiography, *The Street Where I Live*, was published in 1978.

Brigadoon ran for 581 performances on Broadway, beginning in 1947. Cheryl Crawford produced and Robert Lewis directed the musical about a cynic who discovers love in a charming Scottish village that went to sleep in 1754 and wakes for one day each century. It starred David Brooks and Marion Bell.

Brigadoon (1954, MGM, 108m/c, **VHS/DVD**) ☆☆½ **Sc:** Alan Jay Lerner. **D:** Vincente Minnelli. **P:** Arthur Freed. **Cam:** Joseph Ruttenburg. **Cast:** Gene Kelly, Van Johnson, Cyd Charisse, Elaine Stewart, Barry Jones, Hugh Laing, Albert Sharpe, Virginia Bosler, Jimmy Thompson, Tudor Owen, Owen McGiveney, Dody Heath, Eddie Quillen, Hugh Boswell, Hank Mann, Stuart Whitman, George Chakiris. The lifelessness of this uninspired production during MGM's musical heyday ranks it as one of that studio's biggest disappointments of the 1950s.

- *"Curiously flat and out-of-joint, rambling all over creation and seldom generating warmth or charm...pretty weak, synthetic Scotch."* (Bosley Crowther, The New York Times)

- *"MGM was having an economy drive, and this adaptation...[was] scheduled to be shot on location in Scotland, was instead done in the studio. Also by executive decree, the director, Vincente Minnelli, had to do it in CinemaScope—which for dance, in studio settings, was disastrous. Probably the material was too precious and fake-lyrical to have worked in natural surroundings, either, but the way it has been done it's hopeless stagy."* (Pauline Kael, 5,001 Nights at the Movies)

Brigadoon (1966, ABC Special, 90m/c) ☆☆☆ **Tp:** Ernest Kinoy. **D/P:** Fielder Cook. **Cast:** Robert Goulet, Peter Falk, Sally Ann Howes, Marilyn Mason, Thomas Carlisle, Linda Howe, Rhys Williams, Edward Villella, Finlay Currie. This was one of ABC's ambitious series of specials adapted from the stage in the mid-to-late 1960s.

- *"With songs like these neither the tyranny of time nor the harsh realities of commercials can destroy the fragile beauty of* Brigadoon. *It would be difficult to imagine a better Fiona than Sally Ann Howes. Robert Goulet was in fine voice, but his acting was a little dry and his manner too sophisticated for a man who discovers love in an enchanted village."* (George Gent, The New York Times)

Camelot was based by Lerner on T.H. White's novel *The Once and Future King*. King Arthur marries Guinevere, but she falls in love with Sir Lancelot, while the evil Mordred would prefer to run a saw through the Round Table. The 1960 smash hit starred Richard Burton, Julie Andrews, Robert Goulet, and Roddy McDowall.

Camelot (1967, Warner Bros., 179m/c, **VHS/DVD**) ☆☆☆ **Sc:** Alan Jay Lerner. **D:** Joshua Logan. **P:** Jack L. Warner. **Cam:** Richard H. Kline. **Cast:** Richard Harris, Vanessa Redgrave, Franco Nero, David Hemmings, Lionel Jeffries, Laurence Naismith, Estelle Winwood, Pierre Olaf, Gary Marshal, Anthony Rogers, Peter Bromilow, Nicholas Beauvy, Gary Marsh, Sue Casey, Gene Merlino. One of the overproduced film musical flops of the late 1960s, it was an attempt by Warner to recapture the big-musical success he found with *My Fair Lady* (1964). The film won Oscars for Best Art Direction/Set Decoration, Score (Alfred Newman, Ken Darby), and Costumes, and was nominated for Best Cinematography.

- *"Prototypical…grimly festive, a big show with big stars and score in the first place. Jack Warner envisioned a faithful rendering with the epic made manifest—real castle, jousts and round table, Excalibur resplendent, the sweat of the Middle Ages and the poetry of chivalry….So far, so good, if you enjoy the original's ham-handed reduction of T.H. White's highly textured burlesque-romantic pageant of political-psychological self-hatred….much of it does look right, in the callous gung-ho of the jousting tournament or in the castle's eyries by the hearth. But Richard Harris as Arthur, ranting his songs and lines, makes a tricky part impossible and Franco Nero as Lancelot had to be redubbed…The man who sings 'C'est Moi,' 'If Ever I Would Leave You' and 'I Loved You Once in Silence' is supposed to know why those songs are there; Nero clearly doesn't."* (Ethan Mordden, The Hollywood Musical)

Camelot (1982, Showtime, 150m/c) ☆☆☆½ **Tp:** Alan Jay Lerner. **D:** Marty Callner. **P:** Don Gregory, Mike Merrick. **Cast:** Richard Harris, Meg Bussert, Richard Muenz, Barry Ingham, James Valentine, Richard Backus, William Barry, Thor Fields. The musical was revived in 1980 for an extensive tour, starring, at first, Richard Burton. This program was based on that revival.

- *"The result, which was made to appear as if it were taking place entirely before a theatre audience although 90 percent of it was shot without spectators, was worth the extra effort. The story emerges quite touchingly. Meg Bussert is a nicely melodic queen; Richard Muenz is a convincingly innocent knight. And Richard Harris, reported to have been ill and notoriously out of sorts during the taping, is a memorably majestic and troubled king. He skillfully elevates a serviceable musical to surprisingly moving drama."* (John J. O'Connor, The New York Times)

My Fair Lady (1964, Warner Bros., 170m/c, **VHS/DVD**) ☆☆☆☆☆ **Sc:** Alan J. Lerner. **D:** George Cukor. **P:** Jack L. Warner. **Cam:** Harry Stradling. **Cast:** Rex Harrison, Audrey Hepburn, Wilfrid Hyde-White, Gladys Cooper, Stanley Holloway, Jeremy Brett, Theodore Bikel, Mona Washbourne, Isobel Elsom, Henry Daniell. This legendary Broadway smash, based by Lerner on George Bernard Shaw's *Pygmalion*, debuted on Broadway in 1956, staged by Moss Hart at the Mark Hellinger Theatre starring Harrison, Julie Andrews, Holloway, and Cathleen Nesbitt. It ran for 2,717 performances. The replacement of Andrews with Hepburn because of the latter's box-office clout was one of the more discussed casting changes in the history of play adaptations. Warner's suddenly big-style producing mien in the 1960s, Cukor's consummate care for the material, and each actor and crew specialist working at the top of his or her form all combined to produce superior results. The film was lavishly praised and won Oscars for Best Picture, Director, Actor (Harrison), Cinematography, Art Direction/Set Decoration, Score (Andre Previn), Costumes, and Sound, and was nominated for Best Screenplay, Supporting Actor (Holloway), and Film Editing.

- *"...This independent approach to stage musicals succumbed to a fashion merely to copy and expand the original as a means of retaining the Broadway impact. George Cukor's My Fair Lady set the fashion and skillfully exploited the form's limited potential with a flair few later productions were to achieve....much credit for the film's success clearly goes to its designers; production designer Cecil Beaton, and set director Gene Allen and George James Hopkins. The stately 'Ascot Gavotte' with dancers in elaborately recreated Edwardian costumes of black and white pacing in a stylized representation of polite society shows a respect for style audiences instinctively admired."* (John Baxter, Hollywood in the Sixties)
- *"The Lerner and Loewe musical staggers along...The film seems to go on for about 45 minutes after the story is finished. Audrey Hepburn is an affecting Eliza, though she is totally unconvincing as a guttersnipe, and is made to sing with that dreadfully impersonal Marni Nixon voice that has issued from so many other screen stars."* (Pauline Kael, 5,001 Nights at the Movies)

On a Clear Day You Can See Forever (1970, Paramount, 128m/c, **VHS**) ☆☆ **Sc:** Alan Jay Lerner. **D:** Vincente Minnelli. **P:** Howard W. Koch. **Cam:** Harry Stradling Sr. **Cast:** Barbra Streisand, Yves Montand, Bob Newhart, Jack Nicholson, Larry Blyden, Simon Oakland, John Richardson, Pamela Brown, Irene Handl, Roy Kinnear, Byron Webster, Peter Crowcroft, Mabel Albertson, Leon Ames, Laurie Main. Robert Lewis directed the Broadway original at the Mark Hellinger Theatre with Barbara Harris and John Cullum in the leading roles. Streisand played a woman hypnotized by a psychiatrist who finds she can access her previous incarnations. The psychiatrist eventually falls in love with one of them. The film, perhaps Minnelli's worst musical, makes the plot seem like chopped up malarkey, and a fine cast was wasted. The songs include the title tune, "Come Back to Me," "Hurry, It's Lovely Up Here," and "Melinda."

- "...let director Vincente Minnelli exploit his eye for décor in the pre-incarnation scenes, but a sleepwalking Yves Montand so taxed the action that the picture was slashed into chaos, losing some of Minnelli's best work and leaving—because he shares the romance with Streisand—mainly Montand. Disaster." (Ethan Mordden, The Hollywood Musical)

Paint Your Wagon (1969, Paramount, 166m/c, **VHS/DVD**) ☆☆½ **Sc:** Paddy Chayefsky. **D:** Josua Logan. **Cam:** William A. Fraker. **Cast:** Lee Marvin, Clint Eastwood, Jean Seberg, Ray Walston, Harve Presnell, John Mitchum, Tom Ligon, Alan Dexter, Benny Baker, Eddie Little Sky, Alan Baxter, Robert Easton, Terry Jenkins, Roy Jensen, William O'-Connell, H.B. Haggerty, Paula Trueman. Two miners are linked by both a gold mine and a wife in the 1850s in the California Sierra Nevadas. The 1951 hit, based on the Bret Harte story, "The Millionaire of Rough and Ready," starred James Barton and Olga San Juan. This film, made on location in Oregon for $25 million, was the third most expensive movie made up to its time and the leads were all miscast. Marvin overplayed, Eastwood sang "I Talk to the Trees," and the frontier seemed to have done nothing to blemish Seberg's from-the-beauty-parlor look.

- "...the clink of the money they dropped rings yet. Paint Your Wagon, the first all-talking, no-singing, no-dancing musical...Lee Marvin, Clint Eastwood, Jean Seberg, little story, weak comedy, and lots of songs with no lead to sing them. Based on a Lerner-Loewe western with a grand score and three splendid Agnes de Mille ballets, Paint Your Wagon became a film embarrassed to be a musical. When Seberg, holding Marvin at bay with a pistol, likens him to her father, 'born under a...wanderin' star,' an allusion to one of the songs, she blushes at the musical-comedy silliness. No; you have to believe in it or not do it. Or: when Harve Presnell's baritone rips into 'They Call the Wind Maria,' a drugged audience stirs in confusion—what's he doing here?" (Ethan Mordden, The Hollywood Musical)

Ira Levin

Born: August 27, 1929, New York, NY.

Better known as a novelist whose works seem to have a knack for transla-
tions to the screen, Ira Levin's position was secured after he triumphed with
the Andy Griffith-fronted *No Time for Sergeants*; first as a 1955 installment
of *The United States Steel Hour*, then as a play the same year, a 1958 film (see
below), and a TV series from 1964 to 1965 with Sammy Jackson replacing
Griffith. Films that have been made from Levin's novels include *A Kiss Before Dying*—twice, in 1956 with Robert Wagner as a society-climbing murderer and in 1991 with Matt Dillon in the role; *Rosemary's Baby* (1968); *The
Stepford Wives* (1975); *The Boys From Brazil* (1978); and *Sliver* (1993).

Critic's Choice (1963, Warner Bros., 100m/c) ☆½ **Sc:** Jack Sher. **D:**
Don Weis. **P:** Frank P. Rosenberg. **Cam:** Charles Lang. **Cast:** Bob Hope,
Lucille Ball, Marilyn Maxwell, Jessie Royce Landis, Jim Backus, John
Dehner, Marie Windsor, Richard Deacon, Lurene Tuttle, Jerome
Cowan, Ricky Kelman, Stanley Adams. The 1960 Broadway debut was
presented by Otto Preminger at the Ethel Barrymore Theatre with
Henry Fonda, Georgann Johnson, Eddie Hodges, Murray Hamilton, and
Mildred Natwick. A New York newspaper theatre critic's wife's play is
being presented on Broadway.

- *"...a none-too-smooth screen adaptation...There was very little reality to
  Hope's broad portrayal of a theatre critic...Lucy did her darnedest to be sincere...whether dealing with Hope's tired flippancies or the sirenish advances
  of his ex-wife...resisting the flirtations of a bohemian stage director Rip
  Torn...The overblown feature fell apart at the seams most spectacularly in
  the scene in which an inebriated Hope covers the opening night of Lucy's
  play...By opting for inexcusably low slapstick at this strategic point, director
  Don Weis sank the film for good."* (James Robert Parish, The RKO Gals)

Deathtrap (1982, Warner Bros., 115m/c, **VHS/DVD**) ☆☆☆½ **Sc:** Jay
Presson Allen. **D:** Sidney Lumet. **P:** Burtt Harris. **Cam:** Andrzej
Bartkowiak. **Cast:** Michael Caine, Christopher Reeve, Dyan Cannon,
Irene Worth, Henry Jones. The Broadway original was directed by Robert
Moore at New York's Music Box Theatre in 1978 and starred John Wood,
Marian Seldes, and Victor Garber. The three stars keep Levin's secrets as
they deceive each other in an elaborate set of plots and counterplots. It
starts out with playwright Caine, whose newest dud just opened on
Broadway, plotting with his wife in their Connecticut farmhouse to steal
a former student's newly written play and kill him on the grounds.

- *"Deathtrap is not a great film and will not live forever, but if you're an af-*

ficianado of whodunits and haven't seen this one, it'll be a treat. It's more fiendishly complicated than, for example, Caine's similar outing in Sleuth. It plays absolutely fair, more or less, and yet fools us every time, more or less. And perhaps its greatest gift is the sight of three lighthearted comic actors having a good time chewing on the dialogue, the scenery, and each other." (Roger Ebert, Chicago Sun-Times)

Dr. Cook's Garden (1970, ABC, 120m/c) ☆☆½ **Tp:** Art Wallace. **D:** Ted Post. **P:** Bob Markell. **Cast:** Bing Crosby, Blythe Danner, Frank Converse, Barnard Hughes, Thomas Barbour, Fred Burrell, Staats Cotsworth, Bethel Leslie, Abby Lewis, Carol Morley, Jordan Reed, Helen Stenborg. The original Broadway play was produced in 1967 at the Belasco Theatre with Burl Ives and Keir Dullea. One of Crosby's half-hearted returns to the screen late in his career, this piece strangely finds Der Bingle as a seemingly mild-mannered New England physician who is actually performing euthanasia on the sick and elderly in his hometown to keep the place as perfect and disease-free as possible.

- "…the most atypical characterization of his career….An enormously effective horror film…of particular interest because it's the first time the performer ever played a villain….Crosby's performance…is far above other portrayals of screen psychos. His Doctor Cook is neither a raving madman nor a ruthless killer. Instead, Crosby skillfully molds his Doctor Cook into the kind of personable elderly gentleman whom anyone might welcome as an ideal neighborhood physician. Crosby manages to convey beautifully the image of a kind and considerate doctor whose mental sickness is kept quietly under lock and key until the scene in which he attempts to poison the young doctor." (Robert Bookbinder, The Films of Bing Crosby)

No Time for Sergeants (1958, Warner Bros., 119m/bw, **VHS**) ☆☆☆½ **Sc:** John Lee Mahin. **D/P:** Mervyn Le Roy. **Cam:** Harold Rosson. **Cast:** Andy Griffith, Myron Mccormick, Nick Adams, Murray Hamilton, Howard Smith, Will Hutchins, Don Knotts, Sydney Smith, Jean Willes, Bartlett Robinson, Dub Taylor, Malcolm Atterbury, James Milhollin, Jamie Farr. Levin and Mac Hyman's Broadway smash of 1955, which began as an hourlong installment of The United States Steel Hour, was produced for the stage by Maurice Evans and directed by Morton Da Costa with a cast featuring Andy Griffith, Don Knotts, Myron McCormick, Roddy McDowall, and Robert Webber. The film was a big hit, with Griffith's characterization of a physically powerful but largely good-hearted hick who goes to Army boot camp creating a high-water mark in the vein of service comedies.

- "…lacks nothing in the way of comic content…And it has the same marvelous Andy Griffith, who created Will on the stage, to go right on creating chaos with his own staggering simplicity." (Bosley Crowther, The New York Times)

Meyer Levin

Born: October 8, 1905, Chicago, IL. **Died:** 1981.

A journalist for the *Chicago Daily News*, then *Esquire*, Meyer Levin became director for the U.S. Office of War Information during World War II. He later served as a war correspondent who was assigned the task of documenting the fate of European Jewry during the war. His novels include *Frankie and Johnny: A Love Story, The Old Bunch, My Father's House, Eva: A Novel of the Holocaust, The Stronghold, The Harvest,* and *The Architect.* His plays are *The Good Old Days, Anne Frank,* and *Compulsion* (see below). It was Levin, whose writings concentrated on Jewish issues, who brought the Anne Frank story to the attention of producer Cheryl Crawford and Lillian Hellman. They decided that Levin's dramatization was "too Jewish" and gave the play to Frances Goodrich and Albert Hackett to re-tool, which they did, all the way to the Pulitzer Prize. Levin sued and was eventually awarded $15,000 in damages and agreed to a ban on his version of Anne Frank (see **Frances Goodrich & Albert Hackett**).

Compulsion (1960, 20th Century-Fox, 103m/bw, **VHS**) ☆☆☆½ **Sc:** Richard Murphy. **D:** Richard Fleischer. **P:** Richard D. Zanuck. **Cam:** William C. Mellor. **Cast:** Dean Stockwell, Bradford Dillman, Orson Welles, Diane Varsi, E.G. Marshall, Martin Milner, Richard Anderson, Robert F. Simon, Edward Binns, Gavin MacLeod, Russ Bender, Terry Becker. The 1957 Broadway original at the Ambassador Theatre was based on Levin's novel about the events surrounding the 1924 Leopold/Loeb murder case, in which two homosexuals murdered a little girl in Illinois. The play was directed by Alex Segal and starred Stockwell, Roddy McDowall, and Suzanne Pleshette. The film portrays the murder plot, with the actual act occurring off camera, and wraps up with a huge courtroom set piece dominated by Welles as defense lawyer Jonathan Wilk, a stand-in for Clarence Darrow, who argued that the real killers deserved an asylum and not the noose.

- *"On this occasion, the period and the locale are retained, and the film, commandingly shot in black and white CinemaScope, conjures up the Jazz Age to vivid effect. Censorship precluded direct recognition of the homosexual relationship...although the sardonic D.A. is allowed to refer to them as 'a couple of powder boys.' But the emphasis rests more on a grippingly detailed account of the closing of the judicial net around the perpetrators...The concluding courtroom scenes are rescued from any threat of anti-climax by the quality of Welles's invention...and the eloquence of his (successful) plea against capital punishment is all the greater for being made in the context of his clients' unequivocal guilt."* (*Phil Hardy*, The BFI Companion to Crime)

Saul Levitt

Born: March 13, 1911, New York, NY. **Died:** 1977.

Saul Levitt worked uncredited on the screenplay for *The True Glory* (1945), wrote the screenplay for Lamont Johnson's *A Covenant with Death* (1967), one of Gene Hackman's first films, and adapted Daniel Berrigan's play *The Trial of the Catonsville Nine* into the 1972 film produced by Gregory Peck.

The Andersonville Trial (1970, PBS, 150m/c, **VHS**) *Hollywood Television Theatre* ☆☆☆☆☆ **Tp:** Saul Levitt. **D:** George C. Scott. **P:** Lewis Freedman. **Cast:** William Shatner, Richard Basehart, Jack Cassidy, Cameron Mitchell, Martin Sheen, Buddy Ebsen, Albert Salmi, John Anderson, Michael Burns, Whit Bissell, Harry Townes, Wright King. Levitt based his 1959 Broadway hit on MacKinlay Kantor's 1956 Pulitzer Prize-winning novel, *Andersonville*, about the Civil War war-crimes trial of a Confederate captain who ran the prisoner-of-war camp at Andersonville, Georgia, where 14,000 Union soldiers died during the Civil War from malnutrition, wounds, and disease. The 1959 play at New York's Henry Miller Theatre starred the director of this TV version, George C. Scott, was directed by Jose Ferrer, and included in the eclectic ensemble Albert Dekker, Heywood Hale Broun, Vincent Donohoe, and Herbert Berghoff. The TV broadcast became one of the most significant events in PBS history as it won Emmy Awards for Outstanding Single Program of the Year, Adaptation (by Levitt), Technical Direction, and Camerawork, and was nominated for Best Actor (Cassidy). The show won a Peabody Award as well. Scott's direction provides a smorgasbord of opportunities for his fine cast, led by Basehart as the Queeg-like captain.

- "*...superior production...Mr. Scott, to the surprise of absolutely no one, clearly has a new career opening up as a director. His sensitivity and feeling were responsible for the best moments in* Andersonville Trial....*The opening portion resembles a Perry Mason of the Civil War as the procession of witnesses testify to the odious camp conditions. The transition of* The New York Law Journal *to theater really came with the portrayal by Michael Burns of the young Union soldier who has lost his coherence under the ravages of war and confinement, a cameo scene that saw Mr. Scott at his directorial best. From that point on,* The Andersonville Trial *got down to the moral issue of whether the higher demands of civilized behavior should take precedence over a direct military command....In these sequences, Mr. Levitt's dialogue holds the viewer's attention in full measure.*" (Jack Gould, The New York Times)

Howard Lindsay & Russel Crouse

Lindsay:
Born: March 29, 1889, Waterford, NY. **Died:** 1968.

Crouse:
Born: February 20, 1893, Findlay, OH. **Died:** 1966.
Pulitzer Prize-winning play: *State of the Union* (1945)

Howard Lindsay was primarily an actor until he found success as a dramatist when he adapted Edward Hope's novel *She Loves Me Not* into a play. After he teamed with Russel Crouse to write the book of *Anything Goes* in 1934, the team continued on with *Red, Hot and Blue!* (1936) and *Hooray for What!* (1937). In 1939, they created one of the most enduring plays of the 20th century in *Life With Father*, which starred Lindsay as an overbearing 19th century New York patriarch. While the pair continued to write plays, such as *Strip for Action* (1942), they also became theatrical forces as directors, producers, and theatre owners, and produced films and plays of other authors as well. They won the Pulitzer Prize for the political satire, *State of the Union*, which was made into a celebrated film in 1948 and a critically acclaimed TV show in 1954.

Among the films produced by the pair was *The Hasty Heart* (1949) and the plays they produced included *Arsenic and Old Lace* and *Detective Story*. Among the films they wrote that weren't based on their own plays were *The Big Broadcast of 1938* (1938), *Artists and Models Abroad* (1938), and *A Woman's World* (1954). The pair's popularity waned in the late 1950s with the stage musical *Happy Hunting* and the basketball comedy *Tall Story*, even though *The Sound of Music* returned them to great popular success. While Lindsay and Crouse never aspired to literary heights, they were consummate showmen who made a big impact on 20th century theatre.

Anything Goes, about various cases of mistaken identity on a New York-to-Southampton oceanliner crossing, ran for 420 performances on Broadway, beginning in 1934. It was based on a British musical comedy by Guy Bolton and P.G. Wodehouse that Lindsay, the stage director, asked Crouse to help him adapt into an American musical. Cole Porter was engaged to write the score. Starring were William Gaxton and Ethel Merman as Reno Sweeney, with support from Bettina Hall, Victor Moore, and Vivian Vance.

Anything Goes (1936, Paramount, 92m/bw) ☆☆☆ **Sc:** Guy Bolton, P.G. Wodehouse, Howard Lindsay, Russel Crouse. **D:** Lewis Milestone. **P:** Benjamin Glazer. **Cam:** Karl Struss. **Cast:** Bing Crosby, Ethel Merman, Charles Ruggles, Grace Bradley, Ida Lupino, Chill Wills, Arthur Treacher, Margaret Dumont, Edward Gargan, Snub Pollard, Robert McWade, John Carradine, Dennis O'Keefe, Keye Luke, Philip Ahn,

Bess Flowers, the Avalon Boys. The large and eclectic cast contributed sharp performances and the better lines still rang true, even if the production was static. The songs include "Sailor Beware" and "Moonburn."

- *"...Paramount brought Anything Goes to the screen in 1936 with its sharp comedy dulled, its characters prettied, and its Cole Porter score trimmed to 'You're the Top,' 'I Get a Kick Out of You,' and the minor 'There'll Always Be a Lady Fair.'...should have been right for the screen as it was. Letting Bing Crosby and Ida Lupino play the roles originated by William Gaxton and Bettina Hall was good thinking, as Crosby was more amiable and Lupino more exciting than their predecessors, and at least Ethel Merman was held over from Broadway, though setting her in a revolving swing for 'I Get a Kick Out of You' was somebody's very strange anticipation of high-tech camp."* (Ethan Mordden, The Hollywood Musical)

Anything Goes (1950, NBC, 60m/bw) *Musical Comedy Time* ☆☆ **Tp:** John W. Ledon, Sam Moore. **D/P:** Richard Berger. **Cast:** Martha Raye, John Conte, Kathryn Mylrole, Fred Wayne, Billy Lynn, Helen Raymond, Gretchen Hauser, A.J. Herbert, Larry Haynes, Harry Sosnick, Wirlie Birch. This version is set in Europe.

- *"...far from satisfactory despite the stock Porter score being given the treatment by Harry Sosnick's orchestra."* (Variety)

Anything Goes (1954, NBC, 60m/bw) *Colgate Comedy Hour* ☆☆½ **Tp:** Herbert Baker. **D:** Peter Barnum. **P:** Leland Hayward, Jule Styne. **Cast:** Ethel Merman, Frank Sinatra, Arthur Gould Porter, Bert Lahr, Sheree North. The attractive cast made this one of *Colgate's* more memorable offerings with a relaxed Sinatra contrasting to the brassy Merman and the beautiful North.

- *"...a musical comedy that played like one, for TV it marked a triumph!"* (Variety)

Anything Goes (1956, Paramount, 106m/c) ☆☆½ **Sc:** Sidney Sheldon. **D:** Robert Lewis. **P:** Robert Emmet Dolan. **Cam:** John F. Warren. **Cast:** Bing Crosby, Donald O'Connor, Zizi Jeanmaire, Mitzi Gaynor, Phil Harris, Kurt Kaszner, Walter Sande, Richard Erdman, Archer MacDonald, Tracey Roberts, Marcel Dalio, Torben Meyer, Nancy Kulp, James Griffith. This was one of Bing Crosby's returns to dated material during the downswing in his movie popularity, and his last Paramount movie after 24 years and 44 films. This time, a famed musical comedy star is teamed with a brash TV luminary (O'Connor) to find a female co-star abroad.

- *"...bearing little physical resemblance to its [1936] predecessor...For all its activity, Anything Goes is, in the main, standard musical comedy. Mr. Porter's noted ditties have not suffered. They are as bubbly and memorable as ever. Some of the principals are decidedly decorative and talented. The script, however, is transparent and fragile....One of the ladies, Mitzi Gaynor, is a treat to the eye and ear in a beautifully abbreviated costume as she does the titular song-and-dance number....In making his film-directorial debut, Robert Lewis has not come up with a particularly inspired effort."* (A.H. Weiler, The New York Times)

Call Me Madam (1953, 20th Century-Fox, 114m/c) ☆☆☆½ **Sc:** Arthur Sheekman. **D:** Walter Lang. **P:** Sol C. Siegel. **Cam:** Leon Shamroy. **Cast:** Ethel Merman, Donald O'Connor, George Sanders, Vera-Ellen, Billy de Wolfe, Helmut Dantine, Walter Slezak, Steve Geray, Ludwig Stossel. Lindsay and Crouse based their satiric play on the actual activities of Washington socialite Perle Mesta, who was appointed ambassador to Luxembourg under President Harry Truman. The 1950 play, staged by George Abbot, starred Merman, Paul Lukas, and Lilia Skala. The songs include "You're Just in Love." Alfred Newman won the Oscar for his score, and the film was nominated for Best Costuming.

- *"Political satire had been remarkably strong as early as 1953 in* Call Me Madam, *cutting through the jollity of the lightweight Irving Berlin musical....The wisecracks at the expense of President Truman and his family were rather jovial: the movie had a slightly dated quality, because by this tiome Eisenhower was president; but the picture of a brash American female ambassador, distributing largesse to a fictitious European country ('Can You Use Any Money Today?' was a palpable hit), drew astonishingly trenchant contrast from commercial vulgarity on the one hand and pathetic old world dignity on the other. It was light, but not trivial....This was healthy stuff. However, some of the saucier lyrics were omitted, because Hollywood still languished under an antiquated Production Code that was extremely uptight concerning sex."* (Gordon Gow, Hollywood in the Fifties)

- *"Ethel Merman gets more elbow room than usual....Merman has tedious telephone conversations with Truman about his daughter's troubles and her singing career, but the Irving Berlin score has a couple of songs good enough to make the whole apparatus tolerable."* (Pauline Kael, 5,001 Nights at the Movies)

The Great Sebastians (1957, NBC, 90m/c) *Producers' Showcase* ☆☆☆½ **Tp:** Russel Crouse, Howard Lindsay. **D:** Franklin J. Schaffner. **Cast:** Alfred Lunt, Lynn Fontanne, Akim Tamiroff, Anne Francine, Simon Oakland, Arny Freeman, Lisa Ferraday, Eugenia Rawls. A second-rate mind-reading act becomes involved with international intrigue when they are invited to perform for Communist Party officials at a gathering in Prague. The reigning married couple of the American theatre made their TV debut with this Cold War comedy. The Lunts played the Sebastians for more than a year on Broadway starting in 1956.

- *"...Howard Lindsay's and Russel Crouse's hokey comedy melodrama...served as an auspicious entry in the* Producers' Showcase se-

ries....Not that Sebastians *is top theatre. It isn't; but the Lunts are. And the top thespic talents that have carried them through a 33-year stretch (often with flimsy vehicles) were never more skillfully utilized than in the television adaptation of* The Great Sebastians. *It was, for them and for an audience running into the millions, most of whom probably had not seen the Lunts before, a television debut of stature."* (Variety)

Life With Father (1947, Warner Bros., 118m/c, **VHS/DVD**) ☆☆☆½ **Sc:** Donald Ogden Stewart. **D:** Michael Curtiz. **P:** Robert Buckner. **Cam:** J. Peverell Marley, William V. Skall. **Cast:** William Powell, Irene Dunne, Elizabeth Taylor, Edmund Gwenn, ZaSu Pitts, Jimmy Lydon, Emma Dunn, Moroni Olsen, Elisabeth Risdon, Derek Scott, Johnny Calkins, Martin Milner, Monte Blue, Queenie Leonard, Clara Blandick, Clara Reid, Arlene Dahl, Douglas Kennedy, Philip Van Zandt. This play's original 1939 staging was at the Maryland Theatre in Baltimore, directed by Bretaigne Windust and starring Howard Lindsay as the patriarch, Teresa Wright, and Dorothy Stickney. It opened on Broadway the same year.

- *"Rich, careful, rather heavily proficient. Fun, I suppose; but I really can't enjoy laughing at tyrants who are forgiven because of their innocence. William Powell acts, rather than is, Father rather well, but it's strictly an impersonation. Irene Dunne is painfully miscast as Mother..."* (James Agee, The Nation)

- *"William Powell, a favorite of discerning film critics since the early 1920s, received the best notices of his long career for his performance in* Life With Father. *The magnificent role enabled many to see for the first time what an exceptional actor Powell was."* (Chris Francisco, Gentleman: The William Powell Story)

- *"He so utterly dominates the picture that even when he is not on the screen, his presence is felt."* (Bosley Crowther, The New York Times)

Love, Honor and Oh Baby! (1933, Universal, 75m/bw) ☆☆½ **Sc:** Edward Buzzell, Norman Krasna (uncredited). **D:** Edward Buzzell. **Cam:** George Robinson. **Cast:** Slim Summerville, ZaSu Pitts, George Barbier, Donald Meek, Lucille Gleason, Veree Teasdale, Purnell Pratt, Adrienne Dore, Dorothy Granger, Neeley Edwards, Henry Kolker. In the adaptation of the 1930 play *Oh, Promise Me*, co-written by Lindsay and Bertrand Robinson, an attorney concocts a fake lawsuit against a well-heeled roué. Universal's 1940 film of the same name wasn't based on the play, which featured Lee Tracy, Donald Meek, and Mary Philips in its initial Broadway run.

- *"Finding a more unfunny comedy...would come under the heading of thankless tasks. That it had its genesis in the lively stage cartoon* Oh, Promise Me *and that its cast includes such ordinarily persuasive side-splitters as Slim Summerville, ZaSu Pitts...only heighten the embarrassment of the spectator at its aggressive dullness....the script is a disjointed and feeble imitation of the original play."* (Andre Sennewald, The New York Times)

Remains to Be Seen (1953, MGM, 88m/bw) ☆☆½ **Sc:** Russel Crouse, Howard Lindsay, Sidney Sheldon. **D:** Don Weis. **P:** Arthur Hornblow Jr. **Cam:** Robert Planck. **Cast:** June Allyson, Van Johnson, Louis Calhern, Angela Lansbury, Dorothy Dandridge, John Beal, Barry Kelley, Sammy White, Kathryn Card, Paul Harvey, Helene Millard, Charles Lane, Morgan Farley. The 1951 play, about a Park Avenue apartment building's eclectic denizens, was produced by Leland Hayward and ran for 199 performances on Broadway starring Jackie Cooper, Janis Paige, and Lindsay. In the film, Johnson starred as a bashful theatre manager and Allyson played a nightclub singer who's also a sleepwalker.

- *"...a blend of murder and mirth that succeeds in being neither mysterious nor particularly amusing...notable sequence: June Allyson jitterbugging, Van Johnson playing the trap drums, June and Van doing a duet of 'Toot, Toot, Tootsie, Goodbye.'"* (Time)

She Loves Me Not was adapted by Lindsay from Edward Hope's novel of the same name for this 1933 play, which ran for 360 performances starring Burgess Meredith, Caroline Morrison, and John Beal at Broadway's 46th Street Theatre. A Philadelphia nightclub chanteuse hides out on the Princeton University campus and, with the help of roommates, disguises herself as a boy in this sexual flip side to *Charley's Aunt.*

She Loves Me Not (1934, Paramount, 85m/bw) ☆☆½ **Sc/P:** Benjamin Glazer. **D:** Elliott Nugent. **Cam:** Charles Lang. **Cast:** Bing Crosby, Miriam Hopkins, Kitty Carlisle, Edward Nugent, Lynne Overman, Henry Stephenson, Warren Hymer, George Barbier. Hopkins played one of her most outlandish parts as Curley, the nightclub singer.

- *"'Bing,' [Carlisle] said, 'was extremely businesslike...I remember asking him one day, what song in the picture he thought would be a hit. And he said, "My dear, if I knew that, I wouldn't be putting on this toupee and this make-up every day—I'd be a millionaire!"' Again, the cooler side of Bing...If ever She Loves Me Not comes within your scope, watch out for his ears, apart from anything else. Some of the film was shot with them glued back; part with them sticking out. 'They kept coming unstuck under the heat of the lighting,' explains Bing. 'One day they popped out and I said "To hell with it—that's the way they're going to stay." And so they never bothered with the glue again.'"* (Charles Thompson, Bing)

True to the Army (1942, Paramount, 77m/bw) ☆½ **Sc:** Art Arthur, Val Burton. **D:** Albert S. Rogell. **P:** Sol C. Siegel. **Cam:** Daniel L. Fapp. **Cast:** Judy Canova, Alan Jones, Ann Miller, Jerry Colonna, Clarence Kolb, Edward Pauley, William Demarest, Edwin Miller, Arthur Loft, Gordon Jones, Rod Cameron, Eddie Acuff, Mary Treen, Selmer Jackson.

Canova's hotly pursued girl hides out in an Army barracks this time, in this World War II-era flag-waver.

- *"The fine art of tickling the public's rib is being practiced with all the consummate finesse of a longshoreman...as actors, Mr. Jones and Miss Miller are woefully limited. Nor does Judy Canova's lopsided brand of humor make more entertaining the story of a pursued lady who takes refuge in an Army camp and is taken for one of the boys—with the resultant wheezes about medical examinations, etc. As a comedy of errors, True to the Army is full of errors but no comedy."* (The New York Times)

How to Be Very, Very Popular (1955, 20th Century-Fox, 89m/c) ☆☆½ **Sc/D/P:** Nunnally Johnson. **Cam:** Milton Krasner. **Cast:** Betty Grable, Sheree North, Charles Coburn, Robert Cummings, Orson Bean, Fred Clark, Tommy Noonan, Charlotte Austin, Harry Carter, Jesslyn Fax, Mike Lally, Jack Mather, Emory Parnell, Leslie Parish, Alice Pearce, Tony Randell, Milton Parsons, Hank Mann, Emlyn Williams. Two belly dancers hide out from an insane, balding killer in a male college dormitory. Marilyn Monroe turned down the co-starring role, giving North a prime opportunity.

- *"...sets Hollywood's veteran blonde bombshell (Betty Grable) and a current challenger (Sheree North)—both cast as 'interpretive' dancers—in the male dormitory of a rural college and lets them work their way out through 90 minutes of pretty complicated, if familiar, plot....The story comes to an end, fittingly, at commencement, where Sheree interrupts the solemnity with one of the most sizzling dances ever filmed."* (Newsweek)

She's My Weakness (1930, RKO, 75m/c) ☆☆ **Sc:** J. Walter Ruben. **D:** Melville W. Brown. **P:** William LeBaron. **Cam:** Leo Tover. **Cast:** Arthur Lake, Sue Carol, Lucien Littlefield, William Collier Sr., Helen Ware, Alan Bunce, Emily Fitzroy, Walter Gilbert. This film is based on the 1927 play *Tommy* by Howard Lindsay and Bertrand Robinson, which featured Sidney Toler and William Janney. The film concerns a young couple in love whose relationship is complicated by an uncle's shady real estate dealings and another boy who captures the girl's fancy.

- *"...has the flavor of a Booth Tarkington play....There are...complications, one being provided by Arthur Lake...whose adolescent appearance makes him ideal for the part but whose apparent ignorance of what is good acting is appalling....The picture lacks mobility and is little more than a photographed stage play."* (The New York Times)

The Sound of Music (1965, 20th Century-Fox, 172m/c, **VHS/DVD**) ☆☆☆ **Sc:** Ernest Lehman. **D/P:** Robert Wise. **Cam:** Ted D. McCord. **Cast:** Julie Andrews, Christopher Plummer, Eleanor Parker, Peggy Wood, Charmain Carr, Heather Menzies, Marni Nixon, Richard Haydn, Anna Lee, Angela Cartwright, Norma Varden, Nicholas Hammond,

Duane Chase, Debbie Turner, Portia Nelson, Kym Karath. The idyllic world of the Von Trapp family in Austria is interrupted by the Nazis during World War II. A vivacious performance by Andrews, the superb Alpine cinematography, and the songs under the direction of Wise coalesced into one of the all-time Hollywood favorites. Lindsay and Crouse based their 1959 triumph, which ran for 1,443 performances with the music of Rodgers and Hammerstein, on the memoir by Maria Von Trapp. The play starred Mary Martin and Theodore Bikel and included in the ensemble John Randolph, Kurt Kaszner, and Joey Heatherton. The songs included "Climb Every Mountain" and "Do-Re-Mi." The film won Academy Awards for Best Picture, Director, Score (Irwin Kostal), Film Editing, and Sound, and was nominated for Best Actress (Andrews), Supporting Actress (Wood), Cinematography, Art Direction/Set Decoration, and Costumes.

- "And the phenomenon at the center of the monetary phenomenon? Julie Andrews, with the clean, scrubbed look and unyielding high spirits; the good sport who makes the best of everything; the girl who's so unquestionably good that she carries this one dimension like a shield. The perfect, perky schoolgirl, the adorable tomboy, the gawky colt. Sexless, inhumanly happy, the sparkling maid, a mind as clean and well-brushed as her teeth. What is she? Merely the ideal heroine for the best of all possible worlds. And that's what The Sound of Music pretends we live in....the luxuriant falseness of The Sound of Music [is] part of the sentimental American tone that makes honest work almost impossible. It is not only that people who accept this kind of movie tend to resent work which says that this is not the best of all possible worlds, but that people who are gifted give up the effort to say anything. They attune themselves to The Sound of Money," (Pauline Kael, Kiss Kiss Bang Bang)

- "...neither all that great nor all that horrible. It's not sticky-sweet, despite the kids...Andrews is fine in a dull part, Christopher Plummer opposite her is a bore, the score is variable, Robert Wise's direction is excellent for this sort of thing, and so on down the line: okay....less important for what it was than for what it inspired in the industry. Producers...ordered more...but there is no menu for art, even pop art, and instead of Broadway-into-film hits, Hollywood produced the biggest squad of bombs in its history." (Ethan Mordden, The Hollywood Musical)

State of the Union concerns a Republican presidential candidate who asks his estranged wife to come home for the sake of appearances during an election. Ralph Bellamy and Ruth Hussey opened the smash hit on Broadway, which ran for 765 performances, produced by Leland Hayward at the Hudson Theatre.

State of the Union (1948, MGM, 124m/bw, **VHS**) ☆☆☆☆ **Sc:** Anthony Veiller. **D/P:** Frank Capra. **Cam:** George J. Folsey. **Cast:** Spencer

Tracy, Katharine Hepburn, Van Johnson, Angela Lansbury, Adolphe Menjou, Lewis Stone, Howard Smith, Raymond Walburn, Maidel Turner, Pierre Watkin, Carl Switzer, Margaret Hamilton, Tom Pedi, Irving Bacon, Charles Lane, Arthur O'Connell, Tor Johnson, Stanley Andrews, Charles Dingle. The play was transformed into one of the more fondly remembered Tracy-Hepburn vehicles. The then-topical dialogue was lifted from ongoing news reports during production.

- *"It's a shallow but generally entertaining show, with lots of devious characters...doing dirty deeds. Hepburn is wasted in her pillar-of-rectitude role, but she's still such a dervish of a performer, and more fun to watch than just about anybody else who might have played it."* (Pauline Kael, 5,001 Nights at the Movies)

- *"In a very large way, the firm directorial hand of Capra and the strong screen presence of Lansbury and Adolphe Menjou (as a conniving politician) forced Kate into rising above her usual dramatic reach, delivering a performance that was, in the words of Howard Barnes* (New York Herald-Tribune), *'restrained, persuasive, and altogether delightful.'"* (James Robert Parish, The RKO Gals)

State of the Union (1954, NBC, 90m/c) *Producers' Showcase* ☆☆☆☆ **Tp:** Howard Lindsay, Russel Crouse. **D:** Arthur Penn. **P:** Fred Coe. **Cast:** Margaret Sullavan, Joseph Cotten, John Cromwell, Nina Foch, Ray Walston. The second show in the prestigious series was roundly praised. Cromwell, a director, returned to his acting roots for one of the initial collaborations between Coe and Penn.

- *"The magic of the theatre touched television...a fine production...with Margaret Sullavan giving a radiant performance...For 90 minutes the best of Broadway was over at Radio City....There was a play with something provocative to say, the playwrights to say it amusingly, the players to act it and, rarest of all in video, the time to do it. A viewer's minor miracle."* (Jack Gould, The New York Times)

Tall Story (1960, Warner Bros., 91m/bw, **VHS**) ☆☆½ **Sc:** Julius J. Epstein. **D/P:** Joshua Logan. **Cam:** Ellsworth Fredericks. **Cast:** Anthony Perkins, Jane Fonda, Ray Walston, Anne Jackson, Marc Connelly, Murray Hamilton, Elizabeth Patterson. The play's dual concerns follow two professors trying to come up with a foolproof formula at picking basketball game winners and the romance between a man-grabbing cheerleader and an academically weak basketball star. In the 1959 stage production, which was adapted from the Howard Nemerov novel, *The Homecoming Game*, Connelly and Hans Conreid played the profs and Fonda was the cheerleader. The film is interesting as Fonda's perky debut, but Perkins was miscast; he isn't believable as a jock for one moment.

- *"A frantic attempt at sophistication and a steady barrage of jazzy wisecracks about campus sex....The gangly Mr. Perkins jounces around convincingly enough, but near Miss Fonda he generally gapes and freezes, and who can blame him? The pretty newcomer shows charm and promise in her film debut."* (Howard Thompson, The New York Times)

Your Uncle Dudley (1935, 20th Century-Fox, 70m/bw) ☆☆ **Sc:** Allen Birkin, Joseph Hoffman. **D:** Eugene Forde, James Tinling. **P:** Edward T. Lowe Jr. **Cam:** Harry Jackson. **Cast:** Edward Everett Horton, Lois Wilson, John McGuire, Rosina Lawrence, Alan Dinehart, Marjorie Gateson, Florence Roberts, Billy Benedict. The 1929 original Broadway play by Lindsay and Bertrand Robinson at the Cort Theatre starred Walter Connolly and Beatrice Terry. The play is about the congenial and civic-minded Dudley Dixon, who neglects his business to chair several town projects, earning the ire of his nagging sister.

- *"...meager and unassuming little comedy...We cinema reviewers, when films as unobtrusively dull as* Your Uncle Dudley *happen along, make a minor virtue of anemia by applying such kindly adjectives as 'amiable' to them. Although* Your Uncle Dudley *is unpretentious, it is also aggressively commonplace. It seems to have been manufactured for the tail-end of double bills and it barely possesses the laughs for a competent two-reeler."* (Andre Senwald, The New York Times)

Your Uncle Dudley was combined with elements from George Kelly's *The Torchbearers* for the film *Too Busy to Work* (1939; see **George Kelly**). The play was also presented in 1953 on *Broadway Television Theatre*, once again starring Edward Everett Horton and Marjorie Gateson.

Joshua Logan

Joshua Lockwood Logan III
Born: October 5, 1908, Texarkana, TX. **Died:** 1988.

Mostly known as a director of stage and screen works, Joshua Logan wrote or co-wrote four plays that were adapted for film or TV productions, the most popular of them—*Mister Roberts* and *South Pacific*—twice. Eight of his 11 movies as a director were based on stage works. His directorial career sank under the weight of two enormous musical flops, *Camelot* (1967) and *Paint Your Wagon* (1969). A contemporary of James Stewart in the Princeton University theatre program, Logan began in Hollywood as a dialogue director in the late 1930s after stage experience as a performer, director, and producer on Broadway. Among the important shows he subsequently staged were *On Borrowed Time*, *Morning's at Seven*, *Charley's Aunt*, *Annie Get Your Gun*, *Happy Birthday*, *Picnic*, *Middle of the Night*, *Blue Denim*, and *Mr. President*.

Fanny (1961, Warner Bros., 133m/c, **VHS**) ☆☆☆ **Sc:** Julius J. Epstein. **D/P:** Joshua Logan. **Cam:** Jack Cardiff. **Cast:** Charles Boyer, Maurice Chevalier, Leslie Caron, Horst Buccholz, Georgette Anys, Salvatorre Baccaloni, Lionel Jeffries, Victor Francen, Raymond Bussieres. Three Marcel Pagnol films of the 1930s—*Marius*, *Fanny*, and *Cesar*—were converted into a 1938 Wallace Beery vehicle, *The Port of Seven Seas*, by screenwriter Preston Sturges, then retooled by Logan and S.N. Behrman into a 1954 Broadway musical. Produced by Logan and David Merrick and directed by Logan, it ran for 888 performances starring Florence Henderson as Fanny with Walter Slezak, Enzio Pinza, and William Tabbert. This film was originally titled *Joshua Logan's Fanny* until the press made light of it. Harold Rome's songs were stripped out of the film even as Morris Stoloff and Harry Sukman's score retained their melodic spirit. The French setting, the presence of Caron and Chevalier, and the light tone seem as if the film's ancestry goes back to *Gigi* rather than to Pagnol. The film was nominated for Oscars for Best Picture, Actor (Boyer), Cinematography, Musical Score, and Film Editing.

- *"Fanny manifests great spirit and reverence for life. Although it is an American film, it has a distinct European flavor. There is overemphasis on broad comedy...but the truth of the characters that Pagnol created...still asserts itself, and the honesty of their emotions comes through. The acting is uniformly excellent, but does not mesh well....Caron is radiant as Fanny...the beautiful cinematography of Jack Cardiff evokes the Marseilles waterfront to perfection."* (Joan Cohen, Magill's Survey of Cinema)

Higher and Higher (1944, RKO, 90m/bw, **VHS**) ☆☆½ **Sc:** Jay Dratler, Ralph Spence. **D/P:** Tim Whelan. **Cam:** Robert de Grasse. **Cast:** Michele Morgan, Frank Sinatra, Jack Haley, Leon Errol, Marcy McGuire, Victor Borge, Barbara Hale, Mary Wickes, Elisabeth Risdon. Servants attempt to pass a maid off as an heiress in this lightweight fluff. Whelan revamped the play, which featured Vera-Ellen and Jack Haley, and used only one song from the 1940 Rogers and Hart musical. The book by Logan and Gladys Hurlbut survives in the film.

- *"Perhaps music was the strongest element in the 1940s film musical, as the stories were mostly old-hat and the performers too clean cut after that 1930s mob. One even begins to miss Jolson. If he typifies the roughhouse early 1930s, Frank Sinatra typifies the 1940s, with his infinitely engaging vocal quality, smooth delivery and casual self-portrayal. He appears as himself in* Higher and Higher...*and does not quite take part in the plot...Yet without Sinatra,* Higher and Higher *would be half of a film, for his many song spots were the action: music is magic."* (Ethan Mordden, The Hollywood Musical)

Mister Roberts was produced on Broadway by Leland Heyward, directed by Joshua Logan, and starred Henry Fonda, beginning in 1948. Logan and Thomas Heggen derived the play from Heggen's novel. One of the great hits of mid-century theatre, it ran for 1,157 performances. Among those in that initial production were Robert Keith, David Wayne, Ralph Meeker, Jocelyn Brando, Harvey Lembeck, and Steven Hill. The below film also spawned a sequel, *Ensign Pulver* (1964), starring Robert Walker, Jr. and Burl Ives, and was also the basis for the TV series Mr. *Roberts*, starring Roger Smith, which ran on NBC from 1965 to 1966. The story concerns the crew aboard the cargo ship USS Reluctant in the South Pacific during World War II and the ennui of that life, broken by episodes of mischief and the fulminations of a martinet captain.

Mister Roberts (1955, Warner Bros., 123m/c, **VHS/DVD**) ☆☆☆½ **Sc:** Frank Nugent, Joshua Logan. **D:** John Ford, Mervyn LeRoy, Joshua Logan (uncredited). **P:** Leland Hayward. **Cam:** Winton C. Hoch. **Cast:** Henry Fonda, James Cagney, Jack Lemmon, William Powell, Betsy Palmer, Ward Bond, Philip Carey, Martin Milner, Gregory Walcott, James Flavin, Jack Pennick, Ken Curtis, Duke Kahanamoku, Harry Carey Jr., Perry Lopez, Patrick Wayne, Tige Andrews, Nick Adams, Danny Borzage, Shug Fisher. Ford began as the director and had creative differences with Fonda, who had made the part his own. Ford slugged the actor in front of the cast and crew, and was replaced by LeRoy, who shot for a few weeks. The film was then finished by Logan. The film still packs a punch because of the marvelous cast, with Fonda's signature performance of common sense, Cagney in bristling form as the Captain, and Lemmon in his first Oscar-winning role as the skirt-chasing Ensign Pulver.

- *"Now hear this! Another 21-gun salute is hereby accorded* Mister Roberts*…like its predecessors, this version…is a strikingly superior entertainment. Jack Lemmon's Ensign Pulver is a broad delineation of the amorous misfit, anxious to please his idol, Roberts. He exhibits the explosive ebullience of a kid with a live frog in his britches. Henry Fonda does not simply give his role a professional reading. He is Mr. Roberts….a beautifully lean and sensitive characterization, full of dignity and power."* (A.H. Weiler, The New York Times)

- *"The comic and heroic spirit went out of the famous stage success…it's a miserable piece of movie-making—poorly paced and tearjerking."* (Pauline Kael, 5,001 Nights at the Movies)

Mister Roberts (1984, NBC, 100m/c) ☆☆☆ **Tp:** Thomas Heggen, Joshua Logan. **D:** Melvin Bernhardt. **P:** David W. Rintels. **Cast:** Robert Hays, Kevin Bacon, Charles Durning, Howard Hesseman, Marilu Henner, Raye Birk, Joe Pantoliano, Charley Lang. A live production with Hays as Roberts, Bacon as Pulver, Durning as the captain and Hesseman as Doc was filmed in a small theatre in Burbank, California.

- *"In its almost folksy way, Mister Roberts has always been something of an oddity. Its villain is not the 'other side' in the war, but the cargo ship's own captain, a nasty loudmouth...Unfortunately, too much of Mister Roberts has not aged well....has its moments...And Mister Roberts is still attractive as the quintessential nice guy. But, despite the determined efforts of the cast, this production failed to breathe new energy into the play. About the only thing live was the transmission, and that just isn't enough. It never was."* (John J. O'Connor, The New York Times)

South Pacific opened in 1949 at Broadway's Majestic Theatre. Based by Logan and Oscar Hammerstein II on James Michener's historical novel, *Tales of the South Pacific*, the play starred Mary Martin and Enzio Pinza on opening night, ran for 1,925 performances, and won the Pulitzer Prize. The play and film focused on a beautiful U.S. Navy nurse who is romanced by a French plantation owner on a remote Pacific isle during World War II. A race-relations subtext involves the Navy and Pacific Islanders

South Pacific (1958, Magna Theatre, 171m/c, **VHS/DVD**) ☆☆☆½ **Sc:** Paul Osborn. **D:** Joshua Logan. **P:** Buddy Adler. **Cam:** Leon Shamroy. **Cast:** Mitzi Gaynor, Rosanno Brazzi, John Kerr, Ray Walston, France Nuyen, Juanita Hall, Russ Brown, Jack Mullaney, Ken Clark, Floyd Simmons, Candace Lee, Tom Laughlin, Beverly Aadland, Ron Ely, Archie Savage, Doug McClure, Galvan De Leon. Leon Shamroy's glorious color cinematography of the Hawaiian Islands and a game performance by Gaynor and a raft of memorable tunes—"Bali Ha'I," "Some Enchanted Evening," "My Girl Back Home," and "I'm Gonna Wash That Man Right Out of My Hair"—helped make this a great success, even at its lengthy running time. The film won an Oscar for Best Sound and was nominated for Best Cinematography and Score (Alfred Newman, Ken Darby).

- *"In addition to expanding the play, Paul Osborn's script strikes an effective balance between drama and comedy, romance and realism. Osborn knows when to inject humor in order to lighten a mood, but also when to let the full drama emerge for the greatest impact on the audience. Although much dialogue and action are taken directly from the play, certain scenes have been tightened or their order shifted for a more cohesive, compelling story line. With so many elements involved in the making of the picture, Joshua Logan, who coauthored, staged and directed the play, was the suitable choice for its director. Under his caring, capable control everything fits together neatly, and the film moves along fluidly and briskly—seeming far shorter than its nearly three-hour running time....warm, moving, uplifting. Without preaching, it delivers its message of racial tolerance in an opulent, tuneful production filled with charm and humor."* (Libby Slate, Magill's Survey of Cinema)

Rodgers & Hammerstein's South Pacific (2001, ABC, 129m/c) ☆☆½ **Sc:** Lawrence D. Cohen. **D:** Richard Pearce. **P:** Christine A. Sacani.

Cast: Glenn Close, Harry Connick Jr., Jack Thompson, Natalie Jackson Mendoza, Rade Serbedgia, Lori Tan Chinn, Ilene Graff, Simon Burke, Justin Smith, Steve Bastoni, Kimberly Davies, Craig Bell, Ashley Lyons. Close gave it a hearty try, but by 2001 she seemed a bit long in the tooth (54) for this sort of thing.

- *"The tunes are much too good. Yet...often no enchanted evening. Stage shows haven't often transferred well or even interestingly to filmdom, Hair and Jesus Christ Superstar being a pair of exceptions. South Pacific isn't one, a 1958 movie version, with Josh Logan moving behind the camera after directing the show on Broadway, coming up short. Also unevenly successful is this new South Pacific...begins wandering as if lost in the jungle, ceasing to be a musical and instead becoming a tuneless, unrewarding war movie, as if Rodgers and Hammerstein were known for battle scenes instead of plays with indelible melodies and lyrics."* (Howard Rosenberg, Los Angeles Times)

Anita Loos

Born: April 26, 1888, Mount Shasta (Sissons), CA. **Died:** 1981.

Anita Loos wrote or participated in the writing of at least 100 movies for the Biograph Co., going back to company founder D.W. Griffith's *The Musketeers of Pig Alley* (1912). In the silent era, her films included *The New York Hat* (1912), *The Hunchback* (1914), *The Deacon's Whiskers* (1915), *Intolerance* (1916), *The Americano* (1916), *Let's Get a Divorce* (1918), *A Virtuous Vamp* (1919), *Red Hot Romance* (1923), and *Dulcy* (1924). She and her husband, John Emerson, contributed scenarios to Douglas Fairbank's films. In the sound era she wrote *Hold Your Man* (1933) with Jean Harlow and Clark Gable, *Biography of a Bachelor Girl* (1935), *Riffraff* (1936), *San Francisco* (1936), *The Women* (1939), *Susan and God* (1940), and *Blossoms in the Dust* (1941). All of her Broadway plays except *Cheri* were adapted for films. *Gentlemen Marry Brunettes*, the follow-up novel to her wildly successful *Gentlemen Prefer Blondes* (see below), was adapted into a 1955 film starring Jane Russell and Jeanne Crain.

The Fall of Eve (1929, Columbia, 67m/bw) ☆☆ **Sc:** Fanny Hatton, Frederic Hatton, Gladys Lehman. **D:** Frank R. Strayer. **Cam:** Ted Tetzlaff. **Cast:** Patsy Ruth Miller, Ford Sterling, Gertrude Astor, Arthur Rankin, Jed Prouty, Betty Farrington, Fred Kelsey, Hank Mann. The 1926 play, which Loos co-wrote with John Emerson, starred Ruth Gordon on Broadway at the Booth Theatre. One of Columbia's first talking pictures, it concerns marital mistaken identity, but was directed as if the vocal volume were its main subject.

- *"It is a film in which the producers reveal an overwhelming fondness for sound in stentorian volume. And most of the players were equipped with lung power sufficient to meet the desires of the director…It is true that this film has a certain quality of mirth, but how welcome would be an occasional whisper or a soft voice….The dialogue…while it is nothing brilliant, nothing suave or subtle, it often opens up the way to ludicrous incidents….One might say that all the voices…seem to have been treated for carrying power rather than for any tonal nuances."* (Mordaunt Hall, The New York Times)

Gentlemen Prefer Blondes was adapted by Loos from her own novel. It opened on Broadway in 1926 with a cast including June Walker, Katherine Brook, Vivian Purcell, and Grace Hampton. Loos then adapted the material with Joseph Fields into the book for the 1949 Broadway musical starring Carol Channing as Lorelei Lee. Channing reprised the role in the retooled 1974 musical, called *Lorelei*, at Broadway's Palace Theatre. In 1995, K.T. Sullivan played Lorelei Lee in still another rendition, its title returned to *Gentlemen Prefer Blondes*.

Gentlemen Prefer Blondes (1928, Paramount, 75m/bw/silent) ☆☆☆½
Sc: Herman J. Mankiewicz. **D:** Malcolm St. Clair. **P:** Richard Blaydon. **Cam:** Harold Rosson. **Cast:** Ruth Taylor, Alice White, Ford Sterling, Holmes Herbert, Mack Swain, Emily Fitzroy, Trixie Friganza, Blanche Frederici, Eugene Borden, Margaret Seddon, Luke Cosgrave, Chester Conklin, Edward Faust, Yorke Sherwood, Mildred Boyd.

• *"…a splendid pictorial translation…The 'refined' Lorelei is impersonated by Ruth Taylor, who fits Miss Loos's description of her young heroine in surprising fashion….This film is an infectious treat, Malcolm St. Clair has given it just the right touch. The adaptation and the titles were furnished by Miss Loos, and the producers will be forced to admit for once that the co-operation of the author has been of immense assistance."* (Mordaunt Hall, The New York Times)

Gentlemen Prefer Blondes (1953, 20th Century-Fox, 91m/c, VHS/DVD) ☆☆☆½ **Sc:** Charles Lederer. **D:** Howard Hawks. **P:** Sol C. Siegel. **Cam:** Harry J. Wild. **Cast:** Marilyn Monroe, Jane Russell, Charles Coburn, Elliott Reid, Tommy Noonan, George Winslow, Marcel Dalio, Taylor Holmes, Norma Varden, Howard Wendell, Steven Geray, Harry Carey Jr., George Chakiris, Robert Fuller, Larry Kert, Bess Flowers. A huge hit, this glossy soufflé helped confirm Monroe's talent and potent box-office status and reaffirmed Hawks's golden touch.

• *"Some of the East Coast reviews were a bit sniffy about the vulgarization of the material and its having 'gone Hollywood,' but even the starchiest observers had to admit that the gals had something going for them and that Monroe actually might have some talent. It has always been challenging for critics to fit the film into the context of Hawks's career, other than as an example of his extraordinary versatility and his abilities as an entertainer….Ultimately the film can be enjoyed for its very 'unreality' and, of course, for its two lead performances, the musical numbers, and its sheer mythic and camp value." (Todd McCarthy, Howard Hawks: The Gray Fox in Hollywood)*

Gigi (1958, MGM, 119m/c, **VHS/DVD**) ☆☆½ **Sc:** Alan Jay Lerner, Anita Loos (uncredited). **D:** Vincente Minnelli, Charles Waters (uncredited). **P:** Arthur Freed. **Cam:** Joseph Ruttenburg, Ray June (uncredited). **Cast:** Leslie Caron, Louis Jourdan, Maurice Chevalier, Hermione Gingold, Jacques Bergerac, Eva Gabor, Isabel Jeans, John Abbott, Richard Bean, Maurice Marsac, Edwin Jones, Monique Van Vooren. Loos adapted her play from the French novel by Colette, and Audrey Hepburn starred in the 1951 comedy at Broadway's Fulton Theatre. A Parisian virgin is schooled to be a courtesan and her eagerness gets her the richest catch in town. Minnelli's smoothness with the practiced Freed Unit at MGM musicalized the material, making everything look sumptuous and eye-fillingly grand. But the blinders of the 1950s helped audiences overlook the luridness, even though Chevalier's leering "Thank Heaven for Little Girls" brings home the piece's point. The songs include "The Night They Invented Champagne" and "Ah Yes, I Remember It Well." The film won Oscars for Best Picture, Director, Screenplay, Cinematography, Art Direction/Set Decoration, Song ("Gigi"), Score (Andre Previn), Film Editing, and Costumes.

- *"The prize of the era...the capstone of MGM's so-called golden age and one Arthur Freed film that actually exceeds its reputation. Leslie Caron, so winning in...[other films]...at last lucked into a champion: Minnelli at his most imaginative..." (Ethan Mordden, The Hollywood Musical)*

- *"...they've come up with a musical film that bears such a basic resemblance to [the stage version of] My Fair Lady that the authors may want to sue themselves....all in the spirit of good, racy, romantic fun...a charming entertainment that can stand on its own two legs. It is not only a charming comprehension of the spicy confection of Colette, but it is also a lovely and lyrical enlargement upon that story's flavored mood and atmosphere....Perhaps Messrs. Lerner, Loewe and [production designer Cecil] Beaton have stolen Gigi from themselves, but they have no reason to regret or disguise it. They've left their Lady fingerprints for all to see." (Bosley Crowther, The New York Times)*

Happy Birthday (1956, NBC Special, 90m/c) *Producers' Showcase* ☆☆☆ **Tp:** Robert Allsten. **D/P:** Alex Segal. **Cast:** Betty Field, Barry Nelson, Tina Louise, William Harrigan, Enid Markey, Luella Gear, Harry Bellaver, Wynne Gibson, Harold Vermilyen, G. Albert Smith, Parker McCormick. The 1946 Loos play, about a spinster librarian and a bank teller who meet in a Newark bar, and her subsequent crush on him, was played on Broadway by Helen Hayes in a Richard Rodgers and Oscar Hammerstein II production directed by Joshua Logan.

- "...very tepid theatre. The Anita Loos comedy never was much of an example of the art of playwrighting....burdened down with some impossible lines, characterizations and subplots. Its survival depends wholly on the playing of the central role of Addie, the librarian, and Miss Field was perhaps miscast...In appearance and dress she seemed the smartest woman in the tavern, anything but the mousy old maid. Miss Field was not too persuasive in suggesting either the comedy or the poignancy of the plain woman who, under the influence of alcohol finally has her hour as a fairy princess." (Jack Gould, The New York Times)
- "Happy was just such an event for televiewers...served as a joyous vehicle for Betty Field, who gaily romped through the four acts of the Anita Loos play...In her grand tour of acting, Miss Field bridged all the emotional spans with finely shaded performing." (Variety)

The Social Register (1934, Columbia, 71m/bw) ☆☆ **Sc:** Clara Beranger, James Ashmore Creeland. **D:** Marshall Neilan. **Cam:** Merritt B. Gerstad. **Cast:** Colleen Moore, Alexander Kirkland, Charles Winninger, Pauline Frederick, Robert Benchley, Ross Alexander, Margaret Livingston, Mario Braggiotti, Georgette Harvey, Roberta Robinson, Jacques Fray, John Miltern. The 1931 play, co-written and co-directed by Loos and John Emerson at Broadway's Fulton Theatre, featured Sidney Blackmer. A chorus girl counters the prejudices of her boyfriend's family.

- "Good players lost in a trite story." (Variety)

The Whole Town's Talking was a 1923 play about a war veteran who's about to inherit a fortune. To make him seem more attractive, his potential future father-in-law spreads the story that he once romanced a popular film star, who happens to show up in town with her jealous husband. Starring in the original Broadway cast were Alice and Violet Dunn and Grant Mitchell. The 1935 John Ford/Edward G. Robinson film of the same name wasn't based on this play.

The Whole Town's Talking (1926, Universal, bw/silent) ☆☆☆ **Sc:** Raymond Cannon. **D:** Edward Laemmle. **Cam:** Charles J. Stumar. **Cast:** Edward Everett Horton, Virginia Lee Corbin, Trixie Friganza, Otis Harlan, Robert Ober, Aileen Manning, Hayden Stevenson, Margaret Quimby, Dolores Del Rio, Malcolm Waite, August Tollaire. Horton, in one of his last starring roles, was cast as a character who must avoid all excitement, because a war wound left him with a steel plate in his head.

- "...a racy farce with slapstick climax, confidently directed by Edward Laemmle, and well performed..." (Clive Hirschhorn, The Universal Story)

Ex-Bad Boy (1931, Universal, 78m/bw) ☆☆ **Sc:** Fred Niblo Jr., Dale Van Every. **D:** Vin Moore. **Cam:** Jerome Ash. **Cast:** Robert Armstrong, Jean Arthur, Jason Robards Sr., Spencer Charters, Grayce Hampton,

Lola Lane, George Brent, Mary Doran, Grace Cunard, Edward Hearn, Eddie Kane, Tony Stabeneau. An eclectic cast was convened for this schematic and unconvincing nonsense.

- *"...sluggish comedy comprising Jason Robards's attempts to quash an affair between Jean Arthur and Robert Armstrong." (Clive Hirschhorn, The Universal Story)*

Craig Lucas

Born: April 30, 1951, Devon, PA.

Craig Lucas's recent plays include *Three Postcards*. He adapted Jane Smiley's novel *The Age of Grief* into the Alan Rudolph-directed film *The Secret Lives of Dentists* (2002) starring Campbell Scott and Hope Davis. In the 1970s, Lucas performed in the Broadway productions of *Shenandoah*, *Rex*, *On the Twentieth Century*, and *Sweeney Todd*. In 1980, he and director Norman Rene conceived *Marry Me a Little*, a revue of songs dropped from Stephen Sondheim musicals.

Blue Window (1987, PBS, 120m/c) *American Playhouse* ☆☆☆½ **Sc:** Craig Lucas. **D:** Norman Rene. **P:** Lindsay Law. **Cast:** Randy Danson, Matt Craven, Jane Galloway, Margo Skinner, Brad O'Hare, Maureen Silliman, Larry Joshua. The 1984 Off Broadway original traveled to the West Coast where it won the Los Angeles Drama Critics Award for Best Play. It concerns a group of young New Yorkers before, during, and after a tortuous Sunday night dinner party in one of their homes. All but one of the original actors are in the film.

- *"Though the play's West Coast production attracted several movie producers, Mr. Lucas balked at their offers; he didn't feel it could be filmed properly without the help of Mr. Rene. 'Because it was a theatre piece in which seven people talked at the same time, I didn't think it could be done without splitting the screen into seven sections, and that would have been silly,' Mr. Lucas said. 'Then Lindsay Law...approached the two of us with the idea of filming the play for the record. But Norman became intrigued with the idea of making a real film. We managed to preserve some of the simultaneity by overlapping the dialogue, braiding it with various environments, and all of it edited in rapid juxtaposition.'" (Stephen Holden, The New York Times)*

Longtime Companion (1990, PBS, 100m/c, **VHS/DVD**) *American Playhouse* ☆☆☆☆ **Sc:** Craig Lucas. **D:** Norman Rene. **P:** Stan Wlodkowski. **Cast:** Stephen Caffrey, Patrick Cassidy, Brian Cousins, Bruce Davison, John Dossett, Mark Lamos, Dermot Mulroney, Mary-Louise Parker, Michael Schoeffling, Campbell Scott, Robert Joy, Brad O'Hara,

Tanya Berezin, Welker White, Tony Shalhoub. A group of gay men's lives are followed in the early 1980s during the beginnings of the AIDS epidemic. The film was nominated for an Oscar for Best Supporting Actor (Davison).

- *"The movie has been written by Craig Lucas as a series of scenes, sometimes separated by months or years, in the lives of several ordinary homosexual men, and it is the very everyday quality of their lives—work and home, love and cooking, and weekends—that provides the bedrock for this film....The central scene in the film—one of the most emotionally affecting scenes in any film on dying—involves Bruce Davison as the lover of a dying man. The struggle has been long and painful...what Davison has to do is hold the hand of his friend and be with him when he dies....it is about the absolute finality of death, but it is also about why we are alive in the first place....Longtime Companion is about friendship and loyalty, about finding the courage to be helpful, and the humility to be helped."* (Roger Ebert, Chicago Sun-Times)

Prelude to a Kiss (1992, 20th Century-Fox, 105m/c, **VHS/DVD**) ☆☆ **Sc:** Craig Lucas. **D:** Norman Rene. **P:** Michael Gruskoff, Michael I. Levy. **Cam:** Stefan Czapsky. **Cast:** Meg Ryan, Alec Baldwin, Sydney Walker, Ned Beatty, Patty Duke, Kathy Bates, Stanley Tucci, Rocky Carroll, Debra Monk, Ray Gill, Annie Golden, Fern Persons, Richard Riehle. The play received its debut performance at the South Coast Repertory Theatre in Costa Mesa, California, in 1988, and moved to Broadway in 1990 with Timoth Hutton, Mary-Louise Parker, and Barnard Hughes. Baldwin also played the part on Broadway; as a writer who marries a bartender and realizes that, after an obligatory wedding kiss with an old man, she isn't the woman he thought she was.

- *"It's Beauty and the Beast with a wicked twist, in which Beauty becomes a beast and it's a prince of love, not Beauty's, that is put to the test....The novelist Thorne Smith once used such gender switches for gently ribald comic effect, especially in* Turnabout. *Mr. Lucas is interested in more serious things, though he doesn't entirely dismiss the humor....The sad news about this movie adaptation is that it functions as a cruel critique of the problems that, for whatever reason, did not seem important in the stage production....is not only without charm and wit, but it's also clumsily set forth; many people seeing it may wonder what, in heaven's name, is going on....The same dialogue that served well enough on the stage now sounds arch and coy and metaphysically flat."* (Vincent Canby, The New York Times)

Reckless (1995, Goldwyn, 100m/c, **VHS**) ☆☆½ **Sc:** Craig Lucas. **D:** Norman Rene. **P:** Amy J. Kaufman, Lindsay Law. **Cam:** Frederick Elmes. **Cast:** Mia Farrow, Scott Glenn, Mary-Louise Parker, Nancy Marchand, Stephen Dorff, Eileen Brennan, Giancarlo Esposito, Tony

Goldwyn, Deborah Rush, Debra Monk, William Fichtner. The play was initially staged by the South Coast Reperatory in Costa Mesa, California, in 1984. It concerns a woman whose deluded existence spirals into chaos after her husband tells her that he has hired a hit man to kill her during the Christmas holidays.

- "...a fantastical meditation on holidays and forgetfulness and fact-facing and denial, and a disorienting and disturbing film. It doesn't do, exactly, what Home for the Holidays does for Thanksgiving; what writer Craig Lucas and director Rene are after is far darker and morose....It's not a pleasant film, but in its challenging way it makes us look at ourselves a bit differently and it certainly puts a spin on Christmas....Farrow...is quite affecting as Rachel because she mixes vulnerability and self-absorption as few others can." (John Anderson, Los Angeles Times)

Charles MacArthur

Charles Gordon MacArthur
Born: November 5, 1895, Scranton, PA. **Died:** 1956.

Charles MacArthur is best known as one half the legendary writing team he completed with Ben Hecht, and secondarily as the husband of Helen Hayes, the "first lady of the American theatre." The writing pair's barbs, rejoinders, and banter, often using insinuating innuendo, usually came with more sophistication and wit than anyone else's. As Rick Broussard wrote about MacArthur's influence, "He participated in the artistic cross-fertilization of the movie-mills and the New York theatrical dynasty, bringing to each a sensibility of impertinent perfectionism."

MacArthur's first produced play was Miss Lulu Belle in 1926, which he wrote with his uncle, Edward Sheldon. Shortly thereafter, he and Sidney Howard collaborated the next year on Salvation. In 1928, he and fellow former Chicago newspaperman Hecht began their collaboration with the time-honored newspaper comedy, The Front Page, which debuted on Broadway in 1930. MacArthur went west and wrote or contributed to nine screenplays produced in 1930 and 1931, including The Sin of Madeline Claudet, for which Hayes won her first Academy Award.

In 1934, he and Hecht formed a production company and wrote the script for Howard Hawks's Twentieth Century (1934), then co-wrote, co-directed, and co-produced four films—Crime Without Passion (1934), Once in a Blue Moon (1935), The Scoundrel (1935, for which they shared the Oscar for Best Original Story), and Soak the Rich (1936)—and collaborated on two of 1939's great films, George Stevens's Gunga Din and William Wyler's Wuthering Heights.

The pair often wrote their own conversations into some of the most sparkling passages the screen ever heard. In all, the Hecht/MacArthur pedigree of originals and adaptations of their own works and others' appeared on more than 30 motion pictures, including five transmutations of *The Front Page*. Without Hecht, MacArthur's films include *The Senator Was Indiscreet* (1947), which he also directed, and *Lulu Belle* (1948) from his play. Books on MacArthur include *Charlie: The Improbable Life and Times of Charles MacArthur* by Hecht in 1957 (the year after the subject's death), and *Front Page Marriage: Helen Hayes and Charles MacArthur* by Jhan Robbins in 1982.

For collaborations with Hecht and the bulk of MacArthur's output, see **Ben Hecht & Charles MacArthur**. The pair flipped a coin early in their careers to see who would get first billing, and the gods chose to keep it alphabetical.

Lulu Belle (1948, Columbia, 86m/bw) ☆☆½ **Sc:** Everett Freeman, Karl Kamb, **D:** Leslie Fenton. **P:** Benedict Bogeaus. **Cam:** Ernest Laszlo. **Cast:** Dorothy Lamour, George Montgomery, Albert Dekker, Glenda Farrell, Otto Kruger, George McClure, Addison Richards, Charlotte Wynters, Clancy Cooper, Harry Hayes Morgan, Ben Erway, John Indrisano, Bud Wiser. A young lawyer in Natchez, Mississippi, rejects Lulu Belle, his fiancée, when he sees her singing in a dive. He then follows her to a New Orleans club where, in a rage, he stabs a rival in the face with a handful of forks and gets sent to prison. Lulu Belle drifts to New York, where she improbably realizes her heart belongs back in Natchez.

- "... *corny melodrama* ..." (*David Shipman*, The Great Movie Stars 1: The Golden Years)

Archibald MacLeish

Born: May 7, 1892, Glencoe, IL. **Died:** 1982.
Pulitzer Prize-winning play: *J.B.* (1959)

The two-time Pulitzer Prize-winning poet for *Conquistador* (1932) and *Collected Poems 1917–1952* (1952) never saw his Pulitzer Prize-winning verse play, *J.B.*—about Job's travails in a modern setting and idiom—adapted for films or TV. His other plays in verse include *Panic*, *The Fall of the City*, *Air Raid*, and *This Music Crept by Me Upon the Waters*. MacLeish dabbled in films and TV, contributing to *The Spanish Earth* (1937), Joris Ivins's left-wing documentary on the Spanish Civil War that also involved fellow writers Ernest Hemingway, John Dos Passos, Lillian Hellman, Orson Welles, and Prudencio de Pereda; writing the Oscar-nominated 1950 short, *Grandma Moses*; and writing the teleplay for a 1960 *Sunday Showcase* presentation of *The Secret of Freedom*, starring Thomas Mitchell and Kim Hunter.

An Evening's Journey to Conway, Massachusetts (1967, NET, 60m/c) *NET Playhouse* ☆☆☆ **Tp/Narrator:** Archibald MacLeish. **D:** John Desmond. **P:** Jac Venza. **Cast:** Gary Burghoff, Howard Lemay, Paul Benedict, Harriet Rogers, Royal Beal, John McQuade, George Mathews, Edgar Stehli. MacLeish donated this play to his hometown in western Massachusetts during its bicentennial celebration. A teenager who couldn't care less about Conway is taken back through the town's history while significant figures in that history — including Marshall Field, the Chicago merchant — tell him what the town meant to them.

• *"An ennobling appreciation of what the vanishing small town meant for so many years to America...Mr. MacLeish was reminding everyone of the value of roots....As it was, the recourse to the dramatic form was probably much better suited to a village celebration than to the video stage....only occasionally did these soliloquies achieve a moving eloquence. The presence of a representative of today's youth in the midst of the past was very distractingly handled."* (Jack Gould, The New York Times)

David Mamet

Born: November 30, 1947, Chicago, IL.
Pulitzer Prize-winning play: *Glengarry Glen Ross* (1984)

David Mamet is the most prominent American playwright to find film and television as satisfying venues as the stage, and has successfully used all three media to play out his dramas of intellectual deception. While writing screenplays and teleplays for others to direct, he has also built an eclectic body of work as a director of his own work. Profane, off the beaten track, and innovative in their swindles, these films include *House of Games* (1987), *Things Change* (1988), and *Homicide* (1991) — all starring Joe Mantegna — along with the ensemble pieces *The Spanish Prisoner* (1997), *State and Main* (2000), and *The Heist* (2001).

His movies written for others include Bob Rafelson's *The Postman Always Rings Twice* (1981), Sidney Lumet's *The Verdict* (1982), Brian De Palma's *The Untouchables* (1987), Danny De Vito's *Hoffa* (1992), Barry Levinson's *Wag the Dog* (1997), and John Frankenheimer's *Ronin* (1998) under the pseudonym of Richard Weisz. Mamet was Oscar nominated for *The Verdict* and *Wag the Dog*.

Mamet's TV work includes a 1991 adaptation of Anton Chekhov's *Uncle Vanya* with David Warner; the 1992 adaptation of his own radio play, *The Water Engine*, about a 1930s inventor whose titular discovery leads to a proposed buyout by sinister big-money interests; and *Lansky* (1999), a cable biopic of racketeer Meyer Lansky. *Dark Pony*, about a woman who confronts her alcoholic father, was presented on Showtime in 1981 starring Lindsay Crouse, who also starred in the superb *House of Games*.

About Last Night... (1986, MGM, 113m/c, **VHS/DVD**) ☆☆☆ **Sc:** Tim Kazurinsky, Denise DeClue. **D:** Edward Zwick. **P:** Jason Brett, Stuart Oken. **Cam:** Andrew Dintenfass. **Cast:** Rob Lowe, Demi Moore, Jim Belushi, Elizabeth Perkins, George DiCenzo, Robin Thomas, Michael Alldredge, Donna Gibbons, Megan Mullally, Sachi Parker, Rosanna DeSoto. This is the film version of Mamet's hit play, *Sexual Perversity in Chicago*, which brought him his first widespread fame when it was originally staged in 1974. Of the play, Mamet has said, "Voltaire said words were invented to hide feelings. That's what the play is about."

• *"How on Earth can you make a movie out of David Mamet's bleak, bristling, hilariously foul-mouthed play* Sexual Perversity in Chicago? *Well, a group of young Chicagoans...have done it, and in the process have come up with one of the best American films of the year.* About Last Night...*will outrage many of Mamet's fans, who will accuse the movie of sentimentalizing the most savagely antisentimental dramatist of our time. But the filmmakers have understood that Mamet's 1974 play...was less a merciless anatomy of the death of love than a merciful lament for its demise....Zwick beautifully handles his appealing cast...Demi Moore...is a joy to watch....Belushi becomes the Falstaff of singles bars."* (Jack Kroll, Newsweek)

American Buffalo (1996, Goldwyn, 88m/c, **VHS/DVD**) ☆☆☆ **Sc:** David Mamet. **D:** Michael Corrente. **P:** Samuel Goldwyn. **Cam:** Richard Crudo. **Cast:** Dustin Hoffman, Dennis Franz, Sean Nelson. A junk shop owner conspires to steal back a rare coin that he lost in a swindle with the help of a teenage boy, despite the interference of an arrogant card-playing pal. The actors put the material over. Robert Duvall, Kenneth McMillan, and John Savage were in the 1977 Broadway debut, and the 1983 revival starred Al Pacino with James Hayden and J.J. Johnston.

• *"...the direction by Michael Corrente, who seems not so much in charge of his material as deeply in awe of it. There's something cramped and stage-struck about the film, as there was with James Foley's attempt at* Glengarry Glen Ross; *in both cases, I came out of the cinema in need of fresh air. Mamet fans will contend that claustrophobia is part of the deal, but his best lines are meant to coil round your throat."* (Anthony Lane, The New Yorker)

Glengarry Glen Ross (1992, New Line, 100m/c, **VHS**) ☆☆☆☆ **Sc:** David Mamet. **D:** James Foley. **P:** Jerry Tokofsky, Stanley R. Zupnik. **Cam:** Juan Ruiz Anchia. **Cast:** Al Pacino, Jack Lemmon, Ed Harris, Alan Arkin, Kevin Spacey, Alec Baldwin, Jonathan Pryce, Bruce Altman, Jude Ciccolella. The powerhouse cast seizes the inherent kick and fire in Mamet's portrayal of 24 hours in the life of a Chicago real estate office, where the head honchos intend to pick up the pace by offering the top salesman a new Cadillac and new leads, then giving the number two achiever a set of steak knives — and showing all the rest to the door. Lemmon and Pacino delivered performances that are among their finest as, respectively, Shelley "The Machine" Levine and Ricky Roma. The whole cast was excellent. The 1984 Broadway effort starred Joe Mantegna, Robert Prosky, J.T. Walsh, James Tolkin, Lane Smith, Jack Wallace, and Mike Nussbaum.

- *"In reimagining* Glengarry Glen Ross *as a film, Mamet...and director James Foley have slowed the pace, subdued the humor, and emphasized the pathos....Ed Harris and Alan Arkin do well with comparatively underwritten roles....Lemmon strains to display his character's humanity, never letting the audience forget that this is Jack Lemmon giving a powerhouse performance as a weakling....The most impressive performers...are Jonathan Pryce and Al Pacino....His Ricky Roma is...one of Pacino's most powerful performances....*Glengarry Glen Ross *has perhaps been overpraised because so few American films have dealt with the despair of modern life so unflinchingly. Yet Foley's execution of this theme is too often obvious and pedestrian. In the...films that he has both written and directed, Mamet himself has proven to have more cinematic skill than Foley demonstrates here. While Mamet's* Homicide (1991) *is depressing yet exhilarating,* Glengarry Glen Ross *is merely sad." (Michael Adams, Magill's Survey of Cinema)*

A Life in the Theater is a two-person interchange between a hammy old stage actor and his young protégé. As the student becomes older, more skilled and confident, the star of the elder half of the team starts to fade. Mamet wrote it when he was 25 years old and it has endured as a seminal two-character theatrical exercise. The play debuted in New York at the Theatre de Lys in 1977 featuring Peter Evans and Ellis Rabb.

A Life in the Theater (1979, PBS, 90m/c) *Great Performances* ☆☆☆☆ **D:** Kirk Browning, Gerald Gutierrez. **P:** Peter Weinberg. **Cast:** Peter Evans, Ellis Rabb. This bare-bones piece recorded the Broadway originators of the roles going through their paces on San Francisco locations, including the Geary and Kurran theatres.

- *"...a funny, touching, searing portrait of that special ego-obsessed specimen, the actor....They climb in and out of costumes, throwing themselves with scene-stealing gusto into a series of stage performances, allowing Mr. Mamet to spoof Shakespeare, Chekhov, Noël Coward, and a host of pop-*

ular favorites….Mr. Mamet maintains a nicely effective tension between the dreams and the reality." (John J. O'Connor, The New York Times)

A Life in the Theater (1993, TNT, 78m/c, **VHS**) ☆☆☆☆ **Tp:** David Mamet. **D:** Gregory Mosher. **P:** Thomas A. Bliss, Patricia Wolff. **Cast:** Jack Lemmon, Matthew Broderick. This starry acting exercise led to an Emmy nomination for Broderick and a Golden Globe nomination for Lemmon. Mosher, who directed the original play, opened it up with scenes in a gym, bar, hotel, cemetery, and apartment.

- *"…Mamet's taut look at the bittersweet bond…remains as funny and as tender as ever, thanks to triumphant performances by Jack Lemmon and Matthew Broderick. This is one of Lemmon's finest hours. If you've ever thought of Lemmon as a ham, for better or worse, here's a script that uses that quality for all it's worth….Even in the offstage scenes, Lemmon declaims more than his character did in Mamet's original play, thanks to a stock of fancy quotations that Mamet has added to his lines. But Lemmon doesn't lose sight of the man's loneliness—or his integrity." (Don Shirley, Los Angeles Times)*

Oleanna (1994, Goldwyn, 90m/c, **VHS**) ☆☆☆ **Sc/D:** David Mamet. **P:** Sarah Green, Patricia Wolff. **Cam:** Andrzej Sekula. **Cast:** William H. Macy, Debra Eisenstadt, Scott Zigler. A college student accuses one of her professors of sexual harassment, and they debate both sides of the inflammatory issue in a wending and heated conversation set mostly in his office. The excellent performances, Mamet's customarily provocative language, and the red-hot subject make for a fully engrossing experience.

- *"The best part of this invigorating and exasperating film…happens when it's over. No insult intended. It's just that debating the meaning of this sexual bonfire of the vanities with the person you see it with is half the fun. In adapting and directing his two-character drama, Mamet loses some theatrical immediacy but none of his wicked, ferocious talent to provoke….Oleanna shakes up audiences like no movie in years." (Peter Travers, Rolling Stone)*

The Water Engine (1992, TNT, 110m/c, **VHS**) ☆☆½ **Tp:** David Mamet. **D:** Steven Schachter. **P:** Donald P. Borchers, Michael Brandman. **Cast:** Joe Mantegna, John Mahoney, Charles Durning, William H. Macy, Patti LuPone, Joanna Miles, Treat Williams, Mike Nussbaum. Although Mamet wrote this piece as a radio play and it was performed as such, it was eventually produced onstage by the St. Nicholas Theatre Company in Chicago in 1977 with a cast including William H. Macy and Gail Silver. It concerns the fate of one Charles Lang, played by Macy, who invents an engine that runs on water in Depression-era Chicago.

- *"…produces more smoke than energy…plenty of period flavor, with tunes of the time crooned from a radio, a glimpse inside a dime-a-dance joint and snatches of soapbox speechifying. But most of these 90 minutes are devoted to comic book characters acting out a tale whose essential simple-minded-ness is visible through the allegorical fog....Mr. Mantegna's oily perform-ance behind spectacles, high collar, silk scarf and an indeterminate accent, owes a lot to Saturday serials of the 1930s. And so does the plot." (Walter Goodman, The New York Times)*

Bill Manhoff

Born: 1919, Newark, NJ.

A radio and television writer, Bill Manhoff was a graduate of City College of New York who later in life raised Siamese cats in Palm Springs, California. *The Owl and the Pussycat* was his only Broadway play.

The Owl and the Pussycat (1970, Columbia, 96m/c, **VHS/DVD**) ☆☆
Sc: Buck Henry. **D:** Herbert Ross. **P:** Ray Stark. **Cam:** Harry Stradling. **Cast:** Barbra Streisand, George Segal, Robert Klein, Allen Garfield (Goorwitz). A bookshop clerk who fancies himself a writer meets a hooker who fancies herself as a model. As they peel away layers of clothing, they also peel away their characters' facades. The theatrical original had the extra twist of being an interracial exchange. The New York original starred Alan Alda and Diana Sands in a 1964 production at the ANTA Theatre. Streisand's involvement changed the nature and texture of the material considerably.

- *"If computers ever turn out romantic comedies, the results would look like this....She really ought to be called Barbra Strident. She comes on harsh and grating, seeking to win us by being unabashed about seeking to win us. One reason she does it, I think, is panic....In her latest comedy, increas-ingly desperate, she leans on all the crassness she considers sure-fire, like a comic running out of material who can at least drop his pants." (Stanley Kauffmann, The New Republic)*

Emily Mann

Born: April 12, 1952, Bostron, MA.

A director as well as a playwright, Emily Mann has staged such classics as *The Glass Menagerie* and *Hedda Gabler* in addition to her own plays and those by Ntozake Shange and Anna Deavere Smith, among others. Mann's plays often take a documentary-like approach to historical events, such as her *Annulla Allen: An Autobiography* (1977), about a Holocaust survivor; *Still Life* (1980), about a Vietnam War veteran; and

Greensboro: A Requiem (1996), based on the actual 1979 murders of five activists protesting Ku Klux Klansmen and neo-Nazis in North Carolina.

Execution of Justice (1999, Showtime, 98m/c, **VHS**) ☆☆☆☆ **Tp:** Michael Butler. **D:** Leon Ichaso. **P:** Jeff Frellich. **Cast:** Tim Daly, Peter Coyote, Steven Young. Amy Van Nostrand, Khalil Kain, Frank Pellegrino, Trulie McLeod, Shannon Hile, Richard Blackburn, Lisa Rhoden. Mann's 1986 Broadway play, which she directed, starred John Spencer as Dan White, Mary McDonnell, Donal Donnelly, Stanley Tucci, and Wesley Snipes as Sister Boom Boom. Her work was based on the life of San Francisco Supervisor White, who shot and killed openly gay fellow Supervisor Harvey Milk and the city's mayor, George Moscone, in November 1978. White was convicted of involuntary manslaughter and served less than six years, committing suicide eight months after his release. The Oscar-winning documentary, *The Life and Times of Harvey Milk* (1984), covers the same subject.

• *"...intelligent, effective drama...Mr. Daly...gives White a crazy, almost blank stare in all kinds of situations, eyes that convey amorality in a frightening way...Peter Coyote is also wonderful as Milk." (Anita Gates, The New York Times)*

Having Our Say: The Delaney Sisters' First 100 Years (1999, CBS, 100m/c, **VHS**) ☆☆☆½ **Tp:** Emily Mann. **D:** Lynne Littman. **P:** Tony Amatullo. **Cast:** Diahann Carroll, Ruby Dee, Amy Madigan, Lisa Arrindell Anderson, Audra McDonald, Mykelti Williamson, Lonette McKee, Richard Roundtree, Della Reese, Cameron Arnett, Carter Gaston, Micki Grant, Kiara Harris, April Jones, Patty Mack, Bumper Robinson. Based on the book by Sarah L. Delaney, A. Elizabeth Delaney and Amy Hill Hearth, Mann's 1995 play *Having Our Say* premiered at the McCarter Theatre, and was later transferred to Broadway. It was nominated for three Tonys, including Best Play and Best Direction.

• *"In adapting her own play for CBS, Emily Mann rejected her prior, admittedly uncinematic talking-heads approach—cutting away from the aged Delanys to show us their younger selves in flashback. What she seems to have forgotten is that the story didn't capture our hearts so much as the storytellers, and the movie falters whenever they're off screen....Instead of narrative strength, what drives the movie is an increasing desire to spend time with these funny, feisty, enchanting women—so beautifully embodied by Carroll and Dee. The duo could have been unbalanced, but Carroll makes the soft-spoken Sadie hold her own with Dee's louder Bessie. These fine actresses convey the cumulative life experience that resonates through these women's aged voices, a power that's lost when the movie leaves them behind." (Robert Bianco, USA Today)*

Robert Marasco

Born: September 2, 1936, New York, NY. **Died:** 1998.

In addition to *Child's Play*, Robert Marasco's one other screen credit was for *Burnt Offerings* (1976), a horror movie starring Bette Davis in one of her last films.

Child's Play (1972, Paramount, 100m/c) **Sc:** Leon Prochnik. **D:** Sidney Lumet. **P:** David Merrick. **Cam:** Gerald Herschfeld. **Cast:** James Mason, Robert Preston, Beau Bridges, Ronald Weyand, Charles White, Kate Harrington, David Rounds, Jamie Alexander, Brian Chapin, Bryant Fraser. An unpopular disciplinarian schoolmaster at a Catholic boarding school for boys becomes the victim of a plot to discredit him, while the black arts practiced among the boys lead to several mutilations. The play was directed on Broadway by Joseph Hardy in 1970 with a cast featuring Ken Howard, Fritz Weaver, and Pat Hingle. The film was notable for the momentary involvement of Marlon Brando, who was fired by theatrical impressario Merrick. The finished film is heated melodrama.

- *"Unpleasantly tense melodrama, with noisy rattles on the sound track to alert the audience to lurking depravity. Mason's fine performance is marred by an excess of abrupt, badly cropped close-ups." (Pauline Kael, 5,001 Nights at the Movies)*

Donald Margulies

Born: 1954, Brookly, NY.
Pulitzer Prize-winning play: *Dinner With Friends* (2000)

A freelance graphic designer for Hearst Magazines and others, Donald Margulies saw his first play, *Luna Park*, produced in 1982 by the Jewish Repertory Company. His subsequent plays included *Gifted Children*, *Found a Peanut*, *What's Wrong With This Picture?*, *Zimmer*, *Sight Unseen*, *Pitching to the Star*, *The Loman Family Picnic*, *July 7, 1994*, and *Misadventure*. He won the Obie Award for Best Play of 1995 for *The Model Apartment*. Margulies has been the recipient of grants from the Guggenheim Foundation and National Endowment for the Arts. In addition to his work for the stage, Margulies also wrote for the ABC series *Once and Again* and the special *Divorced Kid Blues* (1987).

Collected Stories (2002, PBS, c) **Tp:** Donald Margulies. **D:** Gilbert Cates. **P:** Dennis E. Doty, Gilbert Cates. **Cam:** Robert W. Simmons.

Cast: Samantha Mathis, Linda Lavin. A motherly writing mentor tells an eager apprentice a story in private and it becomes the surprise subject of the younger woman's sensational new novel. Cates directed this cast in the 1999 Geffen Playhouse production in Los Angeles.

• *"In the heated discussion that follows, the issue of ownership of one's 'stories' applies as readily to the parent-child/teacher-student dynamic as to the more obvious type of ethics."* (Daryl H. Miller, Los Angeles Times)

Dinner With Friends (2001, HBO, 94m/c, **VHS/DVD**) ☆☆☆☆ **Tp:** Donald Margulies. **D:** Norman Jewison. **P:** Patrick Markey. **Cast:** Dennis Quaid, Andie MacDowell, Greg Kinnear, Toni Collette, Taylor Emerson, Jake Fritz, Holliston Coleman, Angus T. Jones, Beau Holden, Dina Morrone, Ruth Reichl, Romulo Yanes. A marriage breakup may also break apart a close pair of couples.

• *"...we are all so lucky that HBO has given us a filmed version...four fine actors working on more emotions than you can count. The film...is a model of excellence."* (Anita Gates, The New York Times)

William Mastrosimone

Born: August 19, 1947, Trenton, NJ.

William Mastrosimone has accumulated an eclectic if short list of screen credits, including the film *With Honors* (1994) and the teleplays for *Sinatra* (1992) and director John Frankenheimer's Emmy Award-winning *The Burning Season* (1994), starring Raul Julia as Brazilian rubber tapper and labor leader Chico Mendes.

Bang, Bang, You're Dead (2002, Showtime, 87m/c) ☆☆☆½ **Tp:** William Mastrosimone. **D:** Guy Ferland. **P:** William Mastrosimone, Norman Stephens. **Cam:** Robert Aschmann. **Cast:** Thomas Cavanagh, Ben Foster, Randy Harrison, Janel Moloney, Jane McGregor, David Paetkau, Eric Johnson, Kristian Ayre, Brent Glenen, Gillian Barber, Eric Keenleyside, Glynis Davies, Ryan McDonald, Gary Chalk, Andrew Sabiston, Mitchell Davies, Chad Faust, Mark Holden, Elana Nep. "About a month after the tragedy in Jonesboro, and a week after Springfield," Mastrosimone wrote, "one of my children came home from school and casually mentioned that, upon entering one of his classes, he and other students saw that some anonymous person had written on the blackboard: 'I'm going to kill everyone in this class. And the teacher, too.' Even though the kid who wrote on the blackboard was eventually discovered, I, like every other parent, was shaken to my core because we understood that our kids are no longer safe anywhere; that even though the blackboard phantom said it was a joke, he was copying, he was thinking about it, toying with it, measuring the reaction. That night, unable to sleep, I wrote the first draft of *Bang Bang You're Dead*."

The Beast (1988, Columbia, 111m/c, **VHS/DVD**) ☆☆☆½ **Sc:** William Mastrosimone. **D:** Kevin Reynolds. **P:** John Fiedler. **Cam:** Douglas Milsome. **Cast:** George Dzundza, Jason Patric, Stephen Baldwin, Steven Bauer, Don Harvey, Kabir Bedi, Erick Avari, Chaim Girafi, Shoshi Marciano, David Sherrill, Victor Ken. A cat-and-mouse game of war develops between a Soviet tank crew, led by a tyrant, and a band of Afghan guerrillas during the Soviet/Afghan conflict. The Soviet situation in the film mirrored the American experience in Vietnam.

• "*This visceral action drama was adapted from — believe it or not — a stage play but keeps its feet firmly planted in the war-action genre. Director Kevin Reynolds's second film showcases his aggressive camera work that was featured later, less successfully, in* Robin Hood: Prince of Thieves. *Made directly after the Afghan war, the film was hard to sell in the late 1980s. With the Russians speaking English (and the Afghans their native dialect), the viewer is uncomfortably bonded to the unpopular aggressors. Yet the film reverberates in the sweat and toil of battle, with Patric bringing a more dramatic flair to the role than comes from the usual set of cinematic action heroes.*" (*Doug Thomas,* Amazon.com)

Extremities (1986, Atlantic, 83m/c, **VHS**) ☆☆☆ **Sc:** William Mastrosimone. **D:** Robert M. Young. **P:** Burt Sugarman. **Cam:** Curtis Clark. **Cast:** Farrah Fawcett, James Russo, Diana Scarwid, Alfre Woodard, Sandy Martin, Eddie Velez, Tom Everett, Donna Lynn Leavy, Enid Kent, Micahel Hennessey. A woman's attacker, a day after his initial assault, stalks his victim to her home and tries to attack her again. She fights back and traps him in the fireplace after blinding him with bug spray and scalding him.

• "*Extremities...made a gripping stage play....But it did cross your mind to wonder about the behavior of the heroine's housemates on finding that she had been attacked by an intruder, who was even now corraled in their empty fireplace. This emergency would seem to call for clear-cut action of some sort, particularly with their friend so close to the edge that she is talking about killing the intruder. Instead, the roommates dithered...It was a condescending image...The movie adds a second attempted rape and so should be twice as visceral [as the play]. But observe what this does to the roommate problem. If the heroine's friends know that she has already been attacked in a shopping mall, yet still leave her alone in the house for the day and still behave like idiots when they come home, our attention has got to go to them. Why are they behaving this way? Is it some kind of plot to drive the* heroine, Farrah Fawcett, crazy? Why is she staying with them? Doesn't she have any real friends? Clearly, the screenplay (credited to playwright William Mastrosimone, with 'additional dialogue' by five other people) doesn't have any answers. The camera jumps from one anxious face to another, but we don't know who belongs to each face, and we're about as involved as if this were a cop show. In 'opening up' the story, the movie perversely underlines in crayon what was wrong with the story from the start." (Dan Sullivan, Los Angeles Times)

Edwin Justus Mayer

Born: November 8, 1896, New York, NY. **Died:** 1960.

William Justus Mayer's noteworthy screenplays include those for Dorothy Arzner's *Merrily We Go to Hell* (1932), Henry Hathaway's *Peter Ibbetson* (1935), Cecil B. De Mille's *The Buccaneer* (1938), Mitchell Leisen's *Midnight* (1939), Ernest Lubitsch's *To Be or Not to Be* (1942), and Lubitsch and Otto Preminger's *A Royal Scandal* (1945). Mayer only had a grade-school education, but became a newspaperman and eventually made his way to Hollywood in the silent era as a press agent for Samuel Goldwyn. He wrote titles in the late 1920s and then screenplays, often in collaboration.

Affairs of Cellini (1934, UA, 80m/bw) ☆☆☆½ **Sc:** Bess Meredyth. **D:** Gregory La Cava. **P:** Darryl F. Zanuck. **Cam:** Charles Rosher. **Cast:** Constance Bennett, Fredric March, Frank Morgan, Fay Wray, Jessie Ralph, Lucille Ball, Vince Barnett, Louis Calhern, Jay Eaton, Paul Harvey, Jack Rutherford, Irene Ware, Lionel Belmore, Ward Bond, Lane Chandler, James Flavin. The 1924 play *The Firebrand* starred Edward G. Robinson, Frank Morgan, Joseph Schildkraut, and Nana Bryant in the story of an 18th century womanizing sculptor, the object of his desire, and her jealous husband, the Duke of Florence. Morgan repeated his stage role as this last character in the film, which was a well-received charade. The picture was nominated for Oscars for Best Actor (Morgan), Cinematography, Interior Decoration, and Sound.

- "Benvenuto Cellini, braggart, wastrel and artist, is just the romantic hero of a well costumed musical without the music (here)...Even on the stage...this farcicle account of Florentine life in the days of the Medici was little more than a conventional sex comedy of the bedroom, door-slamming and deceived-husband school, pleasantly decorated by its Renaissance settings and graceful verbiage. In the screen version, carefully acted by such popular performers as Fredric March and Miss Constance

Bennett, it seems to lose some of its grace and dash, if none of its usual visual attractiveness, and emerges something less than a masterpiece of gaiety and wit. As upon the occasion of its stage premiere, it is Frank Morgan, in his original role of the amiably imbecilic Duke of Florence, who walks off with all the acting honors..." (Richard Watts Jr., New York Herald-Tribune)

Carson McCullers

Lula Carson Smith
Born: February 19, 1917, Columbus, GA. **Died:** 1967.

Four of Carson McCullers's five eccentric novels have been adapted into films, with *The Member of the Wedding* being certainly the most successful. *Reflections in a Golden Eye* (1965), about a repressed homosexual Army officer on a Southern base, was converted by director John Huston into an unwieldy smorgasbord of neuroses starring Marlon Brando, Elizabeth Taylor, Julie Harris, and Robert Forster. *The Heart Is a Lonely Hunter* (1968) was another female coming-of-age story in the small-town South, intertwined with the depiction of the hamlet's gentle deaf mute. The perceptive performances of Sondra Locke and Alan Arkin made the material accessible.

   The Ballad of the Sad Cafe (1991), which culminates in a knockdown, dragout fight between Vanessa Redgrave as a hard Southern matron moonshiner and Keith Carradine as her estranged jailbird husband, is certainly the oddest of an odd lot. Edward Albee adapted it into a 1963 play, which Michael Hirst used as the basis for his screenplay (see **Edward Albee**). The one other adaptation of McCullers's prose is the "Dilemma" segment of a made-for-television trilogy movie entitled *Men & Women 2: In Love There Are No Rules* (1991), based on McCullers's short story "A Domestic Dilemma." Ray Liotta played an advertising executive with an alcoholic wife (Andie McDowell) who is under a variety of pressures. McCullers's novel *Clock Without Hands* has yet to be attempted as a film.

The Member of the Wedding was first published as a novel in 1946 and won immediate acclaim in the canons of Southern and coming-of-age fiction. Relating the life and routines of Frankie Addams, a 12-year-old girl in a small Southern town, McCullers illuminates universally human behavior, particularly through Frankie's jealousy of her older brother's pending marriage and the recognition of the passing of adolescence. An instant classic, it coerced the author to become a playwright, and the stage version, starring Harris, Waters, and de Wilde, won the New York Drama Critics Circle Award as the Best Broadway Play of the 1949–50 season.

The Member of the Wedding (1952, Columbia, 91m/bw) ☆☆☆☆ **Sc:** Edna and Edwald Anhalt. **D:** Fred Zinnemann. **P:** Stanley Kramer. **Cam:** Hal Mohr. **Cast:** Julie Harris, Ethel Waters, Brandon De Wilde, Arthur Franz, Nancy Gates, James Edwards, William Hansen, Dick Moore, Danny Mummert. Set mostly in a kitchen, the movie resists the "opening up" that so many filmmakers insist is needed in adaptations of so-called static stage plays. Zinnemann relied on the faces of his actors to carry the themes and emotions. Harris received an Oscar nomination for Best Actress.

- *"The film is successful where so many other filmed plays are not, precisely because, in the sensitive hands of director Fred Zinnemann, specifically cinematic devices are exploited in order to achieve dramatic effect. The entire action of the play takes place in the slightly depressing, ramshackle rear kitchen of the Addams house, and it is here — over the kitchen table, near a cupboard, at the sink — that Frankie and Beatrice and John Henry share their confusions and loneliness, young hopes and old memories, childish confusions and odd flashes of maturity and vision. With little modification, the set for the film was built to match the theatre's three-walled set. Only very occasionally do the three characters leave the kitchen, and when they do, it is not simply to open up the movie. Scenarists Edna and Edward Anhalt have gone back to the novel and adapted key scenes (Frankie's attempt to leave with the wedding party, and her journey into town at night), and these illuminate the human tragicomedy which is articulated so delicately in the kitchen conversations."* (Donald Spoto, Stanley Kramer: Filmmaker)

The Member of the Wedding (1958, CBS, 90m/c/live) *The DuPont Show of the Month* ☆☆½ **Tp:** Jacqueline Babbin, Audrey Gellin. **D:** Robert Mulligan. **P:** David Susskind. **Cast:** Collin Wilcox, Dennis Kohler, Claudia McNeil, Larry Wilcox, Crahan Denton, Stanley Greene, Jo Hurt, Claire Griswold, Catherine Ayres.

The Member of the Wedding (1982, NBC, 120m/c/live) *Live Theater Series* ☆☆½ **Tp:** Carson McCullers. **D:** Delbert Mann. **P:** David W. Rintels. **Cast:** Dana Hill, Pearl Bailey, Benjamin Bernouy, Howard E. Rollins Jr., Lane Smith, Dwier Brown, Bill Cobbs, Sherry Hursey. One of Mann's late-career experiments to recreate the vitality of a live feature-length TV production, this version was well-performed by a solid cast.

- *"NBC wanted an American play of stature, and it's a wonderful piece of writing. It's a personal story that's both unique to theater and tailored to the small-screen intimacy of television. Also, to my knowledge, The Member of the Wedding has not been produced since the...1950s, which means there's a whole new audience out there who has never seen it."* (Delbert Mann in The New York Times)

The Member of the Wedding (1997, USA, 93m/c, **VHS**) ☆☆☆☆ **Tp/P:** David W. Rintels. **D:** Fielder Cook. **Cast:** Anna Paquin, Alfre Woodard, Corey Dunn, Enrico Colantoni, Anne Tremko, Matt Mc-Grath, Alfred Wiggins, Joanne Pankow. This version trimmed off the epilogue about what happened to Frankie Addams in later years, and Rintels, who produced the 1982 TV version (above), wrote this one and took it out of the kitchen—it opens at a carnival.

- *"... the heart of the play remains the intense relationships played out between the woman and the children. The splendid cast never misses a beat: Alfre Woodard...Anna Paquin...and Corey Dunn...Nothing momentous happens in* The Member of the Wedding. *It's a collection of small, beautifully realized perceptions. Huddling together for comfort, the unlikely trio sings, quite movingly, "His Eye Is on the Sparrow." It's a lovely miniature, lovingly revived." (John J. O'Connor, The New York Times)*

Gardner McKay

George Cadogan Gardner McKay
Born: June 10, 1932, New York, NY. **D:** 2001.

Gardner McKay was mostly known as a chiseled-featured actor who starred as the skipper of a freelance schooner in the South Pacific for the ABC series *Adventures in Paradise* from 1959 to 1962. He also sustained the adventurer's image in the breezy films *The Pleasure Seekers* (1964) and *I Sailed to Tahiti With an All Girl Crew* (1968). McKay's *Me,* aka *Untold Damage,* debuted as a teleplay in 1971 on PBS's *Hollywood Television Theatre* starring Geraldine Fitzgerald and Richard Dreyfuss in the tale of a supposedly austistic child who is faking the condition.

Sea Marks (1976, PBS, 90m/c, **VHS**) *Theatre in America* ☆☆☆☆ **Tp:** Gardner McKay. **D:** Ronald F. Maxwell, Steven Robman. **P:** Ronald F. Maxwell. **Cast:** George Hearn, Veronica Castang. This is the story of a reclusive Irish fisherman turned poet and the domineering woman who tries to shape his life to fit her own. This 1976 Manhattan Theatre Club production was opened up by the co-directors with some travelogues shot in Ireland and Liverpool.

- *"The sheer audacity (some might call it gall) of taking a fragile, two-character play like Gardney McKay's Sea Marks and letting it run loose on the beaches of Ireland and the streets of Liverpool is surprisingly well-rewarded...If these are diversions, at least they are artful—and they help to strengthen McKay's story....perfectly cast. George Hearn is so true as the stiff and guileless fisherman-turned-poet that he manages the almost impossible task of communicating his soul-deep love for the sea without striking a false note....Veronica Castang's Timothea is a more complicated character, to which she devotes an amazing amount of subtle energy." (Dick Adler, Los Angeles Times)*

Terrence McNally

Born: November 3, 1939, St. Petersburg, FL.
Tony Award-winning plays: *Love! Valour! Compassion!* (1995), *Master Class* (1996)

Along with his Tony Awards for Best Play, Terrence McNally also won the Tony Award for Best Book of a Musical in 1993 for *Kiss of the Spider Woman*, based on the 1985 screenplay by Leonard Schrader, which was culled from the Manuel Puig novel. McNally's plays include *And Things That Go Bump in the Night* (1964), *Sweet Eros* (1968), *Botticelli* (1969), *It's Only a Play* (1982), and *Lips Together, Teeth Apart* (1991). Among his TV work is the adaptation of John Cheever's short story "The 5:48" for PBS in 1979 and his original teleplay, *Andre's Mother*, in 1990 for PBS's *American Playhouse* starring Sada Thompson, Sylvia Sidney, and Richard Thomas.

Apple Pie (1968, WNET, 90m/c) *New York Television Theatre* ☆☆☆½
Tp: Terrence McNally. **D/P:** Glenn Jordan. **Cast:** Charlotte Rae, John C. Bocher, James Coco, Kevin O'Connor, Roy London. Three one-act plays—*Tour, Next,* and *Botticelli*—provide stark commentary on the United States's involvement in Vietnam. The first is about Americans touring Italy and their thoughts about being ambassadors of good will. *Next* concerns a draftee feigning illnesses. The third piece features soldiers playing cultural trivia while they smoke pot, waiting for a Viet Cong soldier to emerge from his bunker so they can kill him.

• *"Terrence McNally provided a bitingly original look at some American attitudes toward the war in Vietnam....Tour, was an amusing but chilling vignette about the unreality of trivial daily concerns amid the horrors of war....Next...brilliantly played by James Coco as the man who desperately wants to remain a civilian...The final work—and the most successful in purely dramatic terms—was Botticelli." (George Gent, The New York Times)*

Frankie and Johnny (1991, Paramount, 117m/c, **VHS**) ☆☆☆ **Sc:** Terrence McNally. **D:** Garry Marshall. **P:** Michael Lloyd, Charles Mulvehill, Alexandra Rose. **Cam:** Dante Spinotti. **Cast:** Al Pacino, Michelle Pfeiffer, Hector Elizondo, Kate Nelligan, Nathan Lane, Jane Morris, Greg Lewis, K. Callan, Al Fann, Phil Leeds, Dey Young, Tracy Reiner.

First produced in New York in 1987 with a cast topped by Kathy Bates, McNally's *Frankie and Johnny in the Claire de Lune* told of an ex-con who takes a job as short-order cook and begins to fall in love with the slovenly waitress Frankie. Try as she might, Pfeiffer can't possibly sum up the dowdiness required by the part.

- *"One of the things that Terrence McNally did to adapt his play to film was populate the coffee shop with an array of eccentric secondary characters and give Frankie the requisite sympathetic gay neighbor, perhaps with the hope that Frankie truly is a woman to care about despite her hardened, seemingly impenetrable exterior. The problem, however, is that the writer—or is it the director?—has created clichéd types, not characters. McNally does not breathe life into them as he has with Frankie; the author's obvious love for her is evident in the way in which he understands her fear and her pain. Not even Johnny is sketched with such beautifully precise strokes of sympathy....Pacino offers little nuance or shading to Johnny....Marshall relies on his ace-in-the-hole—the power of Pfeiffer's acting ability—to salvage his otherwise weak story."* (Patricia Kowal, Magill's Survey of Cinema)

Love! Valour! Compassion! (1996, Fine Line, 120m/c, **VHS**) ☆☆☆
Sc: Terrence McNally. **D:** Joe Mantello. **P:** Doug Chapin, Barry Krost. **Cam:** Alik Sakharov. **Cast:** Jason Alexander, John Glover, Stephen Bogardus, Randy Becker, John Benjamin Hickey, Justin Kirk, Stephen Spinella. Eight gay men spend several summer weekends at a Victorian retreat in the country, where the gossip, back-biting, sexual liaisons, cheating, and AIDS issues are as prevalent as they are in the city. Glover repeated his Tony Award-winning stage triumph, playing two wildly different twin brothers. The play was first produced Off Broadway at the Manhattan Theatre Club in 1994, then on Broadway at the Walter Kerr Theatre in 1995 with Glover and Nathan Lane.

- *"... the performances are all, save one, remarkable...As cinema, this is a stodgy affair. And although six of the seven members of the original [stage] cast repeat their roles, the part of Buzz, the outrageously flamboyant musical comedy queen, whooped up memorably by Nathan Lane on Broadway, has been given to Jason Alexander...He has no flair for camp; the body language rings false. Miscast, he's a serious liability, as is Harold Wheeler's unrelentingly treacly musical score."* (Elliott Stein, Village Voice)

The Ritz (1977, Warner Bros., 91m/c, **VHS**) ☆☆☆½ **Sc:** Terence McNally. **D:** Richard Lester. **P:** Denis O'Dell. **Cam:** Paul Wilson. **Cast:** Rita Moreno, Jack Weston, Jerry Stiller, Kaye Ballard, Treat Williams, F. Murray Abraham, Bessie Love, George Coulouris. Called *The Tubs* when it was produced at Yale University Theatre in 1974, *The Ritz* was then revised and performed at New York's Longacre Theatre in 1975 with Rita Moreno as Googie Gomez, the hack singer in a gay New York bathhouse, where a garbage man from Cleveland is trying to hide out from his gangster brother-in-law. Moreno won a Tony for her performance.

- *"... good, unclean, superficial fun. A hip descendant of* Ladies' Night in a Turkish Bath *by way of Feydeu farces, McNally's near nonsensical but ultra-savvy comedy...McNally has 'opened-out' his screenplay just enough to add to the frenetic scrambling in and out of the steam room, countless bedrooms and endless stairways....Best of all, the three delights of the Broadway production — Rita Moreno...Jack Weston...Jerry Stiller...augmented by Kaye Ballard as the garbageman's wife...if prudery bars one from enjoying compassionate jokes about fatties, homosexuals, no-talents and dopes — The Ritz is about as good as old-fashioned lowbrow comedy can get."* (Judith Crist, Saturday Review)

Mark Medoff

Born: March 18, 1940, Mount Carmel, IL.

Mark Medoff's varied screenwriting career includes *Good Guys Wear Black* (1978), *Off Beat* (1986), *Clara's Heart* (1988), *City of Joy* (1992), and *Santa Fe* (1997). He also wrote the 1986 TV movie *Apology*. He occasionally acts in productions of his writing, and directed *Children on Their Birthdays* (2002).

Children of a Lesser God (1986, Paramount, 110m/c, **VHS/DVD**) ☆☆☆☆ **Sc:** Mark Medoff, Hesper Anderson. **D:** Randa Haines. **P:** Burt Sugarman, Patrick Palmer. **Cam:** John Seale. **Cast:** William Hurt, Marlee Matlin, Piper Laurie, Philip Bosco, E. Katherine Kerr, Allison Gompf, John F. Cleary, Philip Holmes, Georgia Ann Cline, William D. Byrd, Frank Carter Jr. John Basinger. Matlin won the Best Actress Oscar and the film was nominated for Best Picture, Actor (Hurt), Supporting Actress (Laurie), and Screenplay. Hurt begins teaching at a school for the deaf and he's popular with the students and faculty, but not with a former student who works at the school as a custodian.

- *"Alas, Haines has escaped all the technical pitfalls of bringing a play to the screen only to succumb to the ethical pitfall. She doesn't trust the movie audience to be as intelligent as the theater audience. She doesn't want to get into Sara's attempt to become a spokesman for the deaf. She doesn't want to end the story on a questioning note but on a happy one. Hollywood, she has told an interviewer, is uncomfortable with ambiguity. Granted, Sara's adventures in politics were the cloudiest scenes in Medoff's original play. (He shares credit with Hesper Anderson for the screenplay but was actually dismissed from the project.) But Sara's entry into political activism was more substantial than the vague business that separates the lovers now — until spring and their equally vague reunion.* Children of a Lesser God *was originally a love story that made you think. Now it's a love story that doesn't want you to think. The final danger of making a play into a movie, it appears, is that it will be a Movie of the Week."* (Dan Sullivan, Los Angeles Times)

Homage (1996, Arrow, 97m/c, **VHS**) ☆☆☆ **Sc:** Mark Medoff. **D:** Ross Kagan Marks. **P:** Mark Medoff, Elan Sassoon. **Cam:** Tom Richmond. **Cast:** Blythe Danner, Frank Whaley, Sheryl Lee, Bruce Davison, Danny Nucci, Bob Goen, Raymond Mesa, Arleen Belkin, Harri James, Leon Cox, Lynsey Taylor, Mark Medoff. This film was based on Medoff's play *The Homage That Follows.*

When You Comin' Back, Red Ryder? (1979, Columbia, 118m/c) ☆☆ **Sc:** Mark Medoff. **D:** Milton Katselas. **P:** Marjoe Gortner. **Cam:** Jules Brenner. **Cast:** Candy Clark, Marjoe Gortner, Lee Grant, Hal Linden, Peter Firth, Pat Hingle, Stephanie Faracy, Dixie Harris, Anne Ramsey, Bill McKinney, Audra Lindley, Alex Colon, Sherry Unger, Mark Medoff, Leon Russell, Joe Hernandez, Tiny Wells, Elaine Story.

- *"Mark Medoff's punchy melodrama about the perversion of American heroic myths packed a dramatic wallop onstage, partly because it was confined to a single, inescapable setting. It should have remained there. Medoff and director Milton Katselas have gone to a great length to make their account 'cinematic'—opening up the story, crosscutting jazzily—but the fancy footwork only accentuates the too obvious mechanics of a well-made play....As the crazed, drug-running catalyst Teddy, Gortner...sends off shock waves of artificial energy...he's a hippy Liberace."* (David Ansen, Newsweek)

Thomas Meehan

Born: August 14, 1932, Ossining, NY.

Thomas Meehan has written the books for three Broadway musical adaptations of movies—*I Remember Mama* (1979), *The Producers* (2001), and *Hairspray* (2002)—and his other notable contribution to the Great White Way was *Ain't Broadway Grand* (1993).

Annie (1982, Columbia, 126m/c, **VHS/DVD**) ☆☆½ **Sc:** Carol Sobieski. **D:** John Huston. **P:** Ray Stark. **Cam:** Richard Moore. **Cast:** Aileen Quinn, Albert Finney, Carol Burnett, Ann Reinking, Tim Curry, Bernadette Peters, Geoffrey Holder, Edward Herrmann, Roger Minami, Lara Berk, April Lerman, Toni Ann Gisondi, Peter Marshall, Loni Ackerman, Lu Leonard, Ken Swofford, Shawnee Smith, Janet Jones, Meredith Salenger. More than $25 million was poured into this lumbering musical, including $6.5 million to acquire the screen rights in the highest sum paid up to that time. Most of the cast acquits itself well, including Burnett as the orphanage harpy and Albert Finney as Daddy Warbucks.

- *"Clearly it was hoped that Annie would repeat the success of* The Sound of Music, *but the score is poor, and the book, based on a comic strip about a cute little orphan in the 1930s, includes such dubious conceits as a singing FDR. There are past examples of prestigious directors failing with the musical form, but Huston had always shown himself able to learn from past mistakes, his own included....he has tried to treat its dull 'book' lightly...The numbers...are memorable only for the inefficiency with which they have been staged...Columbia in desperation advertised the film as 'The musical of Tomorrow'—a reference to its only known song—but it assuredly was not."* (David Shipman, The Story of Cinema)

Annie: A Royal Adventure (1995, BBC, 92m/c, **VHS**) **Tp:** Trish Soodik. **D:** Ian Toynton. **P:** Wendy Dytman. **Cast:** Ashley Johnson, Joan Collins, George Hearn, Ian McDiarmid, Emily Ann Lloyd, Camilla Belle, Crispian Bonham-Carter, Perry Benson, George Wood, David Tsi, Carol Cleveland, Ian Redford, Antony Zaki. This is a British TV version.

Annie (1999, Disney, **VHS/DVD**) ☆☆☆ **Tp:** Irene Mecchi. **D:** Rob Marshall. **P:** John Whitman. **Cast:** Alicia Morton, Kathy Bates, Alan Cumming, Audra McDonald, Kristin Chenoweth, Andria McArdle, Victor Garber, Lalaine, Erin Adams, Sarah Hyland, Marissa Rago, Danelle Wilson, Tom Billett.

Stephen Metcalfe

Born: July 4, 1953, New Haven, CT.

A 1983 recipient of a playwriting grant from the National Endowment for the Arts, Stephen Metcalfe has had four plays produced by the Manhattan Theatre Club, including, *Vikings* (1980), *Emily* (1988), and the two discussed below. His screenplays include those for *Cousins* (1989) starring Isabella Rossellini and based on the French film *Cousin, Cousine* (1976), and *Roommates* (1995) with Peter Falk. He contributed episodes to CBS's *The Comedy Zone* in 1984 and wrote a 1990 TV pilot based on the Tom Hanks film *Turner and Hooch* (1989).

Half a Lifetime (1987, HBO, 60m/c, **VHS**) ☆☆☆☆ **Tp:** Stephen Metcalfe. **D:** Daniel Petrie. **Cast:** Keith Carradine, Gary Busey, Nick Mancuso, Saul Rubinek. This adaptation of Metcalfe's 1983 Off Broadway play is about growing out of youth into middle age, re-evaluating priorities, and accepting that life is a process during a poker game.

- *"Adapted for TV by Stephen Metcalfe from his 1983 Off Broadway play, the drama features dynamite performances by Gary Busey, Saul Rubinek, Keith Carradine and Nick Mancuso and a script that crackles with energy and builds like a poker game—easy-going in the beginning but increasingly tense as the stakes grow higher. A series of revealing moments involving each character represent the successive bids, and they are expertly orchestrated by director Daniel Petrie. And, as in poker, the drama climaxes but doesn't offer resolution. Life goes on after the games—poker or other."* (*Lee Margulies*, Los Angeles Times)

Jacknife (1989, Cineplex Odeon, 102m/c, **VHS**) ☆☆☆☆ **Sc:** Stephen Metcalfe. **D:** David Hugh Jones. **P:** Robert Schaffel, Carol Baum. **Cam:** Brian West. **Cast:** Robert De Niro, Ed Harris, Kathy Baker, Sloan Shelton, Tom Isbell, Loudon Wainwright III, Charles S. Dutton, Jordan Lund. This film is based on Metcalfe's play *Strange Snow*, first produced by the Manhattan Theatre Club in 1982.

- *"... represents a breakthrough...one of the first Vietnam films to suggest that the Vietnam veteran can build on the emotional rubble of the past....The film relies wholly on its characterizations, and the performances by lead actors Robert De Niro, Ed Harris and Kathy Baker give* Jacknife *a poignancy that few Vietnam dramas possess....In their scenes together, De Niro and Baker are like two chords in a well-orchestrated symphony of psychic recovery: Their exchanges have the hesitant stop-flow rhythm of two people acclimating themselves to each other, and they never hit a false note."* (*Michael Banka*, Magill's Survey of Cinema)

Arthur Miller

Born: October 17, 1915, New York, NY.
Pulitzer Prize-winning play: *Death of a Salesman* (1949)
Tony Award-winning plays: *Death of a Salesman, The Crucible* (1953)
New York Drama Critics Circle Best Play: *All My Sons* (1947)

Arthur Miller is perhaps the most quintessentially American playwright of the 20th century. His themes and characters evoke and illuminate national ideas and social trends, most pointedly in his two plays that railed against McCarthyism, *An Enemy of the People* and *The Crucible*. His plays about the Great Depression, *A Memory of Two Mondays* and *The American Clock*, also showed an egalitarian take on American history and a great understanding of the "little guy." A great spiritual scion of early-career Clifford Odets, Miller was treated with respect by television, a medium that was more than kind to his work.

His most enduring "little guy," one that has become a touchstone in our cultural history, is Willy Loman in *Death of a Salesman*, Miller's great masterpiece. It has twice been treated to outstanding TV adaptations. Films have been less kind to Miller, as if he were dragged into the business by his tragic ex-wife, Marilyn Monroe.

13 Miller plays have been adapted for film or TV in nearly two dozen versions, including five of *The Crucible*, four of *Death of a Salesman*, and three of *An Enemy of the People*. But only six of the versions have been converted for home viewing, including both the film and TV renderings of *All My Sons*. Conversely, four of the seven film and TV projects not associated with the stage—that either used his source material or with which he was involved directly as a writer—are available for home viewing. On two of these he received no credit: *The Story of G.I. Joe* (1945) and *Let's Make Love* (1960). The others are *The Misfits* (1961) and *Playing for Time* (1980).

Miller originals that debuted on TV include *Fame* (1978) on *The Hallmark Hall of Fame*, which consisted of four vignettes involving Richard Benjamin as an acclaimed playwright. Miller's 1945 novel, *Focus*, set during the waning months of World War II, concerned a man and his wife who are mistakenly identified as Jews by their anti-Semitic Brooklyn neighbors. Suddenly the victims of religious and racial persecution, they find themselves aligned with a local Jewish immigrant in a struggle for dignity and survival. It was adapted for British TV in 1966 with Joss Ackland and into a 2001 film starring William H. Macy.

After the Fall (1974, NBC, 150m/c) ☆☆☆ **Tp:** Arthur Miller. **D/P:** Gilbert Cates. **Cast:** Christopher Plummer, Faye Dunaway, Bibi Andersson, Nancy Marchand, Mariclare Costello, Lee Richardson, Murray Hamilton, Jennifer Warren, Addison Powell. This was Miller's most controversial play, about a man's guilt and his marriage to a booze-guzzling and pill-popping sexpot. It debuted in 1964, two years after the famously mysterious death of the playwright's troubled wife, Marilyn Monroe. Miller was castigated for sullying the memory of Monroe via the play, which contains much sexual detail and includes aside-confessionals to the audience. The stage debut opened the Lincoln Center Repertory in 1964 and the stellar cast included Jason Robards, Jr. as Quentin, Barbara Loden as Maggie, Faye Dunaway, Hal Holbrook, Mariclare Costello, Salome Jens, Zohra Lampert, Ralph Meeker, David Wayne, and Michael Strong. In this TV production, Plummer played the Miller facsimile, a lawyer named Quentin, and Dunaway starred as the thinly-veiled Monroe figure, Maggie, an internationally known pop singer. Quentin speaks asides to the camera as if it's a friend, and brief background dramatizations are lit and darkened to portray flashes of memories.

- *"Strange, but Miller's plays adapt so well to television they could have been written for this medium....for all its lurid implications, the part of Maggie—the Monroe counterpart—is at the heart of the play. And I think Faye Dunaway playing it is the greatest weakness of the production. I don't believe her. She is always an intelligent actress playing a brainless little trollop...Otherwise, Cates has mounted his production well..."* (Cecil Smith, Los Angeles Times)

All My Sons debuted on Broadway in 1947 with Ed Begley and Arthur Kennedy under the direction of Elia Kazan. Named Best Play of the Year by the New York Drama Critics Circle, it concerns a small-town manufacturer, Joe Keller, whose plant produced defective parts for Air Force warplanes during World War II. They were responsible for killing 20-plus pilots, circumstances that shamed one of Joe's sons into suicide. His other son returns from the war and becomes engaged to the daughter of Joe's partner in profiteering.

All My Sons (1948, Universal, 94m/bw, **VHS**) ☆☆☆½ **Sc/P:** Chester Erskine. **D:** Irving Reis. **Cam:** Russell Metty. **Cast:** Edward G. Robinson, Burt Lancaster, Mady Christians, Howard Duff, Louisa Horton, Frank Conroy, Lloyd Gough, Arlene Francis, Henry Morgan, Elisabeth Fraser. A strong performance by Lancaster as the returning son and Robinson's brilliant turn as the misguided and pathetic father fuel this well-mounted family drama.

- *"While there are scenes of fine indignation...realized to the full by Edward G. Robsinson, Burt Lancaster, Mady Christians and Frank Conroy, they do not offset fabricated situations and blurred characterizations."* (Howard Barnes, New York Herald-Tribune)

- *"Perhaps the movie loses something of Miller's bitter comment on the greed and social irresponsibility of war profiteers, but on the other hand brings the personal narrative into closer focus. A fine cast and Irving Reis's direction contribute to a forceful and often eloquent film..."* (Newsweek)

All My Sons (1986, PBS, 122/c, **VHS**) American Playhouse ☆☆☆½ **D:** Jack O'Brien. **P:** Iris Merlis, Michael Brandman. **Cast:** James Whitmore, Aidan Quinn, Joan Allen, Michael Learned, Zeljko Ivanek, Joanna Miles, Alan Scarfe. O'Brien, at the time the artistic director of San Diego's Old Globe Theater, would later direct Miller's version of Henrik Ibsen's *An Enemy of the People* for *American Playhouse*.

- *"Like Willy Loman, Joe will escape through suicide. Mr. Miller was not easy on his fathers. There is much bitterness in All My Sons, and it's explored in powerful confrontations. This is still an unusually moving work....There are no tricks, no exaggerations. The man clearly in charge here is Mr. Miller....Mr. Quinn is especially impressive, displaying once again the special combination of tenderness and strength that was once the almost exclusive trademark of Montgomery Clift."* (John J. O'Connor, The New York Times)

The American Clock (1993, TNT, 90m/c) *Screenworks* ☆☆☆ **Tp:** Frank Galati. **D:** Bob Clark. **P:** Micheal Brandman. **Cast:** Mary McDonnell, Eddie Bracken, Darren McGavin, Yaphet Kotto, Joanna Miles, Estelle Parsons, Loren Dean, John Rubenstein, Kelly Preston, John Randolph, David Strathairn, Rebecca Miller, Jim Dale. Miller's play was inspired by Studs Terkel's *Hard Times*, and presents a panoramic view of American values and ideas during the Great Depression of the 1930s, mostly through the lives of an upper-class New York Jewish family that must move to a Brooklyn flat after the stock market crash of 1929. It was first produced in 1980. The family's travails are at the center of the action, which ranges wide to include loitering jobless folks in shanty towns, prostitutes on the Queen Mary, and votes of confidence in the President. This piecemeal work was given its resonance by a truly eclectic ensemble cast.

- *"Arthur Miller's nominally successful play...has been enlivened and literally rediscovered in its transition from the stage to the screeen...In a rare instance of a major playwright's work finding its more natural form on the TV screen, Miller's mural of the Great Depression now packs the thematic panoramic impact that never quite gelled onstage....moments take your breath away..."* (Ray Loynd, Los Angeles Times)

- *"... a touch scattered, particularly in its early scenes. And it never does make a stimulating connection between America today and in the 1930s and between viewers and anyone on the screen....Mr. Miller is most at home at evoking the perspiring, penny-counting existence in Brooklyn tenements and the radicalism of the times, especially the mixture of idealism, innocence, anger, hope, openheartedness and close-mindedness that went into the making of young, Jewish, big-city Communists. He does not do as well with Wall Street speculators or black radicals..."* (Walter Goodman, The New York Times)

Broken Glass (1996, PBS, 120m/c **VHS**) *Masterpiece Theatre* ☆☆ **Tp:** David Holman, David Thacker. **D:** David Thacker. **P:** Fiona Finlay. **Cast:** Margot Leicester, Mandy Patinkin, Elizabeth McGovern, Henry Goodman. Sylvia, a Jewish woman in Brooklyn, learns of the Nazi reign of terror in Europe in 1938, and becomes inexplicably paralyzed below the waist. While being treated for her condition, she becomes attracted to the doctor attending her, despite her 20-year marriage to a mortgage banker. This production emphasizes the symbolism between the friction overseas and the marriages in limbo of both Sylvia and the doctor. Thacker directed the London stage version, which also starred Leicester.

- *"It's a shame...television appears to be the wrong medium for* Broken Glass. *The intense close-ups and lugubrious music emphasize everything that's soap-operatic about this play—and there's a lot of that....Miller and director David Thacker wield a heavy hand....Patinkin is surprisingly re-*

strained, considering some of his lines. But the play is serious instead of profound, grim instead of galvanizing." (Don Shirley, Los Angeles Times)

- *"...troubling in ways the playwright undoubtedly didn't intend....the story juggles monumental tragedy, namely the Holocaust, with the personally unsettling but relatively trivial spectre of sexual impotence. The juxtaposition is more often jarring than illuminating....Even flawed Miller confronts and provokes powerfully."* (John J. O'Connor, The New York Times)

Clara (1991, A&E, 50m/c) *Playwrights Theater* ☆☆☆½ **Tp:** Arthur Miller. **D:** Burt Brinckerhoff. **P:** Stuart Goodman. **Host:** Lauren Bacall. **Cast:** Darren McGavin, William Daniels, Jennifer Parsons. The title refers to a brutalized corpse found at the outset of this one-act play. A 28-year-old worker in prison-rehabilitation programs, she may have been killed by someone for whom she was making tea. A police detective questions her grief-stricken father for possible clues, taking the viewer into his complex past as both a liberal and a bigot.

- *"... spare and unwavering and, curiously, it even has the tone of 1950s Golden Age television drama....The racial overtones of his daughter's murder and the father's breakdown and wrenching psychological breakthrough finally enable the dad to unblock his repressions. McGavin's pain and turmoil are uncomfortably creditable, but it is Daniels as the world-weary detective who makes the production work."* (Ray Loynd, Los Angeles Times)

The Crucible treated the Salem, Massachusetts, witch trials of 1692 as a parable in the era of McCarthyism, commenting on guilt by association and personal responsibility. The play, starring Arthur Kennedy, opened in 1953 to great critical reception.

The Crucible (1967, CBS, 135m/c) ☆☆☆☆☆ **Tp:** Arthur Miller. **D:** Alex Segal. **P:** David Susskind. **Cast:** George C. Scott, Colleen Dewhurst, Melvyn Douglas, Tuesday Weld, Fritz Weaver, Cathleen Nesbitt, Will Geer, Henry Jones, Catherine Burns, Paula Bauersmith, Dana Elcar, Thayer David, Clarice Blackburn, Kathy Cody, Louise Stubbs. The magnificent performances of the leads fired this TV event. Scott's rip-roaring rendition of John Proctor was protean, rustic, and vociferous. The show was nominated for Emmy Awards for Best Actor (Scott), Actress (Dewhurst), and Director (Segal).

- *"Colleen Dewhurst and George C. Scott together breathed a special life and power into Arthur Miller's essentially unshaded message play. Highly contrasted, yet beautifully coordinated, their performances made a truly special event....Their scenes were rich in unverbalized expressions as they gave the drama power beyond its own bitter irony....Alex Segal...did full justice to the The Crucible and brought home its message with eloquence and force."* (Variety)

The Crucible (1996, 20th Century-Fox, 123m/c, **VHS/Laser**) ☆☆☆☆
Sc: Arthur Miller. **D:** Nicholas Hytner. **Cam:** Andrew Dunn. **Cast:**
Daniel Day-Lewis, Winona Ryder, Paul Scofield, Joan Allen, Bruce
Davison, Jeffrey Jones, Rob Campbell, Peter Vaughan, Karron Graves,
Frances Conroy, Elizabeth Lawrence, George Gaynes, Charlaine
Woodard. Miller was commissioned to reshape the play for the movies.
Its political implications transcend the 1950s to any era in which com-
munity hysteria leads to a "witch trial." The performances are outstand-
ing. The film was nominated for Academy Awards for Best Screenplay
Adaptation (Miller) and Supporting Actress (Allen, as Proctor's wife).

- *"Winona Ryder gives further evidence that she may be the most gifted actress of her generation....the film still speaks intelligently to our times and
  partly for that reason it is one of the very best films of 1996. Very few films
  of such allegorical integrity and moral authority have come out of Hollywood."* (James M. Welch, Magill's Cinema Annual)

- *"The Crucible achieves hurricane force. It's masterful, vibrant, compelling."* (Bruce Williamson, Playboy)

- *"Impassioned and vigorous...The film moves with the dangerous momentum of a runaway train."* (Janet Maslin, The New York Times)

Death of a Salesman is perhaps the quintessential American play. It's
the tragedy of Willy Loman, a longtime salesman who has been fired at
the age of 63 by his young boss, Bernard. He realizes that his two well-
liked sons have turned out to be mediocrities at best, and the meaning-
lessness of his glad-handing life and foolish wishful thinking eventually
shroud him in a grim, suicidal mood. This harrowing family drama was
first performed on the stage in 1949 with Lee J. Cobb as Willy, Mildred
Dunnock as his long-suffering wife, Linda, and Arthur Kennedy and
Cameron Mitchell as the sons, Biff and Happy.

Death of a Salesman (1950, Columbia, 112m/bw) ☆☆☆½ **Sc:** Stanley
Roberts. **D:** Laslo Benedek. **P:** Stanley Kramer. **Cam:** Franz Planer. **Cast:**
Fredric March, Mildred Dunnock, Kevin McCarthy, Cameron Mitchell,
Howard Smith, Royal Beal, Jesse White, Don Keefer, Elizabeth Fraser,
Claire Carleton, Patricia Walker. Roberts practically transferred the
whole play completely intact to the screen. Benedek dramatizes Willy's
walks into the past and back to the present with a deft, theatrical-style
hand. March delivered one of his finest performances, and the whole cast
was exceptional. The film was nominated for five Academy Awards: Best
Actor (March), Supporting Actor (McCarthy), Supporting Actress
(Dunnock), Cinematography (Planer), and Score (Alex North).

- *"March's Willy Loman is a breathtaking figure of pity as the fatal blow of
  success-and-popularity-worship at first unbalances and then destroys him.
  March plays a little man's agony with the enormous passion that expand him*

into a symbol of humanity and therefore a tragic figure, and the contrast of his numerous escapes into visions of the past, where he was a hero to his lithe, promising sons, is a sharp one which is greatly moving." (Otis L. Guernsey, New York Herald-Tribune)

- *"As it was on the stage, the film version is a revealing and deeply affecting study of a little man who had delusions of middle-class grandeur. And like March, the supporting players are near-perfect in their roles: Kevin McCarthy and Cameron Mitchell as Willy's sons; Howard Smith as a prosperous neighbor; Royal Beal as Willy's adventurous brother Ben. Best of all, Mildred Dunnock is back again with her controlled and infinitely touching performance as Willy's understanding and tragically loyal wife."* (Newsweek)

- *"... a bravely uncommon movie to come out of Hollywood, where dreams are the stuff that success is made on. Unhappily, it is also a disappointing picture....On the screen [Willy] is still speaking his disordered thoughts at the top of his lungs. But to the literal eye of the camera, the ranting salesman...seems so appallingly extreme a mental case that it becomes hard to believe that his wife, sons and neighbors would not rush him to an asylum. The madman in Loman, as he is played in this film, is constantly overshadowing the man himself."* (Time)

Death of a Salesman (1966, CBS, 120m/c) ☆☆☆☆☆ **Tp:** Arthur Miller. **D:** Alex Segal. **P:** David Susskind, David Melnick. **Cast:** Lee J. Cobb, Mildred Dunnock, George Segal, James Farentino, Edward Andrews, Gene Wilder, Albert Dekker, Margo Redmond, Bernie Kopell, Stanley Adams, Karen Steele, Joan Patrick, June Foray. Cobb and Dunnock repeated their original 1949 stage roles in this TV benchmark (Dunnock also starred in the 1950 film, above). The ensemble performing led by Cobb, in his most acclaimed role, carried the play's themes to great TV heights. The show won Emmy Awards for Outstanding Dramatic Program of the 1966–67 season, Best Drama Directing (Alex Segal), and for Miller's adaptation, and was nominated for Best Actor in Drama (Cobb) and Best Actress (Dunnock)

- *"An evening of exalted theatre came to television last night in a revelation of Arthur Miller's Death of a Salesman that will stand as the supreme understanding of the tragedy of Willy Loman. For television, the play is a veritable landmark in studio drama, an occasion of power so shattering and poignancy so delicate that there is no earlier parallel to cite. Lee J. Cobb's portrayal of Willy was richer and deeper than it was on the stage. But it was the stoic beauty and pathos of Mildred Dunnock's performance as the salesman's wife that achieved an enlarged and unforgettable nobility on the home screen. It will remain forever a cherished treasure of the acting art."* (Jack Gould, The New York Times)

- *"The cigarette case is a symbol of everything Bernard has won in his life — success, status, wealth — and a mocking sign of all that Willy and his two boys have failed to win. The pain on Mr. Cobb's face as his emotions over-whelm him, the wordless eloquence of his baffled regard for that shining piece of rail that crushed his ego and piecred his boasting—were utterly communicated and shared. I think it was the production's finest moment."* (Robert Lewis Shayon, Saturday Review)

Death of a Salesman (1985, CBS, 135m/c, **VHS**) ☆☆☆☆½ **Tp:** Arthur Miller. **D:** Volker Schlondorff. **P:** Robert F. Colesberry, Dustin Hoffman, Arthur Miller. **Cast:** Dustin Hoffman, Kate Reid, John Malkovich, Stephen Lang, Charles Durning, Louis Zorich. This trans-ference of Hoffman's stage triumph as Willy Loman to the small screen was a television event of the year. The production was dominated by Hoffman while it also managed to showcase Malkovich as Biff, and Reid delivered one of her greatest performances as Linda. This version re-turned to Miller's original intent of Willy as a self-described "little man," literally and figuratively—certain lines were changed when the rangy Cobb signed on for the original New York run. The show won Emmy Awards for Best Actor (Hoffman), Best Supporting Actor (Malkovich), and for Art Direction. It was nominated for Best Drama/Comedy Spe-cial of the 1985–86 season, Director (Schlondorff), and Supporting Actor (Durning).

- *"[Hoffman] played Willy Loman in Death of a Salesman...with a lot more self-pity and whining than I liked. (That production was observed in a fasci-nating 1985 documentary, Private Conversation, directed by Christian Blackwood, which shows how much attention had to be paid to the actor)."* (David Thomson, A Biographical Dictionary of Film)

- *"...as powerful and magnificent a performance of the play as is likely to be seen in this generation....Together, Mr. Miller and the actors have brilliantly distilled the almost mythic aspects of the work, with many of the longer pas-sages, now so familiar, almost taking on the formal structures of operatic arias. At the same time, the performances generate an atmosphere of fresh-ness and spontaneity. This is not simply a showcase for Mr. Hoffman....Kate Reid brilliantly sculpts the character of the clear-eyed but ferociously support-ive wife. And John Malkovich, playing Biff, the son burdened with Willy's most ambitious dreams, creates a riveting figure of boyish sincereity and hope-less weakness, of utter confusion and searing love. And Stephen Lang brings countless shades of surprising color to the other son, Hap, the womanizing lummox."* (John J. O'Connor, The New York Times)

Death of a Salesman (2000, Showtime, 175m/c) ☆☆☆½ **D:** Kirk Browning. **P:** Marc Bauman, Patricia Clifford, Brian Dennehy. **Cast:** Brian Dennehy, Elizabeth Franz, Ron Eldard, Ted Koch, Howard Witt, Kate Buddeke, Steve Pickering, Barbara Eda-Young, Stephanie March, Laura Moss. Dennehy's acclaimed Broadway rendition was preserved here. The show received Emmy Award nominations for Best Actor (Dennehy) and Supporting Actress (Franz).

- *"This new* Salesman *won't, however, give the idiosyncratic 1985 Dustin Hoffman* Salesman *a run for its money....Certain things Dennehy did on-stage become heightened here, and not for the better. He has a tendency to avoid eye contact with other actors, and some of the tortured-psyche gestures—the tugging at the lip, the pulling of the cheek, the latter called for by Miller's own stage directions—indicate distress in obvious ways. But in the big arias, and Miller wrote plenty, Dennehy connects. He's especially shrewd at depicting anger on the cusp of panic. The big scenes give you an idea, at least, of why Elizabeth Franz proved such a revelation as Linda. Ron Eldard and Ted Koch, as Biff and Happy, are terrific throughout, pitch-perfect....In football parlance, more often than not, the formidable Dennehy goes long—and scores."* (Michael Phillips, Los Angeles Times)

An Enemy of the People, Miller's first overt criticism of the McCarthy Era inquisitions, was produced on Broadway in 1951 (*The Crucible* would follow two years later). The Norway-set story of *An Enemy of the People*, which Miller adapted from Henrik Ibsen's 19th century drama of social criticism, tells of Dr. Stockman, a small-town medico who discovers his family's health resort is contaminated and that the townsfolk want him to keep quiet about it to protect their incomes.

An Enemy of the People (1966, NET, 110m/c) *NET Playhouse* ☆☆☆ **Tp:** Arthur Miller. **D:** Paul Bogart. **P:** Jac Venza, Jack Landau. **Cast:** James Daly, Kate Reid, Philip Bosco, James Olson, George Voskovec, William Prince, Barbara Dana, Walter Klavun, Timothy Daly, Earl Hedin.

- *"... a thoroughly worthwhile production that extracted the lasting virtues of Ibsen's convictions from a script that is not totally free from contrivance and serious lapses in forcefulness....Mr. Miller's adaptation is not overburdened with richly articulate scenes of confrontation and many of the subordinate characterizations border on the stereotype. James Daly gave a lucid performance as the doctor...Kate Reid was altogether believable..."* (Jack Gould, The New York Times)

- *"...proved more arresting and to the point than most of the going literature in [tv] or any other medium. It was also more to the point as a merciless indictment of social morality than a season's load of telementary softies via the major [networks]....Foremost was James Daly as the beseiged doctor; but Philip Bosco as his venal brother also was splendid."* (Variety)

An Enemy of the People (1977, First Artists/Warner Bros., 103m/c) ☆☆ **Sc:** Alexander Jacobs. **D/P:** George Schaefer. **Cam:** Paul Lohmann. **Cast:** Steve McQueen, Bibi Andersson, Charles Durning, Eric Christmas, Richard Bradford, Richard A. Dysart, Michael Cristofer, Michael Higgins, Robin Pearson Rose. Jacobs streamlined Miller's adaptation. McQueen—bearded, longhaired, bespectacled, in period dress, 35 pounds overweight—never came close to finding his regular audience. The Ibsen themes and the 19th century trappings were served up with integrity, but without any force. This pet project for the star was dumped by Warner Bros., whose executives bad-mouthed it while it was in production. It has rarely been seen since.

- *"Think of Clark Gable as the tragic Parnell, or Gregory Peck playing Ahab as if he were Abraham Lincoln. Recall Elizabeth Taylor as the Cleopatra of Great Neck. Then add to this list of big-star follies the typical, lean, tight-lipped action hero Steve McQueen. Here, he's plump, bearded and avuncular, a bit like Kris Kringle. For McQueen to play Ibsen's volatile, idealistic intellectual Dr. Stockman is as unusual as it would be for Dr. Carl Sagan to try and play Darth Vader."* (Michael Sragow, Los Angeles Herald-Examiner)

- *"It's a handsomely photographed, solid-looking movie, but it has no juice to it, no life to it at all. There's no way for that picture to make contact with a modern audience. McQueen has no understanding of the play, and it took me 20 minutes to recognize him under all those whiskers."* (Arthur Knight, The Hollywood Reporter)

An Enemy of the People (PBS, 1990, 120m/c) *American Playhouse* ☆☆☆☆ **Tp:** Arthur Miller. **D:** Jack O'Brien. **P:** David Giffiths, Sam Paul, Lindsay Law. **Cast:** John Glover, George Grizzard, Valerie Mahaffey, William Anton, Nina Siemaszko, Richard Easton, Byron Jennings, James Morrison, Robert Phelan, Robert Symonds, Dawn Didawick. The plot changes set the 1882 piece in a Maine village in 1893, with the pollution coming from a tannery. Miller was interviewed outside his Connecticut home by O'Brien, and this brief documentary was attached to the initial broadcast.

- *"As a powerful depiction of social corruption and selfishness, the production provides a fascinating signpost to one major direction that theatre and literature are likely to take in the 1990s: anger is back in fashion....Mr. Glover quite brilliantly and almost recklessly portrays Dr. Stockman as Mr. Miller envisions the character: a holy fool, fanatical, somewhat mad....His fire is perfectly balanced by the ice in Mr. Grizzard's depiction of the calculating Mayor Stockman. In a preface to an earlier adaptation of the Ibsen play, Mr. Miller commented on its outrage at the spectacle of a society refusing to face the truth: 'Those who warp the truth must inevitably be warped and corrupted themselves.' In an age of damage controllers and spin experts, the message is sadly more pertinent than ever."* (John J. O'Connor, The New York Times)

- *"The production's achievement is that it turns what is often staged as a statuesque "problem" play into a throbbing character drama. George Grizzard, particularly, is a terrific foil as the protagonist's older brother and town mayor intent on preserving the baths. Grizzard's irascibility, as opposed to stereotyped oafishness, gives the production sharp counterweight."* (Ray Loynd, Los Angeles Times)

Everybody Wins (1990, Recorded Picture, 97m/c, **VHS**) ☆½ **Sc:** Arthur Miller. **D:** Karel Reisz. **Cam:** Ian Baker. **P:** Jeremy Thomas, Ezra Swerdlow. **Cast:** Nick Nolte, Debra Winger, Jack Warden, Judith Ivey, Will Patton, Frank Military, Kathleen Wilhoite, Frank Converse. This odd piece concerns a moody private eye who falls in love with an unbalanced small-town New England prostitute. She hires him to investigate a murder for which a young man, who she claims to be innocent, has been jailed. Miller substantially retooled his one-act play for this film noir mystery, in which Winger vascillates radically from out-of-date jargon to double entendres to mannered role-playing. No wonder Nolte looked baffled. It's like an asylum kook was the anchor to a standard corrupt-town sojourn. It's undoubtedly the worst film made from Miller material.

- *"Pauline Kael believed Winger was extraordinary in it, playing a schizophrenic, swooping from sexuality to coldness. I felt the picture was incoherent and foolish, and another sign of the actress's lack of technique. No player could be blamed for* Everybody Wins. *The script was the root of the problem. But why had she accepted the part? And how did she seem so undirected?"* (David Thomson, A Biographical Dictionary of Film)

Incident at Vichy (1973, PBS, 120m/c) *Hollywood Television Theater* ☆☆☆½ **D:** Stacy Keach. **P:** George Turpin, Norman Lloyd. **Cast:** Richard Jordan, Barry Primus, Allen Garfield, Rene Auberjonois, Harris Yulin, Andy Robinson, Bert Freed, Curt Lowens, Harry Davis, William Hansen, Joe Hindy, Sean Kelly, Lee Bergere. This World War II piece concerned stragglers rounded up by the French police in 1942 so that they could be examined for circumcision by Nazi "racial anthropologists." It's clear in this 1965 play that they will be shipped to death camps in Poland. Stark sets, threatening shadows, and performances that make you miss the characters once they're escorted through the door make this a distinctive viewing experience. Miller was interviewed on tape at Michigan State University by the show's executive producer, Norman Lloyd, and the interview follows the play.

- *"Miller should love television. It loves his work. Never was this better exemplified than in the powerful production of Miller's* Incident at Vichy...*in no previous production have I felt the emotional intensity generated in this television version, staged with a remarkable free flow of action and ideas by Stacy Keach."* (Cecil Smith, Los Angeles Times)

A Memory of Two Mondays (1971, NET, 90m/c) *NET Playhouse* ☆☆☆☆ **D:** Paul Bogart. **P:** Jacqueline Babbin, Jac Venza. **Host:** Arthur Miller. **Cast:** Jack Warden, George Grizzard, Kristofer Tabori, Estelle Parsons, J.D. Cannon, Barnard Hughes, Cathy Burns, Tony Lo Bianco, Dick Van Patten, Jerry Stiller, Dan Hamilton, Donald Buka, Tom

Bosqui. A *Memory of Two Mondays* is an autobiographical play set in 1933, a time when Miller was working in a Brooklyn auto parts warehouse. A slice-of-life drama among Depression Era working men and their shared sense of quiet panic, it was first staged in 1955 as the curtain-raiser for *A View From the Bridge*. The brilliant ensemble brings this poignant piece to life with Warden outstanding as a husband and worker who is blindsided by tragedy.

- "... *a most rewarding choice....the compassionate character studies of ordinary people reacting to the quiet desperation of their times and their environment was compelling TV fare...Uniformly excellent portrayals brought the Miller characters to life in naturalistic and easily understandable terms....Paul Bogart's direction brought all the ingredients of setting, mood and performance together in a cohesive whole, with an admirable cinematic awareness...*" (Variety)

- "... *filmed in a real Manhattan warehouse under Paul Bogart's direction, [the show] lacked a certain sense of atmosphere that might perhaps have been more easily evoked on the stage, but the acting was generally fine and easy, with a good balance between energy and weariness. Jack Warden plays Gus, a sort of Slavic Falstaff who goes to pieces when his wife dies...*" (Julius Novick, The New York Times)

The Price (1971, NBC, 90m/c) *The Hallmark Hall of Fame* ☆☆☆☆☆
Tp: Arthur Miller. **D:** Fielder Cook. **P:** David Susskind. **Cast:** George C. Scott, Barry Sullivan, Colleen Dewhurst, David Burns. *The Price* concerns two estranged brothers, one a police sergeant who stayed around to help the family, the other a surgeon who went on to accrue wealth. They have an uneasy reunion after 16 years, at a Brooklyn brownstone to discuss the disposition of their recently deceased father's property. The play was first staged on Broadway in 1968. Scott's brilliant performance dominates this practically one-set TV piece, and the ensemble was terrific. Scott, who refused to pick up his Oscar for *Patton* the year before, graciously accepted his Emmy Award for Best Actor, as did Burns for Supporting Actor, playing the appraiser of the goods, and Cook for Best Director. The show was nominated for the Outstanding Single Program of the 1970–71 season and for Best Actress (Dewhurst).

- "*The beleaguered cause of serious drama on TV got a shot in the arm...The Price...lent itself well to the intimate demands of the tube...Fielder Cook's direction concentrated on character revealing close-ups that gave the basically talky script the urgency it needed. His cast of four responded brilliantly, with George C. Scott underplaying the cop with great sensitivity and persuasion. As the surgeon brother, Barry Sullivan amazingly etched a self-centered man reaching out too late for compassion and succor.*" (Variety)

- "*The tight focus of the TV camera captured superbly the agony of two broth-*

ers resurrecting a family portrait with different brushes....Mr. Scott was magnificent as the police officer..." (Jack Gould, The New York Times)

A View From the Bridge (1961, Transcontinental, 117m/bw) ☆☆☆
Sc: Norman Rosten. **D:** Sidney Lumet. **P:** Paul Graetz. **Cam:** Michel Kelber. **Cast:** Raf Vallone, Maureen Stapleton, Carol Lawrence, Jean Sorel, Raymond Pellegrin, Morris Carnovsky, Harvey Lembeck, Vincent Gardenia. First staged in 1955, this play depicts Eddie Carbone, a Brooklyn longshoreman who helps his wife's cousins to illegally immigrate to America. He then explodes after one cousin makes love to his wife's neice, who announces their engagement. His unspoken love for the 18-year-old niece he and his wife have raised undermines his marriage and in his rage he turns the boys over to the authorities. This film was made in France in several languages, even though it's set in Brooklyn. The odd international cast does what it can, especially Vallone, Lawrence, and Carnovsky, who serves as the voice of morality as a lawyer. Eddie is another of Miller's mid-century, middle-aged male walking tragedies, a self-deluded patriarch in the vein of Willy Loman and Joe Keller.

- *"Miller's intention is to create tragedy: But what we see is a man behaving so insanely and stupidly that we keep wondering why he isn't put away or treated. We keep wondering why his wife doesn't have him locked up or the lawyer—played by Morris Carnovsky in his full, rich tones of pear-shaped passion (he seems to be playing Arthur Miller as an old man)—doesn't send him to a doctor. They all just wait for the disaster; we can only assume that they don't want to disturb the tragic inevitability."* (Pauline Kael, I Lost It at the Movies)

- *"The movie's real trouble is that authors Miller and Rosten have invoked the subconscious as a cover for implausibility. The subconscious may prompt men to do things that seem incredible, but it is no license for dramatists to behave the same way."* (Time)

Jason Miller

John Anthony Miller
Born: April 22, 1939, Scranton, PA. **D:** 2001.
Pulitzer Prize-winning play: *That Championship Season* (1973)

Jason Miller became better known to the public as an actor rather than a playwright after his Academy Award nomination for essaying an ill-fated priest in *The Exorcist* (1973). His films as an actor include *Monsignor* (1982), *Light of Day* (1987), and *Rudy* (1993), in which he played former Notre Dame football Coach Ara Parseghian. Miller's TV-movie writing includes *Reward* (1980) with Michael Parks and *A Mother's Courage: The Mary Thomas Story* (1983) starring Alfre Woodard.

That Championship Season depicts a reunion of four former high school basketball players who played on their Scranton, Pennsylvania, school's last state championship team—at the home of their old boorish coach.

That Championship Season (1982, Cannon Group, 110m/c, **VHS**) ☆☆½ **Sc/D:** Jason Miller. **P:** Menahem Golan, Yorum Globus. **Cam:** John Bailey. **Cast:** Robert Mitchum, Martin Sheen, Stacy Keach, Bruce Dern, Paul Sorvino, Arthur Franz, Michael Bernosky, Joseph Kelly, James M. Langan, Tony Santaniello, William G. McAndrew. This production was cast and recast so many times since the play closed that by the time Mitchum came to play the coach, both William Holden and George C. Scott, who at different times had been attached to the role, had moved on to other commitments. Except for Mitchum, the cast is excellent. The film was made on location in Scranton.

- *"Robert Mitchum...seems too strenuously cast against type. From countless memorable performances as the sardonic fatalist, who invariably speaks less than his knowing looks convey...Mitchum brings to the film an image which is sorely at odds with his role as an endlessly exhortative, humorless and ignorant bigot....Miller has followed too slavishly the cardinal rule of filmmaking: do not express verbally what can be expressed visually....The film...begins by defining its world as the larger one of Scranton, Pennsylvania....In relation to this insistently impinging larger world, the return to order and teamwork which the coach verbally imposes in his house seems pointless, and the ending of the film rings hollow....Miller may have made the early part of his story more entertaining...at the cost of a dramatic concentration which he never achieves in the film."* (Terry L. Andrews, Magill's Survey of Cinema)

That Championship Season (1999, Showtime, 126m/c, **VHS**) ☆☆☆½ **Tp:** Jason Miller. **D:** Paul Sorvino. **P:** Steve Greener. **Cam:** Bruce Surtees. **Cast:** Paul Sorvino, Gary Sinise, Vincent D'Onofrio, Terry Kinney, Tony Shalhoub, Joe Bays, Susan F. Carr, Carol Lawrence, Jeff Rogers, Bill Sorvino, Denise Kaye, Gailard Sartain. Wanting to make amends for the above 1982 film version, Sorvino—whose career was boosted by the original stage production—was the driving force behind this production. He directed the film and played the forceful coach. Miller tweaked the script, adding a new opening and updating some of the references.

- *"When Jason Miller's* That Championship Season *emerged in 1972, its subtext spoke volumes to a nation made cynical by Vietnam and the unfolding Watergate melodrama. In a slightly updated film version...it still communicates powerfully—pointing up the ugliness of bigotry even as it extols patriotism, friendship and forgiveness....The result is very much a 'filmed play,' its action confined almost entirely to the coach's Victorian mausoleum of a home. Though momentum lulls occasionally, fine acting keeps powering things along." (Daryl H. Miller, Los Angeles Times)*

Langdon Mitchell

Langdon Elwyn Mitchell
Born: February 17, 1862, Philadelphia, PA. **Died:** 1935.

Langdon Mitchell, the son of author and physician S. Weir Mitchell, trained as a lawyer but turned to writing after his play *Sylvian* was published in 1885. His most notable play was an adaptation of William Thackeray's *Vanity Fair, Becky Sharp* (see below). His books included *Poems, Love in the Backwoods* and *Understanding America.* Seven years before his death, he was named playwrighting chair at the University of Pennsylvania. Other writers have adapted *Vanity Fair* under the original title.

Becky Sharp (1935, RKO, 83m/c) ☆☆☆ **Sc:** Francis Edward Faragoh. **D:** Rouben Mamoulian. **P:** Kenneth Macgowan. **Cam:** Ray Rennahan. **Cast:** Miriam Hopkins, Frances Dee, Cedric Hardwicke, Billie Burke, Alison Skipworth, Nigel Bruce, Alan Mowbray, G.P. Huntley, William Stack, George Hassell, William Faversham, Charles Richman, Doris Lloyd, Colin Tapley, Leonard Mudie, May Beatty, Charles Coleman, Bunny Beatty, Finis Barton, Olaf Hytten, Pauline Garson, James 'Hambone' Robinson, Elspeth Dudgeon, Tempe Pigott, Ottola Nesmith. English dramatist James M. Barrie had previously adapted *Vanity Fair* for the stage, but when a dramatic version of Thackery's novel was first produced in America in 1899, it was Mitchell's version, using the main character's name as the title. The original production starred Mrs. Fiske, Maurice Barrymore, and Tyrone Power (Sr.). The play was selected by John Jay Whitney, part owner of the Technicolor process, to be the first all-Technicolor film. Lowell Sherman was fired three weeks into the production and replaced by Mamoulian.

- "*...too frequently [Hopkins] overacts as though afraid her radiant appearance in many hues will make one miss a gesture or an intonation.*" (*Howard Barnes,* New York Herald-Tribune)

- "*...probably the most significant event of the 1935 cinema...Miriam Hopkins is an indifferently successful Becky, who shares some excellent scenes with many others in which she is strident and even nerve-wracking.*" (*Andre Sennwald,* The New York Times)

Becky Sharp (1949) *Philco Television Playhouse* ☆☆ **P/D:** Fred Coe. **Cast:** Clare Booth Luce.

- "... didn't bring the Victorian story to life, or give it any meaning or distinction...dull and insdistinct from the start, the production continued in that vein. Put this down as a mistake." (Variety)

William Vaughn Moody
Born: July 8, 1869, Spencer, IN. **Died:** 1910.

William Vaughn Moody was described by Laura M. Zaidman as a poet and playwright who "bridge[d] the gap between traditional forms of the 19th century and experimental designs of the 20th century." His themes tended to have a dreamy and mystical quality. After attending Harvard, his poems began appearing in *Scribner's* and *Atlantic Monthly*. His play *A Sabine Woman* was staged in 1906 in Chicago. He rewrote parts of the work and retitled it *The Great Divide*, which hit Broadway the same year. The play contained gender complexity that few plays of its time ever expressed. His other major play was *The Faith Healer*. Moody died of complications from typhoid fever.

The Faith Healer (1921, bw/silent) **Sc:** Z. Wall Covington. **D:** George Melford. **Cam:** Harry Perry. **Cast:** Milton Sills, Ann Forrest, Fontaine La Rue, Frederick Vroom, Loyola O'Connor, Mae Giraci, John Curry, Adolphe Menjou, Edward Vroom, Robert Brower, Winifred Greenwood.

The Great Divide opened at Broadway's Princess Theatre in 1906 featuring Margaret Anglin, Henry B. Walthall, and Laura Hope Crewes. It was revived in 1917.

The Great Divide (1915, V-L-S-E, bw/silent) **Sc:** Anthony Paul Kelly. **D:** Edgar Lewis. **Cam:** Edward Earle. **Cast:** Ethel Clayton, House Peters, Marie Sterling, Hayden Stevenson, Mary Moore, Warner P. Richmond, Fred O'Beck, Ray Chamberlin.

The Great Divide (1925, Metro-Goldwyn, bw/silent) ☆☆☆ **Sc:** Benjamin Glazer, Waldemar Young. **D:** Reginald Barker. **P:** Louis B. Mayer. **Cam:** Percy Hilburn. **Cast:** Conway Tearle, Wallace Beery, Alice Terry, Allan Forrest, George Cooper, ZaSu Pitts, William Orlamond, Huntley Gordon.

- "...makes an entertaining although not a particularly stirring picture. The pace of the story is too slow at times, and Reginald Barker, the director, has not helped matters by dwelling too much here and there on a favorite comedy situation....Conway Tearle impersonates Stephen Ghent, the fierce and impulsive hero. Mr. Tearle delivers a splendid performance...Wallace Beery is excellent..." (Mordaunt Hall, The New York Times)

The Great Divide (1929, First National, 72m/bw) ☆☆½ **Sc:** Fred Myton, Paul Perez. **D:** Reginald Barker. **P:** Robert North. **Cam:** Lee Garmes, Alvin Knechtl. **Cast:** Dorothy Mackaill, Ian Keith, Myrna Loy, Lucien Littlefield, Creighton Hale, Claude Gillingwater, George Fawcett, Roy Stewart, Ben Hendricks Jr., Bill Elliott.

- *"The film's outcome is as obvious as some of its painted backgrounds. One divines that when the wealthy miner carries off the heroine from the city to teach her the ways of pioneers she will love him in Reel Six and fight to protect him ever afterward....Myrna Loy plays the native girl in the same fashion as her many half-caste roles. She dances, sings, slurs her r's in insinuating fashion. Mr. Keith is natural and makes what he can of the hero. Dorothy Mackaill, departing momentarily from the shop-girl-at-Coney Island characterizations, is obnoxiously flippant as the thrill-seeker."* (The New York Times)

Woman Hungry (1931, First National, 65m/bw) ☆☆ **D:** Clarence Badger. **Cast:** Sidney Blackmer, Lila Lee, Raymond Hatton, Fred Kohler, Kenneth Thomson, Olive Tell, David Newell, J. Farrell MacDonald, Tom Dugan, Blanche Frederici.

- *"William Vaughn Moody is described in college courses on the American drama as a playwright of certain mystically beautiful qualities, and* The Great Divide *is on the reading lists as an outstanding example of his work. In bringing this play to the talking screen, First National has kept its faith with the playwright's memory by considerably retitling it* Woman Hungry, *which adequately describes the theme and treatment...a torrid story of the West...Lila Lee and Sidney Blackmer are puppets whose emotional problems never mean anything..."* (The New York Times)

Tad Mosel

Born: May 1, 1922, Steubenville, OH.
Pulitzer Prize-winning play: All the Way Home (1961)
New York Drama Crtics Circle Best Play: All the Way Home

Tad Mosel wrote the screenplays for the films *Dear Heart* (1964) and *Up the Down Staircase* (1967). He became one of the most admired writers during the so-called Golden Age of Television through his association with producer Fred Coe on a variety of drama anthology programs. He adapted Robert E. Sherwood's *The Petrified Forest* for *Producers' Showcase* in 1955 and wrote originals for *Goodyear Television Theatre*, *Studio One*, *Playwrights '56*, *The United States Steel Hour*, and *Westinghouse Presents*. His originals that debuted on *Playhouse 90* were *If You Knew Elizabeth* (1957) with Claire Trevor, *The Playroom* (1957) starring Patricia Neal, *The Innocent Sleep* (1958) with Hope Lange and Buster Keaton, and *A*

Corner of the Garden (1959) featuring Eileen Heckert. He also wrote two installments of the 1976 PBS historical miniseries *The Adams Chronicles*.

All the Way Home was based by Mosel on James Agee's 1958 posthumously Pulitzer Prize-winning autobiographical novel, *A Death in the Family*, which explored early century coming-of-age and family-crisis issues in Knoxville, Tennessee. Producer Fred Coe planned to have it adapted for airing on CBS's *Playhouse 90*, then approached Mosel, who couldn't imagine Agee's poetic prose being broken up by commercials. They then decided to adapt it into a play instead. It had an out-of-town run in New Haven and Boston, then opened on Broadway in 1960 at the Belasco Theatre to great reviews and no business. Coe was going to close the play after a few nights when Ed Sullivan raved about the play in his *New York Daily News* column, then brought the cast onto an installment of TV's *The Ed Sullivan Show*. The move captured the public's attention in a huge way; the play ran for 334 performances and the story won its second Pulitzer Prize, this time for Drama. Arthur Penn directed the stage version starring Arthur Hill, Colleen Dewhurst, and Lillian Gish.

All the Way Home (1963, Paramount, 107m/bw) ☆☆☆½ **Sc:** Philip Reisman Jr. **D:** Alex Segal. **P:** David Susskind. **Cam:** Boris Kaufman. **Cast:** Robert Preston, Jean Simmons, Aline MacMahon, Pat Hingle, Michael Kearney, Thomas Chalmers, John Cullum, John Henry Faulk, Ronnie Claire Edwards, Lylah Tiffany, Georgia Simmons, Edwin Wolfe, Ferdie Hoffman. The film has a great feel for post-turn-of-the-20th-century rural Tennessee and an understated quality via Kaufman's black and white cinematography, but it doesn't grasp the childhood sense of wonder and loss that the made Agee's book fascinating.

- *"Inevitably, some of the poetry and unduplicatable intimacy of Mr. Agee's particular expression was lost in this radical switch [to the stage]…in moving the play of Mr. Mosel into the medium of the screen. And this [refraction] is the one that's all but done for the quality of Mr. Agee's book and twisted it into a moist-eyed ogle that has a standard cinematic character.…in completing the transfer of some very special sentiments to the screen, Philip Reisman Jr., the film's playwright, and Alex Segal, the director, have drained them completely of specialness. Their film…has no sharp cinematic characteristic, no inside-looking-out point of view (which is one of the most important and distinctive things the Agee novel has)."* (Bosley Crowther, The New York Times)

All the Way Home (1971, NBC, 90m/c) *The Hallmark Hall of Fame* ☆☆☆☆ **Tp:** Tad Mosel. **D:** Fred Coe. **P:** David Susskind. **Cast:** Richard Kiley, Joanne Woodward, Eileen Heckert, Pat Hingle, James Woods, Shane Nickerson, Barnard Hughes, Jane Mallett, Betty Garde, Kay Hawtrey, James O'Neill, Nan Stewart, Allen Clowes. This show received a Peabody Award for its heartfelt depiction of alcoholism, family tragedy, and coming-of-age issues. The performances are uniformly excellent.

- "... *watching* All the Way Home *reminds us again that [Coe] was also a first-rate director....And when Grandma is wheeled out onto the lawn of her home at night, it's a beautiful scene with an almost abstract composition. She and her assistant are shown on a hillock above the family members...The background is darkness, bu Grandma is bathed in a kind of celestial light, as if soon destined for heaven.*" (Jon Krampner, The Man in the Shadows: Fred Coe and the Golden Age of Television)

All the Way Home (1981, NBC, 120m/c) NBC *Live Theatre.* ☆☆☆☆ **Tp:** Tad Mosel. **D:** Delbert Mann. **P:** David W. Rintels. **Cast:** Sally Field, William Hurt, Ned Beatty, Murray Hamilton, Polly Holliday, John McIntire, Jeremy Licht, Betty Garrett, Jeanette Nolan, Ann Doran, Ellen Corby, Michael Horton, Francis Lee McCain. This production, with a blue-chip cast, telecast the play live. Mann revisited the world of live TV for the first time since the 1950s and found the experience invigorating. The entire cast was wonderful, especially Field and Hurt.

- "... *good results in capturing double-track of a play in performance: our sense of both the story and the sharing of the story....The level [of adrenalin] was high enough, with their need to pay attention to their characters, the other actors, the cameras and the immediate audience at Bing Theatre, USC. They came through with a genuine ensemble performance, sensitive to everything and shaken by nothing. So private were they on that stage that the audience (I watched a full-scale run-through) could almost imagine the camera crew and sound assistants as 'invisible ' stagehands...Certainly, the actors didn't seem to notice them. Which made them good actors. Even better proof was the number of handkerchiefs pulled out in the audience as death visited Field's and Hurt's family. A couple came out in my house, too, while we watched the play later on TV. Yet it seemed less, somehow, than it had at the Bing.*" (Dan Sullivan, Los Angeles Times)

N. Richard Nash

Nathan Richard Nusbaum
Born: June 8, 1913, Philadelphia, PA. **Died:** 2000.

N. Richard Nash was among the core group of teleplay writers—along with Horton Foote, Paddy Chayefsky, Tad Mosel and others—whose works were mined for TV by producer Fred Coe during the so-called Golden Age of Television. A screenwriter in postwar Hollywood, Nash's movies included *Nora Prentiss* (1947) with Ann Sheridan, *Dear Wife* (1949) with William Holden, *Mara Maru* (1952) with Errol Flynn, Robert Wise's *Helen of Troy* (1956), Otto Preminger's *Porgy and Bess*

(1959), and Gilbert Cates's *One Summer Love* (1976) starring Beau Bridges and Susan Sarandon. Nash was prepared to quit screenwriting when Coe called him in 1953, wanting to produce Nash's *The Happy Rest* for *The Goodyear Theatre*. Coe went on to produce *The Rainmaker* for TV (see below), as well as other scripts by Nash. *The Happy Rest* and *The Young and the Fair* aired in the late 1950s in newly staged versions on *Matinee Theatre*. Nash's TV movies were *The Parade* (1984) with Michael Learned and *Between the Darkness and the Dawn* (1985) with Elizabeth Montgomery as a woman who emerges from a coma after 20 years.

The Rainmaker was first produced on *The Goodyear Theatre* in 1953 and was one of the first dramas of the 1950s TV anthology shows to make the three-media trip, including Broadway and cinema. The hour-long TV piece — set in 1913, about a drifting charlatan who promises rain to a drought-stricken Kansas farm family while he sparks the interest of their spinster daughter — starred Darren McGavin as Starbuck, Joan Potter as Lizzie, and Cameron Prud'homme as her father. The 1954 Broadway play starred McGavin and Shirley Booth. Nash used the play as the basis for Lucille Ball's Broadway musical, *Wildcat* (1960), and then more closely preserved the original story for another Broadway musical, *110 in the Shade* (1964), starring Robert Horton. Nash said that he wrote *The Rainmaker* as a tribute to his older sister, Mae, who helped cure his childhood stuttering by being his attentive listener.

The Rainmaker (1956, Paramount, 121m/c, **VHS/DVD**) ☆☆☆☆ **Sc:** N. Richard Nash. **D:** Joseph Anthony. **P:** Hal B. Wallis. **Cam:** Charles Lang Jr. **Cast:** Burt Lancaster, Katharine Hepburn, Wendell Corey, Lloyd Bridges, Earl Holliman, Cameron Prud'homme, Wallace Ford, Yvonne Lime, Dottie Bee Baker, Dan White, Ken Becker. Lancaster hammed up his role as Starbuck to the maximum, giving his movements a choreographic athleticism and punctuating his vigorous patter with gleaming smiles. The two legendary stars didn't get along, according to many sources, but Hepburn was in her element and excelled as the assertive spinster. The film was nominated for Oscars for Best Actress (Hepburn) and Score (Alex North).

- *"Lancaster has an athletic role, in which he can also be very touching. His conman isn't a simple trickster; he's a poet and dreamer who needs to convince people of his magical powers. Hepburn is stringy and tomboyish, believably plain yet magnetically beautiful. This is a fairy tale (the ugly duckling) dressed up as bucolic comedy and padded out with metphysical falsies, but it is also genuinely appealing in a crude, good-spirited way, though N. Richard Nash, who wrote both the play and the adaptation, aims too solidly at lower-middle-class tastes. Once transformed, the heroine rejects the poet for the deputy sheriff…if there were a sequel, she might be suffering from the drought of his imagination."* (Pauline Kael, 5001 Nights at the Movies)

- *"The film is talky and colorful and a fanciful attempt at an almost fairy-tale-like love affair between two lost and misguided souls....Hepburn and Lancaster's comprehension of their sensitive roles gave the film far more entertainment value than it might have had in lesser hands....Lancaster's character says to the heroine, 'Once in a life you've got to take a chance on a conman.' Many insiders...felt that Hepburn took that chance when she agreed to co-star with the scene-stealing, 'mugging' Lancaster."* (James Robert Parish, The Tough Guys)

The Rainmaker (1982, HBO, 135m/c) HBO Theatre ☆☆☆½ **Tp:** N. Richard Nash. **D:** John Frankenheimer. **P:** Marcia Govons. **Cast:** Tuesday Weld, Tommy Lee Jones, William Katt, Lonny Chapman, James Cromwell, Taylor Lacher, William Traylor. By the time of this performance, the historical framing of the drought year became 1922. Frankenheimer videotaped this purposefully stagy performance in a studio in Provo, Utah, after three and a half weeks of rehearsing—similar to the manner in which the director used to tackle his *Playhouse 90* assignments.

- *"Frankenheimer's staging is clean and confident. The film opens at the back of the theatre moving up over the audience to the curtain, which raises, then onto the stage. Four cameras are used, providing the film or the TV audience with alternate points of view. While the play seems to be taking place on the theatre stage, it was...actually [taped] on a studio interior set...although it seems that we are onstage at all times, we are never stage-bound....Frankenheimer perfectly captures the essence of the play...a fluid stream of visual images. The editing, typical of the director's incisive style, is in keeping with the movements and responses of the actors, making us feel closer to the events than the 'live' audience."* (Gerald Pratley, The Films of Frankenheimer)

The Young and the Fair, a 1948 Broadway play, was produced for an hour-long 1953 presentation on *The Goodyear Theatre* starring Joanne Woodward, with Mildred Dunnock, Louisa Horton, and Jenny Eagon. The play was again staged on *Matinee Theatre* in 1958 with Marian Seldes and Frances Starr.

Marsha Norman

Born: September 21, 1947, Louisville, KY.
Pulitzer Prize-winning play: *'night, Mother* (1983)

Marsha Norman has demonstrated a knack for exploring family and life-changing issues faced by mature women. A former critic and journalist for the *Louisville Times*, she wrote her first play, *Getting Out*, for the Actors' Theatre of Louisville in 1977. It was voted Best New Play of the Year

Produced by a Regional Theatre by the American Theatre Critics Association. For TV, Norman wrote *Face of a Stranger* (1991), which won Gena Rowlands an Emmy Award as a suddenly broke Seattle socialite who befriends a homeless woman (Tyne Daly); *A Cooler Climate* (1999) with Sally Field and Judy Davis in a story of friendship directed by Susan Siedelman; *The Audrey Hepburn Story* (2000) with Jennifer Love Hewitt; and *Custody of the Heart* (2000) with Lorraine Bracco as a successful businesswoman who's sued for the custody of her children by her stay-at-home husband. Norman's plays include *Circus Valentine* (1979) and the Broadway musical *The Secret Garden* (1991)

Getting Out (1994, ABC, 92m/c, **VHS**) ☆☆☆☆ **Tp:** Eugene Corr, Ruth Shapiro. **D:** John Korty. **P:** Robert Halmi Sr., Dorothea G. Petrie. **Cast:** Rebecca DeMornay, Ellen Burstyn, Robert Knepper, Carol Mitchell-Leon, Tandy Cronyn, Richard Jenkins, Norm Skaggs, Sue Bugden, Kevin Dewey, Sean Sweeney, Jack Swanson, Amy Dott, Bruce Evers, Linda Pierce, Suzy Bass. Norman's 1977 play concerns a woman headed home to Macon, Georgia, after eight years in prison for a shooting during a gas station holdup. She wants to see her son, to whom she gave birth while in prison, but finds that her ex-hooker mother gave the child up for adoption. A tough and uncompromising telefilm.

- *"...wallopingly good performances by Rebecca DeMornay and Ellen Burstyn. This is Martha Norman territory...notoriously tough on moms and any male past the age of puberty....Ms. Norman's play is pitch perfect in its depictions of people on the despised rim of society. Ms. Burstyn's gum-chewing, brittle portrayal of an aging tart, now a cabdriver, is a chilling triumph....Ms. DeMornay...here takes an impressive artistic leap with her lascerating portrait...It is indeed a good many notches above the average television movie."* (John J. O'Connor, The New York Times)

The Laundromat (1985, HBO, 60m/c) ☆☆☆☆ **Tp:** Marsha Norman. **D:** Robert Altman. **Cam:** Pierre Mignot. **Cast:** Carol Burnett, Ann Madigan, Michael Wright. Two women meet late at night at a laundromat and share deeply personal secrets with each another. The play was first staged in 1978 in Louisville as *Third and Oak: The Laundromat*.

- *"The difference in HBO's Laundromat...is its cast...and its director... They turn the predictable into the memorable as each woman's dirty laundry eventually comes out...What's splendid about the piece is Burnett's watchful delicacy...played against Madigan's furious, electric outrage."* (Sheila Benson, Los Angeles Times)

'night, Mother (1986, Universal, 96m/c, **VHS**) ☆☆½ **Sc:** Marsha Norman. **D:** Tom Moore. **P:** Aaron Spelling, Alan Greisman. **Cam:** Stephen M. Katz. **Cast:** Sissy Spacek, Anne Bancroft, Ed Berke, Carol Robbins,

Jennifer Roosendahl, Michael Kenworthy, Sari Walker, Claire Malis. Spacek played a middle-aged divorced epileptic unable to keep a job with a son who's a drug-addicted punk. "I'm sick and tired of being sick and tired," she tells her mother, and plans suicide before the next dawn. The Pulitzer Prize-winning play, which is essentially a long one-act piece, was first performed in 1983 starring Kathy Bates and Anne Pitoniak.

- *"Overwrought adaptation...which fails to make the most of its leading ladies. Bancroft in her familiar role as the long-suffering mother is dignified, severe and utterly humorless, and her character sets the movie's tone. Spacek, likewise, seems a little self-important as her suicidal, middle-aged daughter. Director Moore presumably thought his main task was simply to provide a platform for his bravura stars. Unfortunately, by plumping for an inert shooting style, he leaves the actresses looking smug and stolid."* (Geoffrey Macnab, Time Out)

Third and Oak: The Pool Hall (1989, A&E, 60m/c) *American Playwrights Theatre* ☆☆☆ **Tp:** Marsha Norman. **D:** Fielder Cook. **P:** Nederlander Productions. **Cast:** James Earl Jones, Mario Van Peebles, Debra Cole. **Host:** Anthony Quinn. Originally, Norman wrote two one acts that debuted in tandem in 1978 in Louisville and could be staged one without the other, entitled *Third and Oak: The Pool Hall* and *Third and Oak: The Laundromat*, the first concerning men, the other women. Both were set next door to each other in Louisville. Robert Altman made the latter without the Third and Oak framing for TV in 1985 (see above). In this one, Willie, the aging owner of a pool hall, and Shooter, the son of Willie's suicide-ended former best friend, are the only people in the joint. Willie tries to convince Shooter to quit fooling around and be faithful to his wife. The piece was performed live in the short-lived A&E series.

- *"...while modest, the effort is admirable....There are no great surprises in the piece. But as a character study, the play gives Mr. Jones and Mr. Van Peebles an opportunity to play off each other skillfully, prodding and poking with vigor and affection. With the bulk of television devoted to short attention spans and catchy visual effects, it is almost startling to come across a theatre composition that takes its time and pays attention to language as the writer digs beneath surfaces, exploring complexities rather than telegraphing the obvious."* (John J. O'Connor, The New York Times)

Clifford Odets

Born: July 18, 1906, Philadelphia, PA. **Died:** 1963.

Clifford Odets was a founder of the Group Theatre in 1931 along with Harold Clurman, Lee Strasberg, and Cheryl Crawford. Through its auspices, he became one of the most admired playwrights of the 1930s. Pennsylvania-born but Bronx-raised, Odets's first produced play was the one-act *Waiting for Lefty* (1935), about a New York taxi cab strike. *Awake and Sing* came later that year, mining Jewish-American issues during the Great Depression through one family's experiences. *Golden Boy* (1937) was bought by Columbia Pictures and Odets began maintaining careers on both coasts after he married Oscar-winning actress Luise Rainer, whom he divorced in 1940. He would use the Hollywood experiences of a Group Theatre friend, John Garfield, for an acidic attack on the corruption of the studio system in *The Big Knife* (1949).

The playwright's usually acerbic screenplays are a list short on quantity but long on quality, including *The General Died at Dawn* (1936) with Gary Cooper involved in Far Eastern intrigue. Odets directed his *None But the Lonely Heart* (1944), which he also wrote and in which Cary Grant delivered one of his best and toughest performances. The curio *Deadline at Dawn* (1946), Clurman's only film as a director, starred Susan Hayward enmeshed in a murder mystery. *Humoresque* (1947) showed pianist Garfield romancing crackpot socialite Joan Crawford. The sublime Broadway-beat anti-Valentine *Sweet Smell of Success* (1957) starred Burt Lancaster as a scheming Walter Winchell-styled columnist and Tony Curtis a squashed-bug press agent. Other screenplays included *The Story on Page One* (1959) with Rita Hayworth and *Wild in the Country* (1961) with Elvis Presley as an aspiring writer.

Odets's greatest achievement in TV was one for which he received mostly posthumous recognition—as editor-in-chief of *The Richard Boone Show*, a dramatic anthology that was greatly acclaimed but lasted for only 24 installments during the 1963–64 NBC season. Boone hosted and sometimes starred with an ensemble including Robert Blake, Bethel Leslie, Lloyd Bochner, Ford Rainey, Jeanette Nolan, Guy Stockwell, Laura Devon, June Harding, and Harry Morgan. The Odets name signaled quality and the rangy, exacting star was committed to excellence for this unique TV equivalent of a theatrical repertory company. Among other scripts, Odets contributed *Big Mitch* with Boone as a father who can't face his beloved daughter's wedding. The show was nominated for several Emmy Awards, including ones for Outstanding Drama, Best Lead Actor in a Series (Boone), Lead Actress in a Series (Leslie and Nolan), and Drama Adaptation (Walter Brown Newman).

Odets's other plays include *Till the Day I Die*, *Winter Journey*, and *The Flowering Peach*.

Awake and Sing! (1972, PBS, 120m/c, **VHS**) *Hollywood Television Theatre: Special of the Week* ☆☆☆ **Tp:** Clifford Odets. **D:** Norman Lloyd, Robert Hopkins. **P:** Norman Lloyd, Lewis Freedman. **Cast:** Walter Matthau, Ron Rifkin, Martin Ritt, Felicia Farr, Leo Fuchs, Ruth Storey, Robert Lipton, Milton Seltzer, John Myhers. This 1935 play, the first full-length production by the legendary Group Theatre, concerns a Jewish family struggling to survive changing times. The production was mounted at Broadway's Belasco Theatre starring Lou Adler as the outspoken and cynical Moe Axelrod, along with Stella Adler, Jules (John) Garfield, Morris Carnovsky, and Sanford Meisner. This PBS production marked an unexpected return to TV for Matthau during his time as a top movie star, and it also featured a rare late-career return to acting for director Ritt.

- *"Alex Segal, who had been the director, had quit; the starting date was two weeks off, but the challenge was a welcome one, because of the play. A set was designed by the gifted Jan Scott. Walter Matthau agreed to play Moe Axelrod, and Marty Ritt, the director, played Uncle Morty....my first experience with multiple camera tape....the actual shots were called by an associate. For my first experience, I didn't want to call the shots, because I found it very confusing; I wanted to watch the performances."* (Norman Lloyd, Stages: Of Life in Theatre, Film and Television)

The Big Knife (1955, United Artists, 111m/bw, **VHS/DVD**) ☆☆☆½
Sc: James Poe. **D/P:** Robert Aldrich. **Cam:** Ernest Laszlo. **Cast:** Jack Palance, Ida Lupino, Rod Steiger, Shelley Winters, Wendell Corey, Jean Hagen, Ilka Chase, Everett Sloane, Wesley Addy, Nick Dennis, Paul Langton, Bill Walker, Strother Martin, Richard Boone (narrator). This was Odets's Hollywood play, about an idealistic movie star who has been so seduced by studio money that he can be blackmailed into signing a new contract. The 1949 Broadway rendition starred John Garfield in one of his last roles, and Odets partially based the play on the star's experiences. Studio executive Stanley Hoff spends the day at movie star Charlie Castle's ranch-style home to try and convince him to sign a new contract, and the long argument turns to blackmail. A lot of stagy heaving and hollering take place, much of it by Steiger as the pretentious Stanley, while the rangy Palance enacted perhaps his most helpless and indecisive part. Palance's performance, vehemently defended by Aldrich, drew much criticism.

- *"Much of the invective of* The Big Knife *derives from the original Odets play. The film adds a quasi-satirical dimension: Rod Steiger's blubbering, imbalanced Stanley Hoff ('Charlie, Charlie...the pain of this moment!'); Wendell Corey's unctuous press agentry as Smiley Coy; Jack Palance's leering, paranoiac Charlie Castle. The portrayals form an ensemble of not only Hollywood's cliches about itself but also of prototypical Robert Aldrich gargoyles. The unabashed theatrics, the drum rolls, the wildly expressive dialogue, such as, 'You came in here and threw this mess of naked pigeons in my face!,' create the vulgarity and hysteria that are fundamental to Aldrich's stylized, personal interpretation of Hollywood."* (Alain Silver, Film Noir: An Encyclopedic Reference to the American Style)

- *"Over the years* The Big Knife *has developed a cult following. Some admire the film for the courage it displays as an anti-Hollywood film; others take an almost campish delight in the melodrama of the story and the extravagance of the acting. More serious Aldrich critics see the film, along with* Kiss Me Deadly *and* Attack!, *as Aldrich's early trilogy in which he firmly established the themes and concerns heretofore only suggested. The* Big Knife *is one of the most effective and biting satires yet made on Hollywood, more so than the Odets play, which today seems too serious and self-satisfied. Aldrich adds the necessary anger and outrageousness to bring the satire off. Odets approved of Aldrich's work. He called it the best film of any of his plays..." (Edwin T. Arnold and Eugene L. Miller Jr.,* The Films and Career of Robert Aldrich)

Clash by Night is set in Monterey, Calif., where a diligent and somewhat dim commercial fisherman's bored wife strays into a heated affair with the local movie theater's projectionist. In the 1941 Broadway cast, directed by Lee Strasberg, were Tallulah Bankhead, Joseph Schildkraut, Lee J. Cobb, and Robert Ryan.

Clash by Night (1952, RKO, 105m/bw, **VHS**) ☆☆☆☆ **Sc:** Alfred Hayes. **D:** Fritz Lang. **Cam:** Nicholas Musuraca. **P:** Harriet Parsons. **Cast:** Barbara Stanwyck, Paul Douglas, Robert Ryan, Marilyn Monroe, J. Carroll Naish, Keith Andes, Silvio Minciotti, Gilbert Frye. If *The Country Girl* (see below) is the most overrated movie made from Odets's plays, this is the most underrated. Under Lang's hand, the love triangle was enacted by Stanwyck, Douglas, and Ryan with something near sublime senses of reality and complexity—the three were played with light and dark dimension, each with his or her own kind of idiosyncratic loneliness and demons. The working-class, seaside setting was perfectly caught by Musuraca's camera.

- *"This Fritz Lang version of a Clifford Odets melodrama about jealousy never quite comes together; the stylized Odets dialogue seems bizarrely out of place in the setting of a fishing village. But it's a handsome black-and-white setting, and though Barbara Stanwyck (as the adulteress) and Paul Douglas (as the betrayed husband) suffer rather too strenuously, Robert Ryan (as the wife's lover...) is so intensely sexual that the film momentarily achieves real, even if stagy, power." (Pauline Kael,* The New Yorker)

- *"Ryan enacts a...cynical guy who plays every word and gesture halfway into paranoia and with hard-bitten pathos. The role has been played by everyone from Mitchum to Widmark, but Ryan is the first one to give you the sense of an ordinary citizen being destroyed by a neurotic urge to act and admire himself at the same time. With pantomime that gives the sensation of a clock ticking away inside his skull, he is almost always caught in the process of observing himself while seeming to be observing and philosophizing about his friends." (Manny Farber,* The Nation)

Clash by Night (1957, CBS, 90m/bw) *Playhouse 90* ☆☆☆½ **Sc:** F.M. Durkee Jr., Clifford Odets (uncredited). **D:** John Frankenheimer. **P:** Martin Manulis. **Cast:** Kim Stanley, Lloyd Bridges, E.G. Marshall, Edgar Stehli, John Bleifer, Peggy Maurer. CBS and Manulis bought the property at Frankenheimer's urging, and assigned Durkee to the adaptation. Frankenheimer, who directed large-scale TV adaptations of stories by Faulkner, Hemingway, and Fitzgerald, concentrated on *Playhouse 90* in bringing the great American novelists and playwrights to viewers' attention. This was one of those efforts.

- *"Odets's eternal triangle tale is a powerful one intermingling the elements of bitterness, frustration, love and infidelity...trudged too slowly that first half hour....benefited...from excellent performances by Kim Stanley...Lloyd Bridges...and E.G. Marshall...John Frankenheimer's direction was good..."* (Variety)

- *"...Manulis hired a writer to adapt it, but he really messed it up. So I called Odets at home and said, 'There are big problems in the adaptation and I don't want to screw up your play.' He said, 'Come on over and we'll talk about it.' He served lemonade and we talked and eventually spent a week working on the script. I even got* Playhouse 90 *to pay him. He met Kim Stanley, who was in it, and had a long affair with her and directed her in the Paddy Chayefsky film* The Goddess." (*John Frankenheimer*, John Frankenheimer: A Conversation With Charles Champlin)

The Country Girl was the much-celebrated 1950 play about a Broadway marriage between an alcoholic, has-been actor and the supportive wife he abuses, both of whom are buoyed when a flashy young director decides to cast him in a big play. Odets directed the 1950 Broadway play starring Uta Hagen, Paul Kelly, and Steven Hill.

The Country Girl (1954, Paramount, 104m/bw, **VHS**) ☆☆☆ **Sc/D:** George Seaton. **Cam:** John F. Warren. **P:** William Perlberg, George Seaton. **Cast:** Bing Crosby, Grace Kelly, William Holden, Gene Reynolds, Anthony Ross, Jacqueline Fontaine, Eddie Ryder, Robert Kent, Jonathan (Jon) Provost. The big-name cast chewed the scenery, but the piece, as a whole, came off as artificial and stilted. Crosby's song-and-act man Frank Elgin, in a case of art imitating life, plays off the same fear the actor had in this role: He wasn't good enough to pull it off. Kelly, in specs, taking abuse, was also cast against type, and she won the Academy Award for Best Actress while Seaton won for the Screenplay, The film also was nominated for Best Picture, Director, Actor (Crosby), Cinematography, and Art Direction/Set Decoration.

- *"This rather odd movie, derived from a Clifford Odets play, features the least broken-down of actors, Bing Crosby, as a broken-down actor...Rather inexplicably, this sadomasochistic morass was one of the biggest box-office hits of its year, and somewhat inexplicably also, Academy*

Awards were presented...[an] uneven and incoherent screenplay." (Pauline Kael, 5001 Nights at the Movies)

- *"Crosby's performance was hailed as courageous and moving. The truth of the matter is that he remains a glum centerpiece while Kelly and Holden act circles around him. His emotional range is limited and so lumbering that it is often out of synch dramatically....Holden, meanwhile, brings off another demanding role, vitalizing a somewhat stock character and offering an elastic dramatic counterpoint to both Crosby and Kelly....When Grace Kelly was awarded the Oscar that year, he understood that he had assisted well beyond ceremonious nods." (Will Holtzman, William Holden)*

The Country Girl (1974, NBC, 90m/c) *The Hallmark Hall of Fame* ☆☆☆☆ **Tp:** Sidney Carroll. **D:** Paul Bogart. **P:** David Susskind. **Cast:** Jason Robards, Shirley Knight Hopkins, George Grizzard, Larry Haines, John Lithgow, Christopher Murney, Lisa Pelikan. Carroll trimmed much of the opening exposition to establish the characters—the play's fame and the actors' abilities sufficed. The energetic Grizzard's misreading of the marriage is more apparent in this version, as is the character's arrogance—compared to Holden's more movie-star-ish magnetism in the film.

- *"...The Hallmark Hall of Fame at its best, which is saying plenty....The trio of leading actors, Jason Robards, Shirley Knight Hopkins, and George Grizzard, were so good they hardly seemed to be acting at all. The fusion of their skill, Paul Bogart's exquisitely snug direction and Sidney Carroll's lean, uncluttered adaptation so sharply illuminated the characters in this emotion-charged story of backstage theatre that the effect often amounted to eavesdropping. How any of [the three leads] could have been better, I can't imagine." (Howard Thompson, The New York Times)*

The Country Girl (1982, Showtime, 137m/c, **VHS**) ☆½ **D:** Gary Halvorson, Michael Montell. **P:** Thorn-EMI. **Cast:** Dick Van Dyke, Faye Dunaway, Ken Howard, Dann Florek, Harry Groener. Taped at the Ed Sullivan Theater in New York, this purposefully stagebound version features two leads not up to the demands of the material.

- *"Though it was a valiant effort on all our parts, and there were moments that I thought were good and true, the remake fell short of our hopes and certainly of the original. But doing it helped remind me that I do love this business of acting, something the Crawford movie [Mommie Dearest] had come close to making me forget." (Faye Dunaway, Looking for Gatsby)*

Golden Boy (1939, Columbia, 99m/bw, **VHS**) ☆☆☆½ **Sc:** Louis Meltzer, Daniel Taradash, Victor Heeman, Sarah Y. Mason. **D:** Rouben Mamoulian. **Cam:** Nicholas Musuraca, Karl Freund. **P:** William Perlberg. **Cast:** William Holden, Barbara Stanwyck, Lee J. Cobb, Adolphe Menjou, Joseph Calleia, Edward S. Brophy, Sam Levene, Don Beddoe, Charles Halton, Frank Jenks, Clinton Rosemond. Joe Bonaparte, a teenage violinist, becomes an occasional prizefighter to pay for his music education. But his fight handlers use a dame to lure him into a full-fledged ring career in opposition to his music-loving immigrant father's wishes. The 1937 stage production, directed by Harold Clurman for The Group Theatre, starred Luther Adler and Frances Farmer. In 1938, John Garfield starred. Odets's brooding play was watered down for this film and the ending was changed for a Hollywood-styled happy finale. The film made an immediate star of Holden and his raw talent and enthusiasm played right into the part. The film was nominated for an Oscar for Best Musical Score (Victor Young).

- "William Holden — young, sensitive and handsome...in an only semi-reprehensible version of the Clifford Odets play...The role of Lorna Moon was built up to be large enough for Barbara Stanwyck, and the play was softened, rearranged, and wrenched around to provide for a happy ending. Yet the Odets material still has its dramatic pull, and Lee J. Cobb as the boy's father, Sam Levene as his taxi-driver brother-in-law, and Joseph Calleia as the slimy gangster out to corrupt him bring back some of the ambiance of the New York theatre in Odets's impassioned heyday." (Pauline Kael, 5001 Nights at the Movies)

- "William Holden, the newcomer in the title role, has been guilty in scattered scenes, of the exaggerated recoils, lip-bitings and hand-clenchings one associates with the old-time melodramatic school. In sum, however, it has been a good interpretation of an unusual role." (Frank Nugent, The New York Times)

Paradise Lost (1971, PBS, 180m/c) *NET Playhouse* ☆☆☆ **D/P:** Glenn Jordan. **Cast:** Eli Wallach, Jo Van Fleet, Bernadette Peters, Cliff Gorman, Biff McGuire, Fred Gwynn, Mike Kellin, George Voskovec, Sam Groom, Marian Winters, Jay Garner, David Hurst, Dorrie Cavanaugh. This 1935 play staged by The Group Theatre dissects the American middle class through the Gordon household and their acquaintances, living through the rough early years of the Great Depression. Morris Carnovsky, Robert Lewis, and Luther Adler were in the ensemble. This program was the first revival of the play in 25 years, shown in two parts, and was later rebroadcast in 1974 on PBS's *Theatre in America*.

- "Its shortcomings, which are severe, and its attributes, which are considerable, have not really changed. In his time, Mr. Odets was crying out a theme of 1971; the world can be beautiful if only there is love of one another and rejection of uneasy heartbreak and terror....Paradise Lost was not the best of the Odets works in terms of dramaturgy, but it is not hard to see why he had a special affection for the play. Mr. Odets himself was groping for answers in the 1930s as so many are now in 1971. In that context, Paradise Lost provides the patient viewer with an uneven if almost innocent poem of the mood when the world goes awry. Mr. Jordan was wise to do the play as a period piece and to accept the uneasy Odets flirtation with Chekhov." (Jack Gould, The New York Times)

Rocket to the Moon (1986, PBS, 120m/c) *American Playhouse* ☆☆☆
Tp: Wesley Moore. **D:** John Jacobs. **P:** John H. Williams. **Cast:** John
Malkovich, Judy Davis, Eli Wallach, Ian McShane, Connie Booth,
William Hootkins, Edward Wiley. The ensemble—especially Davis and
Wallach—was uniformly brilliant in this British-based production of
one of Odets's least memorable works of romantic idealism. The play depicts a Bronx dentist, Ben Stark, engaged in middle-aged adultery with
his lively if lonely assistant. The tryst is promoted by the father of his
henpecking wife, but Ben's happiness is compromised by the mistakes
and malevolence of his past. The play, directed by Harold Clurman for
the Group Theatre at the Belasco Theatre, debuted on Broadway in
1938 starring Luther Adler, Morris Carnovsky, Eleanor Lynn, Lief Erickson, and Ruth Nelson.

- "*...an exceptionally skillful production featuring several fine performances.
  In the end, though, the play itself is less memorable for its insights than for
  its curious innocence....exactly the kind of project that serious television
  should be encouraging. Even flawed Odets is preferable to the production-
  by-committee pablum typifying the bulk of the ordinary week's television
  schedule....whatever Odets intended, the play really belongs to Cleo, and
  this production is dominated by Judy Davis, who gives the young woman a
  fascinatingly edgy vitality. Miss Davis...is riveting...Failing to be profound,
  or even intellectually tough,* Rocket to the Moon *settles for bittersweet observations.*" (John J. O'Connor, The New York Times)

John O'Hara
John Henry O'Hara
Born: January 31, 1905, Pottsville, PA. **Died:** 1970.

John O'Hara's novels were adapted into the films *Ten North Frederick*
(1958), *From the Terrace* (1960), *Butterfield 8* (1960), which won Elizabeth
Taylor her first Academy Award, and *A Rage to Live* (1965). His short stories were adapted into the films *On Our Merry Way* (1948), and *The Best
Things in Life Are Free* (1956), and the critically acclaimed 1975 TV series
Gibbsville, based on his native Pottsville, Pennsyvania. O'Hara's distinguished novels include *Lovey Childs*, *The Horse Knows the Way*, and *Ap-
pointment in Samarra*, which was adapted into a 1953 installment of *Robert
Montgomery Presents*. O'Hara wrote three screenplays, for the films *He Married His Wife* (1940), *I Was an Adventuress* (1940), and *Moontide* (1942).

Pal Joey (1957, Columbia, 111m/c, **VHS/DVD**) ☆☆½ **Sc:** Dorothy
Kingsley. **D:** George Sidney. **P:** Fred Kolmar. **Cam:** Harold Lipstein. **Cast:**

Frank Sinatra, Kim Novak, Rita Hayworth, Barbara Nichols, Bobby Sherwood, Hank Henry, Elizabeth Patterson, Leon Alton, Isabel Analla, Robert Anderson, Maurice Argent, Tol Avery. On the way to this big-star extravaganza, the 1941 Gene Kelly hit stage musical was considerably laundered, primarily in Joey's character, converting him from a lout into a flawed chum for Sinatra. The character began in a series of fictional articles about Joey's exploits that were signed "Your Pal Joey" in *The New Yorker*. O'Hara converted them into the book for the stage with music by Richard Rodgers and Lorenz Hart. In 1953, the musical was successfully revived in a version starring Harold Lang and was again resurrected on Broadway in 1976 with Christopher Chadman. The songs include "The Lady Is a Tramp," "My Funny Valentine," and "Bewitched, Bothered and Bewildered." The film was nominated for Oscars for Art Direction/Set Decoration, Film Editing, Costumes, and Sound.

• *"Blighted Hollywoodization…with the score purified along with Joey's character. The heel-hero—a hoofer in the Broadway version—is now a crooner, in line with the talents of Frank Sinatra. His singing helps things along, and he does the only acting, though Kim Novak's vacuity is rather touching and isn't as laborious as Rita Hayworth's performance….sad botch…"* (Pauline Kael, 5,001 Nights at the Movies)

Eugene O'Neill

Eugene Gladstone O'Neill
Born: October 16, 1888, New York, NY. **Died:** 1953.
Nobel Literature Laureate: 1936.
Pultitzer Prize-winning plays: *Beyond the Horizon* (1920),
  Anna Christie (1922), *Strange Interlude* (1928),
  Long Day's Journey Into Night (1957)
Tony Award-winning play: *Long Day's Journey Into Night*

As befits America's greatest dramatist, Eugene O'Neill is one of the most adapted playwrights to the big and small screens. His works of melancholy, neurosis, and alcoholism, of unrealized dreams, family strife and haunted Irishmen and sailors, have struck lasting chords with both filmmakers and audiences. Directors usually approached the master's works with a sense of reverence and the acting showcases that emerged are among cinema's greatest, particularly in the film version of *Long Day's Journey Into Night* and the TV versions of *The Iceman Cometh*, *Hughie*, and *A Moon for the Misbegotten*, all starring Jason Robards.

Sidney Lumet directed Robards in O'Neill's two greatest plays to outstanding critical success: *Long Day's Journey Into Night* on film and *The Iceman Cometh* for public television. Roberta Maxwell, Geraldine Fitzgerald,

Richard Backus, James Broderick, John Qualen, Sorrell Booke, Tom Pedi, George Marion, Thomas Mitchell, and Mickey Rooney starred in multiple O'Neill screen versions. Dudley Nichols adapted two and directed one of those. Jose Quintero, who directed 17 productions of O'Neill plays, co-directed two for television. The glaring absentee from home viewing is the John Frankenheimer-directed version of *The Iceman Cometh*. The Laurence Olivier version of *Long Day's Journey Into Night* is also, regrettably, unavailable for home viewing, along with two Robards performances, *Hughie* and the multi-Emmy-nominated *A Moon for the Misbegotten*.

Notable O'Neill plays not yet filmed include *All God's Chillun Got Wings*, *More Stately Mansions*, *The Great God Brown*, *Marco Millions*, *Gold*, *Diff'rent*, *The Dreamy Kid*, *Dynamo*, *The First Man*, *Lazarus Laughed*, *The Fountain*, *Recklessness*, *Before Breakfast*, *Servitude*, *Thirst*, *Fog*, *The Sniper*, *Days Without End*, and *Welded*.

Ah, Wilderness! was the most easygoing of O'Neill's major pieces, an affectionate slice-of-life comedy about a small-town Fourth of July celebration in 1906 enveloping a coming of age story. Unlike anything else by the dark genius of the American stage, it was first produced on the stage in 1933 with an ensemble including George M. Cohan, Elisha Cook, and Gene Lockhart.

Ah, Wilderness! (1935, MGM, 101m/bw, **VHS**) ☆☆☆½ **Sc:** Albert Hackett, Frances Goodrich. **D:** Clarence Brown. **Cam:** Clyde de Vinna. **P:** Hunt Stromberg. **Cast:** Eric Linden, Wallace Beery, Lionel Barrymore, Mickey Rooney, Spring Byington, Aline MacMahon, Charley Grapewin, Eddie Nugent, Bonita Granville. This was an archetypal example of MGM's tendency to romanticize Americana and small-town life. The studio assembled its blue-chip players for the occasion, and Brown's smooth, light touch kept Beery's tippling uncle and Barrymore's grandfatherly mien in check in this, the best film rendition of the play.

- *"...so remote from Eugene O'Neill's life and his other work that it's something of a freak. O'Neill said that the play came to him at night, as a dream, but it seems to be a dream based on Booth Tarkington's world....while not a world-shaker, and rather dim as entertainment, [it] has at least a nice, quiet, comic sense of period."* (Pauline Kael, The New Yorker)

Summer Holiday (1948, MGM, 92m/c, **VHS**) ☆☆½ **Sc:** Irving Brecher and Jean Holloway, from the 1935 screenplay by Albert Hackett and Frances Goodrich. **D:** Rouben Mamoulian. **Cam:** Charles Schoenbaum. **P:** Arthur Freed. **Cast:** Mickey Rooney, Walter Huston, Frank Morgan, Agnes Moorehead, Gloria DeHaven, Marilyn Maxwell, Anne Francis, Butch Jenkins, Selena Royle. This musical version, which was Mamoulian's penultimate film, put Rooney—who played the kid brother in MGM's first version of the play (immediately above)—at center-stage as the love-stricken teen. He was 28 at the time of the film's release, two years after filming. His *c'mon-fellas!* identity from the small-town MGM Andy Hardy series infects this high-gloss Technicolor souffle—he mugs it up. The prominent songs include "It's Our Home Town" and "Stanley Steamer."

- "...*it shattered the ersatz peace of MGM's own* Andy Hardy *series with O'Neill's sharp eye for the details of Growing Up in Smalltown. Here, too, is a safe place, but Mamoulian captures its profound idealism; he shows us what kind of Americans make a safe place....Rooney...remained Andy Hardy, but around him Mamoulian spins a wonderful tour...Everything in the film is commonplace but, viewed with love and wisdom, seems rare.*" (*Ethan Mordden,* The Hollywood Musical)

- "...*essentially ghastly musical...Mamoulian has a heavy touch, and perhaps because of that, Mickey Rooney, in the lead, mugs offensively....disastrous script...undistinguished music...*" (*Pauline Kael,* The New Yorker)

Ah, Wilderness! (1951, ABC, 60m/bw) *Celanese Theatre* ☆☆☆ **Sc:** Joe Schrank. **D/P:** Alex Segal. **Cast:** Roddy McDowall, Thomas Mitchell, Howard St. John, Dorothy Peterson, Sandy Horn, Philip Coolidge. This first TV presentation of the play was the debut installment of the Peabody Award-winning series.

- "...*few dramatic shows on television this year, or in previous years, for that matter, have been treated to a more fluent, full-bodied production....the designing of [the] settings...were one of the delights of the current TV semester....Its comedic quotient is debatable today, and to most people its story value is rather dated.*" (Variety)

Ah, Wilderness! (1959, NBC, 90m/bw) *The Hallmark Hall of Fame* ☆☆½ **Tp:** Robert Hartung. **D:** Robert Mulligan. **P:** Mildred Freed Alberg. **Cast:** Lee Kinsolving, Helen Hayes, Lloyd Nolan, Burgess Meredith, Betty Field, Dolores Sutton, Nicholas Pryor, Abigail Kellogg, Roy Poole, Norman Fell, Truman Smith, Glenn Walken, Sybil Baker, Aina Niemela, Robert Dowdell. The most notable TV adaptation of the play marked the only time that Hayes, the "First Lady of the American Theatre," acted on screen in an O'Neill work.

- "*In terms of [television],* Hallmark's presentation of Ah, Wilderness! *is an American tragedy. It's not frequent that Eugene O'Neill is seen on this medium, and this being his only comedy, it's a pity that it wasn't the joyous event it was slated to be....the major fault in this effort was the extremely slow gait of the show, which seemed to swallow up the shining moments of the cast.*" (Variety)

Ah, Wilderness! (1976, PBS, 120m/c, **VHS**) *Theatre in America* ☆☆☆☆ **D:** Arvin Brown. **P:** Lindsay Law. **Host:** Hal Holbrook. **Cast:** Richard Backus, Joyce Ebert, Geraldine Fitzgerald, Swoosie Kurtz, William Swetland, Victor Garber, Linda Hunt, John Braden. This colorful, taped revival by the Connecticut-based Long Wharf Theatre Company emphasized comedy. The ensemble was uniformly excellent.

- "...a thoroughly charming production, salvaging the play from such past abuses as a musical [stage] production called Take Me Along....With sustained intelligence and sensitivity, the Long Wharf and its artistic director, Arvin Brown, have wrought something of a miracle with Ah, Wilderness!...Geraldine Fitzgerald and William Swetland are splendidly fussy and touching as the parents and a young actress with the name of Swoosie Kurtz is absolutely enchanting. As a celebration of innocence, private and national, Ah, Wilderness! is a startlingly lovely collection of Fourth of Julys, tipsy uncles, books by Shaw and Swinburne, sloe gin fizzes and Manhattans, virgins and swift women." (John J. O'Connor, The New York Times)

Ah, Wilderness! was cut to 60 minutes for a Front Row Center installment in 1955, directed and produced by Fletcher Markle and featuring Robert (Bobby) Driscoll, Leon Ames, Lillian Bronson, Lyle Talbot, Olive Sturgess, and Anne Whitfield.

Anna Christie was first produced on the stage in 1922 starring Pauline Lord, George Marion, and George T. Mack. The play was filmed once as a silent, twice in 1930 talkies with Greta Garbo, and twice for TV. Garbo shot a German version simultaneously with the one listed below, directed by Jacques Feydor with a German supporting cast. The playwright's first Pulitzer Prize winner concerned the title waterfront prostitute and the sailor who wants to marry her.

Anna Christie (1923, Ince, 75m/bw/silent, **VHS**) ☆☆☆ **D:** John Wray. **Cast:** Blanche Sweet, George F. Marion Sr., William Russell, Eugenie Besserer, Chester Conklin, Victor Potel, George Siegmann, Fred Kohler, Sr. This silent arrived a year after the play's Broadway debut, as a vehicle for Sweet via a Thomas H. Ince production. This was reportedly the only screen version of any of O'Neill's works that pleased the playwright.

- "Seldom is the task of writing about a picture approached with the keen enthusiasm we feel for the film version of Anna Christie, which happens to be one of those isolated instances that causes you to forget almost that the story is being told in nothing more than lights and shadows flung upon the screen....Blanche Sweet as Anna Christie makes the shadow impersonation live. In fact it would be difficult to imagine any actress doing better in this exacting role....Miss Sweet does some marvelous acting...a film that is intensely dramatic..." (The New York Times)

Anna Christie (1930, MGM, 90m/bw, **VHS**) ☆☆☆½ **Sc:** Frances Marion. **D:** Clarence Brown. **Cam:** William Daniels. **Cast:** Greta Garbo, Charles Bickford, Marie Dressler, James T. Mack, Lee Phelps, George Marion. This is the picture that introduced Garbo to talkies. The famous advertising lines blared, "Garbo talks!" Her first line: "Give me a whiskey, ginger ale on the side. And don't be stingy, baby." Her Anna is romanced by sailor Bickford and there's a lot of gloomy, ponderous exposition about the evils of the sea in this stagy early talkie that was obviously trapped by immobile microphones. It's the first sound-era O'Neill adaptation. The film received Academy Award nominations for Best Actress (Garbo), Director, and Cinematography.

- *"This is not one of Eugene O'Neill's best plays, and dat-ole-devil-sea stuff is pretty hard to take in this version..."* (Pauline Kael, The New Yorker)

- *"Daniels, eventually to become Garbo's cameraman as Brown was her director, lit Anna Christie with an intensity that partially betrayed the nature of Eugene O'Neill's intramural tragedy, but his work makes it a distinctive film and one of the most striking of the decade's first years....a tour de force [by Garbo]. Ranting, shouting, muttering in almost broken English, she holds one's attention totally."* (John Baxter, Hollywood in the Thirties)

Anna Christie (1952, ABC, 60m/bw) *Celanese Theatre* ☆☆½ **Tp:** Norman Lessing. **D:** Alex Segal. **P:** A. Burke Crotty. **Cast:** June Havoc, Richard Burton, John Qualen, Doris Rich, Art Smith. This initial TV version included one of Burton's few TV appearances and his only association with O'Neill.

- *"...faithful in spirit and mostly in letter to the original. The old TV bogey of trying to beat the rap on condensing a full-blown legiter to an hour (less the commercials) was not as successful....Richard Burton, as Anna's bombastic but simple honest stoker-man intent on marrying her despite her past, was as dynamic as Dr. O'Neill ordered."* (Variety)

Anna Christie (1955, NBC, 60m/bw) *Pond's Theatre* ☆☆☆ **D:** Fred Carney. **Cast:** Constance Ford, Everett Sloan, James Daly, Joseph Sweeney. The series was an offshoot of *Kraft Television Theatre*.

- *"...most effectively directed by Fred Carney. The poetic overtones of the O'Neill work and its understanding of obsessed people were preserved in a production obviously respecting the author's intent...In the title role, Constance Ford caught the elemental beauty behind the girl's seediness....her performance had stature."* (Jack Gould, The New York Times)

Beyond the Horizon (1976, PBS, 90m/c, **VHS**) *Theatre in America* ☆☆☆ **D:** Rick Hauser, Michael Kahn. **Host:** Geraldine Fitzgerald. **Cast:** Richard Backus, James Broderick, Geraldine Fitzgerald, John Houseman, Kate Wilkinson, John Randolph, Maria Tucci. The play, in which two brothers fight over a woman, was O'Neill's Pulitzer Prize-honored debate between the values of hearth-and-home down on the family farm and foreign wanderlust. It was first produced on the stage in 1920 with Richard Bennett.

- *"But a miscalculation of...distressing proportions has been made in the casting of Richard Backus as Robert....simply physical miscasting. Mr. Backus is youthful looking to the point of adolescent blushes. As the years roll by in Beyond the Horizon, he simply refuses to age...Although seriously flawed, this production...merits attention." (John J. O'Connor, The New York Times)*

Desire Under the Elms (1958, Paramount, 114m/bw, **VHS**) ☆☆½ **Sc:** Irwin Shaw. **D:** Delbert Mann. **Cam:** Daniel L. Fapp. **P:** Don Hartman. **Cast:** Sophia Loren, Burl Ives, Anthony Perkins, Pernell Roberts, Frank Overton, Anne Seymour, Jean Willes, Rebecca Welles. First produced on the stage in 1924 with Walter Huston, this play tells of a New England farmer who brings his young foreign bride back to the homestead in 1840, igniting mutual desires between her and his son. This highly charged and uneven melodramatic film used stagy-looking sets, apparently to reflect the origins of the 35-year-old material. It also unleashed Burl Ives, in his rip-roaring screen period, as the father, and he comes off like a dirty old man. Fapp's cinematography, in VistaVision, received the film's lone Oscar nomination.

- *"...a solemn, antiseptic, studio-manufactured version of Eugene O'Neill's stark, spare 1924 drama....It's slow and drab with more melo than drama, and it becomes more dour and ludicrous by each rerun." (Judith Crist, Judith Christ's TV Guide to the Movies)*

- *"There is plenty of kissing in it, without hesitancy; but an inherent fear of joy, a conviction that pleasure must be paid for, haunts the story. The play intends to pluck out the dry demon of Puritanism that it may shrivel in the sunlight, but underneath this, one feels a conviction that even this excision will not improve matters much. In a quite literal sense, life will always be one damned thing after another....Under Delbert Mann's direction, Miss Loren gives considerable evidence of development as an actress....It is in the two principal male performances that the picture falters badly. Anthony Perkins...is miscast...His immaturity is especially evident in the love scenes with Miss Loren. I expected her to brush him aside with the back of her hand. Burl Ives...attempts to perpetuate the myth that he is an actor." (Stanley Kauffmann, The New Republic)*

The Emperor Jones, about a black Pullman porter who escapes a chain gang to become a Caribbean jungle-island king, was written in semi-expressionist style and intended to be presented that way. It was first produced in 1920 at New York's Neighborhood Playhouse starring Jasper Deeter and Christine Ell.

The Emperor Jones (1933, UA, 72m/bw, **VHS**) ☆☆☆ **Sc:** DuBose Heyward. **D:** Dudley Murphy. **Cast:** Paul Robeson, Dudley Digges, Frank Wilson, Fredi Washington, Ruby Elzy, Moms Mabley. The movie is valuable, in retrospect, as the sole chance to see the powerful Paul Robeson on film in an O'Neill work. It was O'Neill who ignited Robeson's passion for acting when the playwright asked him to star in his plays *All God's Chillun Got Wings* and *The Emperor Jones*. The singer/lawyer/athlete proved himself a striking presence, especially in this film. Director Murphy showcased Robeson and emphasized expressionism with austere and painted sets including a fake jungle—artistic tactics that may be lost on modern viewers who think they're just watching a cheap B movie.

- *"It is a distinguished offering, resolute and firm, with a most compelling portrayal by Paul Robeson of the ambitious...Brutus Jones. Although the narrative is slightly amplified, it is developed along intelligent cinematic lines and differs but little from the sum total of the original [play]."* (Mordaunt Hall, The New York Times)

The Emperor Jones (1955, NBC, 60m/bw) *Kraft Television Theatre* ☆☆½ **D/P:** Fielder Cook. **Cast:** Ossie Davis, Rex Ingram, Everett Sloane, Curtis James Dance Troupe. This was one of the long-running series's more attention-getting presentations, with Davis in an early starring role.

- *"A good try, and in spots quite powerful, but it didn't come off with continuity and impact....Ossie Davis, though at times powerful and moving as Jones, couldn't overcome what at times amounted to incoherence in the scripting and staging....rates a bow from the waist for exploring the offbeat and the new in television. More of it is welcome, and better luck next time."* (Variety)

The Emperor Jones (1958, ABC, 75m/bw) ☆☆☆ **Tp:** Terry Southern. **P:** William Kotcheff. **Cast:** Kenneth Spencer, Harry H. Corbett, Connie Smith, Stan Simmons, Van Boolen, Frank Blaine, Harold Holness, Bari Johnson, Jimmy Moore, Cleo Dupont, Rita Lester, Bill Patterson, Raymond McClean, Chief Odongo, Boscoe Holder Dancers.

- *"...hardly the type of program to command and hold a mass audience...the adaptation by Terry Southern and the addition of ballet sequences to illustrate the nightmare of the haunted man hardly eased the way. The dramatic highlight of the production was the performance by Kenneth Spencer in the title role. A man whose stature measured up to the character, he had an authority and presence which enriched the role and gave it depth and meaning....a towering performance."* (Variety)

The Hairy Ape (1944, UA, 90m/bw, **VHS**) ☆☆½ **Sc:** Robert Hardy Andrews, Decla Dunning. **D:** Alfred Santell. **Cam:** Lucien Andriot. **P:** Jules Levy. **Cast:** William Bendix, Susan Hayward, John Loder, Dorothy Comingore, Alan Napier, Roman Bohnen. The title is the pejorative moniker for Yank Smith, a Lisbon-to-New York ship's stoker who decides to kill an elitist female passenger after she recoils from his amorous advances. The play, starring Louis Wolheim and Mary Blair, was first performed in 1922. The plot was dated by the time of this film, which was updated to the World War II years but still had a musty feel. Bendix, though, was successful in the way Garbo was in *Anna Christie* and Paul Robeson was in *The Emperor Jones* in eliciting O'Neill's ideas about self-examination becoming a form of torture. The film received an Oscar nomination for Best Musical Score (Michel Michelet and Edward Paul).

- *"...disappointing...Artily directed by Santell...The play's language was considerably modified and its class-conscious emphases played down in this interesting but unsatisfactory filming."* (Charles Higham and Joel Greenberg, Hollywood in the Forties)

Hughie (1981, Showtime, 60m/c) ☆☆☆½ **D:** Jose Quintero, Terry Hughes. **Cast:** Jason Robards, Jack Dodson. One of O'Neill's posthumously performed works—completed in 1941 but not staged until 1959—the play is essentially a monologue set in the lobby of a dive Broadway hotel in the summer of 1928. The gabber is Erie Smith, whose overly fond and obviously embellished recollections of the deceased title character, the former hotel night clerk, allow both him and the tolerant new night clerk to imagine more satisfying lives than they have lived. Robards acted the definitive Erie Smith in this superb performance. The role was first inhabited by Robards in 1964—with Quintero directing and Dodson co-starring—and has also been subsequently played onstage by Ben Gazzara and Al Pacino. This show was taped at the Hyde Park Festival Theatre in upstate New York. The same production aired on PBS in 1984 on *American Playhouse*.

- *"Erie demands a virtuosic performance, and that is what the role gets from Mr. Robards. [Erie's] bravado is defeated by his mirthless laugh. He whines, cajoles, implores with a mixture of fear and contempt. He is a once-disarming conman reduced to the last roll of the dice. Mr. Robards is almost chillingly on target. This record of his performance is invaluable."* (John J. O'Connor, The New York Times)

The Iceman Cometh, considered a flop when it was first performed on Broadway in 1946 starring James Barton, was revived by the Circle-in-the-Square Theatre in 1956 and elevated to its classical status via the career-making performance of Jason Robards, Jr. The actor played one of his signature O'Neill roles and one of the theatre's great roles as Hickey, the traveling salesman, who tries to talk a New York City barroom full of rummies into ridding themselves of pipe dreams.

The Iceman Cometh (1960, PBS, 208m/bw, **VHS**) *The Play of the Week* ☆☆☆☆☆ **D:** Sidney Lumet. **P:** Lewis Freedman. **Host:** Worthington Miner. **Cast:** Jason Robards, Jr., James Broderick, Myron McCormick, Roland Winters, Robert Redford, Sorrell Booke, Julie Bovasso, Farrell Pelly, Tom Pedi, Michael Strong, Charles White, Hilda Brawner. **Commentary:** Brooks Atkinson. This legendary performance of the nearly four-hour play aired in two parts two weeks apart in November 1960, originating from studios at New York's Channel 13. This was one of Redford's first TV appearances, as Don Parritt, and his only involvement with O'Neill. McCormick was excellent as Larry.

- *"Television drama soared to triumphant, poetic dimensions in the four-hour rendition of Eugene O'Neill's* The Iceman Cometh....*The home screen, usually so filled with formula trivia, seldom has had so many glorious moments. The O'Neill outing...was a landmark for the video medium, a reference point for greatness in TV drama."* (Variety)

- *"A theatrical experience that remorselessly envelops the viewer in the playwright's marathon documentary on doom. It is a superlative triumph."* (Jack Gould, The New York Times)

- *"One of the most electrifying evenings in the history of television drama."* (New York Herald-Tribune)

The Iceman Cometh (1973, American Film Theatre, 239m/c) ☆☆☆☆☆
Sc: Thomas Quinn Curtiss. **D:** John Frankenheimer. **P:** Ely Landau. **Cam:** Ralph Woolsey. **Cast:** Lee Marvin, Fredric March, Robert Ryan, Jeff Bridges, Moses Gunn, Bradford Dillman, Tom Pedi, Sorrell Booke, Clifton James, Evans Evans, John McLiam, Martyn Green, George Voskovec, Bart Burns. Curtiss's job was to trim the play. The film is faithful to the tawdry milieu and the dark-hearted spirit of the playwright, and was unfairly criticized for Marvin's performance by critics who could only recall Robards. But Marvin delivered one of his best performances as Hickey, the insinuation in his foghorn voice giving the character a sardonic edge, and the actor's characteristic expansiveness afforded the dim circumstances moments of light. Ryan received a Special Award from the National Society of Film Critics for his performance as O'Neill's cynical anarchist, Larry Slade, and was named Best Actor by the National Board of Review (a tie with Al Pacino in *Serpico*). When rebroadcast on TV, this film is shown in versions as short as 101 minutes.

- "The Iceman Cometh *is a success indeed. It is not merely the worthy production of a great play; it also posesses moments of its own greatness....The movie belongs most to Robert Ryan, and is an eloquent memorial to his talent."* (Jay Cocks, Time)

- *"A filmed play like this one doesn't offer the sensual excitement that the movies can offer, but you don't go to it for that; you go to it for O'Neill's crude, prosaic virtuosity, which is also pure American poetry, and for the kind of cast that rarely gathers for a stage production....Ryan (who died shorty after) got right to the boozy, gnarled soul of the play."* (Pauline Kael, The New Yorker)

- *"And to crown the work there is Lee Marvin, as Hickey, the salesman-apostle. To put it simply: Marvin was born to play Hickey. He has the perfect understanding of the man and perfect equipment to deal with it....Marvin understands the bumps and sags, and he lifts it all adroitly with gesture, with vaudevillian's esprit, to present both the man who was and who is. Then comes the payoff, the great last act. Marvin is wonderful. I have seen James Barton, the first Hickey, and Jason Robards (along with others), and though they were both unforgettably good, Marvin goes past them—so powerfully that he makes the crux of the play clearer than I have ever found it before, onstage or page." (Stanley Kauffmann,* The New Republic)

Ile, a one-act play first performed in 1917, concerns an 1895 voyage aboard a whaling ship, captained by a tyrannical Ahab-like taskmaster, and carrying his alarmed wife and mutinous crew. It was performed on TV twice in the 1950s. On CBS's *Lux Video Theatre* in 1952, Fielder Cook directed Gene Lockhart and Fay Bainter. On ABC's *Star Tonight* in 1955, the cast included Perry Wilson, Philip Kenneally, Luis Van Rooten, and Bruce Gordon.

Long Day's Journey Into Night depicts 24 hours in an aging matinee idol's family in 1912 Connecticut. This quartet is comprised of the vain James Tyrone, his morphine-addicted wife, and booze-pinching adult sons Jamie, the actor/loafer, and Edmund, the consumption-afflicted seafarer (an O'Neill alter-ego). Produced on Broadway in 1956, three years after the playwright's death, it became a sensation in the embodiments of Fredric March and Florence Eldridge as the parents and Jason Robards Jr. and Bradford Dillman as the sons. The play won a both a Pulitzer Prize a Tony Award, as well as a Tony for March.

Long Day's Journey Into Night (1962, Ely Landau, 174m/bw, **VHS**) ☆☆☆☆☆ Sc/**D:** Sidney Lumet. **P:** Ely Landau. **Cam:** Boris Kaufman. **Cast:** Ralph Richardson, Katharine Hepburn, Jason Robards, Jr., Dean Stockwell, Jeanne Barr. This film remains the standard classical interpretation. The nearly undiluted play was brilliantly interpreted by the great cast and unobtrusively yet reverently lensed in black and white by Lumet and Kaufman. The result has both a near-documentary feel and a museum-piece aspect. The cast was awarded a collective honor as the year's best at the Cannes Film Festival and Hepburn, in what is arguably her greatest performance and one of cinema's great interpretations of drug addiction, received an Oscar nomination for Best Actress.

- "*Mr. Richardson's performance was superb, catching all the celebrated vanity, cruelty and meanness of the man....Jason Robards was absolutely brilliant as the older son...one of the few great American family films.*" (Bosley Crowther, Reruns: 50 Memorable Films)

- "*Perhaps just because of its naked familiarity, its grinding, ludicrous wrestling with expressiveness, Journey is, at last, an American family classic; the usual embarrassments are transcended, and the family theme is raised to mythic heights. This is the best film ever made from an O'Neill play (and it's O'Neill's greatest play)...Hepburn's transitions here — the way she can look 18 or 80 at will — seem iridescent. She surpasses herself: the most beautiful screen comedienne of the 1930s and 1940s becomes our greatest screen tragedienne." (Pauline Kael, The New Yorker)*

Long Day's Journey Into Night (1973, ABC, 175m/c) ☆☆☆☆½ **Sc:** Peter Wood, Michael Blakemore. **D:** Peter Wood. **Cast:** Laurence Olivier, Constance Cummings, Denis Quilley, Ronald Pickup, Maureen Lipman. Olivier starred in a rendition that preserved his performance in the National Theatre of Great Britain stage production. Fussier than most interpretations, it also inferred a snide self-referencing aspect in the matinee idol-gone-to-seed passages. Olivier won the Emmy Award for Best Actor and the show was nominated for Outstanding Single Program of the 1972–73 season.

• *"The performances maintain a rare level of acting excellence. And with Lord Olivier as James Tyrone, that level rises to magnificent. With hair slicked down, sporting a theatrical handkerchief and the air of a gentleman rogue, the former Sir Laurence displays the entire artistic inheritance of his 50 years as an outstanding actor. It is a memorable performance." (John J. O'Connor, The New York Times)*

• *"...wrings the audience like a mop, leaving it drained and exhausted....triumphant...a dazzling individual experience in its own right....shortened by 40 minutes from the stage version...it is Olivier's golden-voiced old James Tyrone that is unforgetable here. That final soliloquy is one of the great triumphs of the modern theatre." (Cecil Smith, Los Angeles Times)*

Long Day's Journey Into Night (1987, Showtime, 169m/c, **VHS**) ☆☆☆☆ **D:** Jonathan Miller. **Cast:** Jack Lemmon, Bethel Leslie, Peter Gallagher, Kevin Spacey. Lemmon's 1987 Broadway rendition of James Tyrone was preserved in this taped version, which was also picked up for airing on PBS's *American Playhouse* in 1988. Spacey was superb as Edmund.

• *"Mr. Miller, who delights in provocation, created something of a stir by having the characters engage in stretches of overlapping readings of the dialogue. They don't so much interpret each other as speak simultaneously, apparently in an effort to simulate what Mr. Miller deems to be normal conversation and, at the same time, to speed up the action....the device quickly becomes an irritating gimmick....[Jack Lemmon delivers] one of the most ambitious and admirable performances of his career." (John J. O'Connor, The New York Times)*

Long Day's Journey Into Night (1982, ARTS) ☆☆☆½ **D:** William Woodman. **Cast:** Ruby Dee, Earle Hyman, Thommie Blackwell, Peter Francis-James. This TV version, with an all-black cast, was filmed in Canada for a Hearst-ABC Alpha Repertory Television Service (ARTS) Showcase presentation that Woodman retooled from a stage version directed by Geraldine Fitzgerald.

- *"The characters of O'Neill's intensely Irish-American world are being played by an entirely black cast of performers. At first, the effect is disconcerting. Everything seems a bit awkwardly self-conscious. But gradually, the sheer power of the play, handled with skill, takes over, and the result is a stunning demonstration of the universality of O'Neill's art. As Mary Tyrone...Ruby Dee gives a luminous performance...with unflagging skill."* (John J. O'Connor, The New York Times)

Long Day's Journey Into Night (1996, Stratford Festival, 174m/c, **VHS**) ☆☆☆½ **Sc:** Eugene O'Neill. **D:** David Wellington. **Cam:** David Franco. **Cast:** William Hutt, Martha Henry, Peter Donaldson, Tom McCamus, Martha Burns. This most recent film version was made in Toronto. Four of the five actors swept the Genie Awards, the Canadian equivalent of the Oscars, and McCamus was also nominated for Supporting Actor. The picture was nominated for the Best Film Genie.

- *"Martha Henry is brilliant...The role almost invites melodrama, yet without diluting its theatricality, Henry reins in the character and makes her real, locating that knife-edge of paranoid wit on which Mary's emotions are so precariously balanced. Her transitions from blithe reverie to stone-cold bitterness are devastating."* (Brian D. Johnson, Maclean's)

The Long Voyage Home (1940, United Artists, 105m/bw, **VHS**) ☆☆☆☆ **Sc:** Dudley Nichols. **D:** John Ford. **Cam:** Gregg Toland. **P:** Walter Wanger. **Cast:** John Wayne, Thomas Mitchell, Ian Hunter, Ward Bond, Barry Fitzgerald, Mildred Natwick, Wilfrid Lawson, Arthur Shields, John Qualen, Joe Sawyer. This is an amalgamation of four one-act plays of the sea, using portions of *The Moon of the Caribees*, *Bound East for Cardiff*, *In the Zone*, and *The Long Voyage Home*, all tied together by the characters of O'Neill's fictional British tramp freighter, the *S.S. Glencairn*. The one-acters dated from between 1916 and 1919. Nichols took his cue from a 1937 production staged by William Challee through the Works Progress Administration's Federal Theatre Project at New York's Lafayette Theatre, with an ensemble that included William Cumberbatch, Canada Lee, and Thurman Jackson. This film amalgam made for one of Ford's most engrossing yet least remembered great works. Filmed along fog-shrouded waterfronts, it deals with sailors on leave from the *S.S. Glencairn*, and the peculiarities of their lives. Character-driven and atmospheric, the film features an exceptional ensemble. The youthful Wayne, in the year after Ford made him a star in *Stagecoach*, proved himself an excellent actor as Ole Olson. The film received Oscar nominations for Best Picture, Screenplay, Black and White Cinematography, Original Score (Richard Hageman), Film Editing, and Special Effects.

- *"...the film was spartanly free of emotional sham or mock heroics. And the performances of all were consistently vibrant and restrained...To be sure, a lot of credit for this picture went to O'Neill, whose poetic philosophy and conception were at the heart of it. But Mr. Ford, Mr. Nichols, the actors and Gregg Toland, the brilliant cameraman, made it all cleanly cinematic and shared the credit for its lasting poetry."* (Bosley Crowther, Reruns: 50 Memorable Films)

- *"The redeeming twitches of idiosyncratic low-life are provided by a strong cast of character actors headed by the ubiquitous bulldog conscience of the era, Thomas Mitchell, and featuring John Wayne in one of the strangest parts of his career as the oafish Scandanavian innocent Ole Olson, who is almost shanghaied by that oddest of all tavern wenches, Mildred Natwick's Freda....the end of the voyage on the fog-shrouded London docks marks also the end of all men's illusions of life on shore. In this respect, Ford and O'Neill are kindred spirits in that they share a tragic vision of life even though that vision is not as keenly articulated as that of the greatest tragedians of the past. It is a uniquely American-Irish-Catholic vision in which guilt, repression and submission play a large part."* (Andrew Sarris, The John Ford Movie Mystery)

A Moon for the Misbegotten (1975, ABC, 150m/c) *ABC Theatre* ☆☆☆☆☆ **D:** Jose Quintero, Gordon Rigsby. **P:** David Susskind, Audrey Maas. **Cast:** Jason Robards, Colleen Dewhurst, Ed Flanders, Edwin J. McDonough, Mary Walsh, John O'Leary. This play follows the drunken Jamie Tyrone, essayed again by Jason Robards, who played Jamie the philanderer in the first play and film presentations of *Long Day's Journey Into Night*. Based by O'Neill on his brother's tragic life, *A Moon for the Misbegotten* was the last full-length play he completed before his illness in 1943. The first performance in 1947 was called by O'Neill biographer Barbara Gelb "a disaster from start to finish," with O'Neill criticizing the lead actors, James Dunn and Mary Welch. The play was published in 1952, and this production was filmed from the 1973–74 Broadway smash revival with the stage cast. This revival became a benchmark in the deepening of the reputations of Quintero and Robards as the quintessential O'Neill interpreters. The entire cast was magnificent. The show was nominated for the Emmy Award for Outstanding Special and Robards and Dewhurst were nominated for Best Actor and Actress. Flanders won the Emmy Award for Best Supporting Actor for his performance as Phil Hogan.

- *"...transferred to TV screens with power, depth and understanding...Dewhurst's magnificent limning of an outsized, earthy farm girl with a great capacity for humor, compassion and love dominated the teleplay...it remains debatable whether O'Neill fare is proper grist for the commercial webs, preoccupied as they are with ratings levels. But if excellence for its own sake remains a criterion of programming, Moon has to stand out as a splendidly acted and executed TV dramatic presentation."* (Variety)

- *"Possibly the [ABC's] chief stage event during the decade...captured the spirit of O'Neill's tortured romanticism. Though clearly taped in a studio, the TV version sought to give the work a realistic feel (there were live pigs in the barnyard and the set looked like a Depression artifact), while still softening its edges with poetic lighting effects. At the show's center was a trio of masterful performances by Colleen Dewhurst, Jason Robards, Jr., and Ed Flanders, that, despite some traces of theatrical stylization, came across with unusual power in closeup. A Moon for the Misbegotten proved to be yet another example of how well O'Neill's dramas play when thoughtfully translated to television."* (Brian G. Rose, Television and the Performing Arts)

Mourning Becomes Electra, an epic trilogy about family tensions in post-Civil War New England, was comprised of three full-length plays, *The Homecoming, The Hunted,* and *The Haunted.* It presented the sexual reversal of sorts of *Desire Under the Elms*, with a mother and daughter vying for the same man. The initial performance in 1931 by the Theatre Guild starred Lee Baker, Alla Nazimova, Alice Brady, and Thomas Chalmers.

Mourning Becomes Electra (1947, RKO, 173m/bw, **VHS**) ☆☆½ **Sc/D/P:** Dudley Nichols. **Cam:** George Barnes. **Cast:** Michael Redgrave, Rosalind Russell, Kirk Douglas, Katina Paxinou, Raymond Massey, Leo Genn, Nancy Coleman, Henry Hull, Thurston Hall, Sara Allgood, Erskine Sanford. Nichols assembled an excellent cast for this RKO/Theatre Guild condensing of the trilogy, but the results are melodramatic and uneven. O'Neill's intention was to parallel the structure of Aeschylus's *Oresteia* in New England. Redgrave and Russell received Oscar nominations for Best Actor and Actress.

- *"...disappointing...Practically a straight photographed play, its bloated mixture of insipient incest, murder, insanity and suicide often proved embarrassingly risible, as when [Paxinou and Redgrave] as mother and son indulge in a window-seat cuddle..."* (Charles Higham and Joel Greenberg, Hollywood in the Forties)

- *"O'Neill's six-hour Freudian-American Greek tragedy accumulates power on the stage, but it merely becomes oppressive in the nearly three hours of this painstaking yet static version....It is apparent from [the cast's] accents that they have only recently become a family."* (Pauline Kael, The New Yorker)

Mourning Becomes Electra (1978–79, PBS, 290m/c, **VHS**) *Great Performances* ☆☆ **Sc:** Eugene O'Neill. **D:** Nick Havinga. **P:** Ann Blumenthal, Jac Venza. **Cast:** Joan Hackett, Roberta Maxwell, Bruce Davison, Josef Sommer, Peter Weller, Jeffrey DeMunn, Roberts Blossom, Deborah Offner, Thomas Hill, Stellar Bennett. This miniseries was composed under the three plays-within-the-play subtitles and performed in five hour-long episodes over five weeks.

- *"...well produced with sporadic glimpses of good acting but, more frequently, amateurish performing, and somewhere the impact of the Greek-O'Neill tragedy was lost in the video translation."* (William Torbert Leonard, Theatre: Stage to Screen to Television)

The Rope (1989, A&E, 60m/c) *American Playwrights Theater* ☆☆☆ **Tp:** Eugene O'Neill. **D:** Lela Swift. **P:** George Manasse. **Host:** Anthony Quinn. **Cast:** Brad Davis, Elizabeth Ashley, Jose Ferrer, Len Cariou, Donna Vivino. Like *Beyond the Horizon*, this is a piece about the return of a prodigal son, this time with the father greeting him with a noose to hang himself. The one-act play was first performed in 1918.

- *"Jose Ferrer turns in a strong, worthy performance that takes full measure of the dramatic potentials as the mentally failing father Abraham in O'Neill's ironic takeoff on the prodigal son story....Ferrer...sustains O'Neill's intentions."* (Variety)

Strange Interlude featured O'Neill's characters speaking their real thoughts in asides to the audience. The story took place over two decades, and involved a woman who fears possible hereditary insanity in her husband's family, causing her to seek an extra-marital stud mate. The Pulitzer Prize winner was first performed in 1928 at New York's John Golden Theatre by Lynn Fontanne, Tom Powers, and Charles Walters.

Strange Interlude (1932, MGM, 110m/bw, **VHS**) ☆☆½ **Sc:** Bess Meredyth, C. Gardner Sullivan. **D:** Robert Z. Leonard. **Cam:** Lee Garmes. **P:** Irving Thalberg. **Cast:** Norma Shearer, Clark Gable, May Robson, Ralph Morgan, Robert Young, Alexander Kirkland, Maureen O'Sullivan, Henry B. Walthall. MGM production chief Thalberg bought the rights to the Pulitzer Prize-winning play as part of his cultural upgrade of the MGM line. He peopled this picture with the best the studio had to offer, including his wife Shearer and Gable in his second year as an actor. Meredyth and Sullivan substituted voiceovers for the asides. The movie either bored or tickled audiences, but it's one of the real curios of its time. If the viewer has no interest in the innovations of the play and the concerns of the playwright, the film appears static despite its racy flavor.

- *"The make-up is excellent, but the make-believe isn't. No question that the devitalization of the O'Neill [play] has much to do with it. The formula cinematic contrivances employed to pitch emotions falsely, to misfit climaxes, are very apparent."* (Variety)

Strange Interlude (1988, PBS, 190m/c, **VHS**) *American Playhouse* ☆☆☆½ **Tp:** Robert Enders. **D:** Herbert Wise. **P:** Philip Barry. **Cast:** Glenda Jackson, Jose Ferrer, David Dukes, Rosemary Harris, Kenneth Branagh, Julie Eccles, Ken Howard, Edward Petherbridge, Jadrien Steele, Elizabeth Kelly. In 1987, British HTV production tackled the material in a 190-minute version. The film arrived on American TV as a two-parter the following year. Jackson essayed the upper-class Nina Leeds, who's juggling the loves of three men. It's the actress's only involvement with the O'Neill canon.

- *"Moving the stage's weighty production to TV's smaller scale doesn't reduce it; the dated, stylized, sometimes unintentionally humorous and awkward, Interlude still provides compelling drama when directed and acted with such fierce professionalism....Besides historic indulgence, [the] play's characters speak their thoughts in asides as others await cues....It takes getting used to....it's Jackson's magnificent interpretation of the neurotic, wounded Nina that makes the production work....All concerned not only preserve the O'Neill play, the first work of his full maturity, for viewers unlikely to get a chance to see it onstage; they also prove* Strange Interlude, *after 60 years, still has an eerie power, that it's more than a museum piece—it's genuine theatre."* (Variety)

The Straw was a 1921 one-act play about a girl who, while confined in a New York tuberculosis sanitarium, falls in love with a newspaper reporter. It aired on *Kraft Television Theatre* in 1955 with a cast topped by Kathleen Maguire, Lin McCarthy, Cliff Hall, and Murray Hamilton.

Three in One: Where the Cross Is Made (1960, CBS, 30m/bw) ☆☆☆ **D:** Tom Donovan. **P:** David Susskind. **Cast:** Art Carney, Frank Conroy, Myron McCormick, Frances Sternhagen. *Where the Cross Is Made* is a 1918 one-act play about a sea captain who may be destined for a mental institution because of his son's machinations. Its performance was the second segment of a 90-minute special showcasing Carney in three one-act plays. The others were Sean O'Casey's *A Pound on Demand* and Noël Coward's *Red Peppers*.

- *"As if he needed to, Art Carney proved again that he is one of television's most versatile performers....[as] a crippled seaman going insane...Of the three sequences, only the O'Neill...was at all affecting."* (Variety)

A Touch of the Poet (1974, PBS, 150m/c, **VHS**) *Theatre in America* ☆☆☆½ **D:** Kirk Browning. **P:** David Griffiths. **Cast:** Fritz Weaver, Nancy Marchand, John Heffernan, Donald Moffat, Roberta Maxwell, Carrie Nye, John Phelan, Howland Chamberlain, Tom Clancy, Humphrey Davis. The play is set in a tavern outside Boston in 1828 during the presidential campaign that pitted Andrew Jackson against John Quincy Adams. One of O'Neill's posthumously produced plays, it examines the culture clash between the then newly immigrant Irish and established Yankees. The initial production in 1957 received a stellar rendering with a cast including Helen Hayes, Eric Portman, Kim Stanley, and Betty Field. One of the best offerings in the *Theatre in America* series, this TV rendition was superbly acted by a brilliant cast, dominated by Fritz Weaver as the boozy old war relic, Conn Melody.

- "Fritz Weaver was the chief beneficiary of a PBS-beamed TV revival of the 1957 Broadway play. His strong portrayal of Conn Melody…was a personal triumph in a play that was otherwise draggy and not top-drawer crafting by Eugene O'Neill. [Weaver] managed to make the old war hero, turned drunken tavern keeper in America, a figure of compassion, despite his outstanding credentials as a buffoon, fraud and sometimes brutal father and husband." (Variety)

Paul Osborn

Born: September 4, 1901, Evansville, IN. **Died:** 1988.

Osborn was nominated for Academy Awards for adapting John Steinbeck's *East of Eden* into Elia Kazan's 1955 film and James A. Michener's *Sayonara* into Joshua Logan's 1957 movie. Osborn's steady course as a screenwriter included the sparkling comedy *The Young in Heart* (1938) with Janet Gaynor; the semi-classic war picture *Cry Havoc* (1943) with Margaret Sullivan; *Madame Curie* (1943) with Greer Garson; *The Yearling* (1947) with Gregory Peck; *Homecoming* (1948) with Clark Gable and Lana Turner; *Portrait of Jennie* (1949) with Jennifer Jones; *Invitation* (1952) with Dorothy McGuire; and *South Pacific* (1958) with Mitzi Gaynor. While that credit list is certainly sufficient to have a lasting impact on American movies, Osborn's most touching, incisive, and exacting work was realized by Kazan for the underrated *Wild River* (1960). It starred Lee Remick, Montgomery Clift, and Jo Van Fleet as an aging rural landowner forced from her property by a dam that raises the level of the Tennessee River. Osborn's teleplays include adapting Robert Louis Stevenson's story *Markheim*, in collaboration with John McGreevey, for a 1956 installment of *Screen Directors' Playhouse* starring Ray Milland and Rod Steiger.

A Bell for Adano is the adaptation of John Hersey's 1945 Pulitzer Prize-winning novel about the occupation of an Italian town in World War II by an American Infantry division commanded by Major Victor Joppolo, who attempts to establish democracy and romances an Italian girl. Osborn's 1944 play starred Fredric March. (The screenplay for the 1945 Henry King film of the same name, starring John Hodiak and Gene Tierney, was adapted by Norman Reilly Raine and Lamar Trotti directly from the Hersey book.)

A Bell for Adano (1956, CBS, 90m/c) *Ford Star Jubilee* ☆☆½ **Tp:** Robert Buckner. **D:** Paul Nickell. **P:** Arthur Schwartz. **Cast:** Barry Sullivan, Anna Maria Alberghetti, Ed Steffe, Frank Yaconelli, Jay Novello, James Howell. After the novel, play, and film came the TV musical. The songs, with music and lyrics by producer Schwartz and Howard Dietz, include the title tune, "I'm Part of You," "O.K. Mr. Major," and "Fish."

• *"In they came and when we asked them each in turn to sing, the little monsters stepped up and tried to be Ethel Merman. They used gestures and mannerisms taught to them by a corps of idiots masquerading as voice teachers. I'd like to get those teachers, line them up on Sunset Boulevard, and run them over, one by one. They're ruining these kids. I settled for acting-trained children who haven't had much voice coaching."* (Paul Nickell to Oscar Godbout, The New York Times)

A Bell for Adano (1967, NBC, 90m/c) *The Hallmark Hall of Fame* ☆☆½ **Tp:** Roger O. Hirson. **D/P:** Mel Ferber. **Cast:** John Forsythe, Murray Hamilton, Kathleen Widdoes, Tom Skerritt, Vito Scotti, Jeff Corey, Frank Puglia, Peter Brandon, Herbert Doland, Bob Ellenstein, Brian Avery. The Vietnam era might have seemed a good time to dust off the original about bringing democracy to a reluctant "host" country with American warfare, but times had changed, and the sentiment of the piece didn't work.

• *"...told with earnestness and care. But the familiarity of the narrative and the limitation of time on the development of such characterization, particularly among the residents of Adano, resulted in 90 minutes of surface drama which suggested that a rerunning of the [1945] film might have been a more rewarding solution....dated undertaking."* (Jack Gould, The New York Times)

A Bell for Adano was also shown in 1955 on *The Lux Video Theatre* with Edmond O'Brien as Major Joppolo.

Morning's at Seven was a popular and much revived comedy of Midwestern family manners and mores originally staged on Broadway at the Longacre Theatre in 1939 by Joshua Logan, starring Jean Adair, Dorothy Gish, and Thomas Chalmers. It was produced on TV on *Celanese Theatre* in 1952 with Aline MacMahon and Patricia Collinge; on *The Alcoa Hour* in 1956 with Dorothy and Lillian Gish, Evelyn Varden, David Wayne, June Lockhart, and Dorothy Stickney; and was restaged—using the same *Alcoa* teleplay by Robert Wallsten—in 1960 on public television's *The Play of the Week* with a cast featuring Beulah Bondi, Chester Morris, Dorothy Gish, and Eileen Heckert.

On Borrowed Time was Osborn and Watkins's adaptation of Lawrence Edward Watkins's book. It concerns an old man who refuses to die and chases death up a tree, because he wants to live until his adopted orphan grandson comes of age so the inheritance won't go to a scheming aunt. The play debuted on Broadway in 1938 starring Dudley Digges.

On Borrowed Time (1939, MGM, 98m/bw, **VHS**) ☆☆☆½ **Sc:** Alice Duer Miller, Frank O'Neill, Claudine West. **D:** Harold S. Bucquet. **P:** Sidney Franklin. **Cam:** Joseph Ruttenberg. **Cast:** Lionel Barrymore,

Bobs Watson, Beulah Bondi, Cedric Hardwicke, Una Merkel, Nat Pendleton, Henry Travers, Grant Mitchell, Truman Bradley, James Burke, Charles Waldron, Ian Wolfe, Philip Terry, Eily Malyon. By this time, Barrymore's identity as an aging curmudgeon was so well established that his name was a substitute for the phrase, and he dominates this MGM treatment.

- *"...a mighty pleasant film, with a deal of warmth and sentiment and just enough ornery human acidity to keep it off the alkaline, or mawkish, side. It has an original theme (for the screen) and a panel of skilled players, and we are reasonably sure almost every one is going to enjoy it. But—and you knew the 'but' was coming—it isn't nearly so effective on the screen as it was on the stage last year...Lionel Barrymore is always too mannered to be anyone but himself...The picture, like the play, is a tender thing and wistful, fantastic in its way, yet firmly rooted in human soil....Mr. Barrymore's Gramps is well enough, we suppose. It's probably unfair to hold his Lionel Barrymorism against him."* (Frank S. Nugent, The New York Times)

On Borrowed Time (1957, NBC, 90m/c) *The Hallmark Hall of Fame* ☆☆☆ **Tp:** James Costigan. **D/P:** George Schaefer. **Cast:** Ed Wynn, Claude Rains, Beulah Bondi, Dennis Kohler, Margaret Hamilton, Larry Gates, William LeMessena, William A. Lee, Mildred Trares, G. Wood, Dorothy Eaton, Robinson Stone, Frank Tweddell. This fantasy stands the test of time, although several of Osborn's original scenes were cut by Costigan and Schaefer to limit the play to 90 minutes, and Warren Clymer's sets, especially the gnarled tree holding Mr. Brink, were quaintly stylized.

- *"...well on its way to the status of a hardy theatrical perennial. This edition, despite several flaws, emerged a gently engaging fantasy which time hasn't hurt very much at all. Strength of this version lies mainly in the elders of the cast—Ed Wynn, Claude Rains, Beulah Bondi and Margaret Hamilton, troupers all. Unfortunately, young Dennis Kohler in the key role of Pud, was unimpressive, a fact which took all the performing skill of the other cast members to overcome....Rains, as Mr. Brink, made Death a most pleasant as well as shrewd fellow."* (Variety)

On Borrowed Time was also broadcast in 1950 on *Ford Theatre Hour* with Henry Hull, and in a more elaborate production in 1952 on *Celanese Theatre* with Alex Segal directing Ralph Morgan, Melville Cooper, Mildred Dunnock, and Billy Chapin.

Point of No Return (1958, CBS, 90m/c) *Playhouse 90* ☆☆☆ **Tp:** Frank D. Gilroy. **D:** Franklin J. Schaffner. **P:** Martin Manulis. **Cast:** Charlton Heston, Hope Lange, Katherine Bard, John Williams, Walter Abel, Russell Collins, Edward Andrews. Osborn based his 1951 play on the John P. Marquand novel of the same name. That Leland Heyward production, directed by H.C. Potter, starred Henry Fonda, Leora Dana, and John Cromwell and ran for 356 performances. Fonda played a bank executive in a subtle but vicious competition with a colleague for a vice presidency. Heston was suitable in the role of a successful man nearing middle age and suddenly faced with self-doubt. He takes a trip down memory lane to review his childhood in his hometown, and questions whether he should be in the VP post at all at middle age.

- *"What Point of No Return lacks in excitement, Playhouse 90 made up for in sharp dialogue, indelible acting and sensitive direction....moved easily, if somewhat leisurely, and without strain, told its story while securely building its characters. Charlton Heston, as Marquand's bewildered hero, was in control all the way, handling the 15-year flashback and resultant personality change with remarkable facility."* (Variety)

The Vinegar Tree was Osborn's 1930 Broadway play concerning a none-too-bright wife, Laura Merrick, who believes that an old flame, Max, has been hanging around because he's still interested in her when, in fact, he's infatuated with her daughter. The play debuted on Broadway in 1930 with Mary Boland as Laura.

Should Ladies Behave? (1933, MGM, 90m/bw) ☆☆½ **Sc:** Sam Spewack, Bella Spewack. **D:** Harry Beaumont. **P:** Lawrence Weingarten. **Cam:** Ted Tetzlaff. **Cast:** Alice Brady, Lionel Barrymore, Conway Tearle, Katherine Alexander, Halliwell Hobbes, Mary Carlisle, William Janney. This film afforded Barrymore another chance to play one of his customized cranky old coots, who nevertheless is aware and thoughtful enough to counsel his daughter on marrying someone twice her age — something his own wife did.

- *"Of the seven characters involved...there is perhaps one who behaves in a reasonably rational fashion. Yet, because of the humorous lines and ludicrous incidents, the film seemed to appeal to an audience..."* (Mordaunt Hall, The New York Times)

The Vinegar Tree was seen under its original title in 1950 on NBC's *Kraft Television Theatre* with a cast led by Raymond Bramley, Bess Winburn, and Edmon Ryan.

The World of Suzie Wong (1960, Paramount, 129m/c, **VHS**) ☆☆ **Sc:** John Patrick. **D:** Richard Quine. **P:** Ray Stark, Hugh Perceval. **Cam:** Geoffrey Unsworth. **Cast:** William Holden, Nancy Kwan, Sylvia Syms, Michael Wilding, Laurence Naismith, Jacqui Chan, Andy Ho, Bernard Cribbins, Yvonne Shima, Lier Hwang, Lionel Blair, Robert Lee, Ronald Eng. Richard Mason's novel, which wasn't quite as sanitized as the play or especially this fraudulent film, was adapted for the stage by Osborn and first produced on Broadway in 1958 with William Shatner and France Nuyen. The story concerns an American painter in Hong Kong who falls for a beautiful local girl. She lies to him about her profession and family while her presence ruins portions of his otherwise serene life.

- *"What ignorance of Hong Kong whores, what cultural illiteracy! Not even fascinating color photography of Hong Kong itself, and the performance of the lovely Sylvia Syms as the spurned English girl, atone for the amorality and commercial venality of this ridiculous film."* (Adelaide Comerford, Films in Review)

- *"Suzie Wong, for all its bustling location footage, is a prettified travesty on the sordid life of prostitution in Hong Kong, with Holden once more snuggling with a woman of easy virtue, played here by Nancy Kwan. Holden's poor showing might have received harder treatment at the hands of the press had it not been for Miss Kwan's glaringly inept whore-with-a-heart-of-plastic, who frisks about, coquettishly displaying her conspicuous behind in one scene after another."* (WIll Holtzman, William Holden)

Dorothy Parker & Arnaud d'Usseau

Parker:
Dorothy Rothschild Parker
Born: August 22, 1893, New York, NY. **Died:** 1967.

d'Usseau:
Born: April 18, 1916. **Died:** 1990.

A dramatic and literary critic with a reputation for sardonic *bons mots* at the expense of others, Dorothy Parker became a poet whose satiric collections were published as *Rope* (1926), *Sunset Gun* (1928), *Death and Taxes* (1931), and the cumulative collection *Not So Deep as a Well* (1936). Her sketches and short stories were collected for *Laments of the Living* (1930) and *After Such Pleasures* (1933). She worked on screenplays with her husband, Alan Campbell, and her movies include *A Star Is Born* (1937), *Trade Winds* (1938), *Saboteur* (1940), and *The Fan* (1949). A legendary personality of her times, Parker was portrayed by Dolores Sutton in the TV movie *F. Scott Fitzgerald in Hollywood* (1976), by Rosemary Harris in *Julia* (1977), and by Jennifer Jason Leigh in *Mrs. Parker and the Vicious Circle* (1994). Parker's one play was the two-act *Ladies of the Corridor*, written with Arnaud d'Usseau.

Arnaud d'Usseau's screenplays include *Lady Scarface* (1941), *Repent at Leisure* (1942), *The Man Who Wouldn't Die* (1942), *Psychomania* (1971), and *Horror Express* (1972).

Ladies of the Corridor (1975, PBS, 120m/c) *Hollywood Television Theatre* ☆☆☆ **Tp:** Dorothy Parker, Arnaud d'Usseau. **D:** Robert Stevens. **P:** Norman Lloyd, George Turpin. **Cast:** Cloris Leachman, Jane Wyatt, Neva Patterson, Zohra Lampert, Barbara Baxley, Mabel Albertson, Mike Farrell, Richard Lenz, Colby Chester, Elaine Giftos, Dick Van Patten,

Gertrude Flynn, Tom Palmer, Pat Hitchcock, Eugene Jackson, Chris Stone, Gary Barton. This play, about the rich and lonely women who inhabit an upscale New York hotel and live through the lives of their children, debuted in 1953 at New York's Longacre Theatre in a production staged by Harold Clurman, starring Betty Field, June Walker, Walter Matthau, Edna Best, and Sheppard Strudwick.

- *"When it was first done on Broadway in the 1950s, it did not do well; it was staged with a turntable moving the sets around, and the changes between scenes were interminable. On television it moved dynamically with cuts from room to room. Robert Stevens did a remarkable job as director, restructuring the piece and giving the work vitality. This impressed Arnaud d'Usseau so much that he thought this production superior to the original."* (Norman Lloyd, Stages: Of Life in Theatre, Film and Television)

John Patrick

John Patrick Goggan
Born: May 17, 1903, Carmel, CA. **Died:** 1995.

A prolific and successful screenwriter of the mid-20th century, John Patrick specialized in popular romances that tended toward the doomed and heavy-handed side. These included a famous pair with William Holden opposite Asian women characters, *Love Is a Many-Splendored Thing* (1955) and *The World of Suzie Wong* (1960), and the adaptation of his Pulitzer Prize-winning play about U.S. servicemen in Okinawa, *The Teahouse of the August Moon* (1956). Patrick also crafted *Enchantment* (1948), *Three Coins in the Fountain* (1954), *High Society* (1956), *Some Came Running* (1958), and the adaptation of Morris West's novel *The Shoes of the Fisherman* (1968), among two dozen others. He produced one film that he also wrote, *The Main Attraction* (1962), starring Pat Boone as a guitar-picking drifter with a European circus. Patrick's plays include *The Curious Savage* (1950) and *Lo and Behold* (1951).

The Hasty Heart was a 1945 play about a bitter and angry Scottish soldier doomed to die during World War II at an Army field hospital in Burma. Almost all of the action takes place in one ward containing six soldiers and a nurse. The Off Broadway production starred John Lund, Anne Burr, and Richard Basehart at the Hudson Theatre in a Howard Lindsay-Russell Crouse production.

The Hasty Heart (1949, Warner Bros., 104m/bw) ☆☆☆½ **Sc:** Ranald MacDougall. **D:** Vincent Sherman. **P:** Howard Lindsay, Russel Crouse. **Cam:** Wilkie Cooper. **Cast:** Richard Todd, Patricia Neal, Ronald Reagan,

Orlando Martins, Howard Crawford, Anthony Nicholls, Ralph Michael, John Sherman, Alfred Bass. Todd, who was new to American audiences at the time and was third-billed to Reagan and Neal, won an Oscar nomination for Best Actor for his performance as the dying Scotsman.

- *"...in many ways Vincent Sherman's most sensitive drama....Despite the fact that the proceedings occur almost entirely in one area,* The Hasty Heart *isn't one bit stagebound. That's quite a feat during a period of emphasis on location work and realistic settings."* (William R. Meyer, Warner Brothers Directors)

- *"Vincent Sherman has done a wonderful job maintaining fluidity in the progress of his drama."* (Otis L. Guernsey Jr., New York Herald-Tribune)

The Hasty Heart (1958, CBS, 90m/c) *The DuPont Show of the Month* ☆☆☆½ **Tp:** Robert Wallsten. **D:** Tom Donovan. **P:** Gordon Duff. **Cast:** Don Murray, Barbara Bel Geddes, Jackie Cooper, Fred Gwynne, Richard Harris, Barry Jones, Rex Everhart, John McCurry. Murray maintained a heavy Scottish accent in a "remarkably versatile and disciplined job," according to *Variety*, which also said:

- *"...a loving and tender television translation...The Patrick play has its weaknesses, to be sure, and these were reflected in Robert Wallsten's adaptation—a second act lull that stretyches too long before the change of pace picks it up, a too-sudden change in character from sullen independence to a revelation in friendship. But these were minor flaws in a wonderfully warm work and a superb presentation. Don Murray set himself a new standard of acting achievement..."* (Variety)

The Hasty Heart (1983, Warner Bros. TV, 100m/c, **VHS**) ☆☆½ **Tp:** John Patrick. **D:** Martin Speer. **Cast:** Gregory Harrison, Cheryl Ladd, Perry King, Jesse Ferguson. This spare TV remake cast Harrison as the Scotsman, who can't understand why his company left him behind, and King, in a Golden Globe-nominated performance in same role Ronald Reagan played earlier.

- *"Either version is good. The accents are better in the original. The content differs slightly. Perry King is great as the Yank. Gregory Harrison plays the surly soldier unaware that he is dying. Well worth seeing. A funny, warm tearjerker."* (Hibree's Reviews)

The Hasty Heart was also presented in 1953 on *Broadway Television Theatre* with a cast led by Hurd Hatfield and John Dall.

The Story of Mary Surratt debuted as a play at Henry Miller's Theatre 1947 and was seen twice on early TV: in 1949 on *Philco Television Playhouse* with Dorothy Gish (a favorite of the playwright) and Kent Smith, and in 1955 on *Kraft Television Theatre* with Doreen Lang, Alexander Scourby, and Bruce Gordon.

The Teahouse of the August Moon was adapted to the stage by Patrick from the novel by Vern Sneider about the postwar American occupation forces encountering Japanese traditions on Okinawa. The 1953 play, produced by Maurice Evans and directed by Robert Lewis, starred David Wayne, John Forsythe, Paul Ford, Mariko Niki, and Larry Gates.

The Teahouse of the August Moon (1956, MGM, 123m/c, **VHS**) ☆☆ **Sc:** John Patrick. **D:** Daniel Mann. **P:** Jack Cummings. **Cam:** John Alton. **Cast:** Marlon Brando, Glenn Ford, Michiko Kyo, Eddie Albert, Henry (Harry) Morgan, Paul Ford, Jun Negami, Nijiko Kiyokawa, Mitsuko Sawamura, Harry Harvey Jr., Shichizo Takeda, Kichizaemon Saramaru, Frank Tokunaga, Aya Oyama. The play is hopelessly of its era, in which its superficial efforts to bridge cultural gulfs are passed off as progressive race relations. Brando's performance, which was considered a lark in its day, is painful to watch as he drops supposedly weighty aphorisms on cue.

- *"Many people thought the play magical, but this MGM version, miserably directed by Daniel Mann, is an almost total mistake. Everybody in it, whether American or Okinawan, seems childish and stupid; the squeals and giggles of the native women are enough to drive one out of the theatre....this whole production is so talky and rhythmless...Glenn Ford grimaces, twitches galvanically, and stutters foolishly. It's the kind of role and the kind of performance that make you hate an actor."* (Pauline Kael, 5,001 Nights at the Movies)

The Teahouse of the August Moon (1962, NBC, 90m/c) *The Hallmark Hall of Fame* ☆☆☆ **Tp:** Robert Hartung. **D/P:** George Schaefer. **Cast:** John Forsythe, David Wayne, Miyoshi Umeki, Paul Ford, William Le Massena, Fred Kareman, Osceola Archer, Mara Kim, Yuki Shimoda, Khigh Dheigh, William Hansen, Teru Masumoto, Sho Onodera.

- *"When Maurice Evans and I produced the stage play, we sold the movie rights before it opened and had nothing to say about the film, which I found disappointing. It's hard to film, because the lead character speaks directly to the audience...We secured the TV rights, but only as a live show, although we actually taped it. We had to destroy the tape afterwards, so no record of this performance exists other than the kinescope. I used our three original leads (David Wayne, John Forsythe and Paul Ford) and made the home audience part of the show. Sakini talked straight at them, which is great on TV but is awkward and false on a big screen."* (George Schaefer, From Live to Tape to Film: 60 Years of Inconspicuous Directing)

Robert Patrick

Born: September 27, 1937, Kilgore, TX.

Robert Patrick saw more than 300 productions of his plays produced Off-Off Broadway in the 1960s and was called in 1972 by major play publisher Samuel French Inc., "New York's most produced playwright." His major publications are the plays *Kennedy's Children* and *T-Shirts* and the seminal novel about underground and gay playwriting, *Temple Slave.* His plays include *Camera Obscura, Judas, Blue Is for Boys, Cheesecake, The Warhol Machine, A Bad Place to Get Your Head, The Arnold Bliss Show, Hymen and Carbuncle,* and *I Came to New York to Write.*

Kennedy's Children (1982, CBS Cable, 180m/c) ☆☆☆☆ **Tp:** Robert Patrick. **D:** Marshall W. Mason. **Cast:** Jane Alexander, Shirley Knight, Lindsay Crouse, Brad Dourif, Charles Harper. Set in a New York dive bar on Valentine's Day 1974, the play inventories the feelings and disillusionment of several souls whose lives had promise during the Camelot White House, including a former actress with Marilyn Monroe-styled career aspirations. The play was first produced in 1975 at Broadway's John Golden Theatre, directed by Clive Donner and starring Shirley Knight and Michael Sacks. This production was reshaped by TV techniques, with Mason using archival footage of Kennedy, Vietnam, Lee Harvey Oswald, and other iconographic imagery in flashbacks. The cast is brilliant.

- *"The play is a grim and tattered Valentine to the 1960s...It's Lindsay Crouse for me, who sticks in your throat, the wild-eyed young revolutionary beaten down again and again and finally out...It's not a pretty play; it's an era seen through the bottom of a dirty wine bottle. It's full of self-pity and simplistic history. But there's a grit in it that is all too real. Turn it on and you won't turn it off."* (Cecil Smith, Los Angeles Times)

S.J. Perelman & Ogden Nash

Perelman:
Sidney Joseph Perelman
Born: February 1, 1904, Brooklyn, NY. **Died:** 1979.

Nash:
Born: August 19, 1902, Rye, NY. **Died:** 1971.

S.J. Perelman was a regular contributor to *The New Yorker* from 1934 onward. The many collections of his fantastic stories that lampoon popular culture are *Parlor, Bedlam and Bath; Westward Ha!; The Ill-Tempered Clavichord;* and *Under the Spreading Atrophy.* His small-screen work includes the script for the 1958 Cole Porter original, *Aladdin,* on *The DuPont Show of the Month* with Cyril Ritchard, Basil Rathbone, and Sal Mineo. He also wrote three short teleplays for a noted 1959 *Omnibus* trilogy under the umbrella title of *Malice in Wonderland: Three Hollywood Cameos,* consisting of "And Thou Beside Me, Yacketing in the Wilderness," "Rent Me, and I'll Come to You," and "Physician, Steel Thyself"

—all with the participation of Keenan Wynn and Julie Newmar. Laura Perelman wrote the screenplays for *Florida Special* (1936) with Sally Eilers and Jack Oakie, *Ambush* (1939) with Lloyd Nolan, *Boy Trouble* (1939) with Charles Ruggles, and *The Golden Fleecing* (1940) with Lew Ayres. Among the plays she wrote with her husband was *The Night Before Christmas* (1941).

Ogden Nash was a poet of light verse whose screenplays included those for *The Shining Hour* (1938) with Joan Crawford and *The Feminine Touch* (1941) with Rosalind Russell. His poetry collections include *The Primrose Path* (1935), *I'm a Stranger Here Myself* (1938), *You Can't Get There From Here* (1957), and *Everyone But Thee and Me* (1962).

Larceny, Inc. (1942, Warner Bros., 95m/bw) **Sc:** Everett Freeman, Edwin Gilbert. **D:** Lloyd Bacon. **P:** Hal B. Wallis. **Cam:** Tony Gaudio. **Cast:** Edward G. Robinson, Jane Wyman, Broderick Crawford, Anthony Quinn, Jack Carter, Edward Brophy, Harry Davenport, John Qualen, Jackie Gleason, Barbara Jo Allen, Andrew Tombes, Grant Mitchell, Fortunio Bononova, George Meeker, Jean Ames, Creighton Hale, Chester Clute, James Flavin, Kitty Kelly, Fred Kelsey. Robinson, Crawford, and Brophy played three ex-cons who want to go straight so they can buy a shop next to a bank. The original play by Laura and S.J. Perelman ran for 22 performances in 1941 with Romney Brent directing Shelley Winters.

• "...Unholy Partners...*turned out to be only passable snarls-and-sneers entertainment. Larceny, Inc....was not much better. The picture was supposed to be a spoof with Edward [G. Robinson] and Broderick Crawford trying to resist temptation to rob banks and mugging superfluously to vitalize the picture. Jack Carson, Edward Brophy and Jackie Gleason supplied the low comedy touch that director Lloyd Bacon felt the audience required to get the salient points of the script.*" (James Robert Parish, The Tough Guys)

One Touch of Venus was a 1943 musical that Perelman and Nash adapted from F. Anatey's story, "The Tinted Venus," about a statue of Venus that comes to life and upsets the humdrum life of a young barber. Starring Mary Martin and Kenny Baker, it ran for 567 performances on Broadway. Kurt Weill wrote some of the melodies and Nash penned the lyrics.

One Touch of Venus (1948, Universal, 82m/bw, **VHS**) ☆☆ **Sc:** Harry Kurnitz, Frank Tashlin. **D:** William A. Seiter. **P:** Lester Cowan. **Cam:** Franz Planer. **Cast:** Ava Gardner, Robert Walker, Eve Arden, Dick Haymes, Tom Conway, Olga San Juan, James Flavin, Sara Allgood. Kurnitz changed the barber to a window dresser in a department store. The film reaffirmed Gardner's draw as the postwar era's top beauty, and its lasting status is based on that. The stars were able to accentuate the essential wit in the piece and the songs include "The Trouble With Women" and "Don't Look Now, But My Heart Is Showing."

- "...an insult to its creators....Robert Walker...didn't succeed in mobilizing her performance or, indeed, his own. The dreariness of the two stars was matched by William A. Seiter's direction...and the dances, by Billy Daniels, were feeble." (Clive Hirschhorn, The Universal Story)

One Touch of Venus (1955, NBC, 90m/c) ☆☆ **Tp:** George Schaefer, John Gerstad. **D:** George Schaefer. **P:** Jack Rayel. **Cast:** Janet Blair, Russell Nype, George Gaynes, Laurel Shelby, Mort Marshall, Iggie Wolfington, Mildred Trares, Adnia Rice, Georgia Simmons, Louis Nye, William LeMassena, Len Doyle. Schaefer purposefully accented the lightness of this thin piece, which wasn't designed for further analysis. The songs include "Speak Low" and "The Trouble With Women."

- "Perhaps time has not been kind to the slight libretto...easy enough on the ears but hard on the credibility....Janet Blair...and Russell Nype...were, indeed, appealing...But the assets were not heavy enough to overcome the numbing effect of an inane storyline. For most of its 90 minutes, One Touch of Venus was labored and dull." (J.P. Shanley, The New York Times)

Paris Interlude (1934, MGM, 72m/bw) **Sc:** Wells Root. **D:** Edwin L. Marin. **P:** Lucien Hubbard. **Cam:** Milton R. Krasner. **Cast:** Madge Evans, Otto Kruger, Robert Young, Una Merkel, Ted Healey, Louise Henry, Bert Roach, George Meeker, Edward Brophy, Richard Tucker. The 1933 play by Laura and S.J. Perelman, *All Good Americans*, ran for 40 performances at Broadway's Henry Miller's Theatre. An American woman in Paris befriends a group of tippling American newspaper correspondents, then falls for an easy charmer while another of the boys falls for her.

- "More episodic than cumulative in drama, this yarn will prove most pleasing to fans who can appreciate a story that is well handled." (Film Daily)

Louis Peterson

Louis Stamford Peterson, Jr.
Born: June 17, 1922, Hartford, CT. **Died:** 1998.

Louis Peterson's reputation was made by *Take a Giant Step*, which opened at Broadway's Lyceum Theatre in 1953. Focusing on the isolation and racial prejudice in the life of an African-American youth in a predominantly white New England town, the play reflected its title in bridging the color barrier on Broadway. Prior to his playwriting career, Peterson studied with Clifford Odets and acted in the touring company of Carson McCullers's *The Member of the Wedding*. Peterson wrote for such TV series as *Goodyear Theatre*, *Dr. Kildare*, and *Wagon Train*, and his later plays include *Crazy Horse* and *Another Show*.

Take a Giant Step (1958, UA, 100m/bw) ☆☆ **Sc:** Louis S. Peterson, Julius J. Epstein. **D:** Philip Leacock. **P:** Julius J. Epstein. **Cam:** Arthur Arling. **Cast:** Johnny Nash, Estelle Hemsley, Ruby Dee, Frederick O'Neal. The play starred Louis Gosset Jr. and ran for 76 performances, earning rave reviews. Nash played the boy in the film, which concentrates on his isolation once he sees that his white boyhood friends are drawn away from him, then his experience with a prostitute. Leacock's direction is stagy.

- *"The concept and writing are straight out of the Golden Age of Television (1950–1958), and, except for...Ruby Dee, it is very badly acted and directed. It is not worth the time of anyone, Negro, white, Oriental or otherwise."* (Stanley Kauffmann, The New Republic)

John Pielmeier

Born: February 23, 1949, Altoona, PA.

John Pielmeier found a career in TV after the great initial success of the play and film of *Agnes of God*. Among his teleplays are *The Shell Seekers* (1989), *The Stranger Within* (1990), *An Inconvenient Woman* (1991), *Original Sins* (1995), *Forbidden Territory: Stanley's Search for Livingstone* (1997), *Happy Face Murders* (1999), *Flowers for Algernon* (2000), and *Sins of the Father* (2002). His plays include *Cheek to Cheek* (1983), *The Boys of Winter* (1985), and *Impassioned Embrace* (1989).

Agnes of God (1985, Columbia, 98m/c, **VHS**) ☆☆☆☆ **Sc:** John Pielmeier. **D:** Norman Jewison. **P:** Patrick Palmer, Norman Jewison. **Cam:** Sven Nykvist. **Cast:** Jane Fonda, Anne Bancroft, Meg Tilly, Anne Pitoniak, Winston Reckert, Gratien Galinas. At a convent, a young nun is accused of secretly birthing a baby and then killing it. The play, which debuted on Broadway in 1982 with Elizabeth Ashley, Geraldine Page, and Amanda Plummer in the leads, affords fireworks in all three roles. The main reason to see the film, outside of its issues relating to Catholicism, is for the performances of the three actresses — Tilly, in particular, is brilliant. The film was nominated for Oscars for Best Actress (Bancroft), Supporting Actress (Tilly), and Score (Georges Delerue).

- *"Agnes of God and A Soldier's Story have nothing in common except Norman Jewison, who has given them a similar ponderousness...Agnes of God is, if anything, the slower and more self-evident of the two. The director's strength again lies in his casting, with Anne Bancroft, Jane Fonda and Meg Tilly sharing what is essentially a three-character melodrama; in unison or in any combination these actresses cannot help but generate in-*

*terest. But the material itself, thoroughly unsurprising on the stage, is if any-
thing even more so on the screen....the claustrophobia of the original material was an advantage, and Mr. Jewison gains nothing by lessening it."*
(Janet Maslin, The New York Times)

David Rabe

Born: March 10, 1940, Dubuque, IA.
Tony Award-winning play: *Sticks and Bones* (1972)

David Rabe's three Vietnam-era productions — *Sticks and Bones* on TV
and the film *Streamers*, both based on his plays, and the screen original
Casualties of War — are rough, complex examinations of soldiers or veterans. All are brilliantly acted and deal with Rabe's often profanity-
laced themes of racial conflict, sexual frontiers, and violent impulses.
These companion pieces haven't had much public profile despite the
reputations of two of their directors, Robert Altman, who made *Streamers*, and Brian De Palma, who crafted *Casualties of War*, which Pauline
Kael has called one of the best films about the war.

    Sticks and Bones, the 1973 TV production of Rabe's Tony Award-win-
ning play, has had a schizophrenic life. First, it was the subject of great
controversy due to its satirical harshness about the life and death of a returning Vietnam veteran, causing CBS to postpone the broadcast. Now
it's a vanished artifact, presumably wasting in a vault, the one curious
absentee from home viewing in the Rabe canon. Among creative associates, Sean Penn played two of his most corroded characters in Rabe
creations — a near demonic rapist/murderer in *Casualties of War* and a
drug-addled Hollywood movie executive in *Hurlyburly*. Notable Rabe
plays not yet filmed are another Army-set piece, *The Basic Training of
Pavlo Hummel*, and *The Orphan*.

Hurlyburly (1998, Fine Line, 122m/c, **VHS/DVD**) ☆☆½ **Sc:** David
Rabe. **D:** Anthony Drazen. **Cam:** Changwei Gu. **P:** Anthony Drazen,
Richard N. Gladstein, David S. Hamburger. **Cast:** Sean Penn, Kevin
Spacey, Robin Wright Penn, Chazz Palminteri, Meg Ryan, Anna
Paquin, Garry Shandling. The 1984 play concerns morally bankrupt
mid-level Hollywood executives driven to hit the big time, and their
pastimes of cocaine snorting and casual sex (including an affair with a
runaway minor). The New York production starred Harvey Keitel,
William Hurt, Sigourney Weaver, Ron Silver, Judith Ivey, Cynthia
Nixon, and Jerry Stiller; a 1988 Los Angeles production starred Sean
Penn and Madonna. Talky and profane, with Penn snorting cocaine almost constantly, the picture is rude, crude, and to the point — con-

stantly to the point. Most of the performances work even if the film doesn't measure up to the play.

- *"They're all great characters, they're just in the wrong movie. These are characters that should be doing something—a heist, a scam, anything— besides just sitting around talking. Watching the film is like talking to someone who just discovered therapy—you just want them to shut up already. Or, as a review in the* Los Angeles Times *was headlined, 'Yo, Hurlyburly, Put a Lid on It.'"* (Jill Hamliton, Magill's Survey of Cinema Annual 1999)

Sticks and Bones (1973, CBS, 120m/c) ☆☆½ **D:** Robert Downey, Sr. **P:** Joseph Papp. **Cast:** Cliff DeYoung, Tom Aldredge, Asa Gim, Anne Jackson, Alan Cauldwell, Brad Sullivan, Joe Fields. Rabe's 1972 Tony Award-winning play was about a blinded Vietnam veteran whose racist Yonkers family derides him: "Shacked up with some yellow pig, weren't you?" he's asked. His mother supplies the basin when he follows through on the family's suggestion that he slit his wrists, and his body is dumped in the garbage. This is the controversial filming of the New York Shakespeare Festival production. The original cast included Aldredge, De Young, and Gim, as well as Elizabeth Wilson, Drew Snyder, and Hector Elias. The TV show was postponed from March to August as CBS assessed the harshness of the piece in deference to returning Vietnam vets. Dumped by the network during the August rerun season, the show wasn't carried by many CBS affiliates, including those in Baltimore, Milwaukee, and Memphis, despite a viewer-discretion disclaimer. The network of the famous sitcom Nelsons changed Rabe's character names for the broadcast from Ozzie, Harriet, David, and Ricky. The show aired again in 1982 on ARTS Showcase.

- *"...[the play] was hideously funny—a grim and bitter charade...But as transposed on tape to TV's small screen...Rabe's play is filled with literal trappings and when you place abstract forms in literal trappings, they are not only bizarre but a little ridiculous....I don't want to put you off completely. This is a powerful and compelling work, highly serious in intent and of immense significance to the timid world of television."* (Cecil Smith, Los Angeles Times)

Streamers (1983, Streamers Int'l, 118m/c, **VHS**) ☆☆☆☆ **Sc:** David Rabe. **D:** Robert Altman. **Cam:** Pierre Mignot. **P:** Robert Altman, Nick J. Mileti. **Cast:** Matthew Modine, Michael Wright, Mitchell Lichtenstein, David Alan Grier, Guy Boyd, George Dzundza, B.J. Cleveland. This 1976 talkfest is set among four infantrymen in a barracks, and the two sergeants in charge during the weekend that they'll all receive their traveling orders to the Vietnam War. The original stage cast featured Paul Rudd, Dolph Sweet, Kenneth McMillan, Arlen Dean Snyder, Dorian Harewood, and Mark Metcalf. Altman spent a decade adapting major plays into small-scale movies, and this is one of his successes. Machismo, race, and the prospects of battle dominate the often booze-fueled talks, which become increasingly intense and eventually explosive. The one-barracks set amplifies this character drama, which is served well by the actors, particularly Wright, Modine, and Lichtenstein.

* *"Even though an overly talky script combined with a stagnant setting is an ever present reminder that this story is better suited for the theatre, this staginess is overshadowed by excellent performances and the film's blunt examination of issues of race, war and machismo."* (Richard Skorman, Off-Hollywood Movies)

Bob Randall

Stanley B. Goldstein
Born: August 20, 1937, New York, NY. **Died:** 1995.

Bob Randall was an advertising copywriter and actor before his literary aspirations were rewarded by the hit success of 6 RMS RIV VU in 1972 on the New York stage. In 1977, his novel The Fan received the Edgar Allan Poe Award, and was later made into the 1981 film of the same name starring Lauren Bacall and James Garner. The Fan was followed by the novels The Next and The Calling. Randall's stage plays include the musical The Magic Show and the comedy revue Annie and the Seven Hoods. For CBS, Randall created the 1977–78 sitcom On Our Own starring Lynnie Green and Bess Armstrong as ad executives.

6 RMS RIV VU (1974, CBS, 90m/c) ☆☆☆½ **Tp:** Bob Randall. **D:** Clark Jones, Alan Alda. **P:** Joe Hamilton, Robert Wright. **Cast:** Carole Burnett, Alan Alda, Millie Slavin, Lawrence Pressman, Maureen Silliman, Francine Beers, Jose Ocasio. Two married strangers meet in an empty apartment by answering the title classified ad in the newspaper. The first production of this enduring comedy (one that can be easily staged among amateur groups and traveling troupes) was in 1972 at New York's Helen Hayes Theatre with F. Murray Abraham, Jane Alexander, Jerry Orbach, and Jennifer Warren. This agreeable TV version, which dovetailed to Alda's romantic-comedy facilities, was taped before a live New York theatre audience.

* *"The plot and characters are New York, undiluted sweet and sour....The old formula is, however, generously spiked with several fresh touches...With two very capable, very attractive performances from Miss Burnett and Mr.*

Alda, the TV production maintains a nimble balance between charmingly light and gently touching." (John J. O'Connor, The New York Times)

Samson Raphaelson
Born: March 30, 1896, New York, NY. **Died:** 1983.

Samson Raphaelson's name will always first be connected to *The Jazz Singer* (1927), the film that brought the greatest attention to the coming of sound to Hollywood movies. But Raphaelson and Ernst Lubitsch forged one of the greatest if largely unsung writer-director partnerships in film history. Lubitsch, the grand master of great light romantic comedies with sparkling dialogue and game performances, found in Raphaelson a master collaborator. The latter wrote or co-wrote *The Smiling Lieutenant* (1931), *One Hour With You* (1932), *Trouble in Paradise* (1932), *The Merry Widow* (1934), *Angel* (1937), *The Shop Around the Corner* (1940), *Heaven Can Wait* (1943), and *That Lady in Ermine* (1948). Raphaelson also wrote *Suspicion* (1941) for Alfred Hitchcock as well as the hits *The Harvey Girls* (1946) and *Green Dolphin Street* (1947).

If anything, Raphaelson's connection with the film revolution brought about by the coming of sound with *The Jazz Singer* obscures his more substantial contributions to the movies. His plays include *Young Love* (1928), *Boolie* (1930), *The Wooden Slipper* (1933), *White Man* (1936), *Jason* (1942), and *The Perfect Marriage* (1944). Several of his short stories were adapted for TV, four for *Matinee Theatre* in the late 1950s, including *Stopover* in 1957 with Barbara Billingsley.

Accent on Youth concerns a middle-aged playwright who is writing a work about an older man leaving his wife for a young girl. His life is turned around when his young lovelorn secretary — whom he truly loves — marries, then finally returns to him after six months. The play opened in 1934 at the Plymouth Theatre in New York starring Nicholas Hannen and Constance Cummings, and played London the following year with Hannen and Greer Garson.

Accent on Youth (1935, Paramount, 77m/bw) ☆☆☆ **Sc:** Herbert Fields, Claude Binyon. **D:** Wesley Ruggles. **P:** Douglas Maclean. **Cam:** Leon Shamroy. **Cast:** Sylvia Sidney, Herbert Marshall, Philip Reed, Astrid Allwyn, Holmes Herbert, Catharine Doucet, Ernest Cossart, Donald Meek, Lon Chaney Jr., Dick Foran, Samuel B. Hinds, Florence Roberts, Laura Treadwell. The one outstanding line in the film, which wasn't in the play, comes after the athletic young husband drags Sidney around his California estate and she pleads to be left alone to read. "Read a book?" he asks incredulously. "In California?"

- *"Samuel Raphaelson's pleasant little stage comedy of middle-aged love spends a good deal of its time being a garrulous bore in its motion picture version...content to be a faithful photographics study of the original...On the surface you might imagine that the love of a sophisticated playwright for his young and healthy secretary might have about it an unpleasant hint of lechery. But Mr. Raphaelson slyly makes his point in the hero's defense by reversing the order of the pursuit....It's a pleasure to have Miss Sylvia Sidney...Her performance...is excellent."* (Andre Sennwald, The New York Times)

Mr. Music (1950, Paramount, 113m/bw, **VHS**) ☆☆ **Sc:** Arthur Sheekman. **D:** Richard Haydn. **P:** Robert L. Welch. **Cam:** George Barnes. **Cast:** Bing Crosby, Nancy Olson, Charles Coburn, Ruth Hussey, Marge Champion, Gower Champion, Peggy Lee, Groucho Marx. This musical rendition, retooled as a Crosby vehicle, has Bing as a middle-aged songwriter who's supplied with a college girl assistant whose secret duty is to keep him creatively productive.

- *"Among the least satisfying [of Crosby films in the 1950s]...an elaborate but weak picture that is a disappointing throwback to the days when the Bingle had to attempt to make the most of silly scripts and threadbare plots....Apart from Crosby's portrayal, however, the film has little to offer. The slow-moving film is also much longer than it should have been."* (Robert Bookbinder, The Films of Bing Crosby)

But Not for Me (1959, Paramount, 105m/bw, **VHS**) ☆☆ **Sc:** John Michael Hayes. **D:** Walter Lang. **P:** William Perlberg, George Seaton. **Cam:** Robert Burks. **Cast:** Clark Gable, Carroll Baker, Lilli Palmer, Lee J. Cobb, Barry Coe, Thomas Gomez. Gable was a bit long in the tooth to be co-starring with the movies's Baby Doll, but the theme still had its vast appeal, even though, overall, this production does it only middling justice.

- *"...But Not for Me wasn't damned or praised, it was one of those run-of-the-mill comedies turned out regularly in those days to keep the studios active. After his long years in the business, Gable could afford now and then to slip in one of these 'bread and butter' flicks. But I was in no such position. I'd taken a giant step backwards, committed a type of professional suicide, and suddenly I was stricken with the horror of what it means to be no longer in demand."* (Carroll Baker, Baby Doll)

Accent on Youth was presented on Kraft Television Theatre in 1950 in a production featuring Melville Ruick and Marilyn Erskine, and again in 1957 on Matinee Theatre.

Hilda Crane (1956, 20th Century-Fox, 87m/c) ☆☆½ **Sc/D:** Philip Dunne. **P:** Herbert B. Swope Jr. **Cam:** Joe MacDonald. **Cast:** Jean Simmons, Guy Madison, Jean-Pierre Aumont, Evelyn Varden, Judith Evelyn, Peggy Knudsen. The title woman, miserable after two marriages, tries it for the third time, still unconvinced that it will work. The original production at New York's Coronet Theatre in 1950 starred Jessica Tandy, Beulah Bondi, Eileen Heckert, and Evelyn Varden. Very much a "woman's picture" of the 1940s dragged into the 1950s, it features Hilda as someone who no one understands, from her mother to men, and it drives her to drink.

- *"Jean Simmons makes a lovely [heroine]...It is no fault of hers that Hilda is still a tough one to understand. Blame that on the original playwright, Samson Raphaelson and writer-director Philip Dunne. The latter has only confused matters thoroughly by having everything turn out ducky in the end. As for the other performers...they all behave like artificial characters in a gaudy CinemaScope soap opera, which this is."* (Bosley Crowther, The New York Times)

The Jazz Singer, based on Raphaelson's magazine story, "The Day of Atonement," concerns Jakie Rabinowitz's desire to become a popular singer over his father's wishes that he become a cantor. On the eve of the musical he's starring in, the father falls ill, and Jakie—who renamed himself Jack Robin in a rejection of his Jewish background—postpones the show to sing "Kol Nidre." The musical eventually opens and his mother says, "He is not my boy anymore. He belongs to the world." The 1925 play became a big hit on Broadway for George Jessel, who was cast in the picture but backed out in a dispute over money.

The Jazz Singer (1927, Warner Bros., 88m/bw, **VHS**) ☆☆☆☆ **Sc:** Alfred A. Cohn. **Titles:** Jack Jarmuth. **D:** Alan Crosland. **P:** Jack L. Warner. **Cam:** Hal Mohr. **Cast:** Al Jolson, Mae McAvoy, Warner Oland, Eugenie Besserer, Otto Lederer, Bobbie Gordon, Richard Tucker, Cantor Josef Rosenblatt, Nat Carr, William Demarest, Anders Randolf, Will Walling, Roscoe Karns, Myrna Loy. This film was the first with sound to capture the imagination of the audience—not the first talking picture, or the first Vitaphone picture, or first all-talking picture, as is often said. Its massive success, which hinged on a scene in which Jolson sings "Mammy" in blackface, made the triumph of sound films inevitable.

- *"The plot was ludicrous, and was treated as such even by contemporary critics, many of whom complained that the story was 'too Jewish.' (Of course, it is worth noting that despite the awfulness of the story, The Jazz Singer has been twice remade [as a film]). What is exciting about the film is its use of sound—not only the interpolated dialogue and songs, but also the musical score and sound effects arranged by Louis Silvers (who skillfully blends elements of popular music with elements of serious music by Tchaikovsky, Debussy and others)."* (Anthony Slide, International Dictionary of Films and Filmmakers—Vol. 1: Films)

The Jazz Singer (1953, Warner Bros., 107m/c) ☆½ **Sc:** Frank Davis, Leonard Stern, Lewis Meltzer. **D:** Michael Curtiz. **P:** Louis F. Edelman. **Cam:** Carl Guthrie. **Cast:** Danny Thomas, Peggy Lee, Mildred Dunnock,

Eduard Franz. Tom Tully, Allyn Joslyn, Alex Geray, Harold Gordon. The resurrection of the property coincided with the first year of Thomas's phenomenal sitcom success on TV as Danny Williams, the nightclub singing father in ABC's *Make Room for Daddy*. Thomas's portrayal in the film is altered from his TV image only in an extra level of blandness.

- *"...Warner Bros....couldn't better their own original with a full sound track, a multi-camera attack and color....Danny Thomas can't show us the compulsion of performance that Jolson had to—does not...Yet that compulsion is what* The Jazz Singer *is based on and what many of the early musicals had, song and dance going off like firecrackers."* (Ethan Mordden, The Hollywood Musical)

The Jazz Singer (1959, NBC Special, 60m/c) *Ford Startime* ☆½ **Tp:** Samson Raphaelson. **D:** Ralph Nelson. **P:** Ernest D. Gluckman. **Cast:** Jerry Lewis, Molly Picon, Eduard Franz, Anna Maria Alberghetti, Barry Gordon, Alan Reed, Joey Faye. This was the most personal project of Lewis's TV career. The comedian changed names of characters to reflect his own upbringing, Jewish heritage, fractured family, and charity Bar Mitzvah. The critics shot Lewis like the proverbial fish in a barrel in one of the more infamous blanket drubbings of the early TV era.

- *"Lewis, is hardly the figure to swing between the double masks of comedy and tragedy with any degree of ease, and there were times when the demands of the role were just too much for him....The spectacle of Lewis singing 'Kol Nidre' in blackface just about 24 hours after the Day of Atonement just didn't sit right along ecclesiastical lines, and looked like a dramatic gimmick of a bygone era."* (Variety)

- *"By 1959—and in the wake of an ill-fated 1950s remake starring Danny Thomas—everyone in Hollywood considered* The Jazz Singer *moldy and sacrosanct at once. Astonishment and wicked anticipatory glee therefore greeted the news that Jerry Lewis would appear in a made-for-TV version...It wasn't a flop on the scale of Neil Diamond's laughable 1980 version...but it was hardly proof to the world of its star's dramatic talents....asked about his recurrent bad luck on television, Jerry sneered to the* New York Post, *'TV is a joke.'"* (Shawn Levy, King of Comedy: The Life and Art of Jerry Lewis)

The Jazz Singer (1980, EMI, 115m/c, **VHS/DVD**) ☆ **Sc:** Herbert Baker, Stephen H. Foreman. **D:** Richard Fleischer. **P:** Jerry Leider. **Cam:** Isidore Mankofsky. **Cast:** Neil Diamond, Laurence Olivier, Lucie Arnaz, Catlin Adams, Sully Boyar, Franklin Ajaye, Ernie Hudson. When the worst bombs in movie history are discussed, this one holds a firm place. Diamond can't act and Olivier overacts. Their scenes together are ludicrous, the religious angle even more unbelievable than in other versions, and the songs unmemorable. This one finally buried the material.

- *"What is jazz to Neil Diamond and what is Neil Diamond to jazz? Old title has nothing to do with music on display here and would seem meaningless to modern audiences."* (Variety)

- *"First question: why is* The Jazz Singer *called* The Jazz Singer *when there's no jazz in it?...second question: why would anyone in his right mind want to update this story of a cantor's son who breaks from his Jewish heritage to become a successful singer? No story is more steeped in the immigrant ethos of the 1920s than Samson Raphaelson's old tale, and the idea that Neil Diamond, of all people, is seriously torn between synagogue and showbiz is, to put it mildly, rather odd....And one look at Laurence Olivier giving one of his vampy sideway glances and pursing his lips in patriarchal grief and you know you're in for another of his sad, take-the-money-and-run performances."* (David Ansen, Newsweek)

Skylark is about the neglected wife of an advertising executive who flirts with a sardonic and hard drinking party guest—who's having an affair with one of her married friends—at her tenth wedding anniversary party. The 1939 stage original at New York's Morosco Theatre starred Gertrude Lawrence, Donald Cook, Glenn Anders, and Vivian Vance.

Skylark (1941, Paramount, 94m/bw) ☆☆ **Sc:** Z. Myers. **D/P:** Mark Sandrich. **Cam:** Charles Lang. **Cast:** Claudette Colbert, Ray Milland, Brian Aherne, Binnie Barnes, Walter Abel, Grant Mitchell, Mona Barrie, Ernest Cossart. This pedestrian run-through of marital discord seems even more clichéd after a half a century of Manhattan upper-crust sitcoms. The stars shine a bit, but it's just not enough.

- *"...a completely forgettable marital comedy."* (David Shipman, The Great Movie Stars 1: The Golden Years)
- *"...a cinema caterer's dream...far from filling, but it is highly palatable fare."* (Bosley Crowther, The New York Times)

Skylark was presented three times on TV, in 1949 on *Ford Theatre Hour* with Faye Emerson and Lee Bowman, in 1951 on *Prudential Family Playhouse* with Gertrude Lawrence and Donald Cook reprising their Broadway success, and in 1956 on *Matinee Theatre* with Sarah Churchill and Gene Raymond.

Muriel Resnik

The one other film made from Muriel Resnik's source material was derived from her novel, *The Girl in the Turquoise Bikini*, which became the romantic comedy *How Sweet It Is!* (1968) starring James Garner and Debbie Reynolds.

Any Wednesday (1966, Warner Bros., 109m/c, **VHS**) ☆☆½ **Sc:** Muriel Resnik, Julius J. Epstein. **D:** Robert Ellis Miller. **P:** Julius J. Epstein. **Cam:** Harold Lipstein. **Cast:** Jason Robards, Jr., Jane Fonda, Dean Jones, Rosemary Murphy, Paula Prentiss. The Broadway hit, staged at the Music Box Theatre in 1964, starred Sandy Dennis as a once-a-week mistress who wants more out of a relationship, and also featured Gene Hackman, Don Porter, and Rosemary Murphy. As the young woman is in danger of losing her apartment, a businessman she meets schemes to add her to his stable of girlfriends by having his company buy the apartment. Unfortunately, his wife and a co-worker both discover her living there.

- "In 1964 Broadway audiences were enthralled by a frothy little sex farce labeled Any Wednesday...In 1966 it became a movie, Jane Fonda took over as the frothy mistress and the froth settled in the stale beer of overproduction, hysterical performance and the spelling out of the no-longer-double-entendres....Miss Fonda is frenetic and Dean Jones, as her beau, looks like the refugee from Disney films that he was at the time and the whole thing looks more clunky-foolish than ever..." (Judith Crist, Judith Crist's TV Guide to the Movies)

Ronald Ribman

Born: May 28, 1932, New York, NY.

Ronald Ribman's distinguished television writing includes the brilliant but almost completely forgotten 1967 CBS *Playhouse* presentation of *The Final War of Olly Winter*, starring Ivan Dixon as a U.S. Army advisor in South Vietnam who forges a friendship with a Vietnamese woman (Tina Chen) across the language barrier after his outfit is wiped out in a Viet Cong ambush. The show, Dixon, Chen, director Paul Bogart, and Ribman received Emmy nominations for their work a scant three years after the Gulf of Tonkin Resolution.. Ribman and Bill Gunn adapted Bernard Malamud's fiction for *The Angel Levine* (1970) with Zero Mostel, and Ribman adapted Saul Bellow's novel *Seize the Day* into an early Robin Williams film. Ribman's plays include *Harry, Noon and Night* (1965), which starred Dustin Hoffman, *Fingernails Blue as Flowers* (1971), *The Poison Tree* (1976), and *The Rug Merchants of Chaos* (1991). He also wrote the original *The Beautiful Fish* for *Foul!*, an anthology of playlets on *NET Playhouse* in 1971 protesting air pollution.

The Ceremony of Innocence (1970, NET, 90m/c) *NET Playhouse* ☆☆☆½ **Tp:** Ronald Ribman. **D:** Arthur A. Seidelman. **P:** Bob Mackell, Jac Venza. **Cast:** Richard Kiley, James Broderick, Larry Gates, Jessie Royce Landis, Elizabeth Hubbard, William Hickey, Gilmer Mc-

Cormick, Ernest Graves, John Horn, Bob Gerringer, Howard Green. The American Place Theater first produced this play in 1968, about King Ethelrod the Unready, who ruled England from 978 to 1016 and preferred to buy off the invading Norwegians and Danes rather than see his countrymen perish at their hands. This program was also shown on PBS's *Theatre in America* in 1974.

- "...*Bob Markell's production demonstrates the greater artistic mobility to be gained through imaginative use of cameras not tied to the perspective of the proscenium arch....It is to the credit of Mr. Markell that he employs the medium with a fluidity that overcomes the hazards of a play written in flashback technique and does not lose a sense of forward narrative movement....reaffirmed that in capable hands TV can be its own art form different from stage or film. The cross-fertilization of media—from the theatre to TV and vice versa—is one of the more intriguing phenomena of the contemporary performing arts.*" (Jack Gould, The New York Times)

The Journey of the Fifth Horse (1966, NET, 60m/c, **DVD**) *NET Playhouse* ☆☆☆☆ **Tp:** Ronald Ribman. **D:** Larry Arrick, Earl Dawson. **P:** Jac Venza. **Cast:** Dustin Hoffman, Michael Tolan, Charlotte Rae, Susan Anspach, William H. Bassett, Jack Aaron, Jim Doerr, Catharine Gaffigan, Martha Greenhouse, Mark Hammer, Susan Lipton. This 1965 Off Broadway play, which won several Obie Awards, was based by Ribman on the novella *The Diary of a Superfluous Man* by Ivan Turgenev. The play and TV show were major steps in the early career of Hoffman, who turned in a spectacular performance as a greedy clerk who defies his former boss's deathbed directive to burn the old man's diary—he instead tries to sell it.

- "...*Dustin Hoffman turns in a powerhouse performance in his first TV starring appearance as Zoditch, a lonely reader at a publishing house who enters the dream world of a writer whose diary he has been given to read overnight.*" (Movies Unlimited)

Elmer L. Rice

Elmer Reizenstein
Born: September 28, 1892, New York, NY. **Died:** 1967.
Pulitzer Prize-winning play: *Street Scene* (1929)

Elmer Rice's limited movie work included the screenplays for *Doubling for Romeo* (1921), *Rent Free* (1922), and the collaboration with Claude Binyon on *Holiday Inn* (1942) for Bing Crosby. He was married to actress Betty Field.

The Adding Machine (1969, Universal, 100m/c) ☆☆½ **Sc/D/P:** Jerome Epstein. **Cam:** Walter Lassally. **Cast:** Milo O'Shea, Phyllis Diller, Sydney Chaplin, Billie Whitelaw, Julian Glover, Phil Brown, Raymond Huntley, Libby Morris. The basic theme of this 1923 play was as relevant in the 1960s as it is today: A lowly and disrespected clerk, Mr. Zero, rebels by killing his boss after he learns that he'll be replaced by a computer. Tried and executed, he spends three decades in heaven, then is "laundered" back into existence as another human schlep. The play starred Dudley Digges and Helen Westley and co-starred Margaret Wycherly and Edward G. Robinson at Broadway's Garrick Theatre. The film, produced two years after Rice's death, is a literal translation that has the potent sting of its theme without Rice's light touch.

- *"...eliminated the expressionist feel of the original play, treating it instead as a* nouvelle vague *fantasy. [Epstein] assembled a cast headed by Phyllis Diller as Mrs. Zero and Milo O'Shea...All appeared uncomfortable in their roles."* (Clive Hirschhorn, The Universal Story)

Counsellor-at-Law starred Paul Muni on Broadway at the Plymouth Theatre in 1931, directed by Rice and co-starring John Qualen and Ned Glass. This is the story of a Jewish lawyer who makes it to the top of his profession, only to be abandoned by the wife who supported him.

Counsellor-at-Law (1933, Universal, 78m/bw) ☆☆☆☆ **Sc:** Elmer Rice. **D:** William Wyler. **P:** Henry Henigson. **Cam:** Norbert Brodine. **Cast:** John Barrymore, Bebe Daniels, Melvyn Douglas, Doris Kenyon, Onslow Stevens, Isabel Jewell, Thelma Todd, Mayo Methot, Richard Quine, John Qualen, Marvin Kline, Vincent Sherman, Conway Washburn, Bobby Gordon, John Hamond Daily, Malka Kornstein, Angela Jacobs, T.H. Manning. Muni, afraid of being typecast in Jewish parts, declined to act on screen the part he originated on stage, opening the door for Lionel Barrymore to play one of his more flamboyant roles.

- *"Seldom has a play been transferred to the screen with such fidelity."* (The New Yorker)

- *"...the 1933 production has by now the patina of a period piece, and what a good movie period it was, full of gold-diggers, social climbers, dedicated radicals, etc. William Wyler directed, and despite his later reputation for such polished works as* The Little Foxes, The Best Years of Our Lives, Roman Holiday *and* The Desperate Hours, *etc., I prefer this earlier Wyler, fresh from more than 50 two-reel westerns, willing to tell his story simply."* (Pauline Kael, Kiss Kiss Bang Bang)

Counsellor-at-Law (1948, NBC, 60m/bw) *Philco Television Playhouse* ☆☆☆ **D/P:** Fred Coe. **Cast:** Paul Muni, Neva Patterson. This was Muni's first TV appearance as he recreated the role that brought him fame on Broadway 17 years earlier.

- *"Muni chose a carefully cut version of* Counsellor at Law. *Muni was fascinated but fearful of the immediacy of live television. Neva Patterson remembers Muni's racking headaches during the* Philco *experience and his extreme nervousness, which somehow miraculously disappeared the moment the camera's little red light flashed on."* (Jerome Lawrence, Actor: The Life and Times of Paul Muni)

Counsellor at Law also aired in 1948 on *Kraft Television Theatre* and in 1951 on ABC's *Celanese Theatre* with Alfred Drake and Ruth Hussey.

Dream Girl concocted a female version of the Walter Mitty syndrome in Georgina Allerton, a well-off but hardly courageous sort whose romantic daydreams are enacted prior to her reckoning with reality at the final curtain. The 1945 play at New York's Coronet Theatre starred Betty Field, Evelyn Varden, Wendell Corey, and James Gregory.

Dream Girl (1948, Paramount, 86m/bw) ☆☆½ **Sc:** Arthur Sheekman. **D:** Mitchell Leisen. **P:** P.J. Wolfson. **Cam:** Daniel L. Fapp. **Cast:** Betty Hutton, Macdonald Carey, Patric Knowles, Walter Abel, Virginia Field, Peggy Wood, Lowell Gilmore. In Paramount's ongoing search to supply Hutton with vehicles, Rice's play became another assembly-line product, even in Leisen's capable hands.

- *"[Betty Hutton's] limitations were clearly exposed by* Dream Girl, *based on Elmer Rice's satire/whimsy, which his wife, Betty Field, had done on Broadway; as the wealthy idealistic book seller...Hutton hangs on to her last syllables like Field and opts, between monotony, for all-out emotions. Mitchell Leisen, who directed, says that she was convinced that she would win an Oscar and was 'devastated' when she wasn't even nominated: her fans, he went on, 'were disappointed when she didn't go around screaming "Murder, He Says" and the rest of the public who couldn't stand her didn't go either.'"* (David Shipman, The Great Movies Stars 1: The Golden Years)

Dream Girl (1955, NBC, 90m/bw) *The Hallmark Hall of Fame* ☆☆½ **Tp:** S. Mark Smith. **D:** George Schaefer. **P:** Maurice Evans. **Cast:** Viviane Blaine, Hal March, Evelyn Varden, Edmon Ryan, Mary Fickett, Priscilla Morrill. Blaine starred as the daydream-afflicted Georgette, and Hal March, best known as the host of the popular *The $64,000 Question*, co-starred as a wisecracking newspaperman.

- *"Elmer Rice's theatrical trifle...was not very good. Responsibility for the disappointment must be attributed in about equal degree to Mr. Rice and to the decision that resulted in the regrettable miscasting of the talented Viviane Blaine...she did not capture the sense of contrast between the real-life and make-believe Georginas, which was what tended to throw the play out of kilter. Whether on or off Cloud 9, Miss Blaine was too much the same person....Hal March quietly walked off with the acting honors."* (Jack Gould, The New York Times)

- *"…a sweet, rather simple story…A lightweight* Hallmark, *it was a lot of fun. I remember the frantic costume changing. I'd be shooting Viviane from the chest up playing some scene while the dressers were putting on a different skirt and preparing her for the next one."* (George Schaefer, From Live to Tape to Film: 60 Years of Inconspicuous Directing)

For the Defense (1922, Paramount, bw/silent) **Sc:** Beulah Marie Dix. **D:** Paul Powell. **Cam:** Harold Rosson. **Cast:** Ethel Clayton, Vernon Steele, ZaSu Pitts, Bertram Grassby, Mayme Kelso, Sylvia Ashton, Mabel Van Buren.

The Grand Tour concerns a New England schoolteacher who, while on a tour of Europe, falls in love with a man whom she later learns is an embezzler.

Holiday (1956, NBC Special, 90m/c) *Max Liebman Presents* ☆☆ **Tp:** Edgar Eager. **D:** Max Liebman, Charles S. Dubin. **P:** Max Liebman. **Cast:** Doretta Morrow, Keith Andes, Kitty Carlisle, Bambi Linn, Rod Alexander, Tammy Grimes, George Irving, Anthony Eisley, Jacques D'Amboise, Charles Weidman. This Liebman spectacular, which has nothing to do with the Philip Barry play of the same name, places the music of Johann Strauss to Rice's *The Grand Tour.* As with Liebman's many "spectaculars," the book suffered at the expense of the music.

- *"Max Liebman's season of spex closed on a low note…The musical was overloaded with 18 numbers, none of them particularly distinguished. Remnants of the story would pop up sporadically, like an unwelcome relative, and hurriedly be shunted away for more music….talent…were wasted in the inferior material….Liebman's producer-director credit was singularly undistinguished. Book was staged by Charles Dubin with equally unsatisfactory results."* (Variety)

The Grand Tour also aired in 1954 on *The United States Steel Hour* with Zachary Scott and Julie Haydon, and in a full-length version on PBS's *The Play of the Week,* with William A. Graham directing Scott McKay and Audrey Meadows.

It Is the Law (1924, Fox, bw/silent) **Sc:** Curtis Benton. **D:** J. Gordon Edwards. **P:** William Fox. **Cam:** George W. Lane. **Cast:** Arthur Hohl, Herbert Hayes, Mona Palma, George Lessey, Robert Young, Florence Dixon, Olaf Hytten, Byron Douglas, Byron Russell, Bijou Fernandez, De Sacia Mooers, Guido Trento. A jilted sailor murders his victorious rival and pins the crime on his spitting image.

Oh, Sailor Behave (1930, Warner Bros., 70m/bw) ☆☆☆ **Sc:** Joseph Jackson, Sid Silvers. **D:** Archie Mayo. **Cam:** Deveraux Jennings. **Cast:** Irene Delroy, Lowell Sherman, Charles King, Vivien Oakland, Noah Beery, Ole Olsen, Chic Johnson, Lotti Loder, Charles Judels, Elise

Bartlett, Lawrence Grant, Gino Corrado, Hallam Cooley. Based on Rice's 1929 play *See Naples and Die*, this travelogue has the protagonists searching for an unknown criminal with a wooden leg by shooting prospects in the leg with a painful pea shooter.

- *"The way-out comedy team of Olsen and Johnson made its film debut in this amusing comedy based on a failed Broadway play by Elmer Rice reworked for the team's talents...The studio recreated the Bay of Naples on its backlot...with amazingly good results."* (J.R. Nash, S.R. Ross, The Motion Picture Guide)

On Trial was first produced on Broadway in 1914 at the Candler Theatre with Frederick Perry and Constance Wolf topping the cast. The story concerns a young attorney who defends a murderer on the grounds that he was protecting his wife's honor.

On Trial (1917, First National, bw/silent) ☆☆½ **Sc/D:** James Young. **Cast:** Barbara Castleton, Sidney Ainsworth, Mary McAllister, James Young, Corene Uzzell, Patrick Calhoun, John Cossar. The future director, W.S. "Woody" Van Dyke, was Young's assistant director on this film.

- *"...only average...It is interesting that the stage production (which was equally mediocre) owed its success to the fact that it used the motion picture technique of the flashback to impress audiences. In 1917 there were few examples of the screen imitating the stage imitating the screen."* (J.P. Nash, S.R. Ross, The Motion Picture Guide)

On Trial (1928, Warner Bros., 91m/bw) ☆☆½ **Sc:** Robert Lord, Max Pollock. **D:** Archie Mayo. **Cam:** Byron Haskins. **Cast:** Pauline Frederick, Bert Lytell, Lois Wilson, Jason Robards (Sr.), Holmes Herbert, Richard Tucker, Johnny Arthur, Vondell Darr, Franklin Pangborn, Fred Kelsey, Edmund Breese, Edward Martindel.

- *"Adaptation is rather weak, but a good cast makes the most of it. The film is of primary interest for its early and unsuccessful use of sound techniques. Muffled dialogue, hissing 'S' sounds, and distracting scratching noises combined, making listening to the Vitaphone sound track a chore."* (J.P. Nash, S.R. Ross, The Motion Picture Guide)

On Trial (1939, Warner Bros., 60m/bw) ☆☆☆ **Sc:** Don Ryan. **D:** Terry O. Morse. **P:** Bryan Foy. **Cam:** L. William O'Connell. **Cast:** Margaret Lindsay, John Litel, Edward Norris, James Stephenson, Sidney Bracey, Nat Carr, Janet Chapman, Earl Dwire, Lola Cheaney, William B. Davidson. This was one of producer "Brynie" Foy's standard-brands, B-picture retoolings of a Warners-owned property that the studio issued for double bills.

- *"...restored to life...at the B-hest of the Warners. Considering its vintage and the fact that it has been screened twice before, it stands up rather well....Mr. Rice may be taxed for taking liberties with the courts — we never thought the trials could be reopened so easily after the jury had retired — but he hasn't missed a melodramatic trick, from the tears of a six-year-old to the exposure of a perjuror. The Warners have filmed it briskly — so briskly, in fact, that one senses a director working with a cost accountant breathing down his neck."* (Frank S. Nugent, The New York Times)

Street Scene offered a look at a panorama of grim life in New York City's tenements in a multi-character display enacted by a large ensemble. The play was a smash success, winning the Pulitzer Prize and running for more than two years on Broadway, beginning at the Playhouse in 1929 in a production staged by Rice with an ensemble that included Beulah Bondi, John Qualen, and Erin O'Brien-Moore.

Street Scene (1931, Goldwyn/UA, 80m/bw, **VHS/DVD**) ☆☆☆☆½
Sc: Elmer Rice. **D:** King Vidor. **P:** Samuel Goldwyn. **Cam:** George Barnes. **Cast:** Sylvia Sidney, William Collier Jr., Beulah Bondi, Max Montor, David Landau, Estelle Taylor, Russell Hopton, Matt McHugh, John Qualen, Tom H. Manning, Greta Grandstedt, George Humbert. As pictorially effective in its mission to display the squalor of urban life as the later *Dead End* (1937) and *One Third of a Nation* (1939), Vidor's film of Rice's play is a largely forgotten landmark. Many of the cast, including Qualen and Bondi, who would become ubiquitous character actors for generations, repeated their stage roles.

- *"...further demonstrated Vidor's mastery in the depiction of character as an extension of environment. Elmer Rice's play had analyzed the conflicting emotions which can exist in a simple tenement building, and Samuel Goldwyn, pursuing as ever his goal of 'cultural' films, saw no great barrier to adapting it to film. Vidor made use of a fluid camera to overcome the static nature of the action, craning dizzyingly to show the ant-like motion of people in the crowded street, tracking in and out of the carefully engineered sets to create the illusion of movement which the original lacked....As a skilful adaptation of an impossible subject,* Street Scene *deserves comparison with Ford's* Arrowsmith *for its ingenuity."* (John Baxter, Hollywood in the Thirties)

Street Scene was produced on TV by Fred Coe in a truncated version in 1948 on NBC's *Philco Television Playhouse* with a cast headed by Betty Field and Erin O'Brien-Moore. *Street Scene* was also produced in 1952, on ABC's *Celanese Theatre* with Alex Segal directing Ann Dvorak, Paul Kelly, Coleen Gray, and Michael Wager. An opera version produced by the BBC also aired in America on PBS's *Great Performances* in 1979.

Jack Richardson

Jack Carter Richardson
Born: February 18, 1935, New York, NY.

At one time, Jack Richardson was portrayed by critic George Wellwarth as the great undiscovered genius of the American theatre. In the 1960s, he was considered in the same category with Edward Albee as one of the finest young playwrights in New York. *The Prodigal*, his first produced play after service in the Korean War and education abroad at Paris and Munich, was an Off Broadway sensation. His plays often concern man's entrapment by society. After winning the Obie Award for Best Play, his subsequent offerings included *Gallows Humor*, *Lorenzo*, and *Xmas in Vegas*. He also wrote the satirical novel *The Prison Life of Harris Filmore*.

The Prodigal (1969, NET special, 90m/c) ☆☆☆ **Tp:** Jack Richardson. **P:** Jac Venza. **Cast:** Kim Hunter, Roy Poole, John Heffernan, Pamela Payton-Wright, Cavada Humphrey. The play, which refracts the Greek legend of the pacifist Orestes through a contemporary 1960s sensibility, was first produced Off Broadway in 1960 at the Downtown Theatre and won the Obie Award for Best Play. In it, Agamemnon returns from the Trojan Wars after ten years to be greeted by a resentful wife, who has taken his cousin as a lover.

• *"...disappointing...flat and uninspiring...With the exceptions of Kim Hunter as Clymenestra and Cavada Humphrey as the witty Trojan seer Cassandra, the principals were not up to Mr. Richardson's heroic intent...But that still does not explain the play's failure to engage the viewer in a continuing dialogue with its author's ideas. And for this, I'm afraid, Mr. Richardson must accept the responsibility. Unlike the Greek dramatists with whom he's obviously familiar and after which he models himself, Mr. Richardson is prolix where they are trenchant, aspires to poetry but rarely rises above rhetoric. Courageously he engages his principals in confrontations and long-winded arguments, but these, unfortunately, while reducing the actors to sputtering elocution, fail to emerge into dramatic insight. Not surprisingly, The Prodigal reads better than it plays."* (George Gent, The New York Times)

Lynn Riggs

Rolla Lynn Riggs
Born: 1899, OK. **Died:** 1954.

An Oklahoma poet and playwright whose works often evoked the folkways, history, and concerns of the pioneers of the Southern

Plains, Riggs's plays included A *Lantern to See By* (1928), *Roadside* (1930), *Green Grow the Lilacs* (1931), *Russet Mantle* (1936), *The Cherokee Night* (1936), and *The Cream in the Well* (1941). His poetry was collected in *The Iron Dish* (1930). One of his unpublished plays, *Out of Dust*, was adapted by John Gay into a 1959 *Playhouse 90* presentation starring Wayne Morris, Uta Hagen, and Charles Bickford.

Green Grow the Lilacs, a folk play set in the Indian Territory of 1900, was intended by Riggs to dramatize the spirit of western folk songs. It was first produced on Broadway by the Theatre Guild in 1931 with Franchot Tone, Helen Westley, June Walker, and Lee Strasberg. *Oklahoma!*, the landmark Broadway musical of 1943, is based on Riggs's play, with a book by Oscar Hammerstein II. The musical starred Alfred Drake and Joan Roberts as the young lovers Curly and Laurey, plus Howard Da Silva and Celeste Holm. It's credited with altering the course of the American musical theatre through the provision of a more-than-substancial book or strong story underneath what had been the usual string of songs.

Oklahoma! (1955, Magna, 145m/c, **VHS/DVD**) ☆☆☆☆½ **Sc:** Sonya Levien, William Ludwig. **D:** Fred Zinnemann. **P:** Arthur Hornblow Jr. **Cam:** Robert Surtees. **Cast:** Gordon MacRae, Shirley Jones, Gloria Grahame, Gene Nelson, Rod Steiger, Charlotte Greenwood, Eddie Albert, James Whitmore, Barbara Lawrence, Jay C. Flippen, Roy Barcroft, James Mitchell, Bambi Linn, Evelyn Taylor, Jennie Workman. This hearty, down-home musical, with its enthusiastic cast and memorable songs, was a great credit to all of those involved, particularly Zinnemann, who was known almost strictly for drama and action films. The songs include "Oh, What a Beautiful Mornin'," "The Surrey With the Fringe on Top," and "People Say We're in Love." The film won Academy Awards for Best Sound Recording and Score (Robert Russell Bennett, Jay Blackton, Adolph Deutsch), and was nominated for Best Cinematography and Film Editing.

- "...*a production that magnifies and strengthens all the charm that it had upon the stage....under the direction of Fred Zinnemann — and, we might add, under the hawk-eyed observation of Messrs. Rogers and Hammerstein — a full-bodied* Oklahoma! *has been brought forth in this film to match the vitality, eloquence and melody any musical this reviewer has ever seen....Agnes De Mille...has made the dances and ballet of the original into eloquent moments that flow beneath the sky....And in Shirley Jones, a strawberry-blonde newcomer, he has a Laurey...so full of beauty, sweetness and spirit that a better Laurey cannot be dreamed....superlative screen entertainment...*" (Bosley Crowther, The New York Times)

Mary Roberts Rinehart & Avery Hopwood

Rinehart:
Born: August 12, 1876, Pittsburgh, PA. **Died:** 1958.

Hopwood:
Born: May 28, 1882, Cleveland, OH. **D:** July 1, 1928.

Mary Roberts Rinehart's stories, novels, and plays often depicted girls and women playing major parts in stories of mystery and suspense, which often used far-fetched plot points. They were the source material for at least 37 films and five TV shows, beginning in 1915 with the conversion of her most famous novel, *The Circular Staircase*. Marguerite Clark starred in three films in 1917 as the continuing character of Bab Archibald, based on Reinhart's stories. Rinehart's novel *Lost Ecstacy* was filmed as *I Take This Woman* (1931) starring Gary Cooper and Carole Lombard. An early Claire Trevor vehicle, *Elinor Norton* (1932) was based on Rinehart's novel *The State vs. Elinor Norton*. Lloyd Bacon directed Joan Blondell in *Miss Pinkerton* (1932), derived from the Rinehart novel. The play *The Bat* (see below), which she wrote with Avery Hopwood, was her most enduring play in popular culture. A regular contributor to *The Saturday Evening Post*, Rinehart was profiled in 1957 on CBS's *Telephone Time*.

The Bat was first produced on the stage in 1920 and was a sensation. A mysterious and energetic thief disguises himself as a giant bat and pulls off daring robberies as the police and others theorize on his identity. The play, which starred Effie Ellsler, was based on Roberts's 1908 novel, *The Circular Staircase*, and was filmed under the same title in 1915. Along with *The Cat and the Canary*, this was the most famous of all the Broadway horror spoofs.

The Bat (1926, UA 81m/bw/silent, **VHS**) ☆☆☆ **Sc:** Julien Josephson, George Marion Jr., Roland West. **D/P:** Roland West. **Cam:** Arthur Edeson, Gregg Toland. **Cast:** Andre de Baranger, Charles Herzinger, Emily Fitzroy, Louise Fazenda, Arthur Houseman, Robert McKim, Jack Pickford, Jewel Carmen, Sojin Kamiyama, Tullio Carminati, Eddie Gribbon, Lee Shumway. This first version of one of the archetypes of the murder-mystery melodrama utilized an eclectic cast and two of the top cameramen of the era.

- "...*will prove entertaining and exciting despite the mechanical twists employed in unfolding the yarn...Roland West has profited by the wide scope of the camera....People in the theatre...were distinctly affected by the spine-*

chilling episodes, and they were relieved by the comedy interludes." (The New York Times)

The Bat Whispers (1930, UA, 82m/bw, **VHS/DVD**) ☆☆☆½ **Sc/D/P:** Roland West. **Cam:** Ray June, Robert Planck. **Cast:** Chester Morris, Una Merkel, Chancer Ward, Grayce Hampton, Maude Eburne, Spencer Charters, Gustav Von Seyffertitz. A stylish retelling of the old dark house chiller used elaborate camera moves for an early talkie and unique sets and models, as West improved on his silent version (see above).

- *"If the material is the routine mixture of screams and laughs, West's direction is often truly startling, with scenes executed in shadowplay, the camera performing stunning arabesques, and one hallucinatory moment when, locked into a candlelit room with the heroine, the Bat can just be seen silhouetted against the wall and spreading his wings before he literally seems to melt into the darkness."* (Phil Hardy, The Encyclopedia of Horror Movies)

The Bat (1958, Allied Artists, 80m/bw, **VHS/DVD**) ☆☆ **Sc/D:** Crane Wilbur. **P:** C.J. Tevlin. **Cam:** Joseph Biroc. **Cast:** Agnes Moorehead, Vincent Price, Gavin Gordon, John Sutton, Lenita Lane, Darla Hood, Eliane Edwards, Harvey Stephens, Mike Steele, John Bryant, Robert Williams, Riza Royce. The disguised title marauder in this version, whose makers learned from other blood-letting, B-league horror pictures of the 1950s, makes it a habit of ripping out his victims' throats with a clawlike hand at a manor house just as he seeks out $1 million in securities stashed there.

- *"As though aware that the hoary formula of prowling maniac, hidden loot and beleaguered household would no longer hold water, the script adds a real bat to terrorize the ladies...Promising performances by Moorehead...and Price...are nipped in the bud by Wilbur's ponderous direction."* (Phil Hardy, The Encyclopedia of Horror Movies)

The Bat (1960, NBC, 60m/bw) *Dow Hour of Great Mysteries* ☆☆½ **Tp:** Walter Kerr. **D/P:** Robert Saudek. **Cast:** Helen Hayes, Jason Robards Jr., Margaret Hamilton, Martin Brooks, Bethel Leslie, Sheppard Strudwick, Karl Light, Mark Satow. **Host:** Joseph N. Welch. Saudek didn't want to update the gimmicky play, but rather present it the way it was presented in 1920. The results for this inaugural installment in the Dow series were lurid and unbelievable.

- *"The Bat is old hat. Robert Saude prided his production in fidelity to the original, let the bodies fall where they may. A lighter touch may have de-vintaged this oldster and made it more palatable to Hitchcock buffs. Not in TV's lifetime has there been such a conglomeration of violence, murder, mayhem and assorted crimes herded into one hour....played with all the sinister markings by Jason Robards Jr. Collectively, the acting was more reflective of [the] period than contemporary theatre."* (Variety)

Seven Days (1925, Producers Distributing, 7reels/bw) ☆☆½ **Sc:** Frank Roland Conklin. **D:** Scott Sidney. **P:** Al Christie. **Cam:** Alex Phillips, Gilbert Warrenton. **Cast:** Lillian Rich, Creighton Hale, Lilyan Tashman, Mabel Julienne Scott, William Austin, Hal Cooley, Rosa Gore, Tim Nilson, Edward Gribbon, Charles Claty.

- *"There is length and feverish action, with a minimum of real comedy, in this film conception…of the stage farce…which caused no little glee when it was presented before the footlights….One of the many failings…is the lack of that all-important factor, suspense. The characters dart hither and thither without much reason, and during certain interludes they engage in slapstick comedy which is not even redeemed by throwing custard pies….It is all the banana peel type of comedy…pretty dull affair."* (Mordaunt Hall, The New York Times)

David W. Rintels
Born: 1939, Boston, MA.

David W. Rintels has been a steadily productive TV writer and producer since his days as an associate producer on the science-fiction series *The Invaders* in the 1960s. His fact-based TV movies include *Fear on Trial* (1975) with William Devane as blacklisted radio personality John Henry Faulk; *Sakharov* (1984) with Jason Robards as the Nobel Peace Prize-winning Russian nuclear physicist; and the miniseries *Andersonville* (1996), about the Georgia Civil War prisoner-of-war camp, and *Nuremberg* (2000), about the World War II war-crimes trials. His one screenplay credit is for *Scorpio* (1972) starring Burt Lancaster, and his great stage contribution was in supplying Henry Fonda with the actor's last great stage role, the one-man *Clarence Darrow*, below.

Clarence Darrow (1974, NBC, 90m/c, **VHS**) ☆☆☆☆☆ **Tp:** David W. Rintels. **D:** John Rich. **P:** Mike Merrick, Don Gregory. **Cast:** Henry Fonda. This Christopher Award-winning production was based by Rintels on his 1974 stage play, adapted from Irving Stone's biography of the famous trial lawyer. The play, directed by John Houseman, starred Henry Fonda in one of his great stage triumphs. His masterful one-man performance carries the audience through Darrow's memories of the Leopold/Loeb trial, Scopes "monkey trial," *Los Angeles Times* bombing trial, and his other courtroom and personal adventures. The program has variously been titled *Clarence Darrow Starring Henry Fonda* and, on PBS reprises, *Henry Fonda as Clarence Darrow*.

- *"Henry Fonda's solo performance...is even more remarkable on television...Fonda's Darrow seems to me funnier on television than he was on the stage—the wit sharper. Or perhaps it's the intimacy of the medium, the intensity of focus....This is a play, not a lecture or performance as Hal Holbrook's Mark Twain or James Whitmore's Will Rogers. Though his stage contains only inanimate things...Fonda fills it with characters, floods it with life....Fonda makes [Darrow] unforgettable."* (Cecil Smith, Los Angeles Times)

Lawrence Roman

Under the Yum Yum Tree was originally the pilot for an unsold NBC series starring Jack Sheldon and Nita Talbot.

Under the Yum Yum Tree (1963, Columbia, 110m/c, **VHS**) ☆☆½ **Sc:** Lawrence Roman, David Swift. **D:** David Swift. **P:** Frederick Brisson. **Cam:** Joseph Biroc. **Cast:** Jack Lemmon, Carol Lynley, Dean Jones, Imogene Coca, Edie Adams, Paul Lynde, Robert Lansing, Bill Bixby. A young couple plans to live together platonically to test their true compatability, so they rent an apartment from a lecherous bachelor who schemes endlessly to chase off the boy and bed the girl. The 1962 play starred Dean Jones, Gig Young, Sarah Church, and Nan Martin.

- *"I can't tell you how* Under the Yum-Yum Tree *ends, because I didn't stay long enough to find out. Nevertheless, I stayed too long for my own good. It's a disgusting comedy, in which we're supposed first to be titilated to hear young people speak of sleeping together and then to be reassured when they carry on and on and on about not quite doing so. I admire Mr. Lemmon and I beg him to turn over a new leaf before it's too late."* (Brendan Gill, The New Yorker)

- *"Lawrence Roman's stage play has been so grossly exaggerated that Lemmon's efforts to portray a lecherous landlord are doubly unbelievable."* (Ellen Fitzpatrick, Films in Review)

Damon Runyon & Howard Lindsay
Runyon:
Alfred Damon Runyon
Born: 1884, Denver, CO. **Died:** 1946.

A legendary Broadway columnist and sports writer, Damon Runyon was best known for his collections of short stories about sports figures and hoodlums, written with snap in the street vernacular of the times. These were collected into the books *Guys and Dolls* (1932), *Take It Easy* (1938), *My Wife Ethel* (1940), *Runyon a la Carte* (1944), *In Our Town* (1946), and *Short Takes* (1946). Jo Swerling and Abe Burrows were inspired by his stories to write the famous 1950 Broadway musical comedy, *Guys and Dolls*, which was filmed in 1955. Howard Brookner and Coleman DeKay wove four of his stories—"Bloodhounds of Broadway," "The Brain Goes Home," "Social Error," and "A Very Honorable Guy"—together in a portrayal of Christmas Eve 1928 for the all-star 1989 *American Playhouse* presentation of *Bloodhounds of Broadway*.

For information on Lindsay, see **Howard Lindsay & Russel Crouse.**

A Slight Case of Murder concerns an illegal beer baron who decides to go legitimate at the close of Prohibition while rival gangsters kill each other in his home.

A Slight Case of Murder (1938, Warner Bros., 85m/bw) ☆☆☆½ **Sc:** Earl Baldwin, Joseph Schrank. **D:** Lloyd Bacon. **P:** Sam Bischoff. **Cam:** Sid Hickox. **Cast:** Edward G. Robinson, Jane Bryan, Willard Parker, Ruth Donnelly, Allen Jenkins, John Litel, Edward Brophy, Harold Huber, Bobby Jordan. After playing variations on the mobster archetype that he invented in *Little Caesar*, Robinson mugged the mug this time in an excellent comic turn. His Remy Marco believes that he's headed for the social register.

- *"One of the funniest and most satisfying farces…out of Hollywood in some time. For Mr. Robinson, the show is a major dispensation. After* The Last Gangster, *it was fairly obvious that straight variations on the* Little Caesar *role had been exhausted.* A Slight Case of Murder *gives him a burlesque underworld big-shot to portray and he handles the assignment with comical efficiency. As a Prohibition needled-beer baron who turns square but forgets to stop needling his beer, he realizes a nice blend of ruthlessness and clowning….Little Caesar has died hard but his passing shouldn't grieve Mr. Robinson unduly if he can get more scripts like this one."* (Howard Barnes, New York Herald-Tribune)

Stop, You're Killing Me (1952, Warner Bros., 86m/c) ☆☆½ **Sc:** James O'Hanlon. **D:** Roy Del Ruth. **P:** Louis F. Edelman. **Cam:** Ted D. McCord. **Cast:** Broderick Crawford, Claire Trevor, Virginia Gibson, Sheldon Leonard, Howard St. John, Bill Hayes, Margaret Dumont, Henry Morgan, Joe Vitale, Charles Cantor, Henry Morgan, Don Beddoe, Stephen Chase, Henry Slate, Ned Glass, Jack Pepper. The wry Runyonesque style was completely leeched from this broadly played and exaggerated reworking.

- *"Maybe it isn't exactly murder that the Warners have performed on their own* A Slight Case of Murder *by turning it into* Stop, You're Killing Me. *But it is an elaborate job of mayhem that the brothers have recklessly done on that memorable travesty on tough guys in the new film…Where the orig-*

inal roughhouse...was a beautiful piece of farcical satire done with a mischievous deadpan, this latest traffic with the same play is a mixture of Technicolored musical and broad-beamed burlesque, thrown together with little inspiration and directed by Roy Del Ruth with a pounding hand." (Bosley Crowther, The New York Times)

Morrie Ryskind

Born: October 20, 1895, Brooklyn, NY. **Died:** 1985.
Pulitzer Prize-winning play: *Of Thee I Sing* (1932) with George S. Kaufman and Ira Gershwin

Ryskind's screenwriting ranged from premium Marx Brothers shenanigans, including *A Night at the Opera* (1935), to the sublime dialogue of *My Man Godfrey* (1936) to the gamut of emotions expressed in *Penny Serenade* (1941). His association with George S. Kaufman included the film adaptation of Kaufman and Edna Ferber's *Stage Door* (1937) and the plays *Strike Up the Band* and *Animal Crackers*. His screenplays include *Palmy Days* (1931) with Eddie Cantor, *Claudia* (1943) with Dorothy McGuire, and *It's in the Bag!* (1945) with Fred Allen.

Animal Crackers (1930, Paramount, 98m/bw, **VHS/DVD**) ☆☆☆☆ **Sc:** Morrie Ryskind. **D:** Victor Herman. **Cam:** George Folsey. **Cast:** Groucho Marx, Chico Marx, Harpo Marx, Zeppo Marx, Margaret Dumont, Lillian Roth, Louis Sorin, Hal Thompson, Margaret Irving, Kathryn Reece, Robert Greig, Edward Metcalf, The Music Masters. The setting is the Rittenhouse manor on Long Island, where the socially-conscious matron, Mrs. Rittenhouse presents two long-awaited events: the unveiling of a painting and the arrival of Capt. Jeffrey T. Spaulding (Groucho) from a tropical African adventure. This second Marx Brothers film was also the second to come from a George S. Kaufman/Ryskind play, and certainly ranks as one of their two or three best.

• *"The Marx Brothers in their pre-Hollywood period...slightly adapted and filmed in Astoria—it looks stagy. But the film is too joyous for cavilling. Arguably the best line: 'Signor Ravelli's first selection will be "Somewhere My Love Lies Sleeping" with a male chorus.'"* (Pauline Kael, 5001 Nights at the Movies)

• *"Their popular brand of comedy pervades the picture. So much, in fact, that there is little footage left for a love plot of any importance. While most of the repartee is nonsense, it gets laughs, and that's what counts."* (Film Daily)

The Cocoanuts (1929, Paramount, 96m/bw, **VHS/DVD**) ☆☆☆½ **Sc:** Morrie Ryskind. **D:** Robert Florey, Joseph Santley. **P:** Walter Wanger.

Cam: George Folsey. **Cast:** Groucho Marx, Chico Marx, Harpo Marx, Zeppo Marx, Margaret Dumont, Mary Eaton, Oscar Shaw, Kay Francis, Cyril Ring, Basil Ruysdael, Sylvan Lee, Gamby-Hale Ballet Girls, Allan K. Foster Girls. The 1925 play featuring the Marx Brothers ran for more than a year on Broadway. Kaufman wrote the original and Ryskind "served a brief cut-and-write apprenticeship" on the out-of-town runs of the play, according to Joe Adamson. Four years later, the Marx Brothers had everything down to a crackpot science in the story of Groucho (Mr. Hammer) owning a 600-room hotel during a land boom in coastal Florida. This was the brothers' first movie.

- *"The Marxes came off handsomely; Groucho's is the first voice I have heard from the screen in swift chatter—not as swift, not as crisp, as his wise-cracking on the stage, but better in these respects than all the other deliveries I have encountered; Chico, who seemed to me to take a giant stride last year, keeps up the pace in this picture; and Harpo is extraordinarily funny and endearing..."* (Gilbert Seldes, The New Republic)

Louisiana Purchase (1941, Paramount, 98m/c, **VHS**) ☆☆½ **Sc:** Jerome Chodorov, Joseph Fields. **D:** Irving Cummings. **P:** Harold Wilson. **Cam:** Harry Hallenberger, Ray Rennahan. **Cast:** Bob Hope, Vera Zorina, Victor Moore, Irene Bordoni, Dona Drake, Raymond Walburn, Maxie Rosenbloom, Frank Albertson, Donald MacBride, Andrew Tombes. The songs were by Irving Berlin. The cinematography was nominated for an Oscar.

- *"...if the picture is more pleasant and less strenuous than most of its type, credit must also be given to the fact that it is a musical comedy with a book, which it follows. There isn't much point and almost no edge to its spoofing of the New Orleans graft ring...It would have been livelier with more point and a lot less of Vera Zorina (a comedy is also something without Vera Zornia in it); but what holds it together is the conception and character of Victor Moore, a Coolidge with likeable qualities and a sense of Humor."* (Otis Ferguson, The New Republic)

Of Thee I Sing (1972, CBS, 90m/c) ☆☆☆½ **Tp:** Arnie Rosen, Don Hinkley, Woody Kling. **D:** Dave Powers. **P:** Arnie Rosen. **Cast:** Carroll O'Connor, Jack Gilford, Cloris Leachman, Michele Lee, Jim Backus, Jesse White, David Doyle, Herb Edelman, Paul Hartman, Garrett Lewis, Shirley Kirkes, Ted Knight. This musical of political satire, which ran for 441 Broadway performances in 1931–32 and won the Pulitzer Prize, was the result of Ryskind's collaboration with the great George S. Kaufman and the musical team of George and Ira Gershwin. In the original cast at the Music Box Theatre were Victor Moore and George Murphy. Of the well-known cast, Jack Gilford stood out as the hapless Vice President Throttlebottom. Otherwise, this production seems tossed together.

- *"The dropoff in quality can hardly be blamed on the ravages of time. With a cadre of production people who generally represented the staff of last year's* The Carol Burnett Show, *the 1972 version of the one-time snappy political satire was a bland, mirthless affair that looked like the output of some amateur community play group staging it at some nearby high school auditorium. With ample viewer bait in Carroll O'Connor and Cloris Leachman, the decision was apparently made to let the good George and Ira Gershwin score carry the proceedings, and after a few scenes suggesting the revered, pithy wit of Kaufman, the laughline content reverted to sitcom level compliance...practically nothing had any political bite in it."* (Variety)

Howard Sackler

Born: December 19, 1929. **Died:** 1982.
Pulitzer Prize-winning play: *The Great White Hope* (1969)
New York Drama Critics Circle Award for Best Play: *The Great White Hope*
Tony Award for Best Play: *The Great White Hope*

Howard Sackler's one outstanding play swept through Broadway in 1969 and resulted in the below film. His two notable associations in films were with Stanley Kubrick and the *Jaws* franchise. Sackler wrote *Fear and Desire* (1953), Kubrick's debut, and worked uncredited on the screenplay for the director's second film, *Killer's Kiss* (1955). For Universal Pictures, Sackler wrote, uncredited, the famous USS Indianapolis monologue performed by Robert Shaw in Steven Spielberg's *Jaws* (1975), then was among the credited trio of writers on *Jaws 2* (1978) and also shared credit on another of the studio's deep-sea epics, *Gray Lady Down* (1978). With novelist Paul Theroux and director Peter Bogdanovich, Sackler also penned the Shanghai-set mood piece about a philosophical pimp, the underrated *Saint Jack* (1979), starring Ben Gazzara.

The Great White Hope (1970, 20th Century-Fox, 103m/c, **VHS**) ☆☆☆½ **Sc:** Howard Sackler. **D:** Martin Ritt. **P:** Lawrence Turman. **Cam:** Burnett Guffey. **Cast:** James Earl Jones, Jane Alexander, Joel Fluellen, Lou Gilbert, Hal Holbrook, Chester Morris, Robert Webber, Moses Gunn. The film was Oscar nominated for Best Actor (Jones) and Actress (Alexander) as the two stars recreated their roles from the 1969 stage production directed by Ed Sherin. The play and film concentrate on a facsimile of turn-of-the-century pugilist Jack Johnson, called Jack Jefferson and played in full-throttle robust style by Jones. The great black boxer faces his downfall because of his love for a white woman. Excellent period flavor helps under Ritt's direction.

- *"How a black prizefighter...is brought down because of white men's fear of the strength of blacks. Martin Ritt's big, noisy production clunks along like a disjointed play; it defeats Jones, and along the way it also inadvertently exposes the clobber-them-with-guilt tactics of the dramatist, Howard Sackler. When it was done onstage, did audiences really accept the beware-the-ides-of-March doom crier and the rag-doll-Ophelia finish of the heroine? In the movie, all this grandiosity makes you squirm."* (Pauline Kael, 5001 Nights at the Movies)

- *"Unfortunately, Sackler's attempt to avoid the curse of cant results in psychological obfuscation and ideological confusion. All the sound and fury of James Earl Jones's performance and all the whimpering and whining of Jane Alexander's, never gets us any closer into the core of their drama together as a doomed couple. Martin Ritt's Philco Playhouse staging of the indoor scenes is so unimaginatively three-wallish that we never feel either privacy or intimacy."* (Andrew Sarris, The Village Voice)

William Saroyan

Born: August 31, 1908, Fresno, CA. **Died:** 1981.
Pulitzer Prize-winning play: *The Time of Your Life* (1939)

William Saroyan's plays were usually marked by a carefree style and faith in the individual spirit abiding bleak circumstances. Only one of his works was adapted for feature films, the Cagney-family version of *The Time of Your Life* (1948). Saroyan won an Academy Award for the original story of *The Human Comedy* (1943), which was autobiographical to the extent that the writer carried telegrams in Fresno just as Mickey Rooney does in a small California town during World War II in the MGM film. Saroyan novelized the screenplay and S. Lee Pogostin later adapted the script for a 1959 *DuPont Show of the Month* presentation starring Michael J. Pollard and Jo Van Fleet. The one-act *Hello Out There* (1942), with Harry Morgan in a lynch-justice piece, was to have been director James Whale's comeback film in 1949. It was never released.

Early television's voracious appetite for material led to several of the playwright's works appearing on the more distinguished dramatic anthology shows. Like many playwrights of the era, Saroyan contributed originals to TV, at least seven in total. For *Omnibus*, he penned *The Christmas Tie* with Helen Hayes and Burgess Meredith in 1952; *Vive* with Burt Lahr and *The Oyster and the Pearl* with Paul Douglas, both in 1953; and *Ah, Sweet Mystery of Mrs. Murphy* with Hugh Griffith and George Grizzard in 1959. Another Saroyan original, *Midsummer Dream*, became the third installment of *Screen Directors' Playhouse* in 1955, with John Brahm directing Keenan Wynn and Kim Hunter.

Saroyan, who was often broke later in life (his Oscar rather infamously turned up in a pawn shop), saw his reputation diminish in the theatre as his loosely structured later plays eroded his prestige with critics until *The Cave Dwellers* (1957). His other more outstanding plays include the often produced long one-act *My Heart's in the Highlands* (1939); *The Beautiful People* (1941); *Get Away, Old Man* (1943), about a screenwriter's run-in with a creepy Hollywood producer; and *Sam the Highest Jumper of Them All* (1960). The writer's stature was upheld by his regard on the prestigious *Omnibus*, which aired *The Boyhood of William Saroyan* in 1955 and *The New Drama as Viewed by William Saroyan* in 1961. The latter show had him discussing avant-garde theatre works by himself, Samuel Beckett, Eugene Ionesco, and Edward Albee. It featured Mike Kellin and Nancy Wickwire in interpretive excerpts, underscoring his 1939 intentions in a love scene in *The Time of Your Life* and then demonstrating how differently it could have been played in 1961. The writer later appeared in the documentaries *Magnificent Armenia: William Saroyan* (1977), a paean to his heritage, and *William Saroyan: The Man, the Writer* (1994).

Making Money and 13 Other Very Short Plays (1970, NET, 60m/c) *NET Playhouse: Theatre in America* ☆☆½ **Tp:** William Saroyan. **P:** Jac Venza. **Cast:** Pat Hingle, Edgar Stehli. Included in this production are *Waiting for the Car* and *The Writers of Great Novels, Plays, Poetry and Philosophy*. National Educational Television presented this rapid-fire assemblage of 13 Saroyan short plays and one by James Saunders, *A Slight Accident*, in an hour.

- *"...such is Mr. Saroyan's ability to go the heart of the characterization that, as representative in the themes of his short plays, he affirmed that a part of the art of writing is not putting everything down on paper. A suggestion of moods in the most sparing of prose allows his audience to be an active collaborator....Oddly, the playlet entitled* Making Money *was the least effective of the 14."* (Jack Gould, The New York Times)

My Heart's in the Highlands told of a poor poet who struggles to maintain his integrity in a materialistic world while living in a shack with his son and mother-in-law, who speaks no English. The initial run of the play was 44 performances in 1939 by the Group Theatre at the Guild Theatre starring Ben Alexander, Sidney Lumet, and Hester Sondergaard.

My Heart's in the Highlands (1956, ABC, 90m/bw) *Omnibus.* ☆☆ **Tp:** William Saroyan. **D:** Charles Dubin. **Cast:** James Daly, Everett Sloan, Dickie Olsen. One third of the show was this clipped adaptation.

- *"...added up to the dullest* Omnibus *outing of a dull season....Longest and least rewarding of the show's components was the performance of the Saroyan play...It's tough enough to swallow the Saroyan pastiche in the the-*

atre, where at least one can be lulled into a happy state of disbelief. But on the home screen the fairy tale fails to register. .. awkward and self-conscious performances....If Omnibus continues with this sort of translation of 'something for everybody,' it will wind up with nothing for nobody." (Variety)

My Heart's in the Highlands was retitled The Man With the Heart in the Highlands in 1949 for a CBS presentation on Actors' Studio starring John McQuade and Butch Cavell. The original title was used for both a 1950 production on CBS's Silver Theater with Howard Da Silva, Byron Foulger, Tommy Pihl, Adelaide DeWalt Reynolds, and Art Smith, and a 1970 opera performance written by Jack Beeson on The NET Festival. See also **Two by Saroyan,** below.

The Time of Your Life centers on a group of eccentrics who converge in a San Francisco saloon. A champagne-drinking philosophical gent and his dim-bulb sidekick chat up the patrons and eventually convince a former prostitute to leave her chippie act and marry the sidekick. The cop who has been trailing her is gunned down by an aging drunk, who's been spinning yarns about his princely deeds in the Old West. The Pulitzer Prize winner was first produced on Broadway in 1939 with Saroyan and Eddie Dowling directing Dowling, Julie Hayden, Gene Kelly, William Bendix, Celeste Holm, and Tom Tully.

The Time of Your Life (1948, UA, 109m/bw, **VHS**) ☆☆☆½ **Sc:** Nathanial Curtis. **D:** H.C. Potter. **Cam:** James Wong Howe. **P:** William Cagney. **Cast:** James Cagney, William Bendix, Wayne Morris, Jeanne Cagney, Broderick Crawford, Ward Bond, James Barton, Gale Page, Paul Draper, Reginald Beane, James Lydon, Tom Powers. This Cagney family affair involved siblings William, Jimmy, and Jeanne converting a labor of love to the screen, preserving the nearly one-set theatricality. It was as faithful and effective a stage-to-screen transference as any in the immediate postwar era. "Saroyan came out of his eccentric funk to shout its praises," claimed Cagney's autobiographical collaborator, Doug Warren, "but it ended up as the only film in Jimmy's long career to lose money"— $500,000—"Jimmy was deeply disappointed, because he felt at the time that this was his most successful attempt at quality movie-making."

• *"The performances—notably those of James Barton, Reginald Beane and James Cagney, are as deft a compromise between stage and screen as you are likely to see. Nevertheless, a good deal which would be as taut and resonant as a drumhead on the stage is relatively dull and slack on the screen. On the other hand, those who have made the picture have given it something very rare. It's obvious that they love the play and their work in it, and their affection and enjoyment are highly contagious. They have done so handsomely by Saroyan that in the long run everything depends on how much of Saroyan you can take....The face on Saroyan's barroom floor has something unas-*

sailably good about the eyes. But the smile is that of a swindling person who is sure his own swindle is for the greater glory of God." (James Agee, Time)

The Time of Your Life (1958, CBS, 90m/bw) *Playhouse 90* ☆☆☆ **Tp:** A.J. Russell. **D:** Tom Donovan. **P:** Gordon Duff. **Cast:** Jackie Gleason, Betsy Palmer, James Barton, Dick York, Dina Merrill, Bobby Van, Jack Klugman, Bert Freed, Terry Carton, Carlos Montalban, Ray McHugh, Billy M. Greene. This version captured attention for Gleason's realistic portrayal at a time when he was considered one of the funniest performers on TV, three years prior to his Academy Award-nominated performance as Minnesota Fats in *The Hustler.*

- *"Playhouse 90 came up with a remarkably faithful reproduction sparked by memorable dramatic and technical contributions...something exceptional. That the show might not have emerged as potent as a nationally marketable video commodity is attributable to the playwright's imaginatively offbeat literary technique...While it may have seemed at first that Jackie Gleason was utterly miscast and uncomfortable as the difficult-to-enact central figure of Joe...he managed in certain scenes and moments to penetrate to the very root of the character...his characterization took on added stature during these moments but much of the time his style was overly self-conscious and forced....The Time of Your Life remains probably Saroyan's finest work, and this revival certainly captured its lofty spirit." (Variety)*

- *"Playhouse 90—now in its third season—has established itself this year as the foremost dramatic program, live or film, on television....A particular delight was 90's boozily poetic production of William Saroyan's The Time of Your Life..." (Frank DeBlois, TV Guide)*

The Time of Your Life (1976, PBS, 120m/c, **VHS**) *Theatre in America.* ☆☆☆ **Tp/Narrator:** William Saroyan. **D:** Jack O'Brien, Kirk Browning. **P:** Lindsay Law, Jac Venza. **Cast:** David Schramm, Kevin Kline, Patti LuPone, Nicolas Surovy, Elaine Hausman, Brooks Baldwin, Benjamin Hendrickson, Robert Bacigalupi, Glynis Bell, Mary Lou Rosato, Norman Snow, James Harper, Gerald Guiterrez. Shot at the Harkness Theatre in New York City, this production featured players from John Houseman's Acting Company.

- *"This is a graceful and charming production of the old play, making no apologies for its sentimentality or its Panglossian philosophy. It's extremely well performed, notably by Nicholas Surovy, a lean, dark young man who reminds you a bit of Bogart, as Joe. David Schramm is a lusty Kit Carson and Patti LuPone a properly ethereal Kitty, the whore with the heart of gold." (Cecil Smith, Los Angeles Times)*

Two by Saroyan aired in 1960 on the public TV mainstay *The Play of the Week* featuring Walter Matthau, who starred here in both the 1950 play *Once Around the Block* and *My Heart's in the Highlands.* Supporting him in the former were Larry Hagman, Orson Bean, and Nina Wilcox, and in the latter were Myron McCormick, Kevin Coughlin, and Eddie Hodges.

Dore Schary

Isidore Schary
Born: August 31, 1905, Newark, NJ. **Died:** 1980.
Tony Award-winning play: *Sunrise at Campobello* (1958)

A journalist, publicist, playwright, and actor in the 1930s, Dore Schary found a niche at MGM as a screenwriter, then a producer. In the 1940s, he went to work with independent David O. Selznick, then moved to RKO, where he clashed with Howard Hughes. He then moved back to MGM, where he was at loggerheads with Louis B. Mayer. He wrote and produced many movies throughout four decades in Hollywood and won an Academy Award for the original story for *Boys Town* (1938), starring Spencer Tracy. His screenplays include *Young and Beautiful* (1934), *Chinatown Squad* (1935), *Silk Hat Kid* (1935), *Mind Your Own Business* (1936), *Young Tom Edison* (1940), and *Lonelyhearts* (1959). Schary's one major contribution to the stage was *Sunrise at Campobello* (1958), which won Tony Awards for Best Play and Best Actor (Ralph Bellamy). For his next and final film following the adaptation of *Sunrise at Campobello*, Schary wrote the screenplay for and directed *Act One* (1963), the pedestrian adaptation of Moss Hart's autobiography starring George Hamilton as Hart and Jason Robards as George S. Kaufman.

Sunrise at Campobello (1960, Warner Bros., 143m/c, **VHS**) ☆☆☆½
Sc/P: Dore Schary. **D:** Vincent J. Donehue. **Cam:** Russell Harlan. **Cast:** Ralph Bellamy, Greer Garson, Hume Cronyn, Jean Hagen, Ann Shoemaker, Alan Bunce, Tim Considine, Zina Bethune, Lyle Talbot, David White, Frank Ferguson, Pat Close, Robin Warga, Walter Sande, Tommy Carty. Schary's lifelong fascination with the life of Franklin Delano Roosevelt culminated in this behind-the-scenes look at FDR's affliction with polio and his efforts to combat his discomfort from 1921 to 1924, when he entered Al Smith's name into contention at the Democratic National Convention. Bellamy won the Tony Award for his 1958 performance opposite Mary Fickett as Eleanor Roosevelt, and repeated it for stage director Vincent J. Donehue in this film. The two leads are superb in this balanced piece of sentiment and courage. Greer Garson captured her final Oscar nomination for her work as Eleanor, perhaps her best performance, and the film also was nominated for Best Art Direction/Set Decoration, Sound, and Costumes.

• *"In the journey from stage to screen...loses none of its poignant and inspi-*

rational qualities, none of its humor and pathos. Dore Schary...can take pride in his grand slam feat. And this satisfaction is to be shared also by Ralph Bellamy, whose brilliant portrayal of Roosevelt, and Vincent J. Donehue, the director, clicked so resoundingly on Broadway." (Variety)

- *"And then, in one startling scene when she attempts to comfort her children by reading to them, she bursts into tears and runs from the room....The raw emotion that Greer displays in this scene...Certainly it is a level of emotion she has never displayed before or after. Slowly, she collects herself in the sequence and, as her strength returns and her back straightens, she informs Howe, 'I won't ever do that again. Not ever.' "* (Michael Troyan, A Rose for Mrs. Miniver: The Life of Greer Garson)

Murray Schisgal

Born: November 25, 1926, Brooklyn, NY.

Murray Schisgal served in the Navy, played jazz, practiced law, and taught in public and private schools before his first plays, *The Typist* and *The Tiger*, were produced in London, then Off Broadway. His outstanding contribution to popular culture was co-writing with Larry Gelbart the screenplay for director Sydney Pollack's gender-bending classic *Tootsie* (1982), in which Dustin Hoffman plays a down-on-his-luck actor who disguises himself as a woman to get a role on a soap opera. Chief among Schisgal's TV originals was *The Love Song of Barney Kempinski* for ABC Stage '67 starring the eclectic combo of Alan Arkin, John Gielgud, Alan King, and Lee Grant in a comedy about a bachelor's last fling through New York City on the eve of his marriage. Schisgal's Off Broadway production of the paired absurdist one-acts, *Fragments* and *The Basement*, featured Gene Hackman. Schisgal's other plays include *The Old Jew*, *Memorial Day*, *Windows*, and *The Chinese*.

Luv (1967, Columbia, 95m/c, **VHS**) ☆☆½ **Sc:** Elliott Baker. **D:** Clive Donner. **P:** Martin Manulis. **Cam:** Ernest Laszlo. **Cast:** Jack Lemmon, Peter Falk, Elaine May, Nina Wayne, Eddie Mayehoff, Paul Hartman, Severn Darden, Harrison Ford. A schlep, believing himself a failure, is about to commit suicide by jumping off the Manhattan Bridge when an old school chum, proclaiming himself a big success, convinces him to come home with him. Mr. Success then tries to palm off his wife on the depressed pal. An outlandishly absurd comedy of its day, which ran for two years on Broadway, this one fizzles into an unimaginative mess on film, despite the trio of stars.

- *"Many of the beguiling qualities are lost in its transference to the screen. Where the legiter was wildly absurd and deliciously outlandish, much of the humor of the picture is forced, proving that a sophisticated stage comedy isn't always ideal for the screen."* (Variety)

- *"There are times when films, like children, will not do what you want them to do, no matter how hard you work at it. Luv, taken from a hit play by Murray Schisgal, was released by Columbia in August 1967 and to this day nobody is sure why."* (Don Windeler, Lemmon, 1975)

The Tiger Makes Out (1967, Columbia, 94m/c) ☆☆☆ **Sc:** Murray Schisgal. **D:** Arthur Hiller. **P:** George Justin. **Cam:** Arthur J. Ornitz. **Cast:** Eli Wallach, Anne Jackson, Bob Dishy, John Harkins, Ruth White, David Burns, Charles Nelson Reilly, Sudie Bond, Bibi Osterwald, Alice Beardsley, Dustin Hoffman, Mariclare Costello, Rae Allen, Remak Ramsey, Elizabeth Wilson, Frances Sternhagen, David Doyle, Edgar Stehli, Kim August, Roland Wood. A schleppy New York postal worker, fed up with his life, decides to kidnap and enslave the first beautiful young girl he can find, but a tough housewife gets in his way. The one-act play debuted as *The Tiger* with Wallach and Jackson originating the starring roles.

- *"...[the] transferring Mr. Schisgal's 30-minute, two-character playlet into a 94-minute, two-star, four-co-star, eight-guest-star film. Pieces of the play are there intact, shards are scattered throughout, and small glittery screen creations have been added. The result? Any number of flawless bits—but gone is the perfection of the original entity....Eli Wallach and Anne Jackson are still perfection...But despite the quality of the actors and the script, the gems are scattered, the design diffuse, the original brilliance sporadic....an attractive and bemusing piece of costume jewelry—but not comparable to the real thing."* (Judith Crist, The Private Eye, the Cowboy and the Very Naked Lady)

The Typists (1971, PBS, 60m/c) *Hollywood Television Theatre* ☆☆☆☆ **Tp:** Murray Schisgal. **D:** Glenn Jordan. **P:** Lewis Freedman. **Cast:** Eli Wallach, Anne Jackson. This new version of the 1963 Broadway play kicked off the third season of the honored PBS series. Sylvia, a veteran at a typing service, is joined by Paul, a new employee. They bicker, reveal their lives, fall in love, then out, all in one day. The performers carry the play.

- *"As an evening of theatre, the Schisgal piece is a bit slight. As less than an hour of television, it works beautifully. With the director, Glenn Jordan, maintaining a remarkably fluid pace, Eli Wallach and Anne Jackson are offering memorable performances—comic, pathetic, touching, all shaded with letter-perfect emotional shifts. Drama, it seems, good drama has returned to television. For that alone, Hollywood Television Theatre and PBS and public television can take several curtain calls."* (John J. O'Connor, The New York Times)

Ntozke Shange

Born: October 18, 1948, Trenton, NJ.

For Colored Girls Who Have Considered Suicide/When the Rainbow Is Enuf (1982, PBS, 78m/c, **VHS/DVD**) *American Playhouse* ☆☆☆☆ **Tp:** Ntozke Shange. **D:** Oz Scott. **P:** Lindsay Law, Jac Venza. **Cast:** Alfre Woodard, Lynn Whitfield, Ntozke Shange, Patti LaBelle, Sarita Allen, Carol Maillard, Crystal Lilly, Trazana Beverley, Laurie Carlos. This "choreopoem" illuminates the epic story of African-American women in America in song, poetry, and dance. The seven women in the cast tell individual stories of tragedy, resourcefulness, and redemption. The play opened in 1976 at the New York Shakespeare Festival produced by Joseph Papp and ran for 742 performances with Shange, Beverley, and Carlos in the original cast.

- *"The words in this dramatized anthology of poems are as exceptional as diamonds — as finely cut, brilliant, and isolating. They constitute some of the richest black-American ever written, with their reticulating syntax, their private alphabet, and fierce black-and-female truths. So when the show airs...it is these words, that fearsome lexicon carved out of the dead a screaming air, that will stand out, no matter how badly served it is by a medium that tends to reduce all imagery to the commonplace."* (Sylvie Blake, Los Angeles Times)

Sam Shepard

Samuel Shepard Rogers
Born: November 5, 1943, Fort Sheridan, IL.
Pulitzer Prize-winning play: *Buried Child* (1979)

A mainstay of the independent and Off Broadway worlds of the 1960s and 1970s, Sam Shepard became a theatrical icon by exploring themes unusual to the New York-centric world of drama. "Sam Shepard is quinessentially American," wrote Harold Clurman in *The Nation*. "...Shepard's plays have a country or grass-roots twang. They are very close to the poorer folk who live on the land outside the big cities. He is a man of the 'road,' that barely charted but widespread territory which we pass through on trains or cars between the main stops. To define him a little more narrowly, one may say that his plays are related to largely unwritten or more or less buried permanent American 'myths,' a kind of itinerant, hobo, open field mystique." Shepard is also a cowboy of the language, and very much interested in the heritage and violence connected to it.

Oblique and edgy, his plays usually aren't as accessible as his Pulitzer

Prize winner, *Buried Child*, which views a family through the eyes of an outsider, a young woman. Shepard directed several of his own plays for the stage, including *Geography of a Horse Dreamer* (1974), *Fool for Love* (1983), *A Lie of the Mind* (1985), and *Simpatico* (1994). Other plays include *Chicago, Icarus's Mother* and *Red Cross* (both 1966), *Operation Sidewinder* (1970), *Mad Dog Blues* (1971), *The Tooth of the Crime* (1972), *Angel City* (1976), *Suicide in B-Flat* (1976), and *States of Shock* (1991). He has won 10 Obie Awards, most of them for Best Play.

Although he played significant roles in such films as *Days of Heaven* (1978), *Resurrection* (1980), and *Raggedy Man* (1981), Shepard's acting increased after his Academy Award nomination as aviation speedster Chuck Yeager in *The Right Stuff* (1983). His films as an actor, to which he usually brings a reedy-voiced understatement, include his former wife Jessica Lange's pictures *Frances* (1982), *Country* (1984), and *Crimes of the Heart* (1986), as well as *Steel Magnolias* (1989), *Thunderheart* (1992), and *The Pelican Brief* (1993). He directed two odd westerns that he wrote for the screen, the contemporary *Far North* (1988), with Lange in her native Minnesota, and *Silent Tongue* (1992) with Richard Harris connected to a Wild West show in 19th century New Mexico. Shepard also co-wrote the films *Me and My Brother* (1967) with Robert Frank, *Zabriskie Point* (1970) for director Michaelangelo Antonioni with several others and *Renaldo and Clara* (1977) with Bob Dylan.

Curse of the Starving Class (1995, Showtime, 102m/c, **VHS**) ☆☆½
Tp: Bruce Beresford. **D:** G. Michael McClary. **P:** William S. Gilmore, Harel Goldstein. **Cam:** Dick Quinlan. **Cast:** James Woods, Kathy Bates, Henry Thomas, Randy Quaid, Louis Gossett Jr., Kristin Fiorella. This 1977 play is the first in a western family trilogy that includes *Buried Child* and *True West*. Shepard presents a farm family slowly destructing from a boozy patriarch, his wife who wants to sell the place, and their directionless teens. This piece, which was made as a theatrical film, then sold to cable TV, is the only American film that Beresford has written but not directed. Longtime Shepard associate Robert Woodruff directed the original play in 1978 at the New York Shakespeare Festival with a cast including James Gammon, Olympia Dukakis, Pamela Reed, Ebbe Roe Smith, and Raymond J. Barry.

- *"Onstage these characters mirror a family of ghosts that might be sprouts off a Eugene O'Neill family tree. But as a movie, the thematic resonance is unfelt, including the great sin of selling off family land to commercial poachers. The result turns grueling. Metaphorically, Shepard was writing about a "starving class" hungry for moral and physical sustenance. Here, they're just snarly, messy farmers. G. Michael McClary's direction misses Shepard's rhythms...Of course, anyone attempting to make a movie out of a Shepard play has to be a touch daft to begin with."* (Ray Loynd, Los Angeles Times)

Fool for Love (1985, Cannon Group, 108m/c, **VHS**) ☆☆ **Sc:** Sam Shepard. **D:** Robert Altman. **P:** Menahem Golan, Yorum Globus. **Cam:** Pierre Mignot. **Cast:** Sam Shepard, Kim Basinger, Randy Quaid, Harry Dean Stanton, Martha Crawford, Louise Egolf, Sura Cox. Shepard adapted and starred in this collaboration with Altman during the director's mid-1980s period of turning theatre pieces into films (*Streamers; Come Back to the 5 and Dime, Jimmy Dean, Jimmy Dean; Secret Honor*). Shepard's Eddie drives 2,000 miles to find his old flame (Basinger) holed up in a delapidated hotel bar, waiting on a date. Stanton, an old man lurking in the background, finally admits that he's father to them both. An extremely slow moving and claustrophobic adaptation. The original 1983 play debuted at the Magic Theatre in San Francisco starring Ed Harris and Kathy Baker.

- "Fool for Love *was as bad as Altman has been—how could Sam Shepard act in the film without realizing that Altman was unsuited to the play's intense, enclosed and mounting explosiveness? (And Shepard had directed* Fool for Love *onstage) Thereafter, Altman's films found little or no release.*" (David Thomson, A Biographical Dictionary of Film)

- "*...a Sam Shepard tour de force....Pierre Mignot's surreal cinematography gives certain scenes a dreamlike, almost poetic quality, while Altman draws top-notch performances from all four main players...Shepard is particularly strong...*" (Richard Skorman, Off-Hollywood Movies: A Film Lover's Guide)

Simpatico (1999, Fine Line, 106m/c, **VHS/DVD**) ☆☆☆ **Sc:** Matthew Warchus, David Nicholls. **D:** Matthew Warchus. **P:** Dan Lupovitz, Timm Oberwelland, Jean-Francois Fonlupt. **Cam:** John Toll. **Cast:** Nick Nolte, Jeff Bridges, Sharon Stone, Albert Finney, Catherine Keener, Shawn Hatosy, Liam Waite, Kimberly Williams. A group of middle-aged friends who pulled a horse racing scam years ago are drawn back into the same world of deceit. The stars give the piece some luster, but even these actors can't enliven the limp noir-ish atmosphere.

- "*While this melodrama of dark secrets and betrayals is sometimes entertaining, it is ultimately a mediocre attempt to bring to the screen a Sam Shepard play that probably was not suited to film in the first place....The main problem...The play's themes of guilt, revenge and the burdens of the past are not handled in a fresh way, and this adaptation cannot rise above the original material. Bridges, Nolte, Stone and Finney are all effective...but the characters themselves do not give the actors much to work with.*" (Peter N. Chumo II, Magill's Cinema Annual 2000)

True West centers on Austin, a screenwriter living outside of Los Angeles whose surly, beer-guzzling brother, Lee, shows up to argue about their father, who's living in a desert hovel. Meanwhile, a Hollywood producer arrives and is more interested in Lee's cliched ideas about a cowboy movie than the script that Austin is preparing for him. The brothers argue and battle in an odd-humored exercise in familial relations, with Lee seemingly taking on his brother's identity by morphing into the boozy, brooding sibling. The play was first performed Off Broadway in 1982 and starred John Malkovich and Gary Sinise

True West (1984, PBS, 110m/c) *American Playhouse* ☆☆☆ **Tp:** Sam Shepard. **D:** Allan Goldstein. **P:** Howard K. Grossman, John H. Williams. **Cast:** John Malkovich, Gary Sinise, Sam Schacht, Margaret Thomson. As much as any production, this fairly static, manifestly two-character banter captures the essence of Sam Shepard's universe.

- *"This is…the almost hermetically sealed world of Sam Shepard. He is a master of menace, spiked with off the wall humor. As Austin and Lee peck away at each other, sometimes actually reverting to physical violence, they command our attention through the sheer intensity of their relationship. At one point, Mr. Shepard hints that they may really be different parts of the same person. In fact, the playwright seems to be talking about himself, with Austin representing his public and accepted persona while Lee reflects his renegade urges. The problem, though, is that the play doesn't go much further than this rather superficial level."* (John J. O'Connor, The New York Times)

True West (2002, Showtime, 107m/c) ☆☆☆½ **D:** Bruce Willis, Gary Halvoson **Tp:** Sam Shepard. **P:** Marc Bauman, Robert Dalrymple, Ayesha Shroff, Mark Zakarin. **Cast:** Bruce Willis, Chad Smith, Andrew Al Burger, Danielle Kennedy, Katrina Kaif, Madhu Sapre, Rodhit Bal, Wendell Rodricks. Willis returned to one of his early stage successes.

- *"…travesty…All the acting is pitched to carry in a theatre. It starts loud and too soon escalates to unremitting yelps and howls…punishingly stagy on TV…Willis acts up such a storm of paranoid bullying, slack-jawed drunkenness and athletic pratfalls that he turns Shepherd's play into something more like 'true Willis,' if only his performance had the ring of truth."* (Robert Horwitt, San Francisco Chronicle)

Martin Sherman

Born: 1939, Philadelphia, PA.

Martin Sherman's first produced play was *A Solitary Thing* in 1963 in Oakland, California. The Actors Studio produced his first New York play, *Fat Tuesday* (1966). Sherman's other plays include *Next Year in Jerusalem* (1968), *Things Went Badly in Wesphalia* (1970), *Passing By*

(1974), *Soaps* (1975), *Messiah* (1982), *When She Danced* (1988), and *Some Sunny Day* (1996). Sherman's biggest success was *Bent*, starring Richard Gere, David Dukes, James Remar, and David Marshall Grant; it was nominated for the Tony Award for Best Play of 1980. Sherman's TV writing includes *Clothes in the Wardrobe* (1992) with Jeanne Moreau, the remake adaptation of Tennessee Williams's novella *The Roman Spring of Mrs. Stone* (2002) with Helen Mirren, and *Callas Forever* (2002) with Jeremy Irons and Fanny Ardant as Maria Callas.

Bent (1997, MGM, 108m/c, **VHS**) ☆☆☆½ **Sc:** Martin Sherman. **D:** Sean Mathias. **P:** Dixie Linder, Michael Solinger. **Cam:** Yorgos Arvanitis. **Cast:** Clive Owen, Lothaire Bluteau, Ian McKellan, Mick Jagger, Jude Law, Nikolaj Coster-Waldau, Brian Webber, Gresby Nash, Suzanne Bertish, David Meyer, Richard Laing, Rupert Graves, Stefan Marling, Cripian Belfrage, Johanna Kirby, Rachel Weisz, Sadie Frost.

• *"Directed with unfailing aplomb by Sean Mathias, Bent is...all but unbearable in its bleakness. Thankfully, it has a saving humor...inspires actors to create towering portrayals...The film moves well, heightened by Phillip Glass's pulsating score..."* (Kevin Thomas, The Los Angeles Times)

Robert E. Sherwood

Robert Emmet Sherwood
Born: 1896, New Rochelle, NY. **Died:** 1955.
Pulitzer Prize-winning plays: *Idiot's Delight* (1936), *Abe Lincoln in Illinois* (1939), *There Shall Be No Night* (1941)

Robert E. Sherwood studied at Harvard and was active in the *Harvard Lampoon*, which his father helped found. He wrote for *Vanity Fair*, *Life*, and *Scribner's*, and became one of the first notable film critics. His first play, *The Road to Rome* (1927), was a success. He had a few less magnetic draws— *The Love Nest* (1927) and the moderately successful *The Queen's Husband* (1928)—before hitting his stride with *Waterloo Bridge* (1930). He then turned out a string of plays that were both popular and critical favorites, winning three Pulitzer Prizes—second-most of all time among playwrights, behind Eugene O'Neill. He was as at home with originals as he was with adaptations, such as his translation from the French, *Tovarich* (1936).

TV originals written by Sherwood include *The Backbone of America*, an hourlong NBC Special satire about an advertising executive searching for "the typical American family" with Yvonne De Carlo and Thomas Mitchell, and two installments of *Robert Montgomery Presents*: *Diary*, the 1954 season debut with Janice Rule and John Cassavetes, and *The Trial of Pontius Pilate* in 1957 with Max Adrian. Sherwood's life up to 1939 is described in critic John Mason Brown's *The Worlds of Robert E. Sherwood* (1965).

Abe Lincoln in Illinois dramatized the future president's campaign for the U.S. Senate and his relationship with the former Mary Todd, along with his famous debates with Stephen Douglas—notable events leading up to his 1861 departure for Washington, DC, to the land's highest office. Raymond Massey and Muriel Kirkland starred as Abe and Mary in the 1938 Broadway production directed by Elmer Rice. In support were Kevin McCarthy and John Payne.

Abe Lincoln in Illinois (1940, RKO, 110m/bw, **VHS**) ☆☆☆½ **Sc:** Robert E. Sherwood, Grover Jones. **D:** John Cromwell. **P:** Max Gordon. **Cam:** James Wong Howe. **Cast:** Raymond Massey, Ruth Gordon, Gene Lockhart, Mary Howard, Dorothy Tree, Harvey Stephens, Minor Watson, Alan Baxter, Howard da Silva, Aldrich Bowker, Louis Jean Heydt, Clem Bevans, Elisabeth Risdon, Harlan Briggs, Charles Middleton, Andy Clyde, Herbert Rudley, Leona Roberts, Florence Roberts, Trevor Bardette, Alec Craig, Peggy Ann Garner, Roger Imhof. The year after John Ford directed Henry Fonda in the popular *Young Mr. Lincoln* (1939), this film of Sherwood's play covered the same history with less cinematic success or popular shelf life on TV or in revival houses. Massey's most memorable and famous moments, both on the stage and in films, were through this play. The film was nominated for Oscars for Best Actor (Massey) and Cinematography.

- *"Massey...grows in stature before our eyes; Wong Howe's lighting and camera placement complete the illusion by strtengthening the gaunt, hungry ambition that has replaced the gawky laziness—particularly in the final sequence with Lincoln standing pensively at the rear of a train taking him east after a moving farewell speech in the gathering dusk..."* (Kingsley Canham, The Hollywood Professionals, Volume 5: King Vidor, John Cromwell, Mervyn LeRoy)

- *"Mainly the production lacks the sense of reality that made John Ford's* Young Mr. Lincoln *so vivid and seeming-true....Ruth Gordon studied her part as Mary Todd some, and I don't imagine intended to be funny...the my-land spinsters parts and haw-hawing yokels, arrive at something—not hamming, which implies some sort of conscious seasoning—suggesting a cross between an animated cartoon and a tray of French pastry....John Cromwell directed from a well-devised if talky script, but he didn't seem to feel it, or to believe it ever really occurred....If you want attitudes, a five-gallon hat, famous incidents, and One Nation Indivisible, they're all here. As a picture, and as a whole, it just doesn't stick."* (Otis Ferguson, The New Republic)

Abe Lincoln in Illinois (1945, NBC, 120m/bw) ☆☆½ **Tp:** Robert E. Sherwood. **D/P:** Edward Sobol. **Cast:** Stephen Courtleigh, Mary Michaels, Morton Stevens, Wendell Phillips, Grandon Rhodes, Ralph

Chambers Vinton Hayworth, Mary Collins, Viola Frane, Harry Bellaver, Lucille Fenton, Earl MacDonald, Kay Renard, Dorothy Emery. The filming of this Broadway revival was another of director/producer Sobol's efforts to perfect TV production in an experimental broadcast.

- *"After the slowdown imposed by the war, NBC's efforts to utilize stage works for its TV programming continued in 1945 with the unusual scheduling of Robert Sherwood's* Abe Lincoln in Illinois, *presented in separate act-by-act installments over the course of a month."* (Brian G. Rose, Television and the Performing Arts)

Abe Lincoln in Illinois (1964, NBC, 90m/c) *The Hallmark Hall of Fame* ☆☆☆½ **Tp:** Robert Hartung. **D/P:** George Schaefer. **Cast:** Jason Robards Jr., Kate Reid, James Broderick, Burt Brinckerhoff, Douglas Watson, Mildred Trares, Hiram Sherman, Roy Poole, Staats Cotsworth, William Hansen, Nan McFarland, Jack Bittner, Tom Slater, Harry Ellerbe. Robards, in a cerebral and tortuous performance, put more of a modern angst into his portrayal than the classical Massey had done.

- *"Jason Robards portrayed a young Lincoln and gave a complex, tortured performance. I don't know whether it's accurate, but Sherwood contends that Lincoln was a miserable young man who didn't want anything to do with politics, didn't want anything to do with the world, was on the verge of suicide, pushed around by the people who believed in him, and driven by his ambitious wife into the life he finally lived. True or not, it made for great drama and I was pleased with our production."* (George Schaefer, From Live to Tape to Film: 60 Years of Inconspicuous Directing)

- *"This is not merely a historical document, but a study of two people, so I focused attention on them while hopefully preserving the play's structure."* (Robert Hartung to Paul Gardner, The New York Times)

Abe Lincoln in Illinois aired in 1950 on ABC's *Pulitzer Prize Playhouse* with Frank Telford directing Raymond Massey in a reprise of his stage triumph opposite Betty Field. Massey returned to his signature role two more times for the cameras, in 1951 for CBS's *Lux Video Theatre* opposite his stage Mary Todd, Muriel Kirkland, and again in a cameo in the star-studded *How the West Was Won* (1962).

Idiot's Delight (1939, MGM, 105m/bw, **VHS**) ☆☆½ **Sc:** Robert E. Sherwood. **D:** Clarence Brown. **P:** Hunt Stromberg. **Cam:** William Daniels. **Cast:** Clark Gable, Norma Shearer, Edward Arnold, Burgess Meredith, Charles Coburn, Joseph Schildkraut, Laura Hope Crewes, Skeets Gallagher, Pat Paterson, Fritz Feld, Virginia Grey, Joan Marsh, Bernadene Hayes. Sherwood's 1936 Broadway play starred Alfred Lunt and Lynne Fontanne among the philosophizing guests at an Alpine winter sports lodge on the eve of World War II. It won the playwright his first Pulitzer Prize.

- *"Robert Sherwood's high reputation as a dramatist was always a little mystifying and never more so than when his windy intellectuality was recorded on film. This allegorical comedy from MGM has Clark Gable as a hoofer and Norma Shearer as a fake Russian countess....there's got to be an antiwar message in it somewhere. Gable isn't bad...but oh, that Shearer. Director Clarence Brown...struggles hopelessly trying to give this stagy material some style and impudence. Sherwood did the adaptation himself, providing early scenes to establish that the hoofer and the 'countess' had had an affair years before (when they were both in vaudeville) and a new, upbeat ending."* (Pauline Kael, 5001 Nights at the Movies)

Jupiter's Darling (1955, MGM, 96m/c, **VHS**) ☆☆½ **Sc:** Dorothy Kingsley. **D:** George Sidney. **P:** George Wells. **Cam:** Charles Rosher, Paul Vogel. **Cast:** Esther Williams, Howard Keel, Marge Champion, Gower Champion, George Sanders, William Demarest, Richard Haydn, Norma Varden, Douglass Dumbrille, Michael Ansara, Henry Corden, Martha Wentworth, Morris Ankrum. Sherwood's 1927 play, *The Road to Rome*, which lampooned Hannibal's march on the city and simultaneously was a peace play, was retooled for this fairly snappy Esther Williams vehicle. It's a significant commentary on the machinations of Hollywood that a Sherwood play could end up as material for the movies' number one mermaid. The film was a flop and helped to end MGM's faith in its line of 1950s big-scale musicals. The songs include "Have a Dream," "I Never Trust a Woman," and "Don't Let This Night Get Away."

- *"Not surprisingly, when the film opened to a disappointing box office, I took the rap. When things go wrong in Hollywood, finger-pointing becomes a blood sport, but this time I was not alone in being gored. While I was saddled with the blame for* Jupiter's Darling, *everyone was condemning Lana Turner for the fact that* The Prodigal, *her costume epic, was a turkey. There was badly concealed glee in the industry over the failure of both films. Everybody was a little too eager to show me the door, and Lana wasn't treated any better. It didn't matter how much money our other films had made for the studio; the disappointing grosses from these movies somehow 'proved' that the fans had abandoned us. The trades ran pieces saying we had come to the end of the line....soon* Time *magazine reported that Lana and I were Hollywood has-beens."* (Esther Williams with Digby Diehl, The Million Dollar Mermaid: An Autobiography)

Miss Liberty aired in 1951 on *Musical Comedy Time*. The 1949 Broadway musical by Sherwood and Moss Hart, featuring lyrics by Irving Berlin, was condensed for this television production.

The Petrified Forest opened on Broadway in 1935 and ran for 181 performances with Arthur Hopkins directing Leslie Howard, Peggy Conklin, Humphrey Bogart, and Blanche Sweet. Bogart's Duke Mantee was one of the stage, screen, and TV's classical gangster interpretations — the boss of several fugitives who hole up at an Arizona roadside cafe holding everyone hostage.

The Petrified Forest (1936, Warner Bros., 83m/bw, **VHS**) ☆☆☆☆ **Sc:** Charles Kenyon, Delmer Daves. **D:** Archie L. Mayo. **P:** Henry Blanke. **Cam:** Sol Polito. **Cast:** Leslie Howard, Bette Davis, Humphrey Bogart, Genevieve Tobin, Dick Foran, Joseph Swayer, Porter Hall, Charley Grapewin, Paul Harvey, Eddie Acuff, Adrian Morris, Nina Campana, Slim Thompson, Constance Bergen, John Alexander. This legendary film gave Bogart his first big break, establishing him as an actor of force and authority, and afforded Davis another high-profile starring role. Using his star clout to help a fellow stage actor, Howard followed through on a promise, making sure that Bogie was hired for the film.

- *"There is a splendid character gallery in Warners's* The Petrified Forest *and it comes to life under the canny but respectful direction that Archie Mayo has given to Mr. Sherwood's play, but it is animate and vital, nevertheless, under the goad of thoughtful writing and the whiplash of melodrama that its author cracked over the back of a conversation piece." (Frank S. Nugent,* The New York Times*)*

- *"[Bogart] plays brilliantly against the gloomy but still vivid Howard, who insisted on having Bogart to enhance his own performance in the film....Bogart's voice, face, body and character all come together to create an unforgettable impression. His startling performance signaled the birth of a major star and kept him in variants of this gangster role till 1942—and beyond." (Jeffrey Meyers,* Bogart: A Life in Hollywood*)*

Escape in the Desert (1945, Warner Bros., 81m/bw) ☆☆ **Sc:** Thomas Job. **D:** Edward A. Blatt. **P:** Alex Gottlieb. **Cam:** Robert Burks. **Cast:** Philip Dorn, Jean Sullivan, Helmut Dantine, Irene Manning, Alan Hale, Samuel S. Hinds, Bill Kennedy, Rudolph Anders, Hans Schumm, Blayney Lewis, Kurt Kreuger. The Warners B-movie machine recycled the play during the World War II years by changing the Duke Mantee gang into German subversives holding captives in the desert.

- *"First thing you know Warners are going to use this same old story so often we'll all be petrified! If we see this picture again, we'll scream! We're warning you, Warners!" (Photoplay)*

The Petrified Forest (1952, ABC, 60m/bw) *Celanese Theatre* ☆☆½ **Tp:** Norman Lessing. **D/P:** Alex Segal. **Cast:** David Niven, Kim Hunter, Lloyd Gough, Dan Matthews, Joe Sweeney, Beverly Roberts, Maurice Burke.

- *"...with top-drawer impact due almost as much to the work of a standout* cast as to the inherent drama in the play itself....[Niven] never registered solidly as the lost idealist, Alan Squire." (Variety)

The Petrified Forest (1955) Producers' Showcase ☆☆☆☆ **Tp:** Tad Mosel. **D:** Delbert Mann. **P:** Fred Coe. **Cast:** Henry Fonda, Lauren Bacall, Humphrey Bogart, Jack Warden, Richard Jaeckel, Jack Klugman, Natalie Schaefer, Joseph Sweeney, Richard Gaines, Paul Hartman, Morris Buchanan, Dick Elliott. After creating Duke Mantee on the stage and screen, Bogart played the role here on TV in one of the prestige shows of its year with a terrific supporting cast.

- "...another hit for Producer's Showcase....successfully caught most of the poignancy and the melodrama of the original....The Cast was both box office and extremely good....direction was uncommonly good..." (Jack Gould, The New York Times)

- "...Flawless in nearly every department....90 minutes of high-voltage realism." (Variety)

The Petrified Forest aired in 1950 on NBC's Robert Montgomery Presents with Norman Felton, Robert Montgomery, Joan Lorring, Herbert Rudley, Ralph Riggs, Glenn Denning, Kitty Kelly, Morton L. Stevens, and Slim Thompson.

The Royal Bed (1931, RKO, 75m/bw, **VHS**) ☆☆☆ **Sc:** J. Walter Ruben. **D:** Lowell Sherman. **P:** William LeBaron. **Cam:** Leo Tover. **Cast:** Lowell Sherman, Mary Astor, Anthony Bushell, Hugh Trevor, Nance O'Neil, Robert Warwick, Gilbert Emery, Alan Roscoe, J. Carroll Naish, Frederick Burt, Nancy Lee Lane, Desmon Roberts, Mischa Auer. Sherwood's 1928 play, The Queen's Husband, starred Roland Young. It concerns a timid king who assumes power during the queen's absence and doesn't, at first, know how to use it. He then comes around to a series of fair-minded decisions when his daughter announces that she will marry a commoner. Sherman, who was in the business of starring and directing in the first years of sound films, put some early zest into this passable interpretation. Astor played his daughter.

- "Lowell Sherman injected some refinement into The Royal Bed...a suggestively titled burlesque that was neither lusty nor particularly humorous....cast Sherman...as the lethargic and henpecked king of a mythical island in the North Sea. The plot begins to simmer after his termagant queen (Nance O'Neil) leaves on a trip to America." (Richard B. Jewell, Vernon Harbin, The RKO Story)

The Queen's Husband was produced twice in 60-minute versions for early TV shows, in 1950 on Kraft Television Theatre with Mercer McLeod, Katherine Meskill and Richard Purdy, and in 1951 on The Pulitzer Prize Playhouse with Roland Young as the king.

Reunion in Vienna is Sherwood's comedic contemplation on the Hapsburgs, in which Prince Maximilian Rudolph rekindles his love for his
former mistress, Elena. Alfred Lunt and Lynn Fontanne starred in the
1931 Broadway production, directed by Worthington Miner and co-starring Henry Travers, Eduardo Ciannelli, and Lloyd Nolan.

Reunion in Vienna (1933, MGM, 100m/bw) ☆☆☆½ **Sc:** Ernest Vajda,
Claudine West. **D:** Sidney Franklin. **Cam:** George Folsey. **Cast:** John
Barrymore, Diana Wynyard, Frank Morgan, May Robson, Eduardo
Ciannelli, Una Merkel, Henry Travers, Nella Walker, Herbert Evans,
Bodil Rosing, Morris Nussbaum, Bela Loblov, Ferdinand Gottschalk.
This was one of Barrymore's finer screen performances.

- *"As sparkling a bit of Viennese charm as ever trinkled across a movie
  screen. Adhering strictly to the Robert Sherwood play with lavish sets, this
  bit of exquisite entertainment dealing with the faded glory of the Hapsburgs
  simply must not be missed."* (Photoplay)

Reunion in Vienna (1952, ABC, 60m/bw) *Celanese Theatre* ☆☆½ **Tp:**
Don Ettlinger. **D:** Alex Segal. **Cast:** Melvyn Douglas, Signe Hasso, Paul
McGrath, Ernest Truex, Evelyn Varden.

- *"The show had a certain sparkle and tempo, but it was more akin to a comic
  opera than the subtle and charmful quality of Sherwood's original."* (Variety)

Reunion in Vienna (1955, NBC, 90m/c) *Producers' Showcase* ☆☆☆
Tp: David Shaw. **D:** Vincent J. Donehue. **P:** Fred Coe, Jean Dalrym-
ple. **Cast:** Greer Garson, Brian Aherne, Robert Flemyng, Peter Lorre,
Cathleen Nesbitt, Horace Cooper, Herbert Berghof, George Voskovec,
Nehemiah Persoff, Gene Saks, Lili Darvas, Tamara Daykarhanova,
Frederic Worlock, Boris Marshalov, Edith Meiser, Donald Marye.
Greer Garson's TV debut showcased her talents in one of the mid-
1950s event-styled series.

- *"...antiquated theatre...Greer Garson's television debut is on the triumphant side. Completely at ease, she sparkled and handled herself like a
  veteran TV trouper....there certainly must be more rewarding vehicles
  around to utilize such gifted talents...."* (Variety)

The Rugged Path was produced in 1952 on *Kraft Television Theatre*
with a cast featuring E.G. Marshall, Carmen Mathews, Philip Kenneally, and Dan Morgan.

There Shall Be No Night (1957, NBC, 90m/bw) *The Hallmark Hall of
Fame* ☆☆☆ **Tp:** Morton Wishengrad. **D/P:** George Schaefer. **Cast:**
Katharine Cornell, Charles Boyer, Ray Walston, Theodore Bikel, Phyl-
lis Love, Bradford Dillman, Val Avery, Karel Stepanek, Gerald Hiken,
Sandor Szabo. This topical production concerned a Hungarian family's

upheaval following the Soviet invasion in 1956. Sherwood's original 1941 play was set among Finnish resistance forces during World War II, and starred Alfred Lunt, Lynn Fontanne, Sydney Greenstreet, Montgomery Clift, Phyllis Thaxter, and Ralph Nelson. This show updated the settting to Budapest with, according to Schaefer, few changes.

- *"I had mixed emotions about the change from live to tape....Ocassionally that was a mixed blessing. In There Shall Be No Night, Katharine Cornell, who was traditionally a very nervous first night actress, held a teacup at one point and the rattling noise was deafening. Not until the second act did she settle down and give a flawless performance. I would have loved to have said, 'Stop. Let's have a cup of coffee, relax, then try it again.' In run-throughs she had been wonderful, a glorious actress — gentle, sweet, a perfectionist. She had been protected most of her acting life by her husband, Guthrie McClintic, who had directed [her] every performance since they were married. She put herself in my hands and I felt very responsible. How I wished we had been taping."* (George Schaefer, From Live to Tape to Film: 60 Years of Inconspicuous Directing)

Tovarich (1937, Warner Bros., 98/bw) ☆☆☆ **Sc:** Casey Robinson. **D:** Anatole Litvak. **P:** Robert Lord. **Cam:** Charles Lang. **Cast:** Claudette Colbert, Charles Boyer, Basil Rathbone, Anita Louise, Melville Cooper, Isabel Jeans, Morris Carnovsky, Maurice Murphy, Montagu Love, Gregory Gaye, Fritz Feld. This 1936 play starring John Halliday and Marta Alba was adapted by Sherwood from Jacques Deval's French original. It concerns a royal Russian husband and wife who flee to Paris during the Bolshevik Revolution and become servants for an eccentric family. The movie is well-dressed, agreeably humored, and largely overrated.

- *"It's the sort of vehicle that comes alive in the theatre, because of the opportunities it affords dazzling technicians, but in the movie version, although Charles Boyer has a devilish cuckoo quality and Claudette Colbert is very charming, the whole thing seems rather attenuated. It's pleasant, but there's no energy in it, and the director, Anatole Litvak, who had demonstrated a highly developed visual style when he worked with Boyer only the year before (in Mayerling), seems paralyzed by the stagy material."* (Pauline Kael, 5,001 Nights at the Movies)

Two Kinds of Women (1932, Paramount, 75m/bw) ☆☆ **Sc:** Benjamin Glazer. **D:** William C. De Mille. **Cam:** Karl Struss. **Cast:** Miriam Hopkins, Phillips Holmes, Wynne Gibson, Stuart Erwin, Edwin Maxwell, Claire Dodd, Irving Pichel, Kent Taylor, Adrienne Ames, Vivienne Osborne, Larry Steers, Robert Emmett O'Connor, June Nash, Lindsay McHarris. Sherwood's play This Is New York was a 1930 Arthur Hopkins production on Broadway with Lois Moran.

- *"...at least agreeable entertainment. Without its humor pic would have been lost in frequently dull love story, some lackluster dialogue and glamour of big city sin that's old stuff by now."* (Variety)

Waterloo Bridge was a 1930 play about a London chorus girl turned prostitute who refuses to give herself to a doughboy during World War I so he can preserve his chivalric ideals.

Waterloo Bridge (1931, Universal, 72m/bw) ☆☆½ **Sc:** Tom Reed, Benn W. Levy. **D:** James Whale. **P:** Carl Laemmle Jr. **Cam:** Arthur Edeson. **Cast:** Mae Clarke, Kent Douglass (Douglass Montgomery), Doris Lloyd, Ethel Griffies, Enid Bennett, Frederick Kerr, Bette Davis, Rita Carlisle.

- *"At Universal, Tom Reed was assigned the job of adapting* Waterloo Bridge *for the screen before James Whale was given the job of directing it....It was Reed who first recast the Sherwood play in filmic terms, taking too seriously a New York stringer's report that the play had 'very little action.' Reed's 62-page adaptation...scuttled the stark intimacy of Sherwood's original and rendered it unrecognizable....gave* Waterloo Bridge *the look and sudden scope of a war picture. Moreover, he hardened the character of Myrna, lessening her appeal, and completely elimated the bridge as a setting. In short, Reed's version of* Waterloo Bridge *was the typical clobbering most plays received in Hollywood."* (James Curtis, James Whale: A New World of Gods and Monsters)

Waterloo Bridge (1940, MGM, 109m/bw, **VHS**) ☆☆☆½ **Sc:** S.N. Behrman, Hans Rameau, George Froeschel. **D:** Mervyn Le Roy. **P:** Sidney Franklin. **Cam:** Joseph Ruttenberg. **Cast:** Vivian Leigh, Robert Taylor, Lucile Watson, Virginia Field, Maria Ouspenskaya, C. Aubrey Smith, Steffi Duna.

- *"A great many people are inexplicably hooked on this weeper. [Leigh] becomes the saddest-eyed fallen woman ever. The director, Mervyn LeRoy, uses candlelight and rain more effectively than he does the actors, although Vivian Leigh does manage to give a beautiful performance....(version[s] in 1931...1956...By far the best version is the parody done by Carol Burnett and Harvey Korman on TV.)"* (Pauline Kael, 5001 Nights at the Movies)

Gaby (1956, MGM, 97m/c) ☆☆½ **Sc:** Albert Hackett, Frances Goodrich, Charles Lederer. **D:** Curtis Bernhardt. **P:** Edwin H. Knopf. **Cam:** Robert Planck. **Cast:** Leslie Caron, John Kerr, Cedric Hardwicke, Tiana Elg, Margalo Gillmore.

- *"...less a* Lili *than a repaint job on* Waterloo Bridge*...a bad idea in its own right and rendered ludicrous by attempts to bring it up to date."* (David Shipman, The Great Movie Stars: The International Years)

Neil Simon

Marvin Neil Simon
Born: July 4, 1927, The Bronx, NY.
Pulitzer Prize-winning play: *Biloxi Blues* (1985)

Neil Simon began his career as a comedy writer in the first decade of TV, usually working in tandem with his brother, Danny Simon. Both were regular contributors to *Your Show of Shows* starring Sid Caesar—Neil from 1950 through 1954. Neil also wrote for *The Admiral Broadway Review* in 1949, *The Tallulah Bankhead Show* from 1951 through 1952, *You'll Never Get Rich* starring Phil Silvers from 1955 through 1959 and *The Garry Moore Show* from 1959 through 1960, among others. Often forgotten is his work, usually in collaboration, for a series of specials in the early and mid-1950s made under the umbrella title of *Max Liebman Presents*.

Among the plays Simon adapted for TV, often with William Friedberg, include *The Desert Song, Dearest Enemy, Best Foot Forward, The Great Waltz, The Merry Widow,* and *Naughty Marietta*. Among Simon's late-career TV efforts was a *Bell Telephone Special* called *The Trouble With People*, a 1972 all-star series of sketches with George C. Scott, Alan Arkin, and Gene Wilder.

Simon's original screenplays include those for *After the Fox* (1966) with Peter Sellers; *The Out-of-Towners* (1970) with Jack Lemmon and Sandy Dennis; *The Heartbreak Kid* (1972) with Cybill Shepherd; the all-star spoofs *Murder by Death* (1976) and *The Cheap Detective* (1978); *The Goodbye Girl* (1977) with Richard Dreyfuss in his Oscar-winning role; *Seems Like Old Times* (1980) with Goldie Hawn; *Max Dugan Returns* (1983) with Jason Robards; *The Slugger's Wife* (1985) with Rebecca DeMornay; *The Marrying Man* (1991) with Kim Basinger and Alec Baldwin; and the remake of *The Out-of-Towners* (1999) with Steve Martin and Goldie Hawn.

A 1972 hourlong NBC special, *The Trouble With People* showcased five short Simon works: "The Greasy Diner" with James Coco, "The Man Who Got a Ticket" with George C. Scott, "The Night Visitor" with Renee Taylor, "The Office Sharers" with Gene Wilder, and "Double Trouble" with Alan Arkin and Valerie Harper. Simon also co-authored *Happy Endings* (1975) and created more adventures for Oscar and Felix with *The Odd Couple: Together Again* (1993) and *Neil Simon's The Odd Couple II* (1998). *Goodbye Doesn't Mean Forever* was a 1982 NBC pilot based on the screenplay of *The Goodbye Girl. The New Odd Couple*, also in 1982, was an African-American take on the classic characters with a cast headed by Demond Wilson and Ron Glass.

Most Simon plays have been converted to films or TV. Those that have yet to be filmed are *Tanamint Revue* (1952), *Catch a Star!* (1955, written with his brother, Danny), *Adventures of Marco Polo: A Musical Fantasy,*

Heidi (1959, a musical of the Johanna Spyri classic), *Little Me* (1962), *Promises, Promises* (1969, the musical based on I.A.L. Diamond and Billy Wilder's *The Apartment*), *The Gingerbread Lady* (1971), *Seesaw* (1973, musical based on William Gibson's *Two for the Seesaw*), *God's Favorite* (1975), *They're Playing Our Song* (1980), *Fools* (1982), and *Rumors* (1988).

Simon often provokes critical ire, but his popular success across all media is unparalleled by any American playwright.

Barefoot in the Park concerns newlyweds in New York City renting a top-floor apartment, who decide to play cupid with the wife's mother and an eccentric neighbor. The celebrated original Broadway cast paired Robert Redford and Jane Fonda and included Herb Edelman and Mildred Natwick under Mike Nichols's direction.

Barefoot in the Park (1967, Paramount, 109m/c, **VHS/DVD**) ☆☆☆ **Sc:** Neil Simon. **D:** Gene Saks. **P:** Hal B. Wallis. **Cam:** Joseph LaShelle. **Cast:** Robert Redford, Jane Fonda, Charles Boyer, Mildred Natwick, Herb Edelman, Mabel Albertson, Fritz Feld, Ted Hartley, James Stone, John Indrisano, Paul E. Burns.

- *"The amount of fun writer Neil Simon can wring out of these rather tired situations is astounding. The cast is a big help. Fonda and Redford work together wonderfully. Mildred Natwick is as appealing as she has ever been, perhaps more so, and Boyer pumps up the gusto."* (Archer Winsten, New York Post)

- *"The hilarious comedy...comes off better on the screen than on the stage. This is the best compliment that can be paid to the film...The improvement in the screen version can be attributed to the camera that movies the action out of a one-set presentation, showing incidents and sights around New York only referred to in the play. Each performance is a gem."* (Kathleen Carroll, New York Daily News)

Barefoot in the Park (1982, HBO, 140m/c) ☆☆½ **Tp:** Neil Simon. **D:** Harvey Medlinsky. **P:** Michael Brandman. **Cast:** Bess Armstrong, Richard Thomas, Barbara Barrie, Hans Conreid, James Cromwell. Thomas and Armstrong fared well as the newlywed Bratters.

Biloxi Blues (1988, Universal, 106m/c, **VHS**) ☆☆☆ **Sc:** Neil Simon. **D:** Mike Nichols. **P:** Ray Stark. **Cam:** Bill Butler. **Cast:** Matthew Broderick, Christopher Walken, Casey Siemaszko, Penelope Ann Miller, Matt Mulhern, Corey Parker, Park Overall, Michael Dolan. Army boot camp is Simon's subject in this third of his autobiographical trilogy about growing up. Broderick, Miller, and Barry Miller starred in the original, which debuted at the Ahmanson Theatre in Los Angeles under Gene Saks's direction. The play and film recollect Simon's 1945 stint in Army boot camp in Mississippi, a time of daily routines, tyrannical sergeants, prejudice, fights, and lousy food. He especially remembers sergeants and a pal who was dishonorably discharged in disgrace. In the end, he allows that he loved it, "because I was young."

- *"The movies made from Neil Simon's plays often tend to be bright and superficial, buzzing with wisecracks like some comedy display window. But* Biloxi Blues *is an exception; it has some marvelous moments....The sentiment may seem sappy, but* Biloxi Blues *lets you share it. Director Mike Nichols—who staged some of Simon's early Broadway hits but none of his movies—helps turn the story into something darker, richer, more underplayed: nostalgia with pinpricks of pain, in a mood of hard-edged reverie. And the actors—especially Matthew Broderick as Eugene Jerome, the Simon surrogate—seize on it."* (Michael Wilmington, Los Angeles Times)

Brighton Beach Memoirs (1986, Universal, 108m/c, **VHS/DVD**) ☆☆½ **Sc:** Neil Simon. **D:** Gene Saks. **P:** David Chasman. **Cam:** John Bailey. **Cast:** Jonathan Silverman, Blythe Danner, Bob Dishy, Judith Ivey, Stacy Glick, Brian Drillinger, Jason Alexander, Lisa Waltz. Matthew Broderick, Joyce Van Patten, Elizabeth Franz, and Zeljko Ivanek starred in the original play directed by Gene Saks.

- *"Buried inside the movie of Neil Simon's semi-autobiographical play* Brighton Beach Memoirs *is a tender, sharp-eyed reminiscence of Brooklyn adolescence: of family squabbles, brotherly bonds, the crises of raging puberty. It's something recognizably Simon's, but more touching than usual. Unfortunately, in the movie it mostly stays buried—or at least lacquered.* Brighton Beach Memoirs *may be one of Simon's best plays, but the film's heart seems to be beating in a plastic wrapper. There's a kind of glace over everything, a sugary show biz coat that dulls your taste buds. Everything is bigger, brighter and broader than it should be—though remnants of that simpler, more honest story often peek through."* (Michael Wilmington, Los Angeles Times)

Broadway Bound (1992, ABC, 90m/c, **VHS**) ☆☆☆ **Tp:** Neil Simon. **D:** Paul Bogart. **Cast:** Jonathan Silverman, Anne Bancroft, Jerry Orbach, Hume Cronyn, Corey Parker, Michele Lee. Gene Saks directed the 1986 stage original at Broadway's Broadhurst Theatre with a cast including Jonathan Silverman, Linda Lavin, John Randolph, Jason Alexander, Phyllis Newman, and Philip Sterling. The other two plays in the trilogy, *Biloxi Blues* and *Brighton Beach Memoirs*, were made as films, and their mediocre box-office performances prompted Simon to make this final part as a TV movie. The play's narration by Eugene Jerome was retained by Simon. Silverman delivers a performance of conviction, but it is Bancroft who steals the film as the mother.

- *"The third and strongest play of Simon's semi-autobiographical trilogy...*Broadway Bound *is not only loyal to its theatrical origins but also acutely felt on the small screen as the intimate, emotional family drama it* *is....the so-called one-liners don't come out of the air but spring naturally from character. It is a deeper, even painful Simon who is portraying the foibles and stresses of his family at a time when he and his brothers were still living at home and beginning their careers as comedy writers....Under Paul Bogart's lucid direction, Bancroft's performance is indelible and memorable as a woman losing her husband's love." (Ray Loynd, Los Angeles Times)*

California Suite (1978, Columbia, 103m/c, **VHS**) ☆☆☆ **Sc:** Neil Simon. **D:** Herbert Ross. **P:** Ray Stark. **Cam:** David M. Walsh. **Cast:** Michael Caine, Jane Fonda, Bill Cosby, Alan Alda, Walter Matthau, Maggie Smith, Richard Pryor, Gloria Gifford, Sheila Frazier. Simon returned to his multi-story idea from *Plaza Suite* (see below) and set it in the Beverly Hills Hotel. The original comedy was staged at the Eugene O'Neill Theatre in 1976 and starred George Grizzard, Tammy Grimes, Jack Weston, and Barbara Barrie, all in multiple roles. Maggie Smith won her second Oscar, in support. Not coincidentally, she played an actress who's nominated for an Academy Award on the eve of the Oscars.

- *"...the 42-year-old Fonda donned a bikini...as the self-assured, independent Hannah Warren, a small but powerful role that compresses a wide range of emotions into a very short time span. Fonda brought an intensity to her encounters with ex-husband Bill (Alan Alda) not evident in the Bill Cosby-Richard Pryor or Walter Matthau-Elaine May segments; only the Michael Caine-Maggie Smith episode seemed on a par with the Fonda-Alda performances." (Les Keyser, Hollywood in the Seventies)*

Chapter Two (1979, Columbia, 127m/c, **VHS**) ☆☆½ **Sc:** Neil Simon. **D:** Robert Moore. **P:** Margaret Booth. **Cam:** David M. Walsh, Richard Kratina. **Cast:** James Caan, Marsha Mason, Valerie Harper, Joseph Bologna, Alan Fudge. The 1977 Broadway original starred Judd Hirsch, Cliff Gorman, Anita Gillette, and Ann Wedgworth. Caan plays a widower writer who falls for Mason.

- *"...when autobiographical romantic comedies became the rage, Neil Simon was ready with* Chapter Two *...starring spouse Marsha Mason in the story of their whirlwind romance and subsequent marital tensions. Never at a loss for good lines guaranteed to generate laughs, Simon was the toastmaster of the 1970s, discreet, only slightly pompous, always insubstantial, but pleasant enough to be endured." (Les Keyser, Hollywood in the Seventies)*

Come Blow Your Horn (1963, Paramount, 115m/c, **VHS**) ☆☆½ **Sc:** Norman Lear. **D:** Bud Yorkin. **P:** Norman Lear, Bud Yorkin. **Cam:** William Daniels. **Cast:** Frank Sinatra, Tony Bill, Lee J. Cobb, Jill St. John, Molly Picon, Barbara Rush, Dan Blocker, Phyllis McGuire, Dean Martin, Eddie Quillan, Grady Sutton, Romo Vincent, Herbie Faye, John Indrisano. The play debuted in 1961 at New York's Brooks Atkinson

Theatre starring Hal March, Arlene Golonka, Warren Berlinger, and Lou Jacobi. Sinatra is in his element as a swinging bachelor initiating his younger brother in worldly ways.

- *"If anything,* Come Blow Your Horn *improves on the stage version, which was a hit....Frankie tries harder this time not just to do his usual walk-through, and in general succeeeds."* (Philip K. Scheuer, Los Angeles Times)

- *"The main thing they have done is throw the play out the window—all but the bones and central situation. (After all, you have to start somewhere.) By shifting the focus from the younger to the older brother, they have strengthened what remains a feeble and familiar story line. But they have also opened it out with gay and inventive business, and paced it with breakneck speed."* (Arthur Knight, The Saturday Review)

The Good Doctor (1978, PBS, 88m/c, **VHS**) *Great Performances* ☆☆
Tp: Neil Simon. **D:** Jack O'Brien. **P:** Lindsay Law, Jac Venza. **Cast:** Richard Chamberlain, Marsha Mason, Lee Grant, Edward Asner, Bob Dishy. Simon adapted stories by Anton Chekhov into a series of mini-playlets, which were originally enacted on the 1973 New York stage by an ensemble including Rene Auberjonois, Marsha Mason, Barnard Hughes, Christopher Plummer, and Frances Sternhagen. Mason seems to relish the opportunity to enact each of *The Three Sisters.*

- *"The result falls awkwardly between gentle Chekhovian satire and clever Simon wisecracks. Neither writer is served to advantage. As 'The Writer' Mr. Chamberlain wanders about attractively, introducing the pieces and acting in some. All concerned, when not overacting in the manner of a Feydeau farce, look terribly smug about their seeming ability to rub elbows with the great Chekhov. The misbegotten adventure is best forgotten."* (John J. O'Connor, The New York Times)

I Ought to Be in Pictures (1982, 20th Century-Fox, 107m/c, **VHS**)
☆☆ **Sc:** Neil Simon. **D:** Herbert Ross. **P:** Herbert Ross, Neil Simon.
Cam: David M. Walsh. **Cast:** Walter Matthau, Ann-Margret, Dinah Manoff, Lance Guest, Lewis Smith, Martin Ferrero, Eugene Butler, Samantha Harper, Santos Morales, David Faustino, Shelby Balik, Michael Dudikoff, Art Le Fleur, Virginia Wing, Bill Cross. The original 1980 Broadway cast starred Ron Liebman, Dinah Manoff, and Joyce Van Patten, directed by Herbert Ross. Manoff won a Tony Award for her performance as a 19-year-old wisecracking Brooklyn girl who is reunited with the father she hasn't seen in 16 years. The father is Herb Tucker, a Hollywood screenwriter with writer's block who's broke from gambling debts and supported by frowzied-down Ann-Margret's hairdresser.

- *"...I found it unbearable. Being so mechanical, so slick and so sentimental, it is, at heart, heartless, and though it has the hyped-up pacing one associ-*

ates with Broadway, it seems longer than Nicholas Nickleby....Mr. *Simon, who can write funny, perceptive lines for self-deceiving adults, especially characters connected to show business...has absolutely no knack for writing words for children. Whether the child is 10, as in* The Goodbye Girl, *or in her mid-teens as in* Only When I Laugh, *or 19, as is Libby Tucker, they all come on like monstrous little Bob Hopes. It's never possible to believe the genuine emotions Mr. Simon assigns them. Because the characters so completely define the performances, the less said the better about the work of Miss Manoff, who seems to be a pretty, intelligent young woman, and Mr. Matthau, who has never given a bad performance in his screen career. Ann-Margret is subdued, willing and drab, and that, I suppose, is acting, though it's a waste of our time and her talent. I Ought to Be in Pictures ought not to be." (Vincent Canby, The New York Times)*

Jake's Women (1996, CBS, 120m/c) ☆☆☆ **Tp:** Neil Simon. **D:** Glenn Jordan. **P:** Glenn Jordan, Robert Halmi Sr. **Cast:** Alan Alda, Anne Archer, Lolita Davidovich, Mira Sorvino, Julie Kavner, Joyce Van Patten, Kimberly Williams, Ashley Peldo, Perry Anzilotti, Steven M. Porter, Yul Vazquez, Aasif Mandvi. Alda starred in the 1992 play with Helen Shaver, Brenda Vaccaro, Kate Burton, Talia Balsam, Joyce Van Patten, and Tracy Pollan. Jake addresses the audience in asides from time to time as he discusses his fear of intimacy with half a dozen women in his life.

- "...[Jordan did a] terrific job in helping me to open it up and make it a film and yet keep it intimate enough for television. I started from page one and treated it as if it were a movie. So I think the changes from stage to film and television helped us enormously. There were things I was never able to do on the stage. I could get out and go to places I wish I would have gone to and which I do in this film version." (Neil Simon to Susan King, Los Angeles Times)

Last of the Red Hot Lovers (1972, Paramount, 98m/c, **VHS**) ☆☆½ **Sc:** Neil Simon. **D:** Gene Saks. **P:** Howard W. Koch. **Cam:** Victor J. Kemper. **Cast:** Alan Arkin, Paula Prentiss, Sally Kellerman, Renee Taylor. The 1969 Broadway original directed by Robert Moore starred James Coco in his career-making performance, Linda Lavin, Marcia Rodd, and Doris Roberts. The plot finds middle-aged restaurateur Barney Cashman wanting to get a piece of the action in the newly permissive society of the early 1970s. But his assignations turn to disaster with a hedonistic Polish-American housewife, his best friend's wife, and a chanteuse.

- "Alan Arkin, as Barney, the homespun hero who can't get the smell of fish off his fingers, plays with the concentration and desperation of a man scared to death he will die without ever experiencing a salacious moment. He almost carries the picture above the level of tame, rib-tickling comedy. But Simon's farces of the familiar need the intimacy of live performers. In cellu-

loid, his figures remain remote, his laughs muffled and his doubts about film-ing his plays confirmed." (Paul D. Zimmerman, Newsweek)

Laughter on the 23rd Floor (2000, Showtime, 102m/c) ☆☆☆ **Tp:** Neil Simon. **D:** Richard Benjamin. **P:** Jeffrey Lampert. **Cast:** Nathan Lane, Saul Rubinek, Mark-Linn Baker, Dan Castellaneta, Richard Portnow, Ardon Bess, Frank Proctor, Sherry Miller, Kristy Angus, Colin Fox, Mackenzie Austin, Victor Garber. Simon's memories of his days writing for Sid Caesar in the 1950s were converted into this treatise on a famous TV comedian named Max Prince, who drives his staff nuts and takes him-self way too seriously. Richard Benjamin, who directed Peter O'Toole to an Oscar nomination in a similar movie about early TV, *My Favorite Year* (1982), in which Joe Bologna was the Caesar figure, also helmed this nos-talgic gem. The show was nominated for an Emmy for Best TV Movie. Lane, Baker, and Lewis J. Stadlin starred in the 1993 Broadway play. Simon himself described his experiences with the Caesar gang, which in-cluded Carl Reiner and Woody Allen, as "a university of comedy."

- "*A modestly funny TV version…The best scene in* Laughter *has oily net-work executives telling Max how much they love his show before ordering him to dumb it down for Peoria…Max's responses to adversity are played broadly, and his goofy writers are an infantile lot, exaggerated behavior bet-ter suited to the stage than the intimate small screen. As a result, Max and his bickering gang are much less funny than grating, no recipe for comedy."* (Howard Rosenberg, *Los Angeles Times*)

London Suite (1996, NBC, 120m/c) ☆☆½ **Tp:** Neil Simon. **D:** Jay Sandrich. **P:** Greg Smith, Robert Halmi Sr. **Cast:** Kelsey Grammar, Julia Louis-Dreyfus, Michael Richards, Jonathan Silverman, Madeline Kahn, Richard Mulligan, Patricia Clarkson, Julie Hagerty, Paxton Whitehead, Kriten Johnston, Margot Steinberg. The 1995 original bowed at New York's Union Square Theatre with Jeffrey Jones, Paxton Whitehead, Kate Burton, and Carole Shelley. Four stories about couples are set in an English hotel in the manner of the playwright's *Plaza Suite* (see below) and *California Suite* (see above).

- "*The news here isn't so much that Simon has extended his* Suite *series…to the small screen but rather that the cast for* London Suite *is a who's who of NBC heavy-hitters…Practically the only thing missing here is the* Friends *cast strutting through the movie's primary setting, the Grosvenor Hotel, with the peacock itself in tow.…The revelations Simon builds…are hardly worth concealing, but suffice it to say that disease and death are not Simon's best subjects. He doesn't feel them genuinely…to put it in [NBC] 'Must see TV' terms, Simon would be a great guest writer on* Seinfeld. *Just keep him away from* E.R.*"* (Robert Koehler, *Los Angeles Times*)

Lost in Yonkers (1993, Columbia, 110m/c, **VHS**) ☆☆☆½ **Sc:** Neil Simon. **D:** Martha Coolidge. **P:** Ray Stark. **Cam:** Johnny E. Jensen. **Cast:** Richard Dreyfuss, Mercedes Ruehl, Irene Worth, David Strathairn, Brad Stoll, Mike Damus, Robert Miranda, Jack Laufer, Susan Merson. Reuhl and Worth repeat their 1991 Broadway roles in Simon's World War II-era tale about two brothers, ages 13 and 15, who are sent to live with relatives after their mother dies and their father goes to find work in the South. The actors are all superb, especially Ruehl, whose depiction of Bella's development creates the emotional arc of Coolidge's film.

- *"...the film...has a special quality to it. All the performances are good, but one of them, by Mercedes Ruehl, casts a glow over the entire film. Ruehl plays Aunt Bella...There is a possibility, subscribed to by everybody but never quite put into words, that she is mentally ill....Only gradually do we begin to understand the darker side of her character, the unhealthy way in which her mother has suppressed her natural exuberance. By the end of the movie, when Aunt Bella is finally able to find a way to live life on her own terms, we're almost surprised how much we've come to care about her."* (Roger Ebert, Chicago Sun-Times)

The Odd Couple (1968, Paramount, 105m/c, **VHS/DVD**) ☆☆☆☆½ **Sc:** Neil Simon. **D:** Gene Saks. **P:** Howard W. Koch. **Cam:** William B. Hauser. **Cast:** Jack Lemmon, Walter Matthau, John Fiedler, Herb Edelman, David Sheiner, Larry Haines, Monica Evans, Carol Sheely, Iris Adrian. The 1965 play starred Art Carney as Felix with Matthau. This benchmark in American comedy claims high places in the histories of stage, film, and TV. It concerns the suddenly shared New York bachelorhood of the compulsively neat Felix, who has left his wife, and the compulsively messy Oscar, a sports writer.

- *"...one of the very best comedies to have emanated from Broadway in recent years....arrived on the screen not only intact but actually enhanced by its transition. As to its enhancement, above all there is Jack Lemmon to make Felix a revolting mass of tics and twitches and fussbudgetry, to hit that fine high of comedic performance that we have long expected from Lemmon but rarely received. The essence of the Felix character is that with all the priggishness and domesticity it be a thoroughly male one—and the slightest hint of camp or flick of wrist could destroy the entire point of the play. Lemmon is pure platinum at long last."* (Judith Crist, New York)

- *"Lemmon, as a definitive hypochondriac, makes a marvelous moment out of clearing his Eustachian tubes, and his compulsive dusting is consistently funny. Matthau, who moves like an arthritic heal-and-toe walker on a sticky treadmill, is beautifully, unyieldingly malevolent in his attitude toward order and his fear that Lemmon, once banished, may yet return as a ghost, 'haunting and cleaning, haunting and cleaning.'"* (Joe Morgenstern, Newsweek)

Only When I Laugh (1981, Columbia, 120m/c, **VHS**) ☆☆☆ **Sc:** Neil Simon. **D:** Glenn Jordan. **P:** Roger M. Rothstein, Neil Simon. **Cam:** David M. Walsh. **Cast:** Marsha Mason, Kristy McNichol, James Coco, Joan Hackett, Kevin Bacon, David Dukes, John Bennett Perry. This melodramatic rehashing of Simonized issues about men, women, and relationships was staged in 1970 as *The Gingerbread Lady* starring Maureen Stapleton, Ayn Ruymen, and Betsy von Furstenberg. A recovering alcoholic actress mends her relationship with her 17-year-old daughter and revives her formerly strained relationships with friends. The film was nominated for Oscars for Best Actress (Mason) and Supporting Actress (Hackett).

- *"Simon is not America's dean of comedy writers by accident He has enough talent, wisdom, foresight and understanding of people to make his comedy work. He also has Marsha Mason, whose dazzling honesty and emotional directness elevated* Chapter Two *and* The Goodbye Girl *above and beyond the confines of comedy. Together, they have now created their most graceful and memorable duet....Everyone in* Only When I Laugh *seems to know that levity is the soul of wit. It isn't crude, vulgar or antisocial. It embraces life. The result is a very sophisticated comedy about very sophisticated people, with an affectionate universality that touches us all."* (Rex Reed, Vogue)

Plaza Suite starred George C. Scott and Maureen Stapleton on Broadway in 1968. Three vignettes take place in the titular New York hotel, and concern a success-driven husband weary of his flaky wife, a loudmouthed Hollywood producer trying to seduce the high school sweetheart he left behind, and the father of a bride-to-be who has locked herself in the bathroom.

Plaza Suite (1971, Paramount, 114m/c, **VHS**) ☆☆½ **Sc:** Neil Simon. **D:** Arthur Hiller. **P:** Howard W. Koch. **Cam:** Jack Marta. **Cast:** Walter Matthau, Lee Grant, Barbara Harris, Maureen Stapleton, Louise Sorel. The playets come across as old-styled, 1960s-era sex farces that, if it weren't for Matthau, would be completely useless.

- *"...reduces the 1968 Broadway smash to 'routine television fare,' and as such it is to be enjoyed. Certainly there's nothing routine in any medium about the presence of four top stars—Walter Matthau in three roles, Maureen Stapleton, Barbara Harris and Lee Grant as his respective partners...The women are perfection and Matthau, donning a variety of wigs rather than personalities, is Matthau all the way."* (Judith Crist, Judith Crist's TV Guide to the Movies)

Plaza Suite (1982, HBO, 120m/c) ☆☆½ **Sc:** Neil Simon. **D:** Harvey Medlinsky. **P:** Richard H. Frank, Maria Govons, Harvey Medlinsky. **Cast:** Jerry Orbach, Lee Grant, Julie Garfield. Like other stage productions in cable's early years, this was filmed before a live audience. A Broadway favorite for years and a Tony Award winner, Orbach hadn't yet achieved TV fame through *Law & Order*. He and Grant each played three roles. Orbach saw the HBO play revivals primarily as a place to make money (see below).

- *"They won't hire people unless they have a certain amount of visibility. But in cases like this (HBO's filming of stage plays) they desperately need people who are used to going through an entire performance in front of an audience without stopping. It's providing us with a new avenue to get in where the money is."* (Jerry Orbach to Kenneth R. Clark, United Press International, Los Angeles Times)

Plaza Suite (1987 ABC, 120m/c) ☆☆½ **Sc:** Neil Simon. **D:** Roger Beatty, Kenny Solms. **P:** Carol Burnett, Kenny Solms. **Cast:** Carol Burnett, Hal Holbrook, Richard Crenna, Dabney Coleman, Erin Hamilton. Burnett played the same roles onstage at the Huntington Hartford Theatre in Los Angeles in 1971, and her woman's take on the three roles with three different men was an obviously good-humored gesture, with middling results.

- *"It's a fitting match of content and form; Simon's sketches wouldn't have been out of place on Burnett's show. This speaks well for the craftsmanship of her show. It doesn't speak well for the depth of Broadway comedy 20 years ago, when Plaza Suite was a big hit....If Simon were writing Plaza Suite today, he might write it directly for television—and he probably wouldn't create three such passive women within one play. The first two of Burnett's housewives are practically needy supplicants, in thrall to domineering men....Still, Burnett...does her best to individuate these women, with her outfits as well as her schtick."* (Don Shirley, Los Angeles Times)

The Prisoner of Second Avenue (1974, Warner Bros., 98m/c, **VHS**) ☆☆☆ **Sc:** Neil Simon. **D/P:** Melvin Frank. **Cam:** Philip Lathrop. **Cast:** Jack Lemmon, Anne Bancroft, Gene Saks, Elizabeth Wilson. An exhausted and fed-up New York advertising executive gets fired, holes up in an apartment, and has a nervous breakdown while his wife tries to take care of him. The play debuted on Broadway in 1971 starring Peter Falk, Lee Grant, and Vincent Gardenia. Lemmon and Bancroft rail at each other for the duration of this better-than-average Simon adaptation.

- *"With a cast whose members appreciate what they're saying and doing, the gnawing 'problems' of Second Avenue become a pleasure. If Melvin Frank's direction is polished but not innovative, he is ably aided by Jack Lemmon and Anne Bancroft, who project forcefully natural characterizations that are as realistic as the authentic Second Avenue and other New York sights. Mr. Lemmon and Miss Bancroft are simply and unromanticized, believable team as recognizable in their comic and serious give-and-take as many of New York's scrambling millions."* (A.H. Weiler, The New York Times)

- *"Vaguely about urban despair, full of bad jokes....Melvin Frank directed in his usual sagging, 1950s style, but probably there isn't a filmmaker in the world who could substancially improve this picture except by throwing out the play altogether." (Pauline Kael, 5001 Nights at the Movies)*

Star Spangled Girl (1971, Paramount, 92m/c, **VHS**) ☆☆ **Sc:** Arnold Margolin, Jim Parker. **D:** Jerry Paris. **P:** Howard W. Koch. **Cam:** Sam Leavitt. **Cast:** Sandy Duncan, Tony Roberts, Todd Sussman, Elizabeth Allen. Connie Stevens starred in the 1966 Broadway original with Anthony Perkins and Richard Benjamin. A patriotic young woman debates politics with two left-wing newspapermen next door.

- *"Sandy Duncan's comic talent shines through—she has a troll-like spark of genius in her timing—and Tony Roberts's and Todd Sussman's talents almost shine through, too, but the material is atrocious Neil Simon. The situations are so contrived that the wisecracks aren't funny even when they're funny. But when they're sour, they're certainly sour. Directed at breakneck speed by Jerry Paris, but the picture can't go by fast enough." (Pauline Kael, 5001 Nights at the Movies)*

The Sunshine Boys starred Jack Albertson and Sam Levene as the old-time comedy team of Lewis and Clark in the 1972 Broadway hit, which co-starred Louis J. Stadlin. Lewis and Clark were Vaudeville partners for 43 years and then enemies who didn't speak for 11 years—until a TV special reunites them.

The Sunshine Boys (1975, MGM, 111m/c, **VHS**) ☆☆☆½ **Sc:** Neil Simon. **D:** Herbert Ross. **P:** Ray Stark. **Cam:** David M. Walsh. **Cast:** Walter Matthau, George Burns, Richard Benjamin, Carol Arthur, Rosetta LeNoire, Sid Gould, Lee Meredith, F. Murray Abraham, Howard Hesseman, Ron Rifkin, Jennifer Lee, Garn Stephens, Fritz Feld, Jack Bernardi, Sammy Smith. The repartee and one-liners fly all over the place. George Burns won the Oscar for Best Supporting Actor.

- *"...even less funny on film than onstage. Neil Simon writes comic turns whose excess needs living but distant presences, and that suffer both by losing one dimension to the screen and by having the other two vastly enlarged. Accordingly, Walter Matthau...plays...as if he were regurgitating a lifetime's worth of chewed up scenery [and] quickly becomes insufferable; whereas George Burns, who meticulously restrains himself as the more silent partner, is a pleasure to see and hear. Richard Benjamin contributes one of his customary greasy performances, while Herbert Ross's direction remains painfully dry." (John Simon, Reverse Angle)*

- *"It's all one-liners; Matthau keeps blasting us with his bullhorn voice; Burns has the repose of a tortoise, his eyes gleaming and alert, and he has a rhythmed formality in his conversation, as an old trouper might....Ross doesn't bring enough invention to the material, and it's just shouting, when it needs to be beautifully timed routines." (Pauline Kael, 5,001 Nights at the Movies)*

The Sunshine Boys (1977, NBC, 60m/c) ☆☆½ **Tp:** Neil Simon. **D:** Robert Moore. **P:** Sam Denoff. **Cast:** Red Buttons, Lionel Stander, Michael Durrell, Bobbie Mitchell, Sarina Grant, George Wyner, Danny Mora, Ann Cooper, Philip Tanzini, Tony Sherman, Bella Bruck, Barra Grant. This was a condensing of the play into an hour-long pilot for a half-hour sitcom envisioned in the Simon/*Odd Couple* tradition, but the show was never sold as a series.

- "*...played well with the laugh content reasonably high.*" (Variety)

The Sunshine Boys (1995, ABC, 120m/c) ☆☆ **Tp:** Neil Simon. **D:** John Erman. **P:** Robert Halmi Sr. **Cast:** Woody Allen, Peter Falk, Michael McKean, Sarah Jessica Parker, Whoopi Goldberg, Edie Falco, Liev Schreiber, Tyler Noyes, Michael Badalucco, Olga Merediz, Andy Taylor. The regime changed at ABC, and this movie, which was greenlighted by the outgoing folks, received a tepid response from the new executives. As it is, these dinner-theatre-styled performances by two aging celebrities never get at the heart of the matter.

- "*No wonder this Neil Simon-scripted TV movie based on his play has been sitting on the shelf since 1995. It's a thoroughly exasperating film devoid of humor or pathos....Falk is especially trying as the stubborn, spiteful half of the team. Best to avoid these* Boys, *whose brand of sunshine can only bring you gloom.*" (*Steve Linan*, Los Angeles Times)

Sweet Charity (1968, Universal, 149m/c, **VHS**) ☆☆☆ **Sc:** Peter Stone. **D:** Bob Fosse. **P:** Robert Arthur. **Cam:** Robert Surtees. **Cast:** Shirley MacLaine, Ricardo Montalban, Sammy Davis Jr., John McMartin, Chita Rivera, Paula Kelly, Stubby Kaye, Barbara Bouchet. Simon based this story of the proverbial prostitute with a heart of gold on Federico Fellini's great film, *Nights of Cabiria* (1957), starring the Italian director's wife, Giulietta Masina. Simon transferred the setting to New York City, where Gwen Verdon starred in the Broadway smash of 1966 along with McMartin, Thelma Oliver, and Ruth Buzzi.

- "*...may have been too ambitious a project for Bob Fosse's debut...The tricky camera effects...are jangling here, and although Shirley MacLaine tries hard, it's obvious that her dancing isn't up to the demands of the role. It's a disaster, but zoom-happy Fosse's choreographic conceptions are intensely dramatic, and the movie has some of the best dancing in American musicals of the period.*" (*Pauline Kael*, 5001 Nights at the Movies)

- "*...its musical portions are stunning. But the stage show was a slick piece of goods that borrowed the plot but none of the spirit of Fellini's* Nights of Cabiria, *and Fosse carried over the faults in the original. Who besides a New Yorker or Woody Allen fan wants to see a musical about crummy New Yorkers using each other?*" (*Ethan Mordden*, The Hollywood Musical)

Bernard Slade

Bernard Slade Newbound
Born: May 2, 1930, St. Catharines, Ontario, Canada.

After an education in Wales and England, Bernard Slade moved to the United States in 1963 and became a prolific sitcom creator and writer. He originated *Bridget Loves Bernie*, *Love on a Rooftop*, and *The Flying Nun* and wrote multiple scripts for *Bewitched* and *The Partridge Family*. "I went into television to make money," he once said, "and it was the labor of love, *Same Time, Next Year*, that made me rich." One of the longest-running plays of all time, it debuted on Broadway in 1975. Slade's other plays include *Special Occasions*, *Fatal Attraction*, *An Act of the Imagination*, *Return Engagements*, *You Say Tomatoes*, *I Remember You*, and *Same Time, Another Year*, a sequel to his greatest hit. Slade's one original screenplay was for a dismal movie about women's lib, *Stand Up and Be Counted* (1972), starring Jacqueline Bisset and Stella Stevens.

Romantic Comedy (1983, MGM, 102m/c, **VHS**) ☆☆ **Sc:** Bernard Slade. **D:** Arthur Hiller. **P:** Walter Mirisch, Morton Gottlieb. **Cam:** David M. Walsh. **Cast:** Dudley Moore, Mary Steenburgen, Frances Sternhagen, Janet Eilber, Ron Liebman, Robyn Douglass. A pair of playwriting partners can't seem to synchronize their talents, even as their personal affair is mostly fulfilling. Slade's autobiographical play originated in New York at the Ethel Barrymore Theatre in 1979, and starred Mia Farrow and Anthony Perkins. The generic title was perfect for this excursion into Neil Simon territory without the one-liners and fun.

- "*...a very optimistic title and fails to deliver. Dudley Moore is strait-jacketed in the guise of a successful Broadway playwright...Their success complicates his marriage. If this sounds more like Neil Simon, you're right. The trouble is that he didn't write the script.*" (Desmond Ryan, *Video Capsule Reviews*)

Same Time, Next Year (1978, Universal, 119m/c, **VHS**) ☆☆☆½ **Sc:** Bernard Slade. **D:** Robert Mulligan. **P:** Walter Mirisch, Robert Mulligan. **Cam:** Robert Surtees. **Cast:** Alan Alda, Ellen Burstyn. A pair of adulterers meet at a resort once a year from 1951 to 1977, and the social changes in America are reflected through their interplay, from mundanities to issues such as feminism and the Vietnam War. The film was Oscar-nominated for Best Actress (Burstyn), Screenplay, Cinematography, and Song ("The Last Time I Felt Like This").

- "*A tepid sweet meal. Genteel lifelong adultery by two ciphers....The gimmick is the way that social changes and fashions in dress and ideas are reflected in these two, and the single joke is that adultery can be regulated and celebrated, just like marriage. Of course it can be, if you remove every ounce of passion and sexual tension from it, which is what the writer, Bernard Slade, and the director, Robert Mulligan, have done. If someone you make the mistake of caring about insists on your going to this movie, take a small flashlight and a book." (Pauline Kael, 5001 Nights at the Movies)*

Tribute (1980, 20th Century-Fox, 122m/c, **VHS**) ☆☆ **Sc:** Bernard Slade. **D:** Bob Clark. **P:** Joel B. Michaels, Garth B. Drabinsky. **Cam:** Reginald H. Morris. **Cast:** Jack Lemmon, Lee Remick, Robby Benson, Colleen Dewhurst, Kim Cattrall, John Marley, Gale Garnett. Slade's 1978 Broadway play starred Lemmon as the glad-handing, tippling good-timer Scottie Templeton, who suddenly discovers that he's dying of cancer. He tries to reconcile what should have been deeper relationships with his family, especially with his son. Lemmon was nominated for an Oscar for his performance.

- *"I am aware that* Tribute *hauls out some of the oldest Broadway cliches in the book, that it shamelessly exploits its melodramatic elements, and that it is not a movie so much as a filmed stage play. And yet if I were to review it just on those grounds, I would be less than honest. In the abstract,* Tribute *may not be a very good film at all. But in its particulars, and in the way they affected me, it is a touching experience....There are long sequences that are obviously just filmed scenes from Bernard Slade's original stage play....The film is mostly Jack Lemmon's...Perhaps the film works better because it's willing to be a bittersweet soap opera." (Roger Ebert, Chicago Sun-Times)*

Anna Deavere Smith

Born: September 18, 1950, Baltimore, MD.

Anna Deavere Smith's rather patriotically themed career as an actress includes the presidential themed *Dave* (1993) and *The American President* (1994) as well as episodes of TV's *The West Wing* and the AIDS drama *Philadelphia* (1993). Two of her acclaimed one-woman stage performances in her own material (see below) were seen on TV.

Fires in the Mirror (1993, PBS, 90m/c) *American Playhouse* ☆☆☆ **Tp/Cast:** Anna Deavere Smith. **D:** George C. Wolfe. Smith presents many views and voices of the Crown Heights tragedy, in the process introducing many ideas about race relations and their complexities in the 1990s. Staged in 1992 at New York's Public Theater, this one-woman show details the responses to the August 1991 unrest between African-Americans and Hasidic Jews in Crown Heights, Brooklyn. Three hours after a vehicle driven by a Hasidic man swerved onto a sidewalk and killed a young black boy, a rabbinical student was murdered in a retaliatory stabbing nearby. Four days of rioting followed.

• *"Although Smith's chameleonic abilities will still blow you away, the characters have been pushed toward caricature. As a result, the common humanity of both the Jews and the African-Americans that is one of the play's points is muted. It's now less about one woman's ability to crawl into the skins of many people, and more about how well she wears different wigs. Smith's consummate skills notwithstanding, the gravitas comes from the fact that the words she is speaking are taken verbatim from what real folks have had to say. Dramatic license enters the picture in the form of shaping and editing: whom Smith has talked to, how she has juxtaposed, distributed and contextualized these excerpts in relation to one another, and most importantly, what bits she has chosen to cull from each interview."* (Jan Breslauer, Los Angeles Times)

Twilight, Los Angeles (2000, PBS, 84m/c) ☆☆☆ **Tp:** Anna Deavere Smith. **D:** Marc Levin. **Cast:** Anna Deavere Smith, Elaine Kim, Ruben Martinez, Paul Parker. Featuring archival footage of such Los Angeles race-relations figures as Rodney King, Daryl Gates, Reginald Denny, Football Williams, and Maxine Waters, this nearly one-woman show again proves Smith to be a marvelous editor and character actor.

• *"...remarkable piece of documentary theatre...on stage, Smith fluidly shifted from character to character by donning representative articles of clothing and changing her body posture. In Marc Levin's film, only a few of these stunning transformations occur on camera. Yet the film gains immediacy from archival footage..."* (Darryl H. Miller, Los Angeles Times)

Aaron Sorkin

Born: June 9, 1961, Scarsdale, NY.

After the success of his play and film *A Few Good Men* (1992), Aaron Sorkin wrote the *The American President* (1995), with Michael Douglas as commander in chief. He took that presidential success to television with the outstanding critical and popular success of *The West Wing*, starring Martin Sheen.

A Few Good Men (1992, Columbia, 138m/c, **VHS/DVD**) ☆☆☆☆ **Sc:** Aaron Sorkin. **D:** Rob Reiner. **P:** David Brown, Rob Reiner, Andrew Scheinman. **Cam:** Robert Richardson. **Cast:** Tom Cruise, Jack Nicholson, Demi Moore, Keifer Sutherland, Kevin Bacon, Kevin Pollak, James Marshall, J.T. Walsh, Wolfgang Bodison, Christopher Guest, J.A. Preston, Cuba Gooding Jr., Noah Wyle, Aaron Sorkin, Matt Craven, Xan-

der Berkeley. Sorkin's 1989 Broadway play starred Tom Hulce, Paul Butler, and Michael Dolan. In peacetime Washington, DC, a U.S. Navy
lawyer is prodded by a legal clerk into defending two Marines accused in
the hazing death of a third Marine at the Guantanamo Naval Air Base
in Cuba. The film was nominated for Oscars for Best Supporting Actor
(Nicholson) and Sound.

- "*Witness Jack Nicholson's vicious, funny, superbly reptilian turn in Rob
  Reiner's entertaining* A Few Good Men...*Mr. Nicholson doesn't steal the
  film, which would mean that he somehow separates himself from everybody
  else in it. Rather, in the course of only a handful of scenes, he seems to suf-
  fuse the entire production, giving it a weight, density and point that might
  not otherwise be apparent. The role, beautifully written, is made to Mr.
  Nicholson's order....The screenplay is a good one...*A Few Good Men *is
  a big commercial entertainment of unusually satisfying order.*" (*Vincent
  Canby,* The New York Times)

- "...*tells you what it's going to do, does it, and then tells you what it did. It
  doesn't think the audience is very bright....an element of surprise is missing
  from the most important moment in the movie, and the key scene by Jack
  Nicholson is undermined, robbed of suspense and made inevitable. That's a
  shame, because in many ways, this is a good film...The flaws are mostly at
  the screenplay level; the film doesn't make us work, doesn't allow us to figure out things for ourselves...*" (*Roger Ebert,* Chicago Sun-Times)

Sam Spewack & Bella Spewack

Sam:
Samuel Spewack (or Spewak)
Born: September 16, 1899, Ukraine, Russia. **Died:** 1971.

Bella:
Bella Cohen
Born: March 25, 1899, Bucharest, Romania. **Died:** 1990.

Tony Award-winning musical: *Kiss Me, Kate* (1948)

Among Bella Spewack's screenplays were *Should Ladies Behave* (1933),
The Gay Bride (1933), *The Chaser* (1938), *My Favorite Wife* (1940),
Weekend at the Waldorf (1945), and a pair of remakes, *Something's Got to
Give* (1962) and *Move Over, Darling* (1963, both based on *My Favorite
Wife*). The couple's most outstanding TV work was writing the 1957
Sidney Lumet-directed song-and-dance special *Mr. Broadway*, starring
Mickey Rooney as George M.Cohan. They also wrote the teleplay for
Enchanted Nutcracker (1961). Aside from her literary achievements,
Bella Spewack is notable as the inventor of the Girl Scout cookie.

Boy Meets Girl is about a pair of fast-talking Hollywood screenwriters whose claims to fame are variations on the title theme. They concoct a plot to create a star out of the yet-unborn child of a ditsy friend. Produced and directed on Broadway in 1935 by George Abbott, the play ran for 669 performances with Allyn Joslyn and Jerome Cowan in the leads with support from Garson Kanin and Everett Sloane.

Boy Meets Girl (1938, Warner Bros., 86m/bw, **VHS**) ☆☆☆½ **Sc:** Bella Spewack, Sam Spewack. **D:** Lloyd Bacon. **P:** George Abbott. **Cam:** Sol Polito. **Cast:** James Cagney, Pat O'Brien, Marie Wilson, Ralph Bellamy, Frank McHugh, Dick Foran, Ronald Reagan, Bruce Lester, James Stephenson, Penny Singleton, John Ridgely, Carole Landis, Pierre Watkin, Curt Bois, Clem Bevans, Paul Clark. A backlot satire with a rapid-fire pace and the Cagney/O'Brien team in good form, this film was a critical and popular hit of its era, and still stands up.

- *"The legend of the culturally moronic mogul became so pervasive in the industry that when a college-educated producer popped up in the front office, his intellectual pretensions were still good for a laugh, as in the caricature of a Walter Wanger-like arriviste in Sam and Bella Spewack's* Boy Meets Girl, *which, like* Once in a Lifetime, *went from stage to screen with most of its anti-Hollywood satiric conceits intact."* (*Andrew Sarris, "You Ain't Heard Nothin' Yet"*)

- *"In the case of* Boy Meets Girl *it is the performing rather than the adaptation or the direction, which has succeeded in changing a popular stage farce into an extremely amusing screen comedy. It seems to me…that it is the irrepressible clowning of James Cagney and Pat O'Brien which gives the show its fine comic flavor. The Messrs. Cagney and O'Brien have been wise, I think, in playing the travesty for straight laughs."* (*Howard Barnes, New York Herald-Tribune*)

Boy Meets Girl (1949, CBS, 60m/bw) *Studio One* ☆☆ **D:** Paul Nickell. **P:** Worthington Miner. **Cast:** Hume Cronyn, Edward Andrews, Sarah O'Connell.

- *"…in completing the three-way entertainment cycle, Studio One's TV version stripped it of humor by rehashing a cold dish and serving it up with poor casting….Sarah O'Connell was a poor runnerup for Marie Wilson while Hume Cronyn and Edward Andrews, as the writing team, weren't too inspired."* (Variety)

Clear All Wires! (1933, MGM, 78m/bw) ☆☆☆½ **Sc:** Delmer Daves. **D:** George W. Hill. **P:** Herman Shumlin. **Cam:** Norbert Brodine. **Cast:** Lee Tracy, Benita Hume, Una Merkel, James Gleason, Alan Edwards, Eugene Sigaloff, Ari Kutal, C. Henry Gordon, Lya Lys, Lawrence Grant, John Melvin Bleifer, Guy Isher. Tracy played Buckley Joyce Thomas, the braggart head of the *Chicago Globe's* foreign service, who traces news across the world with his equally audacious partner, Lefty, played by the irredoubtable Gleason. Thomas's overhyped stories are finally taken to task by *The New York Times*.

- *"It is a good picture with several humorous incidents, but it lacks the sharpness of the play. It has, however, the advantage of the presence of Lee Tracy…his audacity is always diverting. He fancies that most of the population of America hangs on his every written word, and he appears actually to believe what he tells others about himself."* (The New York Times)

Kiss Me, Kate is the Spewacks' backstage farce about stage stars maintaining a heated argument during a performance of Shakespeare's *The Taming of the Shrew*. Alfred Drake and Patricia Morison starred in the 1948 debut production on Broadway, which ran for 1,070 performances.

Kiss Me, Kate (1953, MGM, 109m/c, **VHS**) ☆☆☆ **Sc:** Dorothy Kingsley. **D:** George Sidney. **P:** Jack Cummings. **Cam:** Charles Rosher. **Cast:** Kathryn Grayson, Howard Keel, Ann Miller, Keenan Wynn, Bobby Van, James Whitmore, Bob Fosse, Tommy Rall, Willard Parker, Carol Haney, Jeanne Coyne, Ron Randell, Kurt Kaszner, Claude Allister, Dave O'Brien. MGM gave this one the full, glossy, colorful, 1950s treatment, and the Cole Porter score includes "Why Can't You Behave?," "Always True to You in My Fashion," and "Too Darn Hot."

- *"Grayson's trilling is something to contend with, and so is her busy, amateurish performance, and there's a lot of badly placed rambunctious comedy from just about everybody. But there's also a marvelous Cole Porter score…Howard Keel, with his strong baritone and goodhearted leering…And there's the dancing…'From This Moment On' number, choreographed by [Bob] Fosse, is one of the high points of movie musical history; in its speed and showmanship, one can see the Fosse style in its earliest film realization. This sequence more than balances out the grossly embarrassing moments…"* (Pauline Kael, 5001 Nights at the Movies)

Kiss Me, Kate (1958, NBC, 90m/c) *The Hallmark Hall of Fame* ☆☆½ **Tp:** Sam Spewack, Bella Spewack. **D/P:** George Schaefer. **Cast:** Alfred Drake, Patricia Morison, Julie Wilson, Bill Hayes, Harvey Lembeck, Jack Klugman, Paul McGrath, Robinson Stone, Lee Richardson, Lee Cass, Eva Jessye, Lorenzo Fuller. Drake and Morison, the original Broadway stars, returned to their greatest hit for this TV treatment a decade later.

- *"Much as a viewer may wish for more musicals on the air, this one was quite heavy going. To fit the musical into a 90-minute format, two numbers had to be omitted entirely and a number of others either shortened or speeded up. But these changes probably would not have mattered if there had been lilt and sparkle to the production….the naughtiness and nuances of the original were not conveyed very tellingly. The Spewacks' book is not the easiest thing in the world to stage...George Schaefer's direction was not burdened by many light or fresh touches." (Jack Gould, The New York Times)*

Kiss Me, Kate (1968, ABC Special, 90m/c) *Armstrong Circle Theatre* ☆½ **D:** Paul Bogart. **P:** Norman Rosemont, Robert Goulet. **Cast:** Robert Goulet, Carol Lawrence, Michael Callan, Jessica Walter, Jules Munshin, Marty Ingels, David Doyle, Russell Nype, Lawrence Keith, Tony Hendra, Nick Ullett. The Spewacks so disliked this production that they sued the producers and ABC for punitive damages.

- *"...a disappointingly heavy-handed special — staged and played with barely a trace of sophisticated style of freshness of expression. Goulet''s solo, 'So in Love,' suggested a monument wired for sound." (Jack Gould, The New York Times)*

My Three Angels was based by the Spewacks on the French play *La Cuisine des Anges* by Albert Husson, about three escapees from Devil's Island who hide in a family dry goods store on Christmas Eve and find themselves becoming involved in the family's issues. These include the fact that the avaricious relative who actually owns the store is coming to check the books. It debuted on Broadway in 1953 with Jose Ferrer directing an ensemble including Walter Slezak, Darren McGavin, and Henry Daniell.

We're No Angels (1955, Paramount, 103m/c, **VHS**) ☆☆ **Sc:** Ranald MacDougall. **D:** Michael Curtiz. **P:** Pat Duggan. **Cam:** Loyal Griggs. **Cast:** Humphrey Bogart, Peter Ustinov, Aldo Ray, Joan Bennett, Basil Rathbone, Leo G. Carroll, John Baer, Gloria Talbott, Lea Penman, John Smith. When the cons decide to play Santa Claus for the beleaguered family, the three stars don't quite blend with the material, and the whole show seems forcibly knocked off with little care.

- *"...it's static and laden with leaden talk, with nothing to interest the eye as recompense. Curtiz was going to the dogs at the time, but it's doubtful whether anyone could have worked wonders with such material. Bogart looks particularly ill at-ease and silly." (Geoff Brown, Time Out Film Guide)*

My Three Angels (1959, NBC, 90m/c) *Ford Startime* ☆☆☆ **Sc:** Sam Spewack, Bella Spewack. **D:** Bretaigne Windust, Gordon Rigsby. **P:** Hubbell Robinson, Bretaigne Windust. **Cast:** Barry Sullivan, George Grizzard, Walter Slezak, Carmen Mathews, Henry Daniell, Will Kuluva, Diana Millay, Peter Donat, Ruth Hammond, Byron Sanders. The Spewacks themselves tailored the original play to the needs of TV, cutting very little as the directors pumped the acting along.

- *"...one of the brighter television specials of the season...Bretaigne Windust...and Gordon Rigsby...deserve major credit for the strong and unfaltering pace of the show, a rarity in television comedy plays....the irresistible and impish Slezak as usual stole the show." (Variety)*

We're No Angels (1989, Paramount, 110m/c, **VHS**) ☆☆ **Sc:** David Mamet. **D:** Neil Jordan. **P:** Art Linson. **Cam:** Philippe Rousselot. **Cast:** Robert De Niro, Sean Penn, Demi Moore, Bruno Kirby, Ray McAnally, Hoyt Axton, James Russo, Wallace Shawn, John C. Reilly, Jay Brazeau, Ken Buhay, Elizabeth Lawrence, Bill Murdoch, Jessica Jickels. Shot in Mission, British Columbia, this film is only very distantly related to the Spewacks' material. De Niro and Penn mugged it up as escaped cons in the 1930s, disguised as priests and scheming to cross a bridge to freedom on the other side. Considering the film's pedigree, this is a tepid entertainment.

- *"Pugfaced, slack-jawed and marble-mouthed, De Niro and Penn mug their semi-articulate roles with relish, but as religioso fish out of water, their con game becomes a tiresome joke."* (Variety)

The Solitaire Man (1933, MGM, 68m/bw) ☆☆½ **Sc:** James Kevin McGuinness. **D:** Jack Conway. **P:** Bernard H. Hyman. **Cam:** Roy F. Overbaugh. **Cast:** Herbert Marshall, Elizabeth Allan, Mary Boland, May Robson, Lionel Atwill, Ralph Forbes, Lucille Gleason, Robert McWade. On a Paris-to-London flight, Oliver Lane, a suave safecracker known by the sobriquet of the title, steals a necklace from a competitor en route, but also kills a Scotland Yard inspector. Boland played an American chatterbox who's only quiet when she's exhausted.

- *"...might justly be termed an amusing melodrama, for when persons are slain here, the effect is invariably more humorous than tragic....These episodes are produced with such cleverness that they give a realistic impression of the airplane being in motion, an effect that is heightened by passing clouds and the sound of whirring motors....Miss Boland gives a humorous portrayal. Mr. Marshall is in fine fettle as Lane."* (The New York Times)

Barrie Stavis

Born: 1906, New York, NY.

Barrie Stavis wrote his first full-length play at age 19 while attending Columbia University. His plays wrestle with the large moral and ethical issues that were faced by historical figures, including Gallileo in *Lamp at Midnight*, John Brown in *Harpers Ferry*, labor leader Joe Hill in *The Man Who Never Died*, and George Washington in *The Raw Edge of Victory*. He also wrote a novel, *Home, Sweet, Home!*

Lamp at Midnight (1966, NBC, 76m/c) *The Hallmark Hall of Fame* ☆☆☆½ **Tp:** Robert Hartung. **D/P:** George Schaefer. **Cast:** Melvyn

Douglas, David Wayne, Michael Hordern, Kim Hunter, George Voskovec, Hurd Hatfield, Thayer David, Richard Woods, Roy Scheider, Graham Jarvis, House Jameson, Gaylord Cavallaro, Ralph Clanton, Guy Repp, Hugh Franklin. In the 1947 Off Broadway original about Gallileo's differences with the Roman Catholic Church, Peter Capell played the Italian scientist with Martin Balsam and Leon Janney in support.

- *"We ended that year with a powerful drama...Lamp at Midnight. Melvyn Douglas played Galileo in a remarkably rich performance. David Wayne was the villain, and the Pope was Michael Hordern. This searching play about religion and truth and science has played in 23 countries and holds up very well."* (George Schaefer, From Live to Tape to Film: 60 Years of Inconspicuous Directing)

Joseph Stein

Born: May 30, 1912, New York, NY.
Tony Award-winning musical: *Fiddler on the Roof* (1965).

A former psychiatric social worker who wrote for Sid Caesar's *Your Show of Shows* in the 1950s, Joseph Stein began his playwriting career partnered with Will Glickman for seven musicals, including *Mr. Wonderful* (1956) and *The Body Beautiful* (1958). After winning the Tony Award for *Fiddler on the Roof*, Stein was again nominated for the award for the musical adaptation of *Zorba the Greek* into *Zorba* (1968) with Herschel Bernardi. Stein's other musicals include *King of Hearts* (1978), *The Baker's Wife* (1985), and *Rags* (1986). He was the executive producer of the 1963 sitcom *Harry's Girls* starring Larry Blyden.

Enter Laughing (1967, Columbia, 112m/c, **VHS**) ☆☆½ **Sc/P:** Carl Reiner, Joseph Stein. **D:** Carl Reiner. **Cam:** Joseph F. Biroc, Albert Taffet. **Cast:** Jose Ferrer, Shelley Winters, Elaine May, Jack Gilford, Don Rickles, Janet Margolin, David Opatoshu, Rob Reiner, Michael J. Pollard, Nancy Kovack, Richard Deacon, Reni Santoni, Herbie Faye, Mantan Moreland. Stein's play was based on Carl Reiner's autobiographical novel about his fledgling years in show business.

- *"...hustled rather grossly onto the screen in an uneven film...A clue to what is basically the matter with this spottily funny job...is the fact that four secondary characters are conspicuously overplayed and plugged above the ambitious young hero who should be foremost and more forceful in the show....Ferrer as the aging ham...May as the ham's twitching daughter...Winters as his worrying Bronx mother...Gilford as his wry employer...it appears [Reiner] found Mr. Santoni not up to the demands of his role."* (Bosley Crowther, The New York Times)

Fiddler on the Roof (1971, UA, 181m/c, **VHS/DVD**) ☆☆☆☆ **Sc:**
Joseph Stein. **D/P:** Norman Jewison **Cam:** Oswald Morris. **Cast:** Topol,
Norma Crane, Leonard Frey, Molly Picon, Paul Mann, Rosalind Harris,
Paul Michael Glazer, Neva Small, Michele Marsh, Ray Lovelock, Elaine
Edwards, Zvee Scooler, Louis Zorich, Barry Dennen, Tutte Lemkow.
Sholom Aleichem's book *Tevye's Daughters* and the play he derived from
it, *Tevye der Milkhiker*, were translated by Stein into the libretto of the
long-running smash stage musical. It debuted in 1964 as a Hal Prince
production and ran for 3,242 performances with direction and choreography by Jerome Robbins, music by Jerry Bock, and lyrics by Sheldon
Harnick. The cast was headed by Zero Mostel and included Beatrice
Arthur and Bert Convy. The old-fashioned film, set in a small Russian
village in 1905, pitted the czar's representatives against a Ukrainian village's Jews—the story of why many Russian Jews emigrated to the
United States. Among the songs were "If I Were a Rich Man" and "Sunrise, Sunset." The quaintly yet richly pictorial village is enlivened by
many from the original cast, including Frey and Scooler. The film won
Oscars for Best Screenplay, Score (John Williams), and Sound. It was
nominated for Best Picture, Director, Actor (Topol), Supporting Actor
(Frey), and Art Direction/Set Decoration.

- *"Sentimental in a theatrical way, romantic in the old-fashioned way, nos-*
  talgic of immigration days, affirmative of human decency, loyalty, bravery
  and folk humor…An enormous man with sparkling (not melting) brown
  eyes, Topol has the necessary combination of bombast and compassion, vi-
  tality and doubts. His dialogues with God (and/or the audience) are more
  cautious and less in the chutzpah style of, say, Zero Mostel." (Variety)

- *"The movie offers the pleasures of big, bold strokes; it's American folk*
  opera, commercial style. It's not a celebration of Jewishness; it's a celebra-
  tion of the sensual pleasures of staying alive and of trying to hang onto a bit
  of ceremony, too. Isaac Stern plays the theme (as he does in the solo parts
  throughout the movie) with startling brio and attack, and Topol's Tevye has
  the same vitality and sweetness and gaiety as Stern's music; he's a rough
  presence, masculine, with burly, raw strength." (Paulene Kael, 5,001
  Nights at the Movies)

Mrs. Gibbons' Boys (1962, British Lion, 82m/bw) ☆☆½ **Sc:** Peter
Blackmore, Max Varnel. **D:** Max Varnel. **P:** Henry Halstead. **Cast:**
Diana Dors, Eric Pohlmann, Lionel Jeffries, Milo O'Shea, Kathleen
Harrison, Dick Emery, Peter Hempson, David Lodge, John Le Mesurier.
This film was adapted from the play by Will Glickman and Stein.

- *"…this unhappy farce about a doting mother of three revolting thugs is re-*
  deemed from utter banality by a few slick lines, a few scenes…that are not
  sadistically slapstick and a valiant supporting cast." (Monthly Film Bulletin)

John Steinbeck

Born: February 27, 1902, Salinas, CA. **Died:** 1968.
New York Drama Critics Circle Award, Best Play: *Of Mice and Men* (1938)

John Steinbeck became the seventh American author to be awarded the Nobel Prize in literature, in 1962, during the year when his travelogue of America, *Travels With Charley*, was published. His first novels were *Cup of Gold*, *The Pastures of Heaven* and *To a God Unknown*. He won popular attention with *Tortilla Flat* in 1935. *In Dubious Battle* two years later continued his championing of migrant fruit pickers. The Depression Era tragedy *Of Mice and Men* (1937) illuminated in a classic way the broken lives of drifters. Steinbeck's ultimate take on the economic and social tragedies of the 1930s arrived two years later with *The Grapes of Wrath*, which was awarded the Pulitzer Prize. Steinbeck's other novels include *The Long Valley*, *The Red Pony*, *The Pearl*, *The Moon Is Down*, *East of Eden*, and *The Winter of Our Discontent*. While many of his books have been adapted for TV and the movies, he participated in a stage adaptation only once, the original stage version of *Of Mice and Men* (see below). Horton Foote also adapted the novel for a 1992 play and film directed by and starring Gary Sinise.

Of Mice and Men was originally staged on Broadway in 1937 by George S. Kaufman at the Music Box Theatre, starring Broderick Crawford as Lennie, Wallace Ford as George, Will Geer, Sam Byrd, and Claire Luce.

Of Mice and Men (1939, UA, 106m/bw, **VHS/DVD**)☆☆☆☆½ **Sc:** John Steinbeck, Eugene Solow. **D/P:** Lewis Milestone. **Cam:** Norbert Brodine. **Cast:** Burgess Meredith, Lon Chaney Jr., Betty Field, Charles Bickford, Bob Steele, Roman Bohnen, Leigh Whipper, Noah Beery Jr., Oscar O'Shea, Granville Bates, Leona Roberts, Barbara Pepper, Helen Lynd. Meredith and Chaney deliver definitive performances as the crafty drifter and his huge and dimwitted pal, Lennie, in this poignant classic. The film was nominated for Oscars for Best Picture, Cinematography, Score (Aaron Copeland), Original Score (Copeland), and Sound.

- "...*the screenplay—credited to Eugene Solow, though Milestone claimed it as his own work—is remarkably faithful, beginning in gloom and foreboding and then courting tragedy as it studies some itinerant farmworkers during the Depression. Within the dual themes of the deeply loyal friendship between the simple-minded Lennie...and bright-as-a-button George...and the relationship between the boss's son and his bored wife...there is an honest portrait of life down on the farm: the ca-*

maraderie in the bunkhouse; the gossip in the washroom; the silent, vast meals; the beer-swilling Saturday night hops in town....Milestone's love of the piece is apparent and it was his best film after All Quiet on the Western Front. *Meredith and Chaney never had better roles, and Miss Field is the definitive floozie — not loose, just bored and empty-headed, courting disaster by hanging around the men."* (David Shipman, The Story of Cinema)

Of Mice and Men (1968, ABC, 120m/c) ☆☆☆½ **Sc:** John Hopkins. **D:** Ted Kotcheff. **P:** David Susskind. **Cast:** George Segal, Nicol Williamson, Joey Heatherton, Will Geer, Donald Moffat, Moses Gunn, Don Gordon, Dana Elcar, John Randolph, James Hall.

- *"...remains powerful drama, and that is one big justification for a video re-make....Nicol Williamson and George Segal braved comparison to Lon Chaney Jr. and Burgess Meredith, who were such perfect realizations of Lennie and George in the picture and — laying aside the question of which tandem was best — they were superb....this was far and away the most out-standing effort yet on ABC-TV's part to slow down the movie drain with taped remakes of vintage film scripts."* (Variety)

Michael Stewart

Born: August 1, 1929, New York, NY. **Died:** 1987
Tony Award-winning musicals: *Bye Bye Birdie* (1960),
    Hello, Dolly! (1964).

Michael Stewart began his career in the 1950s working on the same TV staff for Sid Caesar's *Your Show of Shows* with Woody Allen, Neil Simon, and other future luminaries. Stewart was best known as the author of the books for the musicals *Bye Bye Birdie* (1960) and *Hello, Dolly!* (1964) both of which won Tony Awards. Stewart also wrote the books for the musicals *George M!*, *I Love My Wife*, and *Carnival!*, a New York Drama Critics Circle Award winner. Along with writing partner Mark Bramble, he wrote the books for *42nd Street* and *Barnum*. Stewart also wrote the 1977 novel *Belle*.

For *Hello, Dolly!*, see **Thornton Wilder.**

Bye, Bye, Birdie was directed and choreographed on the Broadway stage in 1961 starring Dick Van Dyke, Chita Rivera, Paul Lynde, Kay Medford, and Michael J. Pollard. An Elvis-like heartthrob named Con-rad Birdie gets drafted into the Army. Meanwhile, a songwriter does triple duty, hooking Birdie for *The Ed Sullivan Show*, romancing a new girlfriend, and fending off his meddlesome mother. The show ran for 607 performances, initially at the Martin Beck Theatre.

Bye, Bye, Birdie (1963, Columbia, 112m/c, **VHS/DVD**) ☆☆☆ **Sc:** Irving Brecher. **D:** George Sidney. **P:** Fred Kohlmar. **Cam:** Joseph Biroc. **Cast:** Janet Leigh, Dick Van Dyke, Ann-Margret, Maureen Stapleton, Bobby Rydell, Paul Lynde, Jesse Pearson, Michael Evans, Ed Sullivan, Mary LaRoche, Robert Paige, Kim Darby, Lee Aaker, Frank Albertson, Cyril Delavanti. The wacky aspects are accentuated in this eccentric and exuberant exercise. A hit, it gave career boosts to all involved and became a community theatre favorite for many years.

- *"Credit George Sidney with directing one of the better fun and frolic tune packages. The adaptation of the successful legit musical comedy clearly called for lots of visuals, rather than just dialogue and straight storytelling....Strikingly important...is Ann-Margret. Singer, hoofer and cutie-pie, all wrapped up into one, she has the magnetism of early-vintage Judy Garland....Van Dyke displays a showbiz knowhow far more extensive than his television outings communicate."* (Variety)

Bye, Bye, Birdie (1995, ABC, 135m/c, **VHS**) ☆☆½ **Tp:** Michael Stewart. **D:** Gene Saks. **P:** Tim Bell, J. Boyce Harman Jr., Robert Halmi Sr. **Cast:** Jason Alexander, Vanessa L. Williams, Chynna Phillips, Tyne Daly, George Wendt, Mark Kudisch, Sally Mayes, Jason Gaffney, Blair Slater, Shelley S. Hunt, Brigitta Dau.

- *"...arrives...with its swooning teens, crinolines, bobby socks, and modest pleasures largely intact. Those are thin pleasures, though, that an attempt to prolong them here fails—despite sizzling work by Vanessa Williams in a key role—and they end well before the show does...[leaves] yawns for last."* (Howard Rosenberg, Los Angeles Times)

Preston Sturges
Edmond P. Biden
Born: August 29, 1898, Chicago, IL. **Died:** 1959.

Preston Sturges was educated in Germany and Switzerland and managed a store in Deauville, France, selling his mother's cosmetics line. At the outbreak of World War I, he joined the Air Corps. Following the war, he tried inventing, including the creation of "kissproof lipstick." He began playwriting during convalescence after the removal of his appendix. His second effort, *Strictly Dishonorable*, was a huge hit in 1929 and he followed its sale to Hollywood, where he became a screenwriter. His films in the early sound era included *The Power and the Glory* (1933) with Spencer Tracy, *We Live Again* (1934) with Fredric March, *Diamond Jim* (1935) with Edward Arnold and Jean Arthur, *Easy Living* (1937) with Arthur, *If I Were King* (1938) with Ronald Colman, and *Remember the Night* (1940) with Barbara Stanwyck and Fred MacMurray.

Paramount let Sturges direct his own screenplay for *The Great McGinty* (1940) and his success broke ground for his discipline, as John Huston and several other writers soon began directing their own movies. Sturges's run of superbly crafted social comedies filled with rapier wit and sparkling performances was nearly unparallelled in history. The streak included *The Lady Eve* (1941), *Sullivan's Travels* (1941), *The Palm Beach Story* (1942), *The Miracle of Morgan's Creek* (1944), *Hail the Conquering Hero* (1944), and *Unfaithfully Yours* (1948).

Child of Manhattan (1933, Columbia, 70m/bw) ☆☆½ **Sc:** Gertrude Purcell. **D:** Edward Buzzell. **P:** Harry Cohn. **Cam:** Ted Tetzlaff. **Cast:** John Boles, Nancy Carroll, Warburton Gamble, Clara Blandick, Jane Darwell, Betty Grable, Charles (Buck) Jones Gary Owen, Luis Alberni, Jessie Ralph, Tyler Brooke, Betty Kendall. Sturges's play about a pregnant nightclub taxi dancer who has an affair with a millionaire, then marries him, includes the death of the infant at birth, her Mexican divorce, the arrival of another suitor, and the millionaire's reclamation of his wife. The film —based on Sturges's 1932 play produced at New York's Fulton Theatre by Peggy Fears and featuring Dorothy Hall and Reginald Owen—obviously slipped under the wire before the Production Code was enforced in 1933.

- *"...has nothing new to report on the whirligig of metropolitan life. Nancy Carroll invests her role with flashes of good acting, but her performance is an individual triumph in a tiresome and routine film."* (Mordaunt Hall, The New York Times)

Strictly Dishonorable, which Sturges wrote in six days, was the most popular comedy of the 1929–30 Broadway season. It starred Carl Anthony, Edward J. MacNamara, and Muriel Kirkland under the direction of Brock Pemberton. It concerned a lecherous opera singer who has a whirlwind overnight affair with a naïve girl.

Strictly Dishonorable (1931, Universal, 91m/c)☆☆½ **Sc:** Gladys Lehman. **D:** John M. Stahl. **P:** Carl Laemmle Jr. **Cam:** Jackson Rose. **Cast:** Paul Lukas, Sidney Fox, Lewis Stone, George Meeker, Sidney Toler, William Ricciardi, Carlo Schipa.

- *"...[Lukas] was...oddly loaned to Universal and cast as Gus in the film version of Preston Sturges's great hit Strictly Dishonorable...He had difficulty with several of the brighter lines, but his comedic timing and sly humor put the part across, although the play was well laundered for the cinema."* (James Robert Parish, William T. Leonard, Hollywood Players: The Thirties)

Strictly Dishonorable (1951, MGM, 94m/bw) ☆☆ **Sc/D/P:** Norman Panama, Melvin Frank. **Cam:** Ray June. **Cast:** Enzio Pinza, Janet Leigh, Millard Mitchell, Maria Palmer, Gale Robbins, Esther Minciotti, Silvio Minciotti, Arthur Franz, Sandro Giglio, Hugh Sanders. After Pinza tanked in MGM's initial attempt to launch his stardom with the bomb *Mr. Imperium*, this remake was the studio's careful second step. The Production Code required the couple to marry after meeting.

- *"...the script, which the writers have freely and forcibly contrived from the old Preston Sturges comedy, virtually a classic of the stage, is not what you'd call exactly a masterpiece of wit and comic art. Where Mr. Sturges kept his saga of a most enchanting evening confined to a 'speakeasy' in the West 40s and to an overnight courtship between a panting Italian opera singer and a delicate flower of the South, the Messrs. Frank and Panama range more widely and perforce are more discreet....pure and polite domestic 'tease' in which the young wife, with the help of hubby's mama, tries to lure him as her spouse in more than name. With all due regard for the stern precepts of piety which compelled such restraint, we cannot regard this milky nonsense as a match for Mr. Sturges's bright play."* (Bosley Crowther, The New York Times)

Booth Tarkington
Newton Booth Tarkington
Born: July 29, 1869, Indianapolis, IN. **Died:** 1946.

Booth Tarkington was one of the great portrayers of Midwestern life and sensibility in two centuries and one of the most prolific and successful prose and play stylists in American letters. Two of the first four Pulitzer Prizes in Fiction went to Tarkington for his evocative works, *The Magnificent Ambersons* in 1919 and *Alice Adams* in 1922. He was published in six different decades and wrote 30 novels or novellas, 19 plays, and 171 short stories as well as movie scenarios and radio dramas and also contributed illustrations. James Woodress wrote of him, "Although he had more talent than most of his contemporaries, his work never quite achieved major significance, and he had to be content with a large rather than a discriminating audience."

Tarkington occasionally wrote plays in tandem, usually with Harry Leon Wilson, and also adapted some of his own fiction for the stage, as in the cases of *Monsieur Beaucaire* and *The Gentleman From Indiana*. Much of Tarkington's fiction was converted to the big and little screens, including memorable adaptations of the Pulitzer Prize winners—*Alice Adams* (1935) with George Stevens directing Katharine Hepburn and Fred MacMurray, and especially the critically resurrected *The Magnificent Ambersons* (1942) with Orson Welles directing an ensemble including Anne Baxter and Agnes Moorehead. More than a dozen films have been made from Tarkington's fiction, including at least four by Warner Bros. from his "Penrod" stories for children and young adults, lastly for *By the Light of the Silvery Moon* (1953) starring Doris Day.

Tarkington wrote several photoplays in the silent era, including the "Edgar" series: *Edgar and the Teacher's Pet* (1920), *Edgar's Hamlet* (1920), *Edgar, the Explorer* (1921), and *Get Rich Quick, Edgar* (1921). Tarkington's screenplays also included *Pied Piper Malone* (1924) and *The Man Who Found Himself* (1925).

Cameo Kirby concerns a Mississippi riverboat gambler who enters a crooked card game to help a girl's father, who's being taken advantage of by sharpies, and cleans out everyone, including the old man. But before he can make restitution, the father commits suicide, complicating his romantic relationship with the girl. The 1909 Broadway presentation starring Dustin Farnum ran for only 24 performances at the Hackett Theatre.

Cameo Kirby (1914, Paramount, bw/silent) **Sc:** Clara Beranger, William de Mille. **D:** Oscar Apfel, Cecil B. DeMille. **P:** Jesse L. Lasky. **Cast:** Dustin Farnum, Fred Montague, James Neill, Jode Mullally, Winifred Kingston, Dick Le Reno, Ernest Joy.

Cameo Kirby (1923, Fox, bw/silent) ☆☆☆½ **Sc:** Robert N. Lee. **D:** John Ford. **P:** William Fox. **Cam:** George Schneiderman. **Cast:** John Gilbert, Gertrude Olmstead, Alan Hale, Eric Mayne, Jean Arthur, W.E. Lawrence, Richard Tucker, Phillips Smalley, Jack McDonald, Eugenie Forde, Frank Baker. This film was significant as both a major stepping stone in Ford's career and as the first substantial role played by Arthur.

• "*Cameo Kirby is interesting if only for the reason of its being the first film credited to John Ford rather than the earlier, pulpier Jack Ford.* Motion Picture World *commented: 'Director John Ford has been especially skillful in framing each scene to artistic advantage.' Jean Mitry regards* Cameo Kirby *as a turning point in Ford's career...And certainly at least vestiges of* Cameo Kirby *survived for Ford in John Carradine's courtly Hatfield in* Stagecoach." (Andrew Sarris, The John Ford Movie Mystery)

Cameo Kirby (1930, Fox, bw) ☆☆☆ **Sc:** Marion Orth. **D:** Irving Cummings. **Cam:** George Eastman, L. William O'Connell. **Cast:** J. Harold Murray, Norma Terris, Douglas Gilmore, Myrna Loy, Robert Edeson, Stepin Fetchit, George MacFarlane, John Hyams, Carrie Daumery, Beulah Hall Jones. The musical version took advantage of new sound-recording techniques. Murray sang "Romance," "After a Million Dreams," "Tankard and Bowl," and "Home Is Heaven."

• "*There is an easygoing charm about the scenes in the audible pictorial conception of* Cameo Kirby...*affords genuine entertainment with its colorful glimpses of life in 1850 New Orleans and aboard river steamboats...There is an abundance of beauty in the scenes of the carnival and in the flashes of the paddle-wheel boats. Mr. Murray's agreeable singing is sometime accompanied by a chorus of voices...*" (Mordaunt Hall, The New York Times)

Clarence (1937, Paramount, 64m/bw) ☆☆ **Sc:** Grant Garett, Seena Owen. **D:** George Archainbaud. **Cam:** George T. Clemens. **Cast:** Roscoe Karns, Eleanor Whitney, Eugene Pallette, Johnny Downs, Inez Courtney, Spring Byington, Charlotte Wynters, Theodore von Eltz. A mysterious stranger drifts into the lives of a wealthy family, influencing one and all in various ways.

- *"A lightweight aimed for double bills,* Clarence *will have a tough climb to reach that level…pic itself won't roll any audiences in the aisle. About all that can be said for it is it keeps the screen occupied for 60 minutes — occupied but not alive."* (Variety)

The Country Cousin (1919, Selznick, bw/silent) **Sc:** R. Cecil Smith. **D:** Alan Crosland. **Cam:** William F. Wagner. **Cast:** Elaine Hammerstein, Margaret Seddon, Lumsden Hare, Genevieve Tobin, Reginald Sheffield, Walter McGrail, Bigelow Cooper, Helen Montrose, Gilbert Rooney. This was an adaptation of the 1916 play that Tarkington wrote with Julian Street called *The Ohio Lady*, published the same year as *The Country Cousin*, and produced again in New York under that title in 1917.

The Gentleman From Indiana (1915, Paramount and Julia Crawford Ivers, bw/silent) ☆☆☆☆ **Sc:** J.C. Ivers, Frank Lloyd. **D/P:** Frank Lloyd. **Cam:** Fred Dobson. **Cast:** Dustin Farnum, Elsie Cort, Juan de la Cruz, Howard Davies, Helen Jerome Eddy, C. Norman Hammond, Winifred Kingston, Page Peters, Joe Ray, Herbert Standing. Tarkington's original novel was his reaction to East Coast snobbishness toward supposedly "backwoods" Indiana. The story became a best seller and a hit play.

- *"A more sympathetic and interesting picturization of a famous story seldom has been offered to photoplay patrons, for which the author of the scenario, the director, and the able cast headed by Dustin Farnum may divide the credit…admirable production."* (Lynde Denig, The Moving Picture World)

The Magnolia, Tarkington's play of the old South that was bowlderized for many future adaptations, was originally produced on Broadway in 1923 and starred James Bradbury and Leo Carillo.

The Fighting Coward (1924, Paramount, 66m/bw/silent) ☆☆☆ **Sc:** Walter Woods. **D/P:** James Cruze. **Cam:** Karl Brown. **Cast:** Ernest Torrence, Mary Astor, Noah Beery, Cullen Landis, Phyllis Haver, G. Raymond Nye, Richard Neill, Helen Dunbar.

- *"…regrettably, a disappointment…Mr. Cruze seems to have missed the point…Mr. Cruze has exaggerated sentiment at the expense of drama. Hereafter I shall cultivate a gloomy outlook upon the film industry as a whole. I shall expect nothing. And, as a result, what merit I do encounter will be just so much velvet."* (Robert E. Sherwood, The New Yorker)

River of Romance (1929, Paramount, 78m/bw) ☆☆☆ **Sc:** Ethel Doherty, Joseph L. Mankiewicz, Don Totheroh, John V.A. Weaver. **D:** Richard Wallace. **Cam:** Victor Milner. **Cast:** Charles "Buddy" Rigers, Mary Brian, Wallace Beery, Henry B. Walthall, June Collyer, Fred Kohler, Natalie Kingston, Walter McGrail, Anderson Lawler.

- "...*cumbersome at first, due to satirical thrust at the old code of the South, but once it hits its stride, the picture moves rapidly, boasting some fine comedy supplied by the inimitable Wallace Beery. It's good entertainment.*" (Film Daily)

Mississippi (1935, Paramount, 80m/bw) ☆☆☆½ **Sc:** Claude Binyon, Jack Cunningham, Francis Martin. **D:** A. Edward Sutherland. **P:** Arthur Hornblow Jr. **Cam:** Charles Lang. **Cast:** Bing Crosby, W.C. Fields, Joan Bennett, Gail Patrick, Queenie Smith, Claude Gillingwater, John Miljan, Fred Kohler, Edward Pawley, Theresa Maxwell Conover, King Baggot, Elizabeth Patterson, Ann Sheridan. Crosby played the suitor of a plantation lass in the old South. He refuses to duel the girl's former beau and ends up singing on rascally Fields's riverboat.

- "*Visually a handsome production, with stylish groupings and interesting camera angles...the film is more than a little disjointed, certain sequences tailing off abruptly or failing to build as promised, so that one suspects a good deal of post-production editorial tampering. Possibly it was thought that the mixture of charm and subtlety (from the original) and the more traditional Fieldsian humor didn't mix, and in view of the great personal success that Crosby was scoring, attempts may have been made to divert the film even more in his direction.*" (*William K. Everson,* The Art of W.C. Fields)

Mister Antonio (1929, Tiffany-Stahl, bw) ☆☆ **Sc:** Fanny Hatton, Frederic Hatton. **D:** James Flood, Frank Reicher. **P:** John M. Stahl. **Cam:** Ernest Miller **Cast:** Leo Carillo, Virginia Valli, Gareth Hughes, Frank Reicher, Eugenie Besserer, Franklin Lewis, Viola Louie. Carillo plays an organ grinder who falls in love with the daughter of a corrupt mayor.

- "...*will do great with the kids, but it's hardly a picture for adults...too illogically old fashioned, and maybe monotonous.*" (Variety)

Monsieur Beaucaire, one of Tarkington's first efforts, was serialized in *McClure's* in 1899, published as a novel in 1900, and adapted for the stage in 1901 by Tarkington and Evelyn Greenleaf Sutherland. The play was revived in 1904 and 1912. Tarkington's original story was set in 18th century Bath, England, where the Duke of Orleans poses as a barber to expose British gentry as snobbish.

Monsieur Beaucaire (1924, Paramount, 106m/bw/silent) ☆☆☆ **Sc:** Forrest Halsey. **D/P:** Sidney Ollcott. **Cam:** Harry Fischbeck. **Cast:** Rudolph Valentino, Bebe Daniels, Lois Wilson, Doris Kenyon, Lowell

Sherman, Paulette Duval, John Davidson, Oswald Yorke, Flora Finch, Louis Waller, Ian Maclaren, Templar Powell, H. Cooper Cliffe, Downing Clarke, Yvonne Hughes, Harry Lee, Florence O'Denishawn.

- "...*unquestionably a 'money' picture...For those who think this film star has lost his drawing power,...Valentino has contributed as neat a piece of work as he has ever done before a camera.*" (Variety)

Monte Carlo (1930, Paramount, 90m/bw) ☆☆☆ **Sc:** Ernest Vajda, Vincent Lawrence. **D/P:** Ernst Lubitsch. **Cam:** Victor Milner. **Cast:** Jeanette MacDonald, Jack Buchanan, Claud Allister, ZaSu Pitts, Tyler Brooke, John Roche, Lionel Belmore, Albert Conti, John Garden, Billy Bevan, David Percy, John Carroll. This production combined elements from *Monsieur Beaucaire* with those from the Hans Muller play *The Blue Coat*. The film is about a broke countess fleeing her husband-to-be who checks into the Monte Carlo Hotel. She hires a gent she believes is a hairdresser to do her hair, who immediately develops a crush.

- "...*mainly notable for [Lubitsch's] staging of 'Beyond the Blue Horizon,' sung by Jeanette MacDonald in a train, its music synchronized to the train's movements and those of peasants in the fields—who join in with the singer. As the count who poses as a valet—to be near the lady—Jack Buchanan is no Chevalier, the ideal exponent of Lubitsch's conception of witty and charming male lust.*" (David Shipman, The Story of Cinema)

Monsieur Beaucaire (1946, Paramount, 93m/bw) ☆☆☆ **Sc:** Melvin Frank, Norman Panama. **D:** George Marshall. **P:** Paul Jones. **Cam:** Lionel Lindon. **Cast:** Bob Hope, Joan Caulfield, Patric Knowles, Marjorie Reynolds, Cecil Kellaway, Joseph Schildkraut, Reginald Owen, Constance Collier, Hillary Brooke, Fortunio Bonanova, Douglass Dumbrille, Mary Nash, Leonid Kinskey, Howard Freeman.

- "*Booth Tarkington fans, who are legion, and Bob Hope fans, who are more so, can be invited, urged, even exhorted, to attend...this period comedy...it's an expensively and expertly produced travesty on the Tarkington novel, hilariously funny at its peak and dull only long enough and at appropriately spaced intervals, for an audience to get its breath back.*" (Motion Picture Herald)

Samuel Taylor

Samuel Albert Tanenbaum
Born: June 13, 1912, Chicago, IL. **Died:** 2000.

Samuel Taylor's plays include *The Happy Time* (1950), which he adapted from Robert Fontaine's novel, as well as *No Strings* (1962), *Beekman*

Place (1964) and *Legend* (1976). He was fortunate to have Billy Wilder adapt two of his plays into movies (see below).

Avanti! (1972, UA, 144m/c, **VHS**) ☆☆½ **Sc:** Billy Wilder, I.A.L. Diamond. **D/P:** Billy Wilder. **Cam:** Luigi Kuveiller. **Cast:** Jack Lemmon, Juliet Mills, Clive Revill, Edward Andrews, Gianfranco Barra, Franco Angrisano, Pippo Franco, Giselda Castrini. Wilder went back to a Taylor play nearly two decades after his success with *Sabrina Fair* (see below). *Avanti!* ran for only 21 performances on Broadway in 1968 in a production starring Robert Reed, Jennifer Hilary, and Betsy von Furstenberg. The story concerns an American blueblood who discovers that his father's island vacations are really staged to continue an extramarital tryst. The son proceeds to fall in love with the mistress's daughter. Not one of the better Wilder/Lemmon offerings, this film was notable for having the stars appear nude.

- *"Romantic comedy from another time...The moment the stage is set, we can creak our way to the ending, which arrives an eternity of 144 minutes later. Jack Lemmon, as the chap who thaws within his own limits; Juliet Mills as the charmingly, womanly girl with an endearing (at least to me) weight problem, and Clive Revill, as the all-understanding hotel manager, are all admirable..." (Judith Crist, New York)*

The Happy Time (1952, Columbia, 94m/bw) **Sc:** Earl Felton. **D:** Richard Fleischer. **P:** Stanley Kramer. **Cam:** Charles Lawton, Jr. **Cast:** Charles Boyer, Louis Jourdan, Marsha Hunt, Linda Christian, Kurt Kasznar, Bobby Driscoll, Maurice Marsca, Marcel Dalio, Eugene Borden, Jeanette Nolan, Richard Erdman, Marlene Cameron. The play, which Taylor based on the novel by Robert Fontaine, debuted in 1950 and ran for 614 performances featuring Claude Dauphin, Eva Gabor, Kurt Kasznar, Marlene Cameron, and Richard Hart. Fleischer directed this unsentimental and frank—for its era—picture as a sort of postwar antidote to the *I Remember Mama* school of family portraiture as a 12-year-old boy comes of age in 1924 Ottawa, Canada.

- *"A further problem with* The Happy Time *is the baldness of the options presented: we and the boy seem faced with either unbridled but damnably good-natured lasciviousness on the one hand, or a sort of angry repression on the other. Against these extremes, Boyer, as the embodiment of balanced wisdom and—although we can only infer this—of sane experience, shows his son The Enlightened Way to grow up: seeing sex as Part of Life, whereas Uncle Desmonde, it is implied, sees life as part of sex, and grandpa sees life and sex as virtually synonymous. (Never has so old and frail an actor as Dalio seemed weighted with such an affliction as this astonishingly geriatric case of satyriasis.)" (Donald Spoto, Stanley Kramer: Filmmaker)*

Promise at Dawn (1970, AVCO Embassy, 101m/c, **VHS**) ☆☆½ **Sc/D/P:** Jules Dassin. **Cam:** Jean Badal. **Cast:** Melina Mercouri, Assaf Dayan, Francois Raffoul, Despo, Fernand Gravey, Perlo Vita (Jules Dasson), Jean Martin, Elspeth March, Rene Clermont, Maria Machado, Jacqueline Porel, Julie Dassin, Carol Cole. Taylor's 1961 play, *First Love*, was based on Romain Gary's autobiographical novel, *Promise at Dawn*, about his own childhood and adolescence. The film focuses on his resourceful mother, an actress. The film marked the seventh teaming of the married couple Dassin and Mercouri. Dassin used elements from both the novel and the play.

- *"Jules Dassin has tried to turn Romain Gary's nostalgic celebration of his loving mother into a vehicle for Melina Mercouri. But she seems, as usual, to be playing a normal, hearty, hot nymphomaniac. The different parts of the past run together in a blur in this generally unsatisfying film."* (Pauline Kael, 5,001 Nights at the Movies)

Sabrina Fair was a hit of the 1953 Broadway season, starring Joseph Cotten and Scott McKay as the multimillionaire Larabee brothers—the older, business-oriented Linus and the younger playboy, David. Both of them become smitten with their chauffeur's lovely daughter, played by Margaret Sullavan, after she returns from school in Europe.

Sabrina (1954, Paramount, 113m/bw, **VHS/DVD**) ☆☆☆☆ **Sc:** Billy Wilder, Samuel Taylor, Ernest Lehman. **D/P:** Billy Wilder. **Cam:** Charles Lang. **Cast:** Humphrey Bogart, Audrey Hepburn, William Holden, Walter Hampden, John Williams, Martha Hyer, Joan Vohs, Marcel Hillaire, Marcel Dalio, Nella Walker, Francis X. Bushman, Ellen Corby, Marjorie Bennett, Emory Parnell, Nancy Kulp, Paul Harvey, Marion Ross, Kay Riehl. The luster of the star trio and Wilder's deft touch helped put over one of the biggest box-office hits of its year. Hepburn is Hepburn, Bogart avoids Bogie-isms and plays the role of the industrialist, and Holden's playboy act appears as effortless as it probably was. A sparkling, glossy, romantic comedy, for which Bogart was cast against type as a last-minute replacement for Cary Grant.

- *"Sabrina is the prick that bursts the fair bubble that was Audrey Hepburn in Roman Holiday. Surely the vogue for asexuality can go no further than this weird hybrid with butchered hair. Of course none of this would really matter if the charm and grace were sincere, but I am afraid she is letting her calculation show....[Bogart] is a frail, lisping old man."* (Clayton Cole, Films and Filming)

- *"This is never less than a glittering entertainment, but somehow a certain measure of lead has found its way into the formula."* (Time)

Sabrina (1995, Paramount, 127m/c, **VHS/DVD**) ☆☆½ **Sc:** David Rayfiel, Barbara Benedek. **D:** Sydney Pollack. **P:** Sydney Pollack,

Scott Rudin. **Cam:** Giuseppe Rotunno. **Cast:** Harrison Ford, Julia Ormond, Greg Kinnear, Nancy Marchand, Angie Dickinson, John Wood, Richard Crenna, Lauren Holly, Fanny Ardant, Dana Ivey, Miriam Colon, Elizabeth Franz, Paul Giamatti, Ira Wheeler, Ronald L. Schwary. This film was more of a Hollywood attempt to have Ford anchor a three-cornered romantic comedy to box-office glory the way he did with *Working Girl* (1988) than anything else, but the results came up short. Glossy and slick, it doesn't have the beneath-the-skin reach of the Wilder film. A better supporting cast is seen in this version, but to middling effect.

- *"I'm doing a remake for the first time, which may be the dumbest thing I've ever done...I wanted to work with Harrison Ford and that's finally what it came down to....it's a film I said no to several times and then Harrison called me personally and I couldn't say no to him. I think he's marvelous, particularly in love stories. I like to do love stories and that's the other reason I guess I agreed to it."* (*Sydney Pollack in* The Directors: Take One *by Robert J. Emery*)

Samuel Taylor & Cornelia Otis Skinner

Taylor:
Born: June 13, 1912, Chicago, IL. **Died:** 2000.

Skinner:
Born: May 30, 1901, Chicago, IL. **Died:** 1979.

A writer, actress, director, and producer, Cornelia Otis Skinner's roots in the American theatre go back to *Blood and Sand* (1921), in which she performed alongside her father, the matinee idol Otis Skinner. As a playwright, she wrote *The Wives of Henry VIII* (1931), *The Loves of Charles II* (1933), *Mansion on the Hudson* (1935), *Empress Eugenie* (1937), *Edna His Wife* (1937), and *Paris '90* (1952). As an actress, she starred in the New York stage productions of *Lady Windermere's Fan*, *Major Barbara*, *The Searching Wind*, and *Candida*. Renowned for her wit, Skinner wrote a number of humorous books about her life, of which the most famous was *Our Hearts Were Young and Gay*. She wrote biographies of Sarah Bernhardt (*Madame Sarah*) and the playwriting team of Howard Lindsay and Russel Crouse (*Life with Lindsay and Crouse*).

The Pleasure of His Company (1961, Paramount, 115m/c) ☆☆½
Sc: Samuel Taylor. **D:** George Seaton. **P:** William Perlberg. **Cam:**

Robert Burks. **Cast:** Fred Astaire, Debbie Reynolds, Lilli Palmer, Tab Hunter, Gary Merrill, Charles Ruggles, Harold Fong, Elvia Allman. When a San Francisco debutante accepts the hand of a Napa Valley rancher, her estranged father shows up and appears to want to woo back his ex-wife, who's remarried. The play opened on Broadway at the Longacre Theatre in 1958 directed by and starring Cyril Ritchard with Skinner, George Peppard, Charles Ruggles, Dolores Hart, Walter Abel, and Jerry Fujikawa. The Perlberg/Seaton team tried for a polished, Philip Barry-styled approach with the film, but the Taylor/Skinner material, which was written as a stage vehicle for her and Ritchard, was just too thin.

- *"...Fred Astaire's ageless vitality and urbanity...manage to keep a stagy, static, drawing-room comedy bouncing along to its anticlimax — with a major asset, by the way, Lilli Palmer, a high-stakes contender herself in the enduring charm department. So slickly pro are Astaire and Miss Palmer, in fact, that you might not even notice Debbie Reynolds being just a bit long in the tooth for the ingenue act as Astaire's young daughter."* (Judith Crist, Judith Crist's TV Guide to the Movies)

John-Michael Tebelak
Died: 1985.

Godspell (1973, Columbia, 103m/c, **VHS/DVD**) **Sc/D:** David Greene. **P:** Edgar Lansbury, Kenneth Utt. **Cam:** Richard G. Heimann. **Cast:** Victor Garber, Katie Hanley, David Haskell, Merrell Jackson, Robin Lamont, Jerry Sroka, Joanne Jonas, Gilmer McCormick, Lynne Thigpen, John-Michael Tebelak. A modern-day version of the Gospel According to Matthew begins with John the Baptist gathering young New Yorkers together to follow Jesus, and they become a roving troupe enacting parables through song and dance.

- *"I went to Godspell with some distaste and left with some, but in between there were moments of real pleasure....sounded like a dehydrated (just add holy water) version of Jesus Christ Superstar. In effect this musical is just that: it works up bits of Gospel (St. Matthew) in pop music, pop culture, and pop attitudes; but it's less offensive than JCS, because it transposes the story to the present...In anything remotely resembling something that could begin to be called a religious sense, Godspell is a zero; it's just Age of Aquarius Love fed through a quasi-Godspell funnel, with a few half-hearted supernatural touches."* (Stanley Kauffmann, The New Republic)

Howard Teichmann

Born: January 22, 1916, Chicago, IL. **Died:** 1987.

Both of Howard Teichmann's main successes as a writer involved his friend, the legendary George S. Kaufman, with whom he co-wrote the 1953 Broadway smash *The Solid Gold Cadillac* and about whom he wrote the biography *George S. Kaufman: An Intimate Portrait* in 1972, 11 years after the great playwright's death. The book started him on a new career late in life and his subsequent biographies were *Smart Aleck: The Wit, World and Life of Alexander Woollcott, Alice: The Life and Times of Alice Roosevelt Longworth,* and *Fonda: My Life; As Told to Howard Teichmann.* Teichmann's plays include the adaptation of Nathaniel West's novel *Miss Lonelyhearts, The Girls in 509, A Rainy Day in Newark,* and *Smart Aleck: Alexander Woollcott at 8:40.* A prolific radio writer of the 1940s, Teichmann wrote for *Mercury Theatre of the Air, Texaco Star Theatre, Helen Hayes Theatre, Gertrude Lawrence Review,* and *Ford Theatre of the Air,* among others.

Lonelyhearts (1958, UA, 108m/bw, **VHS**) ☆☆☆ **Sc/P:** Dore Schary. **D:** Vincent J. Donohue. **Cam:** John Alton. **Cast:** Montgomery Clift, Robert Ryan, Myrna Loy, Dolores Hart, Maureen Stapleton, Frank Maxwell, Jackie Coogan, Mike Kellin, Onslow Stevens, Frank Overton, Charles Wagenheim. Teichmann adapted Nathanael West's novella *Miss Lonelyhearts* into a 1957 play that ran for 12 performances at Broadway's Music Box Theatre starring Henderson Forsythe, Pat O'Brien, William Hickey, Fritz Weaver, Anne Meara, and Pippa Scott. In the film, Clift is a would-be reporter who's assigned to what used to be called a "sob-sister" column, and he becomes too deeply involved in his subjects' problems.

- *"Clift is fascinating in this jumbled film as he plays a man of emotional indecision who must arbitrate the emotional destinies of nameless others. Donahue does a commendable job with a meaningful but multi-directional script."* (J.R. Nash, S.R. Ross, The New York Times)

The Solid Gold Cadillac (1956, Columbia, 99m/c, **VHS**) ☆☆☆ **Sc:** Abe Burrows. **D:** Richard Quine. **P:** Fred Kohlmar. **Cam:** Charles Lang. **Cast:** Judy Holliday, Paul Douglas, John Williams, Fred Clark, Hiram Sherman, Neva Patterson, Arthur O'Connell, Ralph Dumke, Ray Collins, George Burns, Madge Blake, Suzanne Alexander, Richard Deacon. This Kaufman/Teichmann satire of big business, about a small shareholder in a large corporation who begins asking disconcerting questions, became one of Holliday's more agreeable star turns.

- *"...needed to be no more than brisked along, sustained by its dialogue and satire...Judy Holliday crackled as the small investor...Hardly too sharp as*

commentary on capitalism, it was a merry study in underdoggery rampant."
Gordon Bow, Hollywood in the Fifties)

Steve Tesich

Stoyan Tesich
Born: September 29, 1942, Uzice, Yugoslavia. **Died:** 1996.

Steve Tesich's plays include *Division Street* (1980) and *The Speed of Dark-*
ness (1991). He arrived in the United States at the age of 14 and settled
with his father in East Chicago, Indiana. Tesich began writing plays
while studying at Columbia University. He received an Academy Award
for writing the screenplay for the Midwestern coming-of-age bicycling
movie *Breaking Away* (1979). His screenplays include those for *Eyewit-*
ness (1981) with Sigourney Weaver, Arthur Penn's *Four Friends* (1981),
the adaptation of John Irving's *The World According to Garp* (1982) with
its remarkable ensemble led by Robin Williams and Glenn Close, *Amer-*
ican Flyers (1985), and *Eleni* (1985) with John Malkovich.

The Carpenters (1974, PBS, 60m/c) *Hollywood Television Theatre* ☆☆½
Tp: Steve Tesich. **D:** Norman Lloyd. **P:** Norman Lloyd, George Turpin.
Cast: Vincent Gardenia, Joseph Hardy, John Korkes, Kitty Winn,
Marge Redmond. The play was first produced at St. Clement's Church
in New York City in 1970. It concerns the generation gap in a family liv-
ing in the Pacific Northwest.

- *"It was a very tough play, seemingly naturalistic but very much influenced*
  by Gunther Grass, which became evident when the house started listing
  and flooding." (Norman Lloyd, Stages: Of Life in Theatre, Film and
  Television)

Nourish the Beast (1974, PBS, 90m/c) *Hollywood Television Theatre* **Tp:**
Steve Tesich. **D/P:** Norman Lloyd. **Cast:** Eileen Brennan, John Randolph, John Beck, Pamela Bellwood, Will Lee, Randy Kim, Geoffrey
Scott, Kenneth Tigar, James Green. Tesich's play was first presented on
the stage in 1973. It concerns the black-caped Goya, a woman who has
buried three husbands and whose fourth is convinced he's dying while
she interviews prospects to be the fifth. Her noisy household—hysterical daughter, whining grandfather, depressed adopted son—occasionally stops to check out an apparently huge dog outside the window
known as the "beast," which howls off screen.

- *"Mr. Tesich's comedy of Saroyanesque eccentricities is often very*
  funny....Mr. Tesich, who was born and raised in Yugoslavia, never stops
  treating his characters as little more than amusing and mildly interesting

specimens. They [mill] about with neither artistic or philosophical anchor. They are reduced to routines. Some work. A lot don't....Goya goes about her organizing, badgering and lecturing with zany relish. But in terms of television, Maude *does it better on her weekly series, and is usually more to the comedic point."* (John J. O'Connor, The New York Times)

- *"As rash a bunch of eccentrics as can be imagined—it is as if the spirit of Kaufman and Hart has found its reincarnation in Tesich's oddball comedy work—there seems little that binds them together....Tesich's play is also full of ominous touches—like the monstrous dog Dodo that howls off screen—and muddled meanings, which are probably best ignored in deference to its sense of lunatic fun."* (Gregg Kilday, Los Angeles Times)

Ernest Thompson

Born: November 6, 1950, Bellows Falls, Vermont.

Ernest Thompson won the 1981 Academy Award for adapting his own play *On Golden Pond* to the screen. His other screenplays include those for the 1988 movies *Sweet Hearts Dance* with Don Johnson and Susan Sarandon and *1969*, which he also directed. He wrote the made-for-TV movies *Take Me Home Again* (1994), *The West Side Waltz* (1995), and *Out of Time* (2000). An occasional actor, he played roles in the 1974 TV movie *F. Scott Fitzgerald and the Last of the Belles* and Bob Fosse's *Star 80* (1983).

On Golden Pond spends a summer with the Thayer family at their lakeside summer cottage in Pennsylvania. The family is tightened by the fading cantankerous patriarch's friendship with a young boy and his reconciliation with his adult daughter. The 1979 play featured Tom Aldredge, Frances Sternhagen, and Barbara Andres.

On Golden Pond (1981, ITC/IPC, 109m/c, **VHS/DVD**) **Sc:** Ernest Thompson. **D:** Mark Rydell. **P:** Bruce Gilbert. **Cam:** Billy Williams. **Cast:** Henry Fonda, Katharine Hepburn, Jane Fonda, Doug McKeon, Dabney Coleman. The film's pedigreed cast guilds the material, which is often warm and funny. In a case of art imitating life, Henry Fonda died the summer after his performance earned him the Oscar for Best Actor. The film also won Oscars for Best Actress (Hepburn, her fourth win) and Screenplay and was nominated for Best Picture, Director, Supporting Actress (Jane Fonda), Score, and Cinematography.

- *"In any season,* On Golden Pond *would be welcome....addresses itself seriously and intelligently without sermon or sociology to an inescapable human issue: in this case finding a decent ending for a life."* (Time)
- *"The movie...is still American cheese, but its stars...add more than color to this pasteurized product.* On Golden Pond *now has the bite of good old*

cheddar....Miss Fonda, a brisk comedienne when her lines are good and a no-nonsense actress even when they aren't, survives her not-great role in On Golden Pond, *even the kind of awful family reconciliation scene that happens with far more frequency in second-rate domestic dramas than in life.*" (Vincent Canby, The New York Times)

- "*This isn't material for actors, no matter what their age. It's material for milking tears from an audience. Hepburn and Fonda are playing America's aged sweethearts—A Married Couple for All Seasons.*" (Pauline Kael, The New Yorker)

On Golden Pond (2001, CBS, 100m/c) **Tp:** Ernest Thompson. **D:** Martin Pasetta Jr., Ernest Thompson. **P:** Samuel J. Paul. **Cast:** Julie Andrews, Christopher Plummer, Glenne Headly, Sam Robards, Brett Cullen, Will Rothhaar. The show, which was broadcast live, was nominated for an Emmy for its Art Direction.

- "*...I had a nightmare flash: Will we be watching this again in 20 years with Mel Gibson and Michelle Pfeiffer as lovable old coots? Then again, 20 years later, with Johnny Depp and Gwyneth Paltrow? This mediocre play does seem indestructible—and irresistable to actors of a certain age and to audiences...At least Julie Andrews and Christopher Plummer, with admirable finesse, brought a crisp astringency to the proceedings, which made the play's sentimentality bearable....The live production gimmick seemed beside the point....The piece had neither the deliberate artifice of theatre nor the burnished authenticity of film.*" (Julie Salamon, The New York Times)

James Thurber & Elliott Nugent

Thurber:
James Grover Thurber
Born: December 8, 1894, Columbus, OH. **Died:** 1961.

Nugent:
Born: September 20, 1896, Dover, OH. **Died:** 1980.

Primarily a humorist and cartoonist, long associated with *The New Yorker*, James Thurber's "most serious work, though a comedy," according to Martin Seymour-Smith, was his play written with Elliott Nugent, *The Male Animal* (see below). He wrote the seminal send-ups *Is Sex Necessary?* (1929), with E.B. White, lampooning sexology, and *Let Your Mind Alone* (1937), a grapple with psychoanalysis. Collections are *The Thurber Carnival* (1945) and *The Thurber Album* (1952).

Thurber's short pieces were adapted more than a dozen times for TV. *The Catbird Seat* was done three times and *The Greatest Man in the World* twice, the latter version, starring Brad Davis and Carol Kane, aired on

PBS's *American Short Story* series. Thurber's TV originals included *This Little Kitty Stayed Cool* with Carol Channing for *Omnibus* in 1953. A whimsical series of 25 episodes based on Thurber stories was *My World —and Welcome to It*, which aired on NBC from 1969 to 1970 and starred William Windom as a Thurber-like character.

Elliott Nugent directed 31 movies, acted in 18, and wrote nine. He was involved in more than two dozen Broadway productions as a producer, director, writer, and actor.

The Male Animal was written by Thurber in tandem with Elliott Nugent, who also directed the first film adapted from it. The 1940 Broadway play featured Nugent as a college professor who faces two crises: his jealousy over his wife's fawning treatment of an old college football star, and his insistence on reading a politically controversial treatise to his students for solely its literary quality against the administration's wishes. The play co-starred Gene Tierney, Leon Ames, and Don DeFore.

The Male Animal (1942, Warner Bros., 101m/bw) ☆☆☆ **Sc:** Julius J. Epstein, Philip G. Epstein, Stephen Morehouse Avery. **D:** Elliott Nugent. **P:** Wolfgang Reinhardt. **Cam:** Arthur Edeson. **Cast:** Henry Fonda, Olivia De Havilland, Joan Leslie, Jack Carson, Hattie McDaniel, Don DeFore, Eugene Pallette, Herbert Anderson.

- *"...combines Fonda's two major images of the period: the pathetically comical, stepped-upon character and the man forced by circumstances to becomes champion of human rights...Fonda sparkles in his bemused sarcasm toward football, his uncontrollable jealousy, and his long drunk scene in which he extols behaving toward women and rivals like a 'male animal,' then ineffectually attempts to fight Carson. But while the film is a good satire of athlete worship and machismo, it can't support its serious pretensions about academic freedom..."* (Michael Kerbel, *Henry Fonda*)

She's Working Her Way Through College (1952, Warner Bros., 101m/c) ☆☆½ **Sc:** Peter Milne. **D:** H. Bruce Humberstone. **P:** William Jacobs. **Cam:** Wilfrid M. Cline. **Cast:** Virginia Mayo, Ronald Reagan, Phyllis Thaxter, Gene Nelson, Don DeFore, Patrice Wymore, Roland Winters, Raymond Greenleaf, Norman Bartold, Amanda Randolph, Henrietta Taylor, Eve Miller, Hope Sansbury. In this musical version of Thurber's play, Mayo is the stripper Garters Gertie, who aspires to be a writer. She enrolls in college, where a professor observes his wife warming up to her old beau, a former football star. A sequel, *She's Back on Broadway* (1953), reteamed Mayo and Nelson.

- *"Although possessing little of the intellectual and sentimental impact of* The Male Animal, *the musical version is diverting entertainment, which manages to retain the original's plea for academic rights, while parading several pleasing but unmemorable song-and-dance routines. Ronald Reagan ap-*

pears to advantage as the mild-mannered professor, and he is especially good in the protracted drunken sequence played by Fonda in the previous film. Reagan admits that the picture was really a showcase for the musical abilities of the delightful Virginia Mayo..." (Tony Thomas, The Films of Ronald Reagan)

The Male Animal (1958, CBS, 90m/c) *Playhouse 90* ☆☆☆ **Tp:** Don M. Mankiewicz. **D:** Vincent Donohue. **Cast:** Andy Griffith, Ann Rutherford, Edmond O'Brien, Charles Ruggles, Gale Gordon, Dick Sargent. This was one of the initial comedy productions on CBS's prestige series, which was mostly known for its dramas. O'Brien played the former football star.

- "*...delightful frolic with all the inherent values of natural humor....dated comedy doesn't necessarily stale in its appreciation and here was a case in point raised to a high level of wit and raillery by the expertness of its provocateur and sharp direction of Vincent Donohue....Andy Griffith was as perfect a foil for the role as the authors...would have chose themselves. The play revolves around him and he kept it spinning with high RPM speed....For Griffith, it was a romp...*" (Variety)

The Male Animal was also produced in a 60-minute version in 1950 for an installment of *Robert Montgomery Presents* starring co-author Nugent and Martha Scott.

Tom Topor

Born: 1938, Vienna, Austria.

A former newspaperman who wrote for the *New York Daily News*, *The New York Times*, and *The New York Post*, Tom Topor began seeing his one-act plays produced in 1969 with the Off-Off Broadway productions of *The Playpen* and *Up the Hill*. *Answers* was staged in 1973. He wrote the screenplay for *The Accused* (1988), which he reconstructed from an actual New England gang-rape incident, and for which Jodie Foster, as the victim, won her first Academy Award for Best Actress. Topor also wrote and directed the acclaimed *Judgment*, a 1990 TV movie about Catholic parents who hire a lawyer, played by Jack Warden, when they begin to believe a popular new priest may have molested their son.

Nuts (1987, Warner Bros., 116m/c, **VHS**) **Sc:** Tom Topor, Darryl Ponicsan, Alvin Sargent. **D:** Martin Ritt. **P:** Barbra Streisand. **Cam:** Andrzej Bartkowiak. **Cast:** Barbra Streisand, Richard Dreyfuss, Maureen Stapleton, Karl Malden, Eli Wallach, Leslie Nielsen, James Whitmore, Robert Webber, William Prince, Hayley Taylor Block. A high-priced hooker tries to prove her sanity when she's tried in a manslaughter case while her parents want to see her institutionalized. A well-directed courtroom drama with Streisand a bit overbearing and over-aged for the role. The original play starred Anne Twomey as Claudia at New York's Biltmore Theatre.

- "...a classic example of A-list liberal Hollywood turning out what it thinks is Important Entertainment." (David Ansen, Newsweek)

- "She acted in Nuts...and effectively revealed her limits as an actress — she has a fierceness of her own that does not easily give way to other characters now." (David Thomson, A Biographical Dictionary of Film)

Alfred Uhry

Born: December 12, 1936, Atlanta, GA.
Pulitzer Prize-winning play: Driving Miss Daisy (1988)

Before Driving Miss Daisy won the Pulitzer Prize and the film won the Academy Award for Best Picture, Alfred Uhry was best known as a stage lyricist, particularly for productions of Terrence McNally's Here's Where I Belong (1968), The Robber Bridegroom (1975), and Conn Fleming's Swing (1980). Uhry worked with composer Frank Loesser from 1960 to 1963 and taught English and drama at New York University. He also wrote the screenplays for the ensemble pieces Mystic Pizza (1988), a coming-of-age saga set in Connecticut that gave Julia Roberts her first major role, and Rich in Love (1988), an adaptation of Josephine Humphreys's novel for a Bruce Beresford-directed film with Albert Finney as the head of a contemporary South Carolina clan deserted by its matriarch.

Driving Miss Daisy (1989, Warner Bros., 99m/c, **VHS/DVD**) ☆☆☆☆☆ **Sc:** Alfred Uhry. **D:** Bruce Beresford. **P:** Richard Zanuck, Lili Fini Zanuck. **Cam:** Peter James. **Cast:** Jessica Tandy, Morgan Freeman, Dan Aykroyd, Patti LuPone, Esther Rolle. Uhry's play is a quiet character study about the relationship between an elderly, well-off Jewish matron and her black chauffeur in Atlanta in the 1950s. This outstanding film featured superb performances and an effusive sense of time and place without overt attention to the larger contexts of the social and racial fulmination of the era. The film won Oscars for Best Picture, Actress (Tandy), Screenplay, and Makeup and was nominated for Best Actor (Freeman), Supporting Actor (Aykroyd), Art Direction/Set Decoration, and Costumes. Oddly, Beresford wasn't nominated. Freeman originated the role of Hoke Colburn onstage in the 1987 Off Broadway production co-starring Dana Ivey and Ray Gill.

- *"Plays, especially small ones, do not always open up with ease on the big movie screen, but* Driving Miss Daisy *carries most of its cinematic options with great style. It is the most successful stage-to-screen transition since Stephen Frears turned Christopher Hampton's* Liaisons Dangereuses *into* Dangerous Liaisons....Mr. Uhry's job was easier than the task most playwrights face when doing stage-to-screen adaptations. His play is comparatively free of form...a minimum of props...To a certain extent, his play was already opened up. Even so, there is an exhilirating, singularly theatrical lightness of touch that is often lost when these settings are made manifest in a movie. Mr. Beresford and Mr. Uhry, working in concert, see to it that the essential spirit of* Driving Miss Daisy *shines through...The two actors manage to be highly theatrical without breaking out of the realistic frame of the film."* (Vincent Canby, The New York Times)

- *"...prejudice hovers around the edges of the world of the film and subtly affects its tone. It is another of Beresford's small films, a work of intense concentration that focuses on a microcosm of the modern world and which, in its unfolding, explores broad human as well as social issues."* (Charles P. Silet, International Dictionary of Films and Filmmmakers — Vol. 2: Directors)

Jane Wagner

Born: February 2, 1935, TN.

Aside from writing Lily Tomlin's one-woman show *The Search for Signs of Intelligent Life in the Universe* (see below), Jane Wagner wrote the monologue *Appearing Nightly*, which ran for 96 appearances at Broadway's Biltmore Theatre and was also composed specifically for Tomlin.

The Search for Signs of Intelligent Life in the Universe (1991, Orion Classics, 120m/c, **VHS**) **Sc:** Jane Wagner. **D/Cam:** John Bailey. **P:** Paula Mazur. **Cast:** Lily Tomlin, Clay Walker. Written specifically for Lily Tomlin, this examination of a dozen characters takes a broad look at feminism, sexual liberation, husbands, and commitments. Wagner directed the 1986 stage production, which ran for 396 performances; it was revived by Tomlin and Wagner in 2000 and ran for 184 more performances. Among the characters are teenager Agnes Angst, prostitutes Brandy and Tina, and bag lady Trudy, who divulges that she's working as a consultant on the human condition for some space aliens.

- *"...transferred to the screen, amplified but more or less intact. Though the experience of watching it is different, the show is pretty much all there. On the screen as on the stage...breezily convoluted, pertinent and sometimes hi-*

larious...Throughout the stage performance, Ms. Tomlin wore gray slacks and a blue shirt...minimal set...only the most necessary props....through the sometimes questionable magic of the cinema...Ms. Tomlin is seen in heavy makeup and costume. The effect is not entirely successful. Ms. Tomlin is no less a wizard than she ever was, but the kind of gross makeup jobs that work in variety-show sketches don't do justice either to her talent as an actress and a monologist or to Ms. Wagner's material. The movie...has trouble finding a method....On the stage she didn't need help." (Vincent Canby, The New York Times)

Joseph A. Walker

Born: February 23, 1935, Washington, DC.
Tony Award-winning play: *The River Niger* (1972)

Joseph A. Walker has taught at the City College of the City University of New York and at Howard University in his native Washington, DC He has acted onstage in productions of *A Raisin in the Sun* and *Purlie Victorious*, and on TV on *NYPD*. Walker's plays, many of which were associated with the Negro Ensemble Company, include *The Believers* (1968, written with Josephine Jackson), *The Harangues* (1969), *Ododo* (1972), *Antigone Africanus* (1975), and *District Line* (1984).

The River Niger (1976, Cine Artists, 105m/c, **VHS**) ☆☆ **Sc:** Joseph A. Walker. **D:** Krishna Shah. **P:** Sidney Beckerman, Ike Jones. **Cam:** Michael Margules. **Cast:** James Earl Jones, Cicely Tyson, Glynn Turman, Louis Gossett Jr., Roger E. Mosely, Jonelle Allen, Hilda Haynes, Theodore Wilson, Charles Weldon, Ralph Wilcox, Shirley Jo Finney, Ed Crick, Tony Burton. The Negro Ensemble Company play opened Off Broadway in 1972 and later had a successful Broadway run. This slice-of-life family play concerns the everyday foibles of a black house painter who's also a poet, his wife, and their son, who has just returned home from the Air Force.

• *"...virtually an abject lesson in how not to make a movie out of a theater piece....The people who made* The River Niger *have opened it up, all right, then left it opened up—exposed and sort of gaping—so that while actors act, the director directs and the cameraman practices tricks used better by other cameramen, the life of the work has passed on to that great theatrical warehouse in the sky....a total lack of cohesive style and cinematic intelligence. The actors have the air of people who have arrived at a party where there's no host. They are on their own. Mr. Jones, one of our finest actors, plays it big, sometimes explosively so...a major disappointment."* (Vincent Canby, The New York Times)

Dale Wasserman

Born: November 2, 1917, Rhinelander, WI.

A multimedia writer, director, and producer, Dale Wasserman wrote more than 35 TV dramas in the 1950s and 1960s, including an adaptation of *The Citadel* (1959), *I, Don Quixote* (1960), and *The Lincoln Murder Case* (1961). At about the same time his TV work was drawing attention for its dramatic quality, Wasserman began making his mark as a screenwriter with *World of Strangers* (1954), *The Vikings* (1958), *Two Faces to Go* (1959), and the much ballyhooed and derided Joseph M. Mankiewicz production of *Cleopatra* (1963) starring Elizabeth Taylor. His big-screen pictures from that point on tended to be flops, despite their talent pools: Delbert Mann's *Mister Buddwing* (1966) with James Garner, John Huston's *A Walk With Love and Death* (1969) with Anjelica Huston, and the film version of his own *Man of La Mancha* (1972, see below)—the source of his greatest fame in the theatre through the late 1960s. Wasserman adapted Ken Kesey's novel *One Flew Over the Cuckoo's Nest* for the Broadway version of 1963, starring Kirk Douglas as McMurphy. Wasserman's other plays include *Living the Life*, *The Pencil of God*, and 998.

Man of La Mancha (1972, UA, 132m/c, **VHS**) ☆☆½ **Sc:** Dale Wasserman. **D/P:** Arthur Hiller. **Cam:** Giuseppe Roytunno. **Cast:** Peter O'-Toole, Sophia Loren, James Coco, Harry Andrews, Brian Blessed, Ian Richardson, John Castle, Rosalie Crutchley, Julie Craig, Dorothy Sinclair, Marne Maitland, Dominic Barto, Miriam Acevedo, Gino Conforti. The play is one of Broadway's all-time great hits, running for 2,328 performances beginning in 1965 with Richard Kiley in his signature stage triumph. The film is a labor to get through, hampered by a cast that can't sing. The screenplay mingles events from Miguel de Cervantes's life with the events of his novel as he tells Don Quixote's story from a jail cell. Laurence Rosenthal's score was nominated for an Oscar. The songs include "The Impossible Dream," "I'm Only Thinking of Him," and "Barber's Song."

- *"...comes across like an animated Classic Comic of the great Cervantes novel. Director Arthur Hiller and screenwriter Dale Wasserman have pitched this screen version of the celebrated Broadway musical as low as possible without sinking it beneath the screen altogether. Their Don Quixote resembles an enfeebled scoutmaster emeritus, spewing laundry lists of virtues that might have been taken from the troop manual. As Quixote, Peter O'Toole is made to look like a foolish Milquetoast with an enormous freckled forehead overlooking eyes that seem afflicted with conjunctivitis. O'Toole does his best to ennoble this debased don, but Hiller uses him mainly for sport....The whole production is basted in the cheapest sentiment." (Paul D. Zimmerman, Newsweek)*

Wendy Wasserstein

Born: October 18, 1950, Brooklyn, NY.
Pulitzer Prize-winning play: *The Heidi Chronicles* (1988)

A graduate of Mount Holyoke College and the Yale School of Drama, Wendy Wasserstein received a Guggenheim Fellowship and a National Education Association playwriting grant. For TV, Wasserstein adapted the John Cheever short story "The Sorrows of Gin" for the 1979 PBS presentation of *3 by Cheever*, wrote a segment of *Triple Play: Sam Found Out* (1988) starring Liza Minnelli, and penned the PBS production *Kiss-Kiss, Dahlings!* (1992) with Blythe Danner and Nancy Marchand. Wasserstein wrote the screenplay for *The Object of My Affection* (1998) with Jennifer Anniston. Her plays include *Isn't It Romantic* and *Miami*.

An American Daughter (2000, Lifetime, 120m/c, **VHS/DVD**) ☆☆
Tp: Wendy Wasserstein. **D:** Sheldon Larry. **P:** Wendy Wasserstein, Abby Adams, Robert Schwartz, Chad S. Hoffman. **Cam:** Bert Dunk. **Cast:** Christine Lahti, Tom Skerritt, Jay Thomas, Mark Feuerstein, Lynne Thigpen, Stanley Anderson, Blake Lindsley. Wasserstein based this play—about a Washington, DC, physician who comes under media scrutiny when she is nominated for U.S. surgeon general—on the experiences of Zoe Baird and Kimba Wood, two unsuccessful nominees for attorney general. The 1997 Broadway play starred Kate Nelligan, Hal Holbrook, Peter Riegert, Penny Fuller, Cotter Smith, and Lynn Thigpen. The show was retitled *Trial by Media* for video.

- *"The characters are cartoonish....Certainly Ms. Wasserstein knows how to write a funny scene, but the speechifying overwhelms the satire....Ms. Lahti rises to the occasion when she's given one. Though Ms. Wasserstein wants us to empathize with Lyssa's plight, she does not really seem to like her own creation very much. When Lyssa finally decides to defend herself on television, she ends up whining."* (Julie Salamon, The New York Times)

The Heidi Chronicles (1995, TNT, 94m/c, **VHS**) ☆☆☆☆ **Tp:** Wendy Wasserstein. **D:** Paul Bogart. **P:** Michael Brandman. **Cast:** Jamie Lee Curtis, Tom Hulce, Kim Cattrall, Peter Friedman, Shari Belafonte, Eve Gordon, Sharon Lawrence, Julie White, Roma Maffia, Debra Eisenstadt. Heidi Holland graduates from high school in the 1960s, and the next 25 years take her through feminine epiphanies, the Vietnam War, John Lennon's death, and her own relationships. The 1988 Pulitzer Prize-winning play was originally staged that year by the Seattle Repertory Theatre with Sarah Jessica Parker in several roles, then opened on Broadway in 1989 with Joan Allen as Heidi. In this TV movie, Curtis delivers perhaps her finest moments.

- *"...a faithful representation...a rare example of the medium's capacity to entertain and inform while generating deep currents of emotion....Curtis—in a splendid, career-boosting display of craft and skill—creates a Heidi who is simultaneously complex, emphatic, and eminently believable....The translation of a stage piece into the small-screen boundaries of TV often produces a reduction of dramatic thrust in favor of action and movement. Bogart and executive producer Michael Brandman, however, have been straight-arrow true to Wasserstein's work. The result is a revelatory, humorous, shrewdly insightful look at a changing era in American life."* (Don Heckman, Los Angeles Times)

Uncommon Women...and Others (1978, PBS, 90m/c, **VHS/DVD**) *Great Performances: Theatre in America* ☆☆☆½ **Tp:** Wendy Wasserstein. **D:** Steve Robman, Merrily Mossman. **P:** Phyllis Geller, Jac Venza. **Cast:** Meryl Streep, Jill Eikenberry, Swoosie Kurtz, Ann McDonough, Alma Cuervo, Ellen Parker, Josephine Nicholas, Cynthia Herman, Anna Levine. Wasserstein's first play centers on a seven-year reunion among five former classmates at Mount Holyoke College, who assess whether they have achieved the goals of their youth. They re-live their senior year and the influences that shaped their characters. The play's life began as a one-act that played New Haven, Connecticut, in 1975 and then became an Off Broadway hit in 1977 at the Phoenix Theatre with a cast including all of the above except Streep, whose role was played by Glenn Close.

- *"...riddled with flaws yet crammed with more insight and energy than most plays of the well-made variety....Some of the play's flaws are structural. The character of Carter, for instance, is really little more than a catatonic blob serving as a sounding board or wailing wall against which others can reveal their sins and neuroses....Elsewhere the flaws are in performance, with what seemed to be an inordinate number of momentarily flubbed lines....Rita, played to a superbly dizzy and touching frazzle by Miss Kurtz, is perhaps the most noticeable of the lot. Her fantasies are as vivid as Dr. Pepper commercials."* (John J. O'Connor, The New York Times)

Louis Weitzenkorn

Born: 1894, Wilkes-Barre, PA. **Died:** 1943.

Louis Weitzenkorn was a reporter and editor on the *New York Tribune*, *The New York Times*, and *New York Call* before his experiences as editor of the tabloid *New York Evening Graphic* from 1924 to 1929 inspired him to write *Five Star Final* (see below). His other plays include *And the Sun Goes Down* and *First Mortgage*. His other screenplays include *24 Hours* (1931), *Ladies of the Big House* (1931), *The Devil Is Driving* (1932), *Finishing School*

(1934), and *King of the Newsboys* (1938). Weitzenkorn was killed in a fire at his Wilkes-Barre home in 1943 and the death was ruled accidental.

Five Star Final is the story of a muckraking newspaper editor who digs up a 20-year-old scandal and serializes it to lure prurient readers. A girl who is about to be married had been shielded from any knowledge of her parents' involvement in the scandal. When they commit suicide, she nearly kills the editor, Joe Randall, and he resigns with a new conscience. The 1930 play starred Arthur Byron.

Five Star Final (1931, First National, 89m/bw) ☆☆☆½ **Sc:** Byron Morgan. **D:** Mervyn LeRoy. **P:** Hal B. Wallis. **Cam:** Sol Polito. **Cast:** Edward G. Robinson, H.B. Warner, Marian Marsh, Anthony Bushell, Aline MacMahon, Boris Karloff, Frances Starr, Ona Munson, George E. Stone, Oscar Apfell, Purnell Pratt, Robert Elliott, Gladys Lloyd, Harold Waldbridge, David Torrence. The portrayals of the flotsam and jetsam that drift in and out of the newspaper office are superb, including Munson as a prostitute, MacMahon as Robinson's wry secretary, and Karloff as T. Vernon Isopod, a lout about whom Robinson snaps, "You're the most blasphemous thing I've ever seen—it's a miracle you've not been struck dead!" MacMahon and Robinson make the most of Weitzenkorn's pungent dialogue.

- *"Edward G. Robinson gives another strong performance as the editor of a muck-raking tabloid in the pictorial translation of Louis Weitzenkorn's play....It is a picture which in a matter of production and acting takes its place beside the film of* The Front Page*....With a big cigar in the corner of his mouth most of the time,...Robinson as Randall, the editor of the* New York Gazette, *makes the most of every line."* (The New York Times)

- *"...one of his best roles in one of his finest (and favorite) films...Some four and a half decades after its release,* Five Star Final *still packs a wallop, due mainly to its crackling dialogue and a wonderful rogues gallery of performers...But it is Edward G. Robinson who makes the film sparkle."* (James Robert Parish, The Tough Guys)

Two Against the World (1936, Warner Bros., 64m/bw) ☆☆ **Sc:** Michael Jacoby. **D:** William McGann. **P:** Bryan Foy. **Cam:** Sid Hickox. **Cast:** Humphrey Bogart, Beverly Roberts, Helen MacKellar, Henry O'Neill, Linda Perry, Carlyle Moore Jr., Virginia Brissac, Robert Middlemass, Clay Clement, Harry Hayden, Claire Dodd, Hobart Cavanaugh, Frank Orth, Howard Hickman, Bobby Gordon. The setting was taken out of a newspaper office and put in a radio station, which serializes a sensationalistic murder case that's 20 years old. The sordid tale jeopardizes the marriage of the daughter of the jury-exonerated Martha Carstairs, who can't bear to re-live the case. One of Bogart's earliest starring roles.

- *"Humphrey Bogart was used, all right. Used again and again.* Two

Against the World *was a recycling of a previous Warner feature that starred Edward G. Robinson, with a title borrowed from an old Constance Bennett release. It was ground out in three weeks. Bogart played the cynical manager of a radio station…The ads showed Bogart's face luridly lit opposite display type screaming: 'The cold-blooded gangster of* The Petrified Forest *finds a new way to kill!'"* (A.M. Sperber, Eric Lax, Bogart)

Five Star Final (1954, NBC, 60m/c/live) *Lux Video Theatre* ☆☆☆ **Tp:** Sanford Barnett. **D:** Earl Ebi. **P:** Carl Kuhl. **Cast:** Edmond O'Brien, Mae Clarke, Joanne Woodward, Dayton Lummis, Marvin Bryan, Frances Mercer, Louise Arthur, Pierre Watkin, Ernestine Barrier, George Eldredge, Liam Sullivan, Ken Christy, Benny Sullivan, Joe Granby. **Host:** James Mason. Pared to an hour, the play's tempo was speeded up. O'Brien was a natural for a scheming newspaper editor and Woodward's career was just taking off when this aired.

- *"It's still packed with power and pathos, generated with high voltage by Edmond O'Brien, Mae Clarke, and Joanne Woodward….O'Brien was superb in all of his stentorian growling and gave a performance that must have ranked with Edward G. Robinson's portrayal in the WB picture back in 1931….For Miss Clarke it should open a door to a new career. For director Earl Ebi, it was a triumphant note in the entire series and must be rated with the best of the live shows done in Hollywood."* (Variety)

Elie Wiesel

Born: September 30, 1928, Sighet, Romania.

Liberated from Buchenwald Concentration Camp in 1945 by advancing Allied troops, Elie Wiesel was taken to Paris, where he studied at the Sorbonne and worked as a journalist. In 1958, he published his first book, *La Nuit*, a memoir of his experiences in the concentration camps. He has since authored nearly 30 books, made his home in New York City, and is now a United States citizen. He was chairman of the United States Holocaust Memorial Council from 1980 to 1986, the year he won the Nobel Peace Prize. His one produced play is *Zalman or the Madness of God* (see below).

Zalman or the Madness of God (1975, PBS, 120m/c) *Theatre in America.* ☆☆☆ **Tp:** Elie Wiesel. **D:** Alan Schneider, Peter Levin. **P:** Ken Campbell, Jac Venza. **Cast:** Joseph Wiseman, Richard Bauer, Robert Prosky, Mark Hammer, Howard Witt, Dianne Wiest, Gary Bayer, John Koch Jr., Sanford Seeger, Lieb Lensky, Michael Mertz, David Reinhardsen, Leslie Carr. The Arena Stage production filmed for this presentation was the American premiere of the play with the same cast.

The play was written in 1966 after Wiesel visited the Soviet Union. The setting is the eve of Yom Kippur in a rural Russian synagogue, where the caretaker urges the rabbi to question God and explore "obscure zones of truth."

- *"Both the play and the production are flawed, but the total experience is profoundly haunting. It is one that will stick in memories....It is an awkward play, its characters squeezed into convenient dialectics. Dramatic fullness is secondary to convincing argument. But it is also an absorbing and extremely moving play, dealing with some of the most important issues of our age, of any age. It spares no one, yet brings to all concerned an element of understanding. As the rabbi, Joseph Wiseman gives a performance in the best traditions of the Yiddish theatre, made up to perfection and declaiming with controlled passion....not material for commercial TV. It is precisely the kind of project that public television should be all about."* (John J. O'Connor, The New York Times)

Thornton Wilder

Thornton Niven Wilder
Born: 1897, Madison, WI. **Died:** 1975.
Pulitzer Prize-winnning plays: Our Town (1938), The Skin of Our
    Teeth (1943)
Tony Award-winning play: Our Town (1989)

Thornton Wilder won his first Pulitzer Prize for the novel *The Bridge of San Luis Rey* (1928), which was produced as a mostly silent film in 1929 with Lila Damita and Ernest Torrence, again in 1944 with Lynn Bari and Nazimova, and on television in a 1958 *DuPont Show of the Month* production with Rita Gam, Judith Anderson, Hume Cronyn, and Eva La Gallienne. His one other novel adapted for film was *Mr. North* (1988), which was prepared by John Huston and starred Anthony Edwards, Robert Mitchum, and Lauren Bacall.

Wilder's two audience-friendly Pulitzer Prize-winning plays were, as John J. O'Connor wrote, "models of theatrical clarity, stripped down to the essences of narrative and theatricality. In *Our Town*, a stage manager appears and, with a few chairs, conjures up an entire generation living in [a] small town. In *The Skin of Our Teeth*, the actors are themselves as well as the characters they are depicting, occasionally stepping forward to explain the play wryly to the audience."

Two Plays by Thornton Wilder was a 1949 installment of *Academy Theatre* in which the Wilder originals *Love and How to Cure It* and *Such Things Only Happen in Books* debuted. The author contributed to the screenplay of Alfred Hitchcock's *Shadow of a Doubt* (1943), which was remade for TV in 1991, and worked uncredited on Howard Hawks's *We Live Again* (1934)

The Happy Journey, which was derived from *The Happy Journey to Trenton and Newark*, was Wilder's play set during an automobile ride by a family. It was produced four times on network TV within a five-year span: in 1951 on *Pulitzer Prize Playhouse* with Spring Byington, Jack Lemmon, and Wanda Hendrix; in 1953 on *Omnibus* with Helen Hayes; in 1954 on *Kraft Television Theatre* with Mildred Dunnock and Frank McHugh; and in 1956 on *Star Tonight* with Elizabeth Wilson.

Infancy and **Childhood** (1968, NET, 60m/c) *NET Playhouse* ☆☆☆ **Tp:** Thornton Wilder. **D:** Joe Layton, Jack Landau. **P:** Jac Venza. **Casts:** Tony Hendra, Nic Ullet, Julie Herrod, Audrey Price, Fred Gwynne, Michael Kearney. The first one-act play features the British comic team of Hendra and Ullet as infants in Central Park whose doubts and feelings are thoroughly adult, while their mother and nanny seem inanely childish. In the second play, children play a game called "funeral."

• *"The Pulitzer Prize playwright employs, of course, highly unorthodox staging techniques to register his incisive comment on the recurring difficulty of establishing meaningful commentary between children and their parents. His bias is all on the side of the youngsters. Their inquiring and inventive minds often are not understood by parents already trapped in the routine of habit and survival....fully reached the NET Playhouse goal of careful preparation of experimental drama." (Jack Gould, The New York Times)*

The Long Christmas Dinner was produced as a segment of an *Ovation* special on the USA Network in 1982.

The Matchmaker, set in late 19th century New York City, concerns a well-heeled widower who consults a matchmaker, Dolly Levi, to find a bride, but the matchmaker has her designs on him. Wilder based an earlier play, *The Merchant of Yonkers*, on a British play called *A Day Well Spent* by John Oxenford, which was staged in London in the 1930s and retooled by Johann Nestroy as a Viennese romp years later. *The Merchant of Yonkers* starred Jane Cowl on Broadway in a 1938 Max Reinhardt production. Wilder later revamped that play and renamed it *The Matchmaker* for 1954 Edinburgh and London productions starring Ruth Gordon, who then took it to Broadway. It was the basis for the 1964 Broadway musical *Hello, Dolly!*, with a book by Michael Stewart and music and lyrics by Jerry Herman, starred Carol Channing.

The Matchmaker (1958, Paramount, 101m/bw, **VHS**) ☆☆☆ **Sc:** John Michael Hayes. **D:** Joseph Anthony. **P:** Don Hartman. **Cam:** Joseph Lang. **Cast:** Shirley Booth, Anthony Perkins, Shirley MacLaine, Paul

Ford, Wallace Ford, Robert Morse, Perry Wilson, Russell Collins, Rex Evans, Torben Meyer, Gavin Gordon. This adaptation is buoyed by the dialogue and Anthony's stylized direction playing up the theatrical farce. Shirley Booth resisted starring in the movie, feeling that Gordon made the role her own, but eventually signed on.

- "...Booth was magnificent...Anthony used stylized elements discreetly, creating a background against which the farcical stuff could be 'played up.' The humor of The Matchmaker has a sentimental core, increasing the director's problem in an intimate medium....Anthony judged to perfection the measure of extravagance that the closer range of cinema would be able to support....All of this was so deft in its blending of hilarity and grace that a musical version of the same subject in the 1960s, Hello Dolly!, seemed otiose." (Gordon Gow, Hollywood in the Fifties)

Hello, Dolly! (1969, 20th Century-Fox, 129m/c, **VHS**) ☆☆☆ **Sc/P:** Ernest Lehman. **D:** Gene Kelly. **Cam:** Harry Stradling. **Cast:** Barbra Streisand, Walter Matthau, Michael Crawford, Louis Armstrong, Marianne McAndrew, E.J. Peaker, Tommy Tune, David Hurst. An enormously costly picture, this is the film that signaled the decline of the gargantuan musical, which hit rock-bottom with *Lost Horizon* (1973). Streisand was on her high horse by this time, but Kelly's direction and Michael Kidd's choreography were excellent. The film won an Oscar for its Score (Lennie Hayton, Lionel Newman) and Art Direction/Set Decoration and was nominated for Best Picture and Cinematography. The songs include the title tune, "Just Leave Everything to Me," "Love Is Only Love," and "Dancing."

- "...the first of the huge disappointments that closed the era of blockbuster musicals. A meticulous recreation of little old New York's 14th Street for a parade sequence was cited as the dead center of overproduction and Streisand, in the name role, was jeered....The kids are delightful, Walter Matthau elegant, and Louis Armstrong unlooked-for benison. What's wrong with Hello Dolly!? Nothing. The press was gunning for Streisand and big musicals, and the public for such events was limited. In any event, it didn't do that badly." (Ethan Mordden, The Hollywood Musical)

Our Town, which won the Pulitzer Prize for 1938, is the slice-of-life story of people living in Grover's Corners, New Hampshire, in the early part of the century. The Stage Manager folksily introduces people and explains the way of life there while the story centers on two teen-age lovers. The play was first presented at the McCarter Theatre in Princeton, New Jersey, in 1938, then the same year at Henry Miller's Theatre on Broadway starring Frank Craven, Martha Scott, and John Craven.

Our Town (1940, UA, 90m/bw, **VHS**) ☆☆☆☆ **Sc:** Thornton Wilder, Frank Craven, Harry Chandlee. **D:** Sam Wood. **P:** Sol Lesser. **Cam:** Bert Glennon. **Cast:** William Holden, Martha Scott, Frank Craven, Thomas

Mitchell, Fay Bainter, Guy Kibbee, Beulah Bondi, Stuart Erwin, Phillip Wood, Ruth Toby, Douglas Gardiner, Spencer Charters, Doro Merande, Arthur Allen, Charles Trowbridge, Dix Davis. Craven repeated his great stage success as the Stage Manager and chipped in on the screenplay while Holden affirmed his stardom, earned the previous year in *Golden Boy*, in this sturdy and appealing realization by Wood.

- *"I believe the fine thing about* Our Town *is its recreation of a mood—a town, a people, a region. You can nearly smell things cooking, and feel the night air; you can certainly see as fine a collection of atrocious lamps and bric-a-brac, good heavy pots and dishes, rail fences and front piazzas, a church, a schoolhouse, a Main Street skyscraper of two stories (as of 1903) as you'd find in a museum. More important…are the local habits as defined and put into everyday action; and especially as put into the mouths of the various local types…It is always very insignificant and everyday stuff, and most delightful because recognized and created as just that."* (Otis Ferguson, The New Republic)

- *"Frank Craven…is the perfect New England Socrates—honest, sincere and profound….We hesitate to employ superlatives, but of* Our Town *the least we can say is that it captures on film the simple beauties and truths of humble folks as very few pictures ever do; it is rich and ennobling in its plain philosophy—and it gives one a passionate desire to enjoy the fullness of life even in these good old days of today."* (Bosley Crowther, The New York Times)

Our Town (1955, NBC, 90m/c) *Producers' Showcase* ☆☆☆ **Tp:** David Shaw. **D:** Delbert Mann. **P:** Fred Coe. **Cast:** Paul Newman, Eva Marie Saint, Frank Sinatra, Ernest Truex, Sylvia Field, Paul Hartman, Peg Hillias, Carol Venzie, Shelley Fabares. The network decided to turn the play into a musical, with Sinatra as the stage manager. The star angered Mann by not showing up for the dress rehearsal and by cocking his hat in Broadway gesture at the close of the play, a move that was very un-*Our Town*. "I was struck speechless," Mann wrote years later, and he never worked with the star again. The songs include "Love and Marriage" and "Wasn't It a Wonderful Wedding?"

- *"…90 minutes of magnificent entertainment….[the producers] decided to add music to the story. The gamble was extremely risky….Mr. Coe, Delbert Mann, the director, and the others did their work remarkably well. The tender narrative of joy and sorrow in the hearts of unspectacular Americans lost none of its charm…complemented splendidly with songs by James Van Heusen and lyrics by Sammy Cahn. Eva Marie Saint…was responsible for a major share of the production's fine quality….She performed brilliantly in a role that demands a great range of acting talent….It is true that Mr. Sinatra was occasionally less at ease than he might have been. And his unconcealed Hobokenese would betray him as an outlander in any part of New England. But he was effectively unobtrusive and his songs were an impor-*

tant contribution to the success of the presentation." (J.P. Shanley, The New York Times*)*

- *"...reached new dramatic heights in the electronic art...The adaptation was so skillfully wrought by David Shaw it made* Town *almost breathe with life and it provided Frank Sinatra, Eva Marie Saint, Paul Newman and a supporting cast of high competence a warm, tender narrative that gave new lustre to their talents."* (Variety)

Our Town (1959, NBC Special, 90m/c) ☆☆☆ **Tp:** Jacqueline Babbin, Audrey Gellen. **D:** Jose Quintero, John Lincoln. **P:** David Susskind. **Cast:** Clint Kimbrough, Kathleen Widdoes, Art Carney, Bibi Osterwald, Dana Elcar, Jerome Kilty, Mary Van Fleet, Roberts Blossom, Ginger MacManus, Martha Greenhouse. This special was produced at the apex of Carney's TV popularity. It marked one of Quintero's rare forays into TV.

- *"...a faithful and lovely revival...rekindled a poignant glow to the work's deep understanding of the little-realized beauties of everyday existence. Mr. Wilder's play is singularly suited to the television medium....The drama's minimum use of props and scenery, which so successfully enlists the imagination of the audience, made a most striking pictorial composition...Mr.Carney's interpretation of the Stage Manager was becomingly straightforward...[but] a shade too crisp and a little wanting in philosophical overtones."* (Jack Gould, The New York Times)

Our Town (1977, NBC Special, 132m/c, **VHS**) ☆☆☆ **Tp:** Thornton Wilder. **D/P:** George Schaefer. **Cast:** Robby Benson, Glynnis O'Connor, Hal Holbrook, Ned Beatty, Barbara Bel Geddes, John Houseman, Ronny Cox, Sada Thompson, Ford Rainey, Don Beddoe, Charlotte Rae, David Cryer, Allen Price, Charles Cyphers, William Lanteau, Elizabeth Cheshire.

- *"It was Wilder's suggestion that instead of using the Stage Manager as one of the characters in the play to use him as a TV host or anchorman, having a direct one-to-one relationship with the home audience. Hal Holbrook as the Stage Manager is interviewing Editor Webb about the politics and culture of Grover's Corners, he is really a talk-show host....Then the Stage Manager shifts the focus and asks the audience, 'Is there anyone out there who would like to ask Editor Webb about the town?' A woman responds, 'Is there much drinking in Grover's Corners?'..."* (Saul Jaffe, The New York Times)

Our Town (1989, PBS Special, 104m/c, **VHS**) ☆☆☆½ **Tp:** Thornton Wilder. **D:** Gregory Mosher, Kirk Browning. **P:** Michael Brandman. **Cast:** Eric Stoltz, Penelope Ann Miller, Spalding Gray, Frances Conroy, James Rebhorn, Marcell Rosenblatt, Roberta Maxwell, Peter Maloney, Lydia Kelly, Shane Culkin, Atticus Brady, Bill Alton, William Duell. Filmed on a bare stage without an audience at the Lyceum Theatre in New York with the cast from the Tony Award-winning revival, this production showcases the play and the actors very effectively.

- *"The genius of Thornton Wilder's* Our Town *is in its simplicity....the scholarly Wilder devised a play drawing on what philosophers call the eternal verities....It is the genius of the Lincoln Center Theatre production, directed by Gregory Mosher...that Wilder's conception has been meticulously respected while the play's darker aspects are confronted unflinchingly....This is a thoughtfully cast production. There are no jarring star turns. I suspect that Spalding Gray's Stage Manager, criticized in some quarters for being a liittle too casual and low-key on the stage, is substantially more effective within the confines of a television screen....Our Town holds a secure place with a handful of lasting masterpieces written for the American theatre in this century. This production brilliantly reminds us why."* (John J. O'Connor, The New York Times)

Our Town was also produced on TV twice in 1950: for an installment of *Robert Montgomery Presents* starring Jean Gillespie and Burgess Meredith, and on *The Pulitzer Prize Playhouse* with Elizabeth Patterson, Charles Dingle, Edward Arnold, and Dorothy Peterson.

The Skin of Our Teeth was a Broadway sensation in 1942 with the stellar cast of Fredric March, Florence Eldridge, Tallulah Bankhead, and a young Montgomery Clift. The 1955 Cold War revival starred Helen Hayes, George Abbott, and Mary Martin. The play is a cautionary tale with the universal theme that the human race in the form of the Antrobus family will always survive, if only by narrow escapes described by the title phrase, through the ice age, flood, and war.

The Skin of Our Teeth (1955, NBC Special, 120m/c) ☆☆☆ **Tp:** Ellen M. Violett. **D:** Alan Scheidner, Vincent J. Donehue. **P:** Fred Coe. **Cast:** Helen Hayes, Mary Martin, George Abbott, Florence Reed, Frank Silvera, Hellen Halliday. This event, a taping and restaging of the starry Broadway revival, which also played Paris, marked one of the few screen opportunities to see writer/director/producer Abbott in a role, as Mr. Antrobus.

- *"The role of Sabina had been written for Tallulah Bankhead....A Tallulah line coming from a Mary Martin-type character doesn't work. I argued and argued but the director was unmovable....Helen Hayes was absolutely marvelous about it. She knew something was wrong....Then a man came to my rescue....Vincent J. Donehue.... 'Vinnie'...had been chosen to direct the television version....He said, 'I think I can help you.' Whereupon I burst into tears and wailed, 'Nobody can help me.' He could and he did. 'Play any actress you want to,' he said. 'Play Tallulah, or play Vivien Leigh...or anybody else you want, but do not play Mary Martin.' My Savior. My ten-minute soliloquy, which had fallen flat before, went on for about 15 minutes because it got such great applause, such spreading laughter, for each great Thornton Wilder line."* (Mary Martin, My Heart Belongs)

The Skin of Our Teeth (1983, PBS, 120m/c) *American Playhouse* ☆☆☆
Tp: Thornton Wilder. **D:** Jack O'Brien. **P:** Thomas Hall, David M. Davis. **Cast:** Sada Thompson, Blair Brown, Harold Gould, John Houseman, Rue McClanahan, Thomas Lacy, Jeffrey Combs, Monique Fowler, Sean Sullivan, Michael Luelders, G. Wood, Renee Brooks, Bill Geisslinger, Larry Drake, Bonnie Britton-Campbell, Diana Bellamy, Susan Hegarty. **Announcer:** Richard Kiley. This live production broadcasted the West Coast revival live from San Diego's Old Globe Theatre.

- *"O'Brien made good use of the screen's enviable ability to articulate the image-flow of a production as precisely as a composer inking a line of notes. Image one: A close-up of Rue McClanahan seeing the deluge in the crystal ball. Image two: A medium shot of some sozzled conventioneers whooping it up on the boardwalk. Think it'll rain? The original show was more legato than that. But by using a real audience, and not stopping to go back, the TV version did carry some of the heat of live performance, with no sense that the actors were overplaying to reach the back of the house."* (Dan Sullivan, Los Angeles Times)

- *"Some of the Wilder techniques, not to mention the jokes, are a bit hokey now, having been absorbed and exploited to death by succeeding waves of avant garde movements. But a few are still remarkably effective....gets better as it moves along....The basic conception holds and the cast is solid."* (John J. O'Connor, The New York Times)

The Skin of Our Teeth was first filmed for a 1951 edition of *Pulitzer Prize Playhouse* starring Peggy Wood, Nina Foch, Thomas Mitchell, and Mildred Natwick.

John Willard

Born: November 28, 1885, San Francisco, CA. **Died:** 1942.

John Willard's one successful play, which endured throughout the 20th century as a favorite of road-show companies and amateur troupes, was the mystery *The Cat and the Canary* (see below). As an actor, Willard appeared in a dozen Broadway shows, including productions of his own plays. His other plays includ *The Blue Flame* (1920), *The Green Beetle* (1924), *Sisters* (1927), *Fog* (1927), and *Adventure* (1928).

The Cat and the Canary was the playwright's one theatrical success. It concerns venal relatives who gather in a mansion to hear the reading of an eccentric relative's will. The play was first performed on Broadway in 1922 with Florence Eldridge, Henry Hull, and Willard in the cast.

The Cat and the Canary (1927, Universal, 84m/bw/silent, **VHS/DVD**)

☆☆☆½ **Sc:** Alfred Cohn, Robert F. Hill. **D:** Paul Leni. **Cam:** Gilbert Warrenton. **Cast:** Creighton Hale, Laura La Plante, Forrest Stanley, Tully Marshall, Flora Finch, Gertrude Astor, Arthur Carewe. This film basically invented the big, old, possibly haunted house genre that became a staple of horror pictures and their spoofs. Done in exceptional style, its archetypal inventiveness created genre standards.

- *"Drawing on his expressionist resources, Leni...works wonders for a while: characters lurching out of the darkness until their backs ominously blot out the entire screen; disembodied hands hovering timidly, curling around doorways, slowly reaching for the heroine's throat; an uncanny resurrection of Caligari as the mysterious, mincing stranger with pebble glasses and limp hands advances to announce 'I am the doctor;' and, most arresting of all, the extraordinary double exposure showing the mechanism of a clock that hasn't struck since old Cyrus died..."* (Phil Hardy, The Encyclopedia of Horror Movies)

The Cat Creeps (1930, Universal, 71m/bw) ☆☆ **Sc:** Gladys Lehman, William Hurlbult. **D:** Rupert Julian. **P:** Carl Laemmle Jr. **Cam:** Jerry Ash, Hal Mohr. **Cast:** Helen Twelvetrees, Raymond Haskell, Neil Hamilton, Jean Hersholt, Montague Love. Mohr, who developed the fluid camera crane that was used on Broadway (1929), again uses the device in the old dark house of this thriller, in which Hersholt plays the evil doctor and Twelvetrees tests the scream quotient level.

- *"Horribly hampered by the laborious dialogue scenes, the film's saving grace is Mohr's effective camerawork..."* (Phil Hardy, The Encyclopedia of Horror Movies)

The Cat and the Canary (1939, Paramount, 72m/bw) ☆☆☆ **Sc:** Walter de Leon, Lynn Starling. **D:** Elliott Nugent. **P:** Arthur Hornblow Jr. **Cam:** Charles Lang. **Cast:** Bob Hope, Paulette Goddard, Gale Sondergaard, John Beal, George Zucco, Nydia Westman, Elizabeth Patterson, John Wray. Bob Hope's first big starring part was in this huge hit, a superbly paced, crafted, and written remake of a durable template.

- *"Elliott Nugent and the authors...played it for laughs, which is the best way to treat the formula of heirs being eliminated one by one in a creaky old mansion. The action was timed with skill, moving from one plateau to the next higher one. The first major film tailored to the talents of Bob Hope, it was crucial to his career."* (Bob Thomas in The Road to Hollywood: My Forty-Year Love Affair with the Movies by Bob Hope and Bob Thomas)

- *"Nugent understood Hope's absolute dependence on the wisecrack as the supreme technical device. He had the sensitivity to recognize that in the role of Wally Hampton, the comedian's screen persona was coming into bloom...Some of the most quotable jokes from the film came in moments of Wally's terror. Once, when he was forced to sleep in a spooky mansion, Nydia Westman asks, 'Don't big, empty houses scare you?' 'Not me,' says*

Wally, 'I used to be in vaudeville.' And, 'Even my goosepimples have goosepimples.'" (William Robert Faith, Bob Hope: A Life in Comedy)

The Cat and the Canary (1960, NBC, 60m/c) *Dow Hour of Great Mysteries* ☆☆½ **Tp:** William Roos, Audrey Roos. **D:** William A. Graham. **P:** Robert Saudek. **Cast:** Collin Wilcox, Andrew Duggan, Sarah Marshall, Telly Savalas, George Macready, Hortense Alden.

- *"...played to the hilt by a competent cast, the play was an hour of well-balanced acting, excitement and fun." (William Torbert Leonard,* Theatre: Stage to Screen to Television)

The Cat and the Canary (1979, Gala/Grenedier, 98m/c, **VHS/DVD**) ☆☆ **Sc/D:** Radley Metzger. **P:** Richard Gordon. **Cam:** Alex Thomson. **Cast:** Honor Blackman, Michael Callan, Wendy Hiller, Olivia Hussey, Carol Lynley, Edward Fox, Beatrix Lehmann, Peter McEnery, Wilfrid Hyde-White. This British production went by the numbers through the cookie-cutter sensibility of former softcore porn maker Metzger.

- *"...an exceptionally ill-advised remake, with some more 'names.'" (David Shipman,* The Great Movie Stars 1: The Golden Years)

Tennessee Williams

Thomas Lanier Williams
Born: March 26, 1914, Columbus, MS. **Died:** 1983.
Pulitzer Prize-winning plays: *A Streetcar Named Desire* (1948),
    Cat on a Hot Tin Roof (1955)
Tony Award-winning play: *The Rose Tattoo* (1951)

Tennessee Williams's name in the last half of the 20th century came to signify sex, neurosis, and violence in the Deep South. As the movies pushed the envelope to portray those aspects of life, his plays became increasingly popular in Hollywood. The poetry of his language, the eccentricities of his often Mississippi-based characters, and his frankness with sexual themes created a genre almost unto itself. His characters became early beneficiaries of the Stanislavsky method promoted by the Actors Studio. Marlon Brando made history as Stanley Kowalski in *A Streetcar Named Desire* and many actors who made excursions into Williams's world on film delivered some of the great performances of the era.

Then again, Williams's world was never the real world, and his themes were often oblique. Many of the plays translated rather oddly to the screen, especially those with homosexual themes, which were at the core of the playwright's interests at a time when gay issues were still closeted. The film versions of *Cat on a Hot Tin Roof* and *Suddenly, Last Summer*, for instance, were crippled by the moratorium Hollywood placed on homosexual material. 24 Williams plays have been adapted to the screen in 35 versions, with 20 of them available for home viewing, including two versions each of *Cat on a Hot Tin Roof*, *Orpheus Descending*, *Summer and Smoke*, and *Sweet Bird of Youth*, and four of *A Streetcar Named Desire*. The original film of this last title is an all-time classic and tops home-viewing recommendations judged for fidelity to the author and the performances. Blythe Danner's performance in *The Eccentricities of a Nightingale* is one of the greatest in the Williams canon.

Elizabeth Taylor and Rip Torn have each appeared in four Williams adaptations. Paul Newman starred in two of the films and directed another. Screenwriters who adapted Williams material more than once were Gore Vidal, Meade Roberts, James Poe, Richard Brooks, Gavin Lambert, and Lanford Wilson. Brooks and Elia Kazan each directed two films based on Williams's work, and Glenn Jordan helmed three such TV productions. James Wong Howe was cinematographer on three films and Boris Kaufman on two. Actors with multiple appearances in Williams material include Katharine Hepburn, Vivien Leigh, Marlon Brando, Richard Burton, Anna Magnani, Joanne Woodward, Jessica Lange, Kim Stanley, Jo Van Fleet, Mildred Dunnock, Karl Malden, and Natalie Wood.

The absentees in home viewing include three of the four versions of *The Glass Menagerie*. The superior 1973 Katharine Hepburn version isn't available while the merely above-par Paul Newman/Joanne Woodward version is on the shelves. It's also curious that the Laurence Olivier version of *Cat on a Hot Tin Roof* has not been made available. The same goes for *Boom!*, the sole ElizabethTaylor/Richard Burton pairing (out of ten films and one TV drama) not yet on tape or disc. Notable Williams plays not yet filmed include *Camino Real* (full-length version), *The Fugitive Kind* (original), *In the Bar of the Tokyo Hotel*, *Something Unspoken*, *Small Craft Warnings*, *The Case of the Crushed Petunias*, *Clothes for a Summer Hotel*, *The Red Devil Battery Sign*, and *Mister Charlie*.

For TV, Williams conceived the original story for *The Migrants*, an unforgettable portrayal of a family of dirt-poor, rootless, Southern farm workers subsisting from job to job, for a 1974 *Playhouse 90* presentation dramatized by Lanford Wilson and produced and directed by Tom Gries. A heartbreaking experience, *The Migrants* is as close as TV has come to emulating the sorrows of the hardscrabble road traveled by the disenfranchised fruit pickers in *The Grapes of Wrath* and approaches the authenticity of Edward R. Murrow's great documentary *Harvest of Shame*. Cloris Leachman, Sissy Spacek, Ron Howard, Cindy Williams, Ed Lauter, Claudia McNeil, Brad Sullivan, and Dolph Sweet were all superb and the show was nominated for six Emmys.

Williams's 1953 novella, *The Roman Spring of Mrs. Stone* was converted into a 1961 film by screenwriter Gavin Lambert, director Jose Quintero, and a cast led by Vivien Leigh and Warren Beatty. It became a European travelogue with Leigh as an aging actress who finds lust in

Rome with a young Italian gigolo. Williams's first book of poetry was *In the Winter of Cities* (1956).

Boom! (1968, Universal, 110m/c) ☆☆ **Sc:** Tennessee Williams. **D:** Joseph Losey. **P:** John Heyman, Norman Priggen. **Cam:** Douglas Slocombe. **Cast:** Richard Burton, Elizabeth Taylor, Noel Coward, Joanna Shimkus, Michael Dunn, Romolo Valli, Fernando Piazza. *The Milk Train Doesn't Stop Here Anymore* was a 1962 one-act play adapted from Williams's *Mademoiselle* magazine piece, "Man Bring This Up Road." The story featured a vagabond poet noted as a harbinger of death who stumbles onto a leukemia-afflicted matriarch's posh villa and presides over her waning days. The play debuted in 1964 with Tallulah Bankhead and Tab Hunter in the principal roles at the Brooks Atkinson Theatre, and closed after four performances. This occasionally incomprehensible film allegory is a meditation on advancing death, well-heeled arrogance, and disenfranchised artists. Rejected by audiences and critics in its day, it was considered a huge failure for all concerned, although fans of Losey defend it. Williams's themes of the haves being callous to the have-nots and human warmth thawing cold hearts are detectable. This was the eighth of 11 Burton/Taylor on-screen pairings and was shot on Sardinian locations.

- *"[Burton] is not good enough, either at acting or acting tactics, to carry a sub-average film actress like Miss Taylor through whole movies; they simply fall down on top of each other. Meanwhile, we have the prospects of many more classics fumbled through and rendered slightly boring, interspersed with outright junk like Boom! Richard Burton's knack for reading poetry has perhaps led him to overrate his own literary taste. At least, his choice of contemporary scripts is medium to awful. The Milk Train Doesn't Stop Here Anymore...is not only one of Tennessee Williams's worst plays, but one in which the leading actress is obliged to make a campy fool of herself throughout—hardly the role for Miss Taylor at this ever-delicate stage of her career." (Wilfrid Sheed, Esquire)*

Cat on a Hot Tin Roof follows the attempted reconciliation of sex-starved wife Maggie the Cat and disaffected, boozy husband Brick in a Mississippi plantation mansion, on the occasion of the announcement of domineering Big Daddy's terminal illness and the resultant in-family inheritance squabbles. The play was adapted once for the cinema and twice for TV—with all-star casts in each case. The Pulitzer Prize-winning play of 1955 starred Barbara Bel Geddes as Maggie, Ben Gazzara as Brick, Burl Ives as Big Daddy, and Mildred Dunnock as Big Mamma.

Cat on a Hot Tin Roof (1958, MGM, 108m/c, **VHS/DVD**) ☆☆☆ **Sc:** Richard Brooks, James Poe. **D:** Richard Brooks. **P:** Lawrence Weingarten. **Cam:** William Daniels. **Cast:** Elizabeth Taylor, Paul Newman, Burl Ives, Judith Anderson, Jack Carson, Madeleine Sherwood, Larry Gates, Vaughn Taylor. Brooks toned down the homosexual overtones in the play between Brick and his recently interred best friend, Skipper. The actors are excellent and the film rides along with them. The film was nominated for six Oscars: Best Picture, Actor (Newman), Actress (Taylor), Director (Brooks), Adapted Screenplay (Brooks and Poe), and Color Cinematography (Daniels).

- "*Much hocus-pocus about the reasons [Brick doesn't want to have sex with Maggie]; when the 'true' reason is revealed it sounds the hokiest. But Taylor looks very desirable, and the cast is full of actors whooping it up with Southern accents.*" (*Pauline Kael*, The New Yorker)

- "*Williams's least worthy long play to date....it lacks resonance beneath its action; its writing is sometimes stilted, some of its motivations are insufficient, and its resolution is feeble. These faults are all italicized in the film...which manages to add one more fault....the matter of the son's imputed homosexuality is watered down by an explanation of a special friendship with his dead teammate so complicated and cautious that one wonders how the actors kept straight faces....Paul Newman's performance...is genuinely creative—the kind of acting in which buried smoldering is made manifest and in which the thought processes between the lines are clear and interesting.*" (*Stanley Kauffmann*, The New Republic)

Cat on a Hot Tin Roof (1976, ABC, 120m/c) *ABC Theatre* ☆☆☆
Tp: Tennessee Williams. **D:** Robert Moore. **Cast:** Natalie Wood, Robert Wagner, Laurence Olivier, Maureen Stapleton, Jack Hedley, Mary Peach, David Healy, Sean Saxon, Heidi Rundt. In this initial offering of Olivier's "Tribute to the American Theatre" for ABC, much of the interest was in the icon's version of Big Daddy. His portrayal was less bombastic than most interpretations, yet more comic and tragic, too, as he casually exposes Big Daddy's redneck past in gestures and vocal tones, contrasting that with his waning days as a big-style Southern gentleman. This was also one of the few on-screen pairings of spouses Wagner and Wood.

- "*The language and attitudes no longer have the shock value of the past, leaving the viewer with a talky squabble among unpleasant characters that hardly seemed worth the effort of watching. With only Natalie Wood and Maureen Stapleton achieving a degree of believability in the key roles, the Williams drama, with its preposterous character names and its murky explanation of Robert Wagner's retreat into the bottle, seemed little more than a contentious tirade of quarrelsome Southern caricatures, projecting their own self-interests in torrents of boring dialogue—often at the top of their voices. Olivier was as forceful as usual, but never convincing...lacked dramatic tension...*" (Variety)

- *"Unlike the great stars whose glitter dims all that surrounds them, Olivier enhances and elevates both the play and the players with his own artistry."* (Judith Crist, TV Guide)

- *"Even with the bravura hamminess of Laurence Olivier's Big Daddy, the program was marred by its soap opera style (intense closeups, cramped direction, excessive musical underlining) and the weak performances of Robert Wagner and Natalie Wood, who, try as they might, never skimmed below the surfaces of their roles."* (Brian G. Rose, Television and the Performing Arts)

Cat on a Hot Tin Roof (1985, PBS, 122min/c, **VHS/DVD**) American Playhouse ☆☆☆ **D:** Jack Hofsiss. **Cast:** Jessica Lange, Tommy Lee Jones, Rip Torn, Kim Stanley, Penny Fuller, David Dukes. Lange made a substantial mark in Williams country with this performance as Maggie the Cat and, a decade later, as Blanche du Bois in *A Streetcar Named Desire* (see below). She had wonderful support from a terrific ensemble, including Torn, who tears the hinges off the role of Big Daddy; Jones, who limps around as the self-tortured Brick; Stanley as the at-first flustered and matronly Big Mamma, and Fuller as "Sisterwoman" Mae, presiding over her "little no-neck monsters." The show was nominated for two Emmys for Best Supporting Actress (Stanley, Fuller).

- *"Once again...decked out in a promising production and, once again, the teleplay itself founders....Imposing credits, all in all, but the seriously flawed play eludes their efforts....Unfortunately, the play seems to be more evasive than ever, coming perilously close to sinking in the same mendacity it pretends to implore. Ironically, the performances are more honest than the play....Mr. Torn captures much of the natural viciousness and sheer vulgarity of [Big Daddy]...Ms. Stanley retains the practical shrewdness behind Big Mama's flighty hysterics..."* (John J. O'Connor, The New York Times)

Dragon Country: Two Plays by Tennessee Williams (1970, NET, 80m/c, **VHS**) New York Television Theatre ☆☆½ **Tp:** Tennessee Williams. **D/P:** Glenn Jordan. **Cast:** Kim Stanley, William Redfield, Alan Mixon, Lois Smith. The two one-act plays were *I Can't Imagine Tomorrow* with Stanley and Redfield, about a dying woman and a shy schoolteacher ruminating on human isolation, and *Talk to Me Like the Rain and Let Me Listen* with Mixon and Smith. The former received its debut on TV in this production and the latter was produced by the West Side Actors Workshop in 1967.

- *"...made for a dreary evening....talky and maudlin. Miss Stanley's expert performing was the program's saving grace, her face and inflections imparting greater depth to her role than the mere words provided. Lois Smith had her moments in the shorter play, but the men were shortchanged, per Williams's fashion. Dragon Country...was more burnt out than firebreathing."* (Variety)

Four by Tennessee Williams was a two-hour installment of NET's *The Play of the Week* in 1961 with a stellar cast including Jo Van Fleet, Eileen Heckert, Anne Revere, Maureen Stapleton, Mike Kellin, Alfred Ryder, Vivian Nathan, Leueen McGrath, and Thomas Chalmers. The four one-act plays were *I Rise in Flame, Cried the Phoenix; Hello, From Bertha; The Lady of Larkspur Lotion;* and *The Purification.* Some of the actors assembled for the production appeared in more than one play. The plays were originally produced in 1959, 1961, 1947, and 1959, respectively. The initial one-act is about the death of D.H. Lawrence, one of Williams's great literary inspirations.

The Glass Menagerie, one of Williams's greatest plays, concerns a domineering St. Louis mother, Amanda Wingfield, lost in the rhapsodies of her past as a fetching belle, and her affect on her adult offspring. These are Tom, the brooding and caustic narrator, and the shy, clubfooted Laura. The original 1944 New York cast featured Laurette Taylor, Eddie Dowling, Julie Haydon, and Anthony Ross.

The Glass Menagerie (1950, Warner Bros., 107m/bw) ☆☆½ **Sc:** Tennessee Williams, Peter Berneis. **D:** Irving Rapper. **P:** Jerry Wald, Charles K. Feldman. **Cam:** Robert Burks. **Cast:** Gertrude Lawrence, Arthur Kennedy, Jane Wyman, Kirk Douglas, Ralph Sanford, Ann Tyrell, John Compton. The initial filming of the play is especially effective in the performances of Kennedy and Wyman as the siblings. The former's glowering and his acidic delivery of Williams's dialogue was a perfect match for the restless Tom, while Wyman's quietude is flush with the playwright's intent. Lawrence seems to have contempt for Amanda while Douglas is a shallow Gentleman Caller.

- *"The first Tennessee Williams film can serve as a textbook demonstration of how insensitive compromises can ruin an adaptation....The primary failure of the film was the producers' insistence upon a happy ending....Actually, the film reduces the complexity of all of the characters....the film fails to develop an equivalent for the poetic techniques of the play....the cast of big names did not meet the artistic needs of the play....Something distinctive and extremely personal has been converted into something simple and prosaic, the standard romantic melodrama. Williams rightly declares it 'the most awful travesty of the play I've ever seen...horribly mangled...'"* (Maurice Yacowar, Tennessee Williams and Film)

The Glass Menagerie (1966, CBS, 120m/bw) *CBS Playhouse* ☆☆☆½ **Tp:** Paul Boules, Tennessee Williams. **D:** Michael Elliott, **P:** David Susskind. **Cast:** Shirley Booth, Hal Holbrook, Barbara Loden, Pat Hingle. Booth received the role of Amanda as a reward from her network for the excellent ratings her *Hazel* sitcom was receiving. Holbrook played the goaded Tom, assigned to find a Gentleman Caller, with deep sarcasm. The program received Emmy nominations for Outstanding Drama of the 1966–67 season and Best Actress in a Drama (Booth).

- "...a scene involving a crippled girl who had retreated from the world of people and a gentleman caller who momentarily brings her back to it — was television at its most sublime. That climactic and most memorable scene...with its delicate pitch and fragile symbolism, was actually heightened by the intimacy of the medium and was given moving performances by Barbara Loden and Pat Hingle...easily the high point of the current TV season. Instead of nagging, prodding and railing corrosively, Miss Booth was merely gabby....Hal Holbrook as the narrator and entrapped brother, was first-rate" (Variety)

The Glass Menagerie (1973, ABC, 120m/c) ☆☆☆☆☆ **Tp:** Tennessee Williams. **D:** Anthony Harvey. **P:** David Susskind. **Cast:** Katharine Hepburn, Sam Waterston, Joanna Miles, Michael Moriarty. The teleplay used for this 1973 production is Williams's own adaptation and is often cited as the best screen interpretation of the play. Hepburn burned into memory all of Amanda's neurotic foibles while not forgetting the embers of her humanity. Waterston was more analytic and passive than most interpretations of Tom. The show won Emmy Awards for Best Supporting Actor (Moriarty) and Supporting Actress (Miles). Hepburn was also nominated for Best Actress.

- "Seldom are TV-flick audiences, let alone moviegoers, offered a film of such quality in every sense of the word...enhanced by first-rank performance, direction and cinematography. This made-for-television production gives us excellence (in place of the more usual and disastrous reverence) from start to finish under the direction of Anthony Harvey....Katharine Hepburn leads a quintet of brilliant performers...Sam Waterston is simply stunning...Miles...Moriarty...The sum of their work is a triumph among television films..." (Judith Crist, TV Guide)

- "Topflight performances by its four-member cast made the latest TV version...memorable...Hepburn's finely etched performance...was one of those tours de force that make a basically unsympathetic role bearable and interesting by the sheer force of the interpretation." (Variety)

The Glass Menagerie (1987, Cineplex, 134min/c, **VHS**) ☆☆☆ **D:** Paul Newman. **P:** Burtt Harris, Joe Carcciolo. **Cam:** Michael Ballhaus. **Cast:** Joanne Woodward, John Malkovich, Karen Allen, James Naughton. This film provided the opportunity for Newman to direct his wife as Amanda. Malkovich played Tom, Allen was Laura, and Naughton portrayed the Gentleman Caller. This is the most dark-hearted version of the play, with Malkovich a bitter Depression Era Tom and Allen a bruised and pitiful Laura. But the piece belongs to Woodward, who swirls in a maelstrom of neuroses, haunting her adult offspring with her overbearing insistence that the family's present should reflect the gilded memory of her yesterdays. The film was the official United States entry in the Cannes Film Festival.

- *"It's a serious and respectful adaptation, but never an incendiary one, perhaps because the odds against its capturing the play's real genius are simply too great. In any case, this* Glass Menagerie *catches more of the drama's closeness and narrowness than its fire."* (Janet Maslin, The New York Times)

The Last of the Mobile Hot-Shots (1970, Warner Bros., 108m/c) ☆☆½ **Sc:** Gore Vidal. **D/P:** Sidney Lumet. **Cam:** James Wong Howe. **Cast:** James Coburn, Lynn Redgrave, Robert Hooks, Perry Hayes, Reggie King, Patricia Zipprodt. Williams's play was published in 1968 as *Kingdom of Earth* and first performed as *The Seven Descents of Myrtle* the same year at the Ethel Barrymore Theatre with Estelle Parsons, Brian Bedford, and Harry Guardino. It is the story of an interracial love triangle set on a crumbling plantation on the eve of a flood in Depression Era Alabama. The insensitive Myrtle moves between the rough outcast, Chicken, and the impotent and boozy patriarch, Jeb. This was an ill-advised return to Williams territory for both Lumet and Vidal with a very loose adaptation of the play. Making the material more topical for the times, Vidal converted Chicken—a mullato in the play—to black, and Lumet cast Hooks in the part. Still, nothing seems to be beneath this talky sex melodrama, except the rising water. When the Motion Picture Association of America rated the film X for its sexual frankness (prior to the ratings code changes of 1984), Warner Bros. released it to a few theaters, closed it quickly, and never sold it to ancillary markets.

- *"All in all, the film is a provocative minor work by a major director. It may be illuminating to compare the film to the specifics of the original. For instance, Williams ended the play with the spirited couple retreating to the rooftop, but Lumet takes them further. He shows them on the roof, huddled under Chicken's chicken-yellow raincape, shrinking to a yellow speck as the camera draws back for a long view of the flooded landscape. Typically, Lumet refers his characters to their physical and social settings. His characters are emblems of a time in American social history, more specifically than Williams's were. Indeed, one might suggest that the film is more deeply related to Lumet's* The Pawnbroker *(1965), both in theme and technique, than it is to Williams's play, which is nowhere as topical as the film."* (Maurice Yacowar, Tennessee Williams and Film)

Lord Byron's Love Letter was produced on *Omnibus* in 1953 starring Ethel Barrymore, Patricia Collinge, and Nydia Westman.

The Night of the Iguana was a 1961 play that tells the story of an earthy hotelier, a New England spinster, and a teen-aged nymphet who vie for the attentions of a free-boozing, defrocked priest who operates bus tours in the backcountry of Mexico. The 1961 Broadway presentation at the Royale Theatre starred Bette Davis, Patrick O'Neal, James Farentino, Margaret Leighton, and Christopher Jones.

The Night of the Iguana (1964, MGM/Seven Arts, 125m/bw, **VHS**) ☆☆☆½ **Sc:** Anthony Veiller, John Huston. **D:** John Huston. **P:** Ray Stark. **Cam:** Gabriel Figueroa. **Cast:** Richard Burton, Deborah Kerr, Ava Gardner, Sue Lyon, Grayson Hall, Skip Ward, Cyril Delevanti, Gladys Hill, Mary Boylan. Dismissed by the playwright, the film demands attention for its pedigree and the central issue of Burton surviving his despair over the hypocrisies he sees in his own religion. Huston instills verve, optimism, and humor in what had been a very dark play. The film won an Oscar for its Costume Design (Dorothy Jeakins), and was nominated for Best Supporting Actress (Hall), Black and White Cinematography, and Art Direction/Set Decoration.

- *"...undoubtedly the best screen adaptation of a Tennessee Williams work...a penetratingly and affectingly compassionate exploration of human agony. More literal but not less literate than the 1961 play, with a vitality and cohesion to compensate, this...production is an intense and painful exploration of loneliness among the hag-ridden, the bedeviled, the misfits, and the captives of their own and others' passions....beautiful performances, chief among them those of Deborah Kerr, Ava Gardner, and Grayson Hall." (Judith Crist, TV Guide)*

Orpheus Descending is a 1957 reworking of Williams's first professionally presented play, *Battle of Angels* (1940). It concerns a drifting guitarist, Val Xavier, sporting a trademark snakeskin jacket, who has an affair with a crippled storekeeper's middle-aged wife in a small Mississippi town. The tryst incites the town to violence. The 1957 production was directed by Harold Clurman at the Martin Beck Theatre, with a cast led by Cliff Robertson as Val Xavier, Maureen Stapleton and Lois Smith, and co-starring Robert Webber, R.G. Armstrong, and Charles Tyner.

The Fugitive Kind (1960, United Artists, 122m/bw, **VHS**) ☆☆☆ **Sc:** Tennessee Williams, Meade Roberts. **D:** Sidney Lumet. **P:** Martin Jurow, Richard A. Shepherd. **Cam:** Boris Kaufman. **Cast:** Marlon Brando, Anna Magnani, Joanne Woodward, Maureen Stapleton, Victor Jory, R.G. Armstrong, John Baragrey, Emory Richardson, Lucille Benson. The potent star troika—with Woodward as a drunken slattern—upholds the interest in this hothouse stew about life-battered Mississippians, but Jory delivers the best performance, as the cripple Jabe. The movie took its title from an earlier Williams play entitled *The Fugitive Kind*, which had no connection to this story, but was more to the filmmakers' liking.

- *"Is there a future for Tennessee Williams? Or is there nothing ahead but his past?...Williams may be turning into a theatrical Erskine Caldwell—*

whose novels continue to make a mountain of money long after they ceased to be good because his name is a guarantee of mattressy sex. One hoped — and still hopes — for more from Williams. There was ample cause to believe that he would grow along Strindbergian or even Chekhovian lines. There is cause now to fear that he is trapped by the facility with which he can rework the same vein — possibly convinced that by refusing to move into new areas he is being true to himself — and that he is also trapped, perhaps unconsciously and insidiously, by the public's present image of him." (Stanley Kauffmann, The New Republic)

Orpheus Descending (1990, TNT, 117m/c, **VHS**) ☆☆☆☆ **Sc:** Peter Hall, Tennessee Williams. **D:** Peter Hall. **P:** George Manasse. **Cast:** Kevin Anderson, Vanessa Redgrave, Anne Twomey, Miriam Margolyes, Brad Sullivan, Sloan Shelton, Patti Allison, Pat McNamara, Michael McCarty, Doyle Richmond, Peg Small. This cable version of the 1989 Broadway revival opens up the play with period cars and location shooting near Jacksonville, Florida, to approximate Williams's "Two River County, Mississippi." Vanessa Redgrave's performance as the Italianate Lady Torrance is one of her most memorable.

• *"...remarkably effective film...Sir Peter [Hall] carefully retains a sense of theatricality. This Williams play is, like most of the others, not naturalistic. Most of the elements, from the language to the imagery, are heightened. This is surrealistic territory, and the balance here is virtually perfect. By the time this film was started...Miss Redgrave's understanding of Lady had become profound. That priceless asset is used here to powerful effect, making this a far more memorable experience than the [1960 film]...this is as fine and perceptive an* Orpheus Descending *as Williams admirers are likely to get for a long, long time." (John J. O'Connor,* The New York Times)

Period of Adjustment (1962, MGM, 112m/bw, **VHS**) ☆☆½ **Sc:** Isobel Lennart. **D:** George Roy Hill. **P:** Lawrence Weingarten. **Cam:** Paul C. Vogel. **Cast:** Tony Franciosa, Jane Fonda, Jim Hutton, Lois Nettleton, John McGiver, Jack Albertson, Mabel Albertson. The actors, all experts in light comedy, seem to convert the playwright's themes into a one-of-a-kind marital comedy about a young couple who helps another couple with marriage woes — caused by the Korean War veteran husband's impotence. The politics of sex, family, and community commingle in this 1960 work. For the original 1960 production at New York's Helen Hayes Theatre, Hill directed James Daly, Barbara Baxley, Robbert Webber, and Rosemary Murphy. The film is significant as Hill's movie debut and one of Fonda's early hits. It was nominated for an Oscar for its Art Direction/Set Decoration.

• *"Williams chose director George Roy Hill on the strength of his musical,* Greenwillow. *The choice proved unfortunate, because Hill failed to develop the shadows and depths that lay beneath Williams's comedy; at least in Hill's film version, the play was trivialized." (Maurice Yacowar, Tennessee Williams and Film)*

Portrait of a Madonna was presented in 1948 on ABC's *Actors Studio* with Hume Cronyn directing Jessica Tandy. This very first telecast of *Actors Studio* showcased Tandy as another of the playwright's aging, delusional Southern belles. The actress was convinced by director and life partner Cronyn to take the part in a 1946 production at the Actors Laboratory Theatre in Los Angeles—even though she didn't feel that she was right for it. Her performance led directly to Williams and Elia Kazan casting her in the stage version of *A Streetcar Named Desire*, with which they all made theatrical history.

The Rose Tattoo (1955, Paramount, 117m/bw, **VHS**) ☆☆☆½ **Sc:** Tennessee Williams, adaptation by Hal Kanter. **D:** Daniel Mann. **P:** Hal B. Wallis. **Cam:** James Wong Howe. **Cast:** Anna Magnani, Burt Lancaster, Marisa Pavan, Ben Cooper, Jo Van Fleet, Virginia Grey. This play was written by Williams as a vehicle for Anna Magnani. But it opened on Broadway in 1951 with Maureen Stapleton instead, because the Egyptian-born and Italian-raised Magnani shied away from the demands of the English language. Magnani then acquiesced for the 1955 film version and played the delusional Gulf Coast widow, whose fond memories of her husband almost prevent her from being wooed by a dim-bulb, half-loony stevedore. The pungency of the Southern atmosphere is caught by Howe's cinematography, and Magnani is excellent in conveying Williams's themes. In his most overtly comic performance, Lancaster plays the Italian stevedore and it's tough to accept him as a dolt. The film won Oscars for Best Actress (Magnani), Cinematography (Howe), and Art Direction/Set Decoration. It was also nominated for Best Picture, Supporting Actress (Pavan), Dramatic Score (Alex North), Film Editing, and Costume Design.

- *"Magnani's virtuoso display of vitality makes it almost frighteningly clear that her husband's perfection was his sexual potency. The weakness of the material is that the reduction of all human needs to sex is handled only semi-comically. Burt Lancaster is rather embarrassing as Serafina's not-too-smart suitor." (Pauline Kael, The New Yorker)*
- *"One perhaps might argue that the film must be taken as a kind of short-hand, in which by convention 'marriage' means 'passion.'...So the film may fairly represent the events of the play, but it lacks Williams's challenge to familiar, domestic morality. In this respect, the film actually subverts the play. And it fails to preserve the resonance of Williams's ambiguous vision. This dilution may be due to director Daniel Mann, whose film work was solidly in the tradition of stolid domestic realism...Mann*

was not at ease with Williams's subtleties and irony....in the filming of The Rose Tattoo, *the poetic turned to prose."* (Maurice Yacowar, Tennessee Williams and Film)

A Streetcar Named Desire concerns a crumbling Southern beauty, Blanche Du Bois, who comes to New Orleans to stay with her sister, Stella, and is both attracted and repulsed by her aggressive, earthy brother-in-law, Stanley Kowalski, who treats her with indignation, and eventually rapes her. She is also initially wooed by Stanley's pal, Mitch. The play, a sensational hit, was adapted into a groundbreaking film, then into two TV productions several decades later. Performing in the landmark 1947 play, directed by Elia Kazan at the Ethel Barrymore Theatre, were three members of the initial film cast: Marlon Brando, Kim Hunter, and Karl Malden. Jessica Tandy, who played Blanche, won the Tony Award for Best Actress of 1948.

A Streetcar Named Desire (1951 Warner Bros., 122m/bw, **VHS**) ☆☆☆☆☆ **Sc:** Tennessee Williams (with Elia Kazan, Oscar Saul). **D:** Elia Kazan. **P:** Charles K. Feldman. **Cam:** Harry Stradling. **Cast:** Vivien Leigh, Marlon Brando, Kim Hunter, Karl Malden, Rudy Bond, Nick Dennis, Peg Hillias, Wright King. The play and this film were instrumental in introducing Method acting to the American public via Brando's powerful performance. A major event in the theatre, it was the same on film, for the advance in acting as well as for the force in Williams's language and candor with sexual themes. The film won Oscars for Best Actress (Leigh), Supporting Actress (Hunter), Supporting Actor (Malden), and Art Direction/Set Decoration. It was also nominated for Best Picture, Director (Kazan), Actor (Brando), Screenplay (Williams), Black and White Cinematography, Score (Alex North), Costume Design, and Sound Recording.

- *"For all of its unanswered questions, minor lapses and ambiguities, A* Streetcar Named Desire *was even more powerful as a film than it was as a play, and Blanche DuBois was a character to set alongside Anna Karenina and Tess of the d'Urbervilles."* (Bosley Crowther, Reruns: 50 Memorable Films)

- *"Elia Kazan's direction is often stagy, the sets and arrangements of actors are frequently too transparently 'worked out,' but who cares when you're looking at two of the greatest performances ever put on film and listening to some of the finest dialogue ever written by an American?"* (Pauline Kael, The New Yorker)

- *"Brando was used by director Elia Kazan to steal part of the play from Tennessee Williams's vision. In its debut,* Streetcar *was more about Stanley and less about Blanche than it ever would be again. Brando was established for a generation of Americans as a great actor."* (David Thomsen, A Biographical Dictionary of Film)

A Streetcar Named Desire (1984, ABC, 154m/c, **VHS**) ☆☆☆☆ **Tp:** Tennessee Williams, adapted by Oscar Saul. **D:** John Erman. **P:** Keith Barish, Marc Trabulus. **Cast:** Ann-Margret, Treat Williams, Beverly D'Angelo, Randy Quaid, Rafael Campos, Erica Yohn. Ann-Margret took her turn as Blanche and delivered what may be her greatest performance, plumbing a well of vulnerability and delusion. The script is the same one used for the 1951 film. This show aired the year after the playwright's death. The show received 11 Emmy Award nominations, including those for Outstanding Drama Special, Director, Best Actress (Ann-Margret), Supporting Actress (D'Angelo), Supporting Actor (Quaid), Cinematography (Bill Butler), Art Direction/Set Decoration, Costume Design, Editing, Sound Editing, and Sound Mixing.

- *"It is a play that creates stars but does not require them, and Ann-Margret now can be considered one of the handful of superior actresses available to films, tv and stage....Ann-Margret is just right as Blanche, the madness in her working its way slowly to the surface and then ebbing just when you think she has gone over the edge. It is a straightforward and poignant performance, naked to the kind of tricks and mannerisms that come easily to the role....Randy Quaid brought just the right amount of sweetness to the role of Mitch, a part, once again, that is as critical to the clockwork structure of this play as any....Beverly D'Angelo was equally as good..."* (Variety)

A Streetcar Named Desire (1995, CBS, 156m/c, **VHS**) *The Hallmark Hall of Fame* ☆☆☆½ **Tp:** Tennessee Williams. **D:** Glenn Jordan. **Cam:** Ralf D. Bode. **Cast:** Jessica Lange, Alec Baldwin, Diane Lane, John Goodman, Jerry Hardin, Patricia Herd, Carlos Gomez. Another starry rendition allowed Lange and Baldwin to repeat their 1992 stage performances from the Broadway revival. Lange brings a modern sensibility and innate sense of toughness to her interpretation of Blanche. This production used Williams's original play, replete with sordid details. The show won an Emmy Award for Art Direction/Set Decoration and was nominated for Best Actor (Baldwin), Actress (Lange), and Supporting Actor (Goodman). Lange also won a Golden Globe for this part.

- *"...far more faithful to the original play than the 1951 Elia Kazan film...there is no mistaking here that this is a stage play, not concerned with penny ante 'realism' of the average made-for-television movie. The world of Williams is a hothouse clutter with eccentric blossoms...Ms. Lange's Blanche is not nearly so fragile [as Vivien Leigh's]. Behind her looming nervous breakdown is a steely bitchiness....intensely sultry version of the play...Ms. Lane perfectly captures the painful ambiguities of Stella...what an admirable thing for a network to do. Cheers to a noble gesture!"* (John J. O'Connor, The New York Times)

- *"Streetcar may be off-putting to viewers used to naturalistic drama, but Blanche is speaking for the playwright when she says, 'I don't want realism; I want magic!' The magic is not quite achieved. Lange's performance is halting and mannered to the point of being irritating. But Baldwin is terrific. He passes the crucial test—he never reminds you that this is the role made famous by Marlon Brando, and he brings a sneaky humor to the part."* (Entertainment Weekly)

Suddenly, Last Summer tells the story of a woman tortured by her memory of seeing her homosexual cousin killed and partially cannibalized by North African boys upon whom he had been preying. Meanwhile, the dead boy's rich, overbearing mother tries to convince a neurosurgeon to lobotomize the memory, erasing the evidence of what was then considered socially aberrant behavior. The play was first presented in 1958 with another one-acter, *Something Unspoken*, under the umbrella title *The Garden District*, starring Hortense Alden, Robert Lansing, and Anne Meacham.

Suddenly, Last Summer (1959, Columbia, 114m/bw, **VHS/DVD**) ☆☆☆ **Sc:** Gore Vidal. **D:** Joseph L. Mankiewicz. **P:** Sam Spiegel. **Cam:** Jack Hildyard. **Cast:** Elizabeth Taylor, Katharine Hepburn, Montgomery Clift, Mercedes McCambridge, Albert Dekker, Mavis Villiers, Gary Raymond. This decadent bit of Williams strangeness is done with the full Hollywood treatment, including well-charged performances from the two female stars. The play is a one-act flight of allegorical fever dream, and completely unrealistic. Vidal and Mankiewicz retain the strong suggestion of the homosexual angle disguised behind the cannibalism, and use flashbacks depicting Taylor on North African beaches. Clift, as the investigating doctor, seems confused, and the two leads realize they're in something of a horror film. The film was nominated twice for Oscars for Best Actress (Taylor, Hepburn) and for its Art Direction/Set Decoration.

- *"This is basically a foolish, unrewarding work, but it could not have been conceived or written except by a dramatist of extraordinary talent. What has happened presumably is that Williams has in this piece plunged so far into its nether reaches after an idea that he has lost his sense of relevancy....he has created an exercise in Grand Guignol. To make it worse, he has plunged with such blind fervor that he has not composed a good Guignol....The film script is simply an arbitrarily prolonged question to which we are finally given the answer."* (Stanley Kauffmann, The New Republic)

Suddenly, Last Summer (1992, PBS, 75m/c) *Great Performances* ☆☆☆½ **D:** Richard Eyre. **P:** Simon Curtis. **Cast:** Natasha Richardson, Maggie Smith, Rob Lowe, Gillian Raine, Richard E. Grant, Moira Redmond, C.P. Wilson, Rosaleen Linehan. The playwright's one-act play was expanded for this special, which retained the force of the original. Smith, as the despicably determined Violet Venable —perhaps Williams's most morally bankrupt controlling mother—

delivers one of her best performances. She was nominated for an Emmy Award as Best Actress in a Miniseries or Special.

- *"...Richard Eyre...carefully treats the one-act play as if it were preserved under glass, safe from any gusts of invention that may prove fatal....written at a time when gay men in literature still had to be punished severely for what was perceived as their transgressions,* Suddenly, Last Summer *is, in a sense, very much a period piece. This is the overall approach taken, rather too solemnly, in this handsome television production."* (John J. O'Connor, The New York Times)

- *"Director Richard Eyre...manages to wring every drop of drama out of the play...In a series titled* Great Performances, *this is one of the few shows in which the performances really do stand out...Ms. Smith delivers a bravura turn..."* (Robert Goldberg, The Wall Street Journal)

Summer and Smoke, first performed in 1948 with Margaret Phillips and Ralph Theadore, is about the spinsterish Alma Winemiller, a minister's daughter in a small Mississippi town who's given a last chance at love with the boozy and dissipated town doctor. It was adapted once for film and once, after substantial retooling by the playwright, for TV.

Summer and Smoke (1961, Paramount, 118m/c, **VHS**) ☆☆☆½ **Sc:** James Poe, Meade Roberts. **D:** Peter Glenville. **Cam:** Charles Lang Jr. **Cast:** Geraldine Page, Laurence Harvey, John McIntire, Una Merkel, Pamela Tiffin, Rita Moreno, Thomas Gomez, Earl Holliman, Lee Patrick, Casey Adams, Malcolm Atterbury. This film afforded the chance for Page to preserve her 1952 Broadway rendition of Alma in a touching performance. The film was nominated for Oscars for Best Actress (Page), Supporting Actress (Merkel), Score (Elmer Bernstein), and Art Direction/Set Decoration.

- *"There's supposed to be something on fire inside Alma, Tennessee Williams's lonely, inhibited preacher's daughter, but from Geraldine Page's performance and Peter Glenville's direction 'taint smoke that rises — just wispy little tired ideas goin' to rejoin the Holy Ghost. Page is all delicate shadings and no surprises, her performance is so meticulously worked out it's dead....Williams's rewritten version,* The Eccentricities of a Nightingale, *was given a far superior production on TV [see below]..."* (Pauline Kael, The New Yorker)

The Eccentricities of a Nightingale (1970, NET, 120M/C, **VHS**) *Theatre America* (formerly *NET Playhouse*) ☆☆☆☆ **D:** Glenn Jordan. **P:** Lindsay Law, Glenn Jordan. **Cast:** Blythe Danner, Frank Langella, Tim O'Connor, Louise Latham, Neva Patterson. In 1964, Williams made changes to Alma's journey to love in *Summer and Smoke,* including the title. Danner's widely praised performance is perhaps her best in filmed media and greatly enhanced her reputation. This version also aired on PBS's *Theatre in America* in 1976.

- *"Blythe Danner's Alma is as much of a television event as Katharine Hepburn's Amanda in* The Glass Menagerie. *Frank Langella is such a warm, dreamy-eyed Dr. Buchanan that the role is reimbursed for the loss of its cynical edge with a smooth romanticism that complements Danner's determined honesty splendidly."* (Tom Shales, The Washington Post)

Sweet Bird of Youth concerns an aging movie actress linking up with alcoholic gigolo Chance Wayne in his Gulf Coast hometown amid the family and political tangles of his old flame's father, Boss Finley. Elia Kazan directed the 1959 Broadway original at New York's Martin Beck Theatre starring Paul Newman, Geraldine Page, Sidney Blackmer, Rip Torn, Diana Hyland, and Madeleine Sherwood.

Sweet Bird of Youth (1962, MGM, 120m/c, **VHS**) ☆☆☆ **Sc/D:** Richard Brooks. **P:** Pandro S. Berman. **Cam:** Milton Krasner. **Cast:** Geraldine Page, Paul Newman, Shirley Knight, Rip Torn, Ed Begley, Mildred Dunnock, Philip Abbott, Madeleine Sherwood, Corey Allen, Dub Taylor, Barry Atwater. Williams film veterans Brooks, Newman, and Page pooled their talents in another toned-down version of the playwright's work, again by Brooks (after *Cat on a Hot Tin Roof*). Chance Wayne's character is more synthesized and the play's culminating castration was, well, cut. Knight co-starred as Heavenly, Newman's longtime sweetheart whose father, Boss Finley, long ago deemed her too good for him. Ed Begley won the Oscar for Best Supporting Actor as harsh politico Boss Finley. The film was also nominated for Best Actress (Page) and Supporting Actress (Knight).

- *"I wish that Tennessee Williams had written fewer or better plays. Having conscientiously wrestled with* Suddenly, Last Summer, The Fugitive Kind, *and* Summer and Smoke, *I am now confronted with Richard Brooks's* Sweet Bird of Youth. *Mr. Brooks has a considerable reputation, one of the many things that I don't understand about movies. So here he bowdlerizes Mr. Williams's play: Chance gave Heavenly not syphilis but a baby; Boss Finley, her father, doesn't rant about white supremacy and his minions don't emasculate Chance, they just mark up his face a little; and a happy ending materializes in the last three minutes—contradicting the logic of the preceding two hours...Miss Page takes over the film as triumphantly as she did the play."* (Dwight Macdonald, Esquire)

Sweet Bird of Youth (1989, NBC, 95m/c, **VHS**) ☆☆½ **Tp:** Gavin Lambert. **D:** Nicolas Roeg. **P:** Fred Whitehead. **Cast:** Elizabeth Taylor, Mark Harmon, Rip Torn, Valerie Perrine, Ruta Lee, Kevin Geer, Michael Wilding Jr., Seymour Cassel, Cheryl Paris, Billy Ray Sharkey, Ruta Lee. Torn, who played Chance Wayne on Broadway and Heavenly's brother in the 1962 film, plays Boss Finley in this 1989 TV vehicle for Elizabeth Taylor. This was a reworking of the play by Lambert based on Williams's notes about changing the material. The finale from the original play is intact here.

- "...by 'opening up' the play, Williams is shut out....Lambert has jettisoned much of Williams's expressive, often searing lingo in favor of a more TV-oriented form of expression. The beautifully orchestrated scenes between Alexandra and Chance have been cut, the poetry and underlying philosophy discarded....The symbolism of the play—which takes place on Easter Sunday—has been bleached out....Disappointing telefilm..." (Variety)

Ten Blocks on the Camino Real (1966, NET, 65m/bw, **VHS**) NET Playhouse ☆☆☆ **D:** Jack Landau. **P:** Jack Landau, Jac Venza. **Cast:** Martin Sheen, Hurd Hatfield, Lotte Lenya, Carrie Nye, Albert Dekker, Janet Margolin, Patricia Neway, Michael Baseleon. This one-act allegory was adapted by Williams into the 1953 full-length play, Camino Real, about Kilroy, the generic American serviceman in an unnamed, dreamlike Latin American country. There, he encounters the spiritless embodied cliches of the macho Latin lover, an earthy Carmen-like woman, a more ethereal female, and others. Sheean (later changed to Sheen) plays Kilroy in this debut installment of NET Playhouse. The 1953 play starred Martin Balsam, Eli Wallach, Hurd Hatfield, Vivian Nathan, Jo Van Fleet, and Nehemiah Persoff.

- "...more a curiosity than the successful literary creation of one of the contemporary masters. On the intimate screen, the atmospheric camino, a kind of pre-death purgatory overhung with tedium and menacing shadows, was superbly realized....Lotte Lenya had a vivid moment as a wry and deceitful Gypsy...As Kilroy, Martin Sheean was suitably naïve and boyishly likable." (Variety)

This Property Is Condemned (1966, Paramount, 109min/c, **VHS**) ☆☆½ **Sc:** Francis Ford Coppola, Fred Coe, Edith Sommer. **D:** Sydney Pollack. **P:** Ray Stark, John Houseman. **Cam:** James Wong Howe. **Cast:** Natalie Wood, Robert Redford, Charles Bronson, Mary Badham, Kate Reid, Jon Provost, Dabney Coleman, Robert Blake, Alan Baxter, John Harding. This play concerns a railroad official sent into a small Mississippi town to close a station and lay off workers. He becomes infatuated with the local strumpet, encouraged in her alluring ways by her mother, a boarding house owner who uses the girl to bait potential male roomers. The star chemistry of the leading players and Pollack's eye for detail help make this an engrossing picture of Depression Era Southern decadence. In another Williams take on sordid matriarchal manipulations, Reid superbly inhabits the controlling boarding house owner. See also Three Plays by Tennessee Williams below.

- "Somewhere in the middle of this horrendous soap opera, Robert Redford *tells an Oriental parable that sort of describes what happened to Williams and his original play when the script writers got through with it. 'A man takes a drink,' said Redford, 'then the drink takes a drink, then the drink takes the man.'...Redford is too good for the movie. So is the photography of James Wong Howe, who imbues the most absurd situations with a glamour and poetic reality they don't deserve."* (Joseph Gelmis, Newsday)

Three Plays by Tennessee Williams (1958, NBC, 60m/bw) *Kraft Television Theatre* ☆☆☆ Tp/Host: Tennessee Williams. D: Sidney Lumet. Cast: Ben Gazzara, Lee Grant, Thomas Chalmers, Gene Saks, Alonzo Bozan, Zina Bethune, Martin Huston. Host: Tennessee Williams. *Mooney's Kids Don't Cry* features Gazzara as a man wants to leave the city for his beloved North Woods, while his wife resists. *The Last of My Solid Gold Watches* features Williams favorite Chalmers as an elderly traveling salesman in the Mississippi Delta confounded by old age and new times. Both plays were performed by the Actors Lab in Los Angeles in 1946, with Vincent Price in the latter. *This Property Is Condemned* had a particularly effective Bethune as the amoral and uncared-for young harlot who entices a railroad executive in a small Mississippi town. It was staged in 1942 at the New School. Williams appeared on screen to introduce these three one-act plays written in the 1930s.

- *"...mixed results, with the author's pen accurately reflecting the turbulence— and squalor—of the 1930s....There were times when Williams's drama had a raw vitality, there were powerful passages with brilliant dialogue; there were other times when he let his characters dwell too long on inconsequentials. Williams's penchant for morbidity was the common denominator connecting the vignettes....Sidney Lumet's direction was excellent..."* (Variety)

27 Wagons Full of Cotton was about a cotton-gin owner with a young, sexy wife who's visited by an Italian American with the title crop for ginning. This sneaky outsider is there to seduce the wife, Baby Doll, as a secret way of seeking vengence. The play was produced on Broadway in 1955 starring Maureen Stapleton and Myron McCormick.

Baby Doll (1956, Warner Bros., 115m/bw, **VHS**) ☆☆☆☆ Sc: Tennessee Williams. D/P: Elia Kazan. Cam: Boris Kaufman. Cast: Carroll Baker, Karl Malden, Eli Wallach, Mildred Dunnock, Lonny Chapman, Rip Torn, Eades Hogue, Noah Williamson. Kazan urged Williams to adapt *27 Wagons Full of Cotton* using plot elements of another one-act play, *The Long Stay Cut Short/or/The Unsatisfactory Supper*, which was copyrighted in 1946 but not produced on the stage until 1971. The film opened with Baker as the saucy teenaged bride, Baby Doll, sleeping in a crib. The image and film were famously attacked by the Catholic Legion of Decency. Baby Doll Meighan is involved in an arranged, unconsummated marriage to an oafish and going-broke Mississippi cotton gin owner, Archie Lee. She becomes attracted to his business rival in what becomes a screwball black comedy. The film retains its sass and contains Malden's most overt performance, replete with bug-eyed hollering and lock-kneed stomping, as well as a helpless melting mode when Archie is in Baby Doll's presence. The film was nominated for four Academy Awards: Best Actress (Baker), Supporting Actress (Dunnock), Adapted Screenplay, and Black and White Cinematography.

- "...the general impact of the drama is Williams's. There is Williams's sense of the cruelty of man (in the fire scene); the need for a fertile outsider (notably, an Italian) to free the stagnant community from its hypocrisy and torpor; and the horror of a marriage that is based upon private humiliation and public lie. Baby Doll is a Williams work in another way, too — it is an extremely funny film. There is horror in the fire scene, fright in the attic chase, sensuality in the posture of Baby Doll, and a stern moral view overall, but the film remains extremely funny....Williams's best film comedy." (Maurice Yacowar, Tennessee Williams and Film)

- "Williams doesn't seem to know how to resolve the movie, but it's wonderfully entertaining. When it came out, the Catholic Legion of Decency and Time said that it was 'just possibly the dirtiest American-made motion picture that has ever been legally exhibited' with 'Priapean detail that might well have embarrassed Boccaccio.' It's not quite all that, but it is a delight." (Pauline Kael, The New Yorker)

27 Wagons Full of Cotton (1990, A&E, 60m/c) American Playwrights Theatre ☆☆☆ **Tp:** Tennessee Williams. **D:** Don Scardino. **Cast:** Lesley Ann Warren, Peter Boyle, Ray Sharkey. **Host:** Anthony Quinn. Warren's low-slung décolletage takes some of the interest away from Williams's play, but this is still an excellent production.

- "It's pure Williams, a warm-up for all his brutal couplings to come, beginning with Blanche and Stanley in A Streetcar Named Desire. Flora is delicate and otherworldly, yet almost hysterically sensual....He is arrogantly contemptuous, stroking her gently and then turning vicious. The focus keeps shifting. Who is the seducer? Who is the victim? It is a riveting conception manipulated by a master....blunt, uncluttered production....Ms. Warren...is terrific...Bursting out of a dress that Al Capp might have designed for Daisy Mae, she tells all with her hands as they flutter nervously to her lips or unthinkingly caress various parts of her torso." (John J. O'Connor, The New York Times)

You Touched Me! is an adaptation of the D.H. Lawrence story of the same name that Williams wrote in collaboration with Donald Windham. It tells of a drunken former sea captain, aided by his adopted son, trying to abort his daughter's retreat from the world. The play, produced by Guthrie McClintic and Lee Shubert at New York's Booth Theatre in 1945, starred Montgomery Clift and Edmund Gwenn.

You Touched Me! (1949, NBC, 60m/bw) *Philco Summer Theatre* (*Philco Television Playhouse*) ☆☆☆ **Tp:** Samuel Carter. **D:** Gordon Duff. **P:** Fred Coe. **Cast:** Dennis King, Mary McCord, William Prince, Margaret Bannerman, Neil Fitzgerald.

- "...*Suitable for fine tele presentation. This Tennessee Williams effort had a short Broadway run, but on [TV] this work served to bring back the quality of this series to its wintertime level. The necessary elements of a worthy adaptation for this medium and an excellent cast gave this play a suitable base for an hour-long display. Adapters ran headlong into a risqué situation in the play....the captain starts telling of a female porpoise who fell in love with him while marooned on an island. Just as the dissertation starts getting spicy, there's a dissolve...This bit could have been left out of [this] version without harming the play.*" (Variety)

You Touched Me! was also produced for TV in 1954 on *Kraft Television Theatre* with Terence Kilburn, Martyn Green, and Catherine Willard, and in 1957 on NBC's *Matinee Theatre* with Oscar Homolka and Joan Tetzel.

Calder Willingham

Calder Baynard Willingham, Jr.
Born: December 23, 1922, Atlanta, GA.

Better known as a novelist and screenwriter, Calder Willingham's one important play, *End as a Man* (see below), captured the fascination of Broadway critics through the manipulative central character of Jocko de Paris and his interpretation by Ben Gazzara. Willingham's novels include *End as a Man*, *Natural Child*, *To Eat a Peach*, *Reach to the Stars*, *Geraldine Bradshaw*, *Eternal Fire*, and *The Big Nickel*. He also wrote *Rambling Rose*, which the author adapted into the 1992 film of the same name. The movie earned the mother/daughter team of Diane Ladd and Laura Dern Oscar nominations and also starred Robert Duvall and Lukas Haas.

Willingham is most famous for co-writing with Charles Webb the screenplay for Mike Nichols's youth-culture benchmark *The Graduate* (1967), which made Dustin Hoffman an immediate star. But Willingham's impressive screenwriting credits also include adapting Humphrey Cobb's antiwar novel into Stanley Kubrick's powerful classic *Paths of Glory* (1957), Marlon Brando's unique western *One-Eyed Jacks* (1961), Arthur Penn's singular *Little Big Man* (1970), and Robert Altman's *Thieves Like Us* (1974). Among Willingham's original teleplays was *Incident in July* for a 1955 installment of *Philco Television Playhouse* starring Maureen Stapleton and Dick York. Willingham also co-wrote with Del Reisman the Delbert Mann-directed *Thou Shalt Not Commit Adultery* (1978) starring Louise Fletcher and Wayne Rogers.

End as a Man debuted in 1953 at New York's Theatre de Lys starring Ben Gazzara as Jocko de Paris, a cruel and controlling student at a Southern military academy. The production featured, under Jack Garfein's direction, Anthony Franciosa, Pat Hingle, Albert Salmi, William Smith, William Smithers, and Arthur Storch. Willingham, whose widely-admired original novel was published in 1947, drew on his personal experiences at The Citadel for his one successful play, which ran for 137 performances. Homosexuality was implicit in the play, and not altogether expunged for the censors in the film version.

The Strange One (1957, Columbia, 100m/bw, **VHS**) ☆☆☆☆ **Sc:** Calder Willingham. **D:** Jack Garfein. **P:** Sam Speigel. **Cam:** Burnett Guffey. **Cast:** Ben Gazzara, George Peppard, Julie Wilson, Pat Hingle, (Peter) Mark Richman, Geoffrey Horne, James Olson, Larry Gates, Clifton James, Arthur Storch. The endemic and usually harnessed control at the center of military life is called into question as the abuses of the system by the sadistic Jocko de Paris become more evident to his fellow cadets, including Peppard's Marquales, who, after considerable angst, leads a revolt against Paris. Excellent film debuts by Peppard and especially Gazzara carry this odd and extremely subversive film, especially for the 1950s.

- *"The entire idea of military training and discipline was called into question...It implied that its chief villain, a sadistic young cadet...was an odd case who would have proved corrupt in any environment but was nurtured in evil by the academy's methods. Fiercely, the movie refuted the glamorized image of cadets, and the implicit admiration of their disciplinary years."* (Gordon Gow, Hollywood in the Fifties)

- *"...serves up Ben Gazzara as the most polymorphous-perverse young sadist of the year. (The competition was keen). This psychopathology of morale in a Southern military academy is a grisly—often effective—fusion of Freud and Actors' Studio."* (Pauline Kael, 5001 Nights at the Movies)

End as a Man also was presented in a 60-minute TV version in 1955 as *The Bold and the Brave* on *Philco Television Playhouse* with a cast including John Kerr, (Peter) Mark Richman and Tom Tully.

August Wilson
Born: April 27, 1944, Pittsburgh, PA.
Pulitzer Prize-winning plays: *Fences* (1987), *The Piano Lesson* (1990)
Tony Award-winning play: *Fences*

August Wilson is, arguably, the greatest African-American playwright. In addition to the awards noted above, he has won New York Drama

Critics Circle Awards for *Ma Rainey's Black Bottom, Fences, Joe Turner's Come and Gone, The Piano Lesson, Two Trains Running*, and *Seven Guitars*. His more recent works include *Jitney* and *King Hedley II*. Many of Wilson's plays evoke mid-century black life in his native Pittsburgh. Perhaps his finest achievement was *Fences*, which starred James Earl Jones in his Tony Award-winning role as a pre-Civil Rights father in 1950s Pittsburgh and Courtney B. Vance as his teenage son. Wilson has been honored with Rockefeller and Guggenheim fellowships in playwriting. The sad Hollywood assumption that the audience for his plays is a limited one has meant that only one of Wilson's plays has been adapted to the screen (see below).

The Piano Lesson (1995, CBS, 99m/c, **VHS**) *The Hallmark Hall of Fame* ☆☆☆☆½ **Tp/P:** August Wilson. **D:** Lloyd Richards. **Cast:** Charles Dutton, Alfre Woodard, Carl Gordon, Tommy Hollis, Lou Myers, Courtney B. Vance, Zelda Harris, Rosalyn Coleman, Tommy Lafitte, Lynne Innerst. The play takes place in Pittsburgh in 1936, and concerns a family heirloom, an ornately configured, 80-year-old upright piano that remains in Uncle Doaker's home under the watchful eye of Berniece. The argumentative Boy Willie returns from Mississippi to convince Berniece to sell it to buy a plot of land where their grandfather had toiled several generations earlier as a slave. The Broadway cast featured Dutton, Gordon, Myers, Hollis, and Coleman. The play originated as a staged reading in 1986 at the Eugene O'Neill Theatre Center in Waterford, Connecticut.

- "...the result is striking: a sweeping arpeggio of exuberance and African-American culture that will reach its widest audience ever...a lovely bit of ethnic magic that mightily deserves this proscenium space on CBS's Hallmark Hall of Fame....It sings, it saddens, it stimulates, but above all, it entertains. There's a lilting, musical grace to this rich, lively tale..." (Howard Rosenberg, Los Angeles Times)

Lanford Wilson

Born: April 13, 1937, Lebanon, MO.

One of the most admired playwrights of the 1960s and 1970s, Lanford Wilson captivated audiences with plays that, as Ann Crawford Dreher described, "typically contain a peculiar, theatrically vital tension which derives from his ability to represent universal truths through widely varying situations and characters. Humor, love, violence, jealousy, greed—all of the secret strivings of the human spirit appear in the fabric of his plays....Although Wilson's plays squarely face the reality of life's pains, laughter and buoyancy ripple through them." Frank Rich wrote in *The New York Times* that "Mr. Wilson's most distinguishing characteristic is his overwhelming compassion," often expressed in stories of misfits.

His plays include *Balm in Galead, The Rimers of Eldritch, Serenading Louie, Lemon Sky,* the enormously popular *Hot l Baltimore, Fifth of July, Talley & Son, Angels Fall, Burn This, Redwood Curtain, Book of Days, Rain Dance,* and *By the Sea by the Sea by the Beautiful Sea.* TV has made up for the fact that the movies have completely steered clear from Wilson's celebrated body of work.

Wilson wrote the one-acter *Stoop: A Turn* for TV, about three women on the stoop of a brownstone building, and it appeared as a segment of *Foul!,* an umbrella title for ten short plays about pollution on *New York Television Theatre* in 1969. Among his projects for TV were the powerful *The Migrants* (1974), which he based on a Tennessee Williams idea (see **Tennessee Williams**); *Taxi!!!* (1978) for *The Hallmark Hall of Fame,* an hour-long, two-character piece set inside the title vehicle starring Martin Sheen and Eva Marie Saint as characters whose shared cab ride to New York's Kennedy Airport changes both their lives; and a segment of *Triple Play: Sam Found Out* (1988) starring Liza Minnelli. *Hot l Baltimore,* about the inhabitants of a seedy hotel, was produced on ABC by Norman Lear as a sitcom (without the benefit of a full TV production of the play) in 1975 starring Conchata Ferrell, James Cromwell, and Al Freeman Jr. Wilson also wrote the libretto for Lee Hoiby's opera version of Tennessee Williams's *Summer and Smoke,* which was telecast on PBS's *Great Performances* in 1982.

Fifth of July (1982, Showtime, 130m/c, **VHS**) ☆☆☆½ **Tp:** Lanford Wilson. **D:** Kirk Browning, Marshall W. Mason. **P:** Samuel Paul. **Cast:** Richard Thomas, Jeff Daniels, Swoosie Kurtz, Jonathan Hogan, Joyce Reehling Christopher, Helen Stenborg, Cynthia Nixon, Danton Stone. Most of the cast recreated their roles from the Circle Repertory Theatre production of 1978. William Hurt and Amy Wright joined the 1980 Broadway cast. This TV co-production between Showtime and WNET in New York was first shown on the cable network, then cut by 20 minutes and aired on PBS's *American Playhouse.* The play, set during Independence Day celebrations in 1977, is part of the trilogy including *Talley's Folly* and *A Tale Told,* both of which take place on July 4, 1944. Thomas played the legless Vietnam War veteran Ken and Daniels his gardening live-in lover. An assortment of activist types from the 1960s visit during the holiday. Aunt Sally (Stenborg) is the connection to the old days and other plays.

- *"It was a pinpointing of Mr. Wilson's strength. Eschewing abstraction, avant-garde experimentation or gimmicky sets, he uses the fairly traditional forms of domestic drama...to create his very own distinctive world of spe-*

cial sensibilities. It is an art he has developed with uncommon skill....Mr. Wilson sets this set of characters spinning, moving them carefully in and out of one another's emotional range...unfortunately, the overall impact of the play has been dissipated in this television adaptation....Television, employing the inevitable close-ups, loses the feeling of the ensemble. The result is a curious imbalance....The performances are still superb. Mr. Thomas is especially impressive..." (John J. O'Connor, The New York Times)

Lemon Sky (1987, PBS, 106m/c) *American Playhouse* ☆☆☆☆ **Tp:** Lanford Wilson. **D:** Jan Egleson. **P:** Marcus Viscidi. **Cast:** Kevin Bacon, Tom Atkins, Lindsay Crouse, Kyra Sedgwick, Casey Affleck, Welker White, Laura White, Peter MacEwan. The play debuted at the Buffalo Studio Arena Theatre in 1970 starring Christopher Walken, Charles Durning, and Bonnie Bartlett. The autobiographical play concerns the Nebraskan teenager Alan, and his visit to his estranged father and stepmother in El Cajon, California. Alan begins to detect odd behavior in his father and the women around him.

- *"...it's terrific....Mr. Wilson's debt here to Thornton Wilder's* Our Town *is obvious but it takes the form of tribute rather than rip-off. Instead of Wilder's Stage Manager, we get Alan, now about 30 and eager to tell us about something that happened back in 1957...Mr. Bacon now clearly demonstrates that he has the solid talent required for the long haul. His performance in* Lemon Sky *is both ingratiating and powerfully affecting....a 'young' play, in a sense Mr. Wilson's equivalent of* The Glass Menagerie*...It is painfully sincere and deeply felt."* (John J. O'Connor, The New York Times)

The Mound Builders (1976, PBS, 90m/c, **VHS**) *Great Performances: Theatre in America* ☆☆☆½ **Tp:** Lanford Wilson. **D:** Marshall W. Mason, Ken Campbell. **P:** Ken Campbell, Jac Venza. **Cast:** Brad Dourif, Trish Hawkins, Tanya Berezin, Jonathan Hogan, Rob Thirkeld, Loren Jacobs, Stephanie Gordon. This play dramatizes the conflict between 20th century values and Native American traditions at a rural archaeological dig, where scientists interact with locals. The 1975 production by New York's Circle Repertory Company was restaged near the Coster dig in southern Illinois.

- *"...Lanford Wilson's most ambitious play. Unfortunately...it is also one of his more disappointing efforts....one of the country's most talented young playwrights. His style, embodied in a kind of lyricism for the gently offbeat, has been beautifully demonstrated in plays going back to the best days of Greenwich Village's Cafe Cino....a younger generation's equivalent to Tennessee Williams, and he has yet to write his* Streetcar. *The Mound Builders strains for that distinction, but the effort is too transparent and curiously muddled....promises insights and delivers ambivalences and, finally, confusions. But even disappointing Wilson offers some very worthwhile television…"* (John J. O'Connor, The New York Times)

New Theatre for Now aired on *NET Playhouse: Theatre in America* in 1968. Wilson's *Wandering* was one of the four playlets enacted by a cast including Marge Champion, Tim O'Connor, Philip Proctor, Gail Kobe, Ed Flanders, Joseph Reala, Anthony Zerbe, and Beverlee McKinsey. The series's first *Theatre in America* installment also included plays by Jean Claude van Itallie and Sam Shepard.

Redwood Curtain (1995, ABC, 100m/c, **VHS**) *The Hallmark Hall of Fame* ☆☆☆☆ **Tp:** Ed Namzug. **D:** John Korty. **P:** Robert W. Christiansen, Mark Rosenberg. **Cast:** Jeff Daniels, Lea Salonga, Catherine Hicks, John Lithgow, Debra Monk, Shirley Douglas, Vilma Silva, Joy Carlin, Steven Anthony Jones, Jarion Monroe, Cab Covay, R. Blakeslee Colby, Jonathan Korty. After its maiden voyage at the Seattle Repertory Theatre in 1993, the play debuted on Broadway the same year, with Marshall W. Mason directing a cast that included Daniels, Monk, and Sung Yun Cho. Geri, a young Asian woman adopted by a wealthy American family, begins searching for her American father, a Vietnam War veteran. Salonga was the original star of *Miss Saigon* on Broadway. Monk won the Tony Award for Best Supporting Actress in the stage version.

• *"Mr. Wilson's play has been expanded. In fact, it has been given an entirely new first act that brings in the character of the girl's adoptive father, Laird Riordan, a demon-driven alcoholic who never appeared in the play.…somewhat slight and predictable, but given this almost flawless production, it is also quite moving. Powerfully repeating their Broadway roles are Jeff Daniels as the disturbed veteran and Debra Monk as Geri's wonderful aunt…Mr. Lithgow and Ms. Salonga deliver exquisite performances, separately and in tandem."* (John J. O'Connor, The New York Times)

The Rimers of Eldritch (1972, PBS, 90m/c) *Playhouse New York* ☆☆☆☆ **Tp:** Lanford Wilson. **D:** Davey Marlin-Jones. **P:** Matthew N. Herman. **Cast:** Will Hare, Frances Sternhagen, Rue McClanahan, Carol Williard, James Staley, Susan Sarandon, K. Callan, Roberts Blossom, Helen Stenborg, Ernest Thompson, Sarah Cunningham, Joanna Roos, Kate Harrington. Wilson's play about a murder in a Midwestern mining town actually used Pittsville, Maryland, locations. The play inventories the cruel small-town characters' thoughts and emotions before, during, and after the murder of a local misfit. The 1966 Off Broadway play was presented at LaMaMa Experimental Theatre Club with a cast including Michael Warren Powell, Claris Erickson, and Frederic Forrest. This filmed production was rebroadcast on PBS on *Theatre in America* in 1974.

- "It mixes humor, compassion, anger, and suspense into a kind of social protest version of Our Town. The play received a first-rate translation to TV film...This is a dialogue play, with very gutsy and unusual insights into human nature against the vast majority of television drama. Yet the play's unique construction, mixing present, past and future in suspenseful unraveling of a local tragedy, present opportunities for solid cinematic treatment which were exploited especially through the location shooting." (Variety)

The Sand Castle and **The Tape Recorder** (1970, PBS, 90m/c) NET Playhouse ☆☆☆ **Tp:** Lanford Wilson. **P:** Jac Venza. **Cast:** Michael Tolan, Inga Swenson, Irene Dailey. The Sand Castle served as something of a warm-up, if you can call it that, for the profundities of Lemon Sky. In The Tape Recorder, set in a California beach house, various family members and friends have complicated relationships.

- "Irene Dailey has the central role and even under difficult circumstances is well worth seeing. But The Sand Castle is one of those dramas that steadily go downhill, and the younger characters in the play are a sick and sordid bunch with nothing of any particular interest to discuss. It strains credulity a bit when a daughter seduces her mother's lover and the mother simply shrugs her shoulders. In The Sand Castle one could hardly blame the cast for switching from Actors Equity to LSD." (Jack Gould, The New York Times)

Meredith Wilson & Franklin Lacey

Wilson:
Robert Meredith Wilson
Born: May 18, 1902, Mason City, IA. **Died:** 1984.
Lacey:
Born: 1917. **Died:** 1988.

Meredith Wilson wrote the book, music, and lyrics for the 1963 musical Here's Love and the music and lyrics for The Unsinkable Molly Brown, which became a 1964 movie that garnered Debbie Reynolds an Oscar nomination. He also composed the music for Charles Chaplin's The Great Dictator (1940).

Franklin Lacey's one other big-screen credit is for supplying the story for Rain for a Dusty Summer (1971) starring Ernest Borgnine.

The Music Man was an enormous smash, running for 1,375 performances beginning in 1957, directed by Morton DaCosta, and starring Robert Preston as con man Harold Hill, who dupes a small Iowa town into creating a band, ostensibly to keep the kids occupied while he's planning on fleecing the local residents.

The Music Man (1962, Warner Bros., 151m/c, **VHS/DVD**) ☆☆☆☆
Sc: Meredith Wilson, Franklin Lacey. **D/P:** Morton DaCosta. **Cam:**
Robert Burks. **Cast:** Robert Preston, Shirley Jones, Buddy Hackett,
Hermione Gingold, Ronny Howard, Paul Ford, Pert Kelton, Monique
Vermont, Al Shea, Vern Reed, Wayne Ward, Bill Spangenberg, Mary
Wickes, Charles Lane, Harry Hickox, Max Showalter. Preston's greatest
fame was for his Harold Hill in this big-style musical, and his enthusi-
asm is contagious. Wilson's legendary songs include "Gary, Indiana,"
"Till There Was You," and "76 Trombones." The film won an Oscar for
Ray Heindorf's score and was nominated for Best Picture, Art Direc-
tion/Set Decoration, Film Editing, Costumes, and Sound. Preston
should have been nominated.

- *"A heavy-footed version…a cheerful, broad piece of Americana…Morton
  DaCosta…isn't comfortable with the camera, and the material seems too
  literal, too practical, too set. But the star, Robert Preston, has a few minutes of fast patter—conmanship set to music—that constitute one of the
  high points in the history of American musicals. This is one of those triumphs that only a veteran performer can have; Preston's years of experience
  and his love of performing come together joyously."* (Pauline Kael, 5,001
  Nights at the Movies)

The Music Man (2003, ABC, 180m/c) **Sc:** Sally Robinson. **D:** Jeff
Bleckner. **P:** John M. Eckert. **Cast:** Matthew Broderick, Jenni Burke,
Kristin Chenoweth, Clyde Alves, David Aaron Baker, Boyd Banks, Juan
Chioran, Victor Garber, Greg Ellwand, Molly Shannon.

- *"It's a bit deflating…to report that Broderick, for all his boyish cheer and
  aura of goodwill, isn't very good…strong production values, excellent costumes and art direction, and a rich color palette that conjures cozy notions
  of small-town America in the early 20th century. It's passable entertainment…"* (Edward Guthmann, San Francisco Chronicle)

Herman Wouk
Born: May 27, 1915, New York, NY.

Herman Wouk's novels were adapted into the films *Slattery's Hurricane*
(1949) with Richard Widmark, *Marjorie Morningstar* (1958) with Natalie Wood, and *Youngblood Hawke* (1964) with James Franciscus. *The
Caine Mutiny* (1954), starring Humphrey Bogart and Jose Ferrer, wasn't
based on the play listed below; producer Stanley Kramer and Wouk
parted company early on the project and Stanley Roberts culled the author's 1952 Pulitzer Prize-winning novel into a 190-page screenplay, according to director Edward Dmytryk. Most famously, Wouk's World War

II novels, *The Winds of War* and *War and Remembrance*, became the biggest TV epics of all time in 1983 and 1989–90, with Robert Mitchum playing globetrotting Navy attaché Captain Victor "Pug" Henry. Wouk's one other TV script was an original for a 1950 *Magnavox Theatre* show called *The Traitor* with Franklin J. Schaffner directing Lee Tracy.

The Caine Mutiny Court-Martial concerned the military trial of the main adjutant to the commander of a minesweeper, the USS Caine, in the Pacific during World War II. He had deemed the commander—the tyrannic, neurotic Captain Queeg—to be unfit in action. The 1954 stage production starred Lloyd Nolan as Captain Queeg and Henry Fonda as Lieutenant Barney Greenwald. The 1954 film version starring Humphrey Bogart wasn't based on Wouk's play.

The Caine Mutiny Court-Martial (1955, CBS, 90m/c) *The Ford Star Jubilee* ☆☆☆☆ **Tp:** Herman Wouk. **D:** Franklin J. Schaffner. **P:** Paul Gregory. **Cast:** Lloyd Nolan, Barry Sullivan, Frank Lovejoy, Ainslie Pryor, Russell Hicks, Robert Gist, Charles Nolte, Herbert Anderson. This production was "supervised" by Charles Laughton, who directed the original 1954 stage production with several of the same actors. Nolan won the Emmy Award for Best Actor for this performance.

- *"…90 minutes of brilliant television theatre, an outstanding achievement of the season in all respects.…retained the absorbing power and intensity of the [stage] original; and in many ways further enhanced those qualities.…In television close-up, [Nolan's] portrayal acquired even added heart-rending dimension and detail, a gripping and poignant study of an individual's disintegration. It was television not readily forgotten.…the play could have been written for TV in the first place.…comes almost tailor-made for the searching and probing eye of the electronic camera.…Widely honored as Mr. Nolan's performance was at the time of his Broadway appearance, it gained magnificence on television."* (Jack Gould, The New York Times)

The Caine Mutiny Court-Martial (1988, CBS, 100m/c, **VHS**) ☆☆☆ **Tp:** Herman Wouk. **D:** Robert Altman. **P:** Robert Altman, John Flaxman. **Cast:** Brad Davis, Jeff Daniels, Eric Bogosian, Michael Murphy, Peter Gallagher, Kevin J. O'Connor, Daniel H. Jenkins, Ken Michaels. Altman's signature camera style clashes with the straightforward military trial piece, but the performances of Bogosian, Daniels, and O'Connor are outstanding.

- *"…misdirected and Queeged out, but still well worth your time.…The tone of Wouk's characters…clash electrifyingly…Director Altman deftly contrasts the irrationality of Queeg with the stiff correctness of the Navy board of investigation.…Altman's staging oozes appealing texture and atmosphere. But his directing is also pretentious and distracting, portraying a stationary event with a fidgety camera. Altman tends to merge foregrounds and backgrounds, an effective tactic in centerless, stream-of-consciousness stories…But here his overlapping and conflicting attention points merely blur and diffuse….a paradoxical exercise in fascinating, absorbing incoherence.*" (Howard Rosenberg, Los Angeles Times)

Philip Yordan
Born: April 1, 1914, Chicago, IL.

Philip Yordan's great contribution to the stage was *Anna Lucasta* (see below), but he was also a prolific screenwriter and producer, who wrote both huge epics and B-pictures, adapted famous plays, and penned spaghetti westerns. He won an Academy Award for writing the original story for *Broken Lance* (1954), which starred Spencer Tracy as a King Lear-like cattle rancher whose family is fracturing into factions, each one seeking control of the empire. During the House Un-American Activities Committee's inquisition of Hollywood, Yordan allowed his name to be used by blacklisted screenwriters.

He enjoyed a fruitful working relationship with director Anthony Mann on *The Man From Laramie* (1955) with James Stewart; *Men in War* (1957) and *God's Little Acre* (1958), both with Robert Ryan; *El Cid* (1961) with Charlton Heston; and the all-star yet little-attended *The Fall of the Roman Empire* (1964). He also worked well with another great cult director, Nicholas Ray, for whom he wrote *Johnny Guitar* (1955), *King of Kings* (1961), and *55 Days at Peking* (1963). Among Yordan's other best-known films as a writer are the adaptation of Sidney Kingsley's play, *Detective Story* (1951), and Humphrey Bogart's final film, *The Harder They Fall* (1956), as well as *The Battle of the Bulge* (1965), *The Royal Hunt of the Sun* (1969), and *Captain Apache* (1971).

Anna Lucasta, which became a favorite of stock companies throughout the last half of the 20th century, concerns a Polish beauty who returns to her small Pennsylvania hometown. Her drunken farmer father schemes to marry her into a wealthy family, but her city life as a prostitute catches up with her. The play was sold to the American Negro Theatre, and Anna was Polish no more. It was such a hit in Harlem that it went to Broadway in 1944 starring Hilda Simms and Canada Lee and became one of the greatest Broadway hits, running for 957 performances.

Anna Lucasta (1949, Columbia, 86m/bw) ☆☆ **Sc:** Philip Yordan, Arthur Laurents. **D:** Irving Rapper. **P:** Philip Yordan. **Cam:** Sol Polito. **Cast:** Paulette Goddard, Oscar Homolka, Broderick Crawford, William Bishop, Gale Page, Mary Wickes. The play was whitewashed by Columbia in more ways than one, returning it to Polish immigrants in Pennsylvania and with the prostitution changed to waitressing. Yordan and

Laurents's toning down leached out the sass that made the play a Broadway legend.

- *"...a major disappointment. What had been dynamite onstage was diffused and flat cinematic melodrama. It certainly did nothing to revitalize Paulette's sagging career. Variety was harsh, stating that Goddard did not have the 'physical accoutrements' meeded for the 'lush requirements of the part.' Most other critics were equally unflattering. The total emphasis placed on Paulette in all advertising and publicity left no doubt that she was the drawing card expected to pull the customers in. She didn't."* (Joe Morella, Edward Z. Epstein, Paulette: The Adventurous Life of Paulette Goddard)

Anna Lucasta (1958, UA, 97m/bw) ☆☆ **Sc:** Philip Yordan. **D:** Arnold Laven. **P:** Sidney Harmon. **Cam:** Lucien Ballard. **Cast:** Eartha Kitt, Frederick O'Neal, Sammy Davis Jr., Henry Scott, Rex Ingram, James Edwards. This all-black version returned the story to the stage production's roots if not the written play's origins, and was an attempt to capitalize on the talents of Kitt.

- *"If somebody dug down into the play-bin and brought up* Bertha the Sewing Machine Girl, *they could probably turn it into a better movie than has been made by Philip Yordan of* Anna Lucasta. *Not only is the basic fustian in this 15-year-old Broadway play about the shame and salvation of a gold-hearted prostitute exposed with embarrassing naïvete in this incredibly artless film. But also it is directed by Arnold Laven as if he were looking out of the window most of the time, and it is played with surprising amateurishness by a big-name Negro cast."* (Bosley Crowther, The New York Times)

Paul Zindel

Born: May 15, 1936, Staten Island, New York.

Pulitzer Prize-winning play: *The Effect of Gamma Rays on Man-in-the-Moon Marigolds* (1971)
New York Drama Critics Circle award, Best Play: *The Effect of Gamma Rays on Man-in-the-Moon Marigolds*

Paul Zindel's most concerted efforts on the big screen were for director Andrei Konchalovsky, for whom he worked on the screenplays for *Maria's Lovers* (1984) and *Runaway Train* (1985), which earned Oscar nominations for Jon Voight and Eric Roberts. Zindel also adapted Anne Richardson Roiphe's novel *Up the Sandbox* into the 1972 film starring Sandy Dennis, and was the screenwriter on the disastrous adaptation of the musical *Mame* (1974), which starred Lucille Ball. For TV, Zindel's adaptations were of traditional fantasies: Irwin Allen's lavish, star-studded, four-hour *Alice in Wonderland* (1985) for CBS, a re-doing of *Babes in Toyland* (1986) with Drew Barrymore and Keanu Reeves, and a fanciful version of *A Connecticut Yankee in King Arthur's Court* (1989) with *Cosby Show* star Keisha Knight Pulliam. He wrote one original for NET *Playhouse* called *Let Me Hear You Whisper* (1969), in which Glenn Jordan directed Ruth White as a woman janitor talking to a dolphin in a research lab. Zindel's plays of diminishing returns included *And Mrs. Reardon Drinks a Little* in 1971 with Julie Harris and *The Secret Affair of Mildred Wild* in 1972 with Maureen Stapleton. The author's novels for young adults include *The Pigman* and *My Darling, My Hamburger*.

The Effects of Gamma Rays on Man-in-the-Moon Marigolds concentrated on a teenage girl who vows to win her school's science fair with the title demonstration, despite the pressures of living with her delusional, alcoholic floozy mother, Beatrice Hunsdorfer, known as "Betty the Loon," and her troublesome sister. The play, which debuted at the Alley Theatre in Houston in 1965, opened Off Broadway at the Mercer-O'Casey Theatre in 1970 starring Sada Thompson. At 819 performances, it's one of the longest-running Off Broadway plays in history. Shelley Winters played Betty at the Biltmore Theatre in 1978.

The Effects of Gamma Rays on Man-in-the-Moon Marigolds (1966, NET, 45m/c) *New York Television Theatre* ☆☆ **Tp:** Paul Zindel. **D:** Melvin Bernhardt. **P:** Jac Venza. **Cast:** Eileen Heckert, Elizabeth Berger, Barbara Dana. This early, short version of the play aired four times in the late 1960s, carried by stage character actress Heckert's intelligent portrayal.

- *"Eileen Heckert's performance...as the bitter and disillusioned mother for whom life had only been a prolonged disappointment rescued Paul Zindel's short play...from the obscurity that otherwise would have been its lot....Thanks to Miss Heckert's presence, the lines never seriously intruded."* (Jack Gould, The New York Times)

The Effects of Gamma Rays on Man-in-the-Moon Marigolds (1972, 20th Century-Fox, 101m/c, **VHS**) ☆☆☆½ **Sc:** Alvin Sargent. **D:** Paul Newman. **P:** Paul Newman, Carl Foreman. **Cam:** Adam Holender. **Cast:** Joanne Woodward, Nell Potts, Roberta Wallach, Judith Lowry, Richard Venture. Following *Rachel, Rachel* (1968), this film was one of Newman's occasional forays into directing his wife, Woodward, in showcase pieces. Betty the Loon is one of her most vivid performances, and she won the Best Actress award at the Cannes Film Festival in 1973 for it. Newman's direction otherwise concentrates on raw emotions and stark realism. Both daughters were played by daughters of theatrical royalty — Potts is the Newmans' daughter, and Wallach is the daughter of Eli Wallach and Anne Jackson.

- *"Although Paul Newman's direction is sensitive and well balanced, the Paul Zindel play is essentially a camp version of the mood-memory plays of Ten-*

nesseee *Williams and William Inge. Woodward has the right sashaying toughness for the role, but it's pretty hard to bring conviction to Betty the Loon's vengeful meanness.*" (Pauline Kael, 5001 Nights at the Movies)

• "*I can't remember when I've been more depressed and more moved on a nearly documentary level than I was with [Marigolds].*" (Joseph Gelmis, Newsday)

• "*...too much theatre and not enough cinema. I screwed up there.*" (Paul Newman, to Time)

Bibliography

Agee, James. *Agee on Film*. Volume 1. New York: Grosset & Dunlap, 1969.

Baxter, John. *Hollywood in the Sixties*. New York: A.S. Barnes & Co., 1972.

——. *Hollywood in the Thirties*. New York: A.S. Barnes & Co., 1968.

Bordman, Gerald. *The Oxford Companion to the American Theatre*. New York: Oxford University Press, 1984.

Brooks, Tim, and Earle Marsh. *The Complete Directory to Prime Time Network TV Shows 1946–Present*. New York: Ballantine, 1988.

Brownlow, Kevin. *The Parade's Gone By*. New York: Ballantine Books, 1968.

Champlin, Charles. *The Movies Grow Up 1940–1980*. Chicago: Swallow Press/Ohio University Press, 1991.

Corliss, Richard. *Talking Pictures: Screenwriters in the American Cinema, 1927–1973*. Woodstock, NY: Overlook Press, 1974.

Craddock, Jim. *Videohound's Golden Movie Retriever 2003: The Complete Guide to Movies on Videocassette and DVD*. Detroit: The Gale Group Inc., 2002.

Crist, Judith. *Judith Crist's TV Guide to the Movies*. New York: Popular Library, 1974.

——. *The Private Eye, the Cowboy and the Very Naked Lady: Movies From Cleo to Clyde*. New York: Holt, Rinehart and Winston, 1968.

Ebert, Roger. *Roger Ebert's Video Companion*. Kansas City, MO: Andrews and McMeel, 1995.

Elley, Derek, and *Variety* staff writers. *Variety Movie Guide*. New York: Prentice Hall General Reference, 1992.

Everson, William K. *The American Silent Film*. London: OUP, 1978.

Farber, Manny. *Negative Space*. New York: Praeger Publishers Inc., 1971.

Frank, Sam. *Buyer's Guide to Fifty Years of TV on Video*. Amherst, NY: Prometheus Books, 1999.

Frankenheimer, John, and Charles Champlin. *John Frankenheimer: A Conversation with Charles Champlin*. Burbank, CA: Riverwood Press, 1995.

Gianakos, Larry James. *Television Drama Series Programming: A Comprehensive Chronicle, 1947–1990*. Metuchen, NJ: The Scarecrow Press, Inc., 1980–92.

Gow, Gordon. *Hollywood in the Fifties*. New York: A.S. Barnes & Co., 1971.

Halliwell, Leslie. *Halliwell's Filmgoer's Companion*. New York: Charles Scribner's Sons, 1985.

Halliwell, Leslie, and John Walker. *Halliwell's Film Guide*. New York: HarperCollins, 1991.

Hardy, Phil. *The Encyclopedia of Horror Films*. New York: Harper & Row, 1987.

Hart, James D., and Phillip Leininger, *The Oxford Companion to American Literature*, Sixth Edition. New York: Oxford University Press, 1996.

Hart, Moss. *Act One*. New York: Random House, 1959.

Higham, Charles, and Joel Greenberg. *Hollywood in the Forties*. New York: Paperback Library, 1970.

Hirschhorn, Clive. *The Hollywood Musical*. New York: Crown, 1981.

——————. *The Universal Story*. New York: Crown Publishers, Inc., 1983.

——————. *The Warner Bros. Story*. London: Octopus Books, 1979.

Holtzman, Will. *William Holden*. New York: Pyramid Publications, 1976.

Jacobs, Lewis. *The Rise of the American Film*. New York: Harcourt Brace, 1939.

Jewel, Richard B., and Vernon Harbin. *The RKO Story*. New York: Arlington House, 1982.

Kael, Pauline. *5001 Nights at the Movies: A Guide from A to Z*. New York: Holt Rinehart and Winston, 1982.

——————. *Kiss Kiss Bang Bang*. New York: Bantam Books, 1969.

Katz, Ephraim, Fred Klein and Ronald Dean Nolan. *The Film Encyclopedia*. New York: Harper Perennial, 1998.

Kauffmann, Stanley. *Before My Eyes: Film Criticism and Comment*. New York: Da Capo Press, 1980.

Kauffmann, Stanley. *A World on Film*. New York: Dell Publishing Co., Inc., 1966.

Keyser, Les. *Hollywood in the Seventies*. San Diego: A.S. Barnes & Co., Inc., 1981.

Krampner, Jon. *The Man in the Shadows: Fred Coe and the Golden Age of Television*. New Brunswick, NJ: Rutgers University Press, 1997.

Leonard, William Torbert. *Theatre: Stage to Screen to Television*. Metuchen, NJ: Scarecrow Press, 1981.

Lloyd, Norman. *Stages: Of Life in Theatre, Film and Television*. New York: Limelight Editions, 1993.

Macdonald, Dwight. *On Movies*. New York: Berkeley Medallion Books, 1969.

Magill, Frank N. *Magill's Survey of Cinema*. Englewood Cliffs, NJ: Salem Press, 1981.

Maltin, Leonard. *The Great Movie Comedians*. New York: Crown Publishers Inc., 1978.

Maltin, Leonard. *Leonard Maltin's TV Movies and Video Guide*. New York: New American Library, 1987.

Maltin, Leonard. *Leonard Maltin's 2003 Movie and Video Guide*. New York: Plume, 2002.

Mann, Delbert, and Ira Skutch. *Looking Back…: At Live Television and Other Matters*. Los Angeles: The Directors Guild of America, 1998.

Martin, Mick, and Marsha Porter. *Video and DVD Guide 2003*. New York: Ballantine, 2002.

Marrill, Alvin H. *Movies Made for Television*. New York: New York Zoetrope Inc., 1987.

Matthews, Charles. *Oscar A to Z: A Complete Guide to More Than 2,400 Movies Nominated for Academy Awards*. New York: Main Street Books, 1995.

McBride, Joseph. *Frank Capra: The Catastrophe of Success*. New York: St. Martin's Griffin, 200.

McCarthy, Todd. *Howard Hawks: The Gray Fox in Hollywood*. New York: Grove Press, 1997.

McNeil, Alex. *Total Television: A Comprehensive Guide to Programming from 1948 to 1980*. New York: Penguin Books, 1980.

Meredith, Scott. *George S. Kaufman and His Friends*. New York: Doubleday.

Meyer, William R. *Warner Brothers Directors*. New Rochelle, NY: Arlington House Publishers, 1978.

Michael, Paul, and James Robert Parish. *The Emmy Awards: A Pictorial History*. New York: Crown, 1970.

Mordden, Ethan. *The Hollywood Musical*. New York: St. Martin's Press, 1981.

Nash, Jay Robert, and Stanley Ralph Ross. *The Motion Picture Guide*. Chicago: Cinebooks, 1985.

The New York Times Directory of the Film. New York: Arno Press, 1974.

The New York Times Directory of the Theatre. New York: Arno Press, 1973.

O'Neil, Thomas. Emmys: *The Ultimate, Unofficial Guide to the Battle of TV's Best Shows and Greatest Stars*. New York: The Berkeley Publishing Group, 1978.

Paris, Barry. *Louise Brooks*. New York: Alfred A. Knopf, 1989.

Parish, James Robert. *The RKO Gals*. New Rochelle, NY: Arlington House, 1974.

——————. *The Tough Guys*. New Rochelle, NY: Arlington House, 1976.

Parish, James Robert, and Don Stanke. The All-Americans. New Rochelle, NY: Arlington House, 1977.

Parkinson, David. *The Graham Greene Film Reader*. New York: Applause Theatre & Cinema Books, 1994.

Patterson, Lindsay. *Black Films and Film-makers: A Comprehensive Anthology from Stereotype to Superhero*. New York: Dodd, Mead, 1975.

Pym, John. *Time Out Film Guide*. New York: Penguin Books, 2000.

Raleigh, John H. *The Plays of Eugene O'Neill*. Carbondale: Southern Illinois University Press, 1965.

Reed, Rex. *Big Screen, Little Screen*. New York: The Macmillan Company, 1971.

Roberts, Jerry. *Mitchum: In His Own Words*. New York: Limelight Editions, 2000.

Roberts, Jerry. *Robert Mitchum: A Bio-Bibliography*. Westport, CT: Greenwood Press, 1992.

Robinson, David. *Hollywood in the Twenties*. Cranbury, NJ: A.S. Barnes & Co., 1968.

Rose, Brian G. *Television and the Performing Arts: A Handbook and Reference Guide to American Cultural Programming*. Westport, CT: Greenwood Press, 1986.

Sarris, Andrew. *The American Cinema: Directors and Directions 1929–1968*. New York: E.P. Dutton, 1968.

——————. *The John Ford Movie Mystery*. Bloomington, IN: Indiana University Press, 1975.

Schaefer, George. *From Live to Tape to Film: 60 Years of Inconspicuous Directing*. Los Angeles: The Directors Guild of America, 1996.

Sennett, Ted. *The Great Movie Directors*. New York: Harry N. Abrams, Inc./AFI Press, 1986.

Seymour-Smith, Martin. *Who's Who in Twentieth Century Literature*. New York: Holt, Rinehart and Winston, 1976.

Shipman, David. *The Great Movie Stars 1: The Golden Years.* Boston: Little, Brown and Company, 1995.

————. *The Great Movie Stars 2: The International Years.* New York: St. Martin's Press, 1973.

————. *The Story of Cinema.* London: Hodder & Stoughton, 1982.

Skorman, Richard. *Off-Hollywood Movies: A Film Lover's Guide.* New York: Harmony Books, 1989.

Silver, Alain, and Elizabeth Ward. *Film Noir: An Encyclopedic Reference to the American Style.* Woodstock, NY: The Overlook Press, 1979.

Simon, John. *Movies Into Film: Film Criticism, 1967–70.* New York: The Dial Press, 1971.

————. *Reverse Angle.* New York: Clarkson N. Potter, Inc./Publishers, 1981.

Spoto, Donald. *Stanley Kramer: Filmmaker.* New York: G.P. Putnam's Sons, 1978.

Thomson, David. *A Biographical Dictionary of Film.* New York: Alfred A. Knopf, 1994.

Wiley, Mason, and Damien Bona. *Inside Oscar: The Unofficial History of the Academy Awards.* New York: Ballantine Books, 1986.

Wilson, Robert. *The Film Criticism of Otis Ferguson.* Philadelphia: Temple University Press, 1971.

Yacowar, Maurice. *Tennessee Williams and Film.* New York: Frederick Ungar Publishing Co., 1977.